Register for Free Membership

Over the last few years, Syngress has published many best-selling and critically acclaimed books, including Tom Shinder's *Configuring ISA Server 2000*, Brian Caswell and Jay Beale's *Snort 2.0 Intrusion Detection*, and Angela Orebaugh and Gilbert Ramirez's *Ethereal Packet Sniffing*. One of the reasons for the success of these books has been our unique **solutions@syngress.com** program. Through this site, we've been able to provide readers a real time extension to the printed book.

As a registered owner of this book, you will qualify for free access to our members-only solutions@syngress.com program. Once you have registered, you will enjoy several benefits, including:

- Four downloadable e-booklets on topics related to the book. Each booklet is approximately 20-30 pages in Adobe PDF format. They have been selected by our editors from other best-selling Syngress books as providing topic coverage that is directly related to the coverage in this book.

- A comprehensive FAQ page that consolidates all of the key points of this book into an easy to search web page, providing you with the concise, easy to access data you need to perform your job.

- A "From the Author" Forum that allows the authors of this book to post timely updates links to related sites, or additional topic coverage that may have been requested by readers.

Just visit us at **www.syngress.com/solutions** and follow the simple registration process. You will need to have this book with you when you register.

Thank you for giving us the opportunity to serve your needs. And be sure to let us know if there is anything else we can do to make your job easier.

SYNGRESS®

CONFIGURING

NetScreen® Firewalls

Rob Cameron   NSA JNCIA-FWV

Christopher Cantrell   NS-IDP

Dave Killion   NSCA, NSCP

Kevin Russell   JNCIS-FWV

Kenneth Tam   NSCP, JNCIS-FWV

Syngress Publishing, Inc., the author(s), and any person or firm involved in the writing, editing, or production (collectively "Makers") of this book ("the Work") do not guarantee or warrant the results to be obtained from the Work.

There is no guarantee of any kind, expressed or implied, regarding the Work or its contents. The Work is sold AS IS and WITHOUT WARRANTY. You may have other legal rights, which vary from state to state.

In no event will Makers be liable to you for damages, including any loss of profits, lost savings, or other incidental or consequential damages arising out from the Work or its contents. Because some states do not allow the exclusion or limitation of liability for consequential or incidental damages, the above limitation may not apply to you.

You should always use reasonable care, including backup and other appropriate precautions, when working with computers, networks, data, and files.

Syngress Media®, Syngress®, "Career Advancement Through Skill Enhancement®," "Ask the Author UPDATE®," and "Hack Proofing®," are registered trademarks of Syngress Publishing, Inc. "Syngress: The Definition of a Serious Security Library"™, "Mission Critical™," and "The Only Way to Stop a Hacker is to Think Like One™" are trademarks of Syngress Publishing, Inc. Brands and product names mentioned in this book are trademarks or service marks of their respective companies.

KEY	SERIAL NUMBER
001	HJIRTCV764
002	PO9873D5FG
003	829KM8NJH2
004	KLNM56332B
005	CVPLQ6WQ23
006	VBP965T5T5
007	HJJJ863WD3E
008	2987GVTWMK
009	629MP5SDJT
010	IMWQ295T6T

PUBLISHED BY
Syngress Publishing, Inc.
800 Hingham Street
Rockland, MA 02370

Configuring NetScreen Firewalls

Printed and bound in the United Kingdom
Transferred to Digital Printing, 2010
ISBN-13: 978-1-932266-39-9
ISBN-10: 1-932266-39-9

Publisher: Andrew Williams	Page Layout and Art: Patricia Lupien
Acquisitions Editor: Jaime Quigley	Copy Editor: Amy Thomson
Technical Editor: C.J. Cui and Thomas Byrne	Indexer: Odessa&Cie
Cover Designer: Michael Kavish	

Distributed by O'Reilly Media, Inc. in the United States and Canada.
For information on rights and translations, contact Matt Pedersen, Director of Sales and Rights, at Syngress Publishing; email matt@syngress.com or fax to 781-681-3585.

Acknowledgments

Syngress would like to acknowledge the following people for their kindness and support in making this book possible.

A special thank you to Tony Cussary at Juniper Networks.

Syngress books are now distributed in the United States and Canada by O'Reilly Media, Inc. The enthusiasm and work ethic at O'Reilly is incredible and we would like to thank everyone there for their time and efforts to bring Syngress books to market: Tim O'Reilly, Laura Baldwin, Mark Brokering, Mike Leonard, Donna Selenko, Bonnie Sheehan, Cindy Davis, Grant Kikkert, Opol Matsutaro, Steve Hazelwood, Mark Wilson, Rick Brown, Leslie Becker, Jill Lothrop, Tim Hinton, Kyle Hart, Sara Winge, C. J. Rayhill, Peter Pardo, Leslie Crandell, Valerie Dow, Regina Aggio, Pascal Honscher, Preston Paull, Susan Thompson, Bruce Stewart, Laura Schmier, Sue Willing, Mark Jacobsen, Betsy Waliszewski, Dawn Mann, Kathryn Barrett, John Chodacki, and Rob Bullington. And a hearty welcome to Aileen Berg—glad to be working with you.

The incredibly hard working team at Elsevier Science, including Jonathan Bunkell, Ian Seager, Duncan Enright, David Burton, Rosanna Ramacciotti, Robert Fairbrother, Miguel Sanchez, Klaus Beran, Emma Wyatt, Rosie Moss, Chris Hossack, Mark Hunt, and Krista Leppiko, for making certain that our vision remains worldwide in scope.

David Buckland, Marie Chieng, Lucy Chong, Leslie Lim, Audrey Gan, Pang Ai Hua, and Joseph Chan of STP Distributors for the enthusiasm with which they receive our books.

Kwon Sung June at Acorn Publishing for his support.

David Scott, Tricia Wilden, Marilla Burgess, Annette Scott, Andrew Swaffer, Stephen O'Donoghue, Bec Lowe, and Mark Langley of Woodslane for distributing our books throughout Australia, New Zealand, Papua New Guinea, Fiji Tonga, Solomon Islands, and the Cook Islands.

Winston Lim of Global Publishing for his help and support with distribution of Syngress books in the Philippines.

Lead Author

Rob Cameron (CCSA, CCSE, CCSE+, NSA, JNCIA-FWV, CCSP, CCNA, INFOSEC, RSA SecurID CSE) is an IT consultant who has worked with over 200 companies to provide network security planning and implementation services. He has spent the last five years focusing on network infrastructure and extranet security. His strengths include Juniper's NetScreen Firewall products, NetScreen SSL VPN Solutions, Check Point Firewalls, the Nokia IP appliance series, Linux, Cisco routers, Cisco switches, and Cisco PIX firewalls. Rob strongly appreciates his wife Kristen's constant support of his career endeavors. He wants to thank her for all of her support through this project.

Technical Editors

C.J. Cui (CISSP, JNCIA) is Director of Professional Services for NetWorks Group, an information security consulting company headquartered in Brighton, Michigan. NetWorks Group provides information security solutions that mitigate risk while enabling secure online business. C.J. leads the technical team at NetWorks Group to deliver information security services to customers ranging from medium-sized companies to fortune 500 corporations. These services touch every part of security lifecycle—from enterprise security management, security assessment and audit to solution design and implementation—and leverage leading edge technologies including firewall/VPN, intrusion prevention, vulnerability management, malicious code protection, identity management and forensics analysis. C.J. holds an M.S. degree from Michigan State University and numerous industrial certifications. He is a board member of ISSA Motor City Chapter and serves as the Director of Operations for the chapter.

Thomas Byrne is a Code Monkey with NetScreen Technologies (now Juniper Networks). He currently does design, planning, and implementation on Juniper's Security Manager, their next-generation network management software. Tom's background includes positions as a UI Architect at ePatterns, and as a senior developer and consultant for several Silicon Valley companies, including Lightsocket.com and Abovenet. Tom is an active developer on several open-source projects and a voracious contributor to several on-line technology forums. Tom currently lives in Silicon Valley with his wife Kelly, and children, Caitlin and Christian.

Contributing Authors

Dave Killion (NSCA, NSCP) is a senior security research engineer with Juniper Networks, Inc. Formerly with the U.S. Army's Information Operations Task Force as an Information Warfare Specialist, he currently researches, develops, and releases signatures for the NetScreen Deep Inspection and Intrusion Detection and Prevention platforms. Dave has also presented at several security conventions including DefCon and ToorCon, with a proof-of-concept network monitoring evasion device in affiliation with several local security interest groups that he helped form. Dave lives south of Silicon Valley with his wife Dawn and two children, Rebecca and Justin.

Kevin Russell (JNCIA-FWV, JNCIA-IDP) is a system engineer for Juniper Networks, specializing in firewalls, IPSEC, and intrusion detection and prevention systems. His background includes security auditing, implementation, and design. Kevin lives in Michigan with his wife and two children.

Chris Cantrell (NetScreen IDP) is a Director of System Engineering – Central Region for the Security Products Group at Juniper Networks. His career has spanned over 12 years, the last 8 focused in network and application security. Chris joined OneSecure in late 2000 where he was an active member of the team who designed and was responsible for the introduction of their intrusion prevention product, the IDP. In 2002, OneSecure was acquired by NetScreen Technologies and most recently acquired by Juniper Networks where Chris continues to manage their security sales engineering team for the Central Region. Chris attended Auburn University at Montgomery where his focus was on business and management information systems. Chris lives in Denver, Colorado with his wife Maria and two children, Dylan and Nikki.

Kenneth Tam (JNCIS-FWV, NCSP) is Sr. Systems Engineer at Juniper Networks Security Product Group (formerly NetScreen Technologies). Kenneth worked in pre-sales for over 4 years at NetScreen since the startup days and has been one of many key contributors in building NetScreen as one of the most successful security company. As such, his primary role has been to provide pre-sale technical assistance in both design and implementation of NetScreen solutions. Kenneth is currently covering the upper Midwest U.S. region. His background includes positions as a Senior Network Engineer in the Carrier Group at 3com Corporation, and as an application engineer at U.S.Robotics. Kenneth holds a bachelor's degree in computer science from DePaul University. He lives in the suburbs of Chicago, Illinois with his wife Lorna and children, Jessica and Brandon.

Johny Mattsson (NCSA, NCSP, SCJP, SCJD) is a senior engineer in Ericsson Australia's IP Centre, where he has been working with NetScreen firewalls for over three years. The Ericsson IP Centre provides global integration and support services for a wide range of IP based telecommunications solutions, including DSL broadband and 3G IP Multimedia Sub-systems (IMS). Johny's main areas of specialization are IP network security and several cutting edge 3G mobile services built on IMS. In addition to making sure things are always working on the technical plane, he is the main interface towards Juniper/NetScreen, working to ensure that the support channels are functioning optimally. Before taking up the role in the Ericsson IP Centre, Johny worked as a system designer for Ericsson in Sweden. There he was involved in the design and implementation of various real-time telecommunications applications, often with a focus on the security aspects. Johny would like to thank Greg Bunt at Juniper/NetScreen, for the many late nights he has spent helping resolve last minute issues, instead of spending time with his family.

Chris Lathem (Network+) is a Security/Network Engineer for NSight Technologies. Nsight, based in Ridgeland, Mississippi, specializes in Internet and network security services. Chris specializes in the support and configuration of firewall appliances from multiple vendors, as well as network design and architecture. Prior to joining Nsight, Chris held the position as Network Engineer for SkyHawke Technologies, where he spent a great deal of time configuring NetScreen Appliances. Chris currently resides in Sebastopol, Mississippi, with his wife Susann and son Miller.

Ralph Bonnell (CISSP, LPIC-2, CCSI, CCNA, MCSE: Security) is a senior information security consultant at Accuvant in Denver, Colorado. His primary responsibilities include the deployment of various network security products and product training. His specialties include NetScreen deployments, Linux client and server deployments, Check Point training, firewall clustering, and PHP web programming. Ralph also runs a Linux consulting firm called Linux Friendly. Before moving to Colorado, Ralph was a senior security engineer and instructor at Mission Critical Systems, a Gold Check Point partner and training center in South Florida.

Kevin Lynn (CISSP) is a network systems engineer with International Network Services (INS). INS is a leading global provider of vendor-independent network consulting and security services. At INS, Kevin currently works within the Ethical Hacking Center of Excellence where he evaluates the security at many of the largest financial corporations. Kevin's more than 12 years of experience has seen him working a variety of roles for organizations including Cisco Systems, IBM, Sun Microsystems, Abovenet, and the Commonwealth of Virginia. In addition to his professional work experience, Kevin has been known to give talks at SANS and teach others on security topics in classroom settings. Kevin currently resides in Rockville, MD with his lovely wife Ashley.

Contents

Appendix A ScreenOS 5.1.0 Enhancements and
New Features **675**
Copyright © Juniper Networks
Reprinted with the consent of Juniper Networks
Authored by Finina Aranez

Appendix B Certification

A complimentary chapter on NetScreen Certification is available from the Syngress Solutions site (www.syngress.com/solutions).

Foreword

You're at home, you've just gotten your first broadband connection, and your computer is hardwired to the Internet. You boot up your computer, and immediately some pit-bull of a virus starts attacking your PC. Or, you go to work, where your (clueless?) IT directory proudly shows off the new HRH brand firewall he's somehow installed between the server and the Cuisinart in the kitchen. You send some e-mail to a co-worker in a remote location, and a hacker with a God complex decides to read it, gets some critical information and ruins your next product release. How about this? You're in charge of your corporation's website running 24/7 and your firewall fails while you're fast asleep, causing thousands or millions of dollars in lost revenue.

These may sound silly, but unfortunately they happen every day. (Well, maybe not the Cuisinart one...) And the thing that most people don't realize is that they're all preventable. With some careful planning and the right equipment, you can avoid all of these scenarios.

A proper product can provide you security, management, high availability, secure VPN's and much more, all with reliability and scalability. If you've bought this book, I think it's safe to assume that you either: a) own a NetScreen device, or b) are considering using one. Either choice shows excellent judgment, given that NetScreen is a proven, award-winning platform that can provide you with all of the above services, and do it very well.

This book will give you the information to install, configure and manage your NetScreen firewalls, whether you are planning to install a single device at your house, or roll out hundreds or thousands of devices into your worldwide network. You will find a lot of information about concepts and implementation of virtually all of the NetScreen's capabilities, enabling you to not just use these amazing devices, but to use all of their abilities to best suit your needs.

This book will cut right to the center of essential functionalities and tell you how to plan for the unexpected, and how to deal with almost all of the pressing issues that confront any IT professional that needs a comprehensive security solution. Whether you are implementing large scale VPN's, an NSRP Cluster, complex routing scenarios or more simplistic Policy based Security and IDP management and logging, you will find concise information enabling you to do so.

This book won't do everything, however. It won't waste your time with unnecessary details. It won't bore you with unneeded information, and it won't let you go until you realize that you can have a secure network, quickly and easily, and that you can have it all in one package, a nice blue package with the NetScreen logo on it.

—Thomas Byrne
Juniper Networks
November 29, 2004

## Chapter 1

Networking, Security, and the Firewall

Solutions in this Chapter:

- Understanding Networking
- Understanding Security Basics
- Understanding Firewall Basics

☑ Summary

☑ Solutions Fast Track

☑ Frequently Asked Questions

Introduction

Every enterprise requires at least one firewall to provide the backbone for its network security architecture. Firewalls are the core component of your network's security. The risks today have greatly increased, so the call for a stronger breed of firewall has been made. In the past, simple packet filtering firewalls allowing access to your internal resources have helped to mitigate your network's risk. The next development was stateful inspection allowing you to monitor network sessions instead of single packets. Today's risks are far greater and require a new generation of devices to help secure our networks' borders from the more sophisticated attacks.

Firewalls police your network traffic. A firewall is a specialized device that allows or denies traffic based upon administratively defined policies. They contain technologies to inspect your network's traffic. This technology is not something that is exclusive to firewalls, but firewalls are designed specifically for inspecting traffic and therefore do it better then any other type of device. Any network can have millions of packets transverse it in a short period of time. It is impossible for a human to directly interact with the network. Even if you were to use a tool to look at the traffic directly it would be impossible for you to decide which traffic is good and which is bad. The need for a specialized device to enforce traffic restrictions has grown over the years. Because security is of such high importance, a specialized device was required to ensure the security of network traffic.

NetScreen firewall appliances have answered this call for a secure enterprise. The NetScreen firewall product line has complete offerings from the home office to the carrier-class networks. In this chapter we will review networking basics. Security requires a strong basic knowledge of networking protocols. In our first section, "Understanding Networking," we will look at networking from a top-down approach. This section starts with the basic ideas of networking models and then works into full networking communications. We will also discuss the components and prerequisites of IP addresses and how they are divided up to make networks.

We will next look at networking in general by breaking it down to a layered approach. This will help you understand the flow of networking. Each specific layer in the networking model has a purpose. Working together, these layers allow for data to seamlessly pass over the network between systems. An example of browsing a website will be used. You will see all of the effort it takes just to fetch a web page. We will focus then on the TCP/IP protocol suite. This is the most commonly used networking protocol and it is the protocol of the Internet. Finally in this chapter, we will look at network security. There are many important concepts to be aware of for information security. This will help you understand some network design considerations and the background behind them.

Understanding Networking

To understand networking is to understand the language of firewalls. A firewall is used to segment resources and limit access between networks. Before we can really focus on what a firewall does for us, we need to understand how networking works. Today in most environments and on the Internet, the protocol suite TCP/IP (Transmission Control Protocol/Internet Protocol) is used to transport data from here to there. We will begin this chapter by looking at networking as a whole with a focus on the Open System Interconnection (OSI) model.

The OSI Model

The OSI model was originally developed as a framework to build networking protocols on. During the time when then Internet was being developed, a protocol suite named TCP/IP was developed. TCP/IP was found to meet the requirements of the Internet's precursor, ARPANET. At this point, TCP/IP was already integrated into UNIX and was quickly adopted by the academic community as well. With the advent of the Internet and its widespread usage, TCP/IP has become the de facto standard protocol suite of internetworking today.

The OSI model consists of seven distinct layers. These layers each contain the fundamental ideas of networking. In Figure 1.1 we can see the way that the seven layers stack on top of each other. The idea is that each upper layer is encapsulated inside of each lower layer. So ultimately, any data communications are transformed into the electrical impulses that pass over the cables or through the air that surrounds us. Understanding the OSI model is understanding the core of networking. In many places throughout this book, the OSI model is used to create a visual representation of networking.

The reality, however, is that the OSI model is just a reference model that protocols are based upon. The next section, called "Moving Data Along With TCP/IP," demonstrates how some of the layers blur together. All in all, the OSI model is a great tool to help anyone understand networking and perform troubleshooting. Over the years, the OSI model has served as a reference for all protocols that have been developed. Almost every book, manual, white paper, or website that talks about networking protocols references the OSI model. It is important to have a baseline when discussing every topic.

For example, let's compare cars and trucks. They are effectively the same device. Both are used to get from here to there, but they are designed very differently. A truck has a sturdier frame to allow it to tow heavy loads. A car is smaller and is designed to be a transport for people. While these devices are very different, they still have common components. They both have wheels, doors, brakes, and engines. This is much like the different components of a network protocol, which is essentially a vehicle for data. Networking protocols have components to help get the data from here to there, like wheels. They have components to control the flow of data, like brakes. These are all requirements of any protocol. Using and understanding the OSI model makes protocol usage and design easier. Whether TCP/IP or IPX/SPX, most protocols are built around the same framework (model).

Figure 1.1 The 7-Layer OSI Model

| 7. Application Layer |
| 6. Presentation Layer |
| 5. Session Layer |
| 4. Transport Layer |
| 3. Network Layer |
| 2. Data Link Layer |
| 1. Physical Layer |

Layer 7: The Application Layer

The application layer contains application data. This is the layer at which applications communicate to one another. The reason for all of the other layers is essentially to transport the messages contained at the application layer. When communicating with each other, the applications use their own language, as specified by that application's standard. A perfect example of an application protocol is Hypertext Transfer Protocol (HTTP). HTTP is used to send and receive web content. When HTTP is used to pass data from server to client, it employs something called HTTP *headers*. HTTP headers are effectively the language of HTTP. When the client wants to request data from a server, it issues a request to get the content from the server. The server then responds with is headers and the data that was requested. All of this is an example of application layer communications. Other examples of application layer protocols are File Transfer Protocol (FTP), Domain Name Service (DNS), Telnet, and Secure Shell (SSH).

Layer 6: The Presentation Layer

The presentation layer controls the presentation or formatting of the data content. At this point in the OSI model there is no data communications per se. The focus of this layer is having a common ground to present data between applications. For example, let's take image files. Billions of image files are transferred every day. Each of these files contains an image that ultimately will be displayed or stored on a computer. However, each image file must be the proper specified file format. This way, the application that reads the image file understands the type of data and the format that is contained in it. A JPEG file and a PNG file may contain the same image, but each uses a separate format. A JPEG file cannot be interpreted as a PNG and vice versa. Additionally, file-level encryption occurs at the presentation layer.

Layer 5: The Session Layer

The session layer controls sessions between two systems. It is important to have sessions, as it is the core of any communications for networking. If you did not have sessions, all communications would run together without any true idea of what is happening throughout the communication. As you will see below, TCP/IP has no session layer, really. In TCP/IP the session layer blends together with the transport layer. Other protocols such as NetBIOS, used on Microsoft networks, use the session layer for reliable communications.

Layer 4: The Transport Layer

The transport layer provides a total end-to-end solution for reliable communications. This layer provides the mechanisms for reliable communications. TCP/IP relies on the transport layer to effectively control communications between two hosts. When an IP communication session must begin or end, the transport layer is used to build this connection. The elements of the transport layer and how it functions within TCP/IP are discussed in more detail later in the chapter. The transport layer is the layer at which TCP/IP ports listen.

Layer 3: The Network Layer

When packets have to get between two stations on a network, the network layer is responsible for the transportation of these packets. The network layer determines the path and the direction on the network in order to allow communications between two stations. The IP portion of TCP/IP rests in this part of the OSI model. IP is discussed in detail in the following section.

Layer 2: The Data Link Layer

Layer two, or the data link layer, is the mechanism that determines how to transmit data between two stations. All hosts that communicate at this level must be on the same physical network. The way in which the transmission of data at this level is handled is based upon the protocol used. Examples of protocols at the data link layer are Ethernet, Point-to-Point Protocol (PPP), Frame Relay, Synchronous Data Link Control (SDLC), and X.25. Protocols such as Address Resolution Protocol (ARP) function at the Data Link Layer.

Layer 1: The Physical Layer

The last but most important layer of the OSI model is the physical layer. The physical layer consists of the objects that connect stations together physically. This layer is responsible for taking the bits and bytes of the higher layers and passing them along the specified medium. There are many examples of the physical layer that you should already have heard of, such as Cat5 cable, T1, and wireless.

Moving Data Along with TCP/IP

On the Internet and most networks, TCP/IP is the most commonly used protocol for passing network data. At the time of its development, TCP/IP used a very advanced design. Decades later, TCP/IP continues to meet the needs of the Internet. The most commonly used version of IP used today is version 4, the version covered in this book. The next generation IP, version 6, is starting to be used much more throughout the world. Many vendors, including Juniper Networks, Cisco, Microsoft, and Apple are developing software that support the new IP version 6 standard.

Over the course of this section, we will cover how systems use TCP/IP to interact, and we will review the IP protocol and how its protocol suite compares to the OSI model. We will also discuss how IP packets are used to transmit data across networks, and we will examine the transport layer protocols TCP and User

Datagram Protocol (UDP) and how they are used to control data communications in conjunction with IP. Finally, we will wrap up the discussion of TCP/IP
with information about the data link layer.

Understanding IP

The Internet Protocol (IP) is used to get data from one system to another. The
IP protocol sits on the third layer of the OSI model, the network layer. When
you need to send data across a network, that data is encapsulated in a packet. A
packet is simply a segment of data that is sent across the network. In TCP/IP
however, there are not seven true layers as there are in the OSI model (see Figure
1.2 for a comparison of TCP/IP and OSI model layers).

    When an application needs to pass its communication to another system on
the network, it passes its information down the protocol stack. This is the process
that creates an IP packet.

Figure 1.2 OSI Model Layers Versus TCP/IP Layers

OSI Model	TCP/IP Model
7. Application Layer	
	5. Application Layer
6. Presentation Layer	
5. Session Layer	4. Transport Layer
4. Transport Layer	
3. Network Layer	3. Network Layer
2. Data Link Layer	2. Data Link Layer
1. Physical Layer	1. Physical Layer

    Lets look at an example of IP connectivity. We will be referencing the
TCP/IP model, as it will be easier to understand for this example. Remember
that the TCP/IP model is a condensed version of the OSI model. Use Figure 1.2
to reference the steps of the OSI model on the left to the TCP/IP model on the
right. You can use your web browser to connect to www.syngress.com and view
the series of events that occur during a network (in this case, the Internet) connection. We will look at the course of action that happens for the first packet
that is created for this connection.

    First, enter the address in the web browser and then press **Enter**. The browser
will make a request to get the data from the server. This request is then given to

the transport layer where it initiates a session to the remote machine. To get to the remote machine, the transport layer sends its data to the network layer and creates a packet. The data link layer's job is to get the packet across the local network. At this point, the packet is called a *frame*. At each junction point between systems and routing devices, the data link layer makes sure that the frame is properly transmitted. The physical layer is used during the entire connection to convert the raw data into electrical or optical impulses.

When the end station receives the packet, that station will convert the packet back to the application layer. The electrical impulses are changed at the physical layer into the frame. The frame is then unencapsulated and converted to individual packets. Because the packet is at its end destination, the network layer and transport portions of the packet are removed and then the application data is passed to the application layer. That sounds like a lot of work for just one packet to transverse the Internet, but all of this happens on a broadband connection in 30 milliseconds or less. This, of course, is the simplified version of how all of this happens. In the following sections, we will expand on this example and show you what happens behind the scenes when two stations have a network conversation.

The following list provides a rundown of the phases of connectivity:

1. The URL www.syngress.com is entered into the browser.

2. The user presses **Enter** and forces the browser to connect to the website.

3. The browser makes a request to the server.

4. The browser request is handed to the transport layer.

5. The transport layer initiates a session to the remote server.

6. The transport layer passes its request to the network layer.

7. The network layer creates a packet to send to the remote server.

8. The data link layer takes the packet and turns it into a frame.

9. The frame is passed over the local network by the physical layer.

10. The physical layer takes the frame and converts it into electrical or optical impulses.

11. These impulses pass between devices.

12. At each junction point or router, the packet is transformed to the data link layer.

13. The packet is taken from the data link layer to the network layer.

14. The router looks at the packet and determines the destination host.

15. The router forwards the packet to the next and all subsequent routers until it reaches the remote system.

16. The end station receives the packet and converts it back through the layers to the application layer.

17. The remote system responds to the client system.

IP Packets

As discussed in the previous sections, IP is essentially used to get data from one system to another. The anatomy of IP is very straightforward. In Figure 1.3 you can see what exactly makes up an IP packet header. An IP packet contains the very important application data that needs to be transported. This data is contained in the last portion of the packet. The IP portion of a packet is called the IP header. It contains all of the information that is useful for getting the data from system to system. The IP header includes the source and destination IP addresses.

Figure 1.3 IP Packet Header Contents

Version	Header Length	Type of Service	Length	
Identification			Flags	Fragment Offset
TTL		Protocol	Header Checksum	
Source IP Address				
Destination IP Address				
Options				
Data				

So the question remains, "how do IP packets actually get from system to system?" Let's reference our previous example of browsing to www.syngress.com. When the IP packet is formed, it includes the source IP address (the IP address of the client system making the request). This is like the return address on an envelope it tells the recipient where to send return mail to. The packet also receives the destination address of the web server being contacted. There are other parts that are set in the IP header, but are not germane to this discussion. After the packet is created, it is sent to the originating system's routing table. The routing table is referenced and then the operating system determines which path to send this packet to. In routing, each system that receives the packet determines the next location or *hop* to send the packet to. So when sending information or requests across the Internet, there may be 15 hops or routers to go through before you get to the final system you are trying to connect to. Simply stated, a router is a system whose primary function is to route traffic from one location to another. As each router receives a packet it determines the next best location to send it to.

This, of course, is very simplified, as there are millions of routers on the Internet. Once the destination system receives the IP packet, it formulates a response. This is then sent back to the client system. The IP header contains the source address of the server that received the first packet and then the destination address of the initiating client machine. This is the fundamental basis of IP communications.

One of the confusing things about IP is that IP packets are not just used to transport data; the IP protocol suite does more than that. If you refer back to Table 1.1, you can see a field called *protocol*. This determines which IP protocol the packet is using. All of the available IP protocols are specified in RFC 1700. Table 1.1 is a short reference of the IP protocols we will be discussing in this book. For example, if the packet was UDP, it would be using IP protocol 17, and if the packet was IP Security (IPSec) ESP, it would be using IP protocol 50.

Table 1.1 IP Protocol Suite

Protocol Number	Name	Protocol
1	ICMP	Internet Control Message Protocol
4	IP	IP to IP Encapsulation
6	TCP	Transmission Control Protocol
17	UDP	User Datagram Protocol
50	ESP	Encapsulating Security Payload
51	AH	Authentication Header

One of the most important protocols in the IP protocol suite is the Internet Control Messaging Protocol (ICMP). ICMP is used as a messaging protocol to give information to the source or destination machine that is engaging in IP communications. Table 1.2 lists all of the commonly used ICMP types and codes. To give an example of ICMP, let's look at the common application *ping*. Ping is an application that is on pretty much any operating system, including ScreenOS. It is used to test if a host is responsive from a network perspective. When you ping a host, an IP packet is generated that has the source IP address of the requesting system and the destination IP address of the system you are trying to contact. This packet then has an ICMP type of eight and a code of zero. The destination system then would receive the packet and recognize that the IP packet is *echo* or *echo request packet*. It then creates an ICMP packet that is a type zero code zero. This is an *echo reply packet*, acknowledging the original request.

Devices use ICMP for other reasons as well. If a system had a route in its routing table that specified a host could be found at a location that did not exist, the router it points to would send an ICMP message to the initiating host. That router would send a type three code zero or code one message specifying that the network or host is not available. Now apply that to the Internet and all of those millions of routers out there. This makes the ICMP protocol very helpful for notifying users when there is a problem with getting IP packets from one location to another.

Table 1.2 ICMP Types and Codes

Type	Name
0	Echo Reply
Codes	Name
0	No Code

Continued

Table 1.2 ICMP Types and Codes

Type	Name
3	Destination Unreachable

Codes	Name
0	Network Unreachable
1	Host Unreachable
2	Protocol Unreachable
3	Port Unreachable

What Does an IP Address Look Like?

IP addresses are thirty-two bits in length. They consist of four eight-bit numbers. An example of an IP address is 1.2.3.4. This looks like a very simple format, but it has a great deal of meaning. Each of the four numbers can contain a value from 0 to 255. IP addresses are allocated in blocks or subnets. A subnet is a grouping of IP addresses based upon a subnet mask. There are three major types of IP address blocks, class A, B, and C. Each class is determined based upon the three leading bits for each number. The class A grouping of IP addresses all start with the binary digit 0. The class B grouping of IP addresses all start with 10. Finally, the class C grouping of IP addresses all start with 110. In Table 1.3 you can see all of the ranges of IP addresses based upon class. There are two other classes of IP addresses, classes D and E, which have special functions that are not covered in this book.

Table 1.3 IP Address Ranges by Class

Class	Address Range
A	0.0.0.0 to 127.255.255.255
B	128.0.0.0 to 191.255.255.255
C	192.0.0.0 to 223.255.255.255
D	224.0.0.0 to 239.255.255.255
E	240.0.0.0 to 255.255.255.255

You can also use your own local computer to look at your IP address. We will use both a Windows system and a UNIX-based system as an example. Open up a DOS window on your Microsoft Windows system, then enter the command **ipconfig**. An example of this is shown in Figure 1.4 below. You can also do the same thing on a UNIX-based system by using the command **ifconfig**. An example of this is shown in Figure 1.5 below.

Figure 1.4 Microsoft Windows ipconfig Output

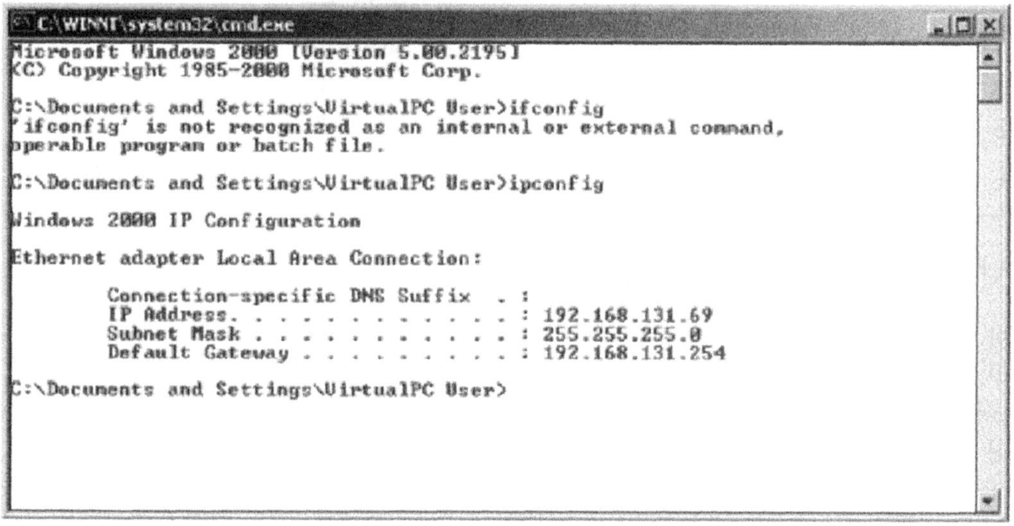

```
C:\WINNT\system32\cmd.exe                                          _|□|x|
Microsoft Windows 2000 [Version 5.00.2195]
(C) Copyright 1985-2000 Microsoft Corp.

C:\Documents and Settings\VirtualPC User>ifconfig
'ifconfig' is not recognized as an internal or external command,
operable program or batch file.

C:\Documents and Settings\VirtualPC User>ipconfig

Windows 2000 IP Configuration

Ethernet adapter Local Area Connection:

        Connection-specific DNS Suffix  . :
        IP Address. . . . . . . . . . . . : 192.168.131.69
        Subnet Mask . . . . . . . . . . . : 255.255.255.0
        Default Gateway . . . . . . . . . : 192.168.131.254

C:\Documents and Settings\VirtualPC User>
```

Figure 1.5 UNIX ifconfig Output

```
en1: flags=8863<UP,BROADCAST,SMART,RUNNING,SIMPLEX,MULTICAST> mtu 1500
        inet 10.6.0.123 netmask 0xffffff00 broadcast 10.6.0.255
        ether 00:0d:93:8c:62:2e
        media: autoselect status: active
        supported media: autoselect
```

IP Address Allocation

When creating a network, deciding on IP address allocation is very important. But with billions of options, how does one decide? The Internet Assigned Numbers Authority, or IANA, is responsible for allocating IP addresses. They determine which organizations get which IP address ranges. They are also responsible for conserving IP addresses and planning for future uses for IP addresses. Does this mean that you need to contact them to get IP addresses? Unless you are starting your own Internet Service Provider (ISP) the size of Qwest or SBC, you do not need to contact them. Your ISP will always assign any Internet or public IP addresses, and for private IP address networks you would use the IP addresses that are specified in RFC 1918. See Table 1.4 for a list of the private IP address ranges. A non–Internet routable IP is an IP address that is not routed on the Internet. If a packet was to leave your network with a source or destination IP address in one of these ranges, it would not get very far.

Table 1.4 RFC 1918 IP Address Ranges

Class	Address Range
A	10.0.0.0 to 10.255.255.255
B	172.16.0.0 to 172.31.255.255
C	192.168.0.0 to 192.168.255.255

NAT and Private IP Addresses

Most companies need to access Internet resources while preserving Internet IP addresses. The solution is Network Address Translation, or NAT. NAT is used to hide your private IP address behind a public IP address. This allows private IP-addressed systems to access publicly addressed systems. NAT also provides a layer of security by hiding the real IP addresses of your internal network. A gateway device such as a NetScreen firewall performs NAT for IP packets that pass through the device. Once the firewall receives an IP packet with the source IP address, it changes the private IP address into a public IP address. When the NetScreen firewall receives the return packet, it translates the new destination address to the private IP address. There are two types of NAT: NAT source, and NAT destination.

TCP Communications

The Transmission Control Protocol is used to control the creation and form of data transfer connections. TCP is one of two transport layer protocols that are used as part of the TCP/IP protocol suite. TCP is designed to provide many functions mostly based on reliability. TCP is used for applications that require reliability over speed. When talking about speed at this level, we are talking about calculations of milliseconds or less. TCP functions as a stateful protocol. This means that during the communications, the connection has specific states in which it functions. There is a clear beginning, middle, and end of a TCP connection.

When a TCP session begins, it goes through a three-way handshaking process. Inside of a TCP header, options (called flags) are set. These flags identify the type of TCP message that has been sent. The three-way handshake process is shown in Figure 1.6. Let's continue to use our earlier example of using your web browser to access www.syngress.com. When your web browser attempts to make its connection to the web server, it attempts to open a connection to TCP port 80. A port is a specific communications channel specific to a particular application. TCP port 80 is the default port for HTTP.

The first packet that is sent to the web server is a SYN packet. A SYN packet is used to synchronize a connection between two hosts. This packet is also sent with a sequence number that is used to identify the packet inside of this connection. This sequence number is to be used for the initiating systems packets. Next, the web server receives the packet acknowledges it. To do this, the server creates and sends a packet with the TCP flags SYN and ACK. A packet that has the ACK (or acknowledgment) flag set is sending a message to the other system that says, "I have received your packet". A sequence number is also given to this packet that is independent of the sequence number that is associated with the initiating system's sequence number. The system that initiated the connection now sends an ACK packet to acknowledge the connection. The ACK packet has a sequence number that is incremented, as it is the second packet that has been sent from this system. The TCP session has now been created and the requested data from the web server can begin to pass to the client.

The data that was requested is divided into packets by TCP. The client sends a TCP packet with the ACK flag for each part of the data. Again, each packet that is sent from the client has a sequence number that is incremented by one. The sequence number is used to identify all of the packets of a TCP exchange. If, for example, a client receives packets with sequence numbers 6, 7, 8, and 10, but never receives packet 9, the client will request that packet nine be resent from the server. On the client, all of the packets would be reordered before passing the data back to the application. When the connection is completed, the server system would send a packet with the FIN flag. This indicates that the connection is finished. The client would then send an ACK packet back to the server acknowledging that the conversation has completed.

Figure 1.6 TCP Session Initialization

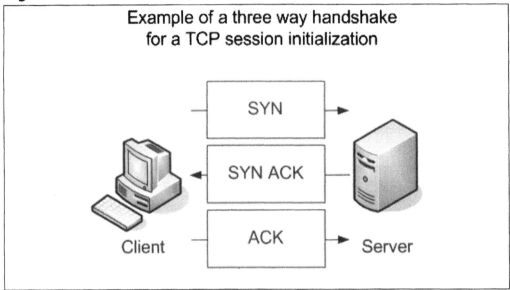

UDP Communications

The User Datagram Protocol is a connectionless protocol that is designed to stream data. When a UDP connection occurs, there is no beginning, middle, or end to the conversation. Data simply begins to flow between the two systems. UDP is a very simple protocol and is used when speed is an issue. UDP packet receipt is not verified. An example of a use of the UDP protocol is DNS queries. When you attempt to use your web browser to access www.syngress.com, it must first resolve the name to an IP address. This would require a DNS query. The query is sent over a single UDP packet. The DNS server would then respond by telling the originating system the IP address of the web server. Because the UDP response is faster than setting up a TCP session, UDP makes sense in these situations. Another example of using UDP is Voice over IP (VoIP). The downfall, of course, is the lack of reliability, so you may have to employ other methods to guarantee delivery.

What is a Port?

Both TCP and UDP support the use of ports. But what exactly is a port? Lets look at an example that can help further explain this. When you turn on your television, you get a picture and sound. Every time you change the channel, each new channel contains different content. This is much like a TCP or UDP port.

Each port contains a specific type of content or application. When you tune to that port, you can access those specific resources. Theoretically, you can put any application on any port, but by specifying specific ports for specific applications, you can always be assured of the type of content you will find on a specific port.

This is why a specification of well-known ports has been established. Table 1.5 gives a list of well-known TCP and UDP ports. Using our earlier television example, this is much like a channel lineup. If television programming could appear on any television channel, there would be a lot of confusion about which programming you were watching. When you use your television, the service provider gives you a channel lineup. This lineup is specified so that you know which channel is which. Most web servers serve data over port 80. Again, they can serve the data over any port, but it would be very hard to get the content if you did not know which port to use.

Table 1.5 Well-Known TCP and UDP Ports

Well-Known TCP Ports		Well-Known UDP Ports	
FTP	21	DNS	53
SSH	22	DHCP-Relay	67
Telnet	23	TFTP	69
SMTP	25	NTP	123
HTTP	80	IKE	500
IMAP	143	Syslog	514
HTTPS	443	H.323	1719

Data Link Layer Communication

The last part of networking we are going to discuss is the data link layer, or layer two. This layer is essentially the protocol that operates on the specific physical medium. Each of the following function differently on the data link layer: Ethernet, ATM, Frame Relay, HDLC, SDLC, PPP, and Serial Line Internet Protocol (SLIP) to name a few. In this section how Ethernet functions will be focused on. As of the time of this writing the main layer two protocol that is used by NetScreen firewalls is Ethernet.

Ethernet is the most commonly used medium today in corporate networks. It is inexpensive to use, easy to set up, and can operate at incredible speeds. The data link layer is used to communicate across the local medium. Figure 1.7 shows the breakdown of the use of layers and where they take place during system-to-system communication. When systems need to talk over Ethernet, they cannot use IP addresses, because Ethernet is at a lower level and it is used to move IP between layer three devices. So each device on an Ethernet segment uses a Media Access Control (MAC) address. When a station needs to have a conversation, the source and destination systems use their MAC addresseses to identify each other. Each manufacturer is assigned a range to use when creating Ethernet adapters. Then each individual adapter is given a unique number to create the MAC address.

Figure 1.7 A Layered Look at Network Communications

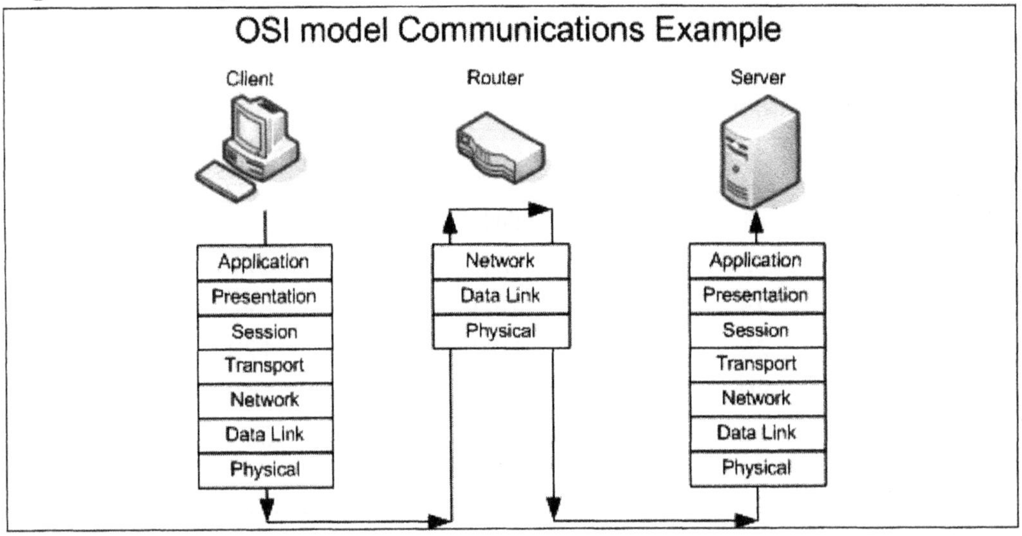

Because systems communicate via IP,but need to talk over Ethernet (which requires the use of MAC addresses),there has to be a way to resolve an IP to a MAC address. The method used is called the Address Resolution Protocol. For example, if system A, which has an IP address of 192.168.1.10, wanted to view the web pages on system B, which has an IP address of 192.168.1.25, before the communications can begin, system A must learn the MAC address of system B. System A broadcasts a request over the local broadcast domain asking who has the IP address 192.168.1.25. A broadcast is a communication that is sent out to every system that is within a broadcast area. All of the systems in the broadcast area get this request and the system with the requested IP address responds with a unicast message that specifies it has the IP address of 192.168.1.25 and also provides its MAC address.

Because almost everyone uses a computer today, a typical company can contain at least twenty computers or more. There are many ways to connect computers together. If you have just two systems, you can connect them with just a crossover Ethernet cable. A crossover cable is an Ethernet cable that allows two systems to directly connect to each other. If you have two to four computers, you could use a hub or bridge. If you have four or more computers, you will likely want to use a switch. A hub or bridge is a device that connects several systems together. When two systems want to access the Ethernet media to transfer data, their communications take up the use of the media while they are talking. If a third system wants to talk over the network, it simply starts talking and the data frames will collide with those of the already ongoing communication. An Ethernet segment where the media is shared between is called a *collision domain.* Switches, however, do not have this problem. When two systems begin a network conversation on a network with a switch, the packets are isolated and the switch prevents packets from colliding. If a system was to broadcast, however, the broadcast would be sent to every system connected to the switch. When the switch sends the data between two hosts, it sends it such a way that other network conversations are not interrupted.

Understanding Security Basics

The first key to understanding network security is understand networking. Hopefully the previous section has started you on the path to understand networking. Just be patent with yourself while reading this book. There may be many new concepts that you have never heard of before. Working with these technologies over time well help solidify your knowledge. In this section, we discuss basic security concepts that will prepare you for the final section about firewalls. In this section, we focus on some of the different aspects of what it takes to have a secure organization. As you will see, there are no hard and fast rules about what it really takes to make your network secure. I have been to many organizations that would fall well below the line I would say is good security. However, some of those same organizations have gone years without a security breach. On the other hand, I have seen other companies spend much more on their security and have more problems with break-ins and data loss. Much like everything in the world, a balance is the best thing you can have for your network.

The Need For Security

Enterprise security is the hottest technology trend today. Every aspect of a company's data infrastructure has the need for security. With ever–growing, ever-evolving networks in every organization, managing security has become harder. For many organizations, the operating budget for security is less than one percent of there total company budget. When it comes down to purchasing security products, firewalls are the core product used to secure the enterprise network. However, firewalls should by no means be the only method used to secure your network, but used effectively, they can mitigate the risks of network security breaches and data loss. With integrated technologies such as anti-virus, deep packet inspection, Uniform Resource Locator (URL) filtering, and Virtual Private Networks (VPNs), the firewall can provide a host of security applications all in one system. As the old saying goes, however, you should never put all of your eggs in one basket.

Introducing Common Security Standards

Security and network professionals use a number of currently accepted procedures and standards to conduct business and ensure that we are following the accepted practices for security and access. Although we have a responsibility as network and systems administrators to try to attain perfection in the availability and integrity of our data, we also have constraints placed on us in accomplishing those tasks. These constraints include budgets, physical plant capability, and training of users and technicians to maintain the security and integrity of the data. These constraints do not relieve us of our responsibility of maintaining the data safely and securely. To that end, we currently employ some accepted standards for security that help us perform our tasks to the best possible level. In this section, we remind you of the common security standards and briefly discuss them:

- **Authentication, authorization, and auditing (AAA)** AAA use is required in security operations for creating and maintaining the method of authenticating users and processes, and validating their credentials prior to allowing access to resources. It is also the method we use to grant access or deny access to the resource. Auditing of activity is a crucial part of this function.

- **Confidentiality, integrity, and availability (CIA)** CIA is the originally defined process that establishes the goals that we have used to try to protect our data from unauthorized view, corruption, or unauthorized modification, and to provide constant availability. Over the past few years, the CIA processes have expanded to include a more comprehensive guideline that also includes the process of defining risk and use of risk management tools to provide a more complete method of protection.

- **Least privilege** This concept is used by the security planners and teams to define the levels of access to resources and the network that should be allowed. From a security standpoint, it is always preferable to be too restrictive with the capability to relax the access levels than to be too loose and have a breach occur.

Remember, too, that the security process involves a three-tiered model for security protection:

- **Computer security**, including the use of risk assessment, the expanded CIA goals, and enterprise planning that extends throughout the entire enterprise, rather than to just a portion of it.

- **Physical security**, in which we must build and include physical access systems and coordinate them with our network access systems.

- **Trusted users,** who become an important cog in maintaining the integrity of our security efforts.

Common Information Security Concepts

A generic dictionary definition of *security* (taken from the American Heritage Dictionary) is, "freedom from risk or danger; safety." This definition is perhaps a little misleading when it comes to computer and networking security, because it implies a degree of protection that is inherently impossible to achieve in the modern connectivity-oriented computing environment.

For this reason, the same dictionary provides another definition specific to computer science: "The *level to which* a program or device is safe from unauthorized use" (emphasis added). Implicit in this definition is the caveat that the objectives of security and accessibility—the two top priorities on the minds of many network administrators—are, by their very nature, diametrically opposed. The more accessible your data, the less secure it is. Likewise, the more tightly you secure your data, the more you impede accessibility. Any security plan is an attempt to strike the proper balance between the two.

Defining Information Security

Over the last couple of decades, many companies began to realize that their most valuable assets were not only their buildings or factories, but also the intellectual property and other information that flowed internally as well as outwardly to suppliers and customers. Company managers, used to dealing with risk in their business activities, started to think about what might happen if their key business information fell into the wrong hands, perhaps a competitor's.

For a while, this risk was not too large, due to how and where that information was stored. *Closed systems* was the operative phrase. Key business information, for the most part, was stored on servers accessed via terminals or terminal emulators and had few interconnections with other systems. Any interconnections tended to be over private leased lines to a select few locations, either internal to the company or to a trusted business partner.

However, over the last five to seven years, the Internet has changed how businesses operate, and there has been a huge acceleration in the interconnectedness of organizations, systems, and networks. Entire corporate networks have access to the Internet, often at multiple points. This proliferation has created risks to sensitive information and business-critical systems where they had barely existed before. The importance of information security in the business environment has now been underscored, as has the need for skilled, dedicated practitioners of this specialty.

We have traditionally thought of security as consisting of people, sometimes with guns, watching over and guarding tangible assets such as a stack of money or a research lab. Maybe they sat at a desk and watched via closed-circuit cameras installed around the property. These people usually had minimal training and sometimes did not understand much about what they were guarding or why it was important. However, they did their jobs (and continue to do so) according to established processes, such as walking around the facility on a regular basis and looking for suspicious activity or people who do not appear to belong there.

Information security moves that model into the intangible realm. Fundamentally, information security involves making sure that only authorized people (and systems) have access to information. Information security professionals sometimes have different views on the role and definition of information security.

The three primary areas of concern in information security have traditionally been defined as follows:

- **Confidentiality** Ensuring that only authorized parties have access to information. Encryption is a commonly used tool to achieve confidentiality. Authentication and authorization, treated separately in the following discussion, also help with confidentiality.

- **Integrity** Ensuring that information is not modified by unauthorized parties (or even improperly modified by authorized ones!) and that it can be relied on. Checksums and hashes are used to validate data integrity, as are transaction-logging systems.

- **Availability** Ensuring that information is accessible when it is needed. In addition to simple backups of data, availability includes ensuring that systems remain accessible in the event of a denial of service (DoS) attack. Availability also means that critical data should be protected from erasure—for example, preventing the wipeout of data on your company's external website.

Often referred to simply by the acronym *CIA*, these three areas serve well as a security foundation. To fully scope the role of information security, however, we also need to add a few more areas of concern to the list. Some security practitioners include the following within the three areas described above, but by getting more granular, we can get a better sense of the challenges that must be addressed:

- **Authentication** Ensuring that users are, in fact, who they say they are. Passwords, of course, are the longstanding way to authenticate users, but other methods such as cryptographic tokens and biometrics are also used.

- **Authorization/access control** Ensuring that a user, once authenticated, is only able to access information to which he or she has been granted permission by the owner of the information. This can be accomplished at the operating system level using file system access controls or at the network level using access controls on routers or firewalls.

- **Auditability** Ensuring that activity and transactions on a system or network can be monitored and logged in order to maintain system availability and detect unauthorized use. This process can take various forms: logging by the operating system, logging by a network device such as a router or firewall, or logging by an intrusion detection system (IDS) or packet-capture device.

■ **Nonrepudiation** Ensuring that a person initiating a transaction is authenticated sufficiently such that he or she cannot reasonably deny that they were the initiating party. Public key cryptography is often used to support this effort.

You can say that your information is secure when all seven of these areas have been adequately addressed. The definition of *adequately* depends, however, on how much risk exists in each area. Some areas may present greater risk in a particular environment than in others.

Insecurity and the Internet

The federation of networks that became the Internet consisted of a relatively small community of users by the 1980s, primarily in the research and academic communities. Because it was rather difficult to get access to these systems and the user communities were rather closely knit, security was not much of a concern in this environment. The main objective of connecting these various networks together was to share information, not keep it locked away. Technologies such as the UNIX operating system and the TCP/IP networking protocols that were designed for this environment reflected this lack of security concern. Security was simply viewed as unnecessary.

By the early 1990s, however, commercial interest in the Internet grew. These commercial interests had very different perspectives on security, ones often in opposition to those of academia. Commercial information had value, and access to it had to be limited to specifically authorized people. UNIX, TCP/IP, and connections to the Internet became avenues of attack and did not have much capability to implement and enforce confidentiality, integrity, and availability. As the Internet grew in commercial importance, with numerous companies connecting to it and even building entire business models around it, the need for increased security became quite acute. Connected organizations now faced threats that they had never had to consider before.

When the corporate computing environment was a closed and limited-access system, threats mostly came from inside the organizations. These *internal threats* came from disgruntled employees with privileged access who could cause a lot of damage. Attacks from the outside were not much of an issue since there were typically only a few, if any, private connections to trusted entities. Potential attackers were few in number, since the combination of necessary skills and malicious intent were not at all widespread.

With the growth of the Internet, *external threats* grew as well. There are now millions of hosts on the Internet as potential attack targets, which entice the now large numbers of attackers. This group has grown in size and skill over the years as its members share information on how to break into systems for both fun and profit. Geography no longer serves as an obstacle, either. You can be attacked from another continent thousands of miles away just as easily as from your own town.

Threats can be classified as structured or unstructured. *Unstructured threats* are from people with low skill and perseverance. These usually come from people called *script kiddies*—attackers who have little to no programming skill and very little system knowledge. Script kiddies tend to conduct attacks just for bragging rights among their groups, which are often linked only by an Internet Relay Chat (IRC) channel. They obtain attack tools that have been built by others with more skill and use them, often indiscriminately, to attempt to exploit vulnerability in their target. If their attack fails, they will likely go elsewhere and keep trying. Additional risk comes from the fact that they often use these tools with little to no knowledge of the target environment, so attacks can wind up causing unintended results. Unstructured threats can cause significant damage or disruption, despite the attacker's lack of sophistication. These attacks are usually detectable with current security tools.

Structured attacks are more worrisome because they are conducted by hackers with significant skill. If the existing tools do not work for them, they are likely to modify them or write their own. They are able to discover new vulnerabilities in systems by executing complex actions that the system designers did not protect against. Structured attackers often use so-called *zero-day exploits*, which are exploits that target vulnerabilities that the system vendor has not yet issued a patch for or does not even know about. Structured attacks often have stronger motivations behind them than simple mischief. These motivations or goals can include theft of source code, theft of credit card numbers for resale or fraud, retribution, or destruction or disruption of a competitor. A structured attack might not be blocked by traditional methods such as firewall rules or detected by an IDS. It could even use non-computer methods such as social engineering.

NOTE

Social engineering, also known as *people hacking,* is a means of obtaining security information from people by tricking them. The classic example is calling up a user and pretending to be a system administrator. The hacker asks the user for his or her password to ostensibly perform some important maintenance task. To avoid being hacked via social engineering, educate your user community that they should always confirm the identity of any person calling them and that passwords should never be given to *anyone* over e-mail, instant messaging, or the phone.

Another key task in securing your systems is closing vulnerabilities by turning off unneeded services and bringing them up to date on patches. Services that have no defined business need present an additional possible avenue of attack and are just another component that needs patch attention. Keeping patches current is actually one of the most important activities you can perform to protect yourself, yet it is one that many organizations neglect.

The Code Red and Nimda worms of 2001 were successful primarily because so many systems had not been patched for the vulnerabilities they exploited, including multiple Microsoft Internet Information Server (IIS) and Microsoft Outlook vulnerabilities. Patching, especially when you have hundreds or even thousands of systems, can be a monumental task. However, by defining and documenting processes, using tools to assist in configuration management, subscribing to multiple vulnerability alert mailing lists, and prioritizing patches according to criticality, you can get a better handle on the job.

One useful document to assist in this process has been published by the U.S. National Institute of Standards and Technology (NIST), which can be found at http://csrc.nist.gov/publications/nistpubs/800-40/sp800-40.pdf (800-40 is the document number).

Also important is having a complete understanding of your network topology and some of the key information flows within it, as well as in and out of it. This understanding helps you define different zones of trust and highlights where re-architecting the network in places might improve security—for example, by deploying additional firewalls internally or on your network perimeter.

Identifying Potential Threats

As you prepare your overall security plan and de-militarized zone (DMZ), it is important that you identify and evaluate the potential risks and threats to your network, systems, and data. You must evaluate your risks thoroughly during the identification process to assign some sort of value to the risks in order to determine priorities for protection and likelihood of loss resulting from those risks and threats if they materialize. In this vein, you should be looking at and establishing a risk evaluation for anything that could potentially disrupt, slow, or damage your systems, data, or credibility. In this area, it is important to assign these values to potential threats such as:

- Outside hacker attacks

- Trojans, worms, and virus attacks

- DoS or Distributed Denial of Service (DDoS) attacks

- Compromise or loss of internal confidential information

- Network monitoring and data interception

- Internal attacks by employees

- Hardware failures

- Loss of critical systems

This identification process creates the basis for your security plan, policies, and implementation of your security environment. You should realize that this is an ongoing evaluation that is subject to change as conditions within your company and partners, as well as employee need for access, change and morph over time. We have learned that security is a process and is never truly "finished." However, a good basic evaluation goes a long way toward creating the most secure system that we can achieve.

Using VPNs in Today's Enterprise

Ensuring that your data arrives safe and sound when it passes through a network is something everyone wants to have. In an ideal world, your data's integrity and confidentiality would be guaranteed. If you believe this all sounds like nothing more then a fantasy, you are wrong. These types of guarantees can be made when you use IPSec VPN technologies. When you use an IPSec connection either between two networks or a client and a network you can ensure that no one looked at the data and no one modified it. Almost every company today uses VPN technologies to secure its data as it passes through various networks. In fact there are many regulations that specify that a VPN connection must be used to pass specific types of data.

IPSec provides integrity checking to ensure that your data was not modified. It also provides encryption ensuring that no one has looked at the data. When two sides create a VPN connection, each side is authenticated to verify that each party is who they say they are. Combined with integrity checking and encryption, you have an almost unbeatable combination.

The Battle for the Secure Enterprise

This book covers the NetScreen firewall product line and focuses on that specific product and technology. A firewall is the core of securing your network, but there are other products out there that should also be implemented in your network. These additional devices help ensure a network that has security covered from all angles. The following technologies are usually the minimum that companies should implement to provide security in the organization.

A *firewall* can contain many different types of technology to increase its importance in your network. Many firewall products today can integrate several different technologies. Almost all firewalls today provide VPN services. This allows secure streams of data to terminate to your firewall. This is usually over the Internet, but also be over other unprotected networks. When the traffic gets to your secured network it no longer requires encryption. You can also force users to authenticate before accessing resources through the firewall. This commonly used practice denies access to systems until the user authenticates. When doing this, clients cannot see the resource *until authentication has occurred*.

URL filtering is another requirement in many organizations. URL filtering provides a way to accept or reject access to specific websites. This allows companies to reduce liability by users accessing inappropriate web content. Many firewalls can integrate with this type of scanning when used with another product.

Anti-virus is a requirement for any organization today. With more viruses being written, the last thing you want to have happen in your network is a virus outbreak. The Windows operating system is built to provide so many different functions that there are many ways that it can be exploited. In recent months, Microsoft has done a great job of coming out with security patches when or before an exploit is discovered. Typically though, when vulnerability is discovered an anti-virus company has a way to stop it much faster than Microsoft. An outbreak on your network can mean disaster, data loss, or loss of your job. Data is a company's most valuable asset today and loss of that data or access to it can cost companies millions of dollars or more per day. Firewalls can be used to perform virus scanning. These devices are usually deployed in a central area on the network. A tiered anti-virus solution is a requirement for any organization.

You should have anti-virus scanning on all of your desktops and servers to stop infections at the source. This will help prevent most virus outbreaks. Also, you should have anti-virus scanning on your Simple Mail Transfer Protocol (SMTP) mail forwarder and should be resident directly on your mail server. Your chances for a virus outbreak should be small as long as you keep all of those devices up to date with the appropriate virus definitions. There are also new technologies such as inline virus scanning in firewalls and other network appliances that can provide extra protection from viruses.

Patch management has become a truly Herculean effort with all of the software that an organization needs to run today. Patching operating systems and applications as soon as a vulnerability occurs is a must. With limited staff and increased software deployed, this task is almost impossible to accomplish. However, by providing an anti-virus system, you can provide a first level of defense against the spreading of malicious software or malware.

No matter what device or security you provide, everything usually comes down to some type of access token, usually a username and password. Using static user names and passwords is not enough anymore. Even fifteen to thirty days may be too long to keep the same password. Two-factor authentication, digital certificates, and personal entropy are leading the march to provide a stronger non-static type of authentication that is hard to break.

Your network has millions of packets transversing it everyday. Do you know what they are all doing? This is where an intrusion detection or intrusion detection and prevention device comes into play. These devices detect application- and network-based attacks. Intrusion detection devices sit on your network and watch traffic. They provide alerts for unusual traffic as well as TCP resets to close TCP sessions. The newer technology of intrusion detection and prevention provide the ability to stop malicious traffic altogether as well as to alert on it. However, heavy tuning of the products is required to make it effective.

Access into your network should be encrypted whenever possible. This ensures that parties that are not authorized to see your data do not get access to it by any means. IPSec VPN clients are one of the most popular ways to do this. This type of client provides strong encryption of your data as well as access to your internal resources without having them be publicly accessible. A new trend in VPN solutions is the Secure Sockets Layer (SSL) VPN. These products allow you to put more behind them and do not require pre deployment of a VPN client.

Making Your Security Come Together

In today's security battlefield it almost seems impossible to win. You must identify the best products and procedures for your organization. If you have all of the suggested security solutions, but not enough staff to manage it, then the solutions may not be effective enough. Simply having the appropriate products is not going to resolve all of your problems; you must effectively understand how to use and configure the products. There is no easy solution regarding the best way to go about securing your organization. This is why companies all over the world spend hundreds of millions of dollars on consulting companies to come in and make security decisions for them.

Understanding Firewall Basics

A firewall is a device that is part hardware, part software and is used to secure network access. Throughout this book, we will cover every aspect of the NetScreen firewall product line, its usage, and configuration. Before we begin to look at the various aspects of the NetScreen firewall, we need to look at some general firewall information. This will give you a better perspective on the pros and cons of the NetScreen firewall. Firewalls have come a long way since the original inception of the idea.

In the first part of this section we discuss the firewall in today's network. We look at the types of firewalls and how its importance has increased as well as there increased deployments in each network. Next, the many types of firewalls are discussed and contrasted and compared. Finally, we will review some common firewall concepts that will be used throughout the book.

Types of Firewalls

In the past, an organization may have had one firewall that protected the edge of the network. Some companies did not have their network attached to the Internet, or may have had perhaps one or two stations that would dial up to the Internet or to another computer that they needed to exchange data with. After the late 1990's, however, the need for the Internet, its information, and e-mail was undeniable.

With the requirement for instantaneous e-mail access comes the requirement for an always-on Internet connection. At first, companies would place their systems directly on the Internet with a public IP address. This, of course, is not a scalable solution for the long term. With limited IP addresses and unlimited threats, a better solution is required. At first, the border router that connected the Internet medium to the local network was used to provide a simple layer of access control between the two networks. With the need for better security, new types of firewalls were developed to meet the new needs for an Internet-enabled office. Better security, the ability for the firewall to provide more secured segments, and the need to thwart newer styles of attacks brought firewalls to where they are today.

Packet Filters

The most basic firewall technology is the packet filter. A packet filter is designed to filter packets based on source IP, destination IP, source port, destination port, and on a packet-per-packet basis to determine if that packet should be allowed through.

The basic security principles of a packet filter, such as allowing or denying packets based upon IP address, provide the minimum amount of required security. So then, where does the packet filter go wrong? A packet filter cannot determine if the packet is associated with any other packets that make up a session. A packet filter does a decent enough job of protecting networks that require basic security. The packet filter does not look to the characteristics of a packet, such as the type of application it is or the flags set in the TCP portion of the packet. Most of the time this will work for you in a basic security setting. However, there are ways to get around a packet filter. Because the packet filter does not maintain the state of exactly what is happening, it cannot determine the proper return packets that should be allowed through the connection.

For example, if you wanted to permit outbound access to DNS on UDP port 53, you would need to allow access for the return packet as well. A packet filter cannot determine what the return packet will in order to let it in. So now you have to allow access inbound for that DNS entry to return. So its source port would be UDP 53 and the inbound destination port would be the source port, which could be 1024-65535. Now add that up with all of the other applications you need to allow through the firewall and you can see the problem.

Because the packet filter has no way to dynamically create an access rule to allow inbound traffic, the packet filter is not effective as a security gateway.

Application Proxy

Application proxies provide one of the most secure types of access you can have in a security gateway. An application proxy sits between the protected network and the network that you want to be protected from. Every time an application makes a request, the application intercepts the request to the destination system. The application proxy initiates its own request, as opposed to actually passing the client's initial request. When the destination server responds back to the application proxy, the proxy responds back to the client as if it was the destination server. This way the client and the destination server never actually interact directly. This is the most secure type of firewall because the entire packet, including the application portion of the packet, can be completely inspected.

However, this is not dominant technology today for several reasons. The first downfall of the application proxy is performance. Because the application proxy essentially has to initiate its own second connection to the destination system, it takes twice the amount of connections to complete its interaction. On a small scale the slowdown will not be as a persistent problem, but when you get into a high-end requirement for many concurrent connections this is not a scalable technology. Furthermore, when the application proxy needs to interact with all of today's different applications, it needs to have some sort of engine to interact with the applications it is connecting to. For most highly used vanilla applications such as web browsing or HTTP this is not a problem. However, if you are using a proprietary protocol, an application proxy might not be the best solution for you.

Stateful Inspection

Stateful inspection is today's choice for the core inspection technology in firewalls. Stateful inspection functions like a packet filter by allowing or denying connections based upon the same types of filtering. However, a stateful firewall monitors the "state" of a communication. So, for example, when you connect to a web server and that web server has to respond back to you, the stateful firewall has the proper access open and ready for the responding connection. When the connection ends, that opening is closed. Among the big three names in firewalls today, all of them use this reflexive technology. There are, as mentioned above, protocols such as UDP and ICMP that do not have any sort of state to them. The major vendors recognize this and have to make their own decisions about what exactly constitutes a UDP or ICMP connection. Overall, though, most uses of stateful technology across vendors have been in use for some time and have worked the bugs out of those applications.

Many companies that implement stateful inspection use a more hybrid method between application proxy and stateful inspection when inspecting specific protocols. For example, if you were to do URL filtering on most firewalls, you may need to actually employ application proxy-type techniques to provide the proper inspection. This, much like application proxy firewalls, does not scale and is not a good idea for a large amount of users. Depending on the vendor and function, your mileage may vary.

Firewall Incarnate

A firewall can function many different ways, but always has the same basic requirements. A firewall is part hardware and part software, and the combination of each makes a huge difference. In this section we will look at the differences between an appliance-based firewall and a standard operating system (OS) running a firewall as an application.

First we will look at the firewall application that sits on an OS. In this case, there is an underlying operating system that runs on a standard computer system. The computer system consists of a processor, memory, and hard disk drive. The operating system will most likely be used for other functions without the firewall application. The operating system may be a multifunction operating system such as Microsoft Windows, Red Hat Linux, or Sun Solaris. To provide the utmost security, the operating system will have to be stripped down either by the end user or the manufacturer before it will be suitable for use as a secure gateway. The firewall software is then installed on top of the operating system and then the OS can be used to provide additional services or resources to other systems or users.

The other scenario is an operating system that has the firewall application integrated with it. In this case, the operating system is not used for any purpose other than to provide the firewall application. The device has a processor, memory, and flash memory for long-term storage. This device is an appliance.

In the first scenario, the device has some clear advantages. It does not require a single purpose device to be used and the underlying hardware most likely can be used for another purpose besides the firewall. This type of firewall can use third-party applications on the system and ultimately the firewall application may be able to have more advanced features because it has so much system behind it.

The firewall application is also limited based upon the limits of the specified hardware it is running upon, as well as the underlying OS. For example, if you wanted to add additional interfaces, it is limited to the specific type of hardware you are running. In most cases you can upgrade your hardware and then simply reinstall your application to upgrade the system.

In the second scenario we have an appliance whose sole purpose is to provide a firewall that willpass packets in and out as fast as possible while inspecting them based upon the defined security policy. The device's hardware is specialized for providing that single application. However, one disadvantage of using this type of firewall is that you cannot load other third-party applications on that system. Furthermore, the device may have some specific limitations, such as limited memory or physical interfaces, and the only way to upgrade the device is to do a forklift upgrade and replace the entire device.

Firewall Ideologies

No matter which type of firewall you choose there are some basic design considerations involved. Placement is usually the biggest question. Where is the most effective location to place my firewall to maximize its effectiveness? Is one firewall enough? How do I protect the servers that I need to make publicly accessible? These and many other questions come to mind when discussing firewall effectiveness. Unfortunately, the answers to all of these questions are beyond the scope of this section.

DMZ Concepts

The use of a DMZ and its overall design and implementation can be relatively simple or extremely complex, depending on the needs of the particular business or network system. The DMZ concept came into use as the need for separation of networks became more acute when we began to provide more access to services for individuals or partners outside the LAN infrastructure. One of the primary reasons that the DMZ has come into favor is the realization that a single type of protection is subject to failure. This failure can arise from configuration errors, planning errors, equipment failure, or deliberate action on the part of an internal employee or external attack force. The DMZ has proven to be more secure and to offer multiple layers of protection for the security of the protected networks and machines. It has also proven to be very flexible, scalable, and relatively robust in its ability to provide the protection we need. DMZ design now includes the ability to use multiple products (both hardware- and software-based) on multiple platforms to achieve the level of protection necessary, and DMZs are often designed to provide failover capabilities as well.

When we are working with a DMZ, we must have a common ground to work from. To facilitate understanding, we examine a number of conceptual paths for traffic flow in the following section. Before we look at the conceptual paths, let's make sure that we understand the basic configurations that can be used for firewall and DMZ location and how each of them can be visualized. In the following figures, we'll see and discuss these configurations. Please note that each of these configurations is useful on internal networks needing protection as well as protecting your resources from networks such as the Internet. Our first configuration is shown in Figure 1.8.

Designing & Planning...

Know What You Want to Secure First

As you begin your DMZ design process, you must first be clear about what your design is intended for. A design that is only intended to superficially limit internal users' access to the Internet, for instance, requires much less planning and design work than a system protecting resources from multiple access points or providing multiple services to the public network or users from remote locations. An appropriate path to follow for your pre-design path might look like this:

- Perform baseline security analysis of existing infrastructure, including OS and application analysis
- Perform baseline network mapping and performance monitoring
- Identify risk to resources and appropriate mitigation processes
- Identify potential security threats, both external and internal
- Identify needed access points from external sources
- Public networks
- VPN access
- Extranets
- Remote access services

Continued

■ Identify critical services

■ Plan your DMZ

Figure 1.8 A Basic Network with a Single Firewall

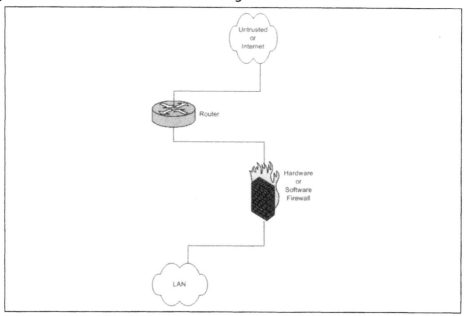

In Figure 1.8, we can see the basic configuration that would be used in a simple network situation in which there was no need to provide external services. This configuration would typically be used to begin to protect a small business or home network. It could also be used within an internal network to protect an inner network that had to be divided and isolated from the main network. This situation could include payroll, finance, or development divisions that need to protect their information and keep it away from general network use and view.

Figure 1.9 details a protection design that would allow for the implementation and provision of services outside the protected network. In this design, it would be absolutely imperative that rules be enacted to not allow the untrusted host to access the internal network. Security of the bastion host machine would be accomplished on the machine itself, and only minimal and absolutely necessary services would be enabled or installed on that machine. In this design, we might be providing a Web presence that did not involve e-commerce or the necessity to dynamically update content. This design would not be used for provision of virtual private network (VPN connections, FTP services, or other services that required other content updates to be performed regularly.

Figure 1.9 Basic Network, Single Firewall and Bastion Host (Untrusted Host)

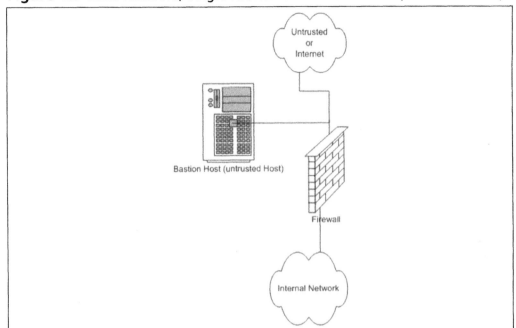

Figure 1.10 shows a basic DMZ structure. In this design, the bastion host is partially protected by the firewall. Rather than the full exposure that would result to the bastion host in Figure 1.9, this setup would allow us to specify that the bastion host in Figure 1.9 could be allowed full outbound connection, but the firewall could be configured to allow only port 80 traffic inbound to the bastion host (assuming it was a Web server) or others as necessary for connection from outside. This design would allow connection from the internal network to the bastion host if it was necessary. This design would potentially allow updating of Web server content from the internal network if allowed by firewall rule, which could allow traffic to and from the bastion host on specific ports as designated.

Figure 1.10 A Basic Firewall with a DMZ

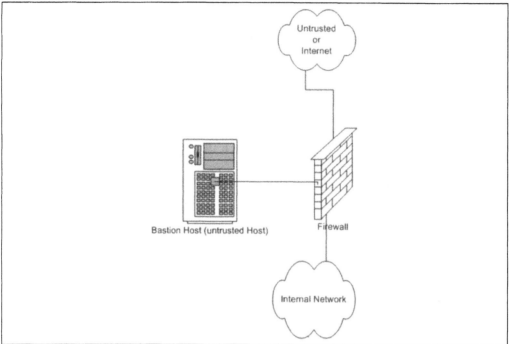

Figure 1.11 shows a generic dual-firewall DMZ configuration. In this arrangement, the bastion host can be protected from the outside and allowed to connect to or from the internal network. In this arrangement, like the conditions in Figure 1.10, flow can be controlled to and from both of the networks away from the DMZ. This configuration and method is more likely to be used if more than one bastion host is needed for the operations or services being provided.

Figure 1.11 A Dual Firewall with a DMZ

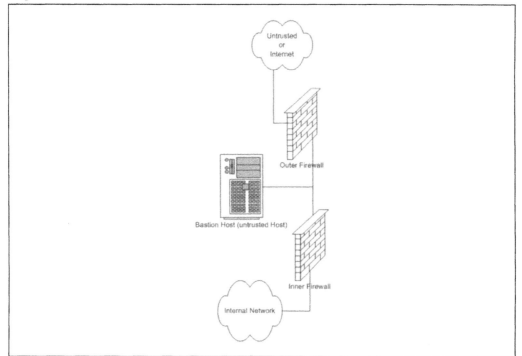

Traffic Flow Concepts

Now that we've had a quick tour of some generic designs, let's take a look at the way network communications traffic typically flows through them. Be sure to note the differences between the levels and the flow of traffic and protections offered in each of them.

Figure 1.12 illustrates the flow pattern for information through a basic single-firewall setup. This type of traffic control can be achieved through hardware or software and is the basis for familiar products such as Internet Connection Sharing (ICS) and the NAT functionality provided by digital subscriber line (DSL) and cable modems used for connection to the Internet. Note that flow is unrestricted outbound, but the basic configuration will drop all inbound connections that did not originate from the internal network.

Figure 1.12 Basic Single-Firewall Flow

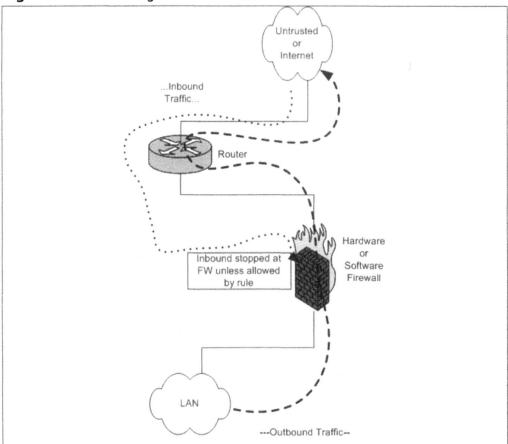

Figure 1.13 reviews the traffic flow in a network containing a bastion host and a single firewall. This network configuration does not produce a DMZ; the protection of the bastion host is configured individually on the host and requires extreme care in setup. Inbound traffic from the untrusted network or the bastion host is dropped at the firewall, providing protection to the internal network. Outbound traffic from the internal network is allowed.

Figure 1.13 A Basic Firewall with Bastion Host Flow

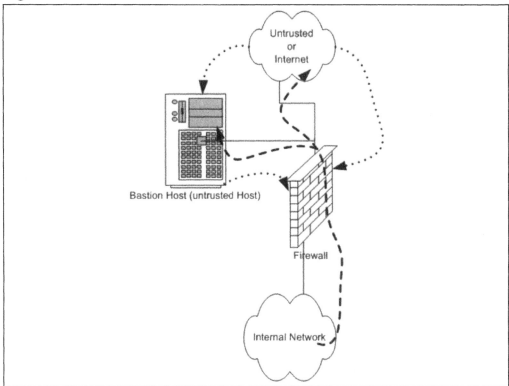

Figure 1.14 shows the patterns of traffic as we implement a DMZ design. In this form, inbound traffic flows through to the bastion host if allowed through the firewall and is dropped if destined for the internal network. Two-way traffic is permitted as specified between the internal network and the bastion host, and outbound traffic from the internal network flows through the firewall and out, generally without restriction.

Figure 1.14 A Basic Single Firewall with DMZ Flow

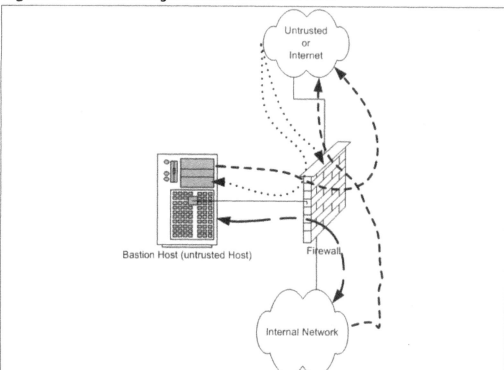

Figure 1.15 contains a more complex path of flow for information but provides the most capability in these basic designs to allow for configuration and provision of services to the outside. In this case, we have truly established a DMZ, separated and protected from both the internal and external networks. This type of configuration is used quite often when there is a need to provide more than one type of service to the public or outside world, such as e-mail, Web servers, DNS, and so forth. Traffic to the bastion host can be allowed or denied as necessary from both the external and internal networks, and incoming traffic to the internal network can be dropped at the external firewall. Outbound traffic from the internal network can be allowed or restricted either to the bastion host (DMZ network) or the external network.

Figure 1.15 A Dual Firewall with DMZ Flow

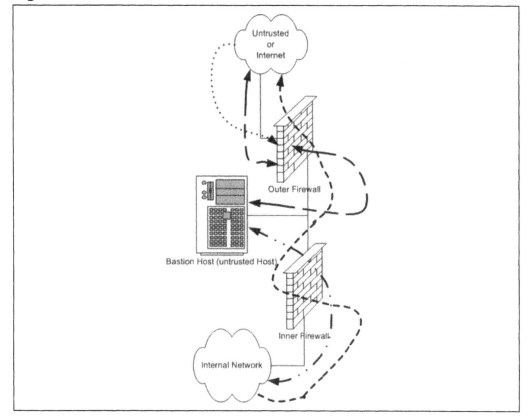

As you can see, there is a great amount of flexibility in the design and function of your protection mechanisms. In the sections that follow, we expand further on conditions for the use of different configurations and on the planning that it done to implement them.

Networks with and without DMZs

As we pursue our discussions about the creation of DMZ structures, it is appropriate to also take a look at the reasoning behind the various structures of the DMZ and when and where we'd want to implement a DMZ or perhaps use some other alternative.

During our preview of the concepts of DMZs, we saw in Figures 1.8 to 1.11 some examples of potential design for network protection and access. Your design may incorporate any or all of these types of configuration, depending on your organization's needs. For instance, Figure 1.8 shows a configuration that may occur in the case of a home network installation or perhaps with a small business environment that is isolated from the Internet and does not share information or need to provide services or information to outside customers or partners. This design would be suitable under these conditions, provided configuration is correct and monitored for change.

Figure 1.9 illustrates a network design with a bastion host located outside the firewall. In this design, the bastion host must be stripped of all unnecessary functionality and services and protected locally with appropriate file permissions and access control mechanisms. This design would be used when an organization needs to provide minimal services to an external network, such as a Web server. Access to the internal network from the bastion host is generally not allowed, because this host is absolutely subject to compromise.

Figure 1.10 details the first of the actual DMZ designs and incorporates a screened subnet. In this type of design, the firewall controls the flow of information from network to network and provides more protection to the bastion host from external flows. This design might be used when it is necessary to be able to regularly update the content of a Web server, or provide a front end for mail services or other services that need contact from both the internal and external networks. Although better for security purposes than Figure 1.9, this design still produces an untrusted relationship in the bastion host in relation to the internal network.

Finally, Figure 1.11 provides a design that allows for the placement of many types of service in the DMZ. Traffic can be very finely controlled through access at the two firewalls, and services can be provided at multiple levels to both internal and external networks.

In the next section, we profile some of the advantages and disadvantages of the common approaches to DMZ architecture and provide a checklist of sorts to help you to make a decision about the appropriate use (or not) of the DMZ for protection.

Pros and Cons of DMZ Basic Designs

Table 1.6 details the advantages and disadvantages of the various types of basic design discussed in the preceding section.

Table 1.6 Pros and Cons of Basic DMZ Designs

Basic Design	Advantages	Disadvantages	Appropriate Utilization
Single firewall	Inexpensive, fairly easy configuration, low maintenance	Much lower security capabilities, no growth or expansion potential	Home, small office/home office (SOHO), small business without need to provide services to others
Single firewall with bastion host	Lower cost than more robust alternatives	Bastion host extremely vulnerable to compromise, inconvenient to update content, loss of functionality other than for absolutely required services; not scalable	Small business without resources for more robust implementation or static content being provided that doesn't require frequent updates
Single firewall with screened subnet and bastion host	Firewall provides protection to both internal network and bastion host, limiting some of the potential breach possibilities of an unprotected bastion host	Single point of failure; some products limit network addressing to DMZ in this configuration to public addresses, which might not be economic or possible in your network	Networks requiring access to the bastion host for updating of information
Dual firewall with DMZ	Allows for establishment of multiple service-providing hosts in the DMZ; protects bastion hosts in DMZ from both networks, allows	Requires more hardware and software for implementation of this design; more configuration work and monitoring required	Larger operations that require the capability to offer multiple types of Web access and services to both the internal and external networks involved

Continued

Table 1.6 Pros and Cons of Basic DMZ Designs

Basic Design	Advantages	Disadvantages	Appropriate Utilization
	much more granular control of resources and access; removes single point of failure and attack		

Configuring & Implementing...

Bastion Hosts

Bastion hosts must be individually secured and hardened because they are always in a position that could be attacked or probed. This means that before placement, a bastion host must be stripped of unnecessary services, fully updated with the latest service packs, hot fixes, and updates, and isolated from other trusted machines and networks to eliminate the possibility that its compromise would allow for connection to (and potential compromise of) the protected networks and resources. This also means that a machine being used for this purpose should have no user accounts relative to the protected network or directory services structure, which could lead to enumeration of your internal network.

DMZ Design Fundamentals

DMZ design, like security design, is always a work in progress. As in security planning and analysis, we find DMZ design carries great flexibility and change potential to keep the protection levels we put in place in an effective state. The ongoing work is required so that the system's security is always as high as we can make it within the constraints of time and budget while still allowing appropriate users and visitors to access the information and services we provide for their use. You will find that the time and funds spent in the design process and preparation for the implementation are very good investments if the process is focused and effective; this will lead to a high level of success and a good level of protection for the network you are protecting. In this section of the chapter, we explore the fundamentals of the design process. We incorporate the information we discussed in relation to security and traffic flow to make decisions about how our initial design should look. Additionally, we'll build on that information and review some other areas of concern that could affect the way we design our DMZ structure.

> **NOTE**
>
> In this section we look at design of a DMZ from a logical point of view. Physical design and configuration are covered in following chapters, based on the vendor-based solution you are interested in deploying.

Why Design Is So Important

Design of the DMZ is critically important to the overall protection of your internal network—and the success of your firewall and DMZ deployment. The DMZ design can incorporate sections that isolate incoming VPN traffic, Web traffic, partner connections, employee connections, and public access to information provided by your organization. Design of the DMZ structure throughout the organization can protect internal resources from internal attack. As we discussed in the security section, it has been well documented that much of the risk of data loss, corruption, and breach actually exists *inside* the network perimeter. Our tendency is to protect assets from external harm but to disregard the dangers that come from our own internal equipment, policies, and employees.

These attacks or disruptions do not arise solely from disgruntled employees, either. Many of the most damaging conditions that occur are because of inadvertent mistakes made by well-intentioned employees. Each and all of these entry points is a potential source of loss for your organization and ultimately can provide an attack point to defeat your other defenses. Additionally, the design of your DMZ will allow you to implement a multilayered approach to securing your resources that does not leave a single point of failure in your plan. This minimizes the problems and loss of protection that can occur because of misconfiguration of rule sets or access control lists (ACLs), as well as reducing the problems that can occur due to hardware configuration errors. In the last chapters of this book, we look at how to mitigate risk through testing of your network infrastructure to make sure your firewalls, routers, switches, and hosts are thoroughly hardened so that when you do deploy your DMZ segment, you can see for yourself that it is in fact secure from both internal as well as external threats.

Designing End-to-End Security for Data Transmission Between Hosts on the Network

Proper DMZ design, in conjunction with the security policy and plan developed previously, allows for end-to-end protection of the information being transmitted on the network. The importance of this capability is explored more fully later in the chapter, when we review some of the security problems inherent in the current implementation of TCP/IPv4 and the transmission of data. The use of one or more of the many firewall products or appliances currently available will most often afford the opportunity not only to block or filter specific protocols but also to protect the data as it is being transmitted. This protection may take the form of encryption and can utilize the available transports to protect data as well. Additionally, proper utilization of the technologies available within this design can provide for the necessary functions previously detailed in the concepts of AAA and CIA, utilizing the multilayer approach to protection that we have discussed in earlier sections. This need to provide end-to-end security requires that we are conversant with and remember basic network traffic patterns and protocols. The next few sections help remind us about these and further illustrate the need to design the DMZ with this capability in mind.

Traffic Flow and Protocol Fundamentals

Another of the benefits of using a DMZ design that includes one or more firewalls is the opportunity to control traffic flow into and out of the DMZ much more cohesively and with much more granularity and flexibility. When the firewall product in use (either hardware or software) is a product designed above the home-use level, the capability usually exists to not only control traffic that is flowing in and out of the network or DMZ through packet filtering based on port numbers but often to allow or deny the use of entire protocols. For instance, the rule set might include a statement that blocks communication via ICMP, which would block protocol 1. A statement that allowed IPSec traffic where it was desired to allow traffic utilizing ESP or AH would be written allowing protocol 50 for ESP or 51 for Authentication Header (AH). (For a listing of the protocol IDs, visit www.iana.org/assignments/protocol-numbers.) Remember that like the rule of security that follows the principle of least privilege, we must include in our design the capability to allow only the absolutely necessary traffic into and out of the various portions of the DMZ structure.

Summary

In this chapter we reviewed the many different fundamental concepts that are important to networking. First we reviewed the OSI model. As you can see, the OSI model is very important to understand. It is used throughout this book and other documentation from Juniper Networks. In fact, almost any documentation referencing networking uses the OSI model as a base to explain how networking functions. An important fact to remember is that the OSI model is just that; a model. As you saw in the explanation of the TCP/IP model, the OSI model does not exactly fit together with TCP/IP. However, once you understand TCP/IP and how it works you will understand it for all platforms and applications.

If you were to truly have a book titled "Understanding Security Basics," it could easily span over a thousand pages. In this chapter we have brought together a concise version of that material to help you begin to understand the expansive world that is security. In the battle for the secure enterprise, the most important thing to remember is that there is no single solution to secure everything. Many products claim to have the silver bullet for securing your network, but this is nothing more than marketing. Each company has different restrictions on resources and has different security requirements.

In the last section we reviewed the basics of firewalls. The evolution of firewalls has been a long and harrowed path. As new threats come to light there will always be new technologies that will be created to stop these threats. The concept of a DMZ is an important one to understand. Segmenting your important hosts is one of the critical things you can do to secure your network.

Solutions Fast Track

Understanding Networking

☑ The OSI model is used as a reference for all networking protocols.

☑ TCP/IP is used as the core networking protocol today on both the Internet and in the enterprise.

☑ The TCP protocol has clear defined points where a session begins and ends.

Understanding Security Basics

☑ Security is a process that is never finished; security needs are constantly changing as well as the needs for new technologies.

☑ There is no single product or solution that can be used to ensure your network's security.

☑ Each organization has its own specific needs to best help it minimize security risks.

Understanding Firewall Basics

☑ NetScreen firewalls use stateful inspection to ensure the security of connections passing though the firewall.

☑ Firewall technology is constantly changing to meet the security needs of today's organizations.

☑ DMZ design depends on the designer's ability to accurately assess the actual risks in order to design an adequate structure.

Frequently Asked Questions

The following Frequently Asked Questions, answered by the authors of this book, are designed to both measure your understanding of the concepts presented in this chapter and to assist you with real-life implementation of these concepts. To have your questions about this chapter answered by the author, browse to **www.syngress.com/solutions** and click on the **"Ask the Author"** form. You will also gain access to thousands of other FAQs at ITFAQnet.com.

Q: If the OSI model does not match the way in which TCP/IP functions, then why is it still used?

A: The OSI model is just that; a model. The OSI model was to be originally used as the model for the development of networking protocols. However, developers found the specifications too rigid for practical use. Most networking protocol suites do not follow the OSI model fully, but do follow the layered concept that was identified first during the development of the OSI model.

Q: Why would I want to use a NetScreen firewall appliance when I could just use Red Hat Linux with ipchains?

A: A NetScreen firewall appliance is built with one thing in mind; security. It doesn't have to provide any other services. There are many more services and applications that run on conventional operating systems that can contain security vulnerabilities. Furthermore, NetScreen does not have a hard drive. This is the most likely part to fail on a computer when running for an extended period of time. Finally, the NetScreen firewall architecture runs on Application-Specific Integrated Circuit (ASIC) chips. These are specifically designed to perform special tasks providing more performance with less horsepower, while general purpose processors are not optimized for networking performance. This requires you to have more horsepower to provide the same function as a lower end NetScreen firewall.

Q: You mention that each organization has different security needs. Why don't you provide a definite answer that can resolve my security issues?

A: Every organization has different types of requirements that they need to provide for their users. Some companies may have hundreds of web servers, others just a few file sharing servers. There are some good baselines that have been outlined that do a good job of securing your resources, such as every organization's need for anti-virus. However, application-level protection may not be required for some organizations.

Q: Do I really need a DMZ? It only confuses my users.

A: Segregated networks are a requirement for any company that has resources that have to be accessible to the Internet or resources that everyone in the company does not need access to. The slight complexities that the DMZ creates simply do not out weigh its benefits.

Q: If I follow your guidelines for security, is this all I will ever need to secure my network?

A: Your organization's security requirements are something that should never be written in stone. You should always be on the lookout for new technologies and methodologies that can provide additional security to your environment.

Q: Why do I need to know so much about networking?

A: Knowing networking allows you to truly understand the risks that can occur in a network. When using networking, the more that you know about it, the more options you give yourself. For example, if you were trying to build a house to provide protection against a hurricane and all you knew was using sticks and straw to build with, your chances of building a successful house are close to zero. However, if you know about several construction styles then you would have more flexibility in choosing methods and materials that would provide you a better chance for creating a better house.

Chapter 2

Dissecting the NetScreen Firewall

Solutions in this Chapter:

- The NetScreen Security Product Offerings
- The NetScreen Firewall Core Technologies
- The NetScreen Firewall Product Line

☑ Summary

☑ Solutions Fast Track

☑ Frequently Asked Questions

55

Introduction

This chapter will introduce you to the NetScreen firewall product. We'll begin by looking at all of Juniper Networks' security products, exploring the wide range of products available, and allowing you to determine which is best suited for your security needs. A well-designed and properly implemented security infrastructure must be multitiered. Juniper Networks offers three separate security product lines (discussed shortly) that can help mitigate your security risks.

Juniper Networks delivers an integrated firewall and virtual private network (VPN) solution, the NetScreen firewall. The firewall product line has several tiers of appliances and systems. This allows you to choose the right hardware for your network, giving the precise fit for your needs. Juniper also offers a Secure Sockets Layer (SSL) VPN product. The Secure Access series offers a clientless remote access solution as well as a collaboration tool. With a clientless VPN approach, you remove the need for software deployment and management of the remote clients. You can easily deploy the SSL portal to thousands of users in mere hours. This is a great boon to any organization.

Also available in the SSL VPN product line is the secure meeting application. This allows for online collaborative meetings where users can share their desktops and engage in chat. These are also secured by SSL. You can use this feature to do presentations or to perform remote support. It's a great tool for any organization.

The last part to the security product line is *intrusion detection and prevention* (IDP). Where some products only allow you to detect incoming malicious traffic, the IDP allows you to fully prevent it from continuing on your network. The IDP is a required device for any network.

We'll be looking at the core technologies of the NetScreen firewalls. These are the frameworks that are used through out this book. This discussion will give you an idea of the features of the NetScreen firewall and will prepare you to actually implement these solutions on the NetScreen firewall. We will look at fundamental concepts such as *zones*. Zones are used to logically separate areas of the network. This allows a more granular approach when you begin to write access rules to allow or deny network traffic.

In the last section of the chapter we will look thoroughly at the NetScreen firewall products. The products range from small office devices that would allow for VPN connectivity into a central location, up to and including the carrier class products that can serve as much as twelve gigabits per second of firewall traffic. That is a gigantic amount of throughput for a firewall. This allows you to take your network to new heights with the options provided in the NetScreen firewall product line.

The NetScreen Security Product Offerings

NetScreen is the fastest growing firewall product line on the market today. It has clinched the number two spot among the worldwide security appliance market. The NetScreen product line is robust and competitive, and is now part of Juniper networks. As of April 16th 2004, Juniper Networks completed its purchase of NetScreen for four billion dollars. Juniper chose to purchase NetScreen to enter the enterprise market space. Previously, Juniper focused on the carrier class market for high-end routers. Juniper is aiming high and attempting to compete directly with Cisco for the spot of number one firewall appliance vendor, as well number one router vendor in the world.

- The NetScreen firewall appliance is Juniper's firewall/VPN solution. Throughout the book, the firewall is referred to as a NetScreen firewall, as Juniper chose to keep the NetScreen firewall product name for brand recognition. The other products in the NetScreen security line all kept their original names as well.

- The NetScreen IDP intrusion detection and prevention product is used to provide protection against network attacks. The IDP can alert you, log events, and capture attacks as they occur. This product offers several modes of operation that allow it to be used in one of several different network designs. It can also prevent against worms, viruses, and Trojans.

- The third part to the NetScreen security product line is the SSL VPN. The NetScreen Secure Access SSL VPN allows for clientless access into your network. The SSL VPN is currently the fastest growing product line for Juniper. The Secure Access SSL VPN appliance is the market leader in its segment with forty-five percent of the market share as of the first quarter of 2004. An offshoot from the SSL VPN product line is the secure meeting product. Secure Meeting can be integrated with the SSL VPN appliance, or it can be run on its own dedicated appliance. It provides web conferencing collaboration to share your desktop and documents over the web.

Firewalls

Juniper Networks' premier security platform is the NetScreen firewall product line. This product line provides integrated firewall and Internet Protocol Security (IPSec) VPN solutions in a single appliance. The NetScreen firewall core is based upon the stateful inspection technology. This provides a connection-oriented security model by verifying the validity of every connection while still providing a high-performance architecture. The NetScreen firewalls themselves are based on a custom-built architecture consisting of Application-Specific Integrated Circuit (ASIC) technology. ASIC is designed to perform a specific task and to do that task at a higher performance level than a general-purpose processor. ASIC connects over a high-speed bus interface to the core processor of the firewall unit a RISC (reduced instruction set computer) CPU.

The firewall platform also contains additional technologies to increase your network's security. First, the products support *deep inspection*. This technology allows you to inspect traffic at the application level to look for application-level attacks. This can help prevent the next worm from attacking your Web servers, or someone from trying to send illegal commands to your SMTP (Simple Mail Transfer Protocol) server. The *deep inspection* technology includes a regularly updated database as well as the ability for you to create your own regular expression-based signatures. All of the appliances include the ability to create IPSec VPNs to secure your traffic. The integrated VPN technology has received both the Common Criteria and the ICSA (wwwicsalabs.com) firewall certifications. This means that the IPSec VPN technologies have a good cross -compatibility as well as standards compliance. Juniper also offers two client VPN solutions to pair with the NetScreen firewall. First, NetScreen-Remote provides the user with the ability to create an IPSec connection to any NetScreen firewall or any IPSec compliant device. The second client product is NetScreen-Security Client. This product cannot only create IPSec tunnels, but also includes a personal firewall to secure the end user's system. The NetScreen firewall product line leverages the technologies of Trend Micro's industry-leading antivirus software. This allows you to scan traffic as it passes directly through the firewall, thus mitigating the risks of viruses spreading throughout your network.

The NetScreen firewall platform provides you with three management options:

- **Command Line Interface (CLI)** The CLI provides the most granular control over the platform through straightforward interaction with the operation system (ScreenOS).

- **Web User Interface (WebUI)** The WebUI is a streamlined web-based application with a user-friendly interface that allows you to easily manage the NetScreen appliance. Both WebUI and CLI are consistent among all of the NetScreen firewall products – this means that once you learn on one firewall model (for example, 5GT), you can easily apply your knowledge to other models (such as 208) in the NetScreen firewall product line.

- **NetScreen Security Manager (NSM)** A centralized enterprise class solution that allows you to manage your entire NetScreen firewall infrastructure. The NSM not only provides a central console to manage your firewalls, it also provides consolidated logging and reporting. This is a great option that allows you to see all of your network's activity from a central location.

SSL VPN

The need for remote access to a company's resources is at an all-time high. The traditional mode in the past was using IPSec VPN clients. However, in many situations, deploying and managing remote VPN clients can be very impractical, especially when you consider that you will need to maintain the software overtime. Juniper Networks offers a product called Secure Access SSL VPN. This product allows you to secure your internal resources behind a single entry point device. The remote users only require a web browser capable of SSL encryption. The user connects to the SSL VPN gateway and begins his or her secure session. At this point the user can access many different types of resources. This provides secure ubiquitous client access, and because you don't have to deploy a client, you can easily deploy access to thousands of users in a matter of hours.

An important feature of the SSL VPN is client-side security. The SSL VPN offers several solutions that provide additional security to the end user's system. First, the Secure Access product offers something called the *host checker*. The host checker performs client-side checks for specific options. It can check to ensure the existence and the validity of any file on the client's system, such as an antivirus scanner or a personal firewall. It can check for the existence of specific registry settings as well. Finally, the host checker can tie into other third-party products and talk to the applications running on the client's system. One example would by the Sygate host integrity-checking client. It can ensure that the client meets or exceeds the company's defined standard for a remote software load. Based on the options that pass or fail, you can give the end user various levels of access.

If the user was to have an antivirus program running on the system, you could allow the user to access network file shares, as well as the first level access of the web mail. If the user has a personal firewall running as well, the user would perhaps be allowed to access servers using Microsoft terminal services, as well as the two other levels of access. The host checking functions allow you to provide granular access to network resources based upon the client's own security. A second security process can run, which is called the *cache cleaner*. The cache cleaner can identify all of the files cached by the web browser and delete them after the client's session is completed. This ensures that no trace of the client's session is left on that remote system.

There are three levels of application access available through the SSL VPN device:

- **Level 1** The first level of access allows you to access web-based and file-based resources. When accessing websites or web-based applications, all of the HTML (Hypertext Markup Language), JavaScript, and Java is rewritten to direct access through the SSL VPN gateway. This ensures that access to all resources can be secured and not directed to another location without the administrator's explicit configuration. In the first level of access you can also access both CIFS/SMB (common Internet fire system/server message block) Microsoft file shares as well as UNIX standards network file system (NFS) shares. Access to these resources is all done through a web interface where you can upload and download files to modify them. Also included is a java-based component that allows you to access systems via either Telnet or secure shell (SSH).

- **Level 2** The second level of access uses a component called *secure application manager*. Secure application manager runs as either a browser-based java component or an Active-X component. This allows you to access resources via a client-initiated Transmission Control Protocol (TCP) or User Datagram Protocol (UDP) unicast connection. You can use this to access various popular applications such as Microsoft Exchange, Citrix, and Microsoft Terminal Services.

- **Level 3** The third level of access allows full network connectivity, allowing the clients to connect into the network as if they were directly on the network. This allows systems to connect back to the client using applications such as X-Windows.

The SSL VPN product also provides a secure collaboration tool called *secure meeting*. Secure meeting allows users to share applications and collaborate from any Internet-connected computer. This is similar to services such as WebEx. It is a powerful tool and can be used on an SSL VPN device or as a standalone solution. The Secure Access products provide application-level logging, allowing you to record exactly what each user has done. The Secure Access product line offers the enterprise a great solution to integrate as a remote access solution.

IDP

Juniper Networks' IDP product provides exemplary intrusion detection and prevention for today's enterprise networks. The IDP is a network appliance that is designed to provide intrusion detection and prevention. It can be deployed in several different configurations to provide its functionality. First, it can be deployed as a non-intrusive network traffic sniffer to provide a method to detect incoming attacks and record them and alert on them. In this mode you can easily install them in your network to provide a network baseline or to quickly replace your other IDS devices. Second, your can install the device in gateway mode. This allows you to use the IDP as an active defense mechanism. In this mode it provides several ways to stop network attacks. It can close the connection or drop the connection on both the client and server sides. It can also capture the session for later analysis. This is great for doing forensic research on the attack.

The IDP platform provides a trademarked multi-method detection (MMD), which combines several detection mechanisms. Different types of applications require different methods of detecting attacks. The applied detection methods ensure that critical attacks are detected, providing you the information you need to identify network threats in your environment. The IDP currently provides nine different mechanisms to detect attacks:

- **Stateful signatures** detect known attack patterns. This mechanism allows you to detect more attacks and reduce the incidence of false positive alerts. A false positive is an alert that falsely detects an attack. A false positive can take away your valuable time and resources.

- **Protocol anomaly detection** reviews the different types of connections that go through the IDP and acknowledges any connections that deviate from the proper protocol standards. This can be used to detect new attacks and expose vulnerabilities.

- **Backdoor detection** looks through interactive traffic for possible malicious communications. A backdoor is an application that resides on a host system unknown to the end user. These malicious applications, when installed on a user's system, can allow attackers to access your network's resources. When using the backdoor detection mechanism on your IDP, you can identify these intrusive connections and then block these connections to eliminate this harmful traffic.

- **Traffic anomaly detection** allows you to look further than a single packet or a single session. It allows you to look across multiple sessions and identify anomalous traffic. An example of this type of traffic is a reconnaissance attack such as a port scan. A port scan is a series of sessions or connections that individually may not raise a red flag. However, when you add many of these probing packets together, this constitutes a traffic anomaly, which can be detected with this mode of operation.

- **Network honeypot** mimics a system's services pretending to be a vulnerable system. This entices an attacker to access these services first, drawing attention away from your critical systems.

- **Layer-2 detection** monitors network traffic on the second layer of the Open Systems Interconnect (OSI) model. This allows you to detect address resolution protocol (ARP)attacks on your network.

- **DoS detection** allows you to detect certain types of Denial of Service (DoS) attacks. Denial of Service attacks can bring your network to its knees and early detection is critical to mitigate these attacks.

- **Spoofing detection** gives you the ability to detect spoofed IP packets, A spoofed IP packet is a packet that seems to be coming from a host, but really is coming from a malicious attacker.

- **Compound signatures** combine multiple detection methods for complex attack detection. Juniper Networks combines stateful signatures and protocol anomaly to create a powerful detection mechanism.

Managing the IDP is made simple with its integrated management system. Logging of attacks is extremely detailed, providing you with extensive information to determine what is happening on your network.

The IDP has a component called the *policy editor*. The policy editor is a graphical interface that allows for granular control over what type of traffic you want to detect and prevent against. Your configuration and signature information is readily available for you to use from within the policy editor, allowing you to easily create effective policies, thus providing detection and prevention from network attacks. The IDP product is an excellent product to use in your network to provide a new layer of security for your organization.

The NetScreen Firewall Core Technologies

The NetScreen firewall platform was designed from scratch, allowing the developers to come up with new ideas for how a firewall should work by combining both conventional and original security approaches. These concepts will be used through out the book time and time again.

Zones

Zones are the core of the NetScreen architecture. A zone can be defined as a logical area. There are several types of zones that can exist on a NetScreen firewall. The first and most commonly used zone is the *security zone*. A security zone is a segment of network space where security measures are applied. These are used to determine the different network locations assigned to a NetScreen firewall. For example, the two most commonly used security zones are *trust* and *untrust*. The *trust zone* is assigned to the internal Local Area Network (LAN) and the *untrust zone* is assigned to the Internet. The name of the zone is arbitrary, but is used to help the administrator determine what the zone is used for. Security zones are used in policy configuration and are a key component of them.

Another zone type is the *tunnel zone*. Tunnel zones are used in conjunction with tunnel interfaces. They are defined as a logical segment to which a VPN tunnel interface is bound. The last type of zone is a *function zone*. An example of a function is the MGT or management zone. It specifies that an interface is to be used only for management traffic and will not allow traffic to be routed over it. A function zone is defined as a physical or logical entity that performs a specific function. The use of zones allows you to clearly define the separation between two or more areas. The NetScreen firewall product line is littered with the use of zones. You will find them used in every chapter of this book.

Virtual Routers

A firewall is nothing more then a glorified router. It essentially sends traffic from one location to another, determining the best path based on its routing table. The firewall has the ability to allow or deny traffic. The NetScreen firewall provides simple routing services, as you would expect, but it also offers much more. A normal device that uses IP has a single routing table. The routing table contains all of the known or learned routes. A NetScreen device uses the concept of the *virtual router*, or VR.

A virtual router is a logical construct within a NetScreen device. It provides you with multiple routing tables on the same device. The virtual router has many uses. Virtual routers are bound to zones, and the zones are bound to interfaces. The NetScreen router will function much like a standard firewall device with one routing table. However, using two separate routing tables gives you the ability to separate your routing domain. For example, if you were to run Open Shortest Path First (OSPF) internally and border gateway protocol (BGP) externally, you would have two separate routing domains. This allows you to securely separate your internally trusted routes with your externally untrusted routes. In chapter five we will discuss the configurations and virtues of virtual routers on NetScreen firewalls in much more depth.

Interface Modes

As we've discussed, a NetScreen firewall, by default, operates initially as a router. It allows for each physical interface to use an IP address, allowing traffic to be forwarded between each interface. A NetScreen firewall, however, is not limited to this traditional type of firewall configuration.

A NetScreen firewall allows its physical interfaces to run in a special mode called *transparent mode*. Transparent mode allows you to put the NetScreen firewall into Layer two mode, which operates at the network layer, allowing a NetScreen firewall to act as a switch, while still providing normal firewall filtering. This serves many purposes. If, for example, you have a flat network with one subnet and no routing, but still want to separate your network and provide security for a few critical devices, you can install a NetScreen firewall in transparent mode.

Policies

A *policy* is a statement that allows or denies traffic based upon a defined set of specifications. The base specifications are source IP address, destination IP address, source zone, destination zone, and service or port. With this information, you can create a policy. There are three types of policies, and they are checked from top down in this order: *inrazone, interzone,* and *global*. By default, there is an invisible global policy that denies any traffic from passing through the NetScreen. So if the traffic is not implicitly allowed by another policy, it is denied. Creating policies allows you to perform one of three actions on the traffic: allow the traffic, deny the traffic from passing, or tunnel the traffic into a VPN. Allowing the traffic is the action you would want to use when the matching traffic is traffic you want to pass through the firewall. You would want to deny traffic when you want to prevent traffic from passing through your firewall. Finally, you would tunnel traffic when you want to permit traffic as well as put the traffic into a VPN tunnel. Each NetScreen device has a limited number of policies. This is a license restriction, as well as a capacity restriction. You are not allowed to create new policies once you reach the maximum amount of policies per device. Juniper does this to ensure the performance numbers that are specified for the specification sheets. It would not make much sense to allow a low-end 5-GT appliance to run 40,000 policies, only to have the performance be at 1Mbps. These restrictions are not modifiable and are restrictions of each platform. There are many different elements involved in configuring an advanced policy. This includes traffic shaping, user authentication, NAT (network address translation), alarms, Uniform Resource Locator (URL) filtering, and scheduling. This provides a great deal of configuration options.

Administering policies can be done in one of three ways: from the WebUI, CLI, or the NetScreen Security Manager. Each method creates the same end result, but performing each task is slightly different. On some competitive firewall products, using access lists can be frustrating. It can be a huge pain to reorder, view, and manage access lists. When the NetScreen platform was designed, it was calculated with those pains in mind. Once you start looking at the configurations in the next chapter, you will begin to understand the power of the NetScreen and its CLI.

VPN

The other half of a NetScreen firewall is a VPN device. It can facilitate both site-to-site VPNs as well as client-to-site VPNs, or as NetScreen calls them, "dial-up VPNs." Juniper's NetScreen firewall supports all of the standard elements you would expect a VPN device to include. It supports Internet key exchange (IKE), authentication header (AH), encapsulating security payload (ESP), tunnel mode, transport, aggressive mode, quick mode, main mode, MD5 (message-digest algorithm 5), SHA-1 (secure hash algorithm 1), DES (data encryption standard), 3DES (triple data encryption standard), AES-128 (advanced encryption standard), and Perfect forward secrecy to name a few. Juniper gives you several options when configuring a firewall on a NetScreen appliance. There are two different methodologies you can use: a route-based or a policy-based VPN.

A *policy-based* VPN allows the creation of a VPN through a policy or rule. This is the traditional method and it is similar to other VPN products. This gives you a simplified method to create VPNs.

A *route-based* VPN uses a special type of virtual interface to connect via a VPN. This virtual interface, called a *tunnel interface*, allows you to provide special types of services. It would allow you to run routing protocols between these two virtual interfaces. You could run OSPF, which requires two devices to be directly connected. This, of course, would not normally be possible over the Internet, but if you create a route-based VPN between two NetScreen firewalls, this limitation for OSPF is removed because of this special virtual interface.

Deep Inspection

Today's firewalls have to provide much more then just your regular Layer 3 and Layer 4 inspection. Filtering your ports, protocols, and IP addresses no longer provides the security necessary for preventing sophisticated attacks. You need the ability to look inside the packet for specific data that indicates an attack. A packet product, such as an IDP, is far more capable of pointing out an attack than a basic firewall. Typically, any device designed to specifically provide a service will do a much better job than a multifunction device. There are many instances where the implementation of application layer inspection can be a great benefit to a network.

A smaller network may not have the same management needs and financial means to gainfully install an IDP device. The integration of application-level inspection may be a better fit. Application-level scanning in an integrated device can also be used provide a second level of protection to your network by blocking specific attacks.

Deep inspection technology is the next step in the evolution of firewalls. Deep inspection allows you to inspect traffic at the application layer, relying on regular expressions (Regex) to determine what content in a packet is malicious. For example, if a worm spreading on the Internet attempts to exploit your IIS (Internet Information Server) Web server vulnerabilities by sending a specific string of characters to your Web server,. a custom signature can be written to identify that attack string. By applying the custom signature to a policy, the traffic in that policy would be inspected for that specific string. Deep Inspection is truly the next jump in evolution for the firewall. Look to the future to provide much more strength in this field for development.

Damage & Defense...

Application-Level Inspection

Firewalls have conventionally focused on layer three and layer four filtering. This means that the connection is only filtered based on IP addressing and TCP and UDP ports and the options set at those layers. This can prevent systems that you do not intend to access your servers from accessing them. What do you do, though, when an attacker can use your firewall configuration against you? Suppose, for example, that your firewall is blocking all ports except for HTTP.

The attacker simply passes right through your allowed port and manipulates your web application without you detecting it on your firewall. It is simply not aware of attacks at the application level. Now even though your Web server is on a separate DMZ (de-militarized zone) than your database server, the attacker uses your web application to access the secured database and takes your customers' credit card information and identities. If you think that this is nothing but a good story, think again. This type of attack goes on every day and many organizations are not aware of this kind of threat. Talented individuals that understand web applications and their designs can easily snake through your applications and extract data from your database.

So does this mean that you need to disable access to your Web server and dismantle your e-commerce efforts? Of course not. You must, however, use security products that provide application-level inspection to attempt to identify these attacks. The best method is to first have a pen-

Continued

www.syngress.com

etration test done on your application to determine what type of vulnerabilities your applications may have. Next, begin implementing products that can determine what are attacks and what is normal traffic. The deep inspection software integrated into the NetScreen firewall can help protect against many of the unstructured attacks that can be damaging to your Web server. However, structured attacks need a stronger tool such as the IDP to mitigate the risks of these attacks.

Using tools such as IDPs and the deep inspection technology is not something that you just turn on and hope for the best. To make this type of application-level inspecting technologies work effectively you need to tune them for your network. This can take a great deal of effort and time to ensure that your network is using these devices effectively. Many times organizations purchase devices like this hoping that they will ensure that a poorly written application will be completely secured. Many times some simple programming techniques can enhance the security of your applications greatly.

Device Architecture

The NetScreen hardware architecture was developed to be a purpose-built device. Developed from the ground up to provide exceptional throughput, the firewall devices provide an amazing device that leads the pack in firewall design. Juniper's NetScreen firewall product line is a layered architecture, as seen in Figure 2.1, designed to provide optimal performance for critical security applications. The top layer of the NetScreen firewall architecture is the integrated security application. This application is integrated with the operating system to provide a hardened security solution. The integrated security application provides all of the VPN, firewalling, denial of service, and traffic management.

The second layer in the NetScreen firewall platform is the operating system. The operating system for the NetScreen firewall product is called ScreenOS. This OS is designed as a *real-time operating system* (RTOS). An RTOS is defined as an operating system that can respond to external world events in a time frame defined by the external world. Because only one task can run at a time for each CPU, the idea is to minimize the time it takes to set up and begin executing a task. A large challenge for RTOS is memory allocation. Allocating memory this takes time, which can slow down the OS from executing a task. ScreenOS prealocates memory to ensure that it will have enough memory to provide a sustained rate of service. ScreenOS is more secure then open source operating systems because the general public cannot review the source code for vulnerabilities. ScreenOS also does not have the exposure of Microsoft Windows. This leads to ScreenOS having exposure to fewer people, thus denying them a chance to learn about the OS or possible exploits for it. The OS on a NetScreen firewall provides services such as dynamic routing, high availability, management, and the ability to virtualize a single device into multiple virtual devices.

The third layer in the NetScreen architecture is the hardware components themselves. The firewall connects all of its components together with a high-speed multi-bus configuration to connect all of the components together. The bus connects together each ASIC with a RISC processor, SDRAM (and the network interfaces. An ASIC is a chip that is designed for a single purpose. This allows that single purpose to be performed much faster then as if you were using a general-purpose microprocessor to compute the task. The NetScreen firewall architecture as you can clearly see has been designed to provide what a firewall running on a general-purpose operating system cannot. It is not limited by connection table limits and processing limits found in firewall designed on general purpose hardware and general purpose operating systems.

Figure 2.1 The NetScreen Device Architecture

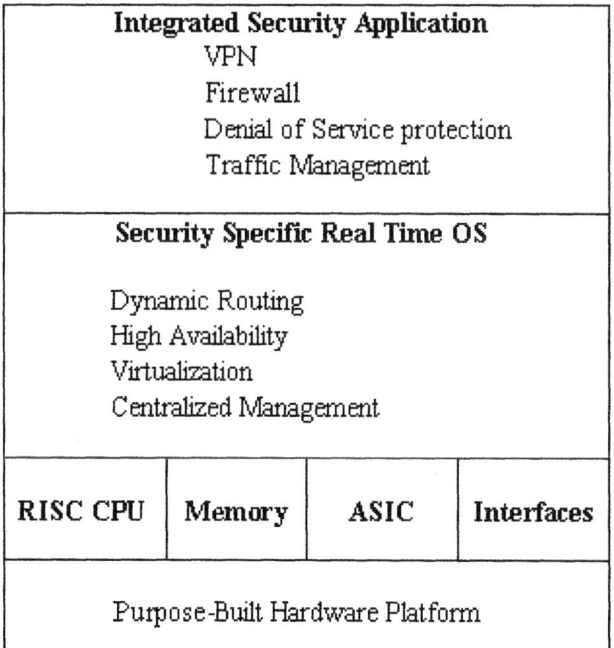

The NetScreen Firewall Product Line

The NetScreen product line has several tiers of products that span over its entire product line. One of the great parts of the NetScreen firewall product line is that no matter what tier of device, the configuration of each device remains similar. This allows you to configure each device as you would the other. Every device supports the same three management options; the WebUI, CLI, and NSM configuration of each device is relatively similar. However, the higher up the firewall product line, the more ports and options you will get to use.

Every firewall device is configured by using the same methods, no matter what tier the device is in. Other vendors offer inconsistent configurations among their devices, but the NetScreen remains unvarying. The architecture on all of the platforms remains very similar, leveraging the power of a RISC processor and ASICs to provide a high-performance operating system. Many systems that you are familiar with, such as Intel-based Pentuim systems, use the less efficient complex instruction set computer (CISC) processor. All of the devices use flash memory as the long-term storage option. None of the firewalls rely on a hard disk to run.

The NetScreen-Security manager provides lasting storage for the firewall devices, eliminating the need for long-term storage on the devices for logs. You can also stream logs to a syslog server for storage.

Product Line

In this section we will review all of the products in the current NetScreen line, starting with the low-end devices, and finishing with the high-end products. At the end of the section we will review the enterprise management options that Juniper Networks has to offer. In Table 2.1 you can see the layout of the product line from the low-end to the high-end.

Table 2.1 The Firewall Product Line Overview

Product Name	Product Class	Max Interfaces	Throughput	Price Range
NetScreen-Remote VPN Client	Remote Client Software	N/A	N/A	$100-$1,000
NetScreen-Remote Security Client	Remote Client Software	N/A	N/A	$350-$20,000
NetScreen-Hardware Security Client	Small Office Home Office	5	50 Mbps	50 Mbps
NetScreen-5-XT	Small Office Home Office	5	70 Mbps	$700-$1200
NetScreen-5-GT	Small Office Home Office	5	75 Mbps	$500-$1800
NetScreen-5-GT-ADSL	Small Office Home Office	5	75 Mbps	$500-$1800
NetScreen-25	Mid Range	4	100 Mbps	$2,800-$3,500
NetScreen-50	Mid Range	4	170 Mbps	$5,000-$6,000
NetScreen-204	High Range	4	400 Mbps	$8,000-$10,000
NetScreen-208	High Range	8	550 Mbps	$12,000-$15,000
NetScreen-500	Enterprise Class	8	700 Mbps	$28,000-$65,000
NetScreen-ISG 2000	Next Gen Enterprise Class	28	2000 Mbps	$33,000-$99,000
NetScreen-5200	Carrier Class	26	4000 Mbps	$70,000-$210,000
NetScreen-5400	Carrier Provider Class	78	12000 Mbps	$130,000-$240,000

Tools & Traps...

Choosing the Right Tool for the Job

When you plan to purchase a NetScreen device, you should put a great deal of thought into your needs. Most of the devices cannot be upgraded in any way. When purchasing a device you need to think about not just today, but tomorrow as well. Realistically, you should look at the life of the product over the next three years. This will provide you for the right amount of growth for your network. Many companies would never need more than the NetScreen-208 product. Providing for eight total interfaces and up to seven hundred megabits per second throughput, it can suffice for most networks.

In many lower end networks where you have just an internal LAN and an Internet connection only four interfaces, a lower amount of throughput would be required. Even the lowest end NetScreen firewall device can easily handle even a hefty DS3 circuit to the Internet providing 45 Mbps. This said, choosing a firewall can be hard work. Because of the low upgrade ability of these devices, many people looking at a device such as NetScreen may think twice. But as you can see with the large selection, a proper selection of a device can easily overcome your cognitive dissidence when choosing a NetScreen firewall.

NetScreen-Remote Client

- NetScreen-Remote VPN Client
- NetScreen-Remote Security Client

Remote access to company resources is a requirement for most organizations. Company resources have to be secured. For remote access security, Juniper offers NetScreen-Remote VPN client and NetScreen-Remote Security client. These products provide an easy-to-use interface to configure and connect to IPSec gateway endpoints. You are not limited to client access of the NetScreen-based VPN firewalls; it is capable of connecting to any IPSec Gateway. Providing standards-based IPSec connectivity is just part of the NetScreen-Remote VPN client. The XAuth Extended Authentication protocol is also supported by

NetScreen Remote. XAuth supports handing out an IP address and DNS (domain name system) settings to a virtual interface on the client. The Remote VPN client is capable of supporting up to one hundred concurrent IPSec VPN tunnels. NetScreen-Remote VPN and Security clients provide easy, secured access to your mobile workforce.

NetScreen-Remote Security client has an integrated client firewall to protect the remote users system. This client allows the end user to connect securely to the enterprise network over the industry standard IPSec. The interface of the client allows the user to quickly configure a VPN connection. It also provides the administrator with the ability to create and then export a VPN policy that can be deployed to all remote users. The crowning feature of the Security client is the integrated firewall. This firewall allows you to protect the end user's system from intrusions and network attacks. Not only does this prevent the end user's system, but it also protects your company's network by preventing malicious attackers from connecting through a VPN client's system into the company's network.

Small Office Home Office

- NetScreen-Hardware Security Client
- NetScreen 5XT
- NetScreen 5GT

For remote locations or remote users with the need for a dedicated security appliance, the Small Office Home Office line of NetScreen firewall appliances provide enterprise class security at a low cost entry point. This product line has a small footprint, but don't let that fool you. These devices still support the easy-to-use CLI and WebUI management interfaces that the high-end appliances and systems do. The Small Office Home Office line of products is illustrated in Table 2.2.

Table 2.2 Small Office Home Office Line

	Hardware Security Client	5-XT	5-XT Elite	5-GT 10 User	5-GT Plus	5-GT Extended
Interfaces	5 10/100 Ethernet	5 10/100 Ethernet	5 10/100 Ethernet	5 10/100 Ethernet	5 10/100 Ethernet	5 10/100 Ethernet
Max IP address behind	5	10	No limit	10	No limit	No limit
Maximum Throughput Firewall	50 Mbps	70 Mbps	70 Mbps	75 Mbps	75 Mbps	75 Mbps
VPN	10 Mbps	20 Mbps	20 Mbps	20 Mbps	20 Mbps	20 Mbps
Maximum Sessions	1,000	2,000	2,000	2,000	2,000	4,000
Maximum VPN Tunnels	2	10	10	10	10	25
Maximum Policies	50	100	100	100	100	100
Virtual Systems	N/A	N/A	N/A	N/A	N/A	N/A
Security Zones	3	3	3	3	3	3
Virtual Routers	2	2	2	2	2	2
VLANs	N/A	N/A	N/A	N/A	N/A	N/A
Routing Protocol Support						
RIP v2	Yes	Yes	Yes	Yes	Yes	Yes
OSPF	Yes	Yes	Yes	Yes	Yes	Yes
BGP	Yes	Yes	Yes	Yes	Yes	Yes

Continued

Table 2.2 Small Office Home Office Line

	Hardware Security Client	5-XT	5-XT Elite	5-GT 10 User	5-GT Plus	5-GT Extended
High Availability	N/A	N/A	N/A	N/A	N/A	N/A
HA Lite						
Active/Passive						
Active/Active						
Active/Active Full Mesh						
Anti-Virus Scanning						
Embedded	Yes	No	Yes	Yes	Yes	Yes
External	No	No	No	No	No	No
Deep Inspection	Yes	Yes	Yes	Yes	Yes	Yes
Throughput	50 Mbps	55 Mbps	55 Mbps	75 Mbps	75 Mbps	75 Mbps

The NetScreen-Hardware Security Client is currently at the low end of NetScreen's firewall product line. This device is designed as a hardware-based version of the remote software client. It still provides huge throughput for being the lowest performing device. This device passes a maximum of fifty megabits per second for its firewall performance, and ten megabits per second for a 3DES VPN. These numbers can easily support the fastest residence-installed broadband connection. Protecting your home users from viruses is made easy with this device. It includes Trend Micro's scan engine embedded directly into the device. This allows for you to scan Post Office Protocol 3 (POP3), SMTP and HTTP Web mail in real time to protect users from viruses. This is a great way to prevent infected home users from spreading viruses to the company's network. The newest firewall technology, Deep Inspection, is supported to help protect against application-level attacks and vulnerabilities. The NetScreen-Hardware security client has to be managed from a NetScreen-Security Manager. Policies cannot be created on the device without the NetScreen-Security Manager.

The next product in the Small Office Home Office product line is the NetScreen 5-XT. This device has many more capabilities then the NetScreen-Hardware security client. It allows up to seventy megabits per second firewall performance, as well as twenty megabits per second triple DES VPN performance. The 5-XT supports the Deep Inspection application level, scanning for attacks at up to a maximum of fifty-five megabits per second. It has a total of five 10/100 Ethernet ports. Up to two of these ports can be used to connect to the Internet to provide redundant Internet connectivity. However, if you require total uptime, the 5-XT also supports the ability to connect an external modem providing dial backup capabilities. The 5-XT does not support any sort of antivirus capabilities, though. This is an older product and is being replaced by the 5-GT.

The NetScreen 5-GT is the answer to your needs if you need a low-end remote appliance. Truly, the only two things that are low-end about this device are the price and the model number. The 5-GT provides a speedy seventy-five megabits per second firewall throughput, a full seventy-five megabits per second Deep Inspection Scanning, and twenty megabits per second triple DES VPN performance. This device is similar in design to the 5-XT and has five 10/100 Ethernet ports. These again allow for a total of two Internet-connected interfaces to provide redundant connectivity in case one Internet service provider experiences a failure. A modem port is provided to allow for dial-up Internet connectivity as well.

The 5-GT has Trend Micro's antivirus engine embedded into it, allowing for inline virus scanning of the POP3, SMTP, and HTTP web mail protocols. This is a separately licensed subscription. The 5-GT has a separate model, which is the same as the features above, but it also contains an asyncronous digital subscriber line (ADSL) port. This model is called the 5-GT ADSL. The 5-GT has several different licensing choices to give you a range of options on this "low-end" appliance:

- **10 User License** Allows for only ten users behind the 5GT to access through the device at one time

- **Unlimited User License** Allows for an unlimited about of users to access through the device at one time

- **5GT Extended** This licensing option provides up to 4,000 concurrent sessions. It allows you to create a DMZ on the firewall through the use of a dedicated DMZ port. The extended license also allows for a two-unit high-availability cluster with two 5GT Extended firewalls.

Mid-Range

- NetScreen-25
- NetScreen-50

The NetScreen-25 and NetScreen-50 are the next step up the NetScreen ladder. These devices are a perfect fit for branch and remote offices, or for medium and small-size companies. The only difference between these two devices is the performance that they provide. Both devices are physically identical. In Table 2.3, you can see the performance benefits of using the advanced feature set.

Table 2.3 The Mid-Range Line

	NS-25 Baseline	NS-25 Advanced	NS-50 Baseline	NS-50 Advanced
Interfaces	4 10/100 Ethernet	4 10/100 Ethernet	4 10/100 Ethernet	4 10/100 Ethernet
Maximum Throughput				
Firewall	100 Mbps	100 Mbps	170 Mbps	170 Mbps
VPN	20 Mbps	20 Mbps	50 Mbps	50 Mbps

Continued

Table 2.3 The Mid-Range Line

	NS-25 Baseline	NS-25 Advanced	NS-50 Baseline	NS-50 Advanced
Maximum Sessions	8,000	16,000	32,000	64,000
Maximum VPN Tunnels	25 Shared	25 Site to Site 100 Dial-Up	100 Shared	100 Site to Site 400 Dial-Up
Maximum Policies	500	500	1,000	1,000
Virtual Systems	N/A	N/A	N/A	N/A
Security Zones	4	4	4	4
Virtual Routers	2	2	2	2
VLANs	0	8	0	8
Routing Protocol Support				
RIP v2	Yes	Yes	Yes	Yes
OSPF	No	Yes	No	Yes
BGP	No	Yes	No	Yes
High Availability				
HA Lite	Yes	Yes	Yes	No
Active/Passive	No	No	No	Yes
Active/Active	No	No	No	No
Active/Active Full Mesh	No	No	No	No
Anti-Virus Scanning				
Embedded	No	No	No	No
External	Yes	Yes	Yes	Yes
Deep Inspection	No	Yes	No	Yes
Throughput	N/A	75 Mbps	N/A	75 Mbps

The NetScreen-25 is the weaker of the two devices in the mid-range category. The NetScreen-25 provides a total of one hundred megabits per second firewall performance, twenty megabits of triple DES VPN performance and up to seventy-five megabits per second of Deep Inspection performance. It has a total of four 10/100 Ethernet ports. It also has a console port and modem port. The console port provides access for console CLI management. The modem port allows you to connect a modem for out-of-band management capabilities. The NetScreen-25 (and all devices upward) allows you to configure the network ports to your liking. This gives you total control over the network, providing for multiple configuration options. You can have a total of four separate security zones for these interfaces. The NetScreen-25 device only allows for high availability (HA) Lite mode. This mode will provide for failover in case of a hardware failure. However, it will not allow you to fail all of your active sessions. All active sessions are lost during the when one device fails over to the backup device when you are using an HA Lite configuration. Antivirus scanning is done only via an external Trend Micro antivirus server. The NetScreen-25 comes in two licensed models: baseline and advanced.

The NetScreen-50 is the performer of the two devices in the mid-range category. The NetScreen-50 provides a total of one hundred and seventy megabits per second firewall performance, forty-five megabits of triple DES VPN performance and up to seventy-five megabits per second of Deep Inspection performance. It has a total of four 10/100 Ethernet ports that you can use. It also has a console port and modem port. The console port provides access for console CLI management. The modem port allows you to connect a modem for out-of-band management capabilities. The NetScreen-50 device allows for high availability in Active/Passive mode. This mode would provide for failover in case of a hardware failure, it would also failover all of your sessions for a seamless failover. Antivirus scanning is done only via an external Trend Micro antivirus server. The NetScreen-50 has two licensed models: the baseline and advanced. In the above table you can see the performance differences between the baseline and the advanced models.

High-Range

- NetScreen-204
- NetScreen-208

The high-range line of NetScreen products is listed in Table 2.4.

Table 2.4 High-Range Line

	NS-204 Baseline	NS-204 Advanced	NS-208 Baseline	NS-208 Advanced	Virtualization License
Interfaces	4 10/100 Ethernet	4 10/100 Ethernet	8 10/100 Ethernet	8 10/100 Ethernet	N/A
Maximum Throughput					
Firewall	400 Mbps	400 Mbps	550 Mbps	550 Mbps	N/A
VPN	200 Mbps	200 Mbps	200 Mbps	200 Mbps	
Maximum Sessions	64,000	128,000	64,000	128,000	N/A
Maximum VPN Tunnels	500	1,000	500	1,000	N/A
Maximum Policies	4,000	4,000	4,000	4,000	N/A
Virtual Systems	N/A	N/A	N/A	N/A	N/A
Security Zones	4	4	8	8	+10
Virtual Routers	2	2	2	2	+5
VLANs	0	32	0	32	+32
Routing Protocol Support					**N/A**
RIP v2	Yes	Yes	Yes	Yes	
OSPF	No	Yes	No	Yes	
BGP	No	Yes	No	Yes	
High Availability					N/A
HA Lite	No	No	No	No	
Active/Passive	Yes	Yes	Yes	Yes	
Active/Active	No	Yes	No	Yes	
Active/Active Full Mesh	No	No	No	Yes	

Continued

Table 2.4 High-Range Line

	NS-204 Baseline	NS-204 Advanced	NS-208 Baseline	NS-208 Advanced	Virtualization License
Anti-Virus Scanning					
Embedded	No	No	No	No	N/A
External	Yes	Yes	Yes	Yes	
Deep Inspection	No	Yes	No	Yes	N/A
Throughput	N/A	180 Mbps	N/A	180 Mbps	

The NetScreen 200 series is the first model of high-end NetScreen features. This is the first series of devices that support an active/active high availability configuration. This allows both of the NetScreen appliances in a high availability cluster to be active at the same time allowing for higher throughput and maximum capacity. This class of firewall is typically required for one of three reasons. The first reason is that you require the use of more than four interfaces, similar to NetScreen-208. The second reason is the higher throughput on these devices. The final reason is for the more advanced features available for the NetScreen-200 series.

The NetScreen-204 has the same genetic make up as the NetScreen-25 and NetScreen-50. The NetScreen-204 provides double the performance of the NetScreen-50, providing four hundred megabits per second firewall performance, two hundred megabits per second triple DES VPN performance, and one hundred and eighty megabits per second of Deep Inspection capability. Much like the other devices of the same form factor, this device provides four 10/100 base-T ports. . It also has a console port and modem port. The console port provides access for console CLI management. The modem port allows you to connect a modem for out–of-band management capabilities. This is the first platform that allows a function in Active/Passive mode or Active/Active mode. Antivirus scanning is done only via an external Trend Micro antivirus server. The NetScreen-204 comes in two licensed models: baseline and advanced. In the table above you can see the performance advantages gained by using the advanced feature set. You can also purchase a virtualization license for this platform. This provides thirty-two additional virtual LANs (VLANs), ten additional security zones, and five additional virtual routers.

The NetScreen-208 comes with a similar one-rack unit form factor but it is the first device to have over four physical interfaces. The NetScreen-208 offers an impressive performance by all security standards. Providing five hundred and fifty megabits per second firewall performance, two hundred megabits per second triple DES VPN performance, and one hundred and eighty megabits per second of Deep Inspection capability, it also offers support to up to one hundred and twenty eight thousand concurrent sessions. The NetScreen-208 has the capabilities to easily support an e-commerce type of deployment. This device provides eight 10/100 base-T ports. It also has a console port and modem port. The console port provides access for console CLI management. The modem port allows you to connect a modem for out of band management capabilities. This enables you to use a Personal Computer Memory Card International Association

(PCMCIA) flash card to back up your configuration. This is the first platform that allows you to have an Active/Passive, Active/Active, and Active/Active Full mesh configuration. Antivirus scanning is done only via an external Trend Micro antivirus server. The NetScreen-208 comes in two licensed models: baseline and advanced. In the table above you can see the performance advantages gained by using the advanced feature set. You can also purchase a virtualization license for this platform. NetScreen-208 provides thirty-two additional virtual LANs (VLANs), ten additional security zones and five additional virtual routers (VRs).

Enterprise Class

- NetScreen-500

If you are looking for a high performance, highly available, and highly expensive platform, then the enterprise class (see Table 2.5) of NetScreen products is where you should start browsing. There are two devices that are similar in design, with one outclassing the other by way of more features. Both systems are the first devices in the NetScreen firewall line to provide redundant power supplies. This is a great option when uptime is crucial. Both devices also have interchangeable interface modules. These modules allow you to have either 10/100 base-T ports or gigabit fiber ports. Copper gigabit ports are not supported at this time. Presently, only fiber connections are supported.

Table 2.5 Enterprise Class Product Line

	NS-500 Baseline	NS-500 Advanced
Interfaces	8 10/100 Ethernet or 8 Mini-GBIC or 4 GBIC	8 10/100 Ethernet or 8 Mini-GBIC or 4 GBIC
Maximum Throughput		
Firewall	700 Mbps	700 Mbps
VPN	250 Mbps	250 Mbps
Maximum Sessions	128,000	250,000
Maximum VPN Tunnels	1,000	5,000 and 5,000 Dial-Up
Maximum Policies	20,000	20,000
Virtual Systems	Up to 25	Up to 25
Security Zones	8	8

Continued

Table 2.5 Enterprise Class Product Line

	NS-500 Baseline	NS-500 Advanced
Virtual Routers	2	2
VLANs	100	100
Routing Protocol Support		
RIP v2	Yes	Yes
OSPF	No	Yes
BGP	No	Yes
High Availability		
HA Lite	No	No
Active/Passive	Yes	Yes
Active/Active	No	Yes
Active/Active Full Mesh	No	Yes
Anti-Virus Scanning		
Embedded	No	No
External	Yes	Yes
Deep Inspection	No	Yes
Throughput	N/A	180 Mbps

The NetScreen-500 is truly an enterprise class device. This tool is capable of providing a highly available firewall scenario. First, it allows you to have redundant power supplies. This is essential when managing a network that requires one hundred percent uptime. Secondly, components, like fans are also redundant to ensure that this device does not overheat. Finally, you can have high availability interfaces to ensure you never have downtime. As far as high availability modes go, the NetScreen-500 supports all three modes: Active/Passive, Active/Active and Active/Active Full Mesh. When using a NetScreen device in high availability mode, you need to have ports dedicated to enable both a heartbeat and the passing of session synchronization information. The NetScreen-500 provides these two ports, which are dedicated only to this purpose.

The NetScreen-500 has very large performance numbers, providing seven hundred megabits per second firewall performance, two hundred and fifty megabits per second triple DES VPN throughput, and an amazing three hundred megabits per second performance while doing Deep Inspection. It supports up to 250,000 concurrent sessions and up to 18,000 new sessions per second. This is the first device in the NetScreen firewall line that can have a modular interface configuration. The

NetScreen-500 can provide up to eight 10/100 base-T Ethernet ports, eight mini-GBIC (SX or LX) ports, or four GBIC (SX or LX) ports. This is not a hugely dense port configuration, but it is the lowest end device to provide for gigabit ports. A feature called Virtual Systems, or VSYS, is supported on this appliance (and all appliances upward). A VSYS allows you to segment a device into several virtual systems. These virtual systems allow you to have a completely separate management domain to truly provide a virtual firewall.

The NetScreen-500 has two separate licensing modes: baseline and advanced. Table 2.5 includes the differences in the devices. You may also purchase virtual systems in three separate options: an upgrade to five virtual systems, upgrades from five virtual systems to ten virtual systems, and from ten virtual systems to twenty-five virtual systems are all available. There is also a second version of the NetScreen-500 called the NetScreen-500 GPRS. This device allows you to secure the general packet radio services (GPRS) protocol as well. The performance of the device is similar to NetScreen-500.

Next Generation Enterprise Class

- NetScreen-ISG 2000

The NetScreen Integrated Security Gateway 2000 or NetScreen ISG-2000 is Juniper Network's next generation firewall. This device is built on fourth-generation ASICs. The chips are specialized for performing specific tasks. This is the newest class of devices in the firewall product line. Its architecture is designed for more then just firewall security purposes. It has four expansion ports. These ports can, of course, be used to add more interfaces. In the future, it will allow users to add products such is the NetScreen IDP to allow for application-level scanning of all traffic. The IDP module will be ASIC-based, and will provide a huge amount of performance while scanning at the application layer. The features of NetScreen's Next Generation Enterprise Class line can be seen in Table 2.6.

Table 2.6 Next Generation Enterprise Class line

	NetScreen-ISG 2000 Baseline	NetScreen-ISG 2000 Advanced
Interfaces	Up to 28 10/100 Ethernet or Up to 8 Mini-GBIC	Up to 28 10/100 Ethernet or Up to 8 Mini-GBIC
Maximum Throughput		
Firewall	2000 Mbps	2000 Mbps
VPN	1000 Mbps	1000 Mbps
Maximum Sessions	256,000	512,000
Maximum VPN Tunnels	1,000	10,000
Maximum Policies	30,000	30,000
Virtual Systems	Up to 50	Up to 50
Security Zones	26	26
Virtual Routers	3	3
VLANs	100	500
Routing Protocol Support		
RIP v2	Yes	Yes
OSPF	No	Yes
BGP	No	Yes
High Availability		
HA Lite	No	No
Active/Passive	Yes	Yes
Active/Active	No	Yes
Active/Active Full Mesh	No	Yes
Anti-Virus Scanning		
Embedded	No	No
External	Yes	Yes
Deep Inspection	No	Yes
Throughput	N/A	300 Mbps

The NetScreen–ISG 2000 is a great look into the future of firewall appliances. This device has two important features that puts it at the top of its class. The first is the enormous throughput of this device. The NetScreen-ISG 2000 provides two gigabits per second firewall through put, one gigabit per second triple DES VPN performance, and three hundred megabits per second Deep

Inspection performance. This is a huge amount of throughput for a firewall device. The second important feature is port density. The NetScreen-ISG 2000 has four expansion slots that allow you to combine any of the following: four-port 10/100 Ethernet module, eight-port 10/100 Ethernet module, or a dual-port mini-GBIC module. That means you could have a maximum of twenty-eight Ethernet ports or eight mini-GBIC modules. For a firewall appliance, that is a huge amount of total ports. This gives you and plethora of options for this device on your network.

The NetScreen-ISG 2000 includes two AC power supplies to start your device for total redundancy. In the advanced license model, the device supports the Active/Passive, Active/Active, and Active/Active Full Mesh high availability configurations. However, with a baseline license, the device only supports an Active/Passive mode HA configuration. A NetScreen device in high availability mode requires you to have ports dedicated to enable both a heartbeat and the passing of session synchronization information. The NetScreen-500 provides these two ports, which are dedicated specifically for this purpose. It can also support up to fifty virtual systems, five hundred and twelve thousand concurrent sessions, and ten thousand concurrent VPN tunnels.

Carrier Class

- NetScreen-5200
- NetScreen-5400

Welcome to the top of the NetScreen firewall product line. These are the true enterprise core class firewalls. These firewall devices are some of the highest performing firewalls in the world. With a colossal amount of throughput and port density, these devices are exactly what you need for a company that has a massive network infrastructure. The Service Provider Class Line features are revealed in Table 2.7.

Table 2.7 Service Provider Class Line

	NetScreen-5200	NetScreen-5400
Interfaces	8 Mini-GBIC or 2 Mini-GBIC and 24 10/100 Ethernet	24 Mini-GBIC or 6 Mini-GBIC and 72 10/100 Ethernet
Maximum Throughput		
Firewall	4,000 Mbps	12,000 Mbps
VPN	2,000 Mbps	6,000 Mbps
Maximum Sessions	1,000,000	1,000,000
Maximum VPN Tunnels	25,000	25,000
Maximum Policies	40,000	40,000
Virtual Systems	Up to 500	Up to 500
Security Zones	16 up to 1,000 additional	16 up to 1,000 additional
Virtual Routers	2 up to 500 additional	2 up to 500 additional
VLANs	4,000	4,000
Routing Protocol Support		
RIP v2	Yes	Yes
OSPF	Yes	Yes
BGP	Yes	Yes
High Availability		
HA Lite	No	No
Active/Passive	Yes	Yes
Active/Active	Yes	Yes
Active/Active Full Mesh	Yes	Yes
Anti-Virus Scanning		
Embedded	No	No
External	No	No
Deep Inspection	Yes	Yes
Throughput	500 Mbps	500 Mbps

Both devices are nearly identical except for two things: port density and throughput. The first device the NetScreen-5200 series appliance can have a maximum of eight mini-GBIC ports, or two mini-GBIC ports and twenty-four 10/100 base-T Ethernet ports. It has a maximum throughput of four gigabits per second firewall inspection. For VPN performance it provides an amazing two

gigabits per second triple DES throughput. The other enterprise class device, the
NetScreen-5400, has even more impressive performance and port density. This
device can have either a maximum of twenty-four mini-GBIC ports, or six
mini-GBIC ports and seventy-two 10/100 base-T Ethernet ports. Without much
explanation needed, you can appreciate the astounding stats on these two
devices.

For the most part these two appliances have identical performance statistics
all around. The NetScreen-5000 product line can support up to one million concurrent sessions. Also they can support up to twenty-five thousand VPN tunnels,
a total of five hundred virtual systems, and up to four thousand VLANs. Both
devices can support all three modes of high availability Active/Passive,
Active/Active and Active/Active Full Mesh. Both devices as well sport the HA
ports to provide both heartbeat and session synchronization.

Enterprise Management

- Unified Management Interface

- Lower Administrative costs

- Centralized Logging

- Simplified VPN deployment

NetScreen offers you two easy-to-use methods for managing a firewall. You
can operate the easy-to-use WebUI, or you can use the command line interface
to control your NetScreen firewall. This is a great way to administer a handful of
NetScreen appliances. However, what if you have the need to manage ten or
perhaps one hundred or maybe even one thousand devices? Managing each individual firewall turns into a great chore. Furthermore, what about all of the logging from these devices? Is it practical to use a simple syslog server to managing
all of those devices? This brings up a definite need for a centralized management
console. Enter the NetScreen-Security manager, or NSM. This product is an all-
in-one solution to manage up to one thousand NetScreen firewall appliances
concurrently. The NetScreen-Security manager is the solution for your needs to
control all of your devices.

Each individual device is entered into the NSM. Once the device has been
imported you can manage each individual aspect of the firewall directly from the
NSM. You can add and delete security zones, create new policies, and tweak
existing policies. If, for example, you have dozens of locations that need to have

the same policy, you can easily deploy that policy to all of those devices. If you then need to make a change to that policy, instead of accessing each device individually, you can simply make the change to the policy and then update all of the policies at once. This simplifies large-scale deployments and allows the administrator to gain more control over the enterprises security as a whole. The NSM also brings together your logging to one central location to store it for historical purposes as well as monitor it in real time. Because sorting through all of that log information can be an extreme hassle, Juniper Networks provides you with a quick reporting system to summarize the top information you need to know. This helps you quickly identify areas of your network that have a need for you're your increased attention.

Deploying all of your devices into a tightly knit VPN solution can be complicated when you have many devices. Verifying that each device has the proper configuration on it can lead to big headaches, especially if you need to make changes to your configuration. If you use the NetScreen-Security Manager, however, deploying large scale VPNs is a snap. You would simply define all of the protected resources that you want to give access to. Then configure your VPN topology, such as which sites are going to be your hubs and spokes. Then simply push the configuration to all of your devices and your VPN is up and running. You can even monitor your enterprise's VPNs with the VPN monitor built into NSM. With one quick look you can see which locations have their VPNs up and connected to each other. This takes the guesswork out determining what is happening to your secured infrastructure.

There are several scenarios in which you may want to use NSM to take total control over your NetScreen infrastructure. If you have all of your devices deployed already, but the need for enterprise management arises, this is an easy task for NSM. Simply import all of your devices' existing configurations into the NSM and then you can begin using NSM. All of your policies, address objects, and VPNs are imported directly into the NSM, allowing you to retain your configurations. Second, if you are doing a new deployment, you can simply preconfigure your devices to contact the NSM. Then once the device is online and can contact the NSM, you can begin managing that device completely from the NSM. Finally, if you are using the legacy Global Pro product, your configuration can easily be imported right into NSM. This allows you to take advantage of newer technologies in the NSM product. For any NetScreen deployment, small or large, the NSM can easily empower the administrator into gaining full control over your network.

Summary

In this chapter we looked at the various components that compose a NetScreen firewall. The NetScreen product may not have been developed by Juniper directly, but it is now a component of that company's product line. With the purchase of NetScreen, Juniper Networks is aiming high and beginning to take Cisco on head-to-head. The NetScreen security product line is just starting to bring out its enterprise class products. The NetScreen product line is only the beginning.

The NetScreen security product line contains an amazing collection of security products. The three core product lines offer the enterprise customer good selections of products for their network. The firewall product line offers a core set of products to secure your network's focal points. To minimize your networks risk, the IDP product gives you the ability to intensely inspect your traffic. With the proper configuration you can block malicious traffic before it affects your systems, possibly compromising them and or creating data loss. The Secure Access SSL VPN product is a new solution to an old problem. Remote access into the company's network has been a long journey to provide an easy-to-deploy, yet secure solution. The NetScreen SSL VPN solution can deploy to thousands of users without the deployment of software. This helps organizations because it does not require a large staff deployment to manage all of the software. These security products provide any company secure options for several facets of the company's needs.

In this chapter we began to look at the core technologies that make up the NetScreen firewall product line. Zones are a core part of the NetScreen firewall. They allow the administrator to divide networks into logical separations. This allows you to simplify the policy creation process by clearly allowing or denying access to different network segments based upon their applied zones. NetScreen truly bends the idea of a firewall with the use of virtual routers. Virtual routers allow you to separate all of your routing domains into separate logical entities. This allows a firewall to employ the firewall as a true router without compromising security. The NetScreen firewall product again bends the traditional look of a firewall by acting as a transparent device in your network, yet still providing full firewalling features. A policy in the NetScreen firewall is the rule base, security policy, or access list of the other competitive products. It can do much more than just allow or deny traffic.

Besides being a firewall gateway, the NetScreen firewall is also a fully integrated VPN gateway, providing the ability to act as a site-to-site gateway and also provide remote VPN access to mobile users. The industry standard IPSec implementation provided by NetScreen gives the enterprise a truly enterprise class VPN solution. Application-level security is a must for every organization today. It provides inspection of the application layer that otherwise could only be provided by a dedicated device such as the IDP product. The amazing design of the hardware architecture shows that the single purpose design can certainly provide for a high-end, high-performance firewall device.

The NetScreen firewall product line provides a complete selection of firewalling products that can cover any company's needs. Each product is tailored to provide exactly what you need for almost every possible solution for an enterprises firewall needs. The NSM product brings all of your firewalls together to be managed under one single solution. It provides all of the various solutions any one would want to centrally manage all of your firewall products.

Solutions Fast Track

The NetScreen Product Offerings

☑ The NetScreen firewall products have both the ICSA and Common Criteria certifications.

☑ Trend Micro Antivirus is used for virus scanning on the firewall product line.

☑ The secure access SSL VPN is a clientless solution that does not require the predeployment of software.

☑ You can deploy the Secure Access SSL VPN product to thousands of users in a matter of hours.

☑ The IDP product allows you to inspect traffic for malicious traffic.

☑ Nine different mechanisms are deployed on the IDP to detect attacks.

The NetScreen Firewall Core Technologies

☑ Zones are used to separate logical areas inside of the firewall.

☑ Virtual routers allow for multiple routing tables in a single device.

☑ You can use a NetScreen firewall in transparent mode, which allows the firewall to act as a switch while still providing its normal firewall functions.

☑ A policy is used to allow or deny traffic that passes through the firewall gateway.

☑ NetScreen firewalls are also integrated VPN devices.

☑ You can use a NetScreen firewall in both site-to-site VPN configurations as well as client-to-site configurations.

☑ There are two different ways to create a VPN in a NetScreen firewall, either route-based or policy-based.

☑ Deep Inspection allows you to look inside of a packet for a specific attacks.

☑ The NetScreen firewall is designed based on ASICs to increase its performance.

The NetScreen Firewall Product Line

☑ The NetScreen VPN clients are only supported on Microsoft Windows operating systems.

☑ The NetScreen 5-GT products contain an internal antivirus scanning engine.

☑ The NetScreen-25 and NetScreen-50 products are perfect solutions for small- to medium-size businesses.

☑ Both of the NetScreen-204 and NetScreen-208 products are good solutions for larger organizations.

☑ The NetScreen-ISG 2000 is a modular device that is of a fourth generation design.

☑ The NetScreen-5400 is the highest performing NetScreen firewall providing twelve gigabits per second of firewall throughput.

Frequently Asked Questions

The following Frequently Asked Questions, answered by the authors of this book, are designed to both measure your understanding of the concepts presented in this chapter and to assist you with real-life implementation of these concepts. To have your questions about this chapter answered by the author, browse to **www.syngress.com/solutions** and click on the **"Ask the Author"** form. You will also gain access to thousands of other FAQs at ITFAQnet.com.

Q: You mention several times that the NetScreen firewall is ICSA certified. Why does this matter?

A: The ICSA certification ensures that the firewall device meets a certain level of criteria. This is important when determining interoperability between different vendors' devices. For example, automotive companies use a special network called the *automotive network exchange*, or ANX for short. They require that you use an ICSA-certified device to ensure that your device will be interoperable with other trading partners on that network.

Q: Security zones seem like a confusing concept. Other vendors get along without them, so why use them?

A: Zones are excellent tools to provide logical separation between multiple areas of your network. As you will see in later chapters when creating policies, zones simplify the process by identifying the two separate areas of your network you want to access each other. This can prevent you from accidentally creating access rules that will allow access to sections of your network that you did not intend.

Q: Deep Inspection seems like a great technology, but in the section about it you seem to have a negative opinion about it, why?

A: I am a firm believer in the Deep Inspection technology. It truly is the next step in the evolution of firewall devices. However, technologies like Deep Inspection should be used as a supplement rather than the only solution for application-level security. Using Deep Inspection only is a great solution for many companies, but it would not be a good idea to use as the only solution for a large e-commerce infrastructure. Security is best served as a layered model.

Q: The 5-XP security product is very similar to the 5-GT product. Why would NetScreen offer it?

A: The 5-XP product is the precursor to the 5-GT. The 5-GT provides better performance as well as the option of integrated antivirus.

Q: Why would NetScreen limit the total amount of policies that each device can have?

A: Each NetScreen device is designed to provide a specific rate of performance. Each NetScreen device could most likely support more policies, but that could degrade its performance. For each policy in the list, the NetScreen firewall checks it from a top-down perspective. Therefore, the longer the list of policies, the more time it takes to transverse the line.

## Chapter 3

Deploying NetScreen Firewalls

Solutions in this Chapter:

- Managing the NetScreen Firewall
- Configuring the NetScreen Firewall
- Configuring Your NetScreen for the Network
- Configuring System Services

☑ Summary

☑ Solutions Fast Track

☑ Frequently Asked Questions

Introduction

In this chapter we will look at the basics of deploying a NetScreen firewall. The "basics" covers a great deal of information. The NetScreen firewall has a large number of configuration options. Before you can deploy a device, you must first understand how to manage it, so in the first section of this chapter we will look at the various methods of managing your NetScreen firewall. Each option and best-known procedure is discussed. Strong system management is important, but no more so than preventing intruder attacks.

There are many management options available on the NetScreen firewall. Of these options, there are effectively two ways to manage the device directly. The first is from the *command line interface* (CLI). Many people still prefer this method of device management. Fully comprehending the command line interface allows you to understand the NetScreen firewall device better. There are specific functions that can only be done from the command line interface, such as setting the flow options. The flow options are specific to the internals of how the firewall works with packets. You most likely will not have to use these commands

The second firewall management option is the *Web User Interface*(WebUI). This streamlined interface is user-friendly and intuitive, allowing anyone to jump in and manage your firewall with ease. Even command line junkies will use the WebUI to reference the configuration or to see a configuration more clearly.

Since a firewall is a core network component of the network, we will focus heavily on how to configure your device to interact with the network. This covers *zone configuration* and *IP address assignment*. Properly configuring the network is crucial to the functionality of your network entity. Each type of zone and interface is documented to explain the different configuration options to you.

Finally, we will configure various system services. These services empower your firewall and stretch its possibilities.

Managing the NetScreen Firewall

The first step in NetScreen firewall execution is learning how to effectively manage them. In this section we will look at all of the various management options. Each option brings certain strengths and weaknesses to the table, so you should never rely on just one method. Instead, take advantage of the range of security options NetScreen offers, and use multiple configurations.

All management access requires authentication, and it's critical that only authorized administrators are permitted to change your firewall's configuration. The last thing that you want to happen is to lose control of your firewall.

There may be times when you mistakenly erase parts of your configuration or lose your configuration altogether. We will review how to recover from these mistakes. Losing access to your device can be devastating. With so many different passwords to remember, you can easily forget how to gain access to your NetScreen firewall. Even the most experienced administrators can find themselves in this scenario, and several methods of recovery have been documented.

Finally, we will look at how to update the operating system on your NetScreen device. Staying current with software revisions is very important. It provides you with security-related fixes as well as new software enhancements. For each type of management option there is a different way to update ScreenOS. Some options may be more effective then others, depending on your needs. At the completion of this section you should be familiar with WebUI and CLI. Knowing this is a requirement for managing your NetScreen firewall.

NetScreen Management Options

Every NetScreen management option centers around two forms of management: the WebUI and the CLI. There is a third type of management, an enterprise class of security, called the NetScreen–Security Manager (NSM). We'll discuss NSM further in Chapter 16.

Serial Console

The *Serial Console* is a 9-pin female serial connection. This option gives you CLI access to the firewall. Serial Console is used to initially connect to your device and to conduct *out-of-band management*. Out-of-band management is management that is not network-based, such as access via a modem. There are certain benefits to using a serial console that you do not get from using any other type of connection. The console provides a secure, physical and dedicated access. Network connectivity issues cannot interrupt this type of connection, and no one can intercept your management traffic. It is completely secured because of its direct connection.

When configuring over a serial port, you are not using any sort of network connectivity. In the case when you need to change Internet Protocol (IP) addressing on the firewall and guarantee connectivity, using the serial console is an excellent option. With, and only with serial console can you view and interact with the booting process. This cannot be accomplished remotely because the OS has not started and it is unable to provide management services. Many devices from UNIX-type servers, as well as other embedded devices, use serial consoles to provide serial console management. On the NetScreen 5XP/5GT/5XP and NetScreen-500, use a DB9 female to DB9 male straight through serial cable to connect for console management. On the NetScreen 25/50/204/208/ISG 2000/5200/5400, use an RJ-45 serial cable with a DB9 female connector. Table 3.1 outlines the proper connection settings when connecting with a serial terminal or serial terminal emulator.

Table 3.1 The Serial Terminal Settings

Setting	Value
Speed	9600 bps
Character Size	8 Bit
Parity	None
Stop Bit	1
Flow Control	None

Telnet

A second form of CLI management is *Telnet*. Telnet is a protocol that has been used for years and is like a network-based version of a serial console. However, it lacks many of the advantages of a serial console. First of all, it is a very unstable connection. The connection is made over the network in clear text. This means that the transmitted data is not encrypted in any way, allowing easy access to your login and password. Most client operating systems provide an easy-to-use Telnet client. A Telnet connection is not an ideal configuration for managing your device from a remote location. You can have a maximum of two Telnet sessions active concurrently.

Secure Shell

The third form of command line management is called *secure shell*, or SSH. Like Telnet, SSH is a remote command line session. Telnet's security concerns are removed when using SSH. Secure Shell provides an encrypted command line session to the NetScreen firewall. It also provides protection from IP spoofing and DNS (Domain Name Service) spoofing attacks. SSH has two different versions: v1 and v2. The versions are not backward-compatible. Version two is considered more popular because of its higher level of security. You are required to have a client that is compatible with the version of SSH you are using. Many UNIX-based operating systems include clients, but Windows based operating systems do not. You can use a client named *putty* for Windows. It is free and easy to use. The putty client can be found at: www.chiark.greenend.org.uk/~sgtatham/putty/download.html.

WebUI

The web user interface is the easiest type of management to use. Because of its simple point-and-click nature, it gives the end user a great jumpstart into the management of the NetScreen firewall. You can see in Figure 3.1 that the interface is very straight-forward. On the left hand side of the browser you have the menu column. From here you can choose from the different configuration options. This menu can be either Dynamic HyperText Markup Language (DHTML)-based, the default, or java-based. The functionality is the same, but the look and feel is slightly different. By default the WebUI is configured to work over just the Hyper Text Transfer Protocol (HTTP). It can, however, be configured to work over Hyper Text Transfer Protocol Secure (HTTPS). This provides a mechanism to secure your web management traffic.

Figure 3.1 Web User Interface

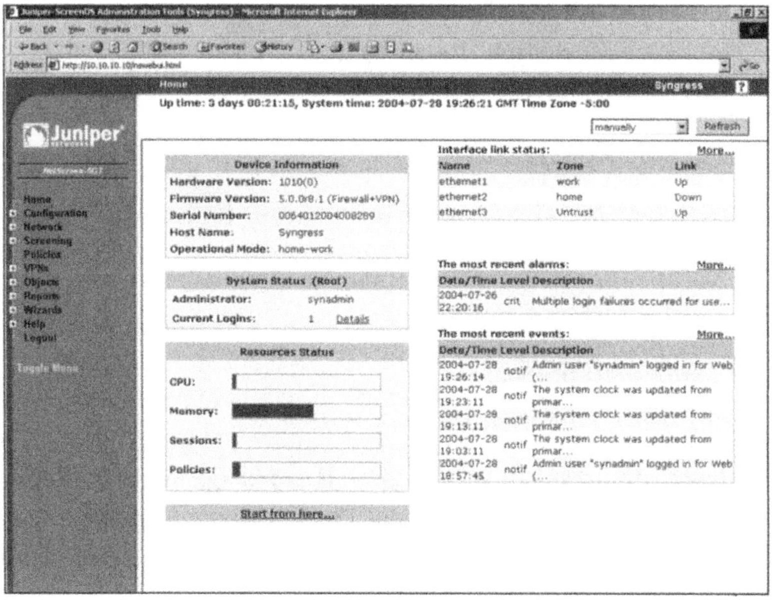

The NetScreen-Security Manager

The NetScreen-Security Manager is a separate tool that can be used to manage a NetScreen firewall device. The NSM is an application that runs on either a Solaris server or a Red Hat Linux server. It requires a separate license, and it is licensed based on how many devices you want to manage. This product is used most effectively if you want to manage several devices at the same time. The NSM product is fully discussed in Chapter 16.

Administrative Users

When connecting to a NetScreen firewall for management, you must always authenticate to the firewall. There are several types of users you can employ to connect a NetScreen firewall. The first user is the *root user*. This user is the principal user of the NetScreen firewall device. The root user has the most power of any user on a NetScreen firewall. There is only one root user per device. By default, the root user's name is *netscreen* and the default password is *netscreen*. It is highly recommended that you change the login name and password immediately. The root user has the most administrative privilege of any device. The *root user administrative privileges* are listed below:

- Add, remove, and manage all other administrators
- Create and manage virtual systems
- Create, delete, and manage virtual routers
- Add, delete, and manage security zones
- Assign security zones to interfaces
- Perform asset recovery
- Set the device to FIPS (Federal Information Processing Standards) mode
- Reset the device to default settings
- Manage the devices firmware
- Load configuration files
- Perform management on the root system

The next level administrator is *read/write*. Read/write is very similar to the root user, however, read/write users cannot create other administrators. This type of access is most useful when you want to distribute administrative privileges to other people. The NetScreen firewall provides a very detailed audit log of what each administrator does. You should capitalize on this by creating administrative users for each person that administers your firewall. This way you can identify which users make which modifications. The read/write administrative privileges include:

- Create and manage virtual systems
- Create, delete, and manage virtual routers
- Add, delete, and manage security zones
- Assign security zones to interfaces
- Perform asset recovery
- Set the device to FIPS mode
- Reset the device to default settings
- Manage the devices firmware
- Load configuration files
- Perform management on the root system

The next type of user is the *read-only* administrator. This user has limited access to the system. As the name suggests, the user can only view the configuration and they are unable to modify the system in any way. This is useful if you want to have someone document your configurations, or if you want to give someone limited access to the device to perform troubleshooting on the network. The following list includes the limited privileges of the read-only administrator.

- Read-only privileges in the root system
- Read-only privileges in all virtual systems

On some devices you can have *virtual systems*. A virtual system acts as its own separate security domain. Virtual system administrators only have permission on a specific system. The following lists the virtual system administrator privileges:

- Create and manage auth, Internet Key Exchange (IKE), Layer 2 tunneling protocol (L2TP), Extended Authentication (Xauth), and Manual Key users
- Create and manage services

- Create and manage policies

- Create and manage addresses

- Create and manage VPNs (virtual private networks)

- Modify the virtual system administrator login password

- Create and remove virtual system read-only administrators

The last type of user is the *virtual system read-only administrator*. They have almost the same privileges as a read-only administrator, but they can only see the configuration of a single specified virtual system. The only privileges that the virtual system read-only administrator has are read-only privileges on the specified virtual system.

Knowing the different types of administrators can give you the options to create an efficient strategy for delegating authority on your system. Don't be afraid to create many different administrative users for your NetScreen device. This will provide you with granular access to your system. Again, all users' actions are logged, providing a detailed list of access for each different user. This can be helpful when determining issues caused by a particular administrator, or in determining if an administrator account has been compromised. Chapter 6 will review the use of external authentication sources for administrative users. This can provide additional security in cases where you use technologies such as SecurID to remove the use of a single static password.

The Local File System and the Configuration File

Each NetScreen firewall device has a similar design for its internal system components. Long-term storage on the device is stored into *flash memory*. Flash memory is a non-volatile type of memory that retains information after the system is turned off. Some devices have a Personal Computer Memory Card International Association (PCMCIA) card slot for external storage. This card is still just flash memory, but it is removable; the internal flash is not. All of the component information that NetScreen needs to store is in flash memory, including ScreenOS log files, license keys, attack databases, and virus definitions.

Each NetScreen device also contains Random Access Memory (RAM). This is a volatile type of memory that is lost whenever the system is powered off or reset. When the NetScreen device powers on, and after the power on self test (POST) is completed, the ScreenOS image is loaded into RAM. After ScreenOS is up and functional, it loads the saved configuration file from flash memory. The configuration that is stored in RAM is called the running configuration.

Whenever you make a change to the configuration, it is always saved to the running configuration. If you did not save your configuration, whenever you reset or rebooted your device, you would lose all of your changes. In those cases you can simply have someone remove power to the device, and then restore power. This will bring you back to the previously saved configuration. When using the CLI, your configuration must be manually saved. This can be done by using the save command. The save command is simple: **save**. By typing that command, your running configuration is saved into the *saved configuration*, which is stored in flash memory. The file system components are shown in Figure 3.2.

Figure 3.2 File System Components

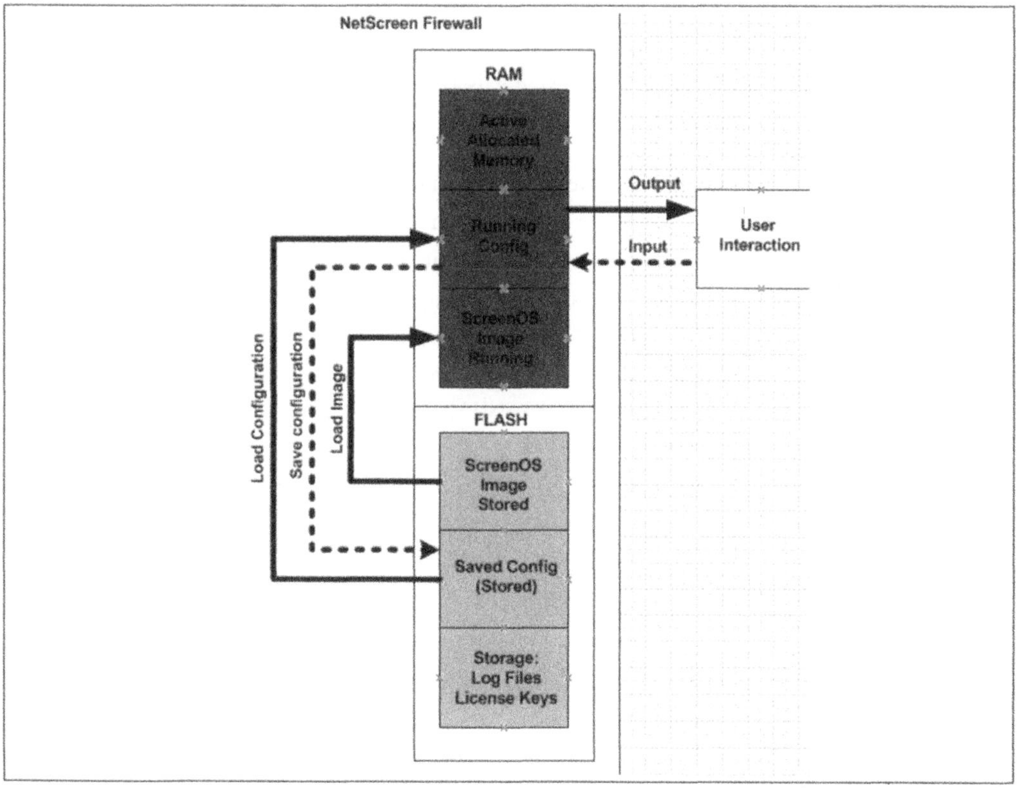

Using the WebUI is even easier. The WebUI automatically saves your configuration after every change. However, when using the CLI, if you exit your session or attempt to reset the device, you are notified that your configuration has changed. At that point you are given the option of saving the configuration. The NetScreen device is much more user-friendly then other devices when it comes to notifying you that your configuration has changed.

There are times when the flash may not provide you with the kind of storage that you need. You may require long-term storage of the log files, or perhaps a backup of your configuration file. There are a couple ways to accomplish this:

- When using the command line you can apply the command **get config** to look at your configuration, then copy and paste it into a simple text document.

- From the command line you can copy the configuration to a TFTP (Trivial File Transfer Protocol) server. TFTP is a simple type of FTP (File Transfer Protocol) server. It requires no authentication, just specification of the filename you are placing on the server. To save your configuration to a TFTP server use the command **save config to tftp** *<a.b.c.d>* *<file>* where *<a.b.c.d>* is the IP address of the TFTP server and *<file>* is the filename you want to save to.

Depending on the data that is being transferred from the file system, you may want a more secure option than TFTP. You can use secure copy (SCP) to transfer files as well. Secure copy is similar to the secure shell. It requires a special client to interact with it. This is included on many UNIX systems. Windows has many clients. I like to use the PSCP software, which is part of the Putty freeware secure shell clients. In the following example we will turn on SCP and copy a file from the NetScreen firewall to our UNIX system.

```
From the CLI:
Syngress-> set scp enable
Syngress-> get scp
SCP is enabled
SCP is ready
Syngress-> get file
    flash:/envar.rec                  98
    flash:/golerd.rec                 1220
    flash:/burnin_log1                10240
    flash:/burnin_log0                10240
    flash:/dhcpserv1.txt              52
    flash:/ns_sys_config              1092
```

```
flash:/dnstb.rec                              1
flash:/license.key                          395
flash:/$lkg$.cfg                            922
flash:/expire.rec                            23
flash:/attacks.sig                       198833
Syngress->
From the UNIX Host:
UNIX-Host:~ syngress$ scp synadmin@10.6.0.1:license.key license.txt
The authenticity of host '10.6.0.1 (10.6.0.1)' can't be established.
DSA key fingerprint is f9:a7:4c:53:4c:0a:cc:5a:50:6b:eb:df:42:42:63:c0.
Are you sure you want to continue connecting (yes/no)? yes
Warning: Permanently added '10.6.0.1' (DSA) to the list of known hosts.
synadmin@10.6.0.1's password:
license.key                             100%  395     4.8KB/s
00:00
UNIX-Host:~ syngress$ cat license.txt
1k=d2f5fb8aa5b9a000&n=capacity_key
k=2JQcSPh1ogana6h82NJeAfDwgb3aiOXT2UFcm9OFQDkuK4iT6YfKefMZjTODboIN2JQ0oWnWWX
+nKkYSMytB8gF1ID7tWXI91vZ11JURDENckexZ7IwtmRmDEh+YT3dJvDSOAYeGuuWFtGYE5tVnPf
Zq6cnlO254GPPm5HJ3qTG4sRBSRR/QFqL6WAnfnoSpByJu/Xr9vxx9GSU4fTMGLFkWsbRP5cVpTG
WmyOBapFfn1qWzu/bMLzDkox8zUHFZ2NcNCOSGOk5PvCMcZwOaADRIFqJj1oh4u7+toY37gdrEM5
sQqmELemAlUi90dhLPl7jsTy1R/V0/ourYn00XcMw==&n=di_db_key
UNIX-Host:~ Syngress$
```

As you can see, we enabled SCP, allowing us to view all of the files stored in flash memory. Next we went over to the UNIX host and copied the file from the NetScreen device to the local UNIX system. Finally, we used the cat command to concatenate the contents of the file so you can see them. SCP can be effective and easy to use for removing files from NetScreen devices.

If you're using WebUI, you can access (**Configuration | Update | Config File**) and then click the button that says **Save To File**. This will allow you to save the configuration to your local PC (Figure 3.3). Alternatively, from this same screen you can select the text in the text window, then copy and paste the configuration to a text file.

Figure 3.3 WebUI Save Screen

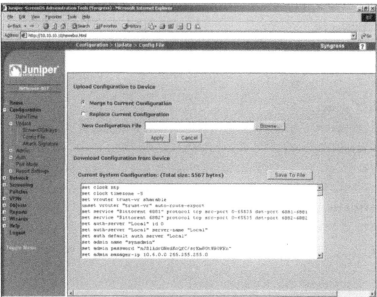

As you have seen from these files, the config files are a bunch of commands. The configuration file operates similarly to manually typing these commands in line-by-line. This is great because it gives you one format to understand. It also allows you to easily modify the configuration files you have saved to reflect new changes you may want to implement. This is one of the reasons I will continue to stress that you understand the CLI. In the next section, "Using the Command Line Interface," we will look at the configuration of the device and what all of these commands mean.

Using the Command Line Interface

The command line interface is essentially the core of configuring your NetScreen firewall device. No matter what method you use to manage your firewall, the CLI commands control the device, and a strong understanding the CLI is crucial. Even the NSM still generates the same CLI commands that you would apply if you were to modify the configuration manually. The CLI commands are straightforward and are easy to learn. Some other devices use very cryptic commands, or commands that seem to do one thing, but actually do something else. When this firewall was designed, the engineers took the need for simplicity into consideration. In Figure 3.4, an example of the help screen is shown. This gives you an idea of the information provided by the help command.

Figure 3.4 Command Line Session Using Help

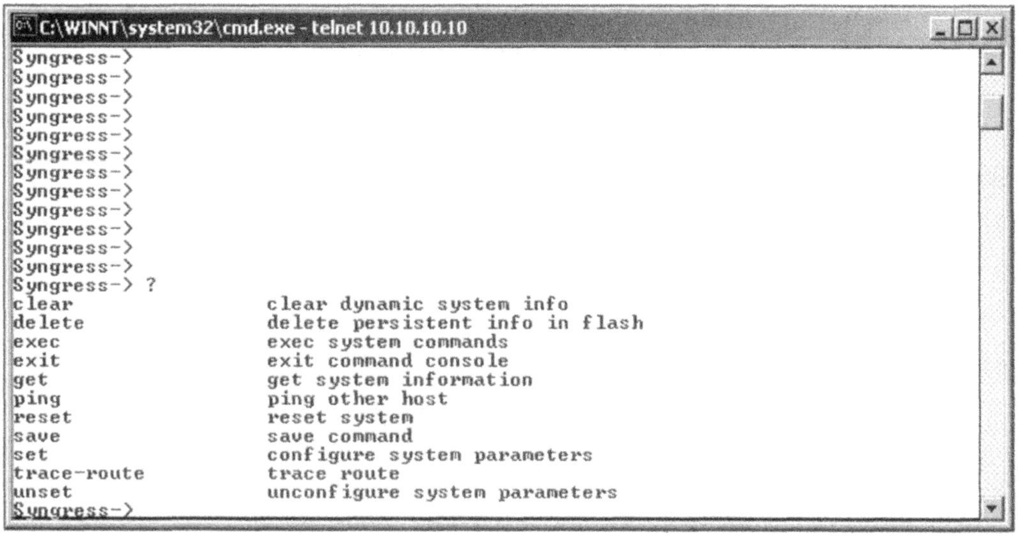

```
C:\WINNT\system32\cmd.exe - telnet 10.10.10.10
Syngress->
Syngress->
Syngress->
Syngress->
Syngress->
Syngress->
Syngress->
Syngress->
Syngress->
Syngress->
Syngress->
Syngress->
Syngress-> ?
clear              clear dynamic system info
delete             delete persistent info in flash
exec               exec system commands
exit               exit command console
get                get system information
ping               ping other host
reset              reset system
save               save command
set                configure system parameters
trace-route        trace route
unset              unconfigure system parameters
Syngress->
```

If you look at Figure 3.4 you can see an example of the command line. The prompt shows the device's current host name. This is very useful if you have several different devices that look very much the same from the command line. Starting from the root of these commands, there are literally thousands of command options. This can be confusing because there are a great number of commands to memorize. Thankfully, there is an easy-to-use built-in help system. From anywhere in the command line simply type **?** to access the help system. This will list most of the available commands. Some commands are not listed; these specific commands will be discussed in later sections.

From here there are several *base commands*, including **clear**, **exec**, **exit**, **get**, **ping**, **reset**, **save**, **set**, **trace-route**, and **unset.** Under each one of these commands are sub-commands.

Let's look at a quick example before continuing. We will first look at the **get** command. This command is used to retrieve information from the device. If we wanted to look at system information from the device such as uptime, serial number, and some configuration information, we would use the **get system** command. At the end of any get command you can do one of three things:

- You can press **Enter** and have the information displayed in your terminal window.

- You can redirect the output to a TFTP server much like we did earlier when we saved the configuration. You would use this command **get system > tftp <*a.b.c.d*> <*string*>** to send the output to a TFTP server, where <*a.b.c.d*> is the IP address of the TFTP server and <*string*> is the filename of the file you want to save to.

- You can also use the pipe (|) to match output. If you were going to use the **get system** command to look for just the serial number of your device you would use the following command: **get system | include "Serial Num"**. This would then display only the serial number and omit the rest of the data. You can also exclude specific information if you wanted to. You would use the same procedure as above but use the term **exclude** instead of **include**. This helps sort though all of the information that can be provided from a get command.

The next command we'll examine is the **set** command. This command is used to set a configuration in the current running configuration. Suppose you wanted to set the hostname to *Syngress*. You would use the following command to set the hostname of your NetScreen device: **set hostname Syngress**. Now your prompt should look like this: **Syngress->**. This again is only in the running configuration, so if you wanted to save this configuration, you would simply use the command **save** to commit the running configuration to the saved configuration. The set command will be used throughout the book, so you will get plenty of exposure to it.

You should familiarize yourself with the *five system-controlling commands*: **save**, **exec**, **exit**, **delete**, and **reset.** Each one of these commands directly performs a system task. The **save** command can be used to perform several other functions. The **save** command is used to save files to and from the local system. The **reset** command is used to reboot the NetScreen device. There are several sub-options that allow you to reboot without prompting you to confirm the configuration. You can also force a reboot, saving the running configuration, or discarding it. This way, when you want to reboot the system you do not have to answer to prompts before doing so. This is very helpful to place inside of a configuration script.

We will now look at the **exec** command. This command is powerful and is multi-purposeful. The **exec** command essentially is like running a command on the system. For example the command **exec save software from flash to tftp 1.2.3.4 CurrentOS.bin** would save the current version of ScreenOS to a TFTP server. So it would be much like copying a file in DOS or UNIX shell from one location to another. This is an example of the type of functions that the exec command can provide.

The command **delete** allows you to manage your local system by deleting several types of stored information. This can range from you local stored SSH information to files on the local flash file system. For example, if you wanted to delete a file named *old_data* that was stored in flash memory, you would use the following command: **delete file flash:old_data**. This would delete that file permanently from flash.

The **exit** command serves only one function: to exit your current session. When you use this command your current CLI session is terminated. If you have made unsaved configuration changes, you will be prompted to save them before you exit.

The **clear** command allows you to clear current data out of memory. This can include dozens of options anywhere from the current local DNS cache to the current sessions that are passing though the firewall. This is useful if you want to remote this information and then you want that data to accumulate again. Sessions are a great example of something that you may need to clear. You would want to clear you session table if you were perhaps troubleshooting a connectivity problem and you wanted to see the session be recreated in your debugging logs. This is as easy as typing **clear session** at the command line and pressing **Enter** to clear out all of the sessions. You could also selectively delete all of your sessions depending upon your situation.

There are two commands that you can use to for troubleshooting purposes. These commands are **ping** and **trace-route**. I am sure you have used these before on other operating systems. Ping is a tool to test connectivity between two systems. You would use ping, for example, if you wanted to verify that your firewall could see a specific host. The **ping** command can be used with other options besides just a host. You can also specify how many ping packets you want to send, as well as the size and the timeout for each packet. To use the ping command, just type **ping** and then the hostname or IP address of device you are trying to contact. The other command is **trace-route**. Trace route is similar to a ping, but it is designed to determine all of the routers' IP addresses and the path across the network you need to take to get to a specified remote host.

When using the command line there are a few special commands that you can use to get around to make things easier for the end user. We already covered the ? command for getting help. This can be used for every sub-command as well as partial commands to tell you what the rest of the available commands are. The help command is very helpful and should be used liberally when you need it. Next is the **TAB** key to provide command completion. For example, you can type **set add** and then press **TAB** to have the command completed for you, resulting in the command **set address**. If there is more then one match to the command, both will be listed. You must type out the command until it is unique for command completion to work. This is universal for the CLI on the NetScreen device, it is the same functionality provided by the UNIX bash shell. If you look at Table 3.2 you can see the rest of the special key combinations that you can use.

Tools & Traps...

Command Line Interface Quandaries

When using the command line there are certain functions that should work, but do not seem to. For example, sometimes **TAB** completion will not work. This can be frustrating, but luckily, there are only a few situations in which this can happen. One is when you attempt to use **TAB** completion with the name of an interface. In this case, each time you press the **TAB** key, you will see the same line again and again. You can still use the question mark to bring up the interface list.

The other situation occurs when you attempt to use **TAB** completion when attempting to complete the name of a zone. You will get the same results as above. When using the command line, you can use truncated commands instead of having to type them out completely. This can be extremely helpful when typing out the full command. It allows you to use shortened commands and can make typing out a long command very simple.

For example, instead of typing out a command **get interface ethernet3** you could use the command **g int e3**. So for the first command we have the letter g. The first command it matches is **get**. Since no other command matches it, ScreenOS interprets this as get. The second command we used is **int**. The third command is **e3**, which matches **ethernet3**. As you use the command line you will learn tricks like this to simplify your experience and make your CLI usage quicker and easier.

As you can see, each command is separated by a space. But what if you want to use a space between two words when entering a command?

Continued

You would simply surround the text with quotes. For example, the command **set snmp location Dearborn, MI** would fail. However, if we used the command **set snmp location "Dearborn, MI"**, the text encompassed in the double quote marks would only count as a single word. This is great for times when you want to use a space in a command.

Table 3.2 Special Key Combinations for the CLI

Special Key	Action
Up Arrow	Recalls previous command
Down Arrow	Recalls next command
Control-A	Brings cursor to beginning of the current line
Control-E	Brings the cursor to the end of the current line
Control-C	This is the escape sequence
Left Arrow	Move cursor back one position
Right Arrow	Move cursor forward one position
TAB	Completes partially typed command
Question Mark (?)	Displays Help and command options

As you can see, the command line has many different options. Once you begin to use these options you can quickly get used to the CLI environment. Many people begin to use the WebUI and then abandon the CLI. At first you may find the WebUI easier to use, but more advanced options can only be carried out from the CLI (such as debugging).

Using the Web User Interface

The Web User Interface is a simple tool to use for managing your NetScreen firewall. It is very intuitive and allows even those with little firewall experience to easily control a NetScreen device. As we continue through the book we will use both the WebUI and the CLI for examples. In Figure 3.1 above, we looked at the main WebUI page following authentication. On the left side is the menu bar, where you can select the different configuration options. On the right-hand side of the screen is the current status of the device. On this screen there are six different boxes: **Device Information**, **System Status**, **Resource Status**, **Interface Link Status**, **The most recent alarms**, and **The most recent events**.

Each of these boxes shows you the current events. The current uptime and the current system time are also displayed (at the top of the screen). The **Device Information** box shows you several different bits of information, including the hardware version, current firmware version, Serial Number, Host name, and its current operational mode. The **System Status** box shows the status for the various systems. It shows the current number of logins to the device and who you are logged in as. The **Resources Status** box shows four different device resources in a bar graph format. If you hover over any of the bar graphs, you will see specific numbers for each graph. The stats that are profiled are CPU, memory, sessions, and policies. These are the core performance metrics of the NetScreen device. As we discussed earlier, the memory bar graph will read higher then you would expect. This is again because ScreenOS pre-allocates memory for performance.

If you look at the box titled **Interface Link Status** you will see all of the interfaces and their link statuses. This is handy for determining which interfaces are up or down. **The most recent alarms** lists the most recent alarms that have occurred. Finally, just as its name implies, **The most recent events** box lists the most recent events. Some boxes in the upper right-hand corner have a **more** hyperlink. This brings you directly to the detail page for each one of those items.

Securing the Management Interface

Now that you are beginning to understand the management of the NetScreen firewall device, it is time to secure the management access to your device. The last thing you want to do is leave the doors wide open for another individual to take over your device. There are some easy things that you can do to prevent this. First, as we mentioned earlier, you should change the root username and password. Everyone who owns a NetScreen firewall is well aware of the default login and password to the device.

Use the following steps to change the root username and password via the WebUI:

1. Select **Configuration | Admin | Administrators**. A screen similar to Figure 3.5 will be displayed.

Figure 3.5 WebUI Administrators Screen

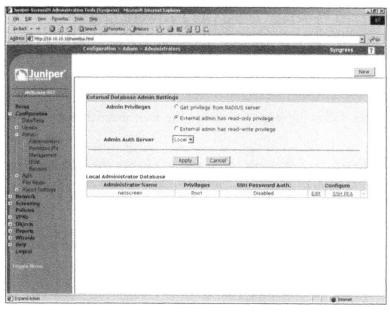

2. Click the **Edit** link for the user with *root* privileges (in our example, the *root* user is the only username entry). A screen similar to that in Figure 3.6 will be displayed. Figure 3.6 below is identical to Figure 3.5 above – the figure below has to be replaced with a screenshot of the Edit screen.

Figure 3.6 Edit Administrator

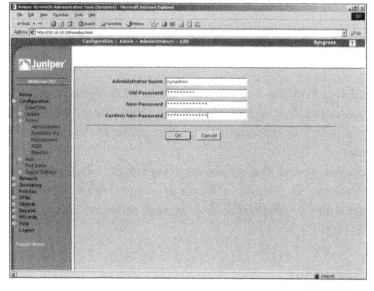

3. Change the **Administrator Name** from **netscreen** to **synadmin**.

4. Enter **netscreen** in the **Old Password** field.

5. Enter the new password in the **New Password** and **Confirm New Password** fields.

6. Click **OK**.

Use the following steps to change the root username and password via the CLI:

1. Enter the following command to change the admin name:

   ```
   Syngress-> set admin name synadmin
   ```

   You will see the following message:

   ```
   Password has been restored to default "netscreen". For security
   reasons, please change password immediately.
   ```

2. Enter the following command to change the password:

   ```
   Syngress-> set admin password password
   ```

3. Use the following command to verify the changes:

   ```
   Syngress-> get admin user
   ```

   You will see an output similar to the following:

   ```
   Name                             Privilege
   -------------------------------- ----------------
   synadmin                         Root
   Syngress->
   ```

The device now has its root users name set to **synadmin** and its password has been changed. It is suggested that you make the password a minimum of eight characters. The maximum allowed number of characters in the password is thirty-one.

It is also suggested that you make a read-write administrator to use for regular maintenance. If that administrator is compromised, there is no direct root access to the device. Use the following steps to create a read-write administrator via the WebUI:

1. Select **Configuration | Admin | Administrators | New**. The screen shown in Figure 3.7 will appear.

Figure 3.7 Administrator Configuration

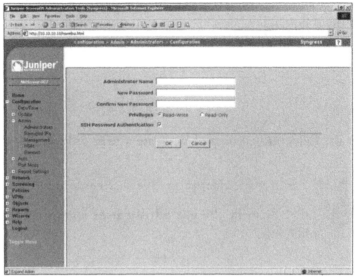

2. Use the **Administrator Name** field to enter the new name (in this example, **backupadmin**).

3. Enter this user's password in the **New Password** and **Confirm New Password** fields.

4. Enable the **Read-Write** option.

5. Click **OK**.

Use the following to create a read-only administrator via the WebUI:

1. Select **Configuration | Admin | Administrators | New**.

2. Use the **Administrator Name** field to enter the new name (in this example, **roadmin**).

3. Enter this user's password in the **New Password** and **Confirm New Password** fields.

4. Enable the **Read-Only** option.

5. Click **OK**.

Enter the following command to create a read-write administrator via the CLI:

```
Syngress-> set admin user backupadmin password %so%back privilege all
```

Verify the entry by using the **get admin user** command. The output will look like the following:

```
Name                             Privilege

-------------------------------  ---------------

synadmin                         Root
backupadmin                      Read-Write
```

Enter the following command to create a read-only administrator via the CLI:

```
Syngress-> set admin user roadmin password n0tru$t privilege read-only
```

Verify the entry by using the **get admin user** command. The output will look like the following:

```
Name                             Privilege

-------------------------------  ---------------

synadmin                         Root
backupadmin                      Read-Write
roadmin                          Read-Only
```

Another option that you should configure is the idle timeout. I have been to many locations where you would simply connect to the console and have a privileged account ready and waiting for you because the previous user had left and not logged out, or not yet returned. This is a bad situation. Anyone with a little know-how can cause trouble on your network this way. Set the idle timeout to something reasonable (the default is ten minutes for the console, Telnet, SSH, and WebUI sessions). Use the following steps to set the console, Telnet, and WebUI sessions to timeout after five minutes via the WebUI:

1. Select **Configuration | Admin | Management**. A screen similar to the one shown in Figure 3.8 will appear.

Figure 3.8 Admin Management

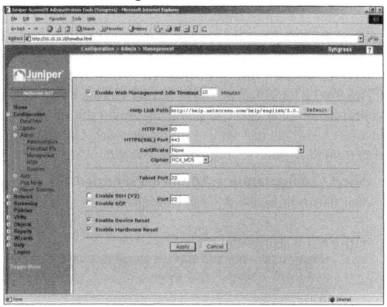

2. Ensure the **Enable Web Management Idle Timeout** option is enabled and enter **5** in the corresponding text field.

3. Click **Apply**.

You can also modify the console timeout option via the CLI by entering **set console timeout 5**. Note that a timeout value of **0** will disable the timeout feature. Use the **get console** command to verify the change. The output will resemble the following:

```
Console timeout: 5(minute), Page size: 22/22, debug: buffer
privilege 250, config was changed and not saved!
ID State   Duration Task Type     Host
 0 Login        660 13433716 Telnet 10.254.5.32:49401
 1 Logout         0 13435768 Local
 2 Logout         0 13424824 Local
 3 Logout         0 13410460 Local
```

To set the admin authentication timeout, enter **set admin auth timeout 5**. Use the **get admin auth** command to verify the setting. The output will resemble the following:

```
Admin user authentication timeout: 5 minutes
Admin user authentication type: Local
```

The next step is to limit the systems that can access your firewall. for management purposes. By specifying *permitted* IP addresses, you can limit which IP addresses are accepted for management services. You are limited to six total entries. This can be for either networks or host entries. Once you enable this setting, it immediately takes effect, so if you are setting this up remotely, ensure that you add your own IP address and/or source network. Use the following steps to create a permitted IP address entry via the WebUI:

1. Select **Configuration | Admin | Permitted IPs**. A screen similar to that shown in Figure 3.9 will be displayed.

Figure 3.9 Permitted IPs

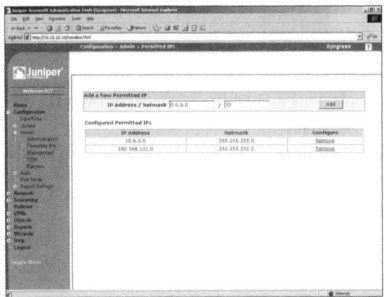

2. Use the available text fields to enter the IP address and netmask, then click **Add**. You can remove an IP address from the list by clicking its **Remove** link.   Note that if the list contains no IP addresses, any IP address will be able to access the firewall.

To add a permitted IP address via the CLI, enter the command **set admin manager-ip** *ipaddress*, where *ipaddress* is the full IP address using dotted quad

(###.###.###.###) notation. You can verify the setting by entering **get admin manager-ip**. To remove an IP address entry via the CLI, enter the command **unset admin manager-ip** *ipaddress*.

Secure Shell is highly suggested over Telnet, as we discussed earlier when we were looking at our different management options. However, SSH must be enabled before you can use it. Again earlier we looked at using SSH version two. In the following code snippet we enable SSH version two in both the WebUI and the CLI. After enabling SSH it may take several minutes for the SSH servers to be enabled. This is because the SSH keys are generating during this time.

Use the following steps to enable SSH via the WebUI:

1. Select **Configuration | Admin | Management**.

2. Enable the **Enable SSH (v2)** option.

3. Click **Apply**.

To enable SSH via the CLI, enter the command **set ssh version v2**. To set version 1 instead of version 2, simply replace **v2** in the command with **v1**.

It is strongly recommended that you use SSL only when using the WebUI. In general, it is very easy to set up and configure. However, there is one task that may prove to be a challenge. You must generate a certificate-signing request (CSR) and submit it back to a certificate authority (CA) to get the certificate signed. Once you have the signed certificate, you can load it back onto your NetScreen device. We will review how to generate the CSR and how to load the certificate. However, signing a certificate varies based upon which certificate authority you use. If you are using your device on your company's network, you should use a certificate purchased from a reputable website such as www.verisign.com or www.godaddy.com. Either site can provide you with a certificate. However if you want to just get a signed certificate for testing purposes go to www.cacert.org to get one for free.

Use the following steps to generate a certificate request. Note that this example includes company-specific information that you should substitute with your own information.

1. Access **Objects | Certificates**. The screen will display the existing certificates (Figure 3.10).

Figure 3.10 Certificates

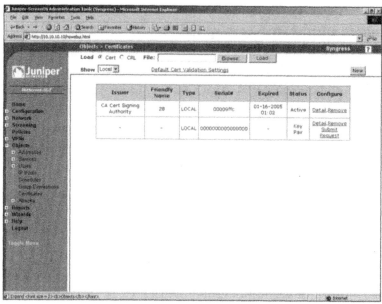

2. Click **New**. The New Request screen will be displayed (Figure 3.11).

Figure 3.11 New Certificate Request

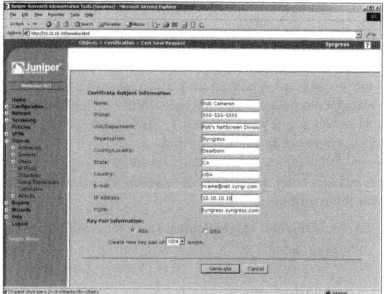

3. Enter your **Name**, **Phone**, **Unit/Department**, **Organization**, **County/Locality**, **State**, **Country**, **E-mail**, **IP Address**, and **FQDN** (Fully Qualified Domain Name).

4. Select the **RSA** option.

5. Select **1024** or **2048** from the **Create new key pair** drop-down list (the higher the number, the more secure the certificate).

6. Click **Generate**. In several minutes a new page will displayed containing a section of text.

7. Copy the text contents from "---BEGIN CERTIFICATE REQUEST---" to "---END CERTIFICATE REQUEST---".

8. Supply this to your certificate authority. They will supply you with a certificate file.

9. Access **Objects | Certificates** and click **Browse**. Choose the certificate file the CA sent you and click **Load**. The certificate is now active and loaded.

10. Now access **Configuration | Admin | Management**. Select the certificate from the **Certificate** field.

Use the following steps to request and set up a certificate via the CLI (use your own personal and company information):

1. Enter the following commands to request a certificate:

```
Syngress-> set admin mail server-name 123.123.123.100
Syngress-> set pki x509 dn country-name US
Syngress-> set pki x509 dn email rob@netscreen.com
Syngress-> set pki x509 dn ip 123.123.123.123
Syngress-> set pki x509 dn local-name "Dearborn"
Syngress-> set pki x509 dn name "Rob Cameron"
Syngress-> set pki x509 dn org-name "Rob's NetScreen division"
Syngress-> set pki x509 dn org-unit-name Books
Syngress-> set pki x509 dn phone 555-555-5555
Syngress-> set pki x509 dn state-name CA
Syngress-> set pki x509 cert-fqdn manage.netscreen.com
Syngress-> set pki x509 dn default send-to rob@netscreen.com
Syngress-> exec pki rsa new-key 1024
```

2. The certificate will be e-mailed to the address you specified. Copy the contents starting with "---BEGIN CERTIFICATE REQUEST---" and ending with "---END CERTIFICATE REQUEST---".

3. Supply this information to your certificate authority. They will supply you with a certificate file. The CA may also supply you with a local certificate and a certificate revocation list (CRL). A CRL contains a list of all of the revoked certificates that the CA has signed that are no longer valid.

4. To import these files, use the following commands:

```
Syngress-> exec tftp 123.123.123.100 cert-name newcer.cer
Syngress-> exec tftp 123.123.123.100 cert-name localpro.cer
Syngress-> exec tftp 123.123.123.100 crl-name notrust.crl
Syngress-> set ssl encrypt 3des sha-1
Syngress-> set ssl cert 1
Syngress-> set ssl enable
```

Now that we have the access restricted to specific hosts there are yet several more options we can do to enhance the security. The first option is to disable unnecessary management services. Management services are bound to individual interfaces. It is important to restrict them to the bare minimum. This can be done easily from both the WebUI and the CLI. In this case, we are using a NetScreen-5GT so we will be modifying the *untrust* interface. We are going to enable the WebUI, SSL for the WebUI, and SSH. We will only use the WebUI with SSL and SSH because they are secured.

Use the following steps to disable unnecessary management services via the WebUI:

1. Access **Network | Interfaces**. Click the **Edit** link for the entry title **untrust** A screen similar to Figure 3.12 will be displayed.

Figure 3.12 Editing Network Interfaces

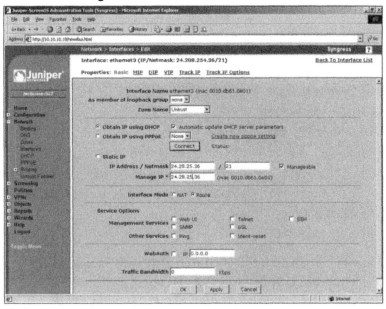

3. Ensure that **WebUI**, **SSH**, and **SSL** are all enabled, and ensure the remaining option are disabled.

4. Click **Apply**.

To disable unnecessary management services via the CLI, enter the following commands:

```
Syngress-> unset interface untrust manage ping
Syngress-> unset interface untrust manage snmp
Syngress-> unset interface untrust manage telnet
Syngress-> set interface untrust manage ssh
Syngress-> set interface untrust manage web
Syngress-> set interface untrust manage ssl
```

Use the **get interface trust** command to verify the settings. The output should resemble the following:

```
Interface untrust:
  number 1, if_info 88, if_index 0, mode route
  link up, phy-link up/full-duplex
  vsys Root, zone Untrust, vr trust-vr
  dhcp client enabled
```

```
PPPoE disabled
*ip 123.208.123.254/24    mac 0010.db61.1231
gateway 123.208.123.1
*manage ip 123.208.123.254, mac 0010.db61.1231
route-deny disable
ping disabled, telnet disabled, SSH enabled, SNMP disabled
web enabled, ident-reset disabled, SSL enabled
webauth disabled, webauth-ip 0.0.0.0
OSPF disabled  BGP disabled  RIP disabled
bandwidth: physical 100000kbps, configured 0kbps, current 0kbps
            total configured gbw 0kbps, total allocated gbw 0kbps
DHCP-Relay disabled
DHCP-server disabled
```

Next, you can change the local port that your management services listen on. This can help prevent your services from being detected if someone was to do a scan looking for open services. Telnet (TCP 23), SSH (TCP 22), WebUI (TCP 80), and WebUI SSL (TCP 443) can all be changed to different ports. Use the following steps to change the ports via the WebUI:

1. Access **Configuration** | **Admin** | **Administrators**.
2. Specify new port numbers for Telnet, SSH, WebUI and WebUI SSL (port numbers must be in the range 1024-32767).
3. Click **Apply**.

Enter the following commands to set the port numbers via the CLI:

```
Syngress-> set admin ssh port 1024
Syngress-> set admin port 32000
Syngress-> set admin telnet port 4000
Syngress-> set ssl port 5000
```

All of the management we have been doing has been to the IP address of the interface. It will be easy for people to determine what the IP address is of the firewall. This can lead them to attempt to connect to it and try and mange your device. You can, however, set up what is called a management IP. This IP address is used only for management. This is configured directly on the interface. For this example we will be using a NetScreen-5GT and we will be modifying the *untrust* interface.

Use the following steps to set up a management IP via the WebUI:

1. Access **Network | Interfaces (List)**. The screen shown in Figure 3.13 will be displayed.

Figure 3.13 Network Interfaces List

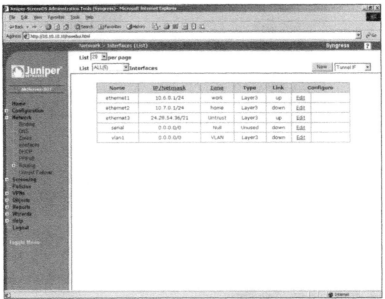

2. Click the **Edit** link for the *untrust* entry. A screen similar to the one shown in Figure 3.14 will be displayed.

3. Use the **Manage IP** * field to enter the new IP address.

Figure 3.14 Edit Network Interface

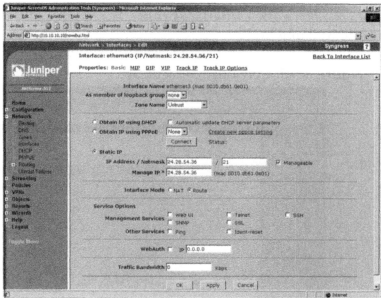

4. Click **Apply**.

To set up a management IP via the CLI, enter the command **set interface untrust manage-ip** *ipaddress*.

For remote command line access you can set up custom login banners. This is useful to give a legal statement or perhaps a help message. This can also identify specific repercussions if someone connects without permission. There are two limitations on using banners, however. First, you are limited to a single line. Second, you are limited to 127 characters. A banner can be configured for both the console and for remote Telnet sessions. This option can be configured from both the WebUI and the CLI.

From the WebUI:

1. Access **Configuration | Admin | Banners**. A screen similar to Figure 3.15 will be displayed.

Figure 3.15 Banners

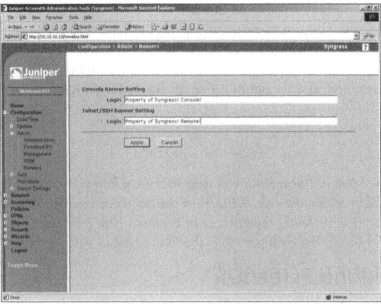

2. Use the **Console Banner Setting Login** field to enter the login banner text that will be displayed for users using the console.

3. Use the **Telnet/SSH Banner Setting Login** field to enter the login banner text that will be displayed for users using Telnet or SSH.

4. Click **Apply**.

Use the following CLI command to set the banner for console users.

```
Syngress-> set admin auth banner console login "Only permitted individuals
are allowed to use this access. If you are not permitted please
disconnect!"
```

Use the following CLI command to set the banner for Telnet users.

```
Syngress-> set admin auth banner telnet login "Authorized users only!!! All
actions are logged!!!"
```

Finally, there are three options that can be configured from the command line only that can enhance your security. Two of these options are not going to save your system, but since they are new to the 5.0 ScreenOS release, they are worth mentioning. First, you can enforce a minimum length for administrative user passwords. Second, you can restrict how many unsuccessful login attempts that a user can have before they are kicked out of the system. The default is three and it does not lock out the user; that same person could attempt to Telnet back in and do it again. Finally, you can restrict the root user to gain access from the console only. This can prevent anyone from gaining root access to the device unless they had physical access to the device.

Use the following CLI commands to set a minimum password length, limit access attempts, and restrict root user access to the console, respectively.

```
Syngress-> set admin password restrict length 8
Syngress-> set admin access attempts 2
Syngress-> set admin root access console
```

The ideas in this section will definitely help you secure your device. Security is all about mitigating risk. With these management security procedures in place you significantly lower the chances of encountering a security problem. You can mix and match the configurations that work best in your environment.

Updating ScreenOS

Juniper Networks is committed to providing a secure and robust operating system for the NetScreen firewall product line. From time to time Juniper will publish new version of ScreenOS. These may include security updates, feature enhancements, or both. It is very important that you maintain the software on your firewall. It is a core component of your network security and it has to be secure. There are several methods that you can use to upgrade ScreenOS. First we will focus on the command line methods. From the command line you can not only update your OS, but you can also back up your operating system. When using the command line you are required to use a TFTP server. Use the following command to back up your software:

```
Syngress-> save software from flash to tftp ipaddress 5.0.0r8.1-5GT.bin
```

      Use the following command to update the software:

```
Syngress-> save software from tftp 1.2.3.4 5.0.0r8.1-5GT.bin to flash
```

You can also use the WebUI to update the firmware. However, as we mentioned before, you cannot download the current software from the WebUI.

1. Access **Configuration | Update | ScreenOS/Keys**. A screen similar to Figure 3.16 will be displayed.

Figure 3.16 ScreenOS/Keys

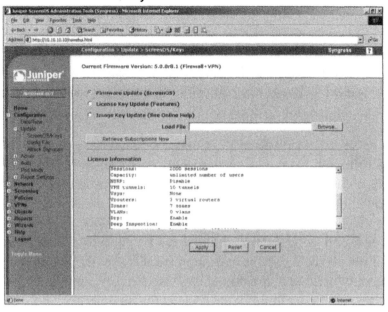

2. Enable the **Firmware Update (ScreenOS)** option.

3. Click **Browse** and locate and select the previously downloaded firmware file (stored on the local system).

4. Click **Apply**. It may take several minutes to update the system with the new OS.

System Recovery

There may be times when your NetScreen firewall runs into problems from which you cannot recover. There are three situations that we will go over in this section. One of the major issues that people run into is configuration management. There may be scenarios that you run into where you are about to make changes that you are unsure of. You may be adding a new route or a new policy that could create havoc on your network, but currently you are running on a successful configuration. In cases where you need a backup copy of a correctly functioning configuration file, you can use the configuration rollback feature.

The configuration rollback feature allows you maintain a backup configuration file that you can use in case your primary configuration file, saved or running, runs into problems. This is a great feature that can get you out of tight squeezes if you run into issues. The configuration rollback cannot be performed from the WebUI. Use the following steps to save your system configuration.

1. Use the command **get file** to get a list of files in flash memory.

2. Enter the command **save config to last-known good**. A new file called lkg.cfg will be created. This file is your rollback configuration file. It is a saved copy of the running configuration at the time you executed the command. That file stays on the system unless you use the **delete** command to remove it. This means that even if you reset the configuration to the defaults, you still will keep this configuration.

To restore a previously saved system configuration, enter the command **exec config rollback**. Note that this process forces your device to reboot.

You can use this restoration process at any time as long as the file exists. There is one additional way to use the configuration rollback. If you are working on a new configuration that could possibly cause you to lose access to your system for whatever reason, configuration rollback can be put into a *watching* mode. In this mode, if the device is reset, it will automatically reset the configuration back to the stored rollback configuration. This is excellent in cases where you need to ensure the safe restoration of your devices provided networking services.

To put the rollback in watching mode, enter the command **exec config rollback enable**. The command prompt will include the text "(rollback enabled)". To turn this mode off, enter **exec config rollback disable**.

Now that we have discussed how to recover your configuration, we now need to look at another scenario. What if you lose your root password? This is a tough scenario to recover from, because you have lost access to the system. There are two methods to recover from this error. Both methods require you to have console access to the device. In the first scenario, you would log into the serial console using the serial number of the device as the username and password. Once you do this, you will be notified that you will lose your configuration and all of your settings. If you have processed proper configuration management, you will be fine. Just as a note; even the configuration rollback file is deleted. So you must have saved your configuration somewhere off of the system if you want to restore it.

The following shows a typical serial number login and the resulting messages.

```
login: 00642120012308289
password:
!!! Lost Password Reset !!! You have initiated a command to reset the
device to factory defaults, clearing all current configuration and settings.
Would you like to continue?  y/[n] y
```

```
!! Reconfirm Lost Password Reset !! If you continue, the entire
configuration of the device will be erased. In addition, a permanent
counter will be incremented to signify that this device has been
reset. This is your last chance to cancel this command. If you
proceed, the device will return to factory default configuration,
which is: System IP: 192.168.1.1; username: netscreen, password:
netscreen. Would you like to continue?  y/[n] y
```

Another way to access a system when you have forgotten the root password is to use the reset button located on the exterior if the system. To use this type of configuration use the following procedure:

1. Locate the reset button on the system. The button is recessed and you would need to use a paper clip or pin to use it

2. Press and hold the button down until the flashing green status light turns red then turns back to flashing green.

3. Release the button and then press it again.

Doing this will reset the system and you will lose all of your configurations. This is done for security reasons. These are both powerful methods to recover your device, however you may want to disable these options. You may not want someone to simply be able to walk up to your device and reset your configuration. You are in luck because both methods can be disabled. However, if you do this the device will be unrecoverable if you lose the root password! So do not lose your root password unless you want to return the device back to Juniper Networks.

To disable the ability to log in using the serial number, enter **unset admin device-reset**. To re-enable this feature, enter **set admin device-reset**. To disable the device's reset button, enter **unset admin hw-reset**. To re-enable this feature, enter **set admin hw-reset**.

In the previous section we looked at ways to upgrade ScreenOS. However, there are many ways in which the image can be corrupted when you upload the file. More then likely your file was previously damaged before you uploaded it. However, there is no reason to worry if your system cannot boot. To restore your system to a functional configuration you need to have serial console access to the system and a TFTP server on the local network to the device. During the boot process a prompt will be displayed four times. The prompt will say, "Hit any key to run loader". Press any key and you will be asked for the file you want to load, the IP address you want to assign to your device, and the IP address of the TFTP server. The interface that gets the IP address you assign is one of the following depending on what type of device you have: Trust, E1, or E1/1. If the file can be found on the TFTP server it will be loaded into flash and then your device will reboot. When the device reboots it will load the new OS image.

```
NetScreen NS-5GT Boot Loader Version 2.1.0 (Checksum: 61D07DA5)
Copyright (c) 1997-2003 NetScreen Technologies, Inc.

Total physical memory: 128MB
    Test - Pass
    Initialization.... Done


Hit any key to run loader
Hit any key to run loader
Hit any key to run loader


Serial Number [0123012123008289]: READ ONLY
HW Version Number [1010]: READ ONLY
Self MAC Address [0010-db61-1230]: READ ONLY
Boot File Name [ns5gt.5.0.0r8.1]:
Self IP Address [192.168.1.1]:
TFTP IP Address [192.168.1.31]:


Save loader config (56 bytes)... Done
```

Configuring the NetScreen Firewall

Now that you are familiar with the basics of managing your NetScreen firewall, it is now time to configure your firewall for the first time. In this section we will look at configuring basic requirements to make your system functional on your network. There are three basics for getting your device running on the network. The first thing you need is a zone. We first touched on zones in the last chapter. In this section we will look at how to use existing zones, create new zones, and binding zones to interfaces. The primary type of zone that exists is the *security zone*, but there are several other types of zones that can be used. It is important to know each type of zone, as they determine how an interface will function. Some zones you many never use, but knowing is half the battle.

There are several types of interfaces on a NetScreen firewall device. You will always have physical interfaces, of course, as they are required to connect to the network. NetScreen also offers several other types of interfaces that you can use. These interfaces provide different functions and are not all actual physical devices. These types of interfaces include subinterfaces, management interfaces, high availability interfaces, and tunnel interfaces. Each type of interface was designed to provide a specific function on the NetScreen device. We will look at each interface type, its function, and how you can leverage their special abilities on your network.

Your newly configured interface will require an IP address if you want it to interact with your network. In Chapter 1 we first discussed IP addressing. I am sure that you are fairly familiar with IP addressing and you have used it on at least one type of system. This process is similar for every device, as each system is implementing the IP standard. A NetScreen firewall is no exception when using IP addressing.

Some Small Office Home Office (SOHO) class devices have a configuration mode called *port mode*. The SOHO devices have five physical interfaces. By default, there is one external untrust interface and four trust interfaces. However, you can change the port mode to modify the distribution of ports. This is a great feature that you can use to extend the value of the SOHO class devices. In this section we will also look at the various options you can use when configuring a network interface and using the built in PPPoE client.

Types of Zones

There are three types of zones on a NetScreen firewall. Each zone provides its own specific function and is used for a specific purpose. The security zone is the most commonly used type of zone. The other two zone types are used much less commonly. One of these types is the tunnel zone. This type of zone is used for creating route-based VPNs. The other type of zone is the function zone. This zone is used for special purposes in high availability. Each type of zone is used to bind to an interface. One exception to this rule will be defined below.

Security Zones

A security zone is used to break your network into logical segments. At a minimum, you need to define two security zones. Most NetScreen firewall devices come with predefined zones that you can use. These zones are usually trust, untrust, and DMZ (de-militarized zone). This varies from device to device. You need to use two zones because this will allow you to separate your network into two parts, usually the two areas you want to separate from each other. Each NetScreen firewall can use only a limited amount of zones. On some devices you can only have a few, while on the higher end firewalls you could have several hundred zones. There is another type of security zone called a layer two zone, covered covered in the chapter, Transparent Mode.

Tunnel Zones

Tunnel zones are used with tunnel interfaces. Tunnel interfaces are a special type of virtual interface that can terminate VPN traffic. Tunnel interfaces are first bound to the tunnel zone. Then the tunnel zone is bound to a security zone, which is in turn bound to a physical interface. Tunnel zones are covered in depth Chapters 11 and 12.

Function Zones

Function zones are used to provide a single type of unique function. There are five types of function zones. The first type is the null zone. The null zone is used as a placeholder for interfaces that are not bound to a zone. The next type of function zone is the MGT (management) zone. This zone is used on out-of-band management interfaces. The HA (high availability) function zone is used for high availability interfaces. There are no configurable options for the HA zone. The self zone is used to host management connections. When using the remote management protocols to connect to your NetScreen device for management you are connecting to the self zone. The last type of zone is the VLAN (virtual local area network) zone. It is used to host the VLAN1 interface. The VLAN1 interface is used to manage a NetScreen firewall that is running in transparent mode.

Virtual Routers

As we have discussed, any device that uses the IP protocol must have a routing table that determines how to send information from one place to another. The NetScreen takes this idea to a whole new level by allowing you to have multiple routing tables called virtual routers. Each virtual router has its own routing table that is a complete separate routing domain from other virtual routers. In this chapter we will only be looking at the trust virtual router and configuring routes in it. A full explanation of routing is covered in the Chapter 5, Routing.

Types of Interfaces

A NetScreen firewall can contain several types of interfaces. An interface allows traffic to enter a zone and leave a zone. If you want an interface to pass traffic, you need to bind it to a zone. Once you bind an interface to a zone, you can apply an IP address to it. There are four types of interfaces: security zone interfaces, function zone interfaces, tunnel interfaces and loopback interfaces. As you can see, each type of interface has a corresponding zone type, except for the loopback interface, which is a special type of interface.

Security Zone Interfaces

Security zone interfaces are used primarily for the passing of traffic from one zone to another. In this category is any type of interface related to physical interfaces or virtual interfaces that are a collection of multiple physical interfaces. This is the most common type interface you will work with on a NetScreen firewall.

Physical Interfaces

Every NetScreen firewall has some sort of physical interface. These interfaces are used to connect the firewall to the network. The naming convention of the physical interfaces varies based upon the platform. On the SOHO class of the NetScreen appliances, the interface names are based upon the zones. For example, the internal interface is named trust and the external interface is named untrust. On the NetScreen-25 up to the NetScreen-208 products, the interfaces are named beginning with the media type *Ethernet* and then specified by the port number, such as "ethernet1". NetScreen firewalls that are systems, including the NetScreen-500, ISG-2000, NetScreen-5200, and NetScreen-5400, are named with the media type, slot number, and then the port number. For example, ethernet2/1 would be an Ethernet interface in slot number two and port number one. Physical interfaces can be assigned a single primary IP address.

There are some situations where you may need to have multiple IP address on an interface. You can add multiple secondary IP addresses on each physical interface. When a secondary IP address is added, the NetScreen firewall automatically adds a route between the two IP address segments. This way you can connect between the two segments. This will automatically remove the route if you delete the secondary IP address. If you want to segment these two networks, you can disable routing between the two. This will just drop packets between the two, but the routing table will not be modified.

Secondary IP addresses have some restrictions as well. First, subnets between the multiple secondary interfaces cannot overlap. Second, interfaces in the untrust zone are unable to use multiple secondary IP addresses. If you choose to manage your firewall with the secondary IP address, it inherits the management properties of the primary interface. The secondary interface is unable to have a gateway, which means anything connecting to that interface must be on that local network.

Subinterfaces

Subinterfaces are used primarily with VLANs. If, for example, you had a network that contained several VLANs, a NetScreen firewall could act as a central point to connect between the separate VLANs. Each subinterface acts just like a physical interface. All of the subinterfaces that are bound to a physical interface can only use the bandwidth that is provided by that interface. So if you have a single 100Mbps interface and several subinterfaces, they can only use the maximum bandwidth of that 100Mbps interface shared amongst them. The properties of a subinterface are otherwise identical to that of a physical interface. However, each subinterface *must* be assigned to a different VLAN and they *must* have a different IP subnet than all of physical interfaces and the other subinterfaces defined on the firewall.

Aggregate Interfaces

When you create an aggregate interface you are binding multiple physical interfaces together to create one super interface. This interface acts as if it was a single physical interface. It provides cumulative bandwidth. So if you bound two 1 gigabit interfaces together, you would have a combined throughput of 2Gbps for that interface. If one of the interfaces was to fail, the remaining interface would continue to carry the traffic. However, that remaining interface can only carry as much traffic as the interface is rated for. So if you had two gigabit interfaces bound together and lost one, you would lower your maximum throughput to 1Gbps. This is a great feature, but is only available on the NetScreen-5200 and the NetScreen-5400 systems.

Redundant Interfaces

The redundant interface is much like the aggregate interface, but only has one of the two benefits of the aggregate interface. Redundant interfaces are unable to combine their bandwidth, and only provide redundancy in case of a failure. This is still a great option to use when redundancy is a requirement.

VLAN1 Interface

The VLAN1 interface is used for one purpose. When you configure a NetScreen firewall to operate in transparent mode, the physical interfaces do not have IP addresses. You will need a way still to manage the firewall and to terminate VPNs. The VLAN1 interface is a virtual security interface that can have an IP address assigned to it. This allows you to remotely manage your firewall and, if need be, have an IP address to terminate VPNs to. Using a NetScreen firewall in transparent mode is covered in Chapter 9.

Virtual Security Interfaces

The last type of security interface is the virtual security interface (VSI). This type of interface is used when two NetScreen devices are used in a high availability configuration. The two firewalls are combined to create a single entity called a virtual security device (VSD). Each device in the cluster defines a physical interface to create a VSI. This VSI has its own MAC address and IP address and operates just like a physical interface. Configuring and using VSIs and VSDs are covered in the Chapter 14, High Availability.

Function Zone Interfaces

Function zone interfaces are special interfaces that are used for a single purpose or task. These interfaces are dedicated to that task and cannot be used to do anything else.

Management Interfaces

Some NetScreen firewalls contain an interface dedicated for management of the device. This interface is called the MGT interface. It allows you to separate the management of the device from rest of the network by using this special interface. It is ensures that you will have bandwidth for management applications. Because the interface does not pass general-purpose traffic, it provides additional security by being dedicated to management.

HA Interfaces

On NetScreen systems (NetScreen-500 and later), each device contains two HA interfaces, HA1, and HA2. These interfaces are used exclusively for high availability. One interface passes control messages to each device. The second HA interface is used for traffic synchronization. If one of the interfaces fails, the remaining HA interface would provide both services. You must use a minimum of 100Mbps interfaces for high availability interfaces.

Some devices that can function in a HA cluster do not have dedicated interfaces for high availability. You can use a virtual HA interface, which is bound to a physical interface. This allows you to use the high availability configurations even though you do not have a dedicated interface to do this.

Tunnel Interfaces

A tunnel interface is used as a gateway to a VPN. This allows you to create a VPN configuration and then bind that VPN to the tunnel interface. If you wanted to pass traffic to the VPN, you would simply create a route on your firewall to point to the tunnel interface for the remote network. The VPN will be automatically established and traffic will be encrypted and sent to the remote gateway. Tunnel interfaces are only used for VPNs. VPNs are explained in the Chapter 12, VPN Usage.

Loopback Interfaces

The last type of interface we are going to discuss is the loopback interface. The loopback interface is a special interface. It is a virtual interface that does not exist except logically inside of the firewall. A loopback interface is assigned to a zone and it is not accessible from other zones unless you specify a policy to permit the traffic. A loopback interface can be used to manage your firewall as well as to manage it.

Configuring Security Zones

The security zones are the core part for creating policies in the NetScreen firewall. Policies are not discussed in this chapter, but are discussed in the next chapter, "Basic Policy Configuration". Here, though, it is important that you become an expert on managing security zones. Once you have the security zones created and configured, it will be much easier for you to effectively create policies. As mentioned before, there will be several predefined security zones on your firewall. These are typically trust, untrust, and DMZ. The trust zone is designed for the internal protected network. The untrust zone is designed typically for the Internet or other undesirable places. The DMZ zone is to be used for your DMZ network. The trust zone and untrust zone have some unique properties that will be discussed later in the chapter. The predefined zones cannot be deleted, but they can be modified.

First, let's look at the zones we have configured on our device. This can be done from both the command line as well as the WebUI. To view the zones using the WebUI, access **Network | Zones**. A screen similar to the one shown in Figure 3.17 will be displayed.

Figure 3.17 Network Zones

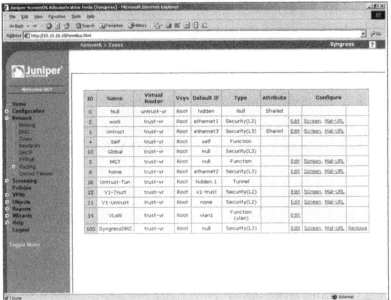

To view the zones using the CLI, enter the command **get zone**. You will see each zone listed in an output similar to the following:

```
Total 10 zones created in vsys Root - 5 are policy configurable.
Total policy configurable zones for Root is 5.
```

ID	Name	Type	Attr	VR	Default-IF	VSYS
0	Null	Null	Shared	untrust-vr	hidden	Root
1	Untrust	Sec(L3)	Shared	trust-vr	untrust	Root
2	Trust	Sec(L3)		trust-vr	trust	Root
4	Self	Func		trust-vr	self	Root
5	MGT	Func		trust-vr	null	Root
10	Global	Sec(L3)		trust-vr	null	Root

```
11  V1-Untrust        Sec(L2)        trust-vr      None         Root

12  V1-Trust          Sec(L2)        trust-vr      v1-trust     Root

14  VLAN              Func           trust-vr      vlan1        Root

16  Untrust-Tun       Tun            trust-vr      hidden.1     Root
--------------------------------------------------------------------
```

Both the WebUI and the CLI look very similar as far as the way that zones are displayed. Both show the following information:

- **ID** The ID is used when doing debugging. It is important to understand where to locate the zone ID.

- **Name** The name is used as a label for the zone.

- **Type** This tells you what type of zone this is. As you can see, there are several of the zone types we have mentioned.

- **Attr** This specifies any additional attributes for the zone. *Shared* means that the zone is shared among all local VSYS. By default, untrust and null are shared.

- **VR** This specifies which virtual router that the zone is operating in.

- **Default-IF** This identifies which interface is bound to the zone by default.

VSYS This lists which VSYS or virtual system the zone is bound to.

It is a simple task to create a new zone. However, before doing so, you should know the following information:

- **Name** What you want to name your zone. It helps to be descriptive. If you have a DMZ for web servers, naming it WebDMZ is more helpful than if you were to just choose DMZ02. This is really a personal preference. If you are creating a layer two security zone, the zone must be prefixed with "L2-"

- **Type of zone** You can create three types of zones; security layer three zones, security layer two zones, and tunnel zones.

This is the minimum information you would need to configure a zone. There are some additional options that can be configured on a zone:

- **SCREEN** SCREEN options are defense options that protect against specific attacks and malicious traffic. This is covered in Chapter 10, Attack Detection and Defense.

- **Malicious URL protection** This feature provides pattern matching for HTTP traffic. It allows you to identify malicious URLs and block those requests. It is fully described in the Chapter 10.

- **Block Intra-Zone Traffic** If this option is selected, it will allow you to block traffic between two interfaces bound to the same zone. This would be called intrazone traffic.

- **If TCP non SYN, send RESET back** This option is only valid for layer three security zones and tunnel zones. If this option is enabled, the NetScreen firewall will send a RESET TCP packet to any host that sends a TCP segment with a TCP flag set other than SYN and that does not belong to an existing session. If you have SYN checking enabled (this is done from the CLI using the command **set flow tcp-syn-check**) the unsolicited SYN packet is dropped and the session initiator is notified to reset the TCP connection without initializing a new session in the session table. If the NetScreen firewall was to skip sending the RESET notice, the system that was attempting to initiate the session would continually send SYN packets until its connection attempt timed out. If SYN checking is disabled, the NetScreen firewall passes the SYN packet to the end system if a policy permits it. This is useful for blocking packets that can be used in different types of network scans. If you are unsure if this will help you, it is best to leave this at the default setting.

- **IP/TCP Reassembly for ALG** (Application Layer Gateway) If this option is selected, the NetScreen firewall will reassemble fragmented HTTP and FTP packets before they are inspected. This will allow for more efficient enforcement for the Mal-URL engine to inspect the traffic. If you are not using the Mal-URL feature, leave this option off.

- **Shared Zone** This option is only available if you have a NetScreen device that supports virtual systems. This option enables the zone to be shared among all of the virtual systems. Once you enable this option, you are unable to disable it. You must either delete the zone or disable all virtual systems first.

- **IP Classification** This option is used with virtual systems only. If this option is selected, the firewall will associate all traffic with this zone to a particular virtual system.

- **WebUI** (layer two zones only) Selecting this option enables management for the WebUI on this zone.

- **SNMP** (layer two zones only) Select this option to enable SNMP (Simple Network Management Protocol) services on this zone.

- **Telnet** (layer two zones only) Select this option to enable Telnet management on this zone.

- **SSL** (layer two zones only) Selecting this option enables SSL WebUI management on this zone.

- **SSH** (layer two zones only) Selecting this option enables SSH management on this zone.

- **NSM** (layer two zones only) Selecting this option enables NSM management on this zone.

- **Ping** (layer two zones only) Selecting this option enables ping from the firewall in this zone.

- **Ident-reset** (layer two zones only) Some services such as SMTP and FTP send an ident, or identification request. If you have Ident-reset enabled, it will reset this ident request and allow you access to that service.

- **WebAuth** (layer two zones only) Selecting this option enables web authentication when passing through the interface that this zone is bound to.

Most of the time you would just define the name for the new zone and what type of zone it is. However, it is always a good idea to know all of the options when creating your new zone. Some of the above options are seldom used, but may serve as a good reference to use in the future.

Next we will go through the actual zone creation process. We will again focus on layer three zones, as the other zone types will be covered in later chapters. Use the following steps to create a zone using the WebUI:

1. Access **Network | Zones** and click **New**. A screen similar to Figure 3.18 will be displayed.

Figure 3.18 Create a New Zone

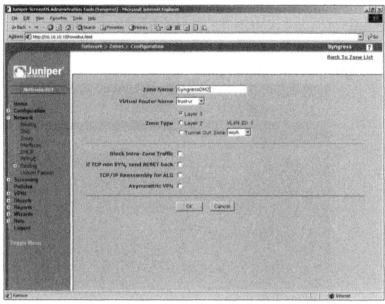

2. Enter the **Zone Name**.

3. Ensure **trust-vr** is selected in the **Virtual Router Name** drop-down list.

4. In the **Zone Type** section, select the **Layer 3** option.

5. Click **OK**.

> To create a zone using the CLI, enter the command **set zone name**
> **name**, where *name* is the name for the zone.

Once a zone is created, you can modify all of its properties except for its name. To change the name, you must delete the zone, then re-create it using the desired name. Use the following steps to delete a zone using the WebUI:

1. Access **Network | Zones** and click the **Remove** link of the zone you wish to delete.

2. Click **OK** to confirm.

To remove a zone using the CLI, enter the command **unset zone *name***, where *name* is the name of the zone you wish to remove.

Use the following steps to modify an existing zone via the WebUI:

1. Access **Network | Zones** and click the **Edit** link of the zone you wish to modify. A screen similar to the one shown in Figure 3.19 will be displayed.

Figure 3.19 Edit a Zone

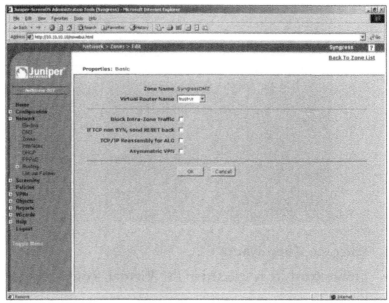

2. Change the desired fields and click **OK**.

Configuring Your NetScreen for the Network

When configuring a NetScreen device, there are several steps you need to perform before it can interact with the network. A physical interface must be first bound to a zone before it can be assigned an IP address. Figure 3.20 depicts the relationship between a zone and an interface. A zone is a parent to a physical interface and the IP address is a child to the physical interface.

Figure 3.20 Zone Interface / IP Relationship

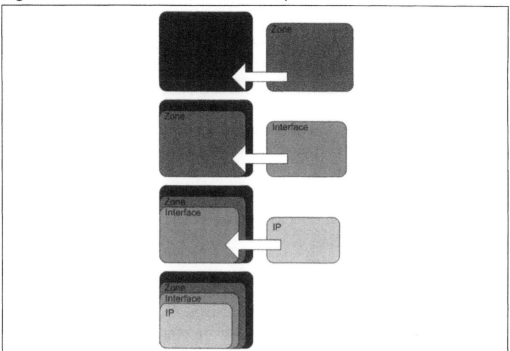

Binding an Interface to a Zone

First let's bind an interface to a zone. In this case we will be using a NetScreen-5GT and we will bind the trust zone to the trust interface. This can be done in both the WebUI and the CLI. However, to change the zone you must first remove the IP address by setting it to **0.0.0.0/0.** Then you can select a new Zone.

From the WebUI:

1. Access **Network | Interfaces**.
2. Click the **Edit** link for the **trust** interface.
3. Select **Trust** from the **Zone Name** drop-down list.
4. Click **OK**.

To bind an interface to a zone using the CLI, enter the command **set interface** *interfacename* **zone** *zonename*, where *interfacename* is the name of the interface you wish to bind and *zonename* is the name of the zone you wish to bind the specified interface to.

Setting up IP Addressing

We will now assign an IP address of 192.168.0.1 with a twenty-four-bit subnet mask to the interface. This can be done in both the WebUI and the CLI. If you wanted to modify the IP address of an interface, it is the same as if you were setting it up for the first time.

From the WebUI:

1. Access **Network | Interfaces** and click the **Edit** link for the **trust** interface (or whichever interface you are binding to).

2. Select the **Static IP** option.

3. Enter **192.168.0.1** (or whatever IP address you want to assign) in the IP address text field, and enter **24** (or another value) in the netmask text field.

4. Click **OK**.

To assign an IP address to an interface using the CLI, enter the command **set interface** *interfacename* **ip** *ipaddress netmask*, where *interfacename* is the name of the interface, *ipaddress* is the IP address you want to assign, and *netmask* is the netmask.

Configuring the DHCP Client

Now let's take our NetScreen-5GT and set the untrust interface to receive an IP address from DHCP. This will allow the NetScreen to be plugged into any cable modem, DSL, or internal network and seamlessly get an IP address.

From the WebUI:

1. Access **Network | Interfaces** and click the **Edit** link for the **untrust** interface (or whichever interface you are configuring).

2. Select the **Obtain IP using DHCP** option.

3. Enable the **Automatic update of DHCP server parameters** option.

4. Click **OK**.

To set this configuration using the CLI, enter the command **set interface** *interfacename* **dhcp client enable**, where *interfacename* is the name of the interface you wish to configure.

Using PPPoE

Some DSL service providers require the use of a protocol called PPPoE, or Point-to-Point Protocol over Ethernet. This requires an additional configuration. You must configure a PPPoE instance and bind to an interface, then configure the interface to use PPPoE to negotiate the connection. You will then get an IP address from PPPoE, just as you would with DHCP.

From the WebUI:

1. Access **Network | PPPoE**. A screen similar to Figure 3.21 will be displayed.

Figure 3.21 Network PPPoE

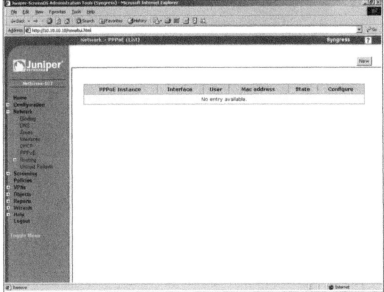

2. Click **New**. A screen similar to the one shown in Figure 3.22 will be displayed

Figure 3.22 Network | PPPoE | Edit

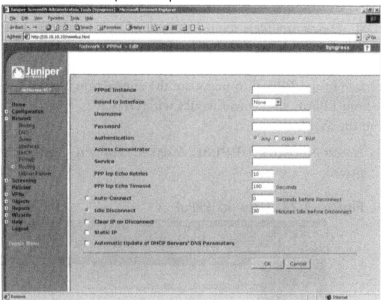

3. Use the PPPoE Instance field to enter the name.

4. Choose **untrust** from the **Bound to Interface** drop-down list (or whichever interface you are binding to).

5. Enter your ISP-provided username and password in the **Username** and **Password** fields, respectively.

6. Select the **Any Authentication** option.

7. Enable the **Automatic Update of DHCP Servers' DNS Parameters** option.

8. Click **OK**.

To create a PPPoE connection via the CLI, enter the command **set pppoe name "*name*" username "*username*" password "*password*"**, ensuring you include the quotes, and where *name* is the name of the interface, *username* is your ISP-provided username, and *password* is your ISP-provided password.

Interface Speed Modes

By default, all of the ports on your NetScreen firewall are auto-sensing. This means they negotiate the Ethernet settings such as speed and duplex. This is great most of the time, but in an ideal world you may want to hard code these settings to ensure that you are getting the proper performance out of your network. This configuration can only be done from the CLI. In the following example, we will hardcode the trust interface port four interface to 100Mbps full duplex.

```
Syngress-> get interface trust port phy
Port 1:  link is down, 10 Mbps, forced to half duplex
Port 2:  link is down, 10 Mbps, forced to half duplex
Port 3:  link is down, 10 Mbps, forced to half duplex
Port 4:  link is up, 100 Mbps, auto negotiated to full duplex
Syngress-> set int trust port 4 phy full 100mb
Syngress-> get interface trust port phy
Port 1:  link is down, 10 Mbps, forced to half duplex
Port 2:  link is down, 10 Mbps, forced to half duplex
Port 3:  link is down, 10 Mbps, forced to half duplex
Port 4:  link is up, 100 Mbps, forced to full duplex
```

Port Mode Configuration

Some devices in the SOHO product line support something called port mode. These devices contain one untrust or external port and four internal ports. By default, the four internal ports are called trust and are bound to the trust zone. However, there are four other modes you can use as well. The *extended* mode requires an additional license. When you change between port modes, this removes your existing configuration. If you clear your configuration by using the **unset all** command, the port mode setting will be unaffected. In Table 3.3 you can see the differences between the different modes.

Table 3.3 Port Modes

Port	Trust-Untrust		Home-Work		Dual Untrust		Combined		Extended	
	Int	Zone	Int	Zone	Int	Zone	Int	Zone	Int	Zone
Untrusted	Untrust	Untrust	Eth3	Untrust	Eth3	Untrust	Eth4	Untrust	Eth3	Untrust
1	Trust	Trust	Eth1	Work	Eth1	Trust	Eth1	Work	Eth1	Trust
2	Trust	Trust	Eth1	Work	Eth1	Trust	Eth2	Home	Eth1	Trust
3	Trust	Trust	Eth2	Home	Eth1	Trust	Eth2	Home	Eth2	DMZ
4	Trust	Trust	Eth2	Home	Eth2	Untrust	Eth3	Untrust	Eth2	DMZ
Modem	Serial	Null	Serial	Null	Serial	N/A	N/A	N/A	Serial	Untrust

You can change the port mode settings from both the WebUI. You can see the port mode WebUI configuration in Figure 3.23.

Figure 3.23 Port Mode Configuration

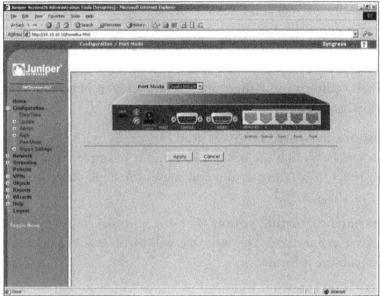

Use the following steps to change the port mode settings via the WebUI:

1. Access **Configuration | Port Mode**.

2. Select the desired mode from the **Port Mode** drop-down list.

3. Click **Apply**, then click **OK** to confirm. Your current configuration will be erased and the device will reboot.

To change modes using the CLI, enter the command **exec port-mode combined** and press **y** to confirm. Your current configuration will be erased and the device will reboot.

Configuring Basic Network Routing

When you want to connect to a remote network, you need to inform your firewall of its location. You would do this by adding network routes on your firewall. These routes tell the firewall where the remote network can be found. In this section we will look at adding a static route to access a remote network. We will also be adding a default route. A default route is also known as the route of last resort. So if a packet on a device needs to get to a location and no other routes on the device are able to identify the next gateway for it to go to, it will use the default gateway. When a system is determining what route to use, it will always use the most specific route first.

In this example we will add a static route on our NetScreen firewall to determine the next hop for the 192.168.1.0/24 network. In this chapter we will only be using the trust-vr. Routing with multiple virtual routers will fully be explained in Chapter 6. Adding routes can be done from both the WebUI and the CLI. When adding a route there are several pieces of information you need to know beforehand:

- **Remote network** First you need to identify what the remote network you will be adding the route for is. In our example we will be using 192.168.1.0/24. You can also add routes for single hosts if you like such as 192.168.1.20/32.

- **Interface or virtual router** For our purposes here we will only be looking at interfaces. The interface will be on what physical interface that gateway is located.

- **Next hop gateway** You need to know which system can take your packets to the specified remote network. This device must be capable of connecting to the remote network, or if not, it must know where the remote network can be located.

- **Metric** The metric is a preference number, with the lowest number having the highest priority. All directly connected networks have a metric of zero. All static routes have a default metric of one. There may be cases in which you need to add the same route twice, the preferred route with the lower metric and the less preferred route with the higher metric. If the first route is unavailable, the firewall will use the next route.

Let's begin with our first example of adding our static route in the WebUI.

1. Access **Network | Routing | Routing Entries**. A screen similar to the one shown in Figure 3.24 will be displayed.

Figure 3.24 Routing Entries

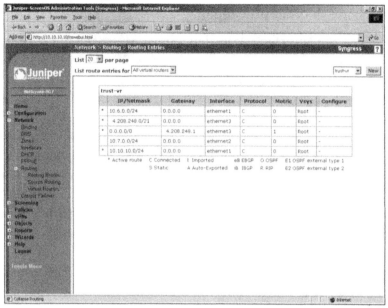

2. Use the drop-down list in the upper right-hand corner to select the virtual router and click **New**. In our example, we will select **trust-vr**. A screen similar to the one shown in Figure 3.25 will be displayed.

Figure 3.25 Configure a Routing Entry

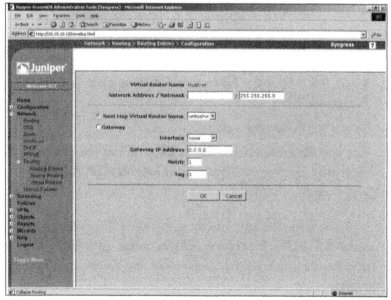

3.   Enter the **Network Address / Netmask**.

4.   Select the **Gateway** option.

5.   Use the **Interface** drop-down list to select the interface (gateway) that is the next hop and use the **Gateway IP Address** field to enter the gateway's IP address.

6.   Click **OK**.

To add a static route using the CLI, enter the command **set route *ipaddress/netmask* interface *interfacename* gateway *gatewayip***, where *ipaddress* is the virtual router's IP address, *netmask* is the cirtual router's netmask, *interfacename* is the next hop gateway, and *gatewayip* is the IP address of the next hop gateway.

To remove a static route via the WebUI, access **Network | Routing | Routing Entries** and click the **Remove** link of the route you wish to delete. Click **OK** to confirm.

The most important and often most used route on a firewall is the default route, or route of last resort. This route is used when no other route matches the traffic. Typically this route will point to your Internet router. If you are running either DHCP or PPPoE, your default route will likely come from that source. However, there may be times when you need to add your own default route. This can be done from both the WebUI and the CLI. It is much like adding a static route, as we did above.

From the WebUI:

1.   Access **Network | Routing | Routing Entries**.

2.   Select your virtual router from the drop-down list in the upper right-hand corner and click **New**.

3.   Enter **0.0.0.0** in the **Network Address** field and enter 0 in the **Netmask** field.

4.   Select the **Gateway** option.

5.   Use the **Interface** drop-down list to select the interface that acts as the next hop gateway and enter the **Gateway IP Address**.

6.   Click **OK**.

To remove the static route using the CLI, enter the command **set route 0.0.0.0/0 interface *interfacename* gateway *gatewayip***, where *interfacename* is the next hop gateway and *gatewayip* is the gateway's IP address.

Configuring System Services

On your NetScreen firewall there are some other notable things to configure. These are important options that you will want to know about. We will first look at configuring the local clock on the device. Configuring the time is very important for being able to correlate information in the logs to a specific time. Also, the firewall executes certain events at given times. If the time is configured improperly, this can cause events to not occur at the correct times.

Most NetScreen firewalls contain a built in DHCP server. Typically, you can have a server on each interface. This allows you to manage your internal IP addressing in a single location. All NetScreen firewalls are able to query DNS servers. This allows them to resolve hostnames to IP addresses just as normal systems do. It is important to have working DNS servers configured on your firewall in case you would use the network to synchronize time to an NTP server.

There is a great deal of information generated by your firewall in the form of logs. Because all NetScreen firewalls have very limited space for storing the logs, you may want to be able to send this logging information to a remote system. We will look at how to configure and use two different remote log repositories. Finally we will look at license keys. These keys unlock the features of your firewall device. We will investigate how license keys work and how to update your license key.

Setting The Time

Every NetScreen device contains an internal clock. This clock continually runs while the device is turned on. You can manually set the clock from both the WebUI and the CLI. Ideally, you want to configure your firewall to contact a timeserver using the Network Time Protocol (NTP). This way the firewall can periodically query the timeserver to ensure that it has the proper time. First we will look at how to manually set the time on your firewall. Figure 3.26 shows the time configuration page from the WebUI.

Figure 3.26 Date/Time Configuration

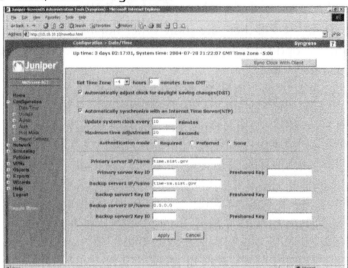

From the WebUI:

1. Access **Configuration | Date/Time**.

2. Use the **Set Time Zone** fields to specify the difference between your time zone and GMT (Greenwich Mean Time).

3. Enable the **Automatically adjust clock for daylight saving changes (DST)** option.

4. Click **Apply**.

5. Click the **Sync Clock With Client** button and click **Yes** to confirm.

   To set the timezone and date/time using CLI, enter the following commands:

```
Syngress-> set clock timezone vv
Syngress-> set clock MM/DD/YYYY hh:mm:ss
```

where vv in the first command is the difference between local time and GMT (expressed as + or -, for example, +3 or −5), and where MM/DD/YYYY is the month, date, and year, and where hh:mm:ss is the hour, minute, and second.

Now we will look at setting up timeservers to sync with the NTP protocol. This protocol allows up to sub-second accuracy for time synchronization. NTP is a free service and every system should use it. The only time you shouldn't use it is when you want your firewall to generate no traffic. NTP can be configured from both the CLI and the WebUI. However, you can only force NTP synchronization from the CLI. Figure 3.25 above shows the time screen, which contains the NTP settings.

From the WebUI:

1. Access **Configuration | Date/Time**.
2. Enable the **Automatically synchronize with an Internet Time Server(NTP)** option.
3. Enter **time.nist.gov** in the **Primary server IP/Name** field.
4. Enter **time-nw.nist.gov** in the **Backup server1 IP/Name** field.
5. Click **Apply**.

To synchronize the time via the CLI, enter the following commands:

```
Syngress-> set ntp timezone -5
Syngress-> set ntp server time.nist.gov
Syngress-> set ntp server backup1 time-nw.nist.gov
Syngress-> set clock ntp
Syngress-> exec ntp update
```

When asked if you want to update the system clock, press **y** for yes.

Finally, you can use something called secure network time protocol (SNTP). This provides MD5-based authentication of each packet to ensure that the packet is from the specified server. If you want to use authentication, you are required to assign a key ID and a preshared key for every timeserver you configure. Additionally, you must configure whether authenticaton is required or simply preferred.

DHCP Server

NetScreen firewall devices can act as a DHCP server. This allows your firewall to control IP address allocation on your network. Any NetScreen device is capable of hosting up to eight DHCP servers. The server can give out IP addresses from a pool or from a reserved list based on MAC address. Another great feature of the DHCP server on the NetScreen firewall is that you can have it determine if another DHCP server is running on the network. This can prevent a conflict between two servers handing out IP addresses. In our example we will set up a DHCP server on the eth2 interface of a NetScreen-5GT. We will assign a pool of IP addresses (as shown in Figure 3.27) and create one reservation based upon MAC address. DHCP servers can be configured from both the WebUI and the CLI.

From the WebUI:

Figure 3.27 DHCP List

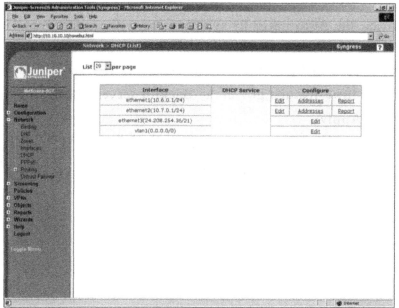

1. Access **Network | DHCP**.

2. Locate the ethernet2 interface and click its **Edit** link. A screen similar to the one shown in Figure 3.28 will be displayed.

3. Enable the **DHCP Server** option.

Figure 3.28 Edit a DHCP Entry

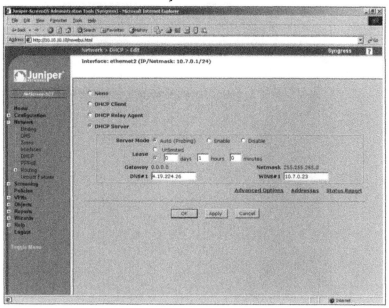

4. For **Server Mode**, enable the **Auto (Probing)** option.

5. In the **Lease** section, click the option button that allows you to enter a specific time period, then enter the desired **days**, **hours**, and **minutes**.

6. Use the **DNS#1** field to enter the IP address of the primary DNS server.

7. Use the **WINS#1** field to enter the IP address of the primary WINS server.

8. Click **OK**. The DHCP list will be displayed.

9. Locate the ethernet2 interface in the list and click its **Addresses** link. A screen similar to the one shown in Figure 3.29 will be displayed.

10. Click **New**.

Figure 3.29 DHCP Server Address List

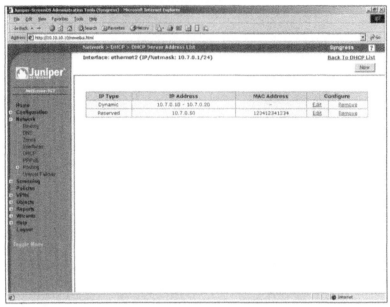

11. Ensure the **Dynamic** option is selected.

12. Use the **IP Address Start** field to enter the first IP address in the address pool.

13. Use the **IP Address End** field to enter the last IP address in the address pool.

14. Click **OK**. The DHCP Server Address List screen will be displayed.

15. Click **New**.

16. Select the **Reserved** option.

17. Use the **IP Address** field to enter the IP address that you wish to reserve.

18. Use the **Ethernet Address** field to enter the MAC address of the device for which you wish to reserve the specified IP address.

19. Click **OK**.

Use the following commands to configure the DHCP server via the CLI:

```
Syngress-> set interface ethernet2 dhcp server auto
Syngress-> set interface ethernet2 dhcp server enable
Syngress-> set interface ethernet2 dhcp server option lease 60
```

```
Syngress-> set interface ethernet2 dhcp server option dns1 10.7.0.23
Syngress-> set interface ethernet2 dhcp server option wins1 10.7.0.23
Syngress-> set interface ethernet2 dhcp server option netmask 255.255.255.0
Syngress-> set interface ethernet2 dhcp server ip 10.7.0.10 to 10.7.0.20
Syngress-> set interface ethernet2 dhcp server ip 10.7.0.50 mac
123412341234
```

DNS

Setting up your NetScreen firewall as a DNS client is fairly simple. The firewall keeps a local cache of DNS entries, and you must decide when you want the cache to be cleared. DNS can be configured from both the WebUI and the CLI. Figure 3.30 shows the WebUI screen for configuring DNS. The hostname and domain name are also set on this page. If you are using a DHCP or PPPoE client on your firewall, the DNS server settings and domain name may be passed down and configured for you.

From the WebUI:

Figure 3.30 DNS Configuration

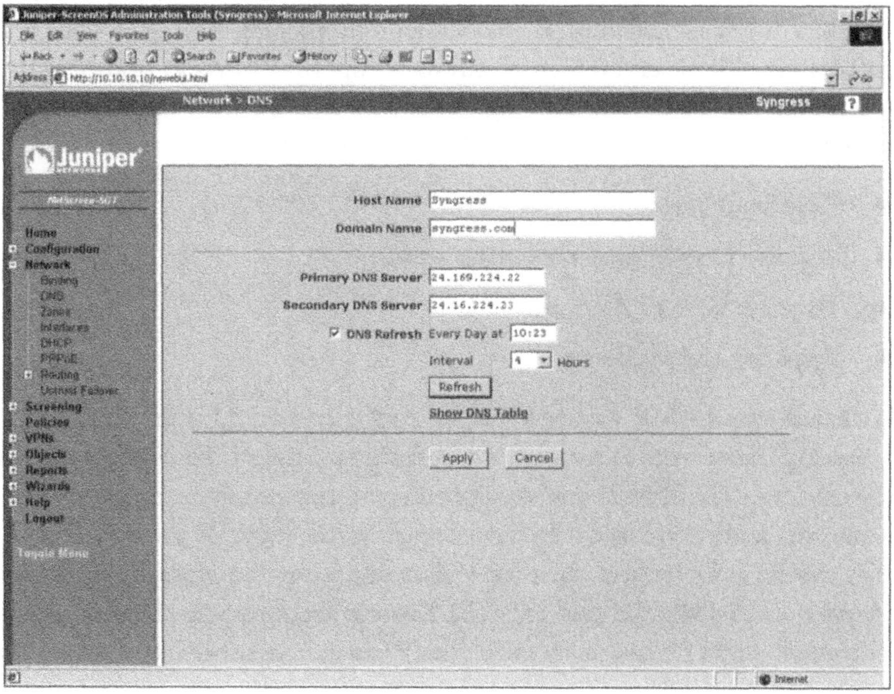

1. Access **Network | DNS**.

2. Enter a **Host Name** and a **Domain Name**.

3. Enter the IP address of the **Primary DNS Server** and the **Secondary DNS Server**.

4. Enable the **DNS Refresh** option and enter the refresh time and frequency.

5. Click **Apply**.

Enter the following commands to configure the DNS server via the CLI:

```
Syngress->set hostname Syngress
Syngress-> set domain syngress.com
Syngress-> set dns host dns1 2.32.23.23
Syngress-> set dns host dns2 2.32.23.24
Syngress-> set dns host schedule 10:23 interval 4
```

SNMP

Simple Network Management Protocol allowsremote administrators to view data statistics on a NetScreen device. It also allows a NetScreen device to send information to a central server. NetScreen firewalls support SNMPv1 and SNMPv2c. It also supports the MIB II, or Management Information Base two standard groups. The SNMP agent supports sending the following traps:

- Cold Start Trap
- Trap for SNMP Authentication Failure
- Traps for System Alarms
- Traps for Traffic Alarms

By default, the SNMP manager has no configuration. This prevents unauthorized viewing of the system based upon default parameters. To configure your NetScreen device for SNMP you must configure community strings, SNMP host addresses, and permissions. In our configuration example we will first set up the basic system information, then we will create a new community. This can be done from both the WebUI and the CLI. You can create up to three communities with up to eight IP ranges in each. An IP range can consist of a single host or a network. If you configure a network those defined IP addresses can only poll the device and not.

Use the following steps to configure SNMP via the WebUI:

1. Access **Configuration | Report Settings | SNMP**. A screen similar to the one shown in Figure 3.31 will be displayed.

Figure 3.31 SNMP Report Settings

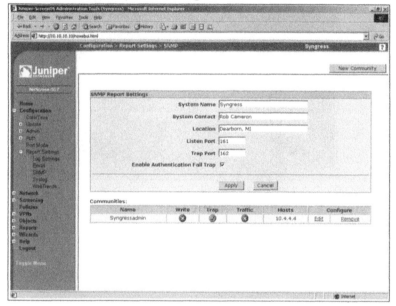

2. Enter the desired **System Name**, **System Contact**, and **Location**.

3. Enter the port numbers of the **Listen Port** and the **Trap Port**.

4. Ensure that the **Enable Authentication Fail Trap** option is enabled.

5. Click **Apply**.

6. Click **New Community**. A screen similar to the one shown in Figure 3.32 will be displayed.

Figure 3.32 New Community

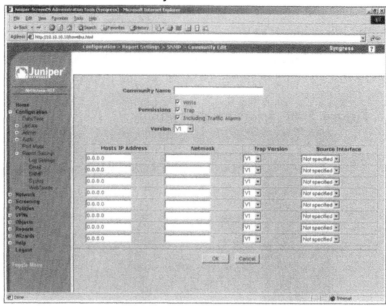

7.   Enter a **Community Name**.

8.   Enable the **Write** option if you want to allow the remote SNMP user to modify this configuration.

9.   Enable the **Trap** option to allow the SNMP agent to send traps to the defined hosts.

10. Enable the **Including Traffic Alarms** option if you wish to force the local SNMP agent to send traffic alarms to the defined hosts.

11. Use the **Version** drop-down list to select the SNMP version that this community will support. The **Any** option will cause the community to support both the v1 and v2c versions.

12. You must define at lease one host or network in the lower portion of the screen. To do so, enter the **Host's IP Address** and **Netmask**. Next, select the **Trap Version** and use the **Source Interface** drop-down list to select the SNMP interface.

13. Click **OK**.

To remove a community, locate it in the community list and click its **Remove** link. Click **OK** to confirm.

To configure SNMP via the CLI, enter the following commands:

```
Syngress-> set snmp name Syngress
Syngress-> set snmp location "Dearborn, MI"
Syngress-> set snmp community Syngressadmin Read-Only version v2c
Syngress-> set snmp host Syngressadmin 10.4.4.4
```

Syslog

NetScreen firewalls generate a great deal of logging. Logged information is contained on the local flash file system using a first-in-first-out method. The first log in will be the first log removed when logging space fills up. If you want to keep your logs for an extended period of time, you must archive them to an external log server. A NetScreen firewall can send information to up to four syslog hosts at a time. Syslog can be configured from both the WebUI and the CLI. Logging will be discussed in depth in the next chapter.

Use the following steps to configure the syslog server via the WebUI:

1. Access **Configuration | Report Settings | Syslog**. A screen similar to the one shown in Figure 3.33 will be displayed.

Figure 3.33 Syslog Configuration

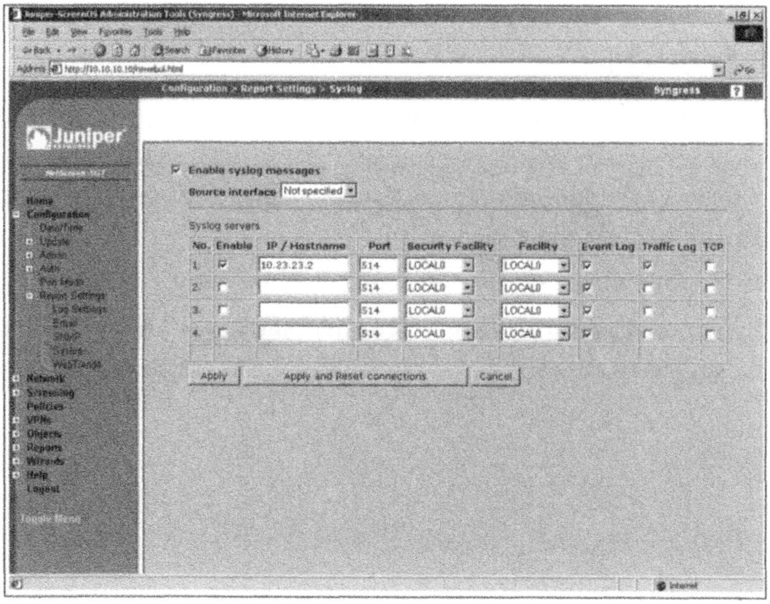

2. Enable the **Enable syslog messages** option.

3. Use the **Source interface** drop-down list to specify the interface from which messages will be sent. If you do not specify an interface here, messages will be sent from the interface closest to the syslog host.

4. In the row labeled **No. 1**, enable the **Enable** checkbox and enter the **IP / Hostname** and **Port** of the remote syslog server.

5. Use the **Security Facility** drop-down list to select the syslog facility to which emergency and critical messages will be sent.

6. Use the **Facility** drop-down list to select the syslog facility to which all other messages will be sent.

7. Enable the **Event Log**, **Traffic Log**, and **TCP** options.

8. Click **Apply**. If you are updating an existing syslog configuration, click **Apply and Reset connections**.

Enter the following commands to configure syslog via the CLI:

```
Syngress-> set syslog config 10.23.23.2 facilities local0 local0
Syngress-> set syslog config 10.23.23.2 port 514
Syngress-> set syslog config 10.23.23.2 log all
Syngress-> set syslog enable
```

WebTrends

WebTrends firewall suite is a product from the company NetIQ. It is a syslog server that collects all of your logs and it allows also you to generate graphical reports from your logs. You can configure a remote WebTrends server from both the CLI and the WebUI.

Use the following steps to configure WebTrends via the WebUI:

1. Access **Configuration | Report Settings | WebTrends**. A screen similar to the one shown in Figure 3.34 will be displayed.

Figure 3.34 WebTrends Configuration

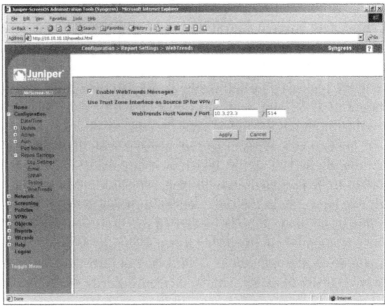

2. Enable the **Enable WebTrends Messages** option.

3. Enter the IP address and port number in the **WebTrends Host Name / Port** fields.

4. Click **Apply**.

Enter the following commands to configure WebTrends via the CLI:

```
Syngress-> set webtrends host-name 10.3.23.3
Syngress-> set webtrends port 514
Syngress-> set webtrends enable
```

Resources

Windows SSH client putty: www.chiark.greenend.org.uk/~sgtatham/putty/
Windows TFTP server Pumpkin: http://kin.klever.net/pumpkin/binaries
Windows Serial/telnet Client Tera Term:
http://hp.vector.co.jp/authors/VA002416/teraterm.html

Summary

In this chapter we covered a great deal of information. The purpose of this chapter was to get you familiar with the initial configuration of your NetScreen firewall. Before you begin using your firewall you must understand how to manage it. We looked at various methods you can use to manage your firewall. It is important to understand each individual option to you. Each option is a different tool you can use to control your firewall.

There are two core types of remote management, the WebUI and the CLI. If you are using the serial console, Telnet, or secure shell, you are using the CLI. It is important to be proficient in both management tools. The WebUI is initially easier to use. However, in the later chapters you will see that advanced troubleshooting techniques can only be carried out from the command line interface. These techniques are invaluable if you intend to do more advanced configuration. We also mentioned a third type of management called the NetScreen-Security Manager. The NetScreen-Security Manager product is an external source of management, covered in chapter 16.

This chapter also discussed configuring your NetScreen firewall to run on the network. Zones are a core part of the NetScreen security infrastructure. The security zone is the most commonly used zone. It is used on every interface and in every policy. Each interface must be bound to a zone. In the next chapter we will focus on basic policy creation and policy theory. In that chapter you will see the application of security zones. We looked at all of the various types of interfaces that the firewall supports. The physical interface will be used on each type of NetScreen device to interact with the network. The firewall can operate in two modes, layer three and layer two. In this chapter we focused on the layer three configuration of the device. In a later chapter (Chapter 9) we focus completely on the layer two mode, called transparent mode.

In the last section of the chapter we looked configuring various system components. Configuring the time on your device is critical. Time is the central reference point used to correlate all events on your firewall. If someone was to break in your network and your logs were off by several hours or days, this could hinder your investigation of the break-in. Configuring your logs to be sent to a separate location is also important if you intend to keep your logs long-term. The syslog server and WebTrends server are both great options. If you use the NetScreen-Security Manager, it also can be used as a central log repository.

Solutions Fast Track

Managing the NetScreen Firewall

☑ There are two types of methods to manage your firewall, the WebUI and the CLI.

☑ Configuration rollback is an important tool to use for saving a working configuration before you implement new changes on your firewall that could possible disrupt your firewall.

Configuring NetScreen

☑ There are three types of Zones: Security, Function Zones, and Tunnel Zones.

☑ Interfaces are bound to zones and function based upon the properties inherited from them.

☑ Device Management is configured per interface.

Configuring your NetScreen for the Network

☑ Security zones are used to identify a logical area of your network.

☑ Physical interfaces can host multiple IP addresses on each interface.

☑ Loopback interfaces are always up when they are configured and they must be bound to a zone like physical interfaces.

Configuring System Services

☑ Setting the system clock is important is crucial as it is your central point of reference for events that occur on your firewall.

☑ If you need to resolve hostnames to IP addresses, you must configure DNS servers.

☑ A NetScreen firewall can only hold so many logs locally, so you must configure an external log server of you want to archive your logs.

Frequently Asked Questions

The following Frequently Asked Questions, answered by the authors of this book, are designed to both measure your understanding of the concepts presented in this chapter and to assist you with real-life implementation of these concepts. To have your questions about this chapter answered by the author, browse to **www.syngress.com/solutions** and click on the **"Ask the Author"** form. You will also gain access to thousands of other FAQs at ITFAQnet.com.

Q: Why does NetScreen use zones on interfaces? I have used this type of configuration on other devices and I did not find it to be very effective.

A: Zones are designed to segment areas of the network from each other. On a NetScreen firewall, using security zones during policy creation allows or disallows traffic from one zone to another. This simplifies policy creation by specifying which zone traffic can go from and to. Furthermore, it removes chances that you accidentally configure access from one system to another. This can easily happen if you use a firewall that does not support zones.

Q: You cover securing the management interface extensively. Are all of those options really required?

A: Because the firewall is such a critical part of your network, you need to ensure its own security as well. Each option may be used in your network, or perhaps a combination of all of the options makes the most sense in your environment. By understanding all of the options you will have the ability to pick and choose among all of them.

Q: I have looked at the command line interface and I do not feel that it is very effective to use. Why should I even use it when the WebUI is easier and quicker?

A: The WebUI is a very useful tool and it should be used in conjunction with the CLI. Both have their own pros and cons. In later chapters you will need to be proficient in using the command line interface and be comfortable with its options. Even if you choose to use the WebUI most of the time, I encourage you to use the CLI from time to time so you are comfortable accessing it.

Q: You have talked about several options like transparent mode and NetScreen-Security Manger. How come you did not give many details on these?

A: These options are complex and deserving of their own discussions. There are dedicated chapters for each of these topics so they can be examined in more depth.

Chapter 4

Policy Configuration

Solutions in this Chapter:

- NetScreen Policies
- Policy Components
- Creating Policies

☑ Summary

☑ Solutions Fast Track

☑ Frequently Asked Questions

Introduction

In a NetScreen firewall, a policy is the fundamental core of access control. In this section we will explore the basic principles of a policy and how to create them. All firewall devices uses some sort of statement that provides access control between two segments of a network. Each product implements access control differently. If you have experience with any firewall product, then NetScreen policies should come easy for you. If you have never had the opportunity to create a network access control policy before, this section will help you understand the principles of access control as well as the methodology of creating a policy.

First we will look at the definition of a policy and what creating one really means. We will also look into the theory of access control and specific methodologies behind allowing or denying access to network resources. In the second part of this section we will review what makes up a policy on a NetScreen firewall. Every policy must have several basic components before it can be created. We will look at each component and how to create them on your firewall.

Much like building a house, NetScreen firewalls use different components to build policies. There are several required components for a policy. In this chapter we will look at these components and how to create them for use in a policy. Components can be created via the Web user interface (WebUI) or the command line interface (CLI). Each method generates the same result, but the process is different. As discussed throughout this book, becoming familiar with both methods will help you better understand the NetScreen firewall platform.

In the final section of this chapter we will take the components we created and use them to form policies. For the first time in this book, we will look at the WebUI and CLI separately, because the methods differ enough that each requires separate attention.

NetScreen Policies

A policy permits, denies, or tunnels specified types of traffic between two points. That is the official definition of a firewall policy according to Juniper Networks. Let's look deeper into that definition. A policy is a single statement defining whether a resource can be accessed and by whom. On a Cisco PIX or router, a policy is the equivalent to a conduit or access list. On a Check Point firewall, a policy is the equivalent of a firewall rule.

A policy does not reference a complete list of rules or the entire embodiment of the access control statements. Nor is a policy referenced as any sort of written statement in this case. A policy is a single access control statement. There are five basic elements of any policy. Any policy you create must contain all five of the following elements.

- **Direction** The first element is direction. The direction is based upon security zones. You must define two security zones in each policy. The first security zone must be the source of the traffic that you want to access a specific resource. The second zone is the destination zone. The destination zone is where the destination system or network is located.

- **Source Address** The next component of a policy is the source addresses. This component defines the source Internet Protocol (IP) address of the source hosts. These hosts must be in the source zone as well. These source IP addresses can access the destination hosts in the destination zone. At a maximum you may use **Any** as the source; this specifies any IP address in the source zone.

- **Destination Address** The destination hosts are the hosts that the source addresses will attempt to access. The destination hosts must be in the destination zone. Destination addresses must have a minimum of a single host. At a maximum, you may use **Any** as the destination; this specifies any IP address in the destination zone.

- **Service** When you define a service, you define which application you want the source address to access. Defining this is based upon both port and protocol. You can allow ICMP (Internet Control Message Protocol), TCP (Transmission Control Protocol), IP, and UDP (User Datagram Protocol) protocols. Each predefined service has these protocols specified. Much like the source and destination address, you can also specify **Any** for the service; this will allow any protocol using any port from the source address to access the destination address through the firewall.

- **Action** The specified action is what you want to happen to the traffic that matches the specified policy. There are three actions that you can impose on traffic that matches the policy. The first action is *permit*. When specifying permit as your action, you are allowing the matching traffic to pass through the firewall. The second action you can select is *deny*. This action denies and drops the traffic if it matches the defined policy. The last action that you can specify is *tunnel*. Tunnel first inherently permits the traffic that is specified by the policy. However, this traffic is only permitted to pass through the specified VPN (virtual private network) tunnel. If you use the action of tunnel then you must specify a VPN tunnel as well.

There are additional items that can be defined for each policy. These additional items include logging, network address translation (NAT), traffic shaping, counting, traffic alarms, antivirus scanning, scheduling, URL (Uniform Resource Locator) filtering, and user authentication.

- **Logging** Logging is an essential tool for both troubleshooting and recording who has accessed your network. We will look at logging in more detail later in this chapter.

- **NAT** NAT allows you to hide your internal IP addresses. It is used in almost every internal network. There are many intricacies of NAT on the NetScreen platform so NAT has its own dedicated chapter in this book.

- **Traffic Shaping** Traffic shaping allows you to control the amount of bandwidth certain traffic can consume. Traffic shaping is covered in more detail in the chapter titled "Advanced Policy Configuration".

- **Counting** When you turn on counting for a policy, the NetScreen firewall creates graphs for the traffic that has passed through the policy. These graphs are displayed in bytes and are useful in determining how much traffic has passed through an interface. Configuring counting is covered in more detail in the chapter titled "Advanced Policy Configuration".

- **Traffic Alarms** Traffic alarms allow you to generate an alert when a specific number of bytes per second or bytes per minute are exceeded. To use traffic alarms you must enable counting. Configuring traffic alarms is covered in more detail in the "Advanced Policy Configuration " chapter.

- **Antivirus Scanning** Using antivirus scanning on your firewall allows you to scan traffic for viruses as the traffic passes through your firewall. Configuring antivirus scanning is covered in the "Attack Detection and Defense" chapter.

- **Scheduling** Configuring scheduling for a policy allows you to create a policy that is in effect only at specific times. This allows you to create a policy that allows your users to browse the Internet only during speci-fied hours. Scheduling is a powerful tool that keeps you from having to enable and disable access at specific times. Scheduling is explained in full detail in the "Advanced Policy Configuration" chapter.

- **URL Filtering** There are times that you may want to allow a user to access the Internet, but require some method of limiting access to appropriate websites. URL filtering allows you to allow or deny access to websites based upon their content. NetScreen has teamed up with the Websense Enterprise Engine product to allow you to do just that. Using URL filtering is covered in the "Advanced Policy Configuration" chapter.

- **User Authentication** User authentication allows you to require authentication to the NetScreen firewall before accessing specified resources in a policy. User authentication and using authentication servers is a large subject, requiring its own chapter. The chapter titled "User Authentication" covers this subject in its entirety.

Theory Of Access Control

The theory of access control is quite simple; allow access to the required resources and deny everything else. On a NetScreen firewall, everything is denied by default unless specifically allowed. This makes creating your access control policies a straightforward process. If you want a resource to be accessed by another system, create a policy to allow access to it. If you do not want access allowed to a system, do not create a policy.

Now that you understand the beginnings of access control on a NetScreen firewall, there are a couple different ideas to add into this mix when creating a policy. When traffic passes through the firewall, policies are checked in a top-down order, so the policy at the top will be checked first and then the second policy in order will be checked and so on. The best thing you can do is to create more specific policies at the top of your policy list and less specific policies as you go down the list.

Let's look at an example. Figure 4.1 shows an example of policy ordering. This is a screenshot of a NetScreen policy. There are three policies in this example. In the first policy you see the source is very specific with only one host (WebMaster) connecting to a single destination (WebServer). This is the most specific policy in this example. The first policy only allows one single system to connect to another single system. In the second policy, any host can connect to the destination WebServer with only HTTP (Hypertext Transfer Protocol). This is a less specific policy as it allows literally any host to connect to WebServer, as long as it uses the proper protocol. In the last policy, any host can connect to the destination "FTP Servers" with the File Transfer Protocol (FTP). This is the least specific policy as it allows any host to connect to the group of FTP servers.

Figure 4.1 Policy Ordering

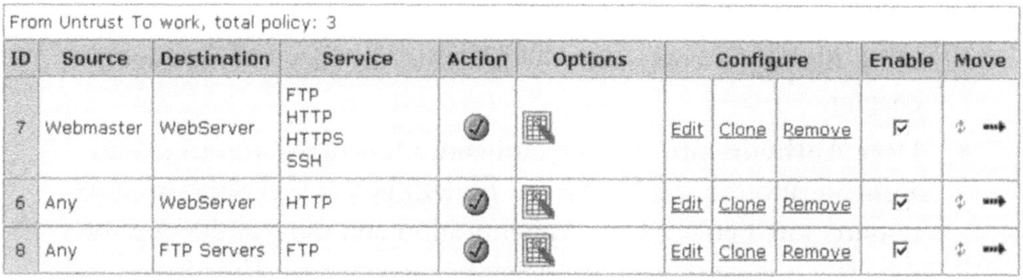

From Untrust To work, total policy: 3

ID	Source	Destination	Service	Action	Options	Configure			Enable	Move
7	Webmaster	WebServer	FTP HTTP HTTPS SSH	✓	🖳	Edit	Clone	Remove	☑	↺ ➡
6	Any	WebServer	HTTP	✓	🖳	Edit	Clone	Remove	☑	↺ ➡
8	Any	FTP Servers	FTP	✓	🖳	Edit	Clone	Remove	☑	↺ ➡

Why does the idea of most specific to least specific matter so much? Let's switch around policy number 6 and number 7 in the example above. 6 is now the top-most policy and 7 is the second policy down. If we were to do this, all connections from "WebMaster" with the HTTP protocol would be logged to policy number 6. This could create havoc when attempting to troubleshoot or for long term purposes of logging. The ID or identification for a policy is automatically generated when you create a policy from the WebUI. When creating a policy from the CLI you get the option of setting the ID if you want or allow the firewall to choose the next available number.

The last component of access control we need to look at is zones. Zones identify the direction a policy works in. Every policy requires a source zone and a destination zone. The source zone is the location from which the source traffic is originating. The destination zone is where the destination traffic is going. When creating a policy you must choose both a source and destination zone. The "Creating Policies" section later in this chapter discusses how to determine which components you need to create a policy.

Types of NetScreen Policies

On a NetScreen firewall, there are three different types of policies. The policies all contain the same five core components. The only difference is the zones that the policy contains. A policy is classified by which source and destination zones are used in the policy. If you look at Figure 4.2, you will see a diagram representing the policy checking order. Before we look at the diagram we will briefly define the three types of policies:

- **Intrazone Policies** An intrazone policy is a policy in which the source and destination zones are the same.

- **Interzone Policies** An intrazone policy is a policy in which the source and destination zones are different.

- **Global Policies** A global policy is a policy in which the source and destination zones are both in the global zone.

Figure 4.2 Policy Checking Order

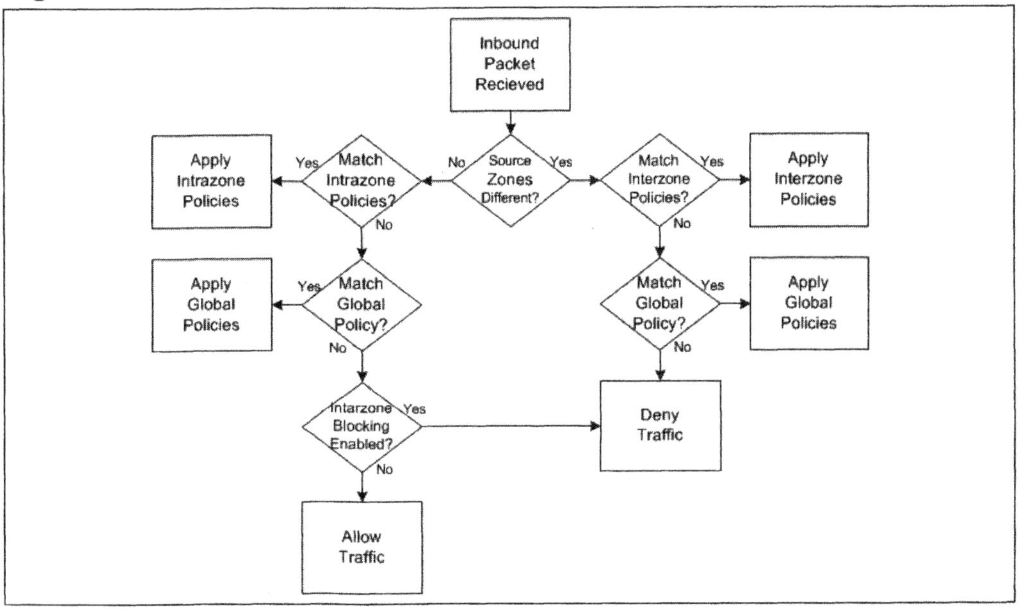

Intrazone Policies

There will be times on your NetScreen firewall when you have multiple interfaces bound to the same zone. By default, traffic within the same zone is not blocked. You have the option of blocking intrazone traffic just as if the traffic was interzone traffic. If you do not enable intrazone blocking, all intrazone traffic is allowed. Use the following command to determine the current zone blocking state, where *zonename* is the name of the zone:

```
zone zonename
```

The status will be listed on the "Intra-zone block" line. For example, the following output indicates that intrazone blocking is *not* enabled:

```
Intra-zone block: Off, attrib: Non-shared, flag:0x0008
```

To enable intrazone blocking, use the following command, where *zonename* is the name of the desired zone:

```
set zone zonename block
```

To disable intrazone blocking, use the following command, where *zonename* is the name of the desired zone:

```
unset zone home block
```

Interzone Policies

An interzone policy (in which the source and destination are in different zones) is the most common type of policy you are going to encounter. There are no configuration changes that you can make to change the behavior of interzone policies.

Global Policies

A global policy is a policy in which the source and destination zone are in the global zone. In Figure 4.2 above, you can see where global policies fall in the policy checking order. Global policies are very useful when you want to allow or deny a specific type of traffic regardless of the type of zone. For example, if you want to allow all zones to be able to get out to browse the Internet with HTTP traffic, but you only want to make one policy, you can do so using a global policy.

Default Policy

NetScreen firewalls have a default out of the box policy that will drop any traffic that does not match any other policies. This default policy is a hidden global policy. Juniper offers this as a security feature to ensure any traffic that you do not want to allow through is automatically dropped. This mitigates the risk of the firewall on the network by dropping any unmatched traffic. It is possible to change the behavior of this traffic from the CLI.

To override the default behavior (and therefore allow all traffic), enter the following command:

```
set policy default-permit-all
```

To change the firewall to deny all traffic by default, enter the following command:

```
unset policy default-permit-all
```

Policy Checking

When a connection is attempted, the NetScreen firewall will receive the source packet on an interface in the source zone. To determine the destination zone, the NetScreen firewall will perform either a route check or an Address Resolution Protocol (ARP) check to determine where the destination zone is. Once the destination zone is determined, the firewall will perform a check against the list of policies that match that zone configuration.

For example, if the source zone is determined as the trust zone and the destination zone is determined as the untrust zone, the firewall will check that list of policies. It will check the matching policy list starting from the first policy at the top of the list down to the bottom policy in that list. The first policy that matches the source IP address, destination IP address, and the service will be applied to that connection. The action of the first matching policy is then applied to that connection. If the connection is permitted, then the connection creates a session in the firewall's internal session table. The allowed session is granted access to pass through the firewall. If the action of the connection is to deny the connection, then the connection is dropped. Finally, if the action on the connection is to tunnel, then the connection is permitted, and a session is created and passed into the applicable VPN connection.

The session table is a table that is stored in memory on the NetScreen firewall. It contains a list of all of the allowed connections that have already passed through the policy and have been allowed. Before a connection is compared against the policy, it is compared against the session table to see if an active session has already been started. If the firewall sees that an existing session matches a session in the session table, then that traffic is allowed through the firewall. For example, if you open your browser and access a website, that entire connection will be stored in one session in the session table. Figure 4.3 shows a condensed version of how a NetScreen firewall determines what to do with network traffic as it passes though the firewall. This topic is fully discussed in the "Troubleshooting" chapter.

Figure 4.3 NetScreen Packet Logic

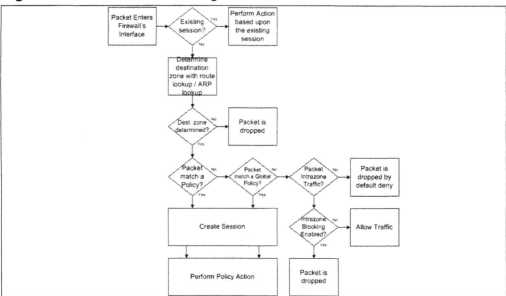

Getting Ready to Make a Policy

Creating policies is actually a very easy process once you have all of your components in place. Much like building a house, you cannot build if you do not have all of the materials. Let's review our steps in creating a policy.

- **Have you determined your source and destination zones?** The source zone is going to be where the originating traffic for your connection is coming from. This is tied into your interfaces. If you can determine which interface the traffic is going to come in, then you can determine which zone the traffic will come in as the interface is tied to the zone. The destination zone is the zone that the traffic will use to exit the NetScreen firewall. You can determine this by identifying which interface the traffic will come out with routing. Look at the configuration of your network and see where the packet will route as it exits your firewall. The interface it exits is bound to a zone, and that zone is your destination zone.

- **Have you determined your source and destination IP addresses?** The source IP address can be a single IP address, multiple IP addresses, or every available IP address. In the interest of security, you should limit the IP addresses to as few as possible. If you are unsure which IP address you want to use, open the source up to a larger pool of IP addresses, then log the traffic as it is goes through the firewall. Over time you can specify a smaller group of IP addresses for the source IP address. When determining your destination, you can use the same procedure by using logging to determine which IP addresses you can limit your traffic to. Ensure that the source and destination addresses have been created as address book entries. If the address book entries have not been created, now is the time to create them.

■ **Have you determined which services you are going to allow in your policy?** Determining the services that you want to use in your policy is a key factor in creating your policies. It is very important that you limit the amount of allowed services to the bare minimum, even if this means you will have 500 services allowed in your policy. This amount of services is much better then allowing all 65535 possible ports. Even policies that are outbound from your internal network should be limited. The more ports you have open, the more risk there is. An example of this would be if a virus was to infect a desktop and then that desktop began sending SMTP (Simple Mail Transfer Protocol) mail out directly to the Internet. Should all desktops be allowed to access the Internet directly with SMTP? These are the questions you should ask yourself as you create your policy.

■ **Which action do you want to perform on matching traffic?** Now that you have narrowed down your traffic to exactly what you want to match, it is now time to determine what you want to do with this traffic. There are three options: permit, deny, or tunnel. When you select to permit traffic, you are allowing the traffic to pass between the two security zones on the firewall. The second option is to deny, or drop the traffic before it passes through your firewall. By default, the firewall blocks all traffic as it attempts to pass through, so creating a policy to deny traffic allows you to apply special properties to the traffic such as logging. The last option is to tunnel the traffic. When you choose to tunnel the traffic, first you are explicitly permitting the traffic, but only to pass into a VPN tunnel. Choosing the tunnel option also forces you to choose a VPN that the traffic must pass into. VPNs are configured in the "Configuring VPNs" chapter.

■ **Where are you going to position your policy?** The position of your policy determines when your policy will take effect. Policies are checked in a top-down order based upon your source and destination zones. Once the source and destination zones are determined, the list of policies that matched the source and destination zone are checked starting from the top policy going to the bottom of the policy list. Once all of the policies in the matching source and destination zone are checked, the global policies are applied to your traffic.

- **Are there any additional options that you want to apply to the traffic?** As we mentioned earlier in the chapter, there are many different options you can apply to your policy beyond the required components. In this chapter we will look at the logging option only. When you turn on logging for a policy, each connection that passes through the firewall is written into the traffic log. In the next chapter, "Advanced Policy Creation," we will look at all of the available options for policy creation.

Policy Components

When you create a policy, you must define five separate components:

- Source Address
- Destination Address
- Service
- Direction
- Action

Zones

When creating a policy, you must first determine the source and destination zones. The source zone will be where the source traffic is going to come from. The destination zone is the location where the destination traffic is going. Because zones are bound to interfaces, you are also inherently choosing which interface the traffic will be using. This may help you when creating a policy, as the concept of zones is different from many other firewall products.

Address Book Entries

The next component that you need to determine when creating a policy is which source systems should be able to access which destination systems – essentially, the source IP addresses and the destination IP addresses for your policy. This is a common firewall concept that you may have come across before. When using the command line interface, you must create all of your address book entries before you make your policies. However, when using the WebUI to create policies, you can create new address book entries as you create the policy. If you choose this latter method of creating address book entries while creating a policy in the WebUI, you can only specify the IP address and netmask for the entry. You will have to go back at a later time and edit the address book entry if you want to associate a name with the address book entry. This idea will become clearer below as we look at some examples of address book entry creation.

Creating Address Book Entries

Figure 4.4 shows the WebUI address entry creation screen. Use the steps below to create an address book entry via the WebUI:

Figure 4.4 Address Book Entry Creation (WebUI)

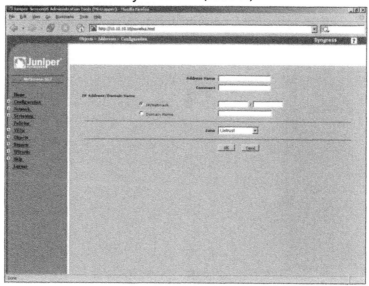

1. Select **Objects | Addresses | List**.
2. Click the **New** button in the upper right-hand corner of the page.

3. Enter the **Address Name**. Refer to the "Naming Convention Errors" sidebar in this chapter to avoid naming errors.

4. If desired, use the **Comment** field to enter additional information about the address book entry.

5. If you wish to identify the address book entry by IP address, select and use the **IP/Netmask** fields to enter the desired IP Address or IP Subnet.

6. If you wish to identify the entry by domain name, rather than by IP address, select the Domain Name option and enter the DNS-resolvable name. Note that your system must have DNS enabled for this feature to work properly.

7. Use the **Zone** drop-down list to specify the zone with which the entry will belong.

8. Click **OK**. The new entry will be displayed in the address book list (Figure 4.5).

Figure 4.5 Address Book List (WebUI)

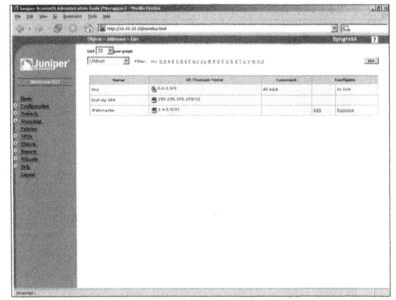

Tools & Traps…

Naming Convention Errors

When creating objects, you can create a big problem for yourself. NetScreen firewalls have no understanding of what you name your objects. This can create confusion for you in the future. When naming objects, no matter if they are address objects, address groups, custom services, or service groups, you should decide upon a naming convention for your organization, otherwise, you may get confused by what the object really does for you. Even if you add a comment to each object, you are unable to see this comment when adding an object to your policy.

For example, you can create an address group with the name "WebServer". When scrolling through address objects to add to your policy, you will see "WebServer" with no other information indicating that this object is a group. You or your colleagues may add this object to a policy without realizing what it actually is. When creating groups, it is a good idea to add the suffix "Grp" so that address groups and service groups can easily be identified.

It is also suggested that you avoid creating objects using the actual policy creation screen because of the long-term confusion it can create for you to have address objects without a name associated with each. Many people find it to be helpful to use only IP addresses for naming their address objects. If this works best for you then go ahead and create your objects with that naming convention. There is one important caveat in doing so. From the object creation screen you can create an object whose name is "10.10.10.10/32" and whose actual IP address is "10.10.10.0/24". So when you attempt to add this to your policy, all the objects that are listed for you to add to your policy are listed by the name and not the actual IP address. So if your name represents an IP address, but that name does not match the actually defined IP address, you could have unexpected results in your policy.

You can also create an address book entry via the CLI. To do so, enter the following command:

```
set address zone name IPaddress "comment"
```

In the command above, *zone* is the zone to which this entry will belong, *name* is the name of the entry, *IPaddress* is the IPaddress/subnet that specifies the range, and *"comment"* is a text string (in quotes) that serves as an optional comment about the entry. For example, the following command specifies that the WebServer entry (at 10.2.2.2/32) belongs to the untrust zone and includes the comment, "This is Darren's Web Server"

```
set address untrust WebServer 10.2.2.2/32 "This is Darren's Web Server"
```

Modifying and Deleting Address Book Entries

You can update existing address book entries via the WebUI. You may wish to do so as servers change IP addresses, or you may want to update the comments about an address object. You can modify everything about an address book entry except its zone. Note that you cannot modify an address object from the CLI; if you wish to change an address object's properties via the CLI, you must first delete it and then recreate it.

Use the following steps to modify an existing address book entry via the WebUI:

1. Access **Objects** | **Addresses** | **List**.
2. Click the **Edit** link of the address entry you wish to modify.
3. Update the desired fields and click **OK**.

Use the following steps to delete an existing address book entry via the WebUI:

1. Access **Objects** | **Addresses** | **List**.
2. Click the **Remove** link of the address entry you wish to delete.
3. Click **OK** to confirm.

Use the following commands to delete and re-create an address book entry (in lieu of being able to modify it directly).

```
unset address domain "name"
set address domain name IPaddress "comment"
```

Address Groups

As you begin to amass many address objects, you will want a method to bring all of these address objects together into logical containers. This is accomplished with the use of address groups. An address group is a logical container that literally groups together address objects. Address groups are very handy when creating policies. Use the following steps to create an address group via the WebUI:

1. Access **Objects** | **Addresses** | **Groups**.

2. Click **New**. A screen similar to the one shown in Figure 4.6 will be displayed.

Figure 4.6 Address Group Creation (WebUI)

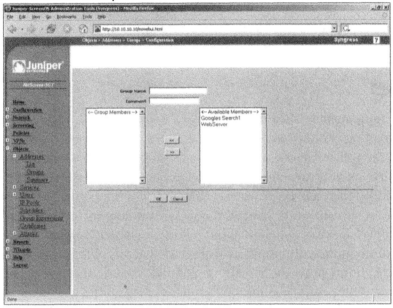

3. Enter the **Group Name** and, if desired, a **Comment**.

4. To place hosts in this group, select them from the list of **Available Members** on the right and click the << button. The host(s) will be placed in the **Group Members** list. To remove a member from the group, click it and click the >> button. Continue this process until the **Group Members** list contains all of the desired hosts.

5. Click **OK**.

To modify a group, access the group list and click its **Edit** button. To delete a group, access the group list and click its **Remove** button, then click **OK** to confirm.

To create an address group using the CLI, enter the following command:

```
Set group address zone groupname comment "commenttext"
```

In the command above, *zone* is the zone to which the group will be placed, *groupname* is the name you wish to give the new group, and *commenttext* is the text you wish to place in the comment field (must be in quotes).

Use the following command to add an address to the group:

```
Set group address zone groupname add addressname
```

In the command above, *zone* is the zone that contains the desired address and group, *groupname* is the name of the group, and *addressname* is the name of the address you wish to place in the specified group.

Services

The next component in creating your policy is using *services*. Services are the protocols that you would use to access a system over the network. Services on a NetScreen firewall are represented by service objects. A service object is used to specify which applications can be used in a policy. Every NetScreen firewall comes with a predefined set of services. The set of services that comes on your firewall varies per version of ScreenOS you are running on your firewall.

Currently, ScreenOS contains about eighty predefined services. These services are some of the more commonly used services that you will use when defining your policies. Some protocols are also predefined because they function in a non-standard way. One example is the FTP protocol. Because FTP sends special port redirects during its communication, Juniper has created a special mechanism to read inside the FTP connection to determine which ports to open up during the communication. Even though the predefined service only allows TCP port 21, the firewall is still able to dynamically allow ports based upon the FTP communication.

It would be impractical for Juniper to create every service that exists. Juniper allows you to create your own custom service objects. These custom service objects can be used just like a predefined service object in your policy.

Creating Custom Services

A service object has several defining properties that tell the firewall how to identify traffic. These properties are specified when defining a new service object. The options that you use when creating a new policy depend on the type of protocol you are creating. Use the following steps to create a custom service via the WebUI:

1. Access **Objects | Services | Custom**.

2. Click **New**. A screen similar to the one shown in Figure 4.7 will be displayed.

Figure 4.7 Service Object Configuration (WebUI)

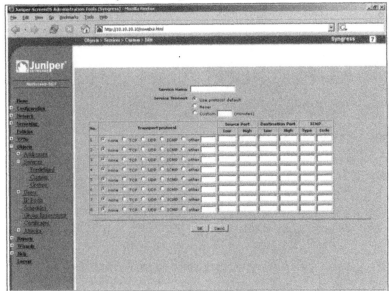

3. Enter the **Service Name**.

4. Use the **Service Timeout** options to specify how long the service session should stay open. The protocol default is thirty minutes for TCP and one minute for UDP. Select **Never** if you do not want to impose a timeout value. To specify your own timeout value, select the **Custom** option and enter the desired number of minutes (up to a maximum of forty minutes).

5. You can define up to eight protocols for this service object. This can be useful in creating a service that uses multiple ports. To define a protocol, select its type from the **Transport Protocol** field. Next, enter the **Low** and **High Source Ports** and the **Low** and **High Destination Ports**. To specify a single port, enter the same number in the **High** and **Low** fields.

6. Click **OK**.

To create a custom service via the CLI, enter the following command:

```
set service servicename protocol protocol src-port srclow-high dst-port
dstlow-high
```

In the command above, *servicename* is the name of the service, *protocol* is the protocol type (TCP, UDP, or ICMP), *srclow-high* is the low and high source port range, and *dstlow-high* is the low and high destination port range.

Tools & Traps…

What exactly is "Any"?

When creating policies on a NetScreen firewall, you will see the option "any" available for the source, destination, and service. This is available here on NetScreen firewalls and on other firewall products. The question always comes down to, "what does *any* actually mean?"

On a NetScreen firewall, *any* literally means any address in the zone (when used as a source or destination address) and any service (when used as a service). This is something important to note, as other firewall products do not always mean "any," even when they say "any."

Modifying and Deleting Services

After creating your service, there may be times when you will want to modify that service or perhaps delete it. Modifying a service is much like creating it. The only difference is that when you come to the editing screen, the portions of the service you have created are already defined for you. From the CLI if you want to add additional protocols to a service you can. However, if you need to edit existing parts of the service, you must delete the service then recreate it.

Use the following steps to modify an existing service via the WebUI:

1. Access **Objects | Services | Custom**.

2. Click the **Edit** link of the service you wish to edit.

3. Make the desired changes to the **Service Name** and/or **Service Timeout** fields.

4. Modify the values for any of the existing protocols. You can add new protocols to this service simply by entering the appropriate data, and you can remove protocols by selecting the **none** option of the protocol you wish to remove.

5. Click **OK**.

To delete a service via the WebUI, access the services list and click the **Remove** link of the service you wish to delete. Click **OK** to confirm. To delete a service via the CLI, enter the following command:

```
unset service "servicename"
```

Service Groups

Even though each individual service can contain up to eight service definitions, you will still want to group services together into logical containers. You can do this through the use of service groups. A service group functions just like an address group, and its creation is nearly identical. Use the following steps to create a service group via the WebUI:

1. Access **Objects | Services | Groups**.

2. Click **New**. A screen similar to the one shown in Figure 4.8 will be displayed.

Figure 4.8 Service Group Creation (WebUI)

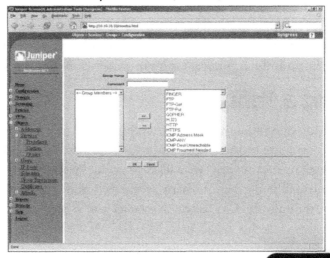

3. Enter the **Group Name** and, if desired, enter a **Comment**.

4. To place hosts in this group, select them from the list of **Available Members** on the right and click the << button. The host(s) will be placed in the **Group Members** list. To remove a member from the group, click it and click the >> button. Continue this process until the **Group Members** list contains all of the desired hosts.

5. Click **OK**.

To modify an existing service group, access the service group list and click the **Edit** link of the group you wish to modify. To delete a service group, access the service group list and click the **Remove** link of the group you wish to delete. Click **OK** to confirm.

Use the following command to create a service group via the CLI, where *groupname* is the name of the new group:

```
set group service "groupname"
```

To add items to the group, enter the following command:

```
set group service "groupname" add item
```

In the command above, *groupname* is the name of the service group and *item* is the name of the service that will be added to the specified group. To delete a service group via the CLI, enter the following command:

```
unset group service "groupname"
```

Creating Policies

Now that you are familiar with the components of creating policies, you can begin actually creating them. Polices are the main reason why you are implementing your firewall in the first place; to control network traffic. In this section we will begin to look at putting together policy components into a policy.

Creating a Policy

In this section we will begin to work with policies. In all of the previous sections of the book we have worked with both the CLI and the WebUI in the same section. However, in this section we will look at the WebUI and the CLI in separate sections. This will bring better clarity to the two different methods of creating a policy. Even though the CLI is not as easy to use as the WebUI, knowing how to use the CLI is crucial. The configuration is always stored as CLI commands, so knowing what each command does will empower your use of the platform.

Creating a Policy via the WebUI

The WebUI is easier to interpret, it allows for easier modification of the policy, and at times can be faster to use. When you start to have over twenty policies on your firewall, the CLI will seem as if all the policies run together, whereas on the WebUI, the icons and coloration of the policies will seem to flow. This is all a matter of preference, but I suggest using whatever tool makes the most sense to you. There is no reason to make the administration of the NetScreen firewall harder on yourself than it has to be. In Figure 4.9, you will see what the main policy page looks like. This page is the root of all policy creation in the WebUI.

Figure 4.9 The Root Of Policy Creation

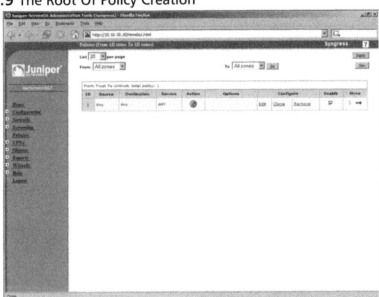

From here we can do everything we need to do with policies. We can create, remove, reorder, search, enable, disable, and clone policies. To access this screen, simply select the **Policies** link from the menu on the left side of the screen. As you can see in Figure 4.9, currently we only have one policy. This policy allows any source to go to any destination via any protocol. The action (indicated by the checkmark in the green circle) is permit. Table 4.1 lists the different icons that may be displayed on this screen, as well as their descriptions.

Table 4.1 Policy Action Icons

Action	Icon	Description
Permit		The permits the traffic specified in the policy.
Deny		This denies the traffic specified in the policy.
Tunnel		The policy permits and then tunnels the matching traffic.
Bi-Directional Tunnel		The policy permits and then tunnels the matching traffic. It also has a matching policy that has the source and destination reversed.
Policy Based NAT		This policy permits the traffic matching the policy but it also performs NAT on the traffic.

These various policy icons are very informative and simple to understand. When defining a new policy from the WebUI, you begin by selecting the source and the destination zones. Once you select the zones and create the new policy, there is no way to change the source and destination zones. If you wish to change the source and destination zones you must delete the undesired policy and then create a new one with the correct zones.

Use the following steps to create a policy via the WebUI:

1. Access the Juniper screen administration tools page and click **Policies** in the menu.

2. Click **New**. A screen similar to the one shown in Figure 4.10 will be displayed.

Figure 4.10 Policy Definition Screen

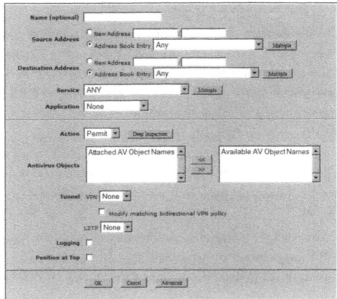

3. Enter the policy **Name**. This should be a descriptive name that will allow you to identify what the policy does.

4. Use the **Source Address** options to specify the source address for the policy. If it is a new address, select the **New Address** option and enter the IP address range. If the address already exists in the address book, select the **Address Book Entry** option and enter the name of the entry. You can select multiple address book entries by clicking the **Multiple** button.

5. Use the **Destination Address** options to specify the source address for the policy. If it is a new address, select the **New Address** option and enter the IP address range. If the address already exists in the address book, select the **Address Book Entry** option and enter the name of the entry. You can select multiple address book entries by clicking the **Multiple** button

6. Use the **Service** drop-down list to specify the services that you want to use in this policy. Select a single service or group of services, or select **ANY**, or click **Multiple** if you wish to specify multiple (but not all) services.

7. Use the **Application** drop-down list to map a custom-defined service to a specific application layer.

8. Use the **Action** drop-down list to specify whether matching traffic will be permitted, denied, or tunneled. If you select **Tunnel**, you must also select an option from the **Tunnel** drop-down list. To apply deep inspection groups to the policy, click the **Deep Inspection** button. Deep inspection is explained in more detail in the "Attack Defense" chapter.

9. The **Antivirus Objects** section allows you to specify which antivirus scanners will be applied to the policy. To select an antivirus object, select it from the **Available AV Object Names** list on the right, then click the << button to place it in the **Attached AV Object Names** list on the left.

10. If you selected **Tunnel** in the **Action** drop-down list, use the **Tunnel VPN** drop-down list to specify the appropriate VPN tunnel. VPN configuration is discussed in greater detail in the "VPNs" chapter.

11. If you wish to turn on logging for this policy, enable the **Logging** checkbox.

12. If you wish to place this policy at the top of the list of policies with matching source and destination zones, enable the **Position at Top** checkbox.

13. Click **OK**.

Reordering Policies in the WebUI

Once you have all of your policies created in the WebUI, there will be many times that you will need to reorder them. Every newly created policy is placed at the bottom of the policies that have the same source and destination zones unless you enabled the **Position at Top** option when creating the policy. Once the policy is created you can modify the policy placement on the Policies list page. Table 4.2 shows the different icons you can use to reorder policies.

Table 4.2 Policy Action Icons

Icon	Description
	Selecting this option allows you to choose the placement of your policy, by policy number. A pop -up window asking you where you want to place your policy based up upon the number of your policy. See figure 4.14 for and example.
	Selecting this option allows you to select where you want to place your policy based upon a selection screen. At the selection screen you can click on a similar arrow to choose where you want to place your policy. See figure 4.15 for an example.

Figure 4.11 Order Policies by Number

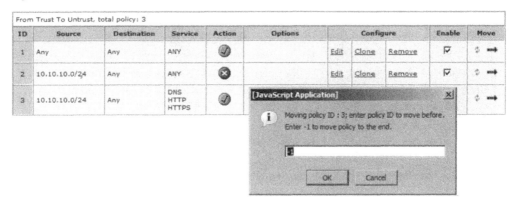

Figure 4.12 Choose Policy Placement

Tools & Traps...

Negation

When creating policies and working with address book entries, you can enable an option called *negate*. This concept is used on several firewall products and can be quite useful depending on what you are attempting to accomplish. The negate option is available for the source and destination addresses. The option is turned on for either source or destination addresses and can be turned on separately for each policy.

Turning on the negate option will apply the following logic: everything except the selected objects. For example, suppose that you created a policy with the following configuration: Source: 10.10.10.0/24 Negated, Destination: Any, Service: FTP, Action: Permit. You are effectively saying, "Allow any source address to FTP, except for 10.10.10.0/24." This can save you time instead of making a policy to deny the 10.10.10.0/24 network to access FTP and then a second policy to allow access to FTP to any.

The negate option can be used in both the WebUI and the CLI. To use this option in the WebUI when you are creating a policy, click on the **Multiple** button for the source or destination address. Once you have selected what you want to negate in the pop-up window, enable the **Negate the following** option, which can be found in the upper left-hand corner of the window. To use this from the command line you must first create the policy, then go into the sub-shell for the policy and negate the source address and destination address. See the command below for an example:

```
Syngress-> set policy id 3

Syngress(policy:3)-> set src-address negate

Syngress(policy:3)-> exit

Syngress-> get policy id 3

name:"none" (id 3), zone Trust -> Untrust,action Permit, status
"enabled"

1 source (negated): "10.10.10.0/24"

1 destination: "Any"

3 services: "DNS", "HTTP", "HTTPS"

Policies on this vpn tunnel: 0
```

Continued

```
nat off, url filtering OFF

vpn unknown vpn, policy flag 0000, session backup: on

traffic shapping off, scheduler n/a, serv flag 00

log no, log count 0, alert no, counter no(0) byte rate(sec/min) 0/0

total octets 0, counter(session/packet/octet) 0/0/0

priority 7, diffserv marking Off

tadapter: state off, gbw/mbw 0/-1

No Authentication

No User, User Group or Group expression set

Syngress->
```

Other Policy Options in the WebUI

There are some additional WebUI options that may be helpful as you begin to create policies. These options are available from the root policies page in the WebUI. These options are displayed in Figure 4.13.

- **Edit** Use a policy's **Edit** link to modify its configuration.

- **Clone** Use this option to create a copy of the policy. The policy's original information will be displayed, but can be edited for your needs. This can save time when creating multiple policies that have only slight differences.

- **Remove** Click a policy's **Remove** link to delete it. The policy will immediately be removed from the firewall.

- **Enable** Use this option to enable or disable the policy.

Figure 4.13 Additional Policy Options

Configure			Enable	Move
Edit	Clone	Remove	☑	↻ ➠

Creating a Policy via the CLI

Even though the point-and-click nature of the WebUI may make policy management easier, the CLI provides the fastest methods of policy management.

Using the CLI requires more memorization of the commands and the order in which you use them. Once you get a grasp of CLI policy management, it will become an effective management tool. There are three basic commands for managing policies. The first command is **set policy** , which is the root of all policy creation. All commands that involve creating and manipulating policies begin here. The second command is **get policy**, which displays information about all or specified policies. Finally, the **unset policy** command is used for removing policies.

```
Syngress-> set policy ?
before                 insert a policy
default-permit-all    permit if no policy match
from                   from zone
global                 set global policy
id                     specify policy id
move                   move a policy
name                   specify policy name
top                    put this policy as the first one in the list
Syngress-> get policy ?
>                      redirect output
|                      match output
<return>
id                     show one policy
all                    show all policies(including global policy)
from                   from zone
global                 show global policies
Syngress-> unset policy ?
<number>               policy id
default-permit-all    permit if no policy match
id                     policy id
Syngress->
```

To view a list of all existing policies, enter the command **get policy**. You can also list policies by specifying the source and destination zones. This is done with the command **get policy from <Src-Zone> to <Dst-Zone>**. A list of all policies matching the specified parameters will be displayed. Use the command **get policy global** to view all of the global policies. Finally, use the command

get policy all to view all of the policies, including the global policies. The **get policy** command supports the following parameter:

ID This is the ID number of the policy. It is a unique number that is used to identify the policy.

From The source zone.

To The destination zone.

Src-address The source address objects.

Dst-address The destination address objects.

Service The service specified for the policy.

Action The action to apply to the traffic that matches the policy.

State Whether the policy is enabled or disabled.

ASTLCB This represents which special properties are turned on in the policy. A = Authentication, S = Scheduling, T = Traffic Shaping, L = Logging, C = Counting, B = HA Backup.

```
Syngress-> get policy
Total regular policies 4, Default deny.
ID From    To         Src-address Dst-address Service Action State    ASTLCB
1  Trust  Untrust Any         Any         ANY     Permit enabled -----X
2  Trust  Untrust 10.10.10.0/ Any         ANY     Deny   enabled -----X
3  Trust  Untrust 10.10.10.0/ Any         DNS     Permit enabled -----X
                                          HTTP
                                          HTTPS
4  Trust  Untrust Any         Any         ANY     Permit enabled -----X
Syngress->
```

You can even look at the configuration of a policy by using the **get policy id <number>** command, where <number> is the policy ID.

```
Syngress-> get policy id 1
name:"none" (id 1), zone Trust -> Untrust,action Permit, status "enabled"
src "Any", dst "Any", serv "ANY"
Policies on this vpn tunnel: 0
nat off, url filtering OFF
vpn unknown vpn, policy flag 0000, session backup: on
traffic shaping off, scheduler n/a, serv flag 00
```

```
log no, log count 0, alert no, counter no(0) byte rate(sec/min) 0/0
total octets 1301676800, counter(session/packet/octet) 0/0/0
priority 7, diffserv marking Off
tadapter: state off, gbw/mbw 0/-1
No Authentication
No User, User Group or Group expression set
```

Creating a policy via the CLI requires the same components as if you were using the WebUI. The full command for creating a policy via the CLI is:

```
set policy from <Src-Zone> to <Dst-Zone> <Src-Address> <Dst-Address>
<Service> <Action>
```

There are five areas in the above example command that you must fill in to complete the policy. The *<Src-Zone>* or source zone, *<Dst-Zone>* or destination zone, *<Src-Address>* or source address book entry, *<Dst-Address>* or destination address book entry, *service*, and *action*. These are the same five minimum options you would use when creating a policy from the WebUI. Once you create the policy, it is give a policy ID or unique identifier. This identifier is used to reference the policy throughout the system. The firewall will return **policy ID = <Identifier>** once the policy has been created.

Notice that this command only allows you to specify one source address, one destination address, and one service. You can add more once the policy has been created by using the **set policy id <ID Number>** to enter the sub-shell that allows you to modify the policy. The sub-shell for policies is the only sub-command shell in the entire firewall.

Once in the policy sub-shell, you have the same options as in the regular shell: set, get, and unset. Using the **set** command, you can add additional source addresses, destination addresses, and services, as well as other policy options. The **unset** command is used to remove parts from the policy, and the **get** command is used to obtain information about the policy. When creating policies from the CLI, you can place a policy in a specific position as it is created by entering the following command:

```
set policy before <ID> from <Src-Zone> to <Dst-Zone> <Src-Address> <Dst-
Address> <Service> <Action>
```

Specify the <ID> as the ID number of the policy you want to place the policy before. If you want to create a policy and place it at the top of the list of policies with the same source and destination zone, you would use the following command:

```
set policy top <Src-Zone> to <Dst-Zone> <Src-Address> <Dst-Address>
<Service> <Action>
```

The following is a snippet of code that shows an example of creating a policy and manipulating it in the sub-shell.

```
Syngress-> set policy from trust to untrust 10.10.10.0/24 any FTP permit
policy id = 6
Syngress-> get policy id 6
name:"none" (id 6), zone Trust -> Untrust,action Permit, status "enabled"
src "10.10.10.0/24", dst "Any", serv "FTP"
Policies on this vpn tunnel: 0
nat off, url filtering OFF
vpn unknown vpn, policy flag 0000, session backup: on
traffic shapping off, scheduler n/a, serv flag 00
log no, log count 0, alert no, counter no(0) byte rate(sec/min) 0/0
total octets 0, counter(session/packet/octet) 0/0/0
priority 7, diffserv marking Off
tadapter: state off, gbw/mbw 0/-1
No Authentication
No User, User Group or Group expression set
Syngress-> set policy id 6
Syngress(policy:6)-> set service DNS
Syngress(policy:6)-> set src-address 10.10.9.0/24
Syngress(policy:6)-> set name "Allow FTP"
Syngress(policy:6)-> set log
Syngress(policy:6)-> exit
Syngress-> get policy id 6
name:"Allow FTP" (id 6), zone Trust -> Untrust,action Permit, status
"enabled"
2 sources: "10.10.10.0/24", "10.10.9.0/24"
1 destination: "Any"
2 services: "DNS", "FTP"
Policies on this vpn tunnel: 0
nat off, url filtering OFF
vpn unknown vpn, policy flag 0000, session backup: on
```

```
traffic shapping off, scheduler n/a, serv flag 00
log yes, log count 0, alert no, counter no(0) byte rate(sec/min) 0/0
total octets 0, counter(session/packet/octet) 0/0/0
priority 7, diffserv marking Off
tadapter: state off, gbw/mbw 0/-1
No Authentication
No User, User Group or Group expression set
Syngress->
```

Other Policy Options Available in the CLI

Once you have all of your policies defined, you can use the CLI to reorder the policies. To move an existing policy above another, use the following command:

```
set policy move <ID1> before <ID2>
```

Specify the policy you want to move with its policy ID as <ID1> and the policy you want to move it before as its policy ID as <ID2>. To move an existing policy after another, use the following command:

```
set policy move <ID1> after <ID2>
```

Specify the policy you want to move with its policy ID as <ID1> and the policy you want to move it after as its policy ID as <ID2>. This may seem like an insignificant option, but if you have ever used a Cisco IOS or Cisco PIX access list you will appreciate this option. Neither Cisco OS allows you to manipulate the policies or access lists this way. Instead, you must first remove all of the applied policies and then add them all back to the firewall. Finally, you can delete policies via the CLI. To delete a policy from the CLI you must know the policy ID of the policy you want to remove, then use either the **unset policy id <ID>** or **unset policy <ID>** command.

Summary

In this chapter we focused on the basics of policy creation. The basics that we looked at are the foundation for much more to come in the way of policies. We looked at policies in this chapter as a primary tool of access control. In the next chapter we will expand on this by looking at various other options that you can apply to policies. When creating a policy on a NetScreen firewall, you must have a minimum of five components. This idea is continually stressed, as it will help you ease into policy creation on a NetScreen firewall.

The first section of the chapter NetScreen Policies took us through the main ideas of policies on a NetScreen firewall. When creating your list of policies you must create policies from least specific to most specific. This will apply the specific policies first to your traffic as the least specific policies may unintendedly match your traffic. Also in the first section, we looked at the three types of polices and how and where they take effect. All three policies are very similar, but they are classified based upon the combination of zones in the policy.

When creating policies on a NetScreen firewall, you build them out of components. These components must be created before you make a policy. Each one of the components for a NetScreen firewall is treated as an object. The components that we looked at in this chapter are the main components for a policy. Address objects represent hosts or subnets of IP addresses. Service objects can be a strange concept. Many competitive firewall products create services as a single protocol. If you want to create several services and represent them as a compilation you must make a group. On a NetScreen firewall, a service object can contain up to eight protocols. This allows you to take an entire suite of protocols and make them into one logical object.

Policy creation is common task for an administrator of a NetScreen firewall. In this chapter we looked at the two methods of policy creation: the WebUI and the CLI. Each has its own merits. The WebUI may be easier to use for looking at policies, while the CLI may be faster for creating policies. The choice is yours, but never limit yourself to a single option. It always pays to be familiar with both options because in the end all policies are stored as CLI commands. If you want to use the CLI to do something, but are unsure of the command, it is most likely possible to do what you need to do from the WebUI. Then look at the configuration from the CLI to see what the commands are to use the CLI in the future.

Solutions Fast Track

NetScreen Policies

☑ A policy on a NetScreen firewall is what other firewall products considered a single rule.

☑ When creating a policy, the policies at the top should start with the most specific access to the least specific access.

☑ There are three types of policies on a NetScreen firewall; intrazone, interzone, and global.

Policy Components

☑ There are five components that are required for creating a policy: Action, direction, source address, destination address, and services.

☑ When naming address objects or service objects, it is best to decide on a naming convention to ease long-term administration.

☑ Service objects can contain up to eight individual protocols.

Creating Policies

☑ The WebUI and the CLI can both be used for creating policies. However, it may be easier for people to use the WebUI because of its GUI nature.

☑ If you want to keep a policy, but not have it stay active, you can disable the policy.

☑ When creating policies via the CLI, you have more choices over where the policy will initially be placed.

Frequently Asked Questions

The following Frequently Asked Questions, answered by the authors of this book, are designed to both measure your understanding of the concepts presented in this chapter and to assist you with real-life implementation of these concepts. To have your questions about this chapter answered by the author, browse to **www.syngress.com/solutions** and click on the **"Ask the Author"** form. You will also gain access to thousands of other FAQs at ITFAQnet.com.

Q: Can you explain the least restrictive to most restrictive policy ordering again?

A: The list of policies with the same matching source and destination zone are checked from the top down. If you were to place less restrictive policies, such as policies allowing entire networks as your source, before individual hosts, the policies with the networks would apply to your traffic first. This may lead to unexpected results if more specific policies are not taking effect first. The NetScreen firewall has no automatic way to determine if the list of policies are listed in the right order. You can, however, use the CLI command **exec policy verify** to see if you have policies overshadowing each other. This still would require you to manually make changes to fix the policy ordering.

Q: Is it possible to use IP address ranges as address objects?

A: When creating address book objects, you can only create objects based on subnetting. Even when you make a single host object, you are making it with a 32-bit mask only allowing for a single host. If you require a range of hosts, see if you can fit it into a subnet. If not, however, you will be required to create each host individually, then place them into a group.

Q: I clearly can make address objects while making policies. I do not understand why you are against this.

A: I firmly believe in creating each part of your policy in order. I think it is best to create all of your objects before you attempt to use them inside of policies. If you need to create a quick address object in a policy then go right ahead. Rename the object to a name that makes sense to you. Everyone has his or her own style of management, so use whatever best suits you.

Q: I am familiar with using other firewall software, and I am confused about why you would bind address objects to zones.

A: Having address objects inside of zones just furthers the zone concept. It is essentially binding that object into the logical location of a zone. Because most other firewall software does not use zones, they essentially have no need to organize address objects in any way other than by type.

Q: What are the differences between service objects and service groups?

A: A service object contains the protocol definition of a service. Each service object allows you to define up to eight protocols in a single service. A service group only contains service objects.

## Chapter 5

Advanced Policy Configuration

Solutions in this Chapter:

- Network Traffic Management
- Advanced Policy Options

☑ Summary

☑ Solutions Fast Track

☑ Frequently Asked Questions

Introduction

In the previous chapter we looked at the most common portions of policy creation. This will be the typical configuration used when creating a policy. As you may have noticed when using the WebUI, there is a button labeled **Advanced** at the bottom of the policy configuration page. You may have also noticed additional options in the CLI. These are the advanced options that you can apply to your policies.

In this chapter, we look at the use and configuration of each of these options. Some options involve more detailed configuration and are discussed in their own separate chapters.

In the first section of this chapter we will look at network traffic management, commonly known as *traffic shaping* or *quality of service* (QoS). This allows you to prioritize traffic on your network and determine which traffic should have access to how much bandwidth. Traffic shaping is a complex configuration that is reviewed in both theory and practice. In the second part of the chapter we review three other advanced policy options including counting, scheduling, and authentication. Counting allows you to monitor the bandwidth utilization on a per policy basis. The scheduling option allows you to specify the time that a policy is active during the day. Policy-based authentication forces a user to authenticate to the firewall before using the access provided in a firewall policy.

Network Traffic Management

Every year the capacity of Local Area Networks (LANs) greatly increases. Most organizations are stretching beyond 100 Megabits per second for their servers by moving into 1 Gigabit per second and beyond. The bandwidth requirement is not just limited for company LANs either; this includes the Internet access requirements as well. The days of companies relying on less than T1 speeds are over. Even today, your average home broadband Internet connection has speeds equal to or faster than a T1. This home broadband access is typically accessed by just one or two people concurrently, versus the multitude of workers at an office.

Many organizations are not familiar with the utilization of their networks. Even fewer can determine which protocols are the most commonly used on their networks. Every network has to be audited to determine what type of traffic is generated on it and how much traffic there is. This information will allow you to understand how your network performs, determine where your network is underperforming, and helps you to plan for future network expansion.

Because of the driving requirements for bandwidth in every organization and the inability to meet these needs, something needs to be done. Network traffic management allows you to create a strategy to prioritize network traffic. Whether used to bolster your Internet performance or ensure the timely delivery of Voice over Internet Protocol (VoIP) traffic on your LAN, QoS is a powerful tool that is included on almost all NetScreen firewalls.

The Benefits of Traffic Shaping

Every network can utilize traffic shaping to enhance network service delivery. There are many applications that are used on your network. Each type of application generates different types of traffic. These various traffic types can affect your network in different ways. Several types of common traffic include:

- **Interactive Applications** Telnet and SSH applications are classified as interactive applications. This is essentially any application where you input information and you gain immediate output. Thus, the application *interacts* with you and what you input. The application should respond to your input immediately.

- **Latency Sensitive** VoIP and H323 applications require that the information be delivered in order and in a timely fashion. These applications can be rendered useless in cases where effective delivery is not possible.

- **Bursty** HTTP (Hypertext Transfer Protocol) and FTP (File Transfer Protocol) applications operate by sending bursts of data instead of streams of data. *Bursty* is Juniper's classification of this traffic.

- **Novelty Traffic** Used by streaming media and peer-to-peer applications, novelty traffic is typically not required on a company's network and it can over-utilize your network resources.

Each type of traffic has different requirements. However, on a typical network this comes down to a first–come-first-serve type of usage, with transport layer protocols struggling to get the most out of the available bandwidth. If you could decide which traffic takes priority in using the available resources, you could make your network more efficient. This is where traffic shaping comes into play. It allows you to determine which traffic gets priority for bandwidth usage.

For protocols that are more susceptible to latency, such as VoIP, you can do two things to ensure that it will be given the proper networking environment to succeed. First, you can set the traffic to a high priority. This will ensure that the traffic is passed in a timely manor. Second, you can guarantee that bandwidth will be available for this protocol. These are two powerful tools for your network to ensure that applications get the bandwidth they need.

Packet Queuing

When using traffic shaping on a NetScreen firewall, incoming packets are put into a queue. As each packet is matched against a policy, traffic shaping rules are applied. Then the different components of traffic shaping are used to determine what happens to the packet. Traffic shaping is configured per policy, so traffic that matches a specified policy will have that policy's traffic shaping configuration applied to it. Below are the various terms that are associated with traffic shaping on a NetScreen firewall:

- **Priority Queuing** There are eight priority queues that can be used on a NetScreen firewall. The higher the priority of the queue, the more likely it will get available bandwidth. Each priority queue is ranked with a number with zero being the highest and 7 being the lowest.

- **Guaranteed Bandwidth** When you configure guaranteed bandwidth, you are specifying that a certain amount of bandwidth will be available for this traffic.

- **Maximum Bandwidth** This option defines the maximum amount of bandwidth that matching traffic can consume.

- **Interface Bandwidth** For the firewall to determine the factors of maximum and guaranteed bandwidth, you must define how much bandwidth is available on each interface. If you do not define the available bandwidth, the firewall will assume the bandwidth of the interface. In many cases this may be 10Mbps or 100Mbps. That, of course, is much more than most organizations' Internet connections.

- **DiffServ Marking** Differentiated Services (DiffServ) allows you to tag packets according to their priorities. This allows you to mark individual packets in the Type of Service (ToS) byte in the IP (Internet Protocol) header. This conforms to Request For Comment (RFC) 2474 and RFC 1349. Table 5.1 below shows a mapping of the DiffServ codes to the traffic priorities configured on a NetScreen firewall.

Table 5.1 DiffServ Mapping to NetScreen Priority Codes

Web	CLI	DiffServ
High	0	000
2nd	1	001
3rd	2	010
4th	3	011
5th	4	100
6th	5	101
7th	6	110
Low	7	111

It is entirely possible to grind your network to a halt with a bad traffic shaping configuration, so it is important to consider all aspects of it before implementing traffic shaping. In the next section we will look at and describe the various rules of traffic shaping.

Guaranteed Bandwidth

Before we jump right into traffic shaping configuration, let's look at the rules of how traffic shaping works. These very specific rules will help you understand the consequences of traffic shaping. Priority queuing contains eight different queue levels ranked from highest to lowest. The higher the queue ranking, the more precedence it gets over the other queues. If there are three policies and each policy was configured with a different priority level, the highest priority traffic would get processed first before the lower priority traffic. This is, however, not a very effective way to work with traffic, as we have not set up any bandwidth restrictions.

If you are considering using traffic shaping, most likely you are looking for two things: a way to guarantee bandwidth to specific traffic, and a way to cap how much bandwidth specific traffic will use. Setting the guaranteed bandwidth and maximum bandwidth settings accomplishes this. These are configured on a per policy basis, directly in the policy. When you configure guaranteed bandwidth you are saying that the defined amount of bandwidth will be available for the traffic. There is no restriction on configuring this. So if you only have a T1 with 1.544Mbps available, but you guarantee 10Mbps then you will have a serious problem. The firewall can over-allocate bandwidth to this traffic. This will leave no bandwidth available for other traffic. When bandwidth is allocated for traffic it is done so in a bidirectional manor. So, if 256Kbps is guaranteed outbound, then the inbound traffic will have the same 256Kbps bandwidth guarantee.

Maximum bandwidth specifies the total amount of bandwidth that can be allocated to the traffic specified in a given policy. This will be the absolute ceiling for the traffic and it cannot be exceeded. This is very useful to specify bandwidth restrictions for protocols such as FTP, streaming media, or HTTP from specific hosts. This will allow you to have hosts still use these bandwidth intensive protocols, but restrict how much bandwidth they can use. The decision about which traffic gets how much bandwidth is based on these three concepts (priority queuing, guaranteed bandwidth, and maximum bandwidth). Figure 5.1 shows a logical diagram of the bandwidth decision process.

Figure 5.1 Bandwidth Allocation

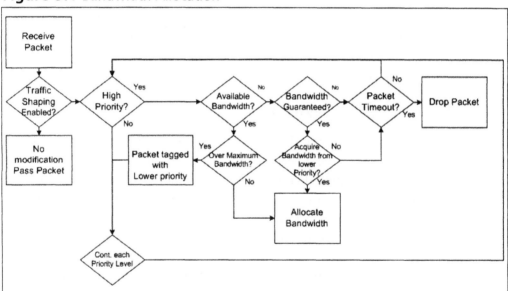

An important factor in bandwidth allocation is what happens to all of the other traffic that matches policies that do not have traffic shaping configured on them. These factors effect what happens to the unmatched traffic in relevance to the traffic that is matched to traffic shaping policies. All traffic that does not match an existing traffic shaping policy will use the following configuration:

- **Guaranteed Bandwidth** No guaranteed bandwidth.
- **Maximum Bandwidth** Unlimited maximum bandwidth.
- **Priority** Lowest priority (priority 7).

Traffic shaping is a very complex process. There are many factors that come into play in regards to designing and effective traffic shaping design. Not only must you consider the effects of guaranteed bandwidth, maximum bandwidth, and priority, you must also consider the protocol you are trying to shape. When shaping a protocol, understand how that protocol works first. If possible, do a study to determine bandwidth usage for each protocol. You may be surprised by how each protocol performs.

One particular protocol is HTTP. I have seen many organizations configure a poor traffic shaping policy around this protocol. Typically the HTTP protocol does not use a great deal of bandwidth as one might assume. If the website you are trying to traffic shape is mainly a text-based site with light images the bandwidth consumption will be relatively low compared to a site delivering many images or multimedia content. When you access a website, you send a small amount of data requesting the content on the page. Then the Web server will deliver the requested information.

The user will review the information by reading the page or looking at the pictures, and can usually then click on a second link on the site to access more content. For this type of website, there is no consistent passing of data, all the data is passed in bursts. Planning for this type of application can be tough because of its inconsistent distribution of data. This is where a study to determine exactly how much bandwidth is used would largely benefit you.

Damage & Defense...

Default Traffic Handling

It is possible for you to determine how the NetScreen firewall handles the rest of the traffic that matches policies without traffic shaping enabled. There are three modes in which you can tell your firewall to handle traffic. The default mode is *auto*. In auto mode, traffic shaping is turned on for all traffic the first time you configure a policy with traffic shaping. In the auto mode, if no traffic shaping is turned on then no traffic shaping is applied.

The second option that you can configure is for traffic shaping to be on all the time. This will enforce traffic shaping to all traffic regardless of whether or not you have configured a policy with traffic shaping. This will

Continued

apply the default traffic shaping options (no guaranteed bandwidth, unlimited maximum bandwidth, and lowest priority) to all traffic.

The last option is to disable traffic shaping on all traffic that is not part of a traffic shaping policy. This mode is how the firewall acts when there is no traffic shaping policies configured. To configure these options you must use the CLI, as these configuration changes cannot be made from the WebUI. In summary:

- **Traffic Shaping Auto** Set traffic shaping mode to **auto**.
- **Traffic Shaping always on** Set traffic shaping mode to **on**.
- **Traffic Shaping always off** Set traffic shaping mode to **off**.

```
Syngress-> get traffic-shaping mode
traffic shaping is set to auto by user
traffic shaping is currently turned off by the system
Syngress-> set traffic-shaping mode on
Syngress-> get traffic-shaping mode
traffic shaping is set to on by user
traffic shaping is currently turned off by the system
Syngress-> set traffic-shaping mode off
Syngress-> get traffic-shaping mode
traffic shaping is set to off by user
traffic shaping is currently turned off by the system
Syngress-> set traffic-shaping mode ?
auto                    automatically turn on/off traffic shaping
off                     turn off traffic shaping
on                      turn on traffic shaping
Syngress-> set traffic-shaping mode auto
Syngress-> get traffic-shaping mode
traffic shaping is set to auto by user
traffic shaping is currently turned off by the system
Syngress->
```

Traffic Shaping Examples

As you have learned already, there are many parts to traffic shaping on a NetScreen firewall. The best way to begin to understand traffic shaping is by example. In this section there are two examples of traffic shaping. These examples will help you better understand the application and use of traffic shaping.

Traffic Shaping Example 1

In this example, we have a simple network setup: we have one firewall with a single trust and untrust interface. The company also has a single T1 with 1.544Mbps bandwidth. On the trust side of the network we have a single IP block with two subnets. The Marketing department uses the 10.1.1.0/25 network and the Research Services department uses the 10.1.1.128/25 network. Each department has different types of requirements. The Sales department has very little use for the Internet besides using e-mail. The Research Services department has to perform research, most of which comes from using the Internet.

We have a possible contention of resources, as the Marketing department has lately been using the Internet for streaming media, as it is inspirational for their work. This has slowed the production of the Research Services department and lowered their important productivity. You have decided to implement a traffic shaping policy to ensure that the Research Services department is getting access to the resources they need. Table 5.2 shows our pseudo policy and what it does for us.

Table 5.2 Example 1 Pseudo Policy

Source	Destination	Service	Guaranteed Bandwidth	Maximum Bandwidth	Traffic Priority
Research Services (10.1.1.128/25)	Any	HTTP HTTPS	512Kbps	Unlimited	High
Marketing (10.1.1.0/25)	Any	Streaming Media	256Kbps	512Kbps	2nd
The entire company (10.1.1.0/24)	Any	Any	512Kbps	Unlimited	Low

We have set up three policies for the company. The first policy allows the Research department to access the Internet with the HTTP and HTTPS (HTTP Secure) protocols. This allows the Research Services department to access the websites to acquire the information they need. We are guaranteeing 512Kbps, or about 1/3$^{rd.}$ of the T1 because of the importance of this action. This traffic is given the high priority tag to ensure that it gets as much bandwidth as possible.

The second policy allows for the Marketing department to access streaming media. We guarantee that they will have 256Kbps for streaming media protocol. However, in this policy we also cap the total bandwidth they use to 512Kbps. This traffic is given the second highest priority because upper management wants to ensure they have access to the streaming media.

The final policy covers the entire company for access to the Internet. On this policy we use the entire network, 10.1.10/24, which encompasses both 10.1.1.0/25 (Marketing), and 10.1.1.128/25 (Research Services). We guarantee 512Kbps for this traffic with no cap on how much bandwidth they can use. This traffic has the lowest possible priority. Let us look at the numbers and how the traffic breaks down for availability.

- **Guaranteed Bandwidth** Total guaranteed bandwidth 512Kbps + 512Kbps + 256Kbps = 1280Kbps. The available floating bandwidth 264Kbps is left from the T1 in cases where all of the policies are using the maximum bandwidth.

- **Maximum Bandwidth** Only one policy is configured with maximum bandwidth. This is to ensure that the marketing department does not consume the entire T1.

- **Traffic Priority** The first policy will always get priority over the rest of the policies for any bandwidth remaining after all of the guaranteed bandwidth is used. The other policies will always get their guaranteed bandwidth regardless of the priority. If the first policy does not use the remaining bandwidth, it will first be available to the second policy, followed by the third policy.

Traffic Shaping Example 2

Because of our excellent use of traffic shaping, the Research Services department has become extremely productive. This has allowed the company to grow and add new departments and, of course, new requirements:

- **Engineering**   Lead researchers Darren, Richard, and Charlie have come up with the new requirements. The research services team needs access to FTP as well to accessing the usual HTTP and HTTPS protocols. Using the FTP protocol will not be as important as the HTTP and HTTPS protocols. Because of the Engineering team has doubled its staff, they now are using the entire 10.1.1.0/24 network for their own department. The team has found the Internet responsive during its use.

- **Marketing Department**   Lisa has scolded the Marketing team for their lack of productivity and has denied them access to the streaming media services. However the Marketing department now requires using the Internet much like Engineering. They require HTTP and HTTPS to identify new ways to be successful. The Marketing department uses the 10.1.2.0/25 network.

- **Human Resources**   Susan heads up the new Human Resources department. This department was created to work with all of the new employees. Susan's only major requirement is to have her Human Resources application download new recruit information over FTP throughout the day. The files they need are small, but must be consistently delivered. The Human Resources department uses the 10.1.2.128/25 network.

We must determine an effective policy to maximize the T1 for this up and coming company. Table 5.3 shows the new policy. We have expanded on our original policy to include more policies.

Table 5.3 Example 2 Policy

Source	Destination	Service	Guaranteed Bandwidth	Maximum Bandwidth	Traffic Priority
Research Services (10.1.1.0/24)	Any	HTTP HTTPS	512Kbps	Unlimited	High
Research Services (10.1.1.0/24)	Any	FTP	128Kbps	128Kbps	High
Marketing (10.1.2.0/25)	Any	HTTP HTTPS	256Kbps	Unlimited	3rd

Continued

Table 5.3 Example 2 Policy

Source	Destination	Service	Guaranteed Bandwidth	Maximum Bandwidth	Traffic Priority
Human Resources (10.1.2.128/25)	Any	FTP	128Kbps	128Kbps	2nd
The entire company (10.1.1.0/24) (10.1.2.0/24)	Any	Any	256Kbps	Unlimited	Low

We continued with the theme of our original policies. The first policy still allows Research Services to access the Internet with the 512Kbps guarantee. The second policy allows for Research Services to FTP to the Internet with a 128Kbps guarantee. Because it is not as important as HTTP and HTTPS, we give FTP less bandwidth. Both of these policies have their traffic labeled as high priority.

The third policy allows the Marketing department to access the HTTPS and HTTP protocols. They have fewer people in their department so they require less bandwidth. We have guaranteed the department 256Kbps of guaranteed bandwidth. The traffic from the Marketing department is not rated as important as either the Research Services or Human Resources traffic, but it is deemed more important than all of the other traffic coming from the company. Because of this we have given this policy third priority.

The fourth policy is used to address the Human Resources department's requirement for FTP. The files for Human Resources are small and require very little bandwidth. We have guaranteed Human Resources 128 Kbps and have specified a maximum bandwidth of 128 Kbps. This will ensure that they get the available bandwidth, but does not allow them to capitalize on the rest of the available bandwidth. The last policy allows the rest of the company to access the Internet, guaranteeing them 256 Kbps. This traffic is not required for the company to function and has been given a low priority.

- **Guaranteed Bandwidth** Total guaranteed bandwidth is 512 Kbps + 128 Kbps + 256 Kbps + 128 Kbps + 256 Kbps = 1280 Kbps. The available floating bandwidth (264 Kbps) is left from the T1 in cases where all of the policies are using the maximum bandwidth.

- **Maximum Bandwidth** We have two separate policies with maximum bandwidth. These policies are used with maximum bandwidth to ensure that they do not use up all of the available floating bandwidth.

- **Traffic Priority** The first two policies will always get priority over the rest of the priorities for any bandwidth remaining after all of the guaranteed bandwidth is used. The Human Resources FTP policy will get second priority to bandwidth. Since this policy is already guaranteed bandwidth and the maximum bandwidth it can use is the same, as the guarantee configuring the priority does not change much because it will already get the bandwidth guaranteed to it. The Marketing policy will be able to use any bandwidth left over that the research services team does not use. The rest of the company gets to use the guaranteed bandwidth of 256 Kbps and gets to use any other bandwidth that is left over.

Configuring Traffic Shaping

So far, we have reviewed the theory of traffic shaping. We will now look at the practical ways to configure the components of traffic shaping. There are two places to configure policy shaping. First, bandwidth must be configured on the interfaces you intend to use traffic shaping on, and second, you must configure traffic shaping on each policy.

Interface Bandwidth

Configuring bandwidth for each interface is a simple process. You must first determine how much bandwidth you have for each connection. Traffic shaping is typically used for the Internet, but it can be used anywhere in the network. If you do not configure the interface bandwidth manually the firewall will assume the interface link as its bandwidth. In Figure 5.2 you can see the WebUI page for configuring bandwidth on the interface.

Figure 5.2 Configuring Interface Bandwidth

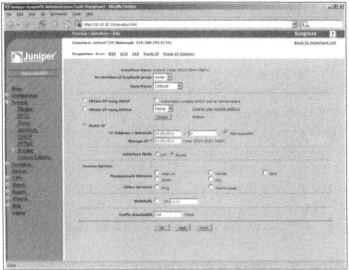

The following steps will guide you through the WebUI configuration:

1. Access **Network | Interfaces**.

2. Click the **Edit** link of the interface you wish to configure.

3. Use the **Traffic Bandwidth** field to enter the speed of the interface (in Kilobytes per second, or kBps).

4. Click **OK**.

Use the following scripts to configure bandwidth via the CLI:

```
Syngress-> get interface untrust
Interface untrust:
  number 1, if_info 88, if_index 0, mode route
  link up, phy-link up/full-duplex
  vsys Root, zone Untrust, vr trust-vr
  dhcp client disabled
  PPPoE disabled
  *ip 214.208.253.9/24    mac 0010.db61.0e01
  *manage ip 214.208.253.9, mac 0010.db61.0e01
  route-deny disable
  ping disabled, telnet disabled, SSH disabled, SNMP disabled
  web disabled, ident-reset disabled, SSL disabled
```

```
   webauth disabled, webauth-ip 0.0.0.0
   OSPF disabled  BGP disabled  RIP disabled
   bandwidth: physical 100000kbps, configured 0kbps, current 0kbps
                total configured gbw 0kbps, total allocated gbw 0kbps
   DHCP-Relay disabled
   DHCP-server disabled
Syngress-> set interface untrust bandwidth 1544
Syngress-> get interface untrust
Interface untrust:
   number 1, if_info 88, if_index 0, mode route
   link up, phy-link up/full-duplex
   vsys Root, zone Untrust, vr trust-vr
   dhcp client disabled
   PPPoE disabled
   *ip 214.208.253.9/24   mac 0010.db61.0e01
   *manage ip 214.208.253.9, mac 0010.db61.0e01
   route-deny disable
   ping disabled, telnet disabled, SSH disabled, SNMP disabled
   web disabled, ident-reset disabled, SSL disabled
   webauth disabled, webauth-ip 0.0.0.0
   OSPF disabled  BGP disabled  RIP disabled
   bandwidth: physical 100000kbps, configured 1544kbps, current 0kbps
                total configured gbw 0kbps, total allocated gbw 0kbps
   DHCP-Relay disabled
   DHCP-server disabled
Syngress->
```

Policy Configuration

Configuring traffic shaping on a policy is a simple process. The hard part is determining the configuration for each policy. In Figure 5.3, you can see the traffic shaping configuration. This is found under the advanced configuration for each policy.

Figure 5.3 Traffic Shaping Configuration (WebUI)

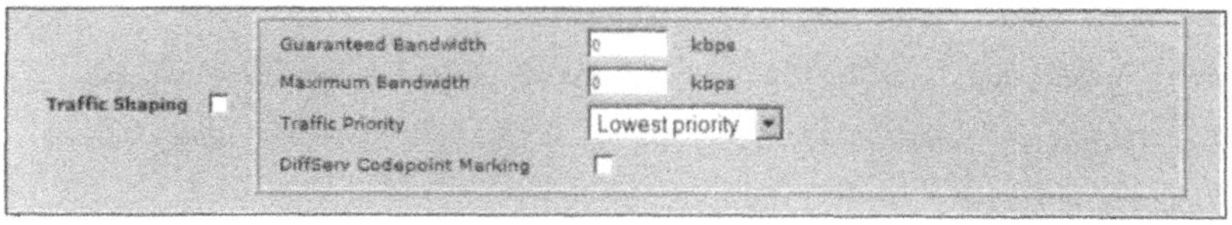

Use the following steps to create a policy configuration via the WebUI:

1. Access the policy List.

2. Click the **Edit** link of the policy you want to modify.

3. Click the **Advanced** button at the bottom of the page (note that you can access the traffic shaping configuration by clicking the **Advanced** button when creating a new policy).

4. Enable the **Traffic Shaping** option.

5. Enter the desired **Guaranteed Bandwidth** (in kbps). A value of **0** indicates that there is no guaranteed bandwidth configured.

6. Enter the desired **Maximum Bandwidth** (in kbps). A value of **0** indicates that there is no maximum bandwidth configured.

7. Use the **Traffic Priority** drop-down list to select the desired priority. If you want to mark packets with DiffServ Codepoint Marking, enable the **DiffServ Codepoint Marking** option.

8. Click **OK**.

NOTE

You can only set traffic shaping on a policy when you create the policy. If you want to modify an existing policy you must first delete it and then recreate it

The following scripts are used for policy configuration via the CLI:

```
Syngress-> set policy from trust to untrust any any HTTP permit traffic gbw
100  priority 0 mbw 200 dscp enable
policy id = 2
Syngress-> get policy id 2
```

```
name:"none" (id 2), zone Trust -> Untrust,action Permit, status "enabled"
src "Any", dst "Any", serv "HTTP"
Policies on this vpn tunnel: 0
nat off, url filtering OFF
vpn unknown vpn, policy flag 4000, session backup: on
traffic shapping on, scheduler n/a, serv flag 00
log no, log count 0, alert no, counter no(0) byte rate(sec/min) 0/0
total octets 0, counter(session/packet/octet) 0/0/0
priority 0, diffserv marking On
tadapter: state on, gbw/mbw 100/200
No Authentication
No User, User Group or Group expression set
Syngress-> set policy from trust to untrust any any FTP permit traffic gbw 0
priority 0 mbw 200 dscp enable
policy id = 3
Syngress-> get policy id 3
name:"none" (id 3), zone Trust -> Untrust,action Permit, status "enabled"
src "Any", dst "Any", serv "FTP"
Policies on this vpn tunnel: 0
nat off, url filtering OFF
vpn unknown vpn, policy flag 4000, session backup: on
traffic shapping on, scheduler n/a, serv flag 00
log no, log count 0, alert no, counter no(0) byte rate(sec/min) 0/0
total octets 0, counter(session/packet/octet) 0/0/0
priority 0, diffserv marking On
tadapter: state on, gbw/mbw 0/200
No Authentication
No User, User Group or Group expression set
Syngress->
```

Advanced Policy Options

There are several options on a NetScreen firewall that are considered *advanced* options. These options are not necessarily more complex, rather they are more like miscellaneous options that do not fit into a particular category. All of these options are invoked directly on the policy much like we configured traffic shaping above.

In this section, we look at counting, scheduling, and authentication. Counting provides the option to track bandwidth that is used on a per policy basis. This can be helpful in determining an effective traffic shaping policy. Scheduling allows you to set times at which a policy is active. Typically, once a policy is created, it is always in effect until you delete it or disable it. Scheduling allows you to specify the times at which a policy is active. Finally, we will review policy-based authentication. Using policy-based authentication forces a user to authenticate to the firewall before the specified policy is active. This forces stricter policy enforcement, as it is applied on a per user level instead of a per system level.

In this section, we cover most of the available advanced options. Some of the features that we do not cover here require more in-depth coverage in their own chapters. One option that is partially covered here is authentication. In this chapter we discuss how to configure policy-based authentication, but not all of the available options with user authentication. Because of the breadth of knowledge involved in the various options of user authentication this has been given its own chapter. Other advanced options omitted from this chapter are NAT (covered in the "NAT" chapter) and URL (Uniform Resource Locator) filtering (covered in the "Damage and Defense" chapter).

Counting

The counting feature allows you to display a graphical view of traffic that passes through the policy. This can be useful in determining traffic usage for a specific policy. It also can assist you in determining effective traffic shaping policies. Counting can be enabled on any policy. When using counting you can also enable something called a *traffic alarm*. A traffic alarm is a threshold for the policy in Bytes per second, kBps, or both. If the threshold is exceeded, a traffic alarm will be generated and can be sent to you via e-mail. The traffic alarm is also logged.

In Figure 5.4, you can see an example of a graph that is generated by configuring counting. At the top of the page there is a drop-down list labeled **Granularity**. This allows you to choose one of the following display units:

- Bytes Per Second
- Kilobytes Per Minute
- Kilobytes Per Hour
- Megabytes Per Day
- Megabytes Per Month

Figure 5.4 Counting Graph Example

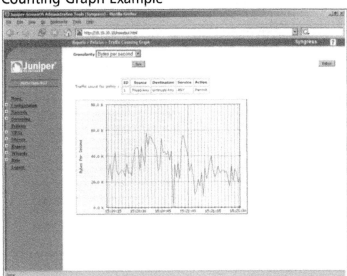

It is also possible to download the data in a text file. An example of the text file is listed below. You can use this text file to generate your own reports with the data.

```
============================================================================

Second Counters Log for Policy:

   (Src = "Any", Dst = "Any", Service = "ANY")

   Current system time is Sat, 16 Oct 2004 15:14:14
============================================================================

                  Time Stamp    Counter ( Bytes )

Sat, 16 Oct 2004 15:14:14    0000036229

Sat, 16 Oct 2004 15:14:13    0000034407

Sat, 16 Oct 2004 15:14:12    0000023846

Sat, 16 Oct 2004 15:14:11    0000029281
```

You can look at traffic alarms from both the WebUI and the CLI. A report is generated for every time period in which the traffic exceeds the set threshold. Figure 5.5 shows an example of an alarm report from the WebUI.

Figure 5.5 Traffic Alarm Report (WebUI)

	ID	Source	Destination	Service	Action
Traffic log for policy :	1	Trust/Any	Untrust/Any	ANY	Permit

Date/Time	Event	Details
2004-10-16 21:42:52	Minute Rate Alarm	Rate = 3578 KBytes/Min. is over threshold.
2004-10-16 21:41:53	Minute Rate Alarm	Rate = 4279 KBytes/Min. is over threshold.
2004-10-16 21:40:54	Minute Rate Alarm	Rate = 4511 KBytes/Min. is over threshold.
2004-10-16 21:39:55	Minute Rate Alarm	Rate = 4200 KBytes/Min. is over threshold.
2004-10-16 21:38:56	Minute Rate Alarm	Rate = 3938 KBytes/Min. is over threshold.
2004-10-16 21:37:57	Minute Rate Alarm	Rate = 3874 KBytes/Min. is over threshold.
2004-10-16 21:36:58	Minute Rate Alarm	Rate = 4127 KBytes/Min. is over threshold.
2004-10-16 21:35:59	Minute Rate Alarm	Rate = 5130 KBytes/Min. is over threshold.
2004-10-16 21:34:29	Minute Rate Alarm	Rate = 2476 KBytes/Min. is over threshold.
2004-10-16 21:33:30	Minute Rate Alarm	Rate = 2387 KBytes/Min. is over threshold.
2004-10-16 21:32:31	Minute Rate Alarm	Rate = 2288 KBytes/Min. is over threshold.
2004-10-16 21:31:32	Minute Rate Alarm	Rate = 2184 KBytes/Min. is over threshold.
2004-10-16 21:30:33	Minute Rate Alarm	Rate = 2362 KBytes/Min. is over threshold.
2004-10-16 21:29:34	Minute Rate Alarm	Rate = 3221 KBytes/Min. is over threshold.

To view a policy's traffic alarm reports via the CLI, click the policy's red alert light, or select **Reports** | **Policies**.

The following traffic alarm scripts were accessed via the CLI:

```
Syngress-> get alarm traffic
Recent Alarm Time      PID Source                Destination
Service
2004-10-16 21:47:57     1 Any                     Any                    ANY
Total entries matched = 1
Syngress-> get alarm traffic detail
PID 1, src Any, dst Any, service ANY
Total alarm entries under this policy = 4095
Date        Time                Rate        Threshold    Unit
2004-10-16 21:47:57             2902                5    KBytes/Minute
2004-10-16 21:46:58             3442                5    KBytes/Minute
2004-10-16 21:45:59             4443                5    KBytes/Minute
2004-10-16 21:44:50             3164                5    KBytes/Minute
2004-10-16 21:43:51             3235                5    KBytes/Minute
2004-10-16 21:42:52             3578                5    KBytes/Minute
2004-10-16 21:41:53             4279                5    KBytes/Minute
2004-10-16 21:40:54             4511                5    KBytes/Minute
2004-10-16 21:39:55             4200                5    KBytes/Minute
```

```
2004-10-16 21:38:56          3938              5    KBytes/Minute

2004-10-16 21:37:57          3874              5    KBytes/Minute

2004-10-16 21:36:58          4127              5    KBytes/Minute

2004-10-16 21:35:59          5130              5    KBytes/Minute

2004-10-16 21:34:29          2476              5    KBytes/Minute

2004-10-16 21:33:30          2387              5    KBytes/Minute

2004-10-16 21:32:31          2288              5    KBytes/Minute

2004-10-16 21:31:32          2184              5    KBytes/Minute

2004-10-16 21:30:33          2362              5    KBytes/Minute

2004-10-16 21:29:34          3221              5    KBytes/Minute

Total entries matched = 19


Syngress->
```

Configuring Counting

Configuring counting is simple. Counting can be enabled or disabled at any time. When you configure counting it is either turned on or off. Figure 5.6 shows the WebUI configuration page of a policy with counting enabled.

Figure 5.6 Configuring Counting (WebUI)

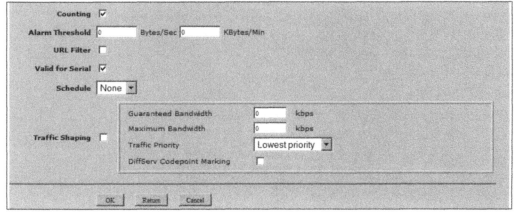

Use the following steps to enable counting via the WebUI:

1. Click the desired policy's **Edit** link.

2. Click **Advanced** at the bottom of the page.

3. Enable the **Counting** option.

4. Click **OK**.

Use the following scripts to enable counting via the CLI:

```
Syngress-> set policy from trust to untrust any any HTTP permit count
policy id = 2
Syngress-> get policy id 2
name:"none" (id 2), zone Trust -> Untrust,action Permit, status "enabled"
src "Any", dst "Any", serv "HTTP"
Policies on this vpn tunnel: 0
nat off, url filtering OFF
vpn unknown vpn, policy flag 0000, session backup: on
traffic shaping off, scheduler n/a, serv flag 00
log no, log count 0, alert no, counter yes(2) byte rate(sec/min) 0/0
total octets 0, counter(session/packet/octet) 0/0/2
priority 7, diffserv marking Off
tadapter: state off, gbw/mbw 0/-1
No Authentication
No User, User Group or Group expression set
Syngress-> set policy id 2
Syngress(policy:2)-> unset count
Syngress(policy:2)-> exit
Syngress-> get policy id 2
name:"none" (id 2), zone Trust -> Untrust,action Permit, status "enabled"
src "Any", dst "Any", serv "HTTP"
Policies on this vpn tunnel: 0
nat off, url filtering OFF
vpn unknown vpn, policy flag 0000, session backup: on
traffic shaping off, scheduler n/a, serv flag 00
log no, log count 0, alert no, counter no(0) byte rate(sec/min) 0/0
total octets 0, counter(session/packet/octet) 0/0/0
priority 7, diffserv marking Off
tadapter: state off, gbw/mbw 0/-1
No Authentication
No User, User Group or Group expression set
Syngress-> set policy id 2
Syngress(policy:2)-> set count
```

```
Syngress(policy:2)-> exit
Syngress->
```

In Figure 5.7, you can see the icon that is added to your policy. You can click on this icon to access the counting graph. The counting graph is represented as an hourglass You are only able to view the graphs from the WebUI. If you are using the CLI, you can see the stored counter information in its raw form, but it is of very little help in actually determining the traffic usage.

Figure 5.7 Policy with Traffic Shaping Configured (WebUI)

From Trust To Untrust, total policy: 1									
ID	Source	Destination	Service	Action	Options		Configure		Enable	Move
1	Any	Any	ANY	✓	⏳))	Edit	Clone	Remove	☑	⇕ ⇥

The following is an example of raw counter information, obtained via the CLI:

```
Syngress-> get counter policy 1 second
PID: 1, Interval: Second, Unit: Byte/Sec, End Time: 16 Oct 2004 16:14:39
000-005: 0000039654 0000035190 0000034479 0000042527 0000029679 0000047886
006-011: 0000033058 0000034236 0000042506 0000032629 0000041460 0000042747
012-017: 0000045812 0000051081 0000067825 0000057319 0000055379 0000043726
018-023: 0000061160 0000072803 0000058361 0000066299 0000073356 0000072003
024-029: 0000076061 0000091056 0000084565 0000064143 0000047321 0000061755
030-035: 0000051065 0000062170 0000046592 0000060783 0000057485 0000079750
036-041: 0000053997 0000044322 0000045913 0000000000 0000056328 0000061494
042-047: 0000052587 0000041281 0000048066 0000055305 0000048326 0000045536
048-053: 0000043505 0000043834 0000047886 0000049541 0000050748 0000048746
054-059: 0000051015 0000067368 0000039355 0000041967 0000039633 0000047315
060-065: 0000066774 0000060505 0000054568 0000046993 0000051292 0000054856
066-071: 0000061414 0000044580 0000035620 0000035112 0000043073 0000041217
072-077: 0000046928 0000055871 0000050939 0000033101 0000035341 0000032518
078-083: 0000031710 0000035645 0000036502 0000042580 0000047418 0000031568
084-089: 0000045538 0000045069 0000048985 0000055465 0000036345 0000055489
090-095: 0000063875 0000049474 0000050028 0000037453 0000040042 0000036762
096-101: 0000028722 0000042958 0000040367 0000000000 0000052461 0000041931
102-107: 0000044813 0000038372 0000049706 0000050366 0000046635 0000036129
108-113: 0000041911 0000042353 0000038854 0000030692 0000037721 0000028314
114-118: 0000040465 0000025109 0000056224 0000040654 0000053751
Syngress->
```

Configuring Traffic Alarms

To configure traffic alarms, first determine what values you want to monitor. You can choose to use Bytes per second, Kilobytes per minute, or both. Use **0** for any option that you do not wish to use. Traffic alarms can be configured from both the CLI and the WebUI. In Figure 5.8, you can see the red alarm icon that shows that traffic alarms are configured for that policy. You can click on this icon to access the report for that policy. If you are using the CLI, you can configure traffic alarms both during policy creation, or after the policy has been created. Note that you must have counting enabled in order to enable traffic alarms.

Figure 5.8 Traffic Alarm Configured on a Policy (WebUI)

ID	Source	Destination	Service	Action	Options	Configure			Enable	Move
From Trust To Untrust, total policy: 1										
1	Any	Any	ANY	✅	🕰️🚨	Edit	Clone	Remove	☑	⇕ ➡

Use the following steps to configure traffic alarms via the WebUI:

1. Click the **Edit** link of the policy you want to modify.

2. Click **Advanced**.

3. In the **Alarm Threshold** section, use the **Bytes/Sec** field to enter the bytes per second you wish to monitor. If you do not wish to use this option, leave the field blank

4. Use the **KBytes/Min** field to enter the Kilobytes per minute you wish to monitor. If you do not wish to use this option, leave the field blank.

5. Click **OK**.

Use the following scripts to configure traffic alarms via the CLI:

```
Syngress-> set policy from trust to untrust any any FTP permit count alarm
0 256
policy id = 2
Syngress-> get policy id 2
name:"none" (id 2), zone Trust -> Untrust,action Permit, status "enabled"
src "Any", dst "Any", serv "FTP"
Policies on this vpn tunnel: 0
nat off, url filtering OFF
vpn unknown vpn, policy flag 0000, session backup: on
```

```
traffic shapping off, scheduler n/a, serv flag 00

log no, log count 0, alert no, counter yes(2) byte rate(sec/min) 0/256

total octets 0, counter(session/packet/octet) 0/0/2

priority 7, diffserv marking Off

tadapter: state off, gbw/mbw 0/-1

No Authentication

No User, User Group or Group expression set

Syngress-> set policy id 2

Syngress(policy:2)-> unset count

Syngress(policy:2)-> set count alarm 500 512

Syngress(policy:2)-> exit

Syngress-> get policy id 2

name:"none" (id 2), zone Trust -> Untrust,action Permit, status "enabled"

src "Any", dst "Any", serv "FTP"

Policies on this vpn tunnel: 0

nat off, url filtering OFF

vpn unknown vpn, policy flag 0000, session backup: on

traffic shapping off, scheduler n/a, serv flag 00

log no, log count 0, alert no, counter yes(2) byte rate(sec/min) 500/512

total octets 0, counter(session/packet/octet) 0/0/2

priority 7, diffserv marking Off

tadapter: state off, gbw/mbw 0/-1

No Authentication

No User, User Group or Group expression set

Syngress->
```

Scheduling

When you create a policy on a NetScreen firewall, you immediately activate that policy into the running configuration. If you do not want to use that policy you can either disable it or remove it manually. Scheduling is a function that allows you to have a policy that is active only at specific times. You would create a schedule object based upon a single time, day, or reoccurring time.

For example, you may want to allow your users to browse the Internet after 5pm. By creating a schedule object you can define a time or times that you want to allow this activity. A schedule object can be created to occur at a single time or on a recurring schedule. When configuring scheduling, the time is based upon the local time of the firewall.

Configuring Scheduling

Configuring a policy to schedule is a two-step process. First you must create a schedule object. Next, you must apply the schedule object to a policy. You can apply the scheduling object to an existing policy or to a policy as it is being created. You can create and apply scheduling objects from both the CLI and the WebUI. In Figure 5.9, you can see the schedule object creation screen in the WebUI.

Figure 5.9 Schedule Object Creation (WebUI)

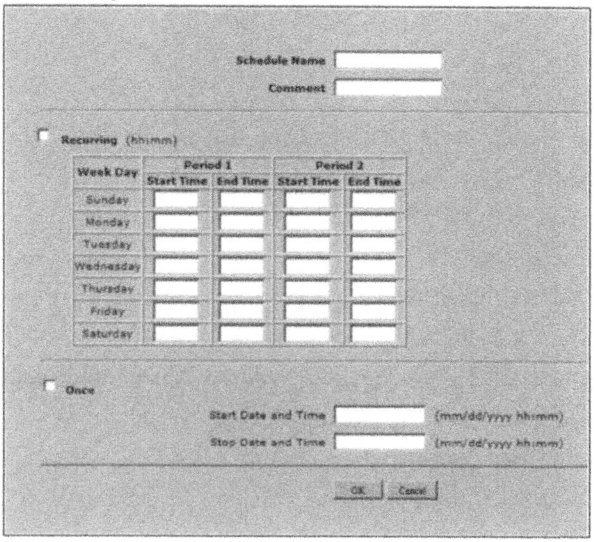

Creating a schedule object requires the use of a name and the definition of either a recurring or one time instance. If you configure a recurring time you can configure two different periods per day. Any days that you do not want to apply a schedule to, leave those days blank. To configure a single occurrence you must configure a start and stop time along with a start and stop date.

Use the following steps to add a schedule object via the WebUI:

1. Click **New**.

2. Enter the name of the object in the **Schedule Name** field.

3. Enter a brief description in the **Comment** field.

4. Select either **Recurring** or **Once**.

5. Enter the start and end times for the schedule object.

6. Click **OK**.

Use the following steps to edit an existing schedule object:

1. Access **Objects | Schedules**.

2. Click the **Edit** link of the schedule you wish to edit.

3. Make the desired changes and click **OK**.

To remove a schedule object, access **Objects | Schedules** click the
Remove link of the schedule object you wish to delete. Click **OK** to
confirm. Note that you cannot delete an object that is used in a policy.
The following scripts are used for configuring scheduling via the CLI:

```
Syngress-> set scheduler "Upgrade Period" once start 08/02/2004 12:00 stop
11/14/2004 12:00 comment "The will allow for contractor access"
Syngress-> get scheduler
One-time Schedules:

Name                    Start Time              Stop Time              Comments
Upgrade Period          08/02/2004 12:00        11/14/2004 12:00       The will
allow f


Syngress-> set scheduler "After Hours" recurrent monday start 17:00 stop
19:00  Syngress-> set scheduler "After Hours" recurrent tuesday start 17:00
stop 19:00
Syngress-> set scheduler "After Hours" recurrent wednesday start 17:00 stop
19:0Syngress-> set scheduler "After Hours" recurrent thursday start 17:00
stop 19:00Syngress-> set scheduler "After Hours" recurrent friday start
17:00 stop 19:00
Syngress-> get scheduler
One-time Schedules:

Name                    Start Time              Stop Time              Comments
Upgrade Period          08/02/2004 12:00        11/14/2004 12:00       The will
allow f


Recurrent schedules:

Name            Weekday         Start1   Stop1   Start2   Stop2   Comments
After Hours     Monday          17:00    19:00   N/A      N/A
After Hours     Tuesday         17:00    19:00   N/A      N/A
After Hours     Wednesday       17:00    19:00   N/A      N/A
After Hours     Thursday        17:00    19:00   N/A      N/A
After Hours     Friday          17:00    19:00   N/A      N/A
Syngress->
```

> **NOTE**
>
> Even though it seems as if there are multiple objects named "After Hours" they all represent the same object.

Once you have created your service objects, you can now apply them to your policy. In Figure 5.10 you can see the activation of a schedule object on a policy. In Figure 5.11 you will see two policies. The top policy (ID 2) is grayed out. This policy has a schedule applied to it and it is not currently active. The bottom policy (ID 1) has a schedule applied to it and is active. If a policy has a schedule, but the policy is currently active, there is no way to tell if the policy has scheduling configured from the main policies page. The only way is to drill down on the policy to the advanced configuration page.

Figure 5.10 Scheduled Policy Configuration (WebUI)

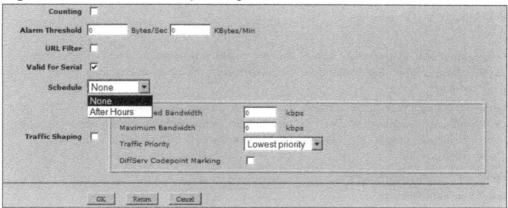

Figure 5.11 Non-Active Scheduled Policy (WebUI)

From Trust To Untrust, total policy: 2										
ID	Source	Destination	Service	Action	Options		Configure		Enable	Move
2	Any	Any	HTTP	✅		Edit	Clone	Remove	☑	↕ ➡
1	Any	Any	ANY	✅		Edit	Clone	Remove	☑	↕ ➡

Use the following steps to apply scheduling to a policy via the WebUI:

1. Click the **Edit** link of the policy you want to modify.
2. Click **Advanced**.

3. Use the **Schedule** drop-down list to select the schedule object you want to apply to the current policy.

4. Click **OK**.

The following scripts are used for configuring a policy for scheduling via the CLI:

```
Syngress-> set policy from trust to untrust any any HTTP permit schedule
"After Hours"
policy id = 3
Syngress-> get policy id 3
name:"none" (id 3), zone Trust -> Untrust,action Permit, status "enabled"
src "Any", dst "Any", serv "HTTP"
Policies on this vpn tunnel: 0
nat off, url filtering OFF
vpn unknown vpn, policy flag 0000, session backup: on
traffic shapping off, scheduler After Hours(off), serv flag 00
log no, log count 0, alert no, counter no(0) byte rate(sec/min) 0/0
total octets 0, counter(session/packet/octet) 0/0/0
priority 7, diffserv marking Off
tadapter: state off, gbw/mbw 0/-1
No Authentication
No User, User Group or Group expression set
Syngress->
NOTE: From the CLI the only way to remove scheduling is to delete and
recreate the policy
```

Authentication

Creating policies allows users to access resources by their IP addresses. This does not prevent specific users from accessing resources, only from accessing systems. So, if your administrator workstation had additional access to resources and someone else used that system or spoofed your IP address, they would have equal privileges. The engineers at Juniper have already thought of a solution to this. You can configure policies to require users to authenticate before they access resources.

There are two methods by which you can force a user to authenticate. Firewall authentication or *in-line authentication* allows you to prompt users for authentication when they attempt to use a specific protocol. These protocols are very limited due to the nature of how various protocols work. You can use FTP,

HTTP, or Telnet to offer authentication intermediation. Once a user attempts to access one of those three protocols through the firewall, he or she is prompted for authentication. The user would then authenticate to the firewall and be allowed to access the end resource. Within these same policies you could also grant access to other protocols. However, the user would first be required to authenticate to FTP, HTTP, or Telnet first.

The second method you can use is called *WebAuth authentication*. This forces the user to access the WebAuth IP address on the firewall. From here the user would authenticate to the firewall. If the authentication was successful, the user would be allowed to access the hosts and services in the policies that require authentication. This is obviously slightly harder to use because it is not automatic. Some users may balk at the requirement to do this. There are some really good ways to use this option. One example would be for remote administration. You can set up a policy to allow access for remote administration, but force authentication first. This way, you can access the WebAuth IP address from home, authenticate, and then perform your administrative tasks.

The WebAuth IP address is an IP that is tied to a specific interface on the firewall. This IP address is separate from the actual interface IP address. The only purpose this IP address serves is to authenticate users. When defining your policy you can choose which type of authentication you want to access. In this section of the chapter we are only going to explain how to configure authentication on a policy. The other functions, such as adding and removing users, will be covered in the chapter called "User Authentication". Both options are configured in the advanced section of the policy configuration.

Configuring Authentication

Configuring authentication is simply a matter of enabling the appropriate option in the advanced section of the policy configuration. In Figure 5.12, you can see the options that are available in the WebUI when configuring authentication on a policy. There are several options:

- **Authentication** This section is where we will turn on authentication for this policy. To enable authentication for the policy you must check the box labeled **Authentication**. You can then choose one of the following two authentication options:

    - **Auth Server** Selecting this option turns on in-line authentication. When you select this option you must also determine which authentication server you want to use. You can choose the default server or select from other available servers.

- **WebAuth** This option uses the user database that is selected on the WebAuth page.

- **User Group** This drop-down list allows you to choose a specific group of users that are allowed to authenticate using this policy.

- **User** Allows you to specify which individual user can authenticate for this policy. If using an external database you must select an external user from the drop-down list, and then enter the username in the **External User** field.

- **Group Expression** Allows you to choose a group expression object.

Figure 5.12 Authentication Configuration (WebUI)

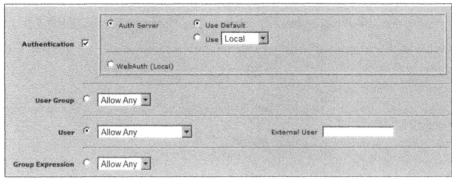

Use the following steps to configure authentication via the WebUI:

1. Click the **Edit** link of the policy you want to modify.
2. Click **Advanced**.
3. Enable the **Authentication** option.
4. To use in-line authentication, select the **Auth Server** option. To use Web authentication, select the **WebAuth (Local)** option.
5. If you select the **Auth Server** option, you must specify which authentication server to use. To use the default authentication server, select the **Use Default** option. To use another available authentication server, select the **Use** option and select the desired server from the drop-down list.

6. Next you must specify which user(s) or group(s) can authenticate to this policy:

    ■   To specify a group, select the **User Group** option and use the drop-down list to select the desired group (select **Allow Any** to allow all groups to authenticate).

    ■   To specify a user, select the **User** option and use the drop-down list to specify the desired user (select **Allow Any** to allow all users to authenticate). If the user is not local, enter the user's name in the **External User** field.

    ■   To specify a group expression, select the **Group Expression** option and select the desired group expression from the drop-down list (select **Allow Any** to allow all group expressions).

7. Click **OK**.

Use the following scripts to configure authentication via the CLI:

```
Syngress-> set policy from trust to untrust any any HTTP permit auth
policy id = 5
Syngress-> get policy id 5
name:"none" (id 5), zone Trust -> Untrust,action Permit-Auth, status
"enabled"
src "Any", dst "Any", serv "HTTP"
Policies on this vpn tunnel: 0
nat off, url filtering OFF
vpn unknown vpn, policy flag 0000, session backup: on
traffic shapping off, scheduler n/a, serv flag 00
log no, log count 0, alert no, counter no(0) byte rate(sec/min) 0/0
total octets 0, counter(session/packet/octet) 0/0/0
priority 7, diffserv marking Off
tadapter: state off, gbw/mbw 0/-1
Authenticate as per default auth settings
No User, User Group or Group expression set
Syngress-> set policy from trust to untrust 10.10.10.0/24 any HTTP permit
webauth
policy id = 6
Syngress-> get policy id 6
name:"none" (id 6), zone Trust -> Untrust,action Permit-Auth, status
"enabled"
```

```
src "10.10.10.0/24", dst "Any", serv "HTTP"

Policies on this vpn tunnel: 0

nat off, url filtering OFF

vpn unknown vpn, policy flag 0000, session backup: on

traffic shapping off, scheduler n/a, serv flag 00

log no, log count 0, alert no, counter no(0) byte rate(sec/min) 0/0

total octets 0, counter(session/packet/octet) 0/0/0

priority 7, diffserv marking Off

tadapter: state off, gbw/mbw 0/-1

Authenticate via WebAuth Server: Local

No User, User Group or Group expression set

Syngress-> set policy from trust to untrust any any HTTP permit auth ?
<return>

attack                 specify attack detection

count                  enable counting

group-expression       specify group expression for this policy

log                    enable logging

no-session-backup      disable session backup

schedule               set scheduler

server                 specify authentication server for this policy

traffic                traffic parameters

url-filter             enable URL-filtering for this policy

user                   specify user name for this policy

user-group             specify user group name for this policy

Syngress->
```

Once you have completed the authentication configuration, you will be able to see the authentication icon in the WebUI (see Figure 5.13).

Figure 5.13 Authentication Icon

From Trust To Untrust, total policy: 2										
ID	Source	Destination	Service	Action	Options		Configure		Enable	Move
4	Any	Any	FTP	✓	📷	Edit	Clone	Remove	☑	⇕ ➡
3	Any	Any	ANY	✓		Edit	Clone	Remove	☑	⇕ ➡

WebAuth Authentication

When configuring WebAuth authentication, you must additionally specify an IP address to use for the WebAuth IP address. This can be done from either the WebUI or the CLI. Figure 5.14 shows the configuration for the WebAuth IP address in the WebUI.

Figure 5.14 WebAuth IP Address Configuration

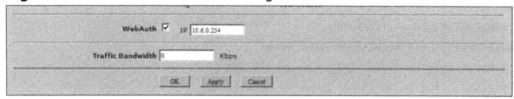

Use the following steps to configure WebAuth authentication via the WebUI:

1. Click the **Edit** link of the interface for which you will be configuring the WebAuth IP address.

2. Enable the **WebAuth** option.

3. Use the **IP** field to enter the WebAuth IP address.

4. Click **OK**.

Use the following scripts to configure a WebAuth IP address via the CLI:

```
Syngress-> set interface trust webauth
Syngress-> set interface trust webauth-ip 10.6.0.254
Syngress-> get interface trust
Interface trust:
  number 2, if_info 176, if_index 0, mode nat
  link up, phy-link up/full-duplex
  vsys Root, zone Trust, vr trust-vr
  dhcp client disabled
  PPPoE disabled
  *ip 10.6.0.1/24    mac 0010.db61.0e02
  *manage ip 10.6.0.1, mac 0010.db61.0e02
  secondary subnet: 10.10.10.10/24
  route-deny disable
  ping enabled, telnet enabled, SSH enabled, SNMP enabled
  web enabled, ident-reset disabled, SSL enabled
```

```
webauth enabled, webauth-ip 10.6.0.254

OSPF disabled  BGP disabled  RIP disabled

bandwidth: physical 100000kbps, configured 0kbps, current 210kbps

             total configured gbw 0kbps, total allocated gbw 0kbps

DHCP-Relay disabled

DHCP-server enabled, status on.

Syngress->
```

The last part you can configure for WebAuth is to choose the authentication server you want to use and the message you want to pass to the user's browser after a successful authentication. These are both configured from the same page in the WebUI. Figure 5.15 shows screen for configuring the WebAuth banner settings.

Figure 5.15 WebAuth Banner Settings

Use the following steps to configure the WebAuth banner settings via the WebUI:

1. Use the **WebAuth Server** drop-down list to select the authentication type.

2. Use the **Success Banner** text field to enter the banner text that users will see upon successful authentication. Note that the banner can be a maximum of 220 characters in length.

3. Click **Apply**.

Use the following scripts to configure the WebAuth banner settings via the CLI:

```
Syngress-> set webauth server Local

Syngress-> set webauth banner success "You have successfully authenticated"

Syngress-> get webauth

Webauth settings:
```

```
Webauth via Server:
Id     :   0                      Auth Server   : Local
Type   : Local                    Timeout       :   10
Syngress-> get webauth banner
You have successfully authenticated
Syngress->
```

Auth Server Banner Configuration

When using Auth server authentication you can customize the banners that show up for the various protocols. These are the banners that are used during the intermediation for HTTP, FTP, and Telnet. The HTTP banner is used for both In-line authentication and WebAuth authentication. The FTP and Telnet authentication are only used for the In-line authentication. The WebUI or the CLI can be used to configure the banners. In Figure 5.16 you can see an example of the WebUI configuration page.

Figure 5.16 Auth Server Banner Configuration

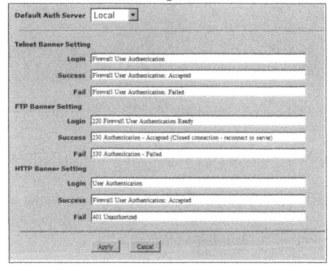

Use the following steps to configure Auth server banner settings:

1. Use the **Default Auth Server** drop-down list to select the default server.

2. Enter the **Login**, **Success**, and **Fail** banner text for **Telnet**, **FTP**, and **HTTP** protocols.

3. Click **Apply**.

Use the following scripts to configure Auth server banner settings via the CLI:

```
Syngress-> set auth banner ftp success "230 Your FTP authentication was
successful"
Syngress-> set auth banner ftp fail "530 Your FTP authentication was
unsuccessful"  Syngress-> set auth banner ftp login "220 Please
authenticate to the FTP Auth "
Syngress-> set auth banner telnet success "Your Telnet authentication was
succesSyngress-> set auth banner telnet fail "Your Telnet authentication
was unsuccessSyngress-> set auth banner telnet login "Please authenticate
to the Telnet Auth"
Syngress-> set auth banner http success "Your HTTP authentication was
successful"
Syngress-> set auth banner http fail "Your HTTP Authentication was
unsuccessful"Syngress-> set auth banner http login "Please authenticate for
HTTP Auth"
Syngress-> get auth banner
Banners:
Telnet :
Login  : Please authenticate to the Telnet Auth
Success: Your Telnet authentication was successful
Fail   : Your Telnet authentication was unsuccessful
FTP    :
Login  : 220 Please authenticate to the FTP Auth
Success: 230 Your FTP authentication was successful
Fail   : 530 Your FTP authentication was unsuccessful
HTTP   :ß
Login  : Please authenticate for HTTP Auth
Success: Your HTTP authentication was successful
Fail   : Your HTTP Authentication was unsuccessful
Syngress->
```

Summary

In this chapter we looked at the various advanced policy options. As mentioned at the beginning of the chapter, these are more like miscellaneous options than options that are truly advanced or complex.

Traffic shaping is what should be considered an advanced feature. To successfully implement traffic shaping you must research your exact requirements for each policy you implement. A poor configuration with traffic shaping can be as bad in some cases as not using traffic shaping at all. We looked at the use of guaranteed bandwidth, traffic prioritization, and maximum bandwidth restrictions. These three components of traffic management allow you to ensure that the available bandwidth is allocated to the policies that need it.

Counting, although simple to configure, can yield some powerful results. Using counting can help you identify traffic patterns on a per policy basis. This can help you identify which policies require more bandwidth and which use less bandwidth. You can use this information to make more informed decisions when configuring traffic shaping.

Policies are typically in one of two states, enabled or disabled. When using scheduling you can create schedule objects to specify which times the policies will be enforced and for how long policies are effective. This allows for access or denial of resources in your network based upon the time of day, allowing you to have a more dynamic set of firewall policies.

Policy-based authentication forces a user to authenticate before using network resources. This can be implemented in one of two ways. First, by forcing a user to authenticate to a specific IP address before he or she can access the resources matching the policy, and second, by using in-line authentication to automatically prompt a user to authenticate when attempting to use HTTP, FTP, or Telnet through the firewall. Using authentication on a policy not only authenticates the system by requiring the source IP address to match the policy, but also forces the user to authenticate to the firewall to ensure the right user is accessing the resources.

Solutions Fast Track

Network Traffic Management

☑ To create an effective traffic shaping policy, it will take time and research to properly utilize the features of traffic shaping.

☑ Guaranteed bandwidth is always allocated first, even on the lowest priority level.

☑ Bandwidth that is allocated is always allocated bidirectionally.

☑ Maximum bandwidth allows you to put a cap on how much total bandwidth a policy can use.

☑ By applying a priority to traffic matched to a policy, you are deciding for the firewall which traffic should be allocated more bandwidth and which traffic is non-essential.

Advanced Policy Options

☑ Counting can assist in creating an effective traffic shaping policy.

☑ Using authentication in your policies allows you to help ensure the person using the policies resources is authorized to use them.

☑ Scheduling allows you to configure a policy that is effective during specific times during the day.

☑ WebAuth authentication is great when you want to require authentication in a more discreet manner.

☑ Using traffic alarms for counting can let you know when you are getting close to utilizing all of your bandwidth for your Internet link.

Frequently Asked Questions

The following Frequently Asked Questions, answered by the authors of this book, are designed to both measure your understanding of the concepts presented in this chapter and to assist you with real-life implementation of these concepts. To have your questions about this chapter answered by the author, browse to **www.syngress.com/solutions** and click on the **"Ask the Author"** form. You will also gain access to thousands of other FAQs at ITFAQnet.com.

Q: In-line authentication policies, which only allow HTTP, FTP, and Telnet, seem very limited as far as protocol options. Why shouldn't I just use WebAuth instead to get more protocol support?

A: When you create a policy using in-line authentication you can use any protocol you want for services in the policy. However, you must use HTTP, FTP, or Telnet in the policy to use for authentication. Because of the nature of most other protocols, Juniper is unable to create intermediation for other protocols to use them for authentication. Once you authenticate with HTTP, FTP, or Telnet, you will be allowed to use any of the protocols that are in the policy.

Q: Why is traffic shaping so difficult to use?

A: Traffic shaping requires some reasonable planning to use. When you configure traffic shaping you are setting up rules that the firewall must follow when prioritizing traffic. Because the firewall is unable to make cognitive decisions, you must determine all of the decisions that need to be made for traffic shaping up front. This can be difficult because it requires some planning, but once you have tuned an effective traffic shaping configuration on your firewall, the results will be well worth the effort.

Q: Traffic shaping does not seem to be as fully featured as I think it should be. Why would Juniper even use it on their firewalls?

A: The traffic shaping option on the NetScreen firewall is an excellent tool for traffic management. Because it is only one small part of what the firewall product can do, it is not the focus of the product. Many products exist solely to do traffic shaping and those products excel at providing that type of capability. The traffic shaping option on a NetScreen firewall provides the minimum required options to be able to support traffic shaping effectively.

Q: Does the use of counting affect the performance of your firewall?

A: If you enable counting on your firewall it will cause a slight performance decrease because of all the internal operations that the firewall must perform to store the counting information. However, the impact is minimal. The impact would only be noticeable if you are already running your firewall at peak capacity. In most situations counting can be enabled on your policies with little performance detriment.

Q: Scheduling looks like a great tool, but can you use it in a policy to deny traffic?

A: The scheduling option can be enabled on any policy, regardless of what that policy does. The policy can be a deny policy, or even contain VPNs. The action or content of the policy does not affect the ability to enable scheduling on a policy.

Chapter 6

User Authentication

Solutions in this Chapter:

- Types of users
- User databases
- External Auth Servers

☑ Summary

☑ Solutions Fast Track

☑ Frequently Asked Questions

Introduction

User authentication is probably one of the two most important aspects of the Netscreen firewall. Without a method of providing for the authentication of users, the firewall would lack the ability to limit who has access to administrative features or virtual private networks (VPNs). By providing a set of strong user authentication capabilities, the Netscreen firewall helps secure your network. The Netscreen firewall also provides a balance between security and ease-of-use via the many features supported in its authentication mechanisms.

User authentication on the Netscreen firewall can at first seem like a daunting task. With five types of supported users, four ways to store the users—one internal, and three external—and limitations that exist only for some of the users, it's no wonder it seems confusing.

In this chapter, we will discuss the types of users and how they should be used. We will discuss the types of authentication servers, the features that each authentication user has and what limitations you should be aware of. Finally, we will show you how to set up users, authentication servers, and more by using both Netscreen's WebUI and the CLI (command line interface).

Types of Users

The Netscreen authentication system has the following different types of users:

- IKE (Internet Key Exchange)
- Auth
- XAUTH
- L2TP
- Admin

Each different type of user has specific capabilities associated with its use. In the next section, we will discuss the types of users further and what their uses can or should be.

Uses of Each Type

The uses of each type of user are varied and each has its own advantages and disadvantages. The biggest difference between the users lies in the capabilities each has with regard to features and the network layer in which the authentication happens. For example, only Auth users can perform IKE authentication. Furthermore, IKE users authenticate before both XAuth and L2TP users, XAuth users authenticate after IKE, but before the VPN tunnel is established, and L2TP authenticates only after the IPSec (Internet Protocol Security) VPN has been established.

Auth Users

Auth users are users that must authenticate to the firewall before being given authorization to access either the firewall or systems behind the firewall. Authentication users may use any supported authentication server for storage of authentication credentials, whether they are the local database, LDAP (Lightweight Directory Access Protocol) directory, SecurID server, or RADIUS (Remote Access Dial-In User Service) server.

There are two different types of authentication that Auth users are capable of utilizing. Run-time, a setting in which the user is queried for authentication credentials after an attempt to contact a protected host, and WebAuth, a setting where users pre-authenticates themselves to the firewall before attempting to access protected resources.

The authentication steps for **Run-time** are as follows:

1. An unauthenticated user attempts to connect to a server behind the firewall.

2. The Netscreen firewall intercepts the packet, looks at the payload, and because the session is unauthenticated, places the packet in a buffer while sending back a Username/Password prompt to the user.

3. The unauthenticated user enters the appropriate login credentials.

4. Based on whether the authentication server is local or external, the firewall either compares the authentication credentials with those in the local database or sends the credentials to an external authentication server for comparison.

5. If the comparison is successful, the Netscreen firewall announces the completion of authentication, sets an internal policy allowing future access through the firewall, and forwards the buffered packet to the host being contacted.

The authentication steps for **WebAuth** are as follows:

1. An unauthenticated user accesses the WebAuth address and enters the appropriate authentication credentials.

2. Based on whether the authentication server is local or external, the firewall either compares the authentication credentials with those in the local database or sends the credentials to an external authentication server for comparison.

3. If the comparison is successful, the Netscreen firewall sets an internal policy allowing future access through the firewall.

4. The currently authenticated user is now able to access computers behind the firewall.

IKE Users

IKE is a key management protocol designed for secure exchange of encryption keys used by other encryption and authentication schemes. IKE is the key exchange used by the IPSEC protocol and therefore IKE is directly related to VPN technologies used by the Netscreen firewall.

IPSEC has two negotiation phases, the first of which is the IKE key negotiation phase. Authentication happens during the first phase of IKE negotiation. IKE users may be authenticated either by pre-shared key or digital certificate. If using pre-shared keys, the Netscreen firewall stores the keys within its internal database; however, if using digital certificates, the Netscreen must get the IKE ID portion of the authentication credentials from the DN (distinguished name) record within the certificate. In either case, the IKE records may only be stored within the internal Local database.

Damage & Defense...

Avoid Aggressive IKE

The use of IKE in aggressive mode should be discouraged. When aggressive mode is used the username—sometimes called the IKE ID—is transmitted on the network in clear text. Therefore, you should not use aggressive mode because it may allow an attacker to gain access to sensitive information about your Netscreen VPN.

To do this on Netscreen firewalls, you select **Main Mode** versus **Aggressive Mode** within the **Advanced** button in **VPNs|Gateway objects**.

L2TP Users

L2TP is a data link layer VPN tunneling protocol published and proposed as a standard in 1999. L2TP originated as an extension to the PPP protocol—L2TP was meant to act as a tunnel through which PPP and other protocols could travel. Unlike IPSEC, because L2TP functions at such a low layer in the OSI model it is ideal for tunneling other protocols through as well as IP (Internet Protocol).

L2TP is not a secure VPN technology because it only supports tunneling and does not provide for privacy via encryption. L2TP should be combined with an IPSEC VPN for complete security. The biggest reason that L2TP is still in active use is because it supports addressing of IP, DNS (Domain Name Service), and WINS (Windows Internet Naming Service) as well as tunneling of many other protocols such as Appletalk, IPX, SNA, and more.

Unlike IKE, Netscreen firewalls are capable of performing L2TP authentication from not just the local database but also SecurID, RADIUS, LDAP, or a combination thereof. Although L2TP authentication may be done by one or a combination of authentication sources, it's important to recognize that it cannot perform addressing of IP, DNS, and WINS without using RADIUS and the Netscreen dictionary file for RADIUS, nor can it perform encryption of the data.

XAuth Users

XAuth is a VPN tunneling protocol that allows for a greater level of assurance that the data being transmitted is coming from the correct user. Unlike IKE, XAuth authenticates via a username and password instead of a pre-shared key. Also unlike IKE, XAuth is capable of tunneling more than the IP protocol and is also capable of performing addressing functions for IP, DNS, and WINS by assigning a virtual adapter and tunneling all traffic via the network adapter.

NOTE

XAuth and L2TP compete for addressing and authentication. You should not attempt to use them together.

Admin Users

Admin users are users capable of viewing or modifying the Netscreen device either via the WebUI or via the CLI. Admin users may be stored on the internal local database or on external authentication servers. Admin users stored on external SecurID or LDAP devices must have privileges assigned on the Netscreen firewall. The only exception to his is admin users stored in RADIUS. If the Netscreen dictionary file is loaded on the RADIUS server, then the admin user can use the RADIUS server for both authentication and authorization.

Vsys admin users have the same capabilities as the Admin users mentioned above.

User Databases

In the next section, we discuss the five different types of user authentication and authorization databases, and the appropriate use of each. This section has been divided into two subsections, local database and external Auth servers for ease of understanding.

Local Database

The local database is the default database used by the Netscreen firewall appliance. The local database is the only database that supports all user and authentication types except for group expressions.

Types of Users

Users supported by the Local database include:

- Admin
- Auth
- IKE
- L2TP
- XAuth

Features

Features supported by the Local database include:

- Admin privileges
- User groups
- WebAuth

> **NOTE**
>
> The local database is the only supported storage of authentication credentials without the installation of external authentication servers. Therefore, if you have few users or don't want to install and maintain an external server, an excellent choice is to keep using the local database.

External Auth Servers

Netscreen devices support a variety of external authentication servers. These authentication servers—including RADIUS, SecurID, and LDAP—allow a properly configured Netscreen firewall to perform authentication and authorization against an externally maintained and configured database of users.

When set to use an external authentication server, upon receipt of an event requiring authentication, the Netscreen device first requests the username/password combination, then forwards the user-supplied credentials to the authentication server. The authentication server verifies the credentials and sends the appropriate response to the Netscreen firewall. The Netscreen firewall then sends a message of success or failure back to the client and finishes establishing the connection with the server.

Object Properties

When created, each authentication server becomes an object on the Netscreen firewall. In order to reference the object when used in rules and VPN endpoints, each object has a set of properties that define pieces of info used when communicating with the external authentication server.

A list of common object properties is as follows:

- **Name** The name of the object.

- **IP/Domain Name** IP or domain name address of the external authentication server.

- **Backup1** IP or domain name address of the backup external authentication server.

- **Backup2** IP or domain name address of the second backup external authentication server.

- **Timeout** An integer value for the number of seconds until timeout during authentication.

- **Account Type** Will be one of either Auth, L2TP, Admin, or Xauth.

    In addition to the above object properties, you may also see these additional object properties:

- **Radius Port** The port number used by the RADIUS server.

- **Retry Timeout** Number of seconds until timeout for the RADIUS server.

- **Shared Secret** Visibility protected shared secret used for securing the connection between the Netscreen firewall and the RADIUS server.

- **Client Retries** Number of client retries to attempt.

- **Client Timeout** Time in seconds before timeout and retry.

- **Authentication Port** The port that the external SecurID server listens for connections on.

- **Encryption Type** The type of encryption used for communication between the Netscreen firewall and the SecurID server.

- **LDAP Port** The port the LDAP server listens on for connections.

- **Common Name Identifier** The record name for common names within the LDAP directory.

- **Distinguished Name** The distinguished name—also known as root DN of the server —comes immediately after the cn.

Auth Server Types

In the following sections you will find descriptions of the three different external authentication servers supported by Netscreen. In addition, you will find both WebUI and CLI directions for configuring a Netscreen firewall to use an external authentication server. Finally, directions to make an external authentication device the default device for authentication are provided.

RADIUS

RADIUS is a protocol developed by Livingston—now Lucent Technologies—that provides for user authentication, authorization, and accountability from a centralized server. Originally developed based on an RFI from Merit, RADIUS quickly grew into the de-facto standard for user authentication of dial-in systems. Being an easily extensible standard, RADIUS lent itself to modification and over time emerged as a robust authentication, authorization, and accountability solution.

Notes rom the Underground...

Enable SSL Encryption or Shared-secrets for Auth Servers

Virtually all modern authentication servers support the ability to transport text in both clear and encrypted formats. Although setup and testing is often done in clear text, many people forget to enable the encryption features. Fortunately, in order to use RADIUS you supply both the client and

Continued

server with a shared secret. Although not necessarily as strong as authentication via certificates like those used in SSL (Security Sockets Layer), shared secrets provide a good level of security when properly protected. In addition, the use of shared secrets allows the use of symmetric cryptography, which in turn means a lower overhead on the processor.

Types of Users

Netscreen's RADIUS implementation supports the following types of users:

- Auth
- XAuth
- L2TR
- Admin

Features

Netscreen's RADIUS implementation supports the following features:

- Auth
- L2TP – Auth & Remote
- Admin – Auth & Privileges
- XAuth – Auth & Remote
- User Groups
- Group Expressions

How to Configure

To configure RADIUS under Netscreen's WebUI:

1. From the WebUI, select **Configuration | Auth | AuthServers**, then click the **New** button.

2. Enter the following fields:

   Name: **radiusserver1**

   IP/Domain Name: **radius1.example.com**

   Backup1:   **radius2.example.com**

   Backup2:   **radius3.example.com**

Timeout:	**10**
Account Type:	**Any combination of Auth, L2TP, Admin, XAuth**
Radius Port:	**1645**
Retry Timeout:	**3**
Shared Secret:	**secret**

3. Click on the **OK** button.

To configure RADIUS under Netscreen's CLI:

```
set auth-server radiusserver1 account-type auth xauth
set auth-server radiusserver1 server-name radius1.example.com
set auth-server radiusserver1 backup1 radius2.example.com
set auth-server radiusserver1 backup2 radius3.example.com
set auth-server radiusserver1 radius secret MySecret
set auth-server radiusserver1 timeout 10
set auth-server radiusserver1 radius port 1645
set auth-server radiusserver1 radius timeout 3
```

SecurID

RSA SecurID is a two-factor dynamic token authentication and authorization system. SecurID utilizes a hardware token—slightly larger than a credit card—to generate a password token that changes every 60 seconds. The second factor in the SecurID authentication is a PIN number. The PIN number and generated token are entered together to complete the authentication process. Once entered, the values are looked up in the SecurID server and compared to the stored values. If successful, the SecurID server transmits a success message back to the Netscreen firewall. In real world use, SecureID is more secure than RADIUS due to its inability to be compromised without access to both the PIN and hardware token.

Types of Users

Netscreen's SecurID implementation supports the following types of users:

- Auth
- L2TP

- XAuth
- Admin

Features

Netscreen's SecurID implementation supports the following features:

- Auth
- L2TP – Auth
- XAuth – Auth
- Admin – Auth

How to Configure

To configure a SecurID server under Netscreen's WebUI:

1. From the WebUI, select **Configuration** | **Auth** | **AuthServers** and then select **New**.

2. Enter the following fields:

   Name: **aceserver1**

   IP/Domain Name: **ace1.example.com**

   Backup1:   **ace2.example.com**

   Backup2:

   Timeout: **10**

   Account Type: **Any combination of Auth, L2TP, Admin, XAuth**

   Client Retries: **3**

   Client Timeout: **5**

   Authentication Port: **5500**

   Encryption Type: **DES or SDI**

   Use Duress: **No**

3. Click the **OK** button.

To configure a SecurID server under Netscreen's CLI:

```
set auth-server aceserver1 type securid
set auth-server aceserver1 server-name ace1.example.com
set auth-server aceserver1 backup1 ace2.example.com
set auth-server aceserver1 timeout 10
set auth-server aceserver1 account-type admin
set auth-server aceserver1 securid retries 3
set auth-server aceserver1 securid timeout 5
set auth-server aceserver1 securid encr 1
set auth-server aceserver1 securid duress 0
set auth-server aceserver1 securid auth-port 5500
save
```

NOTE

Netscreen supports more than one backup authentication server; however, for simplicity we have only configured one in this instance. Depending on your needs—such as disaster recovery of a critical function—you may wish to configure **backup2** in addition to **backup1**.

LDAP

LDAP is a protocol developed in 1996 by the University of Michigan for accessing information directories. Based on x.500, LDAP was created because the need existed to have a Directory Access Protocol capable of utilizing TCP (Transmission Control Protocol)/IP as the transport mechanism. A directory is structured much like a tree, branching for every different level of the DIT (Directory Information Tree). Figure 6.1 shows an example of the Directory Information Tree:

Figure 6.1 Directory Information Tree

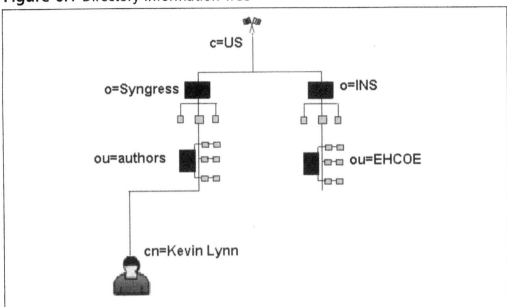

The DIT in Figure 6.1 allows us to follow the DN (distinguished name) with the following branches:

- DN: c=US : c (country) is the first suffix of this DIT.
- DN: o=Sygress, c=US : o (organization) is the name of the organization
- DN: ou=Authors, o=Syngress, c=US : ou (organizational unit) is the name of the group or organization with the organization
- DN: cn=Kevin Lynn, ou=Authors, o=Syngress, c=US : cn (common name) is the name of a person under the DIT.

Notice that each branch of the tree builds on those above it. By specifying a DN with a base of ou=Authors,o=Syngress,c=US, the LDAP directory has a much smaller space to look for the user with the common name of Kevin Lynn2.

Types of Users

Netscreen's LDAP implementation supports the following types of users:

- Auth
- L2TP

- XAuth
- Admin

Features

Netscreen's LDAP implementation supports the following features:

- Auth
- L2TP – Auth
- XAuth – Auth
- Admin – Auth

How to Configure

To configure LDAP under Netscreen's WebUI:

1.   From the WebUI, select **Configuration | Auth | AuthServers** and then select **New**.

2.   Enter the following fields:

Name:	**ldapserver1**
IP/Domain Name:	**ldap1.example.com**
Backup1:	**ldap2.example.com**
Backup2:	**ldap3.example.com**
Timeout:	**10**
Account Type:	**Any combination of Auth, L2TP, Admin, XAuth**
LDAP Port:	**389**
Common Name Identifier:	**cn**
Distinguished Name:	**ou=someorgunit,dc=example,dc=com**

3.   Click the **OK** button.

To configure LDAP under Netscreen's CLI:

```
set auth-server ldapserver1 type ldap
set auth-server ldapserver1 account-type auth
```

```
set auth-server ldapserver1 server-name ldap1.example.com
set auth-server ldapserver1 backup1 ldap2.example.com
set auth-server ldapserver1 backup2 ldap3.example.com
set auth-server ldapserver1 timeout 10
set auth-server ldapserver1 ldap port 389
set auth-server ldapserver1 ldap cn cn
set auth-server ldapserver1 ldap dn c=us;o=Syngress;ou=Authors
save
```

Default Auth Servers

The default authentication server for any Netscreen firewall is the internal Local database. The following is a list of features and types of users the Local database is capable of utilizing:

- Admin
- Auth
- IKE
- L2TP
- XAuth
- Admin privileges
- WebAuth
- User groups
- Group expressions

How to Change

To change the default auth server under Netscreen's WebUI:

Local:

1. Select **VPNs | AutoKey Advanced | XAuth Settings**.

2. Select **Default Authentication Server: Local**, then click **Apply**.

RADIUS:

1. Select **VPNs | L2TP | Default Settings**.

2. Select **Default authentication server: radiusserver1**, then click **Apply**.

   SecurID:

1. Select **Configuration | Admin | Administrator**.
2. Select **Admin Auth Server: aceserver1**, then click **Apply**.

   LDAP:

1. Select **Configuration | Auth | Firewall**.
2. Select **Default Auth Server: ldapserver1**, then click **Apply**.

To change the default auth server under Netscreen's CLI:

```
set xauth default auth server Local
set l2tp default auth server radiusserver1
set admin auth server aceserver1
set auth default auth server ldapserver1
```

When to Use

Deciding on which to authentication server to use depends on your specific needs. If you have few users, don't see yourself making a lot of modifications to the internal Local file, and have only the one Netscreen firewall, then the Local database is probably a good choice. If you have a lot of users, make sure that you are using a more scaleable solution such as RADIUS or LDAP. If security is what you really need then you can't go wrong with the RSA SecurID server.

You should also consider whether you need to use any of the authorization and addressing features of the firewall or just need the authentication features. All of the external authentication servers support the authentication of user credentials; however, only RADIUS supports the loading of a Netscreen dictionary file and the use of RADIUS as a source for external authorization and addressing.

Authentication Types

In the coming sections, we step through the configuration of users in both WebUI and CLI modes. Then, we assign an authentication type to the user. Finally, we set policies to force users to authenticate themselves when accessing the Netscreen device or protected network addresses.

Auth Users and User Groups

In the following example, we first define an Auth user, and then set policies that allow an authenticated user to access hosts inside the firewall.

To set Auth users under Netscreen's WebUI:

1. Select **Objects | Users | Local** then select **New**.

2. Enable the **Authentication User** option.

3. Enter the user password in the **User Password** and **Confirm Password** text fields, then select **OK**.

4. Select **Policies** and set **From: Trust** and **To: Untrust** then select **New**.

5. Enter the following fields:

   Name: **testpolicy**

   Source Address: **10.4.4.1/32**

   Destination Address: **10.50.0.0/16**

6. Select **Advanced** and enable the **Authentication** option.

7. Enable the **Auth Server** and **Use Default** options.

8. Select the **User** option and then **Local Auth User – klynn**.

To set Auth users under Netscreen's CLI:

```
set user klynn password "passw0rd"
set user "klynn" ike-id fqdn "klynn" share-limit 1
set user "klynn" type  auth
set policy id 1 from "Trust" to "Untrust"  "Any" "Any" "ANY" permit
set policy id 2 name "testpolicy" from "Trust" to "Untrust" "10.4.4.1/32"
"10.50.0.0/16" ANY permit auth user klynn
```

Next, create a new address assigned to the Local group, then assign it to a policy. To create a new address and assign it to a policy under WebUI:

1. Select **Objects | Addresses | List** and then click the **New** button.

2. Enter the following text fields:

   Address Name: **1_address**

   IP/Netmask: **10.4.4.1/24**

To set a user group and then assign it to a policy under Netscreen's CLI:

```
set user-group group1 location local
set user-group group1 user klynn
set address trust  1_address "10.4.4.1/24"
set policy top from trust to untrust 1_address Any Any permit auth user-
group group1
```

IKE Users and User Groups

In the next configuration, we create an IKE user, then set policies that allow authenticated users to access hosts inside the firewall.

To create an IKE user under Netscreen's WebUI:

1. Select **Objects | Users | Local** then select **New**.
2. Fill out the text field **User Name: klynn**, enable the **IKE User** option, and click the **Simple Identity** button.
3. Fill out the following fields:

    IKE ID Type: **Auto**

    IKE Identity: **klynn**
4. Enable the **Authentication User** option.
5. Enter the user password under the **User Password**: and **Confirm Password** text fields the select **OK**.
6. Select **Policies** and set **From: Trust** and To**: Untrust** then select **New**.
7. Enter the following fields:

    Name: **testpolicy**

    Source Address: **10.4.4.1/32**

    Destination Address: **10.50.0.0/16**
8. Select **Advanced** and then enable the **Authentication** option.
9. Enable the **Auth Server** and **Use Default** options.
10. Enable the **User** option and then **Local Auth User – klynn**.

NOTE

Groups that have IKE users added automatically become IKE groups.

To create an IKE user under Netscreen's CLI:

```
set user klynn password "passw0rd"
set user "klynn" ike-id fqdn "klynn" share-limit 1
set user "klynn" ike-id ip 10.4.4.201
set user "klynn" type  ike
```

Create a new address assigned to the Local group, and then assign it to a policy. The group automatically becomes an IKE group after an IKE user is added to it.

To create a new address under the local group and assign it to a policy under Netscreen's WebUI:

1. Select **Objects | Users | Local Groups** and then select **New**.

    Group Name: **1_address**

2. Select the user you want to assign and then select the << button to assign the user to the **Group Members** column.

CLI:

```
set user-group group1 location local
set user-group group1 user klynn
set address trust  1_address "10.4.4.1/24"
set policy top from trust to untrust 1_address Any Any permit auth user-
group group1
```

XAuth Users and User Groups

When we're creating XAuth users, first we create an IKE user, and then we create a VPN by creating a new AutoKey Gateway and finally by creating a New AutoKey IKE.

To create an IKE user under Netscreen's WebUI:

1. Select **Objects | Users | Local** then select **New**.

2. Fill out the text field **User Name: klynn**, enable the **IKE User** option, and click the **Simple Identity** button.

3. Fill out the following fields:

    IKE ID Type: **Auto**

    IKE Identity: **klynn**

4. Enable the **Authentication User** option.

5. Enter the user password under the **User Password**: and **Confirm Password** text fields the select **OK**.

6. Enable the **XAuth User** option and enter the following fields:

   IP Pool: **10.4.4**

   Primary DNS IP: **10.4.4.1**

   Secondary DNS IP: **10.4.4.1**

   Primary WINS IP: **10.4.4.1**

   Secondary WINS IP: **10.4.4.1**

Create an AutoKey Gateway with Netscreen's WebUI:

1. Select **VPNs | AutoKey Advanced | Gateway** and then select **New**.

   Gateway Name: **gateway1**

   Security Level: **Custom**

   |Remote Gateway Type: **Static IP Address**

   IP Address/Hostname: **192.168.0.1**

   Preshared Key: **secret**

   Outgoing Interface: **untrust**

Create an AutoKey Gateway with Netscreen's CLI:

```
set user klynn password "passw0rd"
set user "klynn" ike-id fqdn "klynn" share-limit 1
set user "klynn" ike-id ip 10.4.4.201
set user "klynn" type  ike xauth
set user "klynn" remote ippool "10.4.4"
set user "klynn" remote dns1 "10.4.4.1"
set user "klynn" remote dns2 "10.4.4.1"
set user "klynn" remote wins1 "10.4.4.1"
set user "klynn" remote wins2 "10.4.4.1"
set ike gateway "gateway1" address 192.168.0.4 Main outgoing-interface
"untrust" preshare secret sec-level standard
set ike gateway "gateway1" xauth server Local user-group xauthgroup1
```

```
set vpn "ike1" gateway "gateway1" no-replay tunnel idletime 0 proposal
"nopfs-esp-aes128-md5"
```

Create a new address assigned to the Local group, and then assign it to a policy. The group automatically becomes an IKE group after an IKE user is added to it.

To create a new address under Netscreen's WebUI:

1. Select **Objects | Addresses | List** and then select the **New** button.

   Address Name: **1_address**

   IP/Netmask: **10.4.4.1/24**

To create a new address under Netscreen's CLI:

```
set user-group group1 location local
set user-group group1 user klynn
save
```

L2TP Users and User Groups

When we're creating L2TP users, first we create an IKE user, and then we create a VPN by creating a new AutoKey Gateway and finally by creating a New AutoKey IKE.

To create an IKE user under Netscreen's WebUI:

1. Select **Objects | Users | Local** then select **New**.
2. Fill out the text field **User Name: klynn**, enable the **IKE User** option, and click the **Simple Identity** button.
3. Fill out the following fields:

   IKE ID Type: **Auto**

   IKE Identity: **klynn**

4. Enable the **Authentication User** option.
5. Enter the user password under the **User Password**: and **Confirm Password** text fields the select **OK**.
6. Select the L2TP User checkbox and enter in the following fields:

   IP Pool: **10.4.4**

   Primary DNS IP: **10.4.4.1**

Secondary DNS IP: **10.4.4.1**

Primary WINS IP: **10.4.4.1**

Secondary WINS IP: **10.4.4.1**

Create an AutoKey Gateway with Netscreen's WebUI:

1. Select **VPNs | AutoKey Advanced | Gateway** and then select **New**.

    Gateway Name: **gateway1**

    Security Level: **Custom**

    |Remote Gateway Type: **Static IP Address**

    IP Address/Hostname: **192.168.0.1**

    Preshared Key: **secret**

    Outgoing Interface: **untrust**

Create an AutoKey Gateway with Netscreen's CLI:

```
set user klynn password "passw0rd"
set user "klynn" ike-id fqdn "klynn" share-limit 1
set user "klynn" ike-id ip 10.4.4.201
set user "klynn" type  ike l2tp
set user "klynn" remote ippool "10.4.4"
set user "klynn" remote dns1 "10.4.4.1"
set user "klynn" remote dns2 "10.4.4.1"
set user "klynn" remote wins1 "10.4.4.1"
set user "klynn" remote wins2 "10.4.4.1"
set ike gateway "gateway1" address 192.168.0.4 Main outgoing-interface
"untrust" preshare secret sec-level standard
set ike gateway "gateway1" xauth server Local user-group xauthgroup1
set vpn "ike1" gateway "gateway1" no-replay tunnel idletime 0 proposal
"nopfs-esp-aes128-md5"
```

Create a new address assigned to the Local group, and then assign it to a policy. The group automatically becomes an IKE group after an IKE user is added to it.

To create a new address under Netscreen's WebUI:

1. Select **Objects | Addresses | List** and then select the **New** button.

Address Name: **1_address**

IP/Netmask: **10.4.4.1/24**

To create a new address under Netscreen's CLI:

```
set user-group group1 location local
set user-group group1 user klynn
save
```

Admin Users and User Groups

Administrative users at a minimum have the ability to view everything; however, if created with read-write access, the administrator has full administrative privileges. Administrator privileges may be read from a RADIUS database if an external authentication server has been set already.

Add an external authentication server to the Netscreen's configuration and configure the firewall to read admin authentication and authorization credentials from the RADIUS server.

To create an admin user under Netscreen's WebUI:

1. First, Configure a new RADIUS server to hold the Admin credentials:

2. Select **Configuration | Auth | Auth Servers** and then select the **New** button.

3. Enter in the following text fields:

    Name: **radiusserver1**

    IP/Domain Name: **radius1.example.com**

    Backup1:   **radius2.example.com**

    Backup2:   **radius3.example.com**

    Timeout: **10**

    Account Type: **Any combination of Auth, L2TP, Admin, XAuth**

    Radius Port: **1645**

    Retry Timeout: **3**

    Shared Secret: **secret**

4. Click the **OK** button.

Next, Configure the Administrators to get the Admin credentials from RADIUS server:

1. Select Configuration | Admin | Administrators
2. Select **Admin Privileges: Get privilege from RADIUS server**.
3. Select **Admin Auth Server: radiusserver1**.

Finally, Create a new Administrator:

1. Select **Configuration | Admin | Administrators** and click the **New** button.
2. Enter in the following text fields:

Administrator Name:	**admin2**
New Password:	**secret**
Confirm New Password:	**secret**
Privileges:	**Read-Write**

SSH Password Authentication

To create an admin user under Netscreen's CLI:

```
set admin user "admin2" password "nPbcE7r4IayFcqDPis8KX2Mt2BEX4n" privilege
"all"
```

Multi-type Users

Users may be assigned one or more user types during or after creation. Any user may be assigned any user type; however, as a practical rule it's usually better to assign IKE to groups instead of users. The local database has a finite amount of users it is capable of storing. When you assign IKE to groups you use less of the user records the local database is capable of storing. This enables the Netscreen administrators to scale the firewalls

User Groups and Group expressions

Group expressions are Boolean—AND, OR, NOT—expressions that allow a Netscreen administrator to select more than one user, group, or previous group expression. The use of group expressions allows an administrator to select or not select users or groups by following these rules:

The following are some examples of how to create a group expression under Netscreen's WebUI:

1. Select **Objects | Group Expressions** and then click the **New** button.

2. Enter in the following text fields:

Group Expression: **Males_and_Females**

Males AND Females: **True if the current user/group exists in both Males and Females.**

Males OR Females: **True if the current user/group is either Males or Females.**

NOT Females: **True if the current user/group is not Females.**

CLI:

```
set group-expression males_and_females males and females
set group-expression males_or_females males or females
set group-expression only_males not females
```

Summary

In this chapter, we have learned about the types of users and when each user type should be used. We have gone over the types of user database, the uses of the different user database types, the differences between them, and the features or limitations inherent with each. We have learned how to change the default authentication server used, and when you should choose to change the default authentication server. Subsequently, we learned how to set up Auth, IKE, Xauth, L2TP, and Admin users. Finally, we learned that multi-type users are setup automatically when assigning the different users types and that group expressions can be used to place several users or groups inside a broader group for accessing them in the Netscreen's configuration.

Solutions Fast Track

Types of Users

☑ There are 5 different types of users, IKE, Auth, Xauth, L2TP, and Admin. A description of each user type and their use is provided.

User Databases

☑ One Local database, and three external authentication databases, SecurID, LDAP, and RADIUS, are supported.

☑ A description of each type of database and their use is provided.

Configuration and Authentication

☑ A configuration each user and authentication piece is provided for both WebUI and CLI configuration methods.

User Groups and Group Expressions

☑ Group expressions and their use are discussed and examples of their use within both WebUI and CLI are given.

Frequently Asked Questions

The following Frequently Asked Questions, answered by the authors of this book, are designed to both measure your understanding of the concepts presented in this chapter and to assist you with real-life implementation of these concepts. To have your questions about this chapter answered by the author, browse to **www.syngress.com/solutions** and click on the **"Ask the Author"** form. You will also gain access to thousands of other FAQs at ITFAQnet.com.

Q: As a beginner at a small company, which authentication scheme and database type should I use?

A: Each authentication scheme has advantages and disadvantages. For a small company, we recommend the use of the Auth user authentication scheme and the local database. This would allow you to get up and running with a minimal of effort. If you need VPN access, then we suggest the use of IKE authentication for IPSec VPNs.

Q: Can I use an external authentication server and do IKE authentication?

A: No, in order to use IKE authentication you must use IKE user or user-groups. No other authentication server type supports IKE.

Q: Doesn't this make maintenance a headache?

A: IKE authentication being supported only in Auth user authentication does add more overhead in the maintenance process. Fortunately, you can alleviate this problem by defining a group IKE ID and using either pre-shared keys or certificates for user credentials.

Q: Is there an easier way to store authorization information for users than configuring it per user via Auth users?

A: Yes, if you're not using IKE, you may configure authorization information in RADIUS servers by first loading a dictionary containing vendor specific attributes (VSAs). Once loaded, the dictionary configures the Netscreen device to query the RADIUS server for new attributes. You may find the dictionary at the following URL: http://www.juniper.net/customers/csc/research/netscreen_kb/downloads/dictionary/.

Q: If I'm using pre-shared keys for VPN authentication with user-groups, is there a way to force the clients to ask for a username and password as well?

A: Yes, what you want to do in this instance is configure a policy forcing username and password authentication via WebAuth before any access to protected resources is given. Once authenticated correctly, the user would be capable of accessing any of the protected resources—depending on the policies in place of course.

Chapter 7

Routing

Solutions in this Chapter:

- Virtual Routers
- Routing Information Protocol
- Open Shortest Path First
- Border Gateway Protocol

- ☑ Summary
- ☑ Solutions Fast Track
- ☑ Frequently Asked Questions

Introduction

Routing is a fundamental part of any IP (Internet Protocol)-based infrastructure. Every device on an IP-based network uses routes to determine the next hop or location it needs to access the desired host. In many cases, firewalls are just glorified routers. They provide firewall features, but are still a core routing component in many organizations' networks. Routers themselves are usually capable of providing a stateful firewall.

Juniper's NetScreen firewalls are capable of providing routing services above and beyond the average router. NetScreen firewalls can provide the capability to split a normal single routing table into multiple virtual routers. A virtual router is a logical router that can perform all of the tasks a normal routing engine can do. It can contain all of the static routes including the default route. Virtual routers are also capable of supporting dynamic routing protocols.

Most firewall products are very limited in supporting dynamic routing. It is often argued that firewalls should not be integrated into a dynamic routing environment. However, this is often difficult, as firewalls are at the core of most networks. Juniper helps mitigate this risk with virtual routers by allowing you to split your routing domain into multiple virtual routers.

One virtual router can contain all of your outward routes toward the Internet or other untrusted area. A second virtual router can contain all of your internal routes. These routes are contained separate from each other and by default are unknown between each virtual router.

There are three routing protocols that can be used with a NetScreen firewall. The first protocol, Routing Information Protocol (RIP), is an older protocol, but it is the most commonly supported protocol. Open Shortest Path First (OSPF) is an extremely robust protocol. OSPF is an open standard protocol and is used by many organizations for their internal networks. Last, but certainly not least, is Border Gateway Protocol (BGP). BGP is used to run the routing architecture of the Internet. It is often the most misunderstood protocol due to its complexity.

Virtual Routers

Virtual routers provide the capability to split their routing tables into multiple routing tables. A traditional IP routing device contains a single routing table. This routing table contains all routes known to the device. This routing table is known as a *routing domain*. By default, the NetScreen firewall operates as a traditional routing device by using a single virtual router.

A NetScreen firewall, by default, contains two virtual routers. These routers cannot be removed from the firewall. These routers are named *trust-vr* and *untrust-vr*. The trust-vr is the default virtual router. Depending on the device you are using, you may create additional virtual routers. In Chapter 2 we discussed the capabilities of each firewall. Please reference that chapter to see the capabilities of each firewall device.

Using Virtual Routers

Using a virtual router may seem like a complex process at first. However, it is just like using a traditional routing device. Think about having multiple virtual routers in your firewall as having multiple real routers. The virtual routers will function the same way. If you remember from Chapter 3 that zones are bound to virtual routers. This determines which routers are used on your firewall. If your firewall supports it, you can create additional virtual routers.

Creating Virtual Routers

To create a new virtual router, you must be able to provide it with a name. You can choose to name it anything you want; there are no requirements for a prefix or suffix when naming the virtual router. A virtual router's name can contain up to 32 characters, and you can create new virtual routers using both the CLI (command line interface) and the WebUI. Figure 7.1 shows the WebUI virtual router creation screen.

Figure 7.1 Virtual Router Creation (WebUI)

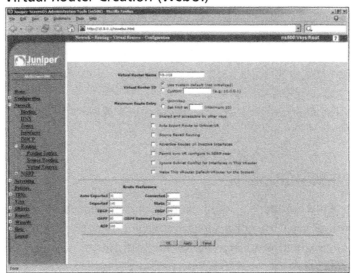

Use the following steps to create a virtual router via the WebUI:

1. Access **Network** | **Routing** | **Virtual Routers**.
2. On the top right-hand side of the page, click the button labeled **New**.
3. A default name (**VR-<number>**)will be generated for you. You can keep this name, or use a different name simply by entering it in the **Virtual Router Name** field.
4. Click **OK**.

Use the following to create a virtual router via the CLI:

```
ns500-> get vrouter
* indicates default vrouter for the current vsys
A - AutoExport, R - RIP, O - OSPF, B - BGP


  ID Name           Vsys           Owner      Routes     Flags
   1 untrust-vr     Root           shared      0/max
*  2 trust-vr       Root           shared      1/max


total 2 vrouters shown and 0 of them defined by user
ns500-> set vrouter name Syngress-WAN
ns500-> get vrouter
* indicates default vrouter for the current vsys
A - AutoExport, R - RIP, O - OSPF, B - BGP


  ID Name           Vsys           Owner      Routes     Flags
   1 untrust-vr     Root           shared      0/max
*  2 trust-vr       Root           shared      1/max
1025 Syngress-WAN   Root           user        0/max


total 3 vrouters shown and 1 of them defined by user
ns500->
```

Route Selection

If your routing table contains a single route to a destination, it will have little difficulty on deciding what route to select. However, with the use of dynamic routing protocols your firewall may be in the position of having to decide the appropriate route. Your NetScreen firewall uses a three-step method to determine which route to select:

- **Most Specific** First, the firewall identifies the most specific route for the host. The most specific route is the route with the smallest possible subnet. The firewall would prefer the route with the most bits in its netmask.

- **Route Preference** The route preference is a table internal to the firewall. The firewall will define a preference based upon the source of the route. The firewall keeps an internal table that defines the preference set for each route. The preference can be modified for all of the route types if so desired. Table 7.1 lists the default route preferences.

- **Route Metric** The metric is the last component checked if there are still two matching routes. The metric is set to zero for all directly connected routes. Static routes receive a metric of one. When adding a route to a NetScreen firewall, you can set the metric manually. In cases where both the route preference and route metric match completely

Table 7.1 Route Preferences

Protocol	Default Preference
Connected	0
Static	20
Auto-Exported	30
EBGP	40
OSPF	60
RIP	100
Imported	140
OSPF External Type 2	200
IBGP	250

Set Route Preference

The route preference can be modified for each of the route types. This is configured for each virtual router separately. This task can be accomplished from both the CLI and the WebUI. Figure 7.2 shows an example of setting the route preference from the WebUI. If you change the route preference on an already learned route, you must wait until the route is relearned until the new preference takes effect.

Figure 7.2 Route Preference Configuration (WebUI)

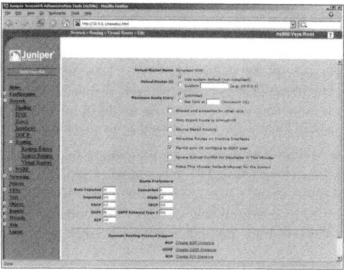

Use the following steps to configure route preference via the WebUI:

1. Access **Network | Routing | Virtual Routers**.

2. Click the **Edit** link of the virtual router you wish to configure.

3. Use the Route Type field to enter the number of the desired route preference.

4. Click **OK**.

Use the following to configure route preference via the CLI:

```
ns500-> get vrouter Syngress-WAN preference
vrouter Syngress-WAN route preference table
--------------------------------------------
Connected Routes:         0
Static Routes:           20
Auto-exported Routes:    30
Imported Routes:        140
RIP Routes:             100
```

```
EBGP Routes:            40
IBGP Routes:            250
OSPF Routes:            60
OSPF External Type-2 Routes:    200
ns500->
ns500-> set vrouter Syngress-WAN preference ebgp 255
ns500-> get vrouter Syngress-WAN preference
vrouter Syngress-WAN route preference table
---------------------------------------------
Connected Routes:       0
Static Routes:          20
Auto-exported Routes:   30
Imported Routes:        140
RIP Routes:             100
EBGP Routes:            255
IBGP Routes:            250
OSPF Routes:            60
OSPF External Type-2 Routes:    200
ns500->
```

Set Route Metric

The route metric is configured when a static route is added into your firewall. This can be done from both the CLI and the WebUI. Figure 7.3 shows an example of the WebUI configuration of a route metric.

Figure 7.3 Route Metric Configuration (WebUI)

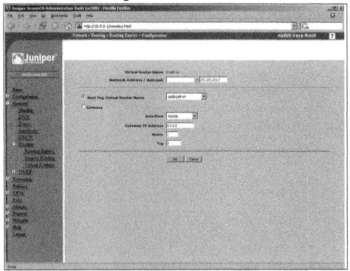

Use the following steps to configure a route metric via the WebUI:

1. Access **Network | Routing | Routing Entries**.

2. Use the available drop-down list in the upper right-hand corner to select the virtual router to which you will add a route. 3.   Click **New**.

4. Configure the properties for the new route.

5. In the text box labeled **Metric**, enter the metric you want to apply to the route.

6. Click **OK**.

Use the following to configure a route metric via the CLI:

```
ns500-> get route
untrust-vr (0 entries)
------------------------------------------------------------------------
C - Connected, S - Static, A - Auto-Exported, I - Imported, R - RIP
iB - IBGP, eB - EBGP, O - OSPF, E1 - OSPF external type 1
E2 - OSPF external type 2
trust-vr (2 entries)
------------------------------------------------------------------------
    ID          IP-Prefix      Interface          Gateway      P Pref      Mtr
Vsys
```

```
-----------------------------------------------------------------------
*    2         10.9.0.0/24          mgt          0.0.0.0   C    0      0
Root
*    3         1.2.3.0/24           mgt          10.9.0.10 S    20     1
Root
Syngress-WAN (0 entries)
-----------------------------------------------------------------------
1099 (0 entries)
-----------------------------------------------------------------------
ns500-> set route 10.123.0.0/24 interface ethernet3/2 metric 20
ns500-> get route
untrust-vr (0 entries)
-----------------------------------------------------------------------
C - Connected, S - Static, A - Auto-Exported, I - Imported, R - RIP
iB - IBGP, eB - EBGP, O - OSPF, E1 - OSPF external type 1
E2 - OSPF external type 2
trust-vr (3 entries)
-----------------------------------------------------------------------
   ID         IP-Prefix      Interface        Gateway   P Pref    Mtr
Vsys
-----------------------------------------------------------------------
    4       10.123.0.0/24       eth3/2        0.0.0.0    S    20     20
Root
*    2       10.9.0.0/24         mgt          0.0.0.0    C    0      0
Root
*    3       1.2.3.0/24          mgt          10.9.0.10  S    20     1
Root
Syngress-WAN (0 entries)
-----------------------------------------------------------------------
1099 (0 entries)
-----------------------------------------------------------------------
ns500->
```

Route Redistribution

Your NetScreen firewall is capable of passing known routes to other devices
using routing protocols. Routes will automatically be distributed if the route was
learned from that same protocol and the route is currently active in the routing

table. You have the option of redistributing learned routes from routing protocol to another routing protocol. To do this you must configure two components.

- **Access List** A route access list specifies a set of matching IP addresses. IP addresses are specified with network prefixes.
- **Route Map** Route maps are a list of conditions listed in a sequential order, much like policies. If a route matches a condition, the action for the route map is then applied to the matching route.

Configuring a Route Access List

Route access lists are configured on specific virtual routers. Each access list contains several configuration components when it is created. Figure 7.4 shows how an access list is configured from the WebUI. An access list can be configured from both the WebUI and the CLI.

- **Access List ID** An access list ID is a unique identifier that is used to reference the access list.
- **Action** The configured action is applied to the routes that match the access list entry. You can choose **Permit** or **Deny** as the action.
- **IP Address/Netmask** The IP address and netmask are used to specify a matching route.
- **Sequence Number** This number is used to determine the sequence in which the access list is checked.

Figure 7.4 Route Access List Configuration (WebUI)

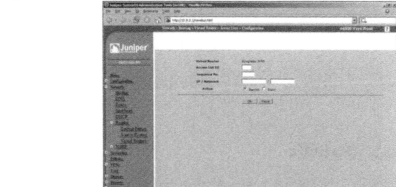

Use the following steps to configure a route access list via the WebUI:

1. Access **Network | Routing | Virtual Routers**.

2. Click the **Access List** link of the router to which you will add the new route access list.

3. Click **New**.

4. Enter the information for the access list in the provided text boxes.

5. Select the action by clicking on the radio button labeled with desired action.

6. Click **OK**.

Use the following to configure a route access list via the CLI:

```
ns500-> set vrouter Syngress-WAN access-list 10 permit ip 10.2.3.0/24 100
ns500-> get vrouter Syngress-WAN access-list
Access list (10)
----------------
Sequence 100: 10.2.3.0/24                     -> Permit
ns500-> get vrouter trust-vr access-list
```

Configuring A Route Map

When configuring a route map, you must choose two components, the match condition and the set attributes.

- **Match Condition** Match conditions are conditions on the route that are matched against. Table 7.2 shows the list of match conditions.

- **Set Attributes** Set attributes are attributes that are set on matched routers. Set attributes are an optional component of route maps. Table 7.3 shows a listing of possible set conditions.

Table 7.2 Match Conditions for Route Maps

Match Condition	Description
BGP AS Path	Matches an AS path access list
BGP Community	Matches a BGP community list
OSPF route type	Matches a type of OSPF route
Interface	Matches a specific interface
IP Address	Matches a specific route access list
Metric	Matches a specific route metric
Next-hop	Matches a specific route access list
Tag	Matches a route tag value or IP address

Table 7.3 Set Conditions for Route Maps

Set Condition	Description
BGP AS Path	Prepends a BGP AS path to the route
BGP Community	Sets the BGP community attribute
BGP Local Preference	Sets the local preference value of the matching route
BGP Weight	Sets the weight of the matching route
OSPF metric	Sets the OSPF metric type of the matching route
RIP offset metric	Sets the offset of the matching route
Metric	Sets the route metric
Next-hop	Sets the next hop of the route
Tag	Sets the tag of the matching route

Tools & Traps…

Distance Vector VS Link State

In this chapter, we use two terms that may be unfamiliar to you. We talk about *link state* routing protocols and *vector* routing protocols. Each routing protocol uses different techniques to accomplish its goals. A distance vector routing protocol requires the router to notify all of its neighbors of the contents of its routing table. The local receiving neighbor identifies the neighbor advertising the lowest cost route for each available route. The router then adds the route into its table and then readvertises it. Because of the constant updates a distance vector protocol is considered "chatty" and inefficient.

A link state routing protocol functions very differently than a distance vector protocol does. Each router participating in a link state routing protocol contains a partial map of the network. When a network link changes state (up to down or down to up), a notification is flooded on the network. All of the routers listening for communications recompute the new routing information. This type of method is typically more reliable and less chatty. It, however, is a more complex protocol and requires more CPU and memory to function.

Routing Information Protocol

The Routing Information Protocol is one of the oldest routing protocols available today. It is highly inefficient, but this of course is made up for with its simple configuration. Almost all routing devices typically support the RIP protocol, even home user Cable/DSL routers. There are two versions of RIP: RIP version one and RIP version two. NetScreen firewalls support RIP version two. Even though the RIP protocol is old, it is mature and functions well in small networks.

RIP Concepts

The RIP protocol sends update messages at regular intervals and when the network changes. This makes RIP a "chatty" routing protocol because it constantly sends information out to the network. RIP uses only one single mechanism to determine the best route. RIP counts a hop or how many hops away a network is. RIP has a limitation of using up to 15 hops of distance. If a route's metric reaches 16 hops, the destination is considered unreachable.

Basic RIP Configuration

RIP is created on a per virtual router basis. To use RIP there are four simple steps you need to configure on your firewall:

- Configure a virtual router ID.

- On the virtual router create a RIP routing instance.

- Activate the new RIP instance.

- Configure the network interfaces to have RIP enabled.

Configuring RIP

In this section we will look at the steps for configuring RIP on your firewall. We will do all steps together for both the WebUI and the CLI.

Use the following steps to configure RIP via the WebUI:

1. Access **Network | Routing | Virtual Router**.

2. Click the **Edit** link of the virtual router you wish to modify.

3. Enable the **Virtual Router ID** option.

4. Use the **Custom** field to enter an ID for the RIP.

5. Click **Apply**.

6. Click **Create RIP Instance**.

7. Enable the **Enable RIP** option.

8. Click **OK**.

9. Access **Network | Interface**.

10. Click the **Edit** link of the interface that you want to enable RIP on.

11. Click the **RIP** link at the top of the page.

12. Enable the **Enable** option.

13. Click **OK**.

Use the following to configure RIP via the CLI:

```
ns500-> get vrouter trust-vr
Routing Table
------------------------------------------------------------------------
C - Connected, S - Static, A - Auto-Exported, I - Imported, R - RIP
iB - IBGP, eB - EBGP, O - OSPF, E1 - OSPF external type 1
E2 - OSPF external type 2
Total 4/max entries
    ID          IP-Prefix      Interface        Gateway     P Pref    Mtr
Vsys
```

```
------------------------------------------------------------------------
----
    5         1.2.3.4/32         eth3/2        0.0.0.0   C    0        0
Root
    4       10.123.0.0/24        eth3/2        0.0.0.0   S   20       20
Root
*   2       10.9.0.0/24           mgt          0.0.0.0   C    0        0
Root
*   3       1.2.3.0/24            mgt         10.9.0.10  S   20        1
Root


Interfaces
------------------------------------------------------------------------
tunnel, hidden.1, self, mgt, ha1, ha2
v1-trust, v1-untrust, v1-dmz, ethernet3/2, ethernet1/2, ethernet2/2
vlan1, ethernet4/1


Auto-exporting:              Disabled
Default-vrouter:             For vsys (Root)
Shared-vrouter:              Yes
--- more ---
nsrp-config-sync:            Yes
System-Default-route:        Not present
Advertise-Inactive-Interface: Disabled
Source-Based-Routing:        Disabled
SNMP Trap:                   Public
Ignore-Subnet-Conflict:      Disabled
ns500-> set vrouter trust-vr router-id 255
ns500-> get vrouter trust-vr
Routing Table
------------------------------------------------------------------------
C - Connected, S - Static, A - Auto-Exported, I - Imported, R - RIP
iB - IBGP, eB - EBGP, O - OSPF, E1 - OSPF external type 1
E2 - OSPF external type 2
Total 4/max entries
    ID         IP-Prefix      Interface        Gateway   P Pref    Mtr
Vsys
```

```
-------------------------------------------------------------------
     5          1.2.3.4/32          eth3/2          0.0.0.0   C    0         0
Root
     4        10.123.0.0/24         eth3/2          0.0.0.0   S   20        20
Root
*    2         10.9.0.0/24           mgt            0.0.0.0   C    0         0
Root
*    3         1.2.3.0/24            mgt          10.9.0.10   S   20         1
Root

Interfaces
-------------------------------------------------------------------
tunnel, hidden.1, self, mgt, ha1, ha2
v1-trust, v1-untrust, v1-dmz, ethernet3/2, ethernet1/2, ethernet2/2
vlan1, ethernet4/1

Auto-exporting:              Disabled
Default-vrouter:             For vsys (Root)
Shared-vrouter:              Yes
--- more ---
nsrp-config-sync:            Yes
System-Default-route:        Not present
Advertise-Inactive-Interface:  Disabled
Source-Based-Routing:        Disabled
SNMP Trap:                   Public
Ignore-Subnet-Conflict:      Disabled
ns500-> set vrouter trust-vr protocol rip
ns500-> set vrouter trust-vr protocol rip enable
ns500-> get vrouter trust-vr
Routing Table
-------------------------------------------------------------------
C - Connected, S - Static, A - Auto-Exported, I - Imported, R - RIP
iB - IBGP, eB - EBGP, O - OSPF, E1 - OSPF external type 1
E2 - OSPF external type 2
Total 4/max entries
```

ID	IP-Prefix	Interface	Gateway	P	Pref	Mtr
Vsys						
5	1.2.3.4/32	eth3/2	0.0.0.0	C	0	0
Root						
4	10.123.0.0/24	eth3/2	0.0.0.0	S	20	20
Root						
* 2	10.9.0.0/24	mgt	0.0.0.0	C	0	0
Root						
* 3	1.2.3.0/24	mgt	10.9.0.10	S	20	1
Root						

```
Interfaces
-------------------------------------------------------------------------------
tunnel, hidden.1, self, mgt, ha1, ha2
v1-trust, v1-untrust, v1-dmz, ethernet3/2, ethernet1/2, ethernet2/2
vlan1, ethernet4/1


Auto-exporting:              Disabled
Default-vrouter:             For vsys (Root)
Shared-vrouter:              Yes
--- more ---
nsrp-config-sync:            Yes
System-Default-route:        Not present
Advertise-Inactive-Interface:  Disabled
Source-Based-Routing:        Disabled
SNMP Trap:                   Public
Ignore-Subnet-Conflict:      Disabled
ns500-> get interface ethernet3/2
Interface ethernet3/2:
  number 10, if_info 82000, if_index 0, mode nat
  link down, phy-link down
  vsys Root, zone Trust, vr trust-vr
  *ip 1.2.3.4/32   mac 0010.db0b.494a
  *manage ip 1.2.3.4, mac 0010.db0b.494a
  route-deny disable
  ping enabled, telnet enabled, SSH enabled, SNMP enabled
```

```
  web enabled, ident-reset disabled, SSL enabled
  webauth disabled, webauth-ip 0.0.0.0
  OSPF disabled  BGP disabled  RIP disabled
  bandwidth: physical 0kbps, configured 0kbps, current 0kbps
            total configured gbw 0kbps, total allocated gbw 0kbps
  DHCP-Relay disabled
ns500-> set interface ethernet3/2 protocol rip enable
ns500-> get interface ethernet3/2
Interface ethernet3/2:
  number 10, if_info 82000, if_index 0, mode nat
  link down, phy-link down
  vsys Root, zone Trust, vr trust-vr
  *ip 1.2.3.4/32   mac 0010.db0b.494a
  *manage ip 1.2.3.4, mac 0010.db0b.494a
  route-deny disable
  ping enabled, telnet enabled, SSH enabled, SNMP enabled
  web enabled, ident-reset disabled, SSL enabled
  webauth disabled, webauth-ip 0.0.0.0
  OSPF disabled  BGP disabled  RIP enabled
  bandwidth: physical 0kbps, configured 0kbps, current 0kbps
            total configured gbw 0kbps, total allocated gbw 0kbps
  DHCP-Relay disabled
ns500->
```

Open Shortest Path First (OSPF)

OSPF is a link state protocol and is considered one of the best protocols to run for your internal network. The open in OSPF represents that it is an open standard protocol. OSPF will only send out periodic updates and is not considered to be a chatty protocol. It is extremely efficient and is supported by most modern routing equipment.

OSPF Concepts

Before we look into the configuration of OSPF on your NetScreen firewall, we will first review a few OSPF concepts. These concepts are common throughout the configuration of OSPF and also across various vendors' devices. Routers are grouped into *areas*. By default, all routers participating in OSPF are grouped in to area **0**, also known as area **0.0.0.0**. There will be occasions when you will want to want to divide your network into multiple areas. This is typically done in large networks.

Each router that participates in an OSPF network is classified as one of four types of routers:

- **Internal Router** A router with all interfaces belonging to the same area.

- **Backbone Router** A router that has an interface in the backbone area. The backbone area is also known as area **0**.

- **Area Border Router** A router that connects to multiple areas.

- **AS Boundary Router** A router that borders another autonomous systems (AS).

Basic OSPF Configuration

Configuring OSPF is similar to configuring RIP, as it is enabled on a per virtual router basis. Each virtual router is capable of supporting one instance of OSPF at a time.

- Configure a virtual router ID.

- On the virtual router, create a OSPF instance.

- Activate the new OSPF instance.

- Configure the network interfaces to have OSPF enabled.

Use the following steps to configure OSPF via the WebUI:

1. Access **Network | Routing | Virtual Router**.

2. Click the **Edit** link of the virtual router for which you will configure OSPF.

3. Enable the **Virtual Router ID** option.

4. Enter an ID in the text box labeled **Custom**, next to the raido button you selected.

5. Click **Apply**.

6. Click **Create OSPF Instance**.

7. Enable the **OSPF Enabled** option.

8. Click **OK**.

9. Access **Network | Interface**.

10. Click the **Edit** link of the interface you want to enable OSPF on.

11. Click the link labeled **OSPF**.

12. Enable the **Enable Protocol OSPF** option.

13. Click **OK**.

Use the following to configure OSPF via the CLI:

```
ns500-> get vrouter trust-vr

Routing Table

--------------------------------------------------------------------------

C - Connected, S - Static, A - Auto-Exported, I - Imported, R - RIP

iB - IBGP, eB - EBGP, O - OSPF, E1 - OSPF external type 1

E2 - OSPF external type 2

Total 4/max entries

    ID          IP-Prefix      Interface         Gateway    P Pref     Mtr
Vsys

--------------------------------------------------------------------------

     5          1.2.3.4/32       eth3/2         0.0.0.0     C   0         0
Root

     4        10.123.0.0/24      eth3/2         0.0.0.0     S  20        20
Root

*    2        10.9.0.0/24         mgt          0.0.0.0     C   0         0
Root

*    3        1.2.3.0/24          mgt         10.9.0.10    S  20         1
Root


Interfaces

--------------------------------------------------------------------------

tunnel, hidden.1, self, mgt, ha1, ha2

v1-trust, v1-untrust, v1-dmz, ethernet3/2, ethernet1/2, ethernet2/2

vlan1, ethernet4/1


Auto-exporting:                 Disabled

Default-vrouter:                For vsys (Root)
```

```
Shared-vrouter:                Yes
nsrp-config-sync:              Yes
System-Default-route:          Not present
Advertise-Inactive-Interface:  Disabled
Source-Based-Routing:          Disabled
SNMP Trap:                     Public
Ignore-Subnet-Conflict:        Disabled
ns500-> set vrouter trust-vr router-id 255
ns500-> get vrouter trust-vr
Routing Table
--------------------------------------------------------------------------
C - Connected, S - Static, A - Auto-Exported, I - Imported, R - RIP
iB - IBGP, eB - EBGP, O - OSPF, E1 - OSPF external type 1
E2 - OSPF external type 2
Total 4/max entries
     ID         IP-Prefix        Interface          Gateway    P Pref     Mtr
Vsys
--------------------------------------------------------------------------
      5         1.2.3.4/32         eth3/2           0.0.0.0    C   0         0
Root
      4       10.123.0.0/24        eth3/2           0.0.0.0    S   20       20
Root
*     2        10.9.0.0/24         mgt             0.0.0.0    C   0         0
Root
*     3        1.2.3.0/24          mgt             10.9.0.10  S   20        1
Root


Interfaces
--------------------------------------------------------------------------
tunnel, hidden.1, self, mgt, ha1, ha2
v1-trust, v1-untrust, v1-dmz, ethernet3/2, ethernet1/2, ethernet2/2
vlan1, ethernet4/1


Auto-exporting:                Disabled
Default-vrouter:               For vsys (Root)
Shared-vrouter:                Yes
nsrp-config-sync:              Yes
```

```
System-Default-route:          Not present
Advertise-Inactive-Interface:  Disabled
Source-Based-Routing:          Disabled
SNMP Trap:                     Public
Ignore-Subnet-Conflict:        Disabled
ns500-> set vrouter trust-vr protocol ospf
ns500-> set vrouter trust-vr protocol ospf enable
ns500-> get vrouter trust-vr
Routing Table
------------------------------------------------------------------------
C - Connected, S - Static, A - Auto-Exported, I - Imported, R - RIP
iB - IBGP, eB - EBGP, O - OSPF, E1 - OSPF external type 1
E2 - OSPF external type 2
Total 4/max entries
    ID         IP-Prefix      Interface          Gateway    P Pref    Mtr
Vsys
------------------------------------------------------------------------
    5          1.2.3.4/32        eth3/2          0.0.0.0    C   0       0
Root
    4        10.123.0.0/24       eth3/2          0.0.0.0    S   20      20
Root
*   2         10.9.0.0/24         mgt           0.0.0.0    C   0       0
Root
*   3         1.2.3.0/24          mgt          10.9.0.10   S   20      1
Root


Interfaces
------------------------------------------------------------------------
tunnel, hidden.1, self, mgt, ha1, ha2
v1-trust, v1-untrust, v1-dmz, ethernet3/2, ethernet1/2, ethernet2/2
vlan1, ethernet4/1

Auto-exporting:                Disabled
Default-vrouter:               For vsys (Root)
Shared-vrouter:                Yes
nsrp-config-sync:              Yes
System-Default-route:          Not present
```

```
Advertise-Inactive-Interface:    Disabled
Source-Based-Routing:            Disabled
SNMP Trap:                       Public
Ignore-Subnet-Conflict:          Disabled
ns500-> get interface ethernet3/2
Interface ethernet3/2:
  number 10, if_info 82000, if_index 0, mode nat
  link down, phy-link down
  vsys Root, zone Trust, vr trust-vr
  *ip 1.2.3.4/32   mac 0010.db0b.494a
  *manage ip 1.2.3.4, mac 0010.db0b.494a
  route-deny disable
  ping enabled, telnet enabled, SSH enabled, SNMP enabled
  web enabled, ident-reset disabled, SSL enabled
  webauth disabled, webauth-ip 0.0.0.0
  OSPF disabled  BGP disabled  RIP disabled
  bandwidth: physical 0kbps, configured 0kbps, current 0kbps
             total configured gbw 0kbps, total allocated gbw 0kbps
  DHCP-Relay disabled
ns500-> set interface ethernet3/2 protocol ospf enable
ns500-> get interface ethernet3/2
Interface ethernet3/2:
  number 10, if_info 82000, if_index 0, mode nat
  link down, phy-link down
  vsys Root, zone Trust, vr trust-vr
  *ip 1.2.3.4/32   mac 0010.db0b.494a
  *manage ip 1.2.3.4, mac 0010.db0b.494a
  route-deny disable
  ping enabled, telnet enabled, SSH enabled, SNMP enabled
  web enabled, ident-reset disabled, SSL enabled
  webauth disabled, webauth-ip 0.0.0.0
  OSPF enabled BGP disabled  RIP disabled
  bandwidth: physical 0kbps, configured 0kbps, current 0kbps
             total configured gbw 0kbps, total allocated gbw 0kbps
  DHCP-Relay disabled
ns500->
```

Border Gateway Protocol

Border Gateway Protocol is the core routing protocol used on the Internet. BGP routing information is not broadcast like RIP or OSPF. Two BGP peers connect to each other and form a TCP (Transmission Control Protocol) session. This session is then used to transmit all of the routing data. BGP is a very complex protocol and in this book we are only focusing on the basic BGP configuration on a NetScreen firewall.

Basic BGP Configuration

Use the following steps to configure BGP via the WebUI:

1. Access **Network | Routing | Virtual Router**.
2. Click the **Edit** link of the virtual router on which you will create a BGP instance.
3. Enable the **Virtual Router ID** option.
4. Enter an ID in the **Custom** field next to the radio button you selected.
5. Click **Apply**.
6. At the bottom of the page, click the **Create BGP Instance** link.
7. Enter the number of your autonomous system in the **AS Number** field.
8. Enable the **BGP Enabled** option.
9. Click **OK**.
10. Access **Network | Interface**.
11. Click the **Edit** link of the interface that you want to enable BGP on.
12. Click the **BGP** link.
13. Enable the **Enable Protocol BGP** option.
14. Click **OK**.

Use the following to configure BGP via the CLI:

```
ns500-> get vrouter trust-vr

Routing Table

-----------------------------------------------------------------------

C - Connected, S - Static, A - Auto-Exported, I - Imported, R - RIP
```

```
iB - IBGP, eB - EBGP, O - OSPF, E1 - OSPF external type 1
E2 - OSPF external type 2
Total 4/max entries
   ID          IP-Prefix        Interface         Gateway    P Pref    Mtr
Vsys
----------------------------------------------------------------------------
    5          1.2.3.4/32         eth3/2          0.0.0.0    C   0        0
Root
    4        10.123.0.0/24        eth3/2          0.0.0.0    S   20       20
Root
*   2        10.9.0.0/24           mgt            0.0.0.0    C   0        0
Root
*   3        1.2.3.0/24            mgt           10.9.0.10   S   20       1
Root


Interfaces
----------------------------------------------------------------------------
tunnel, hidden.1, self, mgt, ha1, ha2
v1-trust, v1-untrust, v1-dmz, ethernet3/2, ethernet1/2, ethernet2/2
vlan1, ethernet4/1


Auto-exporting:              Disabled
Default-vrouter:             For vsys (Root)
Shared-vrouter:              Yes
nsrp-config-sync:            Yes
System-Default-route:        Not present
Advertise-Inactive-Interface: Disabled
Source-Based-Routing:        Disabled
SNMP Trap:                   Public
Ignore-Subnet-Conflict:      Disabled
ns500-> set vrouter trust-vr router-id 255
ns500-> get vrouter trust-vr
Routing Table
----------------------------------------------------------------------------
C - Connected, S - Static, A - Auto-Exported, I - Imported, R - RIP
iB - IBGP, eB - EBGP, O - OSPF, E1 - OSPF external type 1
E2 - OSPF external type 2
```

```
Total 4/max entries
    ID          IP-Prefix        Interface         Gateway    P Pref    Mtr
Vsys
-----------------------------------------------------------------------------
     5          1.2.3.4/32         eth3/2          0.0.0.0    C   0         0
Root
     4       10.123.0.0/24         eth3/2          0.0.0.0    S   20       20
Root
*    2        10.9.0.0/24           mgt            0.0.0.0    C   0         0
Root
*    3        1.2.3.0/24            mgt           10.9.0.10   S   20        1
Root


Interfaces
-----------------------------------------------------------------------------
tunnel, hidden.1, self, mgt, ha1, ha2
v1-trust, v1-untrust, v1-dmz, ethernet3/2, ethernet1/2, ethernet2/2
vlan1, ethernet4/1


Auto-exporting:             Disabled
Default-vrouter:            For vsys (Root)
Shared-vrouter:             Yes
nsrp-config-sync:           Yes
System-Default-route:       Not present
Advertise-Inactive-Interface:   Disabled
Source-Based-Routing:       Disabled
SNMP Trap:                  Public
Ignore-Subnet-Conflict:     Disabled
ns500-> set vrouter trust-vr protocol bgp 10245
ns500-> set vrouter trust-vr protocol bgp enable
ns500-> get vrouter trust-vr
Routing Table
-----------------------------------------------------------------------------
C - Connected, S - Static, A - Auto-Exported, I - Imported, R - RIP
iB - IBGP, eB - EBGP, O - OSPF, E1 - OSPF external type 1
E2 - OSPF external type 2
Total 4/max entries
```

ID Vsys	IP-Prefix	Interface	Gateway	P	Pref	Mtr
5 Root	1.2.3.4/32	eth3/2	0.0.0.0	C	0	0
4 Root	10.123.0.0/24	eth3/2	0.0.0.0	S	20	20
* 2 Root	10.9.0.0/24	mgt	0.0.0.0	C	0	0
* 3 Root	1.2.3.0/24	mgt	10.9.0.10	S	20	1

```
Interfaces
---------------------------------------------------------------------------
tunnel, hidden.1, self, mgt, ha1, ha2
v1-trust, v1-untrust, v1-dmz, ethernet3/2, ethernet1/2, ethernet2/2
vlan1, ethernet4/1


Auto-exporting:                 Disabled
Default-vrouter:                For vsys (Root)
Shared-vrouter:                 Yes
nsrp-config-sync:               Yes
System-Default-route:           Not present
Advertise-Inactive-Interface:   Disabled
Source-Based-Routing:           Disabled
SNMP Trap:                       Public
Ignore-Subnet-Conflict:         Disabled
ns500-> get interface ethernet3/2
Interface ethernet3/2:
  number 10, if_info 82000, if_index 0, mode nat
  link down, phy-link down
  vsys Root, zone Trust, vr trust-vr
  *ip 1.2.3.4/32    mac 0010.db0b.494a
  *manage ip 1.2.3.4, mac 0010.db0b.494a
  route-deny disable
  ping enabled, telnet enabled, SSH enabled, SNMP enabled
```

```
   web enabled, ident-reset disabled, SSL enabled
   webauth disabled, webauth-ip 0.0.0.0
   OSPF disabled  BGP disabled   RIP disabled
   bandwidth: physical 0kbps, configured 0kbps, current 0kbps
              total configured gbw 0kbps, total allocated gbw 0kbps
   DHCP-Relay disabled
ns500-> set interface ethernet3/2 protocol BGP enable
ns500-> get interface ethernet3/2
Interface ethernet3/2:
   number 10, if_info 82000, if_index 0, mode nat
   link down, phy-link down
   vsys Root, zone Trust, vr trust-vr
   *ip 1.2.3.4/32   mac 0010.db0b.494a
   *manage ip 1.2.3.4, mac 0010.db0b.494a
   route-deny disable
   ping enabled, telnet enabled, SSH enabled, SNMP enabled
   web enabled, ident-reset disabled, SSL enabled
   webauth disabled, webauth-ip 0.0.0.0
   OSPF disabled BGP enabled RIP disabled
   bandwidth: physical 0kbps, configured 0kbps, current 0kbps
              total configured gbw 0kbps, total allocated gbw 0kbps
   DHCP-Relay disabled
ns500->
```

Tools & Traps…

Routing Complexities

Using routing protocols is a very efficient way to advertise routes on your network. Many organizations stick to just using static routing on their networks to keep the configuration simple. However, as you may have learned from this chapter, configuring routing protocols is almost as easy as turning on a switch.

Continued

Any time you have two or more routing devices, you may want to consider configuring and using routing protocols. If you have never used routing protocols before, I suggest you at least look into how they work. It may benefit your environment as well as your own learning. Whenever using routing protocols, make sure you fully understand the implications of what you are doing. It is possible, through misconfiguration, to inadvertently take down your network and create an extended outage. Always fully test your configuration to prevent network failures.

Summary

Routing is a powerful tool for any network. In this chapter we presented an overview of routing on a NetScreen firewall. NetScreen firewalls have a very unique implementation of routing with the use of virtual routers. As we discussed earlier, a virtual router is capable of splitting your routing domain into multiple virtual domains. This allows you to securely use routing protocols in your network. Because a typical firewall only contains one routing table, it may be possible to send poisoned or illegitimate routes into your firewall possible creating outages.

However, with the ability to use multiple virtual routers on your firewall you can mitigate this risk. NetScreen firewalls are capable of supporting three different routing protocols. Depending on the model of your firewall, it may not support all three of these protocols. The first protocol is RIP version 2. RIP is supported on many routing devices for a few reasons. First, it is easy to configure; just turning it on enables you to have a RIP infrastructure. Second, it is reliable and contains tried and true algorithms. Finally, because it is not an intensive protocol it does not require a great deal of processing power.

OSPF is an excellent protocol for you to use inside of your network. It is extremely efficient and provides a very robust routing infrastructure. Unfortunately, it has a few downsides. First, it requires additional processing power and additional memory to compute its complex algorithms, and second, it is complex to configure. The third supported protocol is BGP. BGP is typically used on the Internet to provide dynamic routing. BGP can be extremely complex to use. Many firewalls do not support this protocol because of its complexities. Juniper is dedicated to providing top-notch products and the proof of that can be found in the fact that its products support the BGP protocol.

Solutions Fast Track

Virtual Routers

- ☑ Each virtual router contains its own routing domain and routing table.
- ☑ Every NetScreen firewall supports at least two virtual routers.
- ☑ Virtual routers allow you to separate your routing design into separate routing domains on the same device.

RIP

- ☑ RIP is a distance vector protocol.
- ☑ RIP is considered a chatty protocol because it is constantly sending updates.
- ☑ Using RIP is the easiest of all of the dynamic routing protocols supported by the NetScreen firewall.

OSPF

- ☑ OSPF is an efficient routing protocol.
- ☑ OSPF is a link state protocol.
- ☑ OSPF is more complicated to configure than RIP.

BGP

- ☑ BGP is used as the primary routing protocol on the Internet.
- ☑ BGP is very complex and requires careful planning to configure.
- ☑ BGP routes by autonomous systems.

Frequently Asked Questions

The following Frequently Asked Questions, answered by the authors of this book, are designed to both measure your understanding of the concepts presented in this chapter and to assist you with real-life implementation of these concepts. To have your questions about this chapter answered by the author, browse to **www.syngress.com/solutions** and click on the **"Ask the Author"** form. You will also gain access to thousands of other FAQs at ITFAQnet.com.

Q: When would you need more than one virtual router?

A: Most people using NetScreen firewalls today are using only a single virtual router. This makes the NetScreen firewall function like a traditional routing firewall. However, when you want to use dynamic routing protocols on your device, using a virtual router is a great idea. This allows you to separate your two routing domains easily and effectively.

Q: What is the point of virtual routers?

A: Virtual routers are very effective when using dynamic routing protocols. This is typically when they are used.

Q: What are the purposes of using dynamic routing?

A: Dynamic routing allows you to dynamically update your network configuration. It is usually a requirement when using multiple locations with multiple subnets. Integrating it onto your firewall allows for seamless updates to your network and can ensure that resources can be accessed from almost anywhere in case of a link failure.

Q: Why doesn't the NetScreen firewall support IGRP or EIGRP?

A: Both IGRP and EIGRP are Cisco proprietary protocols.

Q: Can you use dynamic routing with VPNs?

A: All of the dynamic routing protocols can be used over VPNs. This would allow for the ability to reroute over a VPN in the case of a link failure. This is a very powerful tool to use in your network.

Chapter 8

Address Translation

Solutions in this Chapter:

- **Purpose of Address Translation**
- **NetScreen NAT Overview**
- **NetScreen Packet Flow**
- **Source NAT**
- **Destination NAT**

Introduction

NetScreen is well known for its firewall and virtual private network (VPN) technologies primarily due to the Application-Specific Integrated Circuit (ASIC)-based design of most of their core features, including address translation. This chapter focuses on how the address translation features of NetScreen products have evolved from a simple physical interface translation (Screen OS 2.5 and below) to a solution capable of handling complex address translation design requirements.

Throughout this chapter are several NetScreen scenarios with different example configurations. The assumption for all of the examples within this chapter assumes the following:

- **Security Zones:** Ethernet3 (Untrust) and Ethernet1 (Trust)

Both security zones are within the Trust virtual router (Trust-VR). The example configurations highlight the key areas that relate to that specific scenario.

Purpose of Address Translation

Network address translation (NAT) is the ability to masquerade one Internet Protocol (IP) address from another. This functionality is completely transparent to the users. For example, Figure 8.1 shows a host on network 10.1.1.*x*/24 traversing through a NAT device. The NAT device then translates the source packet coming from host 10.1.1.100 and going to address 172.16.1.1, which then communicates with host 172.16.1.50. This method is called *source NAT*.

Figure 8.1 All Egress Traffic from 10.1.1.*x* Network will NAT from Source 172.16.1.1

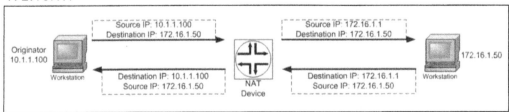

Advantages of Address Translation

Because of the tremendous growth of the Internet in the past decade, there were not enough IP v.4 addresses. NAT was developed to provide an immediate solution to this depletion. Request for Comment (RFC) 1631 was written in 1994 as the short-term solution to address the problem—the long-term solution was IP v.6.

Other ways that NAT is useful:

- **Security** NAT can provide a hidden identity for host(s).

- **Addresses RFC 1918 Private Address Usage on a Routable Network** A NAT device can translate an existing non-public routable subnet to a public routable address(s). Most companies use RFC 1918 addresses for their corporate networks because it helps conserve their routable Internet Assigned Numbers Authority (IANA) public addresses. RFC 1918 addresses are:

  ```
  10.0.0.0 to 10.255.255.255 (10/8 prefix)

  172.16.0.0 to 172.31.255.255 (172.16/12 prefix)

  192.168.0.0 to 192.168.255.255 (192.168/16 prefix)
  ```

- **Addresses Overlapping Networks** NAT can provide a masquerade of different networks when two duplicate networks must be merged

- **Helps Maintain a Cohesive Network** Provides a method of maintaining one cohesive network when needed to communicate with different extranets.

Both the source and destination packets can be translated using NetScreen's NAT functionality.

NetScreen also provides the ability to translate ports from protocols such as Transmission Control Protocol (TCP) and User Datagram Protocol (UDP). Port Address Translation (PAT) provides the translation for the source port and/or the destination port just as a NAT function translates for a source IP and/or destination IP. The ability to utilize source port PAT allows a company with hundreds of computers to access the Internet using only one public IP address. When using source PAT, over 64, 000 concurrent sessions can be generated for just one NAT IP address. Like NetScreen, source PAT usually starts at port 1024 and above; therefore, it is possible to scale up to 64,512 ports (65,535 max number that a TCP/UDP port can reach − 1023 = 64,512) that can be allocated for one NAT IP. The reason that PAT ports start at 1024 and above is because ports 0 through 1023 are reserved and primarily used for well-known services (e.g., TCP port 23 is for Telnet, TCP port 22 is for Secure Shell [SSH], and TCP port 80 is for Hypertext Transfer Protocol [HTTP]). (See RFC 3022 for more information on PAT.)

An example of source PAT is illustrated in Figure 8.2. The image shows the NAT device performing a source NAT and a source PAT from the originator (10.1.1.100). Besides translating the source IP, such as shown in Figure 8.1, the NAT device will also translate the original source port to a random source port, which usually starts at 1024 and above. Notice that the return packet response from 172.16.1.50 is translated back to port 3001.

Figure 8.2 All Egress Traffic from the 10.1.1.*x* Network will NAT from 172.16.1.1 and PAT with a Random Source Port

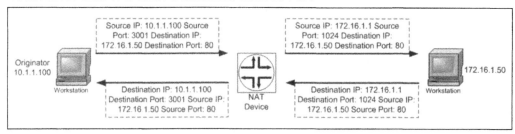

Figure 8.3 shows an example of a destination PAT function. Traffic destined for port 80 from the originator would be translated to a different port. Notice that the return packet response from 172.16.1.50 is translated back to port 80.

Figure 8.3 All Egress Traffic from 10.1.1.x Network will NAT from 172.16.1.1 and Destination PAT from Port 80 to Port 8080

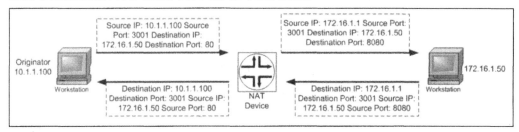

NOTE

The combined use of NAT and PAT is called NAPT, which is a default function on the NetScreen firewalls.

Disadvantages of Address Translation

When using address translation, certain scenarios come with certain concerns. The following is a list of the most common issues found when using NAPT:

- **Security Internet Protocol (IPSec) usage through a NAT device.** See Chapter 12, "VPN Usage," for more information on why NAT causes IPSec to break. There are two workarounds to this:
  - Create a one-to-one NAT and disable PAT
  - Use NAT Traversal

- **Protocol that requires dynamic port allocation.** For example: passive File Transfer Protocol (FTP), Sun Remote Procedure Call (RPC), MS-RPC, Domain Name System (DNS), Voice over Internet Protocol (VOIP), Session Interface Protocol (SIP), and so on. There are workarounds available. Most firewalls implement a feature called Application Level Gateway (ALG) to address applications that require dynamic port opening. NetScreen currently offers this for several protocols, as discussed in Chapter 2.

- **Legacy application or custom application requires that the original packet information be maintained.** This varies from requiring the network address to the port to remain the same. In some cases, disabling NAT, PAT, or both will address this issue. It is generally recommended to disable PAT first, because the majority of these applications relate to restrictive ports.

NetScreen NAT Overview

The NetScreen firewall solution always incorporates NAT functionality; there is always some NAT enhancement with each major ScreenOS release. This section highlights the key NAT features from early ScreenOS to ScreenOS 5.0. It is important to note that some of the older features such as Mapped IP (MIP) and Virtual IP (VIP) can also be performed in the newer ScreenOS releases. These NAT features are covered in detail in the following sections.

- **Source NAT** provides address translation on the source IP address. Source PAT is another functionality that may be performed along with source NAT. Source PAT provides address translation on the source port. There are several methods of Source NAT:

- **Interface-based Source NAT** was the first method of NAT functionality included within NetScreen firewall solutions. It is a typical feature that is normally found with most NAT vendors. This feature provides the ability to NAT ingress traffic received in the defined interface, with NAT enabled with the last known egress interface. Source NAT is also performed by default. (If it cannot be disabled, use an alternative method such as policy-based NAT to over-source PAT, if needed.)

- **MIP** provides a static NAT functionality for one-to-one address translation. This feature can be used for either source or destination NAT capabilities.

- **Policy-based Source NAT** is similar in functionality to Interface-based Source NAT; the configuration is done on a firewall rule rather then a global interface setting. Based on the firewall rule, you can specify certain traffic up to a Layer 4 definition on whether or not to perform address translation on the source IP address.

- **Destination NAT** provides address translation on the destination IP address. Destination PAT is another feature set that can be enabled at the same time, which provides address translation for the destination port. There are several methods of destination NAT:

  - **VIP** provides one-to-many address translation functionality. This feature can be used to translate the destination IP and the destination port at the same time.

  - **MIP** can also be used in a destination one-to-one address translation and can be used for either source or destination NAT capabilities.

  - **Policy-based Destination NAT** is similar in functionality to Policy-based Source NAT except that it performs address translation on the destination IP or destination port on a per-firewall rule definition.

NetScreen Packet Flow

This section highlights the address translation portion of the NetScreen packet flow. Understanding how NetScreen handles a packet flow provides a good base to understanding how address translations are triggered and also makes troubleshooting and debugging a problem much easier. Figure 8.4 shows a high-level overview of how a NetScreen firewall handles packets flowing into their devices.

Figure 8.4 NetScreen Packet Flow

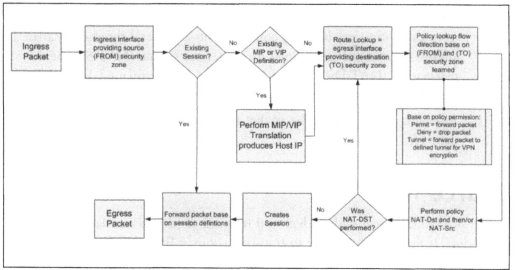

The process steps are as follows:

1. Based on the arriving ingress packet, the NetScreen device notes the incoming interface and the bonded security zone to that interface. (For the purposes of this book, the ingress security zone is considered the FROM zone.) The interface can be a physical Ethernet interface, a subinterface, a VPN tunnel interface, or a VPN tunnel zone. At this point, the NetScreen screening functions are performed. The screening function detects any anomalous traffic behavior such as denial of service (DOS) attacks. The screen options are configurable at the security zone level.

2. Check to see if the session exists. If it does, forward the packet based on the session definition. If the session does not exist, check to see whether a MIP or VIP entry exists. If one does exist, perform a MIP or VIP translation.

3. Next, the route lookup is performed. Based on the destination packet IP address, the route lookup determines which egress interface the packet will eventually leave from. When you know the egress interface you will also know the egress security zone (remember, the security zones are

bonded to an interface). (For the purposes of this book, the egress security zone is considered the TO zone.)

4. Now that you know the FROM and TO security zones, you can apply
them to a policy lookup. At a minimum, a policy performs a permit or
deny or pushes the packet through a VPN tunnel. Other miscellaneous
operations can also be performed such as traffic shaping, deep inspection, authentication, logging, counters, anti-virus, and threshold alarms. If
address translations are defined for either the source (NAT-Src) or the
destination (NAT-Dst), those functions are also performed. If NAT-Dst
is performed, another route lookup is required.

5. A session is created and the packet is forwarded to the egress interface as
defined.

Source NAT

Source NAT is the most widely deployed method of address translation provided
by vendors. It provides the ability to translate a source IP address to another IP
address (as illustrated in Figure 8.1). By default (NetScreen solution), source NAT
is enabled on the interfaces using the Trust security zone (see Figure 8.5).

Figure 8.5 Web UI Screenshot of Interface-based Source NAT Shown
Enable5

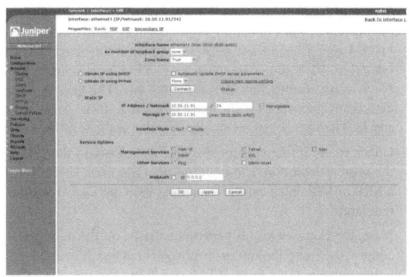

Interface-based Source Translation

Interface-based source translation provides the ability to launch NAT off of a physical interface or a logical interface (e.g., a sub-interface). The interface with NAT mode enabled will perform NAPT by default for the ingress traffic. The source IP address used for translation will be the egress interface. In other words, whichever interface the packet exits from is the interface IP address that will be used as the translated source IP address. Figure 8.6 shows what address translation looks like for a packet sourcing from a host behind Ethernet1 on the Trust zone with NAT enabled.

Figure 8.6 Source 10.1.1.100 will Source NAT from the Egress Interface Untrust

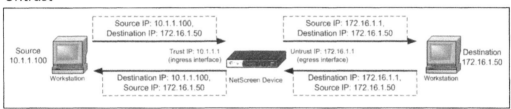

The egress interface used is determined via the NetScreen packet flow (see Figure 8.4). The key area is the route table lookup for the destination.

> **NOTE**
>
> Prior to ScreenOS 5.0, communication from a host on the Untrust zone to a host on the Trust zone with interface set for NAT was not possible unless a MIP or VIP was defined. With the current ScreenOS release, this communication is possible as long as there is a firewall rule defined to allow it.

> **TIP**
>
> Here are some rules and limitation on interface-based NAT:
>   1. The egress interface *must* be bonded to the Untrust zone.
>   2. When a user-defined zone is bonded to the ingress interface with NAT enabled, that user-defined security zone must be defined on a different virtual router than the Untrust zone

3. Interface-based NAT will not work between the Trust zone and a user-defined defined zone
4. Interface-based NAT does not work on an interface bonded to the Untrust zone, even though it can be enabled.

MIP

MIP provides the ability to perform a one-to-one mapping translation, which is referred to as *Static NAT*. This setting ensures that a host gets the same NAT every time traffic traverses the firewall, whether it's ingress or egress traffic. A MIP definition only performs NAT (no PAT), thus the IP address changes but the protocol ports remain the same. MIP(s) are defined on an interface that can be the physical Ethernet interface, a sub-interface, a tunnel interface, or a loop-back interface. Once a MIP is defined, a firewall rule is needed to allow access to the MIP.

Besides one-to-one mapping, a MIP can also be created to a subnet. In a MIP-to-subnet definition, it is important to define the subnet mask properly. The host range used for the MIP should not be used elsewhere on the NetScreen device.

All MIP definitions are placed within a global zone no matter which security zone originally defined the MIP. Once a MIP has been defined, a firewall rule must be set up to allow for traffic destined for the MIP address. Within the firewall rule creation, the destination MIP selection can be from a global zone or the zone the MIP address was originally defined in.

MIP Limitations

There are a limited number of MIPs that can be performed on a NetScreen firewall. The following matrix shows the MIP capacity as of ScreenOS 5.0. These numbers are the same for both basic and advanced license models:

Table 8.1 MIP Capacity Matrix

Product Name	MIP Capacity
NetScreen HSC	5
NetScreen 5XT	100
NetScreen 5GT	100
NetScreen 25	500
NetScreen 50	1,000

Continued

Table 8.1 MIP Capacity Matrix

Product Name	MIP Capacity
NetScreen 204/208	4,096
NetScreen 500	4,096
NetScreen ISG 2000	8,192
NetScreen 5200/5400	10,000

Policy-based NAT can perform the same functions as a MIP; however, there are a couple of advantages to using a policy-based NAT for one-to-one mapping. Using one form of translation such as policy-based translation over older features such as interface-based translation, MIP, and VIP provides a more unified way of managing your NAT functions. Another advantage of using policy-based NAT is that the only limitation is the number of policies you can create, which far exceeds any MIP capacity. The following matrix shows the policy capacity for each firewall platform:

Table 8.2 Policy Capacity Matrix

Product Name	Policy Capacity
NetScreen HSC	50
NetScreen 5XT	100
NetScreen 5GT	100
NetScreen 25	500
NetScreen 50	1,000
NetScreen 204	4,000
NetScreen 208	4,000
NetScreen 500	20,000
NetScreen ISG 2000	20,000 base/30,000 adv
NetScreen 5200/5400	40,000

MIP Scenarios

This section covers some real-world scenarios where MIP is useful. Each scenario provides a figure showing a visualization of the general concept and Web UI example steps for configuring the scenario. It is assumed that you have the necessary basic settings pre-defined on your firewall such as security zone definitions on interfaces, IP address definitions on interfaces, route definitions, and so on.

Scenario 1

This example shows a typical MIP scenario. MIP is defined for you to access a Web server located on your private network from the Internet.

The following Web UI configuration example is illustrated in Figure 8.7:

1. To define the MIP on the Untrust interface (Ethernet3), go to **Network | Interface | Ethernet3 | MIP | New**.

2. Fill in the following:

   Mapped IP: 2.2.2.10

   Netmask: 255.255.255.255

   Host IP Address: 10.1.1.10

   Host Virtual Router Name: Trust-VR

3. Define the firewall rule to permit traffic to the MIP. Go to **Policies | FROM | Untrust | TO | Trust | New**.

4. Fill in the following:

   Source Address: Any

   Destination Address: MIP (2.2.2.10)

   Services: HTTP

   Action: Permit

Figure 8.7 NetScreen with MIP Definition to a Host on the RFC 1918 Network

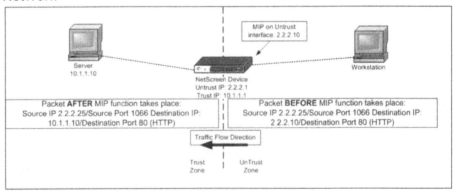

Scenario 2

The following example shows how a host defined within a MIP definition always uses the translated MIP address when originating traffic.

The configuration for this example is not very complicated. In fact, it can be as simple as defining an outgoing "permit all" rule. Note that there is no incoming rule (Untrust to Trust) because the 10.1.1.10 server is *initiating* the traffic. Because NetScreen is a stateful firewall, the response packet back is handled based on the session that was originally created from this server (see Figure 8.4, Step 2).

The following Web UI configuration example is illustrated Figure 8.8:

1. To define the MIP on the Untrust interface (Ethernet3) Go to **Network | Interface | Ethernet3 | MIP | New**.

2. Fill in the following:

   Mapped IP: 2.2.2.10

   Netmask: 255.255.255.255

   Host IP Address: 10.1.1.10

   Host Virtual Router Name: Trust-VR

3. Define the firewall rule to permit traffic to the MIP. Go to **Policies | FROM | Trust | TO | Untrust | New**.

4. Fill in the following:

   Source Address: Any

   Destination Address: Any

   Services: Any

   Action: Permit

Figure 8.8 MIP Outbound Traffic from Internal Host

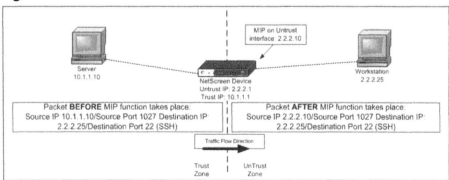

Again, you can always create a more granular rule for this scenario. Change the source address to 10.1.1.10/32 and the destination address to 2.2.2.25/32, and change the servers to SSH. Notice that there is no need to choose the MIP (2.2.2.10) for either the source or destination, because the translation occurs automatically (see Figure 8.4, Step 2).

Scenario 3

There may be certain scenarios where you have to create a route to reach the original host once a MIP translation occurs. Going back to NetScreen packet flow, a MIP translation occurs before a route lookup and a policy lookup. If the MIP translation to the original host route is not defined within the routing table(s), the packet either gets dropped or is sent to a default route, assuming one exists.

The following example scenario shows the need to create a route in order for the MIP translation to work. Figure 8.9 shows a diagram of MIP host 172.16.1.10 behind a different segment from the Trust side of the NetScreen firewall.

To reach the server on the 172.16.1.*x* network segment after MIP translation occurs, a static route is needed on the NetScreen device. This route would consist of the following:

Destination: 172.16.1.0/24

Interface: Trust (Ethernet1)

Gateway: 10.1.1.254

1. To define the static route, go to **Network | Routing | Routing Entries | Trust-VR | New**.

2. Fill in the following:

   Network Address/Network: 172.16.1.0/255.255.255.0

   Select Gateway:

   Select Interface: Ethernet1

   Gateway IP Address: 10.1.1.254

   Metric: 1

Figure 8.9 MIP Host Behind Another Network Segment

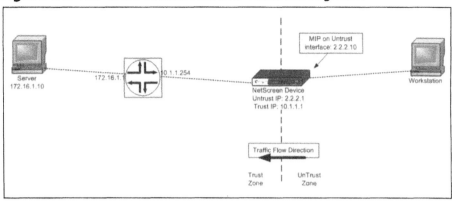

> **TIP**
>
> The MIP address needs to be on the same subnet as the interface's subnet, but cannot overlap with another IP(s) within the same subnet (i.e., you cannot use a MIP address from an IP address already defined within an existing dynamic IP [DP] pool). However, there are two advantages if the interface is set up on the Untrust zone:
>
> 1. On smaller appliances (HSC, 5XT, 5GT) the existing interface IP that is bonded to the Untrust zone as a MIP address can be used.
>
> 2. A MIP address on a subnet different than the Untrust interface is allowed. This requires that a route be defined to indicate that traffic destined for that MIP address subnet must go through the NetScreen Untrust interface.

Policy-based Source NAT

Policy-based source translations are accomplished by creating a firewall rule with source NAT enabled. By default, the outbound interfaces' or egress interfaces' IP address in the destination zone is used as the newly translated source address. PAT is also enabled by default. Figure 8.10 shows a host behind the NetScreen Trust zone (10.1.1.15) sending a packet out to the Internet via the NetScreen device that is acting as the default gateway. The NetScreen policy is to use source NAT for traffic sourcing from the Trust side to the Untrust side. The source NAT address will be the egress interface IP, in this case the Untrust Ethernet interface. The figure shows the packet before and after translation using the IP address of the egress interface on the Untrust side of 2.2.2.1.

Address objects must be defined before any firewall rule is created. Two address objects are created for this example, one for the Trust zone and one for the Untrust zone.

1. For the Trust zone address definition go to **Objects | Addresses | List | New**.

2. Fill in the following:

    Address Name: 10.1.1.15

    Select IP/Netmask: 10.1.1.15/32

    Zone: Trust

3. For the Untrust zone address definition go to **Objects | Addresses | List | New**.

4. Fill in the following:

    Address Name: 2.2.2.25

    Select IP/Netmask: 2.2.2.25/32

    Zone: Untrust

4   Create the firewall rule to perform the Source NAT using the egress interface. Go to **Policies | FROM | Trust | TO | Untrust | New**.

5. Fill in the following:

    Source Address: 10.1.1.15

    Destination Address: 2.2.2.25

    Services: SSH

    Action: Permit

    Select: Advance

6. Select **Source Translation | None (Use Egress Interface IP)**.

Figure 8.10 Example of Policy-based Source NAT

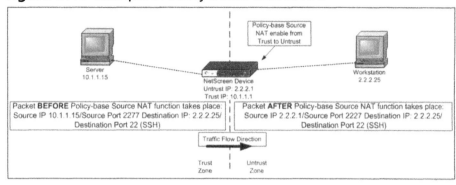

DIP

There are several other methods that can be used to translate the source address via the policy. These methods are primarily due to the functionality of dynamic IP pool definitions (DIP pool). DIP pool definitions are created on interfaces, which can be a physical interface, a sub-interface, a VPN tunnel interface, or a loop-back interface. A DIP can be either a host range definition or a pool of address definitions. If it is a pool of address definitions, the pool must be in consecutive order. Therefore, it is important to note that no other IP(s) within that pool can be used anywhere else (e.g., a MIP definition).

DIP pool definition also offers the option to disable or enable PAT . Since the DIP pool is only used in source NAT scenarios, PAT on the source ports can be utilized to increase the amount of usage for each address within the pool.

Figure 8.11 Policy-based Source NAT Using a DIP Pool

Packet **BEFORE** Policy-base Source NAT function takes place:
Source IP 10.1.1.10/Source Port 3338 Destination IP: 2.2.2.50/
Destination Port 80 (HTTP)

Packet **AFTER** Policy-base Source NAT function takes place:
Source IP 2.2.2.2/Source Port 3338 Destination IP: 2.2.2.50/
Destination Port 80 (HTTP)

Policy-base Source NAT from Trust to Untrust
using DIP Pool with Fix ports (PAT disable)
DIP Pool ID 4: 2.2.2.2 to 2.2.2.10

Workstation
10.1.1.10

Workstation
10.1.1.11

NetScreen Device
Untrust IP: 2.2.2.1
Trust IP: 10.1.1.1

Web Server
2.2.2.50

Packet **BEFORE** Policy-base Source NAT function takes place:
Source IP 10.1.1.11/Source Port 2227 Destination IP: 2.2.2.50/
Destination Port 80 (HTTP)

Packet **AFTER** Policy-base Source NAT function takes place:
Source IP 2.2.2.3/Source Port 2227 Destination IP: 2.2.2.50/
Destination Port 80 (HTTP)

Traffic Flow Direction

Trust
Zone

Untrust
Zone

The following Web UI configuration example shows policy-based source NAT using a DIP pool with PAT disabled and traffic flow from Trust to Untrust. Address objects must be defined before a firewall can be created.

1. For the Trust zone address definition, go to **Objects | Addresses | List | New**.

2. Fill in the following:

   Address Name: 10.1.1.0/24

   Select IP/Netmask: 10.1.1.0/24

   Zone: Trust

3. For the Untrust zone address definition, go to **Objects | Addresses | List | New**.

   4. Fill in the following:

   Address Name: 2.2.2.50

   Select IP/Netmask: 2.2.2.50/32

   Zone: Untrust

5. Create the DIP pool on the egress interface, which in this example is the Untrust (Ethernet3) interface. Go to **Network | Interfaces | Untrust | DIP | New**.

6. Fill in the following:

   ID: 4

   Select IP Address Range: 2.2.2.2 ~ 2.2.2.10

   Uncheck Port Translation

   Select: "In the same subnet as the interface IP or its secondary IPs."

7. Create the firewall rule to perform the Source NAT from a DIP pool. Go to **Policies | FROM | Trust | TO | Untrust | New**.

8. Fill in the following:

   Source Address: 10.1.1.0/24

   Destination Address: 2.2.2.50

   Services: HTTP

   Action: Permit

9. Select **Advance | NAT | Source Translation | DIP ON | 4(2.2.2.2-2.2.2.10)/fix-port**.

A DIP pool can also contain one IP range. For example, when defining the single IP address 2.2.2.2 within a DIP pool, the IP address range would be 2.2.2.2 ~ 2.2.2.2. This is an alternative way of using a different IP address than what is currently defined on the egress interface. It is recommended that you enable PAT within the DIP pool definition when creating for a one IP range.

> **NOTE**
>
> When PAT is disabled in a DIP pool, the IP pool assignment remains the same for the host for all concurrent sessions. When PAT is enabled, the IP pool assignments rotate in a round-robin fashion for each new session.

Sticky DIP

Sticky DIP provides the ability for the translated host to maintain its IP pool assignment. By default, the IP addresses within the DIP pool are rotated in a round-robin fashion for each new session. For example, when there exist a DIP pool of 2.2.2.2 to 2.2.2.10, the host (10.1.1.10) utilizing the DIP pool will have a new NAT IP pool assignment starting at 2.2.2.10 for each new session. Figure 8.11 illustrates the default scenario without Sticky DIP enabled and Figure 8.12 shows the scenario with Sticky DIP enabled. Note that the Sticky DIP setting is a command line only setting.

Figure 8.12 Policy-based Source NAT DIP Pool Usages without Sticky DIP

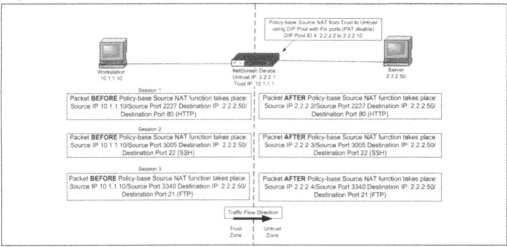

The example in Figure 8.12 shows that the NetScreen device assigns a different IP address from the pool for each new session originated from workstation 10.1.1.10. This pool assignment is done via round-robin fashion.

Figure 8.13 Policy-based Source NAT DIP Pool Usage with Sticky DIP

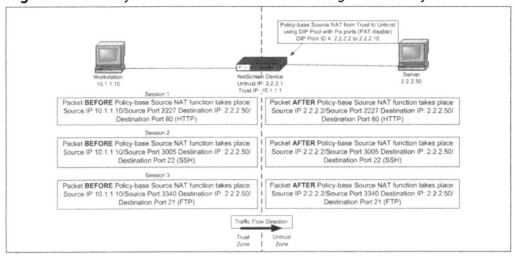

The example in Figure 8.13 shows the same DIP pool usage as shown in Figure 8.12, but with the Sticky DIP feature enabled. The NetScreen device now maintains the same IP address (2.2.2.2) assignment for all sessions generated from 10.1.1.10.

As of this writing, enabling Sticky DIP must be done via the Command Line Interface (CLI). The command to enable Sticky DIP is:

```
set dip sticky
```

DIP Shift

DIP Shift ensures that the translated IP pool assignment ranges are one-to-one mapping with the original host IP ranges requesting the translation. The advantage of this feature is that it provides a predictable translation. For example, if communication takes place to a remote end with another firewall, the administrator can define a more granular source IP access rather than allow a range of addresses to come in. The following example shows a range of hosts from 10.1.1.10 to 10.1.1.12 using a DIP Shift definition to map its one-to-one mapping translations. The DIP shift pool will always be assigned in order from the first mapping original IP. Figure 8.14 shows the one-to-one mapping translation for all traffic generated from the original host IP.

Figure 8.14 Policy-based Source NAT using DIP Shift

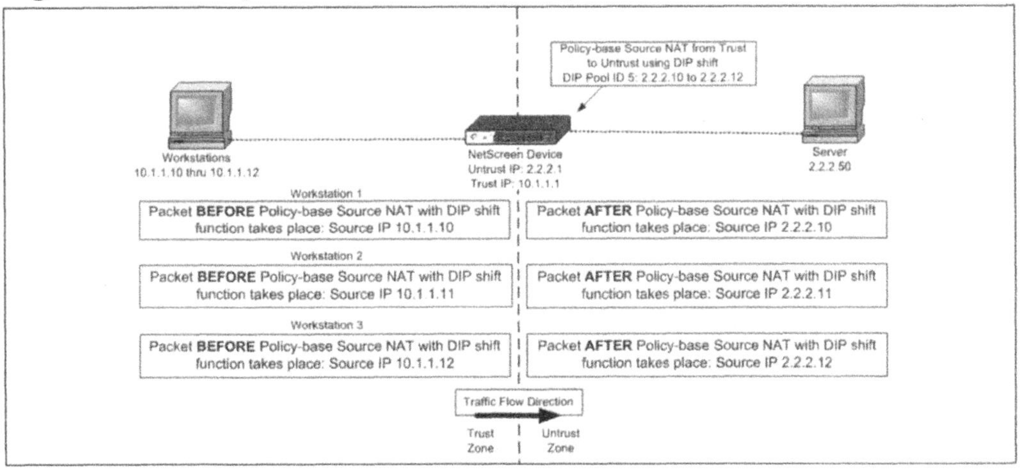

1. Create the DIP pool on the egress interface as defined in Figure 8.14. Go to **Network | Interfaces | Untrust |DIP | New**.

2. Fill in the following:

   ID: 5

   Select IP Shift:

   From: 10.1.1.10

   To: 2.2.2.10 ~ 2.2.2.12

3. Select the same subnet as the interface IP or its secondary IP.

4. Create the firewall rule to perform the Source NAT from the DIP Shift pool defined in the previous step. Go to **Policies | FROM | Trust | TO | Untrust | New**.

5. Fill in the following:

   Source Address: 10.1.1.0/24

   Destination Address: 2.2.2.50

   Services: Any

   Action: Permit

6. Select **Advance | NAT | Source Translation | DIP ON | 5(2.2.2.10-2.2.2.12)/ip-shift**.

NOTE

When DIP Shift is configured, there is no option for PAT.

Destination NAT

The following section illustrates how the NetScreen firewall solution handles destination address translations.

VIP

A VIP provides a one-to-many mapping scenario, whereas a MIP provides a one-to-one mapping. The one-to-many mappings a VIP performs are more related to a combination of destination NAPTs.

VIP definitions are placed into the global zone no matter which interface/security zone it was originally defined in. Once a VIP is defined, a firewall rule must be set up to allow for traffic destined for the MIP address. Within the firewall rule creation, the VIP can be selected from a global zone or the zone that the VIP address was originally defined in (see Figure 8.15).

Figure 8.15 VIP Example

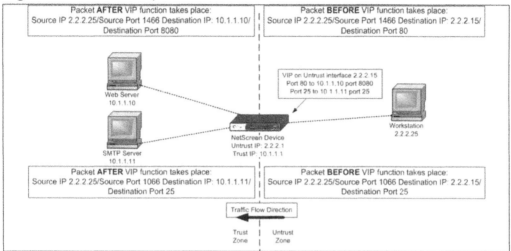

1. To define the VIP go to **Network | Interfaces | Ethernet3 | VIP**.

2. Select **Virtual IP Address**, enter **2.2.2.15**, and click on **Add**.

3. Add the VIP mapping for host 10.1.1.10 by selecting **New VIP Services** on the top left portion of the Web UI.

4. Fill in the following:

   Virtual IP: 2.2.2.15

   Virtual Port: 80

   Map to Service: 8080

   Map to IP: 10.1.1.10

   Server Auto Detection: Enable

5. Add the VIP mapping for host 10.1.1.11 by selecting **New VIP Service**.

6. Fill in the following:

   Virtual IP: 2.2.2.15

   Virtual Port: 25

   Map to Service: 25

   Map to IP: 10.1.1.11

   Server Auto Detection: Enable

7. Define the firewall rule to permit traffic to the VIP definitions. Go to **Policies** | **FROM** | **Untrust** | **TO** | **Trust** | **New**.

8. Fill in the following:

    Source Address: Any

    Destination Address: VIP::1

    Services: Select **Multiple** and move HTTP, SMTP to **Selected Members**

    Action: Permit

TIPS

1. VIP only works on interfaces bonded to the Untrust zone.
2. The VIP address has to be on the same subnet as the Ethernet interface where the VIP is defined.
3. Custom ports can be created for VIP mappings.
4. You can use the existing IP assignment on the Ethernet interface. During your VIP creation select **Same as the Untrusted interface IP address**. This feature is only limited to the HSC, 5XT, 5GT, 25, and 50 models.

Each NetScreen platform can support a very limited capacity of VIP(s).

Policy-based Destination NAT

Policy-based destination NAT is also a subset setting within a firewall rule. Just like the source-based NAT configuration, there is a separate definition in place to define a destination NAT. Unlike source NAT, there are no requirements to predefine settings on the interfaces. For example, you do not need to create a DIP pool before actually creating a destination NAT firewall rule. The address schemes for the newly translated destination are all defined within the firewall rule. Besides destination NAT, a destination PAT can also be defined. The options available to perform destination NAT are as follows:

■ Destination NAT to another IP

■ Destination NAT to another IP with PAT to a different port

■ Destination NAT to an IP range

> **NOTE**
>
> When using destination NAT, it is important to know the NetScreen packet flow. Route lookup on the NetScreen device occurs *before* and *after* policy lookup. Policy lookup also entails policy-based NAT functions. Therefore, there might be a need to create a route *before* or *after* a policy-based NAT function takes place.

Destination NAT Scenarios

The following are some possible scenarios that destination NAT can accomplish.

One-to-One Mapping

A one-to-one mapping scenario illustrates a translation from one host to another host. One-to-one mapping is equivalent to a static NAT or the MIP feature.

The following is a Web UI configuration example for a one-to-one mapping as defined in Figure 8.16.

1. Create the firewall rule to perform the destination NAT. Go to **Policies | FROM | Trust | TO | Untrust | New**.

2. Fill in the following:

   Source Address: 2.2.2.25

   Destination Address: 2.2.2.10

   Services: HTTP

   Action: Permit

3. Select **Advance | NAT | Destination Translation | Translate to IP' | 10.1.1.10**.

Figure 8.16 One-to-one Policy-based Destination NAT

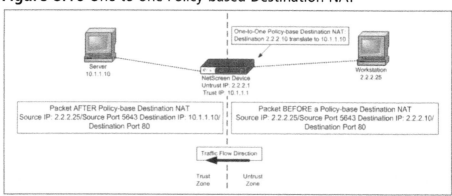

Many-to-one Mapping

A many-to-one mapping scenario illustrates that traffic sent to several different destination can be translated to a single host.

The following Web UI configuration example for a many-to-one mapping is defined in Figure 8.17.

1. Create the address objects of the destination hosts and put them into an address group to be used in the policy-based rule definition. For this example, two address host objects (2.2.2.10/32 and 2.2.2.11/32) are created within the Untrust zone.

2. To create address objects go to **Objects | Addresses | List | New**. (Perform this function twice for each host address.)

3. For 2.2.2.10, fill in the following:

   Address Name: 2.2.2.10/32

   Select IP/Netmask: 2.2.2.10/32

   Zone: Untrust

4. For 2.2.2.11, fill in the following:

   Address Name: 2.2.2.11/32

   Select IP/Netmask: 2.2.2.11/32

   Zone: Untrust

5. Move the two host address objects into an address group. To create an address group go to **Objects | Addresses | Groups | New**.

6. Fill in the following for the address group:

Group Name: Web_Servers

Move **2.2.2.10/32** and **2.2.2.11/32** over to **Group Members**.

7. Create the policy-based NAT rule to perform the many-to-one destination NAT. Go to **Policies | FROM | Trust | TO | Untrust | New**.

8. Fill in the following:

   Source Address: 2.2.2.25

   Destination Address: Web_Servers

   Services: HTTP

   Action: Permit

9. Select **Advance | NAT | Destination Translation | Translate to IP | 10.1.1.10**.

Figure 8.17 Many-to-one Policy-based Destination NAT

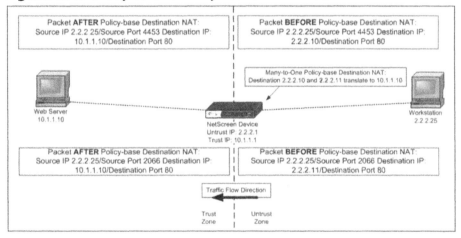

Many-to-Many Mapping

The many-to-many mapping scenario illustrates that traffic sent to several different destinations can be translated to several other destinations.

The following Web UI configuration example is defined in Figure 8.18.

1. Create the address objects of the destination hosts and put them into an address group to be used in the policy-based destination rule definition. For this example, three address host objects (2.2.2.10/32, 2.2.2.11/32, and 2.2.2.12/32) must be created within the Untrust zone.

2. To create address objects go to **Objects** | **Addresses** | **List** | **New**. (Perform this function twice for each host address.)

3. For 2.2.2.10, fill in the following:

   Address Name: 2.2.2.10/32

   Select IP/Netmask: 2.2.2.10/32

   Zone: Untrust

4. For 2.2.2.11, fill in the following:

   Address Name: 2.2.2.11/32

   Select IP/Netmask: 2.2.2.11/32

   Zone: Untrust

5n For 2.2.2.12, fill in the following:

   Address Name: 2.2.2.12/32

   Select IP/Netmask: 2.2.2.12/32

   Zone: Untrust

6. Move the two host address objects into an address group. To create an address group go to **Objects** | **Addresses** | **Groups** | **New**.

7. Fill in the following:

   Group Name: Servers

8. Move **2.2.2.10/32, 2.2.2.11/32, 2.2.2.12/32** to **Group Members**.

9. Create the policy-based NAT rule to perform the many-to-many destination NAT. Go to **Policies** | **FROM** | **Trust** | **TO** | **Untrust** | **New**.

10. Fill in the following:

    Source Address: 2.2.2.50

    Destination Address: Servers

    Services: Any

    Action: Permit

11. Select **Advance** | **NAT** | **Destination Translation** | **Translate to IP Range** | **10.1.1.10 – 10.1.1.12**.

Figure 8.18 Many-to-many Policy-based Destination NAT

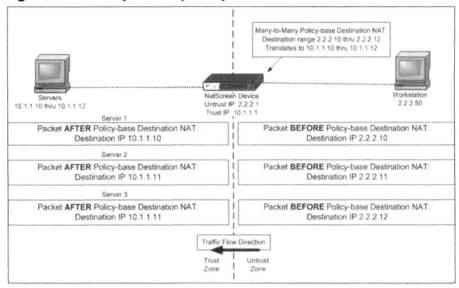

Destination PAT Scenario

Destination PAT provides an alternative destination port from what the original packet is sent to. It can also provide an extra security measure for hiding the original destination port.

The following Web UI configuration example is defined in Figure 8.19.

1. Create the firewall rule to perform the destination NAPT. Go to **Policies | FROM | Trust | TO | Untrust | New**.

2. Fill in the following:

   Source Address: 2.2.2.25

   Destination Address: 2.2.2.10

   Services: HTTP

   Action: Permit

3. Select **Advance | NAT | Destination Translation | Translate to IP | 10.1.1.10 | Map to Port | 8080**.

Figure 8.19 One-to-one Policy-based Destination NAT with
Destination PAT

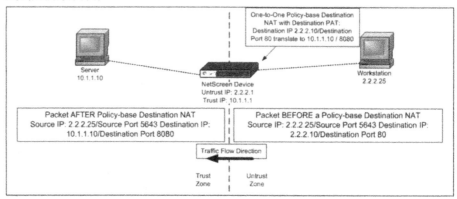

Source and Destination NAT Combined

Source and destination address translation can be combined together in a single
firewall rule. The following example shows a source and destination NAT.

The following Web UI configuration example is defined in Figure 8.20.

1. Create the firewall rule to perform the source and destination NAT. Go
   to **Policies | FROM | Trust | TO | Untrust | New**.

2. Fill in the following:

   Source Address: 2.2.2.25

   Destination Address: 2.2.2.10

   Services: HTTP

   Action: Permit

3. Select **Advance | NAT | Source Translation | DIP ON | None
   (Use Egress Interface IP) | Destination Translation | Translate
   to IP | 10.1.1.10**.

Figure 8.20 Policy-based Source and Destination NAT

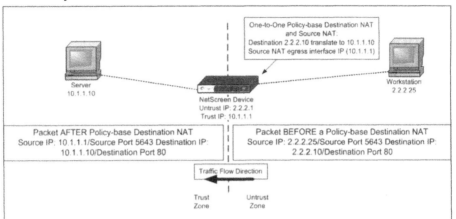

Summary

NAT has always been an essential part of network design. Whether for security reasons or to conserve IP addresses, it is a useful method. NAT provides the ability to hide the originating IP address thus providing an extra layer of security to protect the host's identity. NAT provides a short-term solution to the depleting IP v.4 addresses on the Internet. NAT provides the ability to utilize one IP for several thousand devices thus conserving non–RFC 1918 IP addresses. With the cost of NAT devices going down each year and the increase in Internet usage, it is not surprising that NAT is a widely used feature.

The NAPT features of the Juniper NetScreen products are covered in detail with example scenarios and their respective configurations steps.

One of the original methods used for NAT was the interface-based NAT mode, which is enabled by default on the Ethernet interface bonded to the Trust security zone. It is recommended that the interface-based NAT mode setting be disabled and set to Route mode all the time, thus using policy-based NAT instead. Policy-based NAT provides a more efficient and scalable method than interface-based NAT. As seen with MIP and VIP, there are capacity limitations that restrict the use of these NAPT methods. Policy-based translation can perform the same functions as a MIP or a VIP and also has a much larger capacity support.

It is good to note the tips provided throughout this chapter. The goal of these tips is to provide an understanding of the limitations and capabilities of the Juniper NetScreen firewall address translation features. Knowing how the firewall handles a packet is a key essential for troubleshooting NAT issues.

Solutions Fast Track

Purpose of Address Translation

- ☑ Advantages of address translation:
  - ☑ Conserves IP addresses providing the ability to use non-routable addresses from the RFC 1918 space.
  - ☑ Provides a hidden identity for host(s).
  - ☑ Addresses overlapping subnets.
  - ☑ Maintains a cohesive network.
- ☑ Disadvantages of address translation:
  - ☑ Address translation breaks IPSec traffic – use NAT Traversal as a workaround.
  - ☑ Address translation breaks applications that require dynamic port allocation – most firewall vendors have ALG, which addresses this issue.
  - ☑ Compatibility with legacy-based applications.

NetScreen Packet Flow

- ☑ Understanding how NetScreen handle packets is very important.
- ☑ MIP and VIP translation occurs before a route and policy lookup.
- ☑ A route lookup occurs *before* and *after* a policy-based NAT function.

Source NAT

- ☑ Prior to ScreenOS 5.0 communication, translating from a host on the Untrust zone to a host on the Trust zone with the interface set for NAT was not possible unless a MIP or VIP was defined. With current ScreenOS releases this is possible as long as there is a firewall rule in place to allow it.
- ☑ Interface-base NAT restrictions:
  - ☑ The egress interface *has* to be bonded to the Untrust zone.

☑ When a user-defined zone is bonded to the ingress interface with NAT enabled, that user-defined security zone must be defined on a different virtual router than the Untrust zone.

☑ Interface-based NAT will not work between the Trust zone and a user-defined zone.

☑ Interface NAT does not work on interfaces bonded to the Untrust zone even though it can be enabled.

☑ There are limited amounts of MIP that can be created. To address the scalability of one-to-one mapping use Policy-based NAT.

☑ The MIP address needs to be on the same subnet as the interface's subnet *but* cannot overlap with another IP(s) within the same subnet (i.e., you cannot use a MIP address from an IP address already defined within an existing DIP pool). However, there are two advantages if the interface is setup on the Untrust zone:

☑ On the smaller appliances (HSC, 5XT, 5GT) the existing interface IP that is bonded to the Untrust zone as a MIP address can be used.

☑ A MIP address on a different subnet than the Untrust interface is allowed. This requires that a route is defined to indicate that traffic destined for that MIP address subnet must go through the NetScreen Untrust interface.

☑ When PAT is disabled in a DIP pool, the IP pool assignment remains the same for the host for all concurrent sessions. When PAT is enabled, the IP pool assignments rotate in a round-robin fashion for each new session.

☑ There are no options for PAT in a DIP Shift configuration.

Destination NAT

☑ VIP restrictions:

☑ VIP only works on interfaces bonded to the Untrust zone.

☑ The VIP address has to be on the same subnet as the Ethernet interface where the VIP is defined.

☑ Custom ports can be created for VIP mappings.

☑ The existing IP assignment on the Ethernet interface can be used. During VIP creation select **Same as the Untrusted interface IP address**. This feature is limited to only the HSC, 5XT, 5GT, 25, and 50 models.

☑ When using policy-based destination NAT it is important to understand the NetScreen packet flow, specifically that a route lookup is performed *before* and *after* a policy-based destination NAT.

☑ PAT is not used on the source port during a policy-based destination NAT. PAT can be used for the destination.

Links to Sites

- NAT RFC 1631: www.faqs.org/rfcs/rfc1631.html
- NAPT RFC 3022: www.faqs.org/rfcs/rfc3022.html

Frequently Asked Questions

The following Frequently Asked Questions, answered by the authors of this book, are designed to both measure your understanding of the concepts presented in this chapter and to assist you with real-life implementation of these concepts. To have your questions about this chapter answered by the author, browse to **www.syngress.com/solutions** and click on the **"Ask the Author"** form. You will also gain access to thousands of other FAQs at ITFAQnet.com.

Q: What are the advantages with using NAT?

A: NAT conserves IP addresses, provides a hidden identity for host(s), has the ability to use non-routable addresses from the RFC 1918 space, addresses overlapping subnets, and maintains a cohesive network.

Q: What is the difference between a MIP and a VIP?

A: MIP provides a one-to-one static NAT function whereas VIP provides a one-to-many NAT function.

Q: What are the advantages of using policy-based NAT over interface-based NAT?

A: The number one reason to choose policy-based NAT over interface-based NAT is the scalability. With interface-based NAT you are limited to only performing address translation in one flow direction, only the source address can be translated, you cannot turn off PAT, and it requires all ingress traffic to be translated. With policy-based NAT you can uniquely define address translation on a per-firewall rule definition giving you the ability to control address translation flows and to perform source and/or destination translation, and the ability to turn PAT on/off.

Q: Can interface-based NAT and policy-based NAT configuration co-exist?

A: Yes. Interface-based NAT and policy-based NAT can co-exist together. It is recommended that interface-based NAT be disabled (set to Route mode) and to utilize policy-based NAT for your address translation needs.

Q: What is a DIP?

A: A DIP is used for policy-based source NAT functionality. A DIP can consist of one to many IP ranges.

Q: MIP and VIP methods scale better then policy-based NAT. True or False?

A: False. There are software-set limitations for MIP and VIP on all NetScreen security appliance and system products. This is the same with policy-based NAT, but these limitations far exceed the capacity for MIP and VIP. Instead, the limitation is based on the number of firewall policies that can be created, which usually ranges from to 50 to 40,000.

Chapter 9

Transparent Mode

Solutions in this Chapter:

- Interface Modes
- Understanding How Transparent Mode Works
- Configuring a Device to Use Transparent Mode
- Transparent Mode Deployment Options

☑ Summary

☑ Solutions Fast Track

☑ Frequently Asked Questions

Introduction

As some point in their careers, network administrators will need to reassess their current network deployments and determine if they are designed to meet the needs of their growing companies. Perhaps, when the company was a small startup, it was convenient to have the database, the Web server, and the user community on the same network. But as a company grows and services are added, and additional resources continually exposed to various parts of the internal and external infrastructure, the administrator will probably wonder if this environment is really benefiting the company or just creating unnecessary risk to corporate information assets. Once administrators make this decision, they are confronted with the possibility of added complexity as well as the cost of making the recommended changes.

One solution that can help address these possible issues is the *transparent* mode capability of a NetScreen firewall. Transparent mode provides the capability to convert a NetScreen firewall from a layer 3 device to a layer 2 device. Rather than requiring the administrator to redesign the entire network for physical and network changes to servers and devices, he or she has the option to implement a flexible alternative that can help to simplify deployment efforts and reduce the costs.

Interface Modes

Before we talk about transparent mode, let's quickly review the other interface modes on a NetScreen firewall. The interfaces on a NetScreen firewall can operate in three different modes: NAT (Network Address Translation), route, and transparent. The following is a review of NAT and route modes.

NAT Mode

As described in Chapter 8, NAT can be configured at the interface or through policy. When an interface is placed in NAT mode, the NetScreen device replaces the private, unroutable IP (Internet Protocol) address of the host with the IP address of the interface in the *untrust* zone. Additionally, the source port number is replaced by a random port generated on the firewall. By doing so, NAT provides an additional layer of security by never directly exposing a resource on a trusted zone to one in an untrusted zone.

Figure 9.1 below shows an example of NAT mode. In this example, the packet originating from 10.10.10.150 is translated to the Untrust IP address of

1.1.1.99. All Internet traffic will appear as if it is coming from the translated address.

Figure 9.1 Traffic from Private IP to Internet

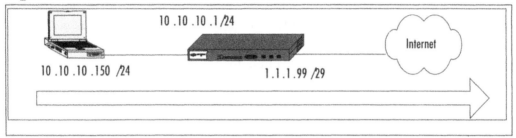

Route Mode

With route mode, the device passes traffic from one zone to another without performing NAT translation. This means that the source IP address and port remains unchanged as a packet passes through one zone to another, as shown in Figure 9.2. In this example, the traffic passing from the trust zone to the DMZ (de-militarized zone) is not translated and the DMZ servers can see the IP address 10.10.10.150 as the source.

Figure 9.2 Traffic from Trust Zone to DMZ Zone

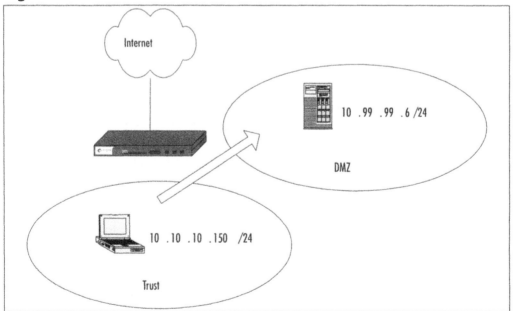

Understanding How Transparent Mode Works

With transparent mode, the NetScreen firewall is converted from a layer 3 device to one that operates at layer 2, essentially becoming a layer 2 bridge. By doing so, the device can be deployed into existing infrastructures without requiring the readdressing that would be required for a routed solution. The IP addresses of the physical interfaces are set to 0.0.0.0/0 and truly make the deployment invisible to the user. Figure 9.3 provides an example for segmenting internal resources using transparent mode.

Figure 9.3 NetScreen Device in Transparent Mode

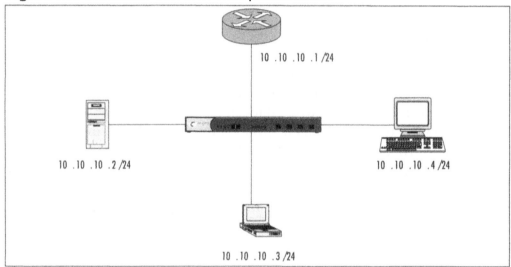

In this example, notice that all of the networked devices are part of the same subnet. By converting the device to transparent mode, an existing subnet can be segmented, providing the ability to secure resources with firewall policy. If the firewall was to remain in layer 3 mode, it would have to route the traffic, which would require subnet and network changes. Transparent mode is the easiest method to use since it requires the fewest infrastructure changes.

How to Transparent Mode Works

Transparent mode converts the firewall device from its default layer 3 route mode to what is essentially a layer 2 bridge. A NetScreen firewall comes predefined with three layer 2 zones, which are applied to the physical interfaces. In addition, there is a single VLAN (virtual local area network) zone that hosts a virtual interface for management and VPN (virtual private network) termination. Once all interfaces have been converted to the layer 2 zones, the device is considered to be in transparent mode. It is important to note that at this time, a NetScreen device cannot operate in a mixed configuration of transparent and route modes.

Layer 2 Zones

The three pre-defined zones included with a NetScreen firewall are V1-Trust, V1-Untrust, and V1-DMZ, and are all part of the same broadcast domain. Also, interfaces assigned to these zones must be a part of the same subnet. It is these zones that are used when defining policy between network resources.

VLAN Zone

A VLAN zone is a predefined zone that hosts the virtual interface named VLAN1. Like the layer 2 zones, the VLAN1 interface is part of the same subnet, but unlike the layer 2 zones, it can be assigned an address for VPN tunnel termination as well as another IP address for management. In addition, the VLAN zone can be used in policy to protect the interface.

Broadcast Methods

It is important to understand how a NetScreen firewall forwards traffic when it is acting as a layer 2 bridge. Without policy, no traffic can pass through the device. Once a policy is applied, it permits traffic to flow based on the permitted services as well as allowing ARP (address resolution protocol) and non-IP-based layer 2 traffic, such as spanning tree. However, IP-based layer 2 traffic and IPSEC are not permitted by default. Managing these services will be discussed later.

When a network host does not know the MAC (media access control) address associated with a particular IP, the host will find the MAC by performing an ARP query. The requesting host will flood all networked devices with the ARP query. The host that owns the MAC address will respond to the requestor with an ARP reply; all other network hosts will drop the packet. Once the requestor receives the reply, it then adds that information to its ARP cache. NetScreen firewalls will also learn which interface is associated with the MAC address based on which interface receives the ARP reply. NetScreen firewalls can use one of two methods for building its ARP table:

- **Flood Method** When a NetScreen device receives an Ethernet frame with a destination MAC address that is not in the MAC table, the device will flood the packet out all interfaces, similar to the way most switches work. When a response is found, the NetScreen device learns which interface is attached to the responding MAC address and adds the MAC and interface to its forwarding table.

- **ARP/Traceroute** When a NetScreen device receives an Ethernet frame with a MAC address that is not in the MAC table, the device performs a series of actions. First, it records the MAC in the initial packet and then drops that packet. Next, the NetScreen device generates two packets, one for an ARP query and another for a traceroute. The ARP query replaces the source MAC address from the initial packet and instead uses the MAC address of the VLAN1 interface. The traceroute packet is an ICMP echo request with a Time To Live (TTL) of 1. The two generated packets are then flooded out to all interfaces except for the one that received the initial packet. If the ARP reply is found on a device in the same subnet, the NetScreen device learns that MAC and forwards traffic to the appropriate interface. If the IP address of the packet exists in a different subnet, the traceroute packet returns with the IP address and MAC of the router that the packet must pass through. The NetScreen device then learns the router's MAC and forwards traffic accordingly.

    ARP/traceroute is considered the most secure broadcast method since it does not flood the initial packet out on all interfaces; rather, the NetScreen device floods the ARP queries and traceroute packets. It should also be noted that the traceroute packet is optional. If it is not used, then the NetScreen will only be able to learn the destination MAC if it is in the same subnet as the received packet. The traceroute option is turned on by default.

Configuring a Device to Use Transparent Mode

By default, a NetScreen firewall is configured as a layer 3 device. Switching to layer 2 is a simple matter of moving the interfaces into the layer 2 zones. However, before the interfaces are moved, it is important to configure the VLAN1 interface. This will ensure that you will be able to manage the device across the network once it has been converted.

VLAN1 Interface

As mentioned, all NetScreen devices have a VLAN1 interface. Using the **get int** command will show a list of all physical and virtual interfaces, including the VLAN1 interface (see Figure 9.4).

Figure 9.4 Interfaces on a NetScreen 204

```
ns204- get int

A - Active, I - Inactive, U - Up, D - Down, R - Ready

Interfaces in vsys Root:
Name       IP Address         Zone       MAC            VLAN State VSD
eth1       192.168.1.1/24      Trust      0010.db32.3500  -    D    -
eth2       0.0.0.0/0           DMZ        0010.db32.3505  -    D    -
eth3       0.0.0.0/0           Untrust    0010.db32.3506  -    D    -
eth4       0.0.0.0/0           HA         0010.db32.3507  -    D    -
vlan1      0.0.0.0/0           VLAN       0010.db32.3501  1    D    -
```

Figure 9.4 displays the default configuration of a NetScreen 204 firewall. As shown, the VLAN1 interface is listed along with its MAC address. Configuring an IP address on VLAN1 is the same as for any other interface. If you are using the command line, enter **set int vlan1 ip 192.168.0.44/24**. If you are using the WebUI, access **Network | Interfaces | VLAN1**, then enter the IP address. Figure 9.5 displays the available VLAN1 options from the WebUI.

Figure 9.5 WebUI Configuration for VLAN1 Interface

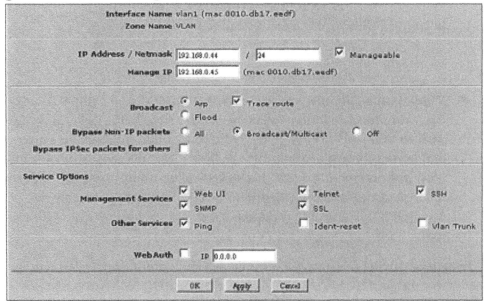

The following discusses the options that are unique to the VLAN1 interface:

- **Broadcast** as previously discussed, this is where the administrator must decide what broadcast method is going to be used. The default method is Flood.

    - From the CLI:

```
set int vlan1 broadcast arp
unset int vlan1 broadcast arp trace-route
set int vlan1 broadcast flood
save
```

- **Bypass Non-IP packets** *All* will permit all non-IP traffic, like IPX, to pass while in transparent mode. *Broadcast/Multicast* will only allow broadcast and multicast to pass, while *off* disables this feature altogether. By default, *Broadcast/Multicast* is selected.

    - CLI:

```
set int vlan1 bypass-non-ip
set int vlan1 bypass-non-ip-all
save
```

- **Bypass IPSec packet for others** By enabling this option, the NetScreen device will allow IPSEC traffic to pass. This would allow a VPN device sitting behind the NetScreen to terminate the traffic.

    - CLI:

```
set int vlan1 bypass-others-ipsec
save
```

- **Vlan Trunk** All other service options are the same as a physical interface, with the exception of Vlan Trunk. By default, if a packet is received with an 802.1q VLAN tag, the NetScreen will drop the traffic. This option must be enabled in order to allow the traffic to pass on a trunk port. It is important to note that a NetScreen cannot currently perform 802.1q tagging while in transparent mode, the tagging can only be passed. If 802.1q tagging is required, the device must be deployed in route mode.

By default, the VLAN1 interface is only accessibly from the V1-Trust zone. In order to manage the device from a zone other than the V1-Trust, management must be enabled on the layer 2 interface of that zone. This can only be accomplished from the command line.

- CLI:

```
set int ip V1-Untrust manage
save
```

Converting an Interface to Transparent Mode

Once the VLAN1 interface is configured, the device is ready to be deployed in transparent mode. This is done by moving all interfaces from layer 3 zones to the layer 2 zones. Before an interface can be moved to the new zone, the IP address on the interface needs to be set to 0.0.0.0/0. Once completed, the interface can then be moved to the layer 2 zone. This will have to be completed for all interfaces that will participate in the subnet. This excludes interfaces dedicated for high availability.

- From the WebUI:

    Go to **Network | Interfaces | ethernet1**

    Select **Zone Name** and enter **V1-Trust**

    In the **IP Address/Netmask** option, fill in **0.0.0.0/0**

    Go to **Manage IP** and fill in **<Blank>**

- From the CLI:

```
unset int eth1ip
set int eth1 zone V1-Trust
save
```

Once all participating interfaces are moved to the layer 2 zones, confirm the device is in transparent mode by entering **get sys** from the command line. A sample output of this command is shown in Figure 9.6.

Figure 9.6 System Information Indicating a NetScreen 204 is in Transparent Mode

```
ns204-> get sys
Product Name  NS204
Serial Number  0029012003000173  Control Number  00000000
Hardware Version  0110(0)-(11)  FPGA checksum  00000000  VLAN1 IP (192.168.0.44)
Software Version  5.0.0r8.0  Type  Firewall+VPN
Base Mac  0010.db32.3500
File Name  ns200.5.0.0r8.0  Checksum  1001eb68


Date 10/17/2004 10:20:41  Daylight Saving Time enabled
The Network Time Protocol is Disabled
Up 0 hours 8 minutes 15 seconds Since 17 Oct 2004 10:12:26
Total Device Resets  0

System in transparent mode.

Use interface IP  Config Port  80
User Name  netscreen
```

From the WebUI, transparent mode can be confirmed by verifying participating interfaces are in layer 2 zones (Figure 9.7)

Figure 9.7 Interface Screen from WebUI Indicating the Interfaces are in Layer 2

Name	IP/Netmask	Zone	Type	Link	Configure
ethernet1	0.0.0.0/0	V1-Trust	Layer2	up	Edit
ethernet2	0.0.0.0/0	V1-DMZ	Layer2	down	Edit
ethernet3	0.0.0.0/0	V1-Untrust	Layer2	down	Edit
ethernet4	0.0.0.0/0	HA	Layer3	down	Edit
vlan1	192.168.0.44/24	VLAN	Layer3	up	Edit

Creating a Custom Layer 2 Zone and Network Object

Creating a custom Layer 2 zone is just like creating a custom layer 3 zone. When naming the zone, the name must be prefaced with **L2-**.

- From the WebUI:

    Go to **Network | Zones | Press New**

    Select **Zone Name** and fill in **L2-Test**

    Go to **Zone Type** ad fill in **Select Layer 2**

- From the CLI:

```
set zone name L2-Test L2 1
save
```

- From the WebUI:

    Go to **Objects | Addresses | List | Select Zone** and press **New**

    In the **Address Name** option, fill in **TestObject**

    Got to **IP/Netmask** and type **10.10.10.40/24**

    Select **Zone**, and fill in **L2-Test**

- From the CLI:

```
set address L2-Test TestObject 10.10.10.40/24
save
```

Transparent Mode Deployment Options

Transparent mode provides a great deal of flexibility by providing additional ways to protect the network with a firewall. The following are examples of several types of deployments along with the steps for configuration.

Network Segmentation

In this first example, let's refer to the example used in the beginning of the chapter. A small company has grown and network resources are exposed to unnecessary risk. Cost and time are factors, so keeping the design simple and effective is critical. Figure 9.8 provides an example of what could this network could look like.

Figure 9.8 A Single Subnet Without Segmentation

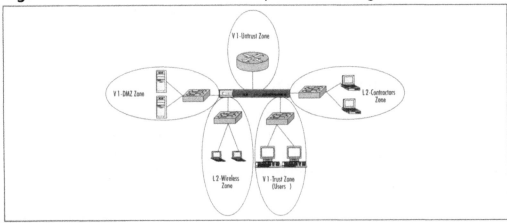

As noted in Figure 9.8, all devices exist in the same subnet, 10.10.10.0/24. There is no policy protecting the Web and database servers from the contractors, wireless, or general user community. The contractors are mobile laptops and provide no way for the administrator to guarantee their security. Wireless devices have their own security issues and allowing these devices open access to the network creates a great risk for company assets. Even though the general user community could have antivirus software running, it does not make them 100% secure from a worm outbreak. Inserting a NetScreen firewall in transparent mode into the mix could help to mitigate the risk, while keeping the required network changes minimal and invisible to the users (Figure 9.9).

Figure 9.9 The Same Subnet with Transparent Mode Segmentation

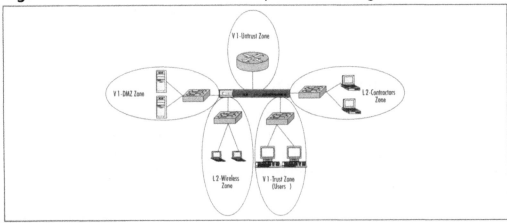

This example makes use of a NetScreen-208 to achieve segmentation. Let's walk through the steps that would be required for this type of configuration.

1. Configure the VLAN1 interface with an IP address of 10.10.10.2 and select the management services for WebUI, Telnet, SSH, and Ping.

■ From theWebUI:

Go to **Network | Interfaces | select Edit for VLAN1**

In **IP Address/Netmask**, type **10.10.10.2/24**

Select **Service Options**, and type **WebUI, Telnet, SSH**

In the **Other Services** section, enter **Ping**

Figure 9.10 VLAN1 Interface

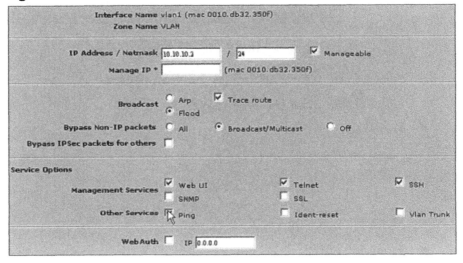

■ From the CLI:

```
set int vlan1ip 10.10.10.2/24
set int vlan1manage web
set int vlan1manage telnet
set int vlan1manage ssh
set int vlan1manage ping
save
```

2. Create custom zones for Wireless and Contractors.

■ From the WebUI:

Go to **Network | Zones | Select New**

Select **Zone Name** and fill in **L2-Wireless**

Select **Zone Type** and type **Layer 2**

Figure 9.11 L2-Wireless Zone

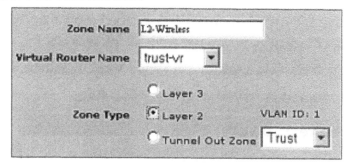

Go to **Network | Zones | Select New**

Select **Zone Name** and fill in **L2-Contractors**

Select **Zone Type** and type **Layer 2**

- From the CLI:

```
set zone name L2-Wireless L2 1
set zone name L2-Contractors L2 1
save
```

3. Move interfaces into Layer 2 zones.

- From the WebUI:

Go to **Network | Interfaces | Select Ethernet 1**

Select **Zone Name** and fill in: **V1-Trust**

In the **IP Address/Netmask** option, type **0.0.0.0/0**

Go to **Network | Interfaces | Select Ethernet 2**

Figure 9.12 Ethernet 1 configured for V1-Trust

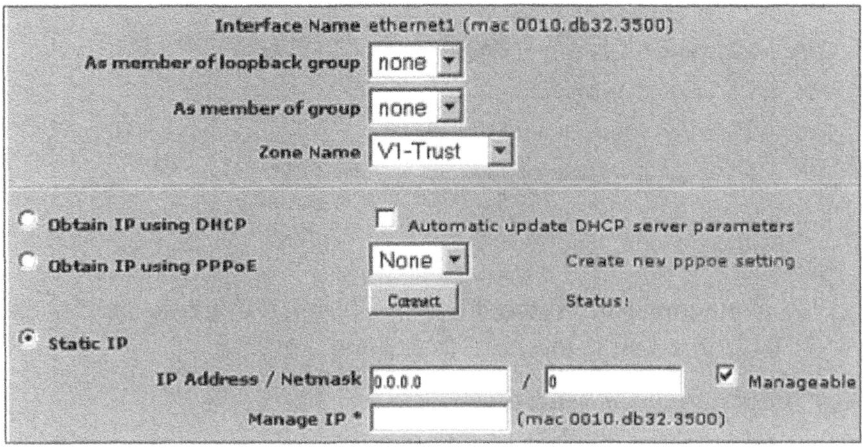

Go to **Zone Name** and fill in **V1-DMZ**

Go to **IP Address/Netmask** and fill in **0.0.0.0/0**

Go to **Network | Interfaces | Select Ethernet 3**

Go to **Zone Name: V1-Untrust**

Go to **IP Address/Netmask: 0.0.0.0/0**

Go to **Network | Interfaces | Select Ethernet 4**

Go to **Zone Name: L2-Wireless**

Go to **IP Address/Netmask: 0.0.0.0/0**

Go to **Network | Interfaces | Select Ethernet 5**

Go to **Zone Name: L2-Contractors**

Go to **IP Address/Netmask: 0.0.0.0/0**

CLI:
```
unset int eth1 ip
unset int eth2 ip
unset int eth3 ip
unset int eth4 ip
```

```
unset int eth5 ip
set int eth1 zone V1-Trust
set int eth2 zone V1-DMZ
set int eth3 zone V1-Untrust
set int eth4 zone L2-Wireless
set int eth5 zone L2-Contractors
save
```

1. Configure policies to allow V1-Trust, L2-Wireless, and L2-Contractors HTTP access to the L2-DMZ zone.

■ Steps from theWebUI:

Go to **Policies | From: V1-Trust, To: V1-DMZ, Select New**

Select **Service** and type **HTTP**

Go to**Policies | From: L2-Wireless, To: V1-DMZ**, Select **New**

Figure 9.13 Policy for V1-Trust to V1-DMZ for HTTP

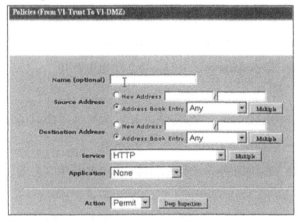

Select **Service** and type **HTTP**

Go to **Policies | From: L2-Contractors, To: V1-DMZ**, Select **New**

Select **Service** and fill in **HTTP**

■ Steps from the CLI:

```
set pol from V1-Trust to V1-DMZ any any http permit
set pol from L2-Wireless to V1-DMZ any any http permit
set pol from L2-Contractors to V1-DMZ any any http permit
save
```

VPNs with Transparent Mode

Even in transparent mode, the NetScreen device is still able to terminate policy-based VPNs. In Figure 9.14, there are two NetScreen 25's establishing a VPN tunnel across the Internet. Firewall A is running in Layer 3 route mode while firewall B is running Layer 2 transparent mode. The following details the steps involved with configuring this scenario.

Figure 9.14 VPN Deployment with a NetScreen Device in Transparent Mode

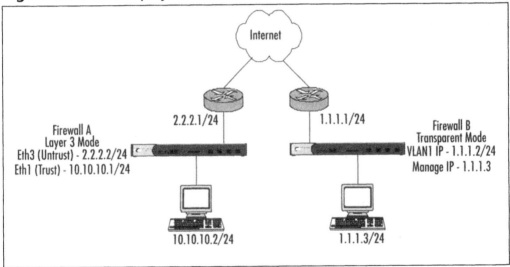

1. Configure interface IP addresses and default route.

From Firewall A:

- Steps from the WebUI:

    Go to **Network | Interfaces | Edit Ethernet 1**. In the **Static IP** option, fill in **10.10.10.1/24**

    Go to **Network | Interfaces | Edit Ethernet 3**. Again, select, **Static IP** and type **2.2.2.2/24**

Go to **Network | Routing | Routing Entries | Select Trust-VR**
and press **New**

Fill in:

Network Address/Netmask: 0.0.0.0/0

Select Gateway

Interface: ethernet3

Gateway IP Address: 2.2.2.1

■ Steps from the CLI:

```
set int eth1 ip 10.10.10.1/24
set int eth3 ip 2.2.2.2/24
set route 0.0.0.0/0 int eth3 gate 2.2.2.1
save
```

From Firewall B:

■ Steps from the WebUI:

Go to **Network | Interfaces | Edit VLAN1**

Select **IP Address/Netmask. Type 1.1.1.2/24**

Select Manage IP. Type 1.1.1.3

Go to **Network | Interfaces | Edit Ethernet 1**

Select **Zone Name. Type V1-Trust**

Select IP Address/Netmask. Type 0.0.0.0/0

Go to **Network | Interfaces | Edit Ethernet 2**

Select **Zone Name. Type V1-DMZ**

Select IP Address/Netmask. Type 0.0.0.0/0

Go to **Network | Interfaces | Edit Ethernet 3**

Select **Zone Name. Type V1-Untrust**

Select IP Address/Netmask. Type 0.0.0.0/0

Go To **Network | Routing | Routing Entries | Select Trust-VR**
and press **New**

Fill in:

Network Address/Netmask: 0.0.0.0/0

Select Gateway

Interface: VLAN1

Gateway IP Address: 1.1.1.1

■ Steps from the CLI:

```
set int vlan1 ip 1.1.1.2/24
set int vlan1 manage-ip 1.1.1.3
unset int eth1 ip
unset int eth2 ip
unset int eth3 ip
set int eth1 zone V1-Trust
set int eth2 zone V1-DMZ
set int eth3 zone V1-Untrust
set route 0.0.0.0/0 int vlan1 gate 1.1.1.1
save
```

2. Configure objects and VPN for both firewalls.

From Firewall A:

■ From the WebUI:

Go to **Objects | Addresses | List | Select Trust** and **New**

Fill in:

Address Name: **FirewallA_Local**

IP/Netmask: **10.10.10.2/32**

Go to **Objects | Addresses | List | Select Untrust** and **New**

Fill in: Address Name: **FirewallB_Remote**

IP/Netmask: **1.1.1.2/32**

Go to **VPNs | AutoKey Advanced | Gateway | Select New**

Fill in:

Gateway Name: p1-VPN

Security Level: Standard

Static IP Address: 1.1.1.2

Preshared Key: netscreen

Outgoing Interface: **ethernet3**

Figure 9.15 VPN Configuration for Gateway (Phase 1)

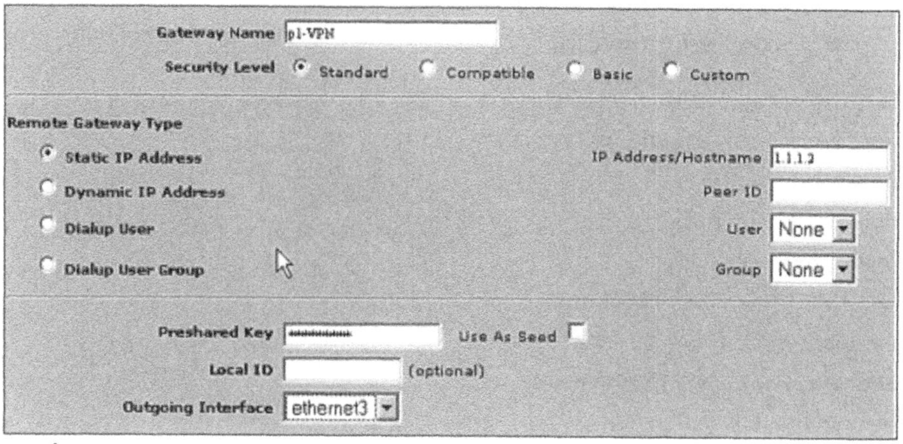

Go to **VPNs | AutoKey IKE | Select New**

Fill in:

VPN Name: p2-VPN

Security Level: Standard

Predefined: p1-VPN

Figure 9.16 VPN Configuration for AutoKey IKE (Phase 2)

- From the CLI:

```
set address trust FirewallA_Local 10.10.10.2/32
set address untrust FirewallB_Remote 1.1.1.2/32
set ike gateway p1-vpn address 1.1.1.2 main outgoing-interface ethernet3
preshare netscreen sec-level standard
```

```
set vpn p2-vpn gateway p1-vpn tunnel sec-level standard
save
```

From Firewall B

- WebUI:

  Go to **Objects | Addresses | List | Select V1-Trust** and **New**

  Fill in:

  Address Name: FirewallB_Local

  IP/Netmask: **1.1.1.3/32**

  Go to **Objects | Addresses |List | Select V1-Untrust** and **New**

  Fill in:

  Address Name**: FirewallA_Remote**

  IP/Netmask: **10.10.10.2/32**

  Go to **VPNs | AutoKey Advanced | Gateway | Select New**

  Fill in:

  Gateway Name: **p1-VPN**

  Security Level: **Standard**

  Static IP Address: **2.2.2.2**

  Preshared Key: **netscreen**

  Outgoing Interface: **V1-Untrust**

  Go to **VPNs | AutoKey IKE | Select New**

  Fill in:

  VPN Name: p2-VPN

  Security Level: **Standard**

  Predefined: **p1-VPN**

- From the CLI:

```
set address V1-Trustrust FirewallB_Local 1.1.1.3/32
set address V1-Untrust FirewallA_Remote 10.10.10.2/32
```

```
set ike gateway p1-vpn address 2.2.2.2 main outgoing-interface V1-Untrust
preshare netscreen sec-level standard
set vpn p2-vpn gateway p1-vpn tunnel sec-level standard
save
```

3. Configure Bi-directional VPN policies for both firewalls
Firewall A

- From the WebUI:

  Go to **Policies | From Trust to Untrust, Select New**

  Fill in:

      Source Address Book Entry: **FirewallA_Local**

      Destination Address Book Entry: **FirewallB_Remote**

      Service: **Any**

      Action: **Tunnel**

      Tunnel VPN: **p2-VPN**

      Modify matching bi-directional policy: Checked

      Logging: Checked

- **Figure 9.17** Policy Configuration for VPN

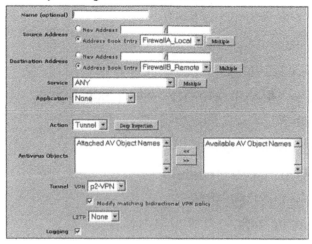

From the CLI:

```
set policy from trust to untrust FirewallA_Local FirewallB_Remote any
tunnel vpn p2-VPN log
```

```
set policy from untrust to trust FirewallB_Remote FirewallA_Local any
tunnel vpn p2-VPN log
```

```
save
```

From Firewall B

- WebUI:

    Go to **Policies | From V1-Trust to V1-Untrust,** Select **New**

    Fill in:

    Source Address Book Entry: **FirewallB_Local**

    Destination Address Book Entry: FirewallA_Remote

    Service: **Any**

    Action: **Tunnel**

    Tunnel VPN: **p2-VPN**

    Modify matching bi-directional policy: Checked

    Logging: Checked

- From the CLI:

```
set policy from V1-Trust to V1-Untrust FirewallB_Local FirewallA_Remote any
tunnel vpn p2-VPN log
```

```
set policy from V1-Untrust to V1-Trust FirewallA_Remote FirewallB_Local any
tunnel vpn p2-VPN log
```

```
save
```

Summary

As demonstrated in this chapter, transparent mode provides a viable and cost-effective method to provide the segmentation that is required in today's networks. Transparent mode can be used to quickly create a DMZ environment and easily secure Web servers and resources, provide internal segmentation, and provide a method to terminate VPN tunnels. From a user perspective, the "invisible hop" removes the pain that can be associated with dramatic changes to the network.

While the overall look and feel of a NetScreen in transparent mode is not significantly different from a device operating in layer 3, it is important to understand what differences exist. NAT and routing are no longer the concern since the device operates within the same subnet as the other existing devices. The zones that are assigned to the interfaces are specifically designed to be layer 2 zones, which are then used in developing policy. The firewall is managed by making use of the virtual interface, VLAN1.

The final section of this chapter provided two examples that show off these capabilities. Referring to these examples, while considering the direction of your network, can provide additional alternatives that may not have been previously considered. Segmentation is extremely important and any advantage that is provided to administrators is greatly welcomed.

Solutions Fast Track

Understand How Transparent mode works

☑ The NetScreen firewall operates at Layer 2.

☑ There are two methods for performing ARP, flood and ARP/traceroute.

☑ The VLAN zone hosts the VLAN1 interface.

Configuring a Device to Use Transparent Mode

☑ The VLAN1 interface is used for managing the device and terminating VPNs.

☑ Interfaces are assigned to layer 2 zones.

☑ Three layer 2 zones are included by default and additional ones can be created.

Transparent Mode Deployment Options

☑ Segment internal subnets with minimal network configuration.

☑ Often used to provide firewall protection for Internet-based resources.

☑ Can be used as a termination point for VPNs.

Frequently Asked Questions

The following Frequently Asked Questions, answered by the authors of this book, are designed to both measure your understanding of the concepts presented in this chapter and to assist you with real-life implementation of these concepts. To have your questions about this chapter answered by the author, browse to **www.syngress.com/solutions** and click on the **"Ask the Author"** form. You will also gain access to thousands of other FAQs at ITFAQnet.com.

Q. What interface modes can a NetScreen firewall be assigned?

A. NAT, route, and transparent modes.

Q. How is a NetScreen device converted to transparent mode?

A. The interfaces are placed in layer 2 zones. By default, the layer 2 zones included with a NetScreen device are V1-Trust, V1-Untrust, and V1-DMZ.

Q. How does is ARP managed?

A. NetScreen firewalls have two methods for supporting ARP, flood and ARP/traceroute. Simply put, flood sends the ARP query out all interfaces and learns the destination based on which interface receives the reply. The ARP/traceroute method searches for the destination by using the MAC address of the VLAN1 interface, while the traceroute provides the router destination if the packet is not part of the local subnet.

Q. What is the VLAN1 interface?

A. This is the virtual interface used to manage the NetScreen firewall and terminate VPNs when in transparent mode. Management services are turned off and on just like on an interface that is running in layer 3. Like a physical interface, a management IP address can also be assigned.

Q. With transparent mode, how is policy developed?

A. Rather than using layer 3 zones, policy is simply applied by using the layer 2 zones.

Chapter 10

Attack Detection and Defense

Solutions in this Chapter:

Introduction to the ScreenOS Security Features

This chapter will cover the nuts and bolts of the security features in Juniper Networks' NetScreen firewall products. As you've no doubt already discovered, these devices are packed with features that make life easier for administrators—easy to configure VPNs (virtual private networks), built-in DHCP (Dynamic Host Control Protocol) servers, advanced Network Address Translation (NAT) functionality, support for a wide range of routing protocols, and much more. But a firewall's primary responsibility has always been security—keeping the bad bits out, and letting the good bits in.

In addition to the strong feature set found for network administration is an equally strong set of protective tools. NetScreen firewalls have always protected owners from classic attacks such as Land, Teardrop, and other network layer-based attacks. These defensive SCREEN features allow for zone-specific settings based upon the risk factor of the facing network segment.

And while protecting at the network layer is both important and efficient, in today's world of application layer-specific attacks, it's not sufficient security coverage all by itself. Starting with tentative steps for application layer coverage in ScreenOS 4.0 with the Malicious URL feature, NetScreen firewalls now have full application layer coverage for typical Internet-facing protocols with Deep Inspection (DI), found in ScreenOS version 5.0 and later.

Combine the application layer gateway features with the advanced filtering features and antivirus (AV) protection, and a complete coverage picture emerges. But what are we protecting ourselves from?

Understanding the Anatomy of an Attack

There are almost as many different ways of attacking a network as there are hackers who try it, but the majority of attack methods can be categorized as one of the following: manual attacks and automated attacks. Manual attacks are generally still performed by a piece of code or other script, but the attack itself is initiated at the request of a live user, who selects his or her targets specifically. Automated attacks cover the kinds of attacks made by self-propagating worms and other viruses. There's also a question of the competence of an attacker or complexity of an automated attack, which we'll discuss.

The Three Phases of a Hack

Most hack attacks follow a series of phases:

1. **Reconnaissance** Initial probing for vulnerable services. Can include direct action against the target, such as port scanning, OS (operating system) fingerprinting and banner capturing, or it can be performing research about the target.

2. **Exploit** The attempt to take control of a target by malicious means. This can include denying the service of the target to valid users. Generally, the ultimate goal is to achieve root, system or administrator level access on the target.

3. **Consolidation** Ensuring that control of the target is kept. This usually means destroying logs, disabling firewalls and antivirus software, and sometimes includes process hiding and other means of obfuscating the attacker's presence on the system. In some extreme cases, the attacker may even patch the target against the exploit he used to attack the box, to ensure that no one else exploits the target after him.

While each step may have more or less emphasis, depending on the attacker, most hack attacks follow this pattern of progression.

Script Kiddies

For manual attacks, the majority of events are generated by inexperienced malicious hackers, known both in the industry and the hacking underground as "Script Kiddies". This derogatory reference implies both a lack of maturity ("just a kid") as well as a lack of technical prowess (they use scripts or other pre-written code instead of writing their own). Despite these limiting factors, what they lack in quality, they more than make up for in quantity. Under a hail of arrows, even the mightiest warrior may fall. These sorts of attacks will generally be obvious, obnoxious, and sudden, and will usually light up your firewall or IDP (Intrusion and Detection Prevention) like a Christmas tree.

The majority of these attacks have no true intelligence behind them, despite being launched by a real person. Generally the reconnaissance phase of these sorts of attacks will be a 'recon-in-force' of a SYN packet and immediately transition to phase two by banging on your front door like an insistent vacuum cleaner salesman. Script Kiddies (also "Skr1pt Kiddies", "Newbies", or just "Newbs/Noobs") glean through security websites like Security Focus (www.securityfocus.com), Packet Storm Security (http://packetstormsecurity.nl), and other sites that provide proof of concept code for exploits for new scripts to try out. Once they have these scripts, they will blindly throw them against targets. Very few of these amateurs understand exactly how these hacking tools work or how to change them to do something else. Many sites that provide code realize this, and will purposely break the script so that it doesn't work right, but would with a simple fix after a walk-through of the code by an experienced security professional.

Unfortunately, that only stops the new, inexperienced, or unaffiliated hacker. More commonly, hacking groups or gangs form with a few knowledgeable members at its core, with new inept recruits joining continuously. The people themselves need not live near each other in real life, but rather meet online in Internet Relay Chat (IRC) chat rooms and other instant messaging forums. These virtual groups will amass war chests of scripts, code snippets, and shellcode that work, thanks to the work of the more experienced members. Often, different hacking groups will start hacking wars, where each side attempts to outdo the other in either quantity or perceived difficulty of targets hacked in a single time span. Military targets in particular are seen as more difficult, when in fact generally the security of these sites is often well below corporate standards. Mass website defacements are the most common result from these intergroup hacking wars, with immature, lewd, or insulting content posted to the sites.

A bright side to this problem is that many times a successful breach by these amateurs is not exploited to its fullest, since many of these hackers have no clue to exactly what sort of system they have gained access to, or how to proceed from there. To them, *owning* (a successful hack which results in a root, administrator, or system-level account) a *box* (a server), and modifying its presented webpage for others to see and acknowledge is generally sufficient. These sorts of attacks commonly do not proceed to phase three, consolidation.

From a protection standpoint, to defend against these sorts of attacks, it is important to keep DI and IDP signatures updated, and all systems patched, whether directly exposed to the Internet or not. Defense-in-depth is also key to ensure that a successful breach does not spread. The motivation behind these groups is quick publicity, so expect hard, fast, obvious, but thorough strikes across your entire Internet-facing systems.

Black Hat Hackers

Experienced malicious hackers (sometimes called "Black Hat" hackers or just "Black Hats") tend to have a background of either a Script Kiddy graduating from the underground cyber-gangs or a network security professional or other administrator turning to the 'dark side' or a combination of both. In fact, it is common to call law-abiding security professionals "White Hats", with some morally-challenged, but generally good-intending people termed "Grey Hats". The clear delineation here is intent—Black Hats are in it for malicious purposes, often profit. This hat color scheme gets its roots from old Western movies and early black and white Western TV shows. In these shows, the bad guys always wore black hats, and the good guys wore white hats. Roles and morality were clearly defined. In the real world, this distinction is more muddled.

Black Hats will slowly and patiently troll through networks, looking for vulnerabilities. Generally, they will have done their homework very thoroughly and will have a good idea of the network layout and systems present before ever sending a single packet directly against your network—their phase one preparation is meticulous. A surprising amount of data can be gleaned from simple tools like the WhoIs database and Google or other web search engines for free. Mail lists and newsgroups when data-mined for domains from a target can reveal a lot of good detail about what systems and servers are used by seeing network and system admins asking questions on how to solve server problems or configure devices for their networks, not to mention the wealth of information gleaned for social engineering. Names, titles, phone numbers, and addresses—it's all there to use by a skilled impersonator to make a few phone calls and obtain domain information and even usernames and sometimes passwords!

Notes from the Underground…

Social Engineering

Social engineering is the term used to describe the process by which hackers obtain technical information without using a computer directly to do so. Social engineering is essentially conning someone to provide you with useful information that they should not—whether it's something

Continued

obviously important like usernames and passwords or something seemly innocuous like the name of a network administrator or his phone number.

With a few simple pieces of valid information, some good voice acting and proper forethought, a hacker could convince you over the phone that he or she was a new security engineer, and that CEO is in a huff and needs the password changed now because he can't get to his e-mail or someone's going to get fired. "And that new password is what now? He needs to know it so we can login and check it..."

Be sure to train your staff, including receptionists who answer public queries, to safeguard information to keep it out of the hands of hackers. Have authentication mechanisms to prevent impersonation.

The recon portion of the attack for a cautious Black Hat may last weeks or even months—painstakingly piecing together a coherent map of your network. When the decision to move to phase two and actively attack is finally made, the attack is quiet, slight, and subtle. They will avoid causing a crash of any services if they can help it, and will move slowly through the network, trying to avoid IDPs and other traffic logging devices. Phase three consolidation is also very common, including patching the system from further vulnerability, as they do not want some Script Kiddy coming in behind them and ruining their carefully laid plans.

A Black Hat's motivation is usually a strong desire to access to your data—credit cards, bank accounts, social security numbers, usernames, and passwords. Other times it may be for petty revenge for perceived wrongs. Or they may want to figure out a way to divert your traffic to websites they control, so they can dupe users into providing these critical pieces of information to them—this technique is known as *phishing* (pronounced like *fishing*, but with a twist). Some phishing attacks will merely copy your website to their own, and entice people to the site with a list of e-mails they may have lifted off your mail or database server. Sometimes malware authors will also compromise websites in a manner similar to a Script Kiddy web defacement, but instead of modifying the content on the site, they merely add additional files to it. This allows them to use the website itself as an infection vector for all who visit the site by adding a malicious JPEG file, Trojan horse binary, or other script into an otherwise innocuous website—even one protected by encryption (via Hypertext Transfer Protocol Secure, known simply as HTTPS).

Defense against these sorts of attacks requires good network security design as well as good security policy design and enforcement. Training employees, especially IT and receptionist or other public-facing employees, about social engineering awareness and proper information control policy is paramount. For the network itself, proper isolation of critical databases and other stores of important data, combined with monitoring and logging systems that are unreachable from potentially compromised servers is key. Following up on suspicious activity is also important.

Worms, Viruses, and other Automated Malware

Mentioned in the Notes from the Underground sidebar, the concept for self-propagating programs is nothing new, but the practical application has only been around for the last 15 to 20 years. Since the origins of the Internet are well over 40 years old now, this is significant. Indeed, it's in the last two to three years that malware has taken a rather nasty turn for the worst, and there's a good reason behind it.

Early worms were merely proofs-of-concept, either a "See what I can do" or some sort of glimpse at a Cyber Pearl Harbor or Internet Armageddon, and rarely had any purposefully malicious payload. This didn't keep them from being major nuisances that cost companies millions of dollars year after year. But then some of the more advanced hacking groups started getting the idea that a large group of computers under a single organization's complete control might be a fun thing to have. And the concept of a zombie army was born.

Notes from the Underground

Are You a Zombie?

The majority of machines compromised to make a zombie army are unprotected home users, directly connected to the Internet through DSL lines or cable modems. A recent study showed that while 60% of home Internet users surveyed felt they were safe from hackers, only 33% of them had some sort of firewall. Of that minority of Internet users with firewalls, 72% were found to be misconfigured. This means *less than 10%* of home Internet users are properly protected from attack!

Furthermore, of the users who had wireless access in their homes, 38% of them used no encryption, and the other 62% who did, used wireless encryption schemes with known security flaws that could be exploited to obtain the decryption key. Essentially, every person surveyed

Continued

who used wireless could be a point from which a hacker could attack – and over a third of them effortlessly.

Find out more information from the study online at www.stay safeonline.info/news/safety_study_v04.pdf

Zombies, sometimes also referred to as *Bots* (a group of Bots is a *Bot-net*), are essentially Trojan horses left by a self-propagating worm. These nasty bits of code generally phone home to either an IRC channel or other listening post system and report their readiness to accept commands. Underground hacker groups will work hard to compromise as many machines as they can to build up the number of systems under their command. Bot-nets comprised of hundreds to tens of thousands of machines have been recorded. Typically these groups use the bots to flood target servers with packets, causing a Denial of Service (DoS) attack from multiple points, creating a Distributed Denial of Service (DDoS) attack. Nuking a person or site you didn't like is fun for these people. But the fun didn't last long.

Once the reality of a multi-thousand node anonymous, controllable network was created, it was inevitable that economics would enter the picture, and zombie armies were sold to the highest bidder—typically spammers and organized crime. Spammers use these bots to relay spam through, so that ISPs (Internet service providers) couldn't track them back to the original spammer and shut down their connection. This became so important to spammers that eventually they were contracting ethically challenged programmers to write worms for them with specific features such as mail relay and competitor Trojan horse removal. Agobot, MyDoom, and SoBig are examples of these kinds of worms. Organized crime realizes the simplicity of a cyber-shakedown and extorts high-value transaction networks such as online gambling sites for protection from DDoS attack by bot-nets under the mob's control.

Protection from these tenacious binaries requires defense-in-depth (security checkpoints at multiple points within your network) as well as a comprehensive defense solution (flood control, access control, and application layer inspection). Many of the Script Kiddy defense methods will also work against most worms, since the target identification logic in these worms is generally limited—phase one recon is usually just a SYN to a potentially vulnerable port. This is because there is only so much space for all that the worm needs to do—scanning, connecting, protocol negotiation, overflow method, shellcode, and propagation method, not to mention the backdoor Trojan. Most worms pick targets completely at random and try a variety of attacks against it, whether it's a valid target for the attack or not. To solve the complexity problem, many Trojans are now split into two or more parts – a small, simple propagating worm with a file transfer stub, and a second stage full-featured Trojan horse, with the *phone home*, e-mail spamming, etc. The first stage attacks and infects, then loads the second stage for the heavy lifting. This allows for an effective phase three consolidation.

Information obtained by Honeypot Networks (systems designed to detect attacks) shows that the average life expectancy of a freshly installed Windows system without patches connected directly to the Internet without a firewall or other protection is approximately 20 minutes. On some broadband or dial-up connections it can take 30 minutes or longer to download the correct patches to prevent compromise by these automated attack programs. Using the Internet unprotected is a race you can't win.

Notes from the Underground…

Multi-Vector Malware and the People Who Pay For It

Hacking (the term as used by the media for unauthorized access) is as old as Computer Science itself. Early on, it was mostly innocent pranks, or for learning and exploring. And while concepts for self-replicating programs were bantered around as early as 1949, the first practical viruses did not appear until the early 1980's.

These early malicious software (or malware) applications generally required a user's interaction to spread – a mouse button clicked, a file open, a disk inserted. By the late 1980's, however, fully automated self-replicating software, generally known as worms, were finally realized. These programs would detect, attack, infect, and restart all over again on the new victim without any human interaction. The earliest worms, such as the Morris Worm in 1988, had no purposeful malicious intent, but due to programming errors and other unconsidered circumstances, it still caused a lot of problems.

The earliest worms and hacking attacks targeted a single known vulnerability, generally on a single computing platform. Code Red is a classic example – it targeted only Microsoft Windows Web servers running Internet Information Server (IIS), and specifically a single flaw in the way IIS handled ISAPI (Internet Server App;ication Programming Interface) extensions. And while they did significant damage, a single flaw on a

Continued

single machine tends to confine the attack to a defined area, with a known, specific defense.

Unfortunately, this is no longer the case. Malware is now very complex, and the motivations for malware have changed with it. Early malware was limited to mostly pranks—file deletion, web defacement, CD tray opening, and so on. Later, when commerce came to the Web, and valuable data, like credit card numbers and other personal information were now on-line and potentially vulnerable, greed became a factor in why and how malware authors wrote their code. Recently the culprits are spammers with significant financial clout, who pay programmers to add certain features to their malware, so that spam (unsolicited e-mail), spim (unsolicited instant messages) and spyware can be spread for fun and profit.

NetSky, MyDoom, and Agobot are the newest breeds of these superworms. New versions come out almost weekly, and certainly after any new major vulnerability announcement. They don't target just one vulnerability on one platform—they are multi-vector, self-propagating infectors, and they'll stop at nothing to infiltrate your network. Most exploit at least four different vulnerabilities, as well as brute force login algorithms. These worms even attack each other—NetSky and MyDoom both remove other Trojan horses as well as antivirus and other security programs. A variant of Agobot attempts to overflow the FTP (File Transfer Protocol) server left behind by a Sasser worm infection as an infection vector.

Configuring SCREEN Settings

The SCREEN options on a NetScreen firewall are perhaps the oldest form of protection found on these firewalls. New options and features were added over time to address new threats present on the Internet. In the newer versions of ScreenOS (starting with ScreenOS 3.1, which was a limited-platform release—all devices supported this new feature in ScreenOS 4.0), these options are security-zone specific—each zone may have unique settings applied to it. For all options, these settings are applied as the inspected traffic externally enters the zone—that is, when the stream is read from the interface off the wire, not as it passes through the NetScreen and out another interface.

While NetScreen organizes these attacks by layers and protocols, it's easier to talk about them more generically by their purpose. The two major functions of the SCREEN features are *reconnaissance detection* and Denial of Service protection. See Figure 10.1 for the ScreenOS version 5.1.0r1 SCREEN setting page.

Figure 10.1 SCREEN Settings for ScreenOS 5.1.0r1

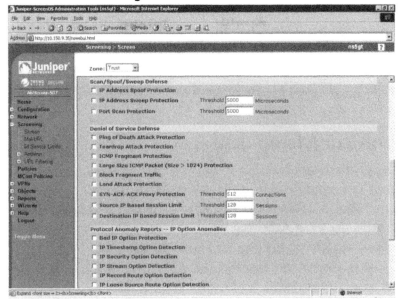

Reconnaissance Detection

As mentioned earlier, an attacker will more than likely perform some initial reconnaissance on your systems before launching an attack. Generally these methods are benign, and so they are therefore easily lost in the clutter of normal traffic.

Port Scans and Sweeps

Port scanning, especially across multiple machines, is the simplest and most common network reconnaissance method. A variety of tools, most notably NMap (www.insecure.org/nmap/), perform port scanning as well as more advanced system identification such as OS fingerprinting and service banner capture.

NetScreens can detect a single system being scanned for ports open (port scan), a single port being scanned across multiple systems (port sweep), or a combination of the two. Configuring NetScreen to detect these attacks can be done via the **IP Address Sweep Protection** and **Port Scan Protection** options in the **Screening | Screens** window. To the right-hand side of these options you'll find a user-definable threshold in microseconds. This value both indicates how quickly ten probes must occur before the detection trips. The default value is 5000 microseconds, or 0.005 seconds. Some protocols can open up several ports in rapid succession. If you find this triggering often from trusted machines that you've verified have no malware running on them, you may need to adjust this threshold higher to weed out these false positives.

You'll most commonly detect scans and sweeps from Script Kiddies or other automated, semi-intelligent attacks. More experienced Black Hats will scan more slowly, generally slow enough to avoid being detected by a firewall. This technique of sending port scanning packets infrequently over a long period of time is known as a *slow scan*.

TCP Protocol Manipulation

Other methods of scanning involve modifying TCP (Transmission Control Protocol) flags to invalid or improper settings. Many stateless routers that are pressed into service as rudimentary firewalls can detect established communications based upon the TCP ACK flag. Scanners will utilize this logic flaw and send *ACK scans* in which the packet sent will have the ACK bit set—this bypasses most ACL (access control list)-based packet filters, but thanks to the stateful inspection feature in ScreenOS, no TCP packet not matching an established session (created with a proper TCP three-way handshake) may pass. Other TCP flag tomfoolery that can be detected and blocked include:

- **SYN Fragment Protection** Protects against initial SYN packets with the fragmentation bit also set. SYN packets generally have no data and therefore cannot be fragmented.

- **TCP Packet Without Flag Protection** Also called a *NULL scan*. This is an invalid flag configuration.

- **SYN and FIN Bits Set Protection** Sometimes called an *open-close scan*. SYN flags begin sessions, while FIN flags generally end them—a single packet that both requests and closes a session is anomalous.

- **FIN Bit With No ACK Bit in Flags Protection** Per RFC, when closing a connection with FIN, you need to acknowledge (ACK) the byte count you received. This detects a packet not matching that requirement.

IP Protocol Manipulation

Other, more obscure methods of network mapping involve detecting Internet Protocol (IP)-layer parameters. ScreenOS supports blocking these probes with a slew of IP option anomalies:

- Bad IP Option Protection

- IP Timestamp Option Detection

- IP Security Option Detection

- IP Stream Option Detection

- IP Record Route Option Detection

- IP Loose Source Route Option Detection

- IP Strict Source Route Option Detection

- IP Source Route Option Filter

If for some reason you have need for these services, generally you'll already know about it. If these do not sound familiar to you, it's a safe bet you don't need them. Most of these activities have no valid use on a network and are generally safe to block.

Flood Attacks

Flooding is one of the oldest, yet still very popular methods of attack. The problem was, connection requests could come in over the network faster than most systems could properly handle them. Thanks to Moore's Law, CPU capacity has outstripped network capacity, and this problem, while not completely mitigated, is considerably reduced. It's still prudent to block these attacks as far out to the perimeter as possible, if for no other reason than to clean up the clutter and keep unnecessary traffic out of your network.

NetScreen offers three different flood protection queues based upon the protocol that they handle:

- ICMP (Internet Control Message Protocol)

- UDP (User Datagram Protocol)

- TCP (SYN flood)

ICMP is the most straightforward of the flood protections. A threshold value of total ICMP packets per second (from all IP addresses) is set, and if that threshold (default of 1000 p/s) is exceeded in a particular second, the remainder of the ICMP packets for that second, as well as all of the ICMP packets for the next second, are dropped. Furthermore, sessions are not made for dropped packets.

UDP flood protection is essentially the same as ICMP flood protection, but uses a separate threshold and queue. It uses a threshold value (default of 1000 p/s) that if exceeded, drops all remaining UDP packets from all IP addresses for that second as well as the next.

TCP SYN flood protection is the most complicated flood protection, due to the NetScreen's ability to proxy the three-way handshake. It allows for a variety of different threshold settings:

- **Attack Threshold** This controls how many packets per second must arrive at a single IP/port pair before the NetScreen begins proxying SYNs, Any SYNs above this threshold for the remainder of that second are proxied, until the proxy queue is full.

- **Alarm Threshold** This controls when an alarm should be logged for a potential SYN flood. This number should be *lower* than your attack threshold – it is a warning that you could be having trouble.

- **Source Threshold** This threshold is separate from the *attack threshold* where the total number of SYN packets from a particular source IP are counted. The *source threshold* setting is very useful for isolating scanning worm infections on end user systems. Set this number relatively low on your user-space segment (see "Zone Isolation" in the "Applying Best Practices" section) and notice that when an infected host tries to open up 100 new connections per second to other targets, attempting to infect them, this feature will throttle that attack to a manageable level.

- **Destination Threshold** This threshold is also separate from the attack threshold, and is similar to source threshold, except the number of sessions compared is for a particular destination IP. This is also measured in packets per second, and should be used for servers or other important machines to keep the overall level of new TCP connections to a set maximum.

- **Timeout** This is how long a SYN should be kept in the proxy queue before being flushed as an invalid connection request. Its default setting is 20 seconds, which is very generous. I would recommend something lower, perhaps as low as 5 to 7 seconds, depending on the latency of your network. Keep in mind that any properly negotiated three-way handshake will automatically clear the entry from the queue.

- **Queue Size** Specifies the number of SYNs that can be proxied and monitored before dropping new SYNs. A larger number uses more memory (since it needs to remember the IP address and port number of the session requested), and also takes longer to scan the queue for completed three-way handshakes, resulting in a higher initial connection latency.

There is a special case when a NetScreen is in *transparent mode* and it needs to proxy the SYN for a session, but the destination MAC (Media Access Control) address hasn't been learned yet, and isn't in the NetScreen's ARP (Address Resolution Protocol) table. This could occur on a large layer 2 network where the destination MAC has aged off of the NetScreen device, or it could be that the destination IP doesn't exist, and therefore the MAC cannot be learned. The **Drop Unknown MAC** option allows to you set the behavior of the NetScreen device when this situation occurs. By default, NetScreen will pass a packet with an unknown destination MAC and *not* proxy it. With this option set, NetScreen will drop the packet instead.

Protocol Attacks

In addition to flood attacks, the SCREEN functions can also block protocol-specific attacks. These are generally legacy attacks—new attacks are blocked with Deep Inspection, discussed below. Protocols and attacks covered:

- **HTTP (Hypertext Transfer Protocol)** Allows the blocking of Java and ActiveX code, as well as ZIP and EXE file downloads.

- **Windows** Allows the blocking of the classic WinNuke (malformed data to port 139) attack.

- **ICMP protocol attacks** Allows the blocking of the *ping of death* (fragment boundary overflow attack), ICMP fragments, and large ICMP packets.

- **TCP protocol attacks** Allows the blocking of *teardrop* (another fragment boundary overflow attack) and *land* (source and destination IP and port are the same) attacks.

Applying Deep Inspection

Juniper Networks' line of NetScreen firewall products have evolved with security requirements to consistently keep up to date with threats that plague network administrators. Deep Inspection is the newest and most comprehensive coverage to date, with even more protocols coming soon. DI takes network security all the way up the stack to the application layer, inspecting traffic as it would be interpreted by the end host application. This answers the problem vexing many Administrators who are used to solving security at layer 3 and 4—"How do I defend from attacks when I need to leave port 80 open?"

Deep Inspection is a subset of Juniper Networks' award-winning NetScreen Intrusion Detection and Prevention, with support for protocols typically considered to be Internet-facing—HTTP, SMTP (Simple Mail Transfer Protocol), DNS (Domain Name System), POP3 (Post Office Protocol v3), FTP, and IMAP (Internet Message Access Protocol). Support for MS-RPC (Microsoft Remote Procedure Call) and SMB (Server Message Block) is available in ScreenOS 5.1, though generally these protocols do not traverse the Internet legitimately.

DI examines all incoming packets and assigns them a session (or in the case of stateless protocols such as UDP or ICMP, a *pseudo-session*). It reassembles fragments, rearranges out-of-order frames, and creates data streams from these packets (errors from overlapping fragments and other tomfoolery are handled by IP layer protocol anomaly inspectors). These streams are then handed off to protocol-specific inspection engines, called *Q modules*, which further inspect and parse the stream into protocol-specific elements (called *contexts*) for signature matching. Protocol-specific anomalies are also detected at this stage. For example, DNS requests are matched to DNS replies to ensure that the answer matches the question—this prevents DNS poisoning.

These contexts are what make DI so accurate. With this level of parsing, a signature writer can specify a more targeted portion of the data stream for inspection—this also has the added benefit of increased performance, since only the relevant portion of the stream is inspected for attacks. Take this hypothetical situation:

Say you have a simple, stateless, in-line Intrusion Detection System (IDS) monitoring your network. A new vulnerability (in this case, a secret backdoor left by the developer) is discovered in the mail server, whereby if an e-mail arrives from a specific user (littlepig@bigbadwolf.com for this example), in addition to forwarding the message to the recipient, it also takes whatever attachments are included with the message and attempts to execute them as programs. Being limited to this stateless IDS, you write a signature that says, "If you see the pattern 'littlepig@bigbadwolf.com' go over TCP port 25 then block it". You then send an e-mail out to all your users, informing them to report any suspicious e-mails that they receive from that address. Later that day, you ask a coworker if he'd received any of the e-mails you were talking about earlier. He gets very confused and asks you what you're talking about. When you start talking about little pigs and big bad wolves, he gets a funny look on his face and mumbles something about being late to a meeting and hurries off. It's only after you check your IDS logs that you realize that *no one* received your e-mail because your own IDS blocked it! It detected the string match based upon the data in your e-mail, and took what it thought was appropriate action.

Take that sample situation and instead use DI's SMTP-From context, and put your string match there. The same e-mail message you sent out to your users would pass through DI unmolested, because it knows the difference between the SMTP command phase of the session and the SMTP data phase of the session. Your e-mail had a matching string in the data portion of the stream, which isn't where the vulnerability lies, so DI ignores it. Later on that day, when a hacker tries to test your security, DI detects the match in the SMTP command phase (specifically, in a SMTP From command) and blocks the message from arriving on your mail server.

But what if you missed the memo? Security issues come up every day, and it's more than a full-time job just to keep abreast of all the details. Is this particular security announcement relevant to your network? Do you run a vulnerable version on any of your servers? Are these servers accessible from the Internet? How does the attack work? What kind of regular expression (RegEx) would detect it? Would your signature trigger on non-malicious traffic (called a *false positive*) and block legitimate traffic? Would your signature fail to trigger on malicious traffic (called a *false negative*) and let attacks through? Did you leave the garage door open this morning?

Since not everyone can be a full-time security researcher, Juniper Networks has the Juniper Engineering Security Team do research for you. With a valid subscription, you can receive a well-stocked signature pack as well as regular and periodic updates as new vulnerabilities are announced. Medium through critical (as defined by CERT/CC − www.cert.org/) severity issues, when possible, are covered by DI.

Getting the Database

NetScreen firewall products need a valid DI license key before DI is used. Your Juniper Customer Service Representative can assist you with obtaining one, as well as helping out if there are problems with loading the key on to the device. The device may need a reboot when adding a new license key. Updating subscriptions to already-activated features generally do not require a reboot. Once the license is on the device, you are ready to load your database.

NOTE

All license keys are tied to the serial number of the device for which the key was granted—there is no such thing as a *universal* key. Trying to load a license key created for one unit and trying to load it on another unit—even the same model—will fail. Additionally, if you ever need to return your unit for replacement under the RMA policy, the new device you receive needs to have new keys issued for it. Support generally will handle this for you automatically, but it's something to check in case something doesn't work with the new unit. Many configuration settings are hidden until a valid license key is loaded to activate those features—loading a configuration from an entitled firewall onto another firewall without entitlements could cause the inactive portions of the config to be dropped.

TIP

With ScreenOS 5.1 you can also use the **Retrieve Subscriptions Now** button in the **Configuration | Update | ScreenOS/Keys** WebUI page for the device to automatically retrieve keys assigned to it from Juniper Networks' entitlement server. Note this requires the firewall to have Web access to the Internet in order to connect to the server. For devices that cannot reach the entitlement server directly, the key file must be loaded on the device by hand.

The database file is a pre-compiled binary database file and can be downloaded by the device directly from the Juniper website if the firewall is attached to the Internet and firewall policies are in place to permit it to do so. This can be configured to automatically occur on a set schedule so that you'll never miss an update. You can also force an update from the Internet via the WebUI.

If the firewall is on a private network, or if access is restricted, the file can be manually downloaded from the Internet, and then either placed on an internal Web server for your firewalls to download from (the URL that specifies the location of the attack file is mostly configurable) or it can be loaded by hand by either using the WebUI via HTTP upload direct from the browser or the command line interface (CLI) via TFTP (Thin File Transfer Protocol) file transfer. For the latter method, a TFTP server is required.

Configuring the Firewall for Automatic DI Updates

One of the more handy features of DI is its ability to automatically check for new signature packs and download them as necessary without user intervention. Configuration for this is easy.

NOTE

Remember that the device has to have HTTPS access to the Internet in order to automatically update. Read below on how to perform a manual update if HTTPS access is not possible.

Using the WebUI, access **Configuration | Update | Attack Signature**. Figure 10.2 shows this screen as shown on ScreenOS 5.1.0r1. The **Database Server** field is used to select the partial URL from which to download (the current default is still apparently **https://services.netscreen.com/restricted/ sigupdates**, although since Juniper acquired NetScreen some time ago now, I expect this URL to be updated sometime soon). I say partial, because the latter half of the complete URL is hard-coded as **/[model-name]/attacks.bin** (for example, /ns500/attacks.bin). As of ScreenOS 5.1.0r1 and 5.0.0r7 (and earlier), there is a bug in which the model name is hard-coded to ns500, regardless of the actual platform type. If you're looking to configure an internal DI update server, you can use HTTP or HTTPS, and be sure to put the newest attacks file in a subdirectory called /ns500 for the update to work.

The section below the URL entry line allows you three update modes: **None, Automatic Notification**, and **Automatic Update. None** turns auto-update off, while **Automatic Notification** checks to see if there is a new file, but does not download and update; rather it puts an entry in the logs that an update is available. If you don't check your logs often, but want to make sure the device always has the most current coverage, you can select **Automatic Update**, which checks for new signature updates and, when available, automatically downloads and installs them.

The remainder of the options for this screen are fairly self-explanatory and include settings for when the device will auto-update (daily, weekly, or monthly), and what time of day to update. There's also a handy **Update Now** button that allows you to test your settings.

Figure 10.2 Automatic DI Signature Update Settings

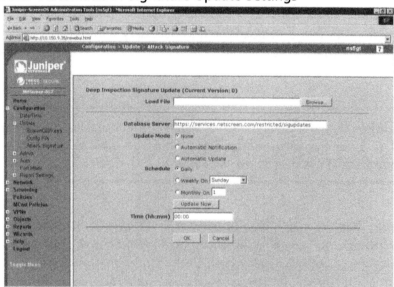

Loading the Database Manually

Sometimes due to architectural decisions, a firewall may not have direct access to the Internet. In these circumstances, an automatic update may not be possible. Manual updates require you to obtain the update by hand from another system connected to the Internet, then take that image and manually place it on the device in question.

Using the WebUI, manual loading is a straightforward affair. If you have your DI key properly installed, the **Deep Inspection Signature Update** field will be available on the Configuration | Update | Attack Signature screen. This field is hidden if the DI key is not installed. Use the **Load File** field to enter the local path to the signature update file, or use the **Browse** button to locate and select the file location. Once you have specified or selected the file location, click **OK** to update the device from the local file.

To perform this action via the CLI, you'll need to download the signature update to a TFTP server. The syntax for the command is **save attack-db from tftp [server-IP] [path/filename] to flash**. If successful, you'll see a string of dots generated across your console as TFTP packets arrive. Exclamation points (!) mean packet loss or other network error. Missed packets from an otherwise successful stream are present, but if the NetScreen can't connect to your TFTP server, you'll receive a number of beginning exclamation points followed by a TFTP timeout error.

NOTE

While your NetScreen device is signed up for subscriptions, you can update the device as many times as you like. Once your subscription has expired, you'll be ineligible for new updates, but your existing signature pack will continue to work as before. You'll also still be able to create your own custom signatures even if your subscription has run out.

Using Attack Objects

NetScreen-supplied attack objects are organized into groups based upon three criteria: protocol, severity, and type. For ScreenOS 5.0, the only valid severity levels were critical, high, and medium. Beginning with ScreenOS 5.1, the new severity levels of low and info are included. For ScreenOS 5.0, only six protocols were supported: HTTP, FTP, DNS, POP3, SMTP, and IMAP. Beginning with ScreenOS 5.1, this protocol list has expanded to include SMB, MS-RPC, NetBIOS, Gnutella (a popular peer-to-peer file sharing protocol), as well as several instant messaging protocols. For type, there are signatures and anomalies. Signatures are specialized regular expression pattern matching strings applied to contexts that then match malicious or other unwanted traffic in network flows. Protocol anomalies are protocol-specific functions that ensure that the flow adheres to protocol standards or other settings.

Using Attack Groups

Attacks cannot be used individually in a policy—they must be assigned to a group, even if that group contains just a single entry. If a predefined group has entries in it that you do not want to use, you may deactivate them from the group by accessing the **Objects | Attacks | Predefined Groups** window and clicking **View** for the group you wish to edit. You will see a listing of all attacks included in the group. The right-hand column has a checkbox next to each entry. To remove an entry from inspection by the group, remove the check mark from its checkbox.

Changing active entry settings within a group is a global action that affects the entire device for all policies that use that group. Also note that this does *not* remove the entry from inspection, it only removes it for the purposes of action against the event—there is *no* performance improvement for removing signatures from a group. Likewise, there is no performance impact for using DI groups over and over again in different policies. When DI is on, it's *ON*, and when it's off, it's *OFF*. The first time you use DI in a policy, DI inspection automatically turns on. When it is removed from every single policy, DI automatically turns off.

Enabling Deep Inspection with a Policy using the WebUI

In order to use DI, you must first create an access policy. Figure 10.3 shows a ScreenOS 5.1 policy crafting window in the WebUI. Create appropriate entries for **Source Address**, **Destination Address**, and **Service**. To choose which DI groups will inspect the traffic through sessions matching this policy, click on the **Deep Inspection** button.

Figure 10.3 ScreenOS 5.1 Policy Editor, Basic

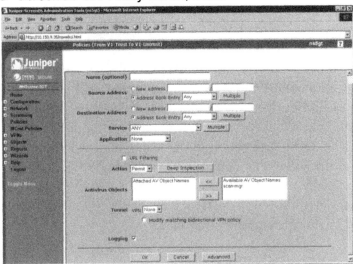

Figure 10.4 shows the Deep Inspection Configuration window.

Figure 10.4 Policy Deep Inspection Configuration

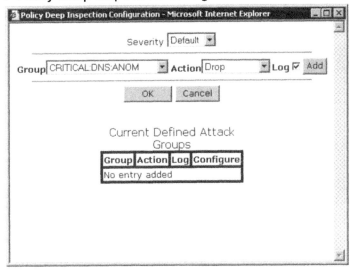

Here you'll find an unsorted, unfiltered drop list of all available Deep Inspection groups. In DI 5.1, you'll have a pick list of at least *58* items. Following that is a drop-down list that allows you to select which **Action** to perform on the selected group, as well as a **Log** option checkbox. Below this you'll find a table showing the **Currently Defined Attack Groups** assigned to this policy. Different groups within a policy can have different action and logging settings. This is useful, since there can be only one policy that matches traffic between two hosts on a port – multiple duplicate policies are not permitted. As in ScreenOS, the first matched policy for a connection is used. Click on the **Add** button to add the selected group with the selected action and log setting to the defined attacks table. Click the **OK** button when you are finished. These DI options will be applied to your policy. Click on the **OK** button in the main policy editing window to apply your changes to the policy. The resulting DI-enabled policy has the DI inspection magnifying glass icon in the **Actions** column of the policy list. Policy ID 2 in Figure 10.5 has Deep Inspection enabled, while policy ID 3 has both Deep Inspection and Trend Micro antivirus enabled.

Figure 10.5 Policy Listing in the WebUI

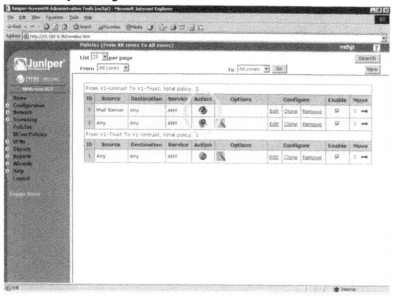

Enabling Deep Inspection with a Policy using the CLI

Creating a policy that inspects traffic using many attack groups is a major chore in the WebUI. My personal recommendation is to create the initial policy in the way you feel comfortable—either WebUI or CLI—and then for bulk DI inspection configuration, use the CLI. You'll find this is a vastly superior method.

If you are managing multiple firewalls and policies, using NetScreen Security Manager (NSM) will make your task many times easier – define an attack and policy once, then simply specify which devices to apply it to.

To get a listing of which attack groups are available, use the **get attack group sort-by name** command:

```
ns5gt-> get attack group sort-by name
Total number of attack groups is 58
```

You should get results similar to the following:

Table 10.1 ScreenOS 5.1 CLI attack groups sample listing

```
ns5gt-> get attack group sort-by name
Total number of attack groups is 58
```

Name	Type	Defined
CRITICAL:DNS:ANOM	group	pre-defined
CRITICAL:DNS:SIGS	group	pre-defined
CRITICAL:FTP:SIGS	group	pre-defined
CRITICAL:HTTP:ANOM	group	pre-defined
CRITICAL:HTTP:SIGS	group	pre-defined
CRITICAL:MSRPC:ANOM	group	pre-defined
CRITICAL:POP3:SIGS	group	pre-defined
CRITICAL:SMB:ANOM	group	pre-defined
CRITICAL:SMB:SIGS	group	pre-defined
CRITICAL:SMTP:SIGS	group	pre-defined
HIGH:DNS:ANOM	group	pre-defined
HIGH:DNS:SIGS	group	pre-defined
HIGH:FTP:ANOM	group	pre-defined
HIGH:FTP:SIGS	group	pre-defined
HIGH:HTTP:ANOM	group	pre-defined
HIGH:HTTP:SIGS	group	pre-defined
HIGH:IMAP:ANOM	group	pre-defined
HIGH:IMAP:SIGS	group	pre-defined
HIGH:MSRPC:ANOM	group	pre-defined
HIGH:NBDS:ANOM	group	pre-defined

Continued

Table 10.1 ScreenOS 5.1 CLI attack groups sample listing

Name	Type	Defined
HIGH:NBNAME:ANOM	group	pre-defined
HIGH:POP3:ANOM	group	pre-defined
HIGH:POP3:SIGS	group	pre-defined
HIGH:SMB:ANOM	group	pre-defined
HIGH:SMB:SIGS	group	pre-defined
HIGH:SMTP:ANOM	group	pre-defined
HIGH:SMTP:SIGS	group	pre-defined
INFO:AIM:ANOM	group	pre-defined
INFO:DNS:ANOM	group	pre-defined
INFO:DNS:SIGS	group	pre-defined
INFO:GNUTELLA:ANOM	group	pre-defined
INFO:HTTP:ANOM	group	pre-defined
INFO:HTTP:SIGS	group	pre-defined
INFO:MSN:ANOM	group	pre-defined
INFO:MSN:SIGS	group	pre-defined
INFO:SMB:ANOM	group	pre-defined
INFO:SMTP:ANOM	group	pre-defined
INFO:YMSG:ANOM	group	pre-defined
INFO:YMSG:SIGS	group	pre-defined
LOW:FTP:SIGS	group	pre-defined
LOW:HTTP:SIGS	group	pre-defined
LOW:SMTP:SIGS	group	pre-defined
MEDIUM:DNS:ANOM	group	pre-defined
MEDIUM:DNS:SIGS	group	pre-defined
MEDIUM:FTP:ANOM	group	pre-defined
MEDIUM:FTP:SIGS	group	pre-defined
MEDIUM:HTTP:ANOM	group	pre-defined
MEDIUM:HTTP:SIGS	group	pre-defined
MEDIUM:IMAP:ANOM	group	pre-defined
MEDIUM:MSRPC:ANOM	group	pre-defined
MEDIUM:NBDS:ANOM	group	pre-defined

Continued

Table 10.1 ScreenOS 5.1 CLI attack groups sample listing

Name	Type	Defined
MEDIUM:NBNAME:ANOM	group	pre-defined
MEDIUM:POP3:ANOM	group	pre-defined
MEDIUM:POP3:SIGS	group	pre-defined
MEDIUM:SMB:ANOM	group	pre-defined
MEDIUM:SMB:SIGS	group	pre-defined
MEDIUM:SMTP:ANOM	group	pre-defined
MEDIUM:SMTP:SIGS	group	pre-defined

```
Total number of attack groups is 58

ns5gt->
```

Cut and paste this output to a text file for handy reference. Now let's edit this policy to add DI. From the command line, type **set policy id [x]** where [x] is the ID number of the policy we're editing, and press Return. This puts us unto policy-edit mode—you'll notice the command prompt has changed, and added a **(policy:x)** to the end of the prompt. This lets us know we're editing policy 'x'. All subsequent commands apply only to our current policy until we use the **exit** command to end policy-edit mode.

From here, it's a simple matter of adding **set attack [attack-group-name] action [action]** to add attack [attack-group-name] to the policy with action of [action]. To enable logging of this group, we need to add another set attack command, this time with logging instead of an action command, like so: **set attack [attack-group-name] logging**. Once you've added all your attack groups, remember to use the **exit** command.

Explanation of Deep Inspection Contexts and Regular Expressions

After using the built-in signatures, I'm sure you're eager to write a few of your own. Before we jump into how to write a signature, we need to cover some basics on how DI looks for patterns, and how to write instructions to make it recognize bad traffic.

As mentioned earlier, Deep Inspection uses contexts to examine relevant portions of network streams for content. In ScreenOS 5.0, a very limited set of DI contexts were exposed to end users. Table 10.1 shows the *only* contexts a user could use to make a signature; many more were available to Juniper signature writers.

Table 10.2 ScreenOS 5.0.0 User-Accessible Contexts

Deep Inspection Protocols	End User Contexts
FTP	ftp-command, ftp-username
HTTP	http-url-parsed
SMTP	smtp-from, smtp-header-from, smtp-header-to, smtp-rcpt

With ScreenOS 5.1, a whole new slew of protocols with new contexts are available, as well as additional contexts for existing protocols (see Table 10.2).

Table 10.3 ScreenOS 5.1.0 User-Accessible Contexts

Deep Inspection Protocols	End User Contexts
AOL Instant Messenger (AIM)	aim-chat-room-desc, aim-chat-room-name, aim-get-file, aim-nick-name, aim-put-file, aim-screen-name
DNS	dns-cname
FTP	ftp-command, ftp-password, ftp-path-name, ftp-username
Gnutella Peer-to-Peer Protocol	gnutella-http-get-filename
HTTP	http-authorization, http-header-user-agent, http-request, http-status, http-text-html, http-url, http-url-parsed, http-url-variable-parsed
IMAP	imap-authenticate, imap-login, imap-mailbox, imap-user
Microsoft Network Chat (MSN)	msn-display-name, msn-get-file, msn-put-file, msn-sign-in-name
Post Office Protocol ver 3 (POP3):	pop3-auth, pop3-header-from, pop3-header-line, pop3-header-subject, pop3-header-to, pop3-mime-content-filename, pop3-user
Server Message Block/Common Internet File System (SMB/CIFS)	smb-account-name, smb-connect-path, smb-connect-service, smb-copy-filename, smb-delete-filename, smb-open-filename

Continued

Table 10.3 ScreenOS 5.1.0 User-Accessible Contexts

Deep Inspection Protocols	End User Contexts
Simple Mail Transfer Protocol (SMTP)	smtp-from, smtp-header-from, smtp-header-line, smtp-header-subject, smtp-header-to, smtp-mime-content-file-name, smtp-rcpt
Transmission Control Protocol (TCP)	stream256
Yahoo! Instant Messenger (YMSG)	ymsg-alias, ymsg-chatroom-message, ymsg-chatroom-name, ymsg-nickname, ymsg-p2p-get-filename-url, ymsg-p2p-put-filename-url, ymsg-user-name

There's not enough space to cover all of these contexts in detail, so in the next section we're going to hit the highlights and give some examples of what you can do with some of the more popular contexts. A complete context reference can be found in the Juniper documentation.

Before we can talk about writing signatures in contexts, we need to cover the pattern matching syntax, also known as DFA (Deterministic Finite Automaton) syntax (see the "Deep Inspection Search Algorithm" sidebar below). NetScreen DFA syntax is similar to regular expression syntax, but not quite the same. Below we'll cover the basics of how NetScreens match patterns.

The most straightforward way of looking for data would be an exact match. For example, to find the exact byte-pattern of **root** in a context, we would simply type **root**. Note that if the context presents any additional data, like **rooter** or, if the capitalization does not match, like **Root** or **rOoT**, then this simple match string will *not* match.

In order to insert special matching commands within a search string, the commands have to be identified as commands instead of just more matching text. This command delineation method is commonly known as *escaping*. In DFA syntax, commands are identified by a preceding backslash (\).

Sometimes, an exact string match is what you want. Most often, however, you want to detect variations and permutations of strings. For a case-insensitive match of alphabetic characters, enclose the string within escaped square brackets. Our earlier search for root with case-insensitive added would be **\[root\]**. Failing to close the case-insensitive range with an ending delimiter will cause the signature to not work.

This is useful, but what if we need to match this string at the beginning of the stream, but more information comes after it (such as in our rooter example above)? For this, we turn to our good friend, dot-star. The dot is used to match any one-byte value (in order to match a literal dot, it must be escaped, like so: \.). Star means *zero or more of the previous match* (again, to match a literal asterisk, it must be escaped like so: *). Put these two elements, dot and star, together, and it will match zero or more of anything, which is quite handy. For example, **\[root\].*** matches **Rooter** and **rooTMan**, but not **iamroot**. For that last match, a dot-star at the beginning is the trick. For example, .*\[root\] matches nicely, as well as .*\[root\].*, which will also match **IamRootMan**. Many Juniper-authored signatures work exactly this way.

NOTE

The dot-star implementation used by Juniper's IDP and DI is different from the common RegEx implementation. Standard (java/perl/grep) RegEx treats .* as a greedy match; if you put dot-star at the beginning it will always match. Juniper's implementation is a bit more intuitive, but may surprise someone who is already familiar with using a posix regep.

While these work great for ASCII character matches, many protocols use non-ASCII bytes. There are two ways to match arbitrary binary data in DI—hexadecimal (hex) and octal representations. For hex, DFA uses an escaped X (for heX) while for Octal, DFA uses an escaped zero (0), which represents the letter O in Octal. Another fundamental difference between these two methods is that an octal match always represents a single byte (so the maximum value is \0377, two bytes would be \0377\0377), while a hex match always represents one or more bytes with \x delimiting the start and end of the range of characters to be evaluated as hex (that is, \xff\x or \x0123456789abcdef\x). White space within the hex range is ignored, so you can space out your match characters by nybbles, bytes, words, etc. For example, you can enter **\x 0123456789ABCDEF \x = \x 01 23 45 67 89 AB CD EF \x = \x 0123 4567 89AB CDEF \x**. Failing to close a hex range with an ending delimiter will cause the signature to not work.

There are times when an attack will have one or more methods for gathering the same results, or perhaps you want to combine similar signatures into a single entry. In order to define elements of a match string, parentheses are used, but they are *not* escaped. To use literal parentheses in a match, you must escape them like so: \(\) or use their ASCII hex or octal values. Don't confuse escaped parentheses with case-insensitive matching brackets that *must* be escaped in order to work so that they are not misinterpreted as a character class (see below). When selecting one or the other of a series of options, we use the pipe (|) character for an *OR* operator. That is, match A or B using the entry **(A|B)**. Several ORs can be chained together—any one of them will match: **(A|BC|DEF)**. Note that they need not be a single byte, nor have the same amount of bytes.

There are times when you might want to match a large range of characters that would make ORing them all together entirely impractical. For example, 'all capital letters' would be **(A|B|C|D|E|F|G** and so on until **|X|Y|Z)** which is way too long, and makes reading difficult. To solve this dilemma, we have the character class feature. Character classes use unescaped brackets with a list of characters or a single character range to match on. **[A–Z]** would solve our 'all capital letters' problem. For an arbitrary character class, merely add the characters within bracket in any order: **[ABCcba]**. Character classes also allow for octal codes for non-printable byte value match: **[\000–\017]** or **[\011\013\020]** etc.

Yet another use of the character class is to define values *not* to match. This is known as a *negate character* class. To negate a character class, merely place a caret (^) as the first character inside the class. This will *not* match on a caret – it will negate the remainder of the character class. In ScreenOS 5.0, only a single character is allowed after the caret, while in ScreenOS 5.1, multiple characters are allowed, for example, **[^A]** or **[^123]**. A common state-saver to the traditional dot-star in the middle of a match string (see the "Deep Inspection Search Algorithm" sidebar) is a not-space-star, or **[^]*** match string.

The question mark (?) makes the directly preceding match optional. For example, **html?** matches both **html** as well as just **htm**. This is also handy for using with parentheses to make an entire element optional. For example, **super(duper)?man** matches both **superman** and **superduperman**.

One final major matching syntax we'll cover before jumping into signature writing is the unicode decoder. Many Windows protocols, like SMB, NetBIOS, and MS-RPC can use either traditional ASCII encoding or the new international-friendly unicode encoding. To convert ASCII to unicode, nulls (\000) are inserted after every character. Traditionally, it was very messy to make a string match both normal ASCII and ASCII in Unicode. For example, to match **Windows** would require **W(\000)?i(\000)?n(\000)?d(\000)?o(\000)?w(\000)?s(\000)?**, which is almost unreadable. The same match using the unicode decoder is merely **\uWindows\u**. Be sure to close your decoder with a second **\u** or the signature will not work.

Table 10.4 includes a quick reference to the match strings described above.

Table 10.4 NetScreen Search String Syntax Summary

Match String	Usage Notes and Syntax
.	The dot character matches any one byte. When a literal dot match is needed, try escaping the dot like so: **www\.juniper\.net**.
*	The asterisk (or star) matches zero or more of the preceding match. When a literal asterisk is needed, try escaping it: *****
.*	Dot-star is a useful combination that matches zero or more of any characters. Place at the beginning of a match string to search anywhere in the context. Place at the end of a match string to ignore any additional data after the matched string. Remember that Juniper's implementation of dot-star is *not* greedy.
+	The plus sign character matches one or more of the preceding match. For example, **AA+** matches **AAA**, but not **AA** or **AAB**.
?	The question mark makes the preceding character/element an optional match. For example, **html?** matches both **htm** and **html**.
\xAB CD\x \XABCD\X	Matches hexadecimal values. Be sure to close your decoder with a second **\x** or the signature will not work.
\0oct	Slash-zero matches a single byte of octal values \000 through \0377. Permitted octal characters are 01234567 only.
\[match\]	Case-insensitive search. Alphabetic characters are compared with both upper and lower case. For example, **\[dog\]** matches **dog**, **DOG**, **Dog**, **dOG**, and **DoG**.
( )	Parentheses are used to group portions of match strings into a single element. Parentheses are also useful with the pipe character for OR comparisons. For example, **AA(AA|BB)BB** matches **AAAABB** or **AABBBB**. For a literal parentheses, try escaping them like so: **\(\)**
[abc123] [a-z] [\0123-\0321]	Character class. Counts as a single byte that matches any symbol or symbol range inside. Cannot be used inside a case-insensitive search. For example, **\[abc[def]ghi\]** is illegal. Instead, try **\[abc\][def]\[ghi\]**. Also note that multiple ranges are not allowed, such as **[a-zA-Z]**. Octal is also supported in order to define non-printable ranges.

Continued

Table 10.4 NetScreen Search String Syntax Summary

Match String	Usage Notes and Syntax
[^ abc] [^] [^ \000]	Negated character class. Counts as any single byte that does *not* match the contents inside the brackets. Note that octal is still supported in negated character classes. ScreenOS 5.0 DFA only supports a single character in a negate character class, while ScreenOS 5.1 DFA supports multiple characters.
\s	New in ScreenOS 5.1 is the white-space character, or slash-s. This matches a single space or tab. For ScreenOS 5.0, in order to match the same value, an octal OR group was used: **(\011|\020)**. This is much easier to read.
\uUnicode\u	New in ScreenOS 5.1 is the unicode decoder, or slash-u. Be sure to close your decoder with a second **\u** or the signature will not work.

For an exhaustive reference to regular expressions, I highly recommend the O'Reilly book *Mastering Regular Expressions, 2nd Edition*, by Jeffrey E. F. Friedl, (ISBN: 0-596-00289-0).

Tools and Traps

Deep Inspection Search Algorithm

NetScreen IDP and DI both use a method of searching traffic for malicious patterns very quickly using a technique known as a Deterministic Finite Automaton. A simple explanation of DFA is a tree of all possibilities the search is looking for, combined into a logical table where similar matches are grouped together and searched simultaneously. When a difference between two unique patterns occurs along the line, the search line forks and each subsequent possibility then gets its own line. The total unique search lines these forks create are known as states.

A DFA with a large number of states takes significantly longer to parse though to find a match. Regular expression symbols that generate a large number of states are the wildcard symbols ., *, and +, and the conditional symbol ?. When placed in the middle of a match, they can expand the number of states exponentially, severely impacting perfor-

Continued

mance and memory. Use these symbols sparingly in the middle of your signatures. Using them at the beginning or end of your signature does not add states and is actually a handy way to scan for a match where the beginning of the stream of information to match is unknown or variable.

Creating Your Own Signatures

Now that we've covered the two major aspects to signature creation – contexts and syntax – let's put them together and write a few signatures! This section will cover a few of the more popular contexts with some RegEx usage on how to get the most out of them.

To make a new custom signature, access **Objects | Attacks | Custom**, and click the **New** button. This will open the signature editor window, which has 5 fields; **Attack Name**, **Attack Context**, **Attack Severity**, **Attack Pattern**, and **Negate**. Also note that custom signature names must start with the string CS (for custom signature). We'll be using this window as we experiment with some of the more common contexts below.

HTTP is the most common protocol, and by far the highest bandwidth consumer. Adding new HTTP signatures impacts the performance of this already heavily burdened protocol, so add new signatures here with care, and try to avoid high-state wildcards (see the "Deep Inspection Search Algorithm" sidebar above) in the middle of signatures and after common matching strings.

To understand how the HTTP contexts work, we need to first examine the HTTP protocol itself. HTTP is a stateless client-server protocol, where a server generally supplies files based upon requests by the client. In addition to the file transfer itself, several protocol-related data exchanges occur, mostly at the beginning, before the actual file transfer – these are known as *HTTP headers* (inspected by the **http-header-user-agent** and **http-authorization** contexts). The client request itself is called a *Uniform Resource Locator*, or URL. The URL itself is generally broken down into two elements: the path/file and the parameters/variables. The path and file includes all characters after the request verb but before the question mark, exclusive. The parameters (also called variables) include everything after the question mark, also exclusive. DI has an **http-url-parsed** context as well as an **http-variable-parsed** context. These contexts take any kind of URL obfuscating encoding and parse it as it would be by the end server and then apply the signature against the result. This allows us to write a nice, clean URL signature without worrying about encoding schemes or other kinds of IDS evasion techniques. If such encoding attacks are what you're looking for, there's also the unparsed **http-url** context for just the URL, or **http-request** for the entire request, completely unparsed. Let's try some practical examples of these contexts using the sample exchange below:

The client requests:
GET /etc/pass%77d?bar=yes HTTP/1.1
User-Agent: HappyBrowser v1.1
Host: www.foo.com
Authorization: Basic dXNlcjpwYXNzd29yZAo=

The server responds:
HTTP/1.1 200 OK
Date: Sat, 25 Dec 2004 00:00:01 GMT
Etc…

Notice the %77 in the URL? That decodes to an ASCII **w**, making the path **/etc/passwd**; someone was trying to hide the true name of the filename he or she was requesting. This is a fairly common evasion method and it's easily defeated by the **http-url-parsed** context, since the context itself normalizes (parses) the URL before inspecting it. To match this attack, merely enter \[/**etc/passwd**\] (remembering to add case-insensitivity to catch further evasion) as the attack pattern with an attack context of **HTTP Decoded HTTP URL**. Name this something useful, starting with the **CS:** identifier, such as **CS:HTTP:ETC-PASSWD**, then assign it a severity (like **Medium**) and you're done! Note we did not need a dot-star at the end of this pattern to account for the **bar=yes** parameter, as the http-url-parsed context stops before the question mark that delineates path from parameter. This is very similar to the Juniper-supplied signature HTTP:INFO-LEAK:HTPASSWD-REQUEST, whose match pattern is .*/\.\[htpasswd\]. The important differences are that this signature is looking for the file .htpasswd at the end of any path, which is covered by the dot-star and a forward slash. The dot in .htpasswd is also escaped for a more accurate match.

Sometimes, you may want to match a particular protocol's (for example, HTTP or FTP) traffic on a port other than the typical ports used by that protocol. This is where the **Application** setting in the policy editor (see figure 10.6) comes in handy. The **Application** setting is a list of all application layer gateways (ALGs) and DI protocols parsed. The **Application** setting activates all ALGs and DI contexts for that protocol on whatever the service (pre-defined or custom) is set to. So, to use FTP (with dynamic-gate ALG support) on a non-standard port, you would merely create a custom service for the command port used, then bind the FTP application setting to it. All traffic permitted by this policy will be inspected for FTP protocol conventions, including PORT commands that will be used to open data connection gates. Additionally, any FTP-based DI anomalies or signatures assigned to the policy in the Deep Inspection editing window will also be applied to this custom service.

Figure 10.6 Policy Editor Application Field

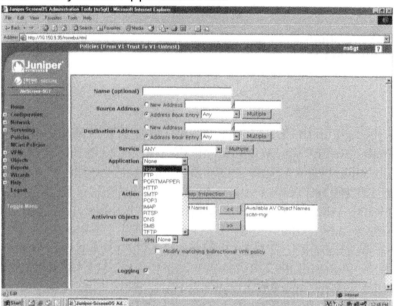

Now let's tackle another protocol – Transmission Control Protocol. "But that's not an Application Layer Protocol!" you shout. And you're quite right. But there is a single context that can be bound to any TCP service supported by DI called *stream256*, and so for lack of a better description, this is a TCP context. Stream256 is a very simple, but very powerful context. It should be used with care. This context is powerful since it gets around the problem that certain useful contexts may not be customer-accessible. It's also useful for inspecting protocols not supported by DI. The downside is that it only inspects the first 256 bytes of the stream, but you'd be surprised what you can do with 256 bytes. It inspects any DI-supported service that bound by policy. In order for stream256 to work, however, an **Application** setting (other than **None** or **Ignore**) *must* be selected.

Be sure *not* to use a dynamic-port protocol like H.323, SIP, PORTMAPPER, MSRPC-EPM or FTP, unless you are specifically writing a signature for these services, since the ALG will try to unnecessarily parse the protocol for dynamic-gate opening, and will slow traffic going through it. That is, if you're writing a stream256 signature for HTTP, be sure to apply the HTTP **Application** setting. For non-DI supported protocols, use an uncommon **Application** setting like TALK to make stream256 work best.

The majority of the other contexts are fairly simple and self-explanatory. A few quick comments on some of the more interesting contexts:

- **dns-cname** examines just the DNS hostname of a DNS request, for example, www.juniper.net.

- **ftp-pathname** includes both the path and the filename. Add a dot-star to the beginning of the search pattern to look for files downloaded via FTP.

- **http-authorization** automatically decodes the Authorization: Basic Base64 code into a username:password format. Use **\[username\]:.*** to look for specific usernames and **.*:password** to look for specific passwords.

- **http-header-user-agent** can be used for browser identification, especially peer-to-peer and spyware applications that use the Web. Quite a few of them aren't clever enough yet to hide their actual program names. Use **Gator.*** to match the Gator spyware program.

- **pop3-user** and **pop3-auth** provide you with username and password, respectively, for POP3 users.

- **smtp-rcpt** is essentially the To: field of an SMTP mail exchange. Good for looking for specific destination e-mail addresses.

- **smtp-mime-content-filename** provides filenames to attachments in e-mails sent via SMTP.

Also recall that signatures cannot be used by themselves; they must be incorporated into an attack group before they can be used. So before we add these attack objects to a policy, we need to make our own custom attack group. Attack groups must begin with the letters **CS:**, for example, **CS:HTTP-ATTACKS**, **CS:FTP-SIGS**, etc. Create a new custom group by accessing **Objects | Attacks | Custom Groups** and clicking the **New** button. Once in the new group creation window, you'll see a **Group Name** field (again, must start with **CS:**), as well as the **Selected Members** and **Available Members** lists. Merely select which custom signatures (Juniper-supplied signatures cannot be assigned to a custom signature group) you want this group to contain and click the **<<** button to move them over to the **Selected Members** list. Remove selected members with the **>>** button. Once you have this new custom signature group, you're ready to use it in a policy, just like any other attack group.

Tools & Traps...

Advanced DI signature writing using an IDP

One of the more powerful features of DI is the ability to write your own signatures for it. But one of frustrating things with this feature is the fact you can't see quite how DI will actually inspect the traffic within its contexts. Does it include the HTTP GET verb? Are the parameters parsed, or just the path?

Since DI is truly a subset of the IDP feature set, if you have an IDP handy, you can use it for advanced DI signature development. This is the same technique used by the actual DI and IDP signature writers at Juniper Networks to develop production signatures. This can be used on a production IDP with minimal impact to network performance, but because of the volume of data provided, you might want this to be done on a lab IDP instead. Also note that the Environment Security Profiler (ESP) feature of the IDP (disabled by default) will have to be turned off before this technique can be used.

To start, log into your IDP remotely via SSH and become the root user. Using the command **scio ccap all** will show you every context that the IDP is parsing against traffic currently flowing through the device and exactly how that traffic is parsed. Press **Ctrl + C** to stop the display. While displaying, this will slow the unit some, especially if there is a lot of traffic. You can either limit the services to be examined by replacing the all with a service limiter command such as **scio ccap svc http** or **scio ccap svc ftp**. The command has a help system to show you valid services, but for the purposes of DI, remember that the services are somewhat limited.

Once you have your ccap (short for Context Capture) running, execute an attack that you're interested in blocking through the IDP, and watch it parse your attack into contexts. At this point you should be able

Continued

to write a regular expression string to match your attack. Keep in mind that some contexts that exist on an IDP are limited in DI and may not be available. Work backwards from the contexts that are available in DI and find out how it is examined using an IDP. Since DI and the IDP view these contexts in exactly the same way, you can be reasonably certain that if it detects it on an IDP, it will work on DI.

Setting up Content Filtering

Juniper Networks' NetScreen firewalls support content filtering through two major methods, URL filtering and antivirus. Of course, Deep Inspection could also be used as a sort of content filtering, but it's not quite as suitable since it doesn't present the end user with an appropriate error page when a violation is detected like the URL filtering feature does.

URL Filtering

URL filtering is the process of examining HTTP requests for content. Requests to inappropriate sites like those that host pornography, racism, or other offensive sites can be blocked using this feature. This works by comparing the requested URL against a database of classified sites. URLs can be categorically permitted or denied with a variety of configuration settings, which depend on the filtering server/service used. These services charge a recurring fee for updates to the database, as new sites are constantly created on the Internet. The URL filtering software provides Internet usage reports and also keeps track of repeat violators.

Starting with ScreenOS 5.1, NetScreen firewalls support the SurfControl Redirect protocol as well as the legacy WebSense Redirect protocol, but not both at the same time. With SurfControl, ScreenOS 5.1 also supports a special *integrated mode* on the NS-HSC, NS-5GT, NS-25 and NS-50. This loads the filter database directly on the device.

WebSense Redirect Mode

This is the only method of URL filtering for ScreenOS 5.0 and earlier. It's fairly straightforward to configure on the NetScreen device – the majority of work required is on the WebSense server side, configuring users, user groups, policies, and exceptions. To use WebSense with ScreenOS 5.1, select this as protocol to use for URL filtering.

WebSense requires a Web server like IIS or Apache in order to operate. Usually that means installing it on Windows 2000 or 2003 Server, although it will run on Windows 2000 or XP Professional with Apache installed. If a Web server is not found, the installation will automatically download and install Apache for you if you permit it to. Setup and installation really is easy. 512 Megabytes of RAM is the minimum requirement, but at least 1 Gigabyte is strongly recommended. See www.websense.com/products/about/Enterprise/ for more product details. They offer a 30-day free trial.

From the firewall side of things, setup is a snap. See Figure 10.7 for an example of a firewall configured for WebSense Redirect Mode. First, enable the **Enable URL Filtering** option. Next, type the IP address (or DNS domain name if configured for your WebSense server, and your NetScreen has a DNS server configured) into the **Server Name** field. Enter the port number that the WebSense server is listening on for URL validation requests in the **Server Port** field (the default port is 15868). Now set a reasonable **Communication Timeout** value (10 is the default, but you may need more if the WebSense server is being accessed via a VPN). At this point, if the server is up and properly configured, a click on the yellow circle next to **Server Connection Status** should show that the server is running. If it doesn't work right away, give it ten to fifteen seconds, and try the yellow circle button again. If the server is still down, check your settings (including DNS!), your routes, and your server. Try to ping the server by IP from a CLI prompt on the NetScreen if you're having trouble getting the system to work.

There's also an option to set the behavior of the firewall in the event that the URL server cannot be contacted. Using this option to either block all HTTP or permit all HTTP is a policy decision you'll have to make on your own, depending on your business requirements and the stability of your WebSense setup.

Figure 10.7 URL Filtering Configuration with WebSense Redirect Mode

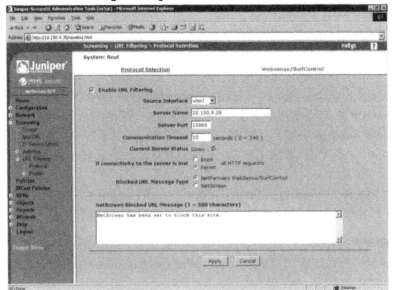

SurfControl Redirect Mode

SurfControl Web Filter for Juniper Networks Security Devices is a competitor to WebSense, and with ScreenOS 5.1 you now have a choice of URL filtering services to select. Like WebSense, SurfControl will work with 512 Megabytes of RAM, but would prefer 1 Gigabyte or more. SurfControl requires either an external MS-SQL database or an internal Microsoft Desktop Engine 2000 (MSDE2000) database. If an MSDE2000 database is not already installed, SurfControl will download and install it for you, similar to how WebSense handles a missing Web server – very handy. Like WebSense they also offer a 30-day free trial. After using both, I found WebSense easier to set up and configure, but unlike WebSense, SurfControl has an Integrated mode that uses public servers (which means no local installation!) that we'll examine below.

Since it's essentially the same concept, the configuration settings for SurfControl Redirect Mode are the same as WebSense Redirect Mode. To use SurfControl with ScreenOS 5.1, you'll first need to select it as the protocol to use for URL filtering. Then fill in the options as you would in WebSense, such as turning on **Enable URL Filtering**, setting a **Server Name**, **Server Port** (the default for the Surf Control Filter Protocol (SCFP) is 62252), and a **Communications Timeout** value. Now it's time to check the server availability. Click on the yellow circle to ensure you've set everything up correctly.

Try some of the troubleshooting tips found above in the WebSense section if things aren't working right.

SurfControl Integrated Mode

This mode is only available on the newer low-to-midrange model NetScreen firewalls—the NS-HSC, NS-5GT, NS-25 and NS-50. SurfConrol Integrated Mode also requires a feature key to activate. To use SurfControl with ScreenOS 5.1, you'll first need to select it as the protocol to use for URL filtering. The protocol used for this mode is the SurfControl Content Portal Authority (SC-CPA) protocol.

Once Integrated Mode is selected, configuration options for this mode appear. See Figure 10.8 for a reference. These options include:

- **Server Name** A drop-down list that allows you to select in which major continent (America, Europe, Asia) the device is located so the closest SurfControl server is selected.

- **Host** The actual hostname for the server to use. This value is automatically filled in from the **Server Name** field, but can be overridden.

- **Port** The port to use for communication with the URL filtering server database. SC-CPA's default port is 9020.

- **Enable Cache** This allows the NetScreen device to cache the results of SC-CPA look-ups, decreasing the response time to end user requests.

- **Cache Size** The size (in kilobytes) allocated for the cache.

- **Cache Timeout** The length of time an entry will age off the cache if not requested.

- **Query Interval** How often the NetScreen device will check with the server for major category updates.

- **Permit** or **Block** Included as a default fallback decision if the server does not respond to a request.

Integrated Mode URL filtering supports the concept of *black lists* (always deny regardless of classification) and *white lists* (always permit regardless of classification) right on the device. These lists, as well as custom URL lists, are created by accessing **Screening | URL Filtering | Profile | Custom List** and clicking the **New** button. In the custom list edit window, add a name to this category (Whitelist, Blacklist, Competitors, etc) and add your first URL and click the

Apply button. The category name will be saved and locked, and the URL added to the list. Add additional URLs (up to a maximum of 20) by entering them in the URL field and clicking the **Apply** button. When you are done adding URLs, click the **OK** button to save.

Figure 10.8 URL Filtering Configuration with SurfControl Integrated Mode

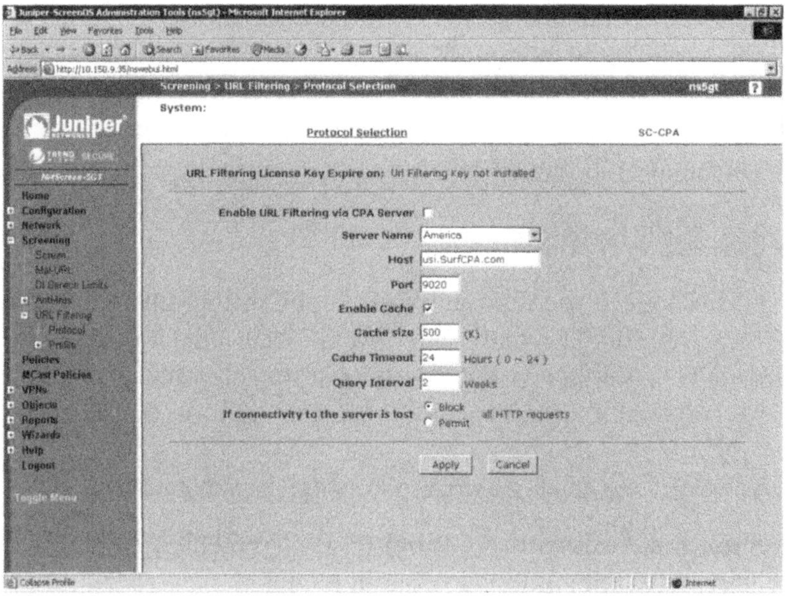

Enforcing URL Filtering

In order to instruct the NetScreen device as to which sources and destinations are to be inspected for URL filtering, a policy definition is required. Refer back to Figure 10.3 for the basic policy editing window. Note that at the top of the second section there is a checkbox to enable URL filtering for the policy.

For Integrated Mode filtering, filter decisions (called a *filter profile*), based upon which category the URL matches, are made on the device itself. If no custom filtering profile exists, then the default *ns-profile* is compared and action is taken. This profile is a read-only template that can be cloned and the resulting copy modified and used. If a custom profile is created, either from scratch or cloned from the ns-profile, the inspection process becomes a little more complicated. As URLs are offered to the NetScreen for inspection, it first checks the user-defined whitelist, then the user-defined blacklist, then the NetScreen checks the URL for categorization. Once it knows the URL's category, it first compares it to the user-defined filtering profile. Any match against the user profile is acted on as configured and the default profile check is skipped. If the URL category matches no defined categories in the user-defined profile, and the user-defined profile default action is set to **Permit**, then a final check against the ns-profile is performed, and whatever action is set for that category is then performed.

For Redirected Mode filtering, filter decisions (based upon which category the URL matches) are handled by the remote filtering server. This allows for advanced policy editing, including the ability to override a profile based upon a user login, or have different profiles based upon the time of day or day of the week. These features are offered by the third-party filtering servers, so check their product sheets for specific filters.

Antivirus Scanning

ScreenOS 5.0 introduced the new antivirus engine from Trend Micro. This feature is supported on middle-to-low-end devices from NS-HSC through NS-208. A license key is required to activate the feature. Files sent via HTTP, FTP, POP3. IMAP, and SMTP are inspected for viruses right on the device.

Configuring Global Antivirus Parameters

Access **Screening | Antivirus | Global** to display the ScreenOS 5.1.0 screen shown in Figure 10.9. The options to configure are:

- **Fail Mode Traffic Permit** If this option is enabled, and for some reason the AV scan fails (either is too large, reaches a compression recursion limit, or some other scan failure), the traffic is still permitted. If the scan is successful, and no virus is found, the traffic is permitted regardless of this setting. If the scan detects a virus, the traffic is dropped, regardless of this setting.

- **AV HTTP Skipmime** If this option is enabled, the following MIME (Multipurpose Internet Mail Extension) types and subtypes are skipped from AV scan:

  - application/x-director

  - application/pdf

  - audio/*

  - image/*

- text/css

- text/html

- video/*

This improves AV scanning performance, since the majority of HTTP traffic uses these MIME types. Until recently this was considered a safe setting, so bypassing is enabled by default. Thanks to recent Microsoft vulnerabilities with JPEG and BMP file formats, this is no longer the case. Unless performance is suffering considerably, do *NOT* enable this option.

- **Keep Alive** If this option is enabled, the NetScreen device will keep the HTTP session open to the server with a keep alive request after the file arrives on the NetScreen device, but before it has finished scanning the file. This decreases overall latency of the connection, but is less secure.

- **Trickling** The method of sending a small portion of the file on to the requesting client so that the client's browser won't timeout the connection. The three options for this are **Disable** (which disables the trickling feature), **Default** (if the received file is larger than 3MB, it will trickle 500 bytes for every 1MB of data scanned) or **Custom**, in which you can set your own trickling settings:

  - **Minimum Length** This sets the minimum file size to start trickling. Files smaller than this will not be trickled at all. Files of this size or larger are trickled according to the following settings.

  - **Trickle Size** This sets the trickle packet size.

  - **Trickle For Every** This sets the amount of traffic sent before a single packet is sent.

These settings handle how the device handles traffic it inspects, but how does the NetScreen get these attacks to match against? For these settings, we need to configure the Scan Manager.

Figure 10.9 ScreenOS 5.1.0 Global Antivirus Parameters

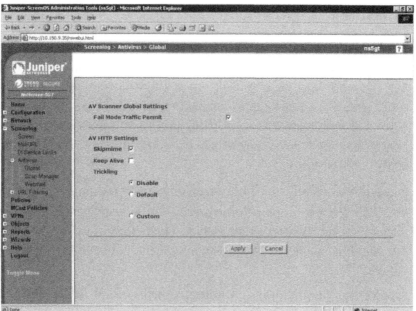

Configuring Scan Manager Settings

An antivirus is only as good as its virus database, so to stay protected you need to stay updated. These settings are found by accessing **Screen | Antivirus | Scan Manager** in your WebUI. Figure 10.10 shows the 5.1.0 version of this screen. This shows important information such as AV license entitlement as well as how current your virus definitions are. Other important features on this screen are:

- **Pattern Update Server** This is the server the device will automatically connect to in order to obtain AV pattern updates from. The default is http://[device-model]-t.activeupdate.trendmicro.com:80/activeupdate/server.ini.

    The **[device-model]-t** portion of the URL for my NetScreen-5GT was **5gt-t**.

- **Auto Pattern Update** This permits or disables the auto-update feature. Leave this option enabled unless you're experiencing problems obtaining the update.

- **Interval** This sets how often (in minutes) it checks for an update, with a default of 60. Don't be concerned if the **Last Updated on:** value doesn't coincide within the current time minus the update time. The date/time group at the top is the date/time of the AV pattern file, and not necessarily when it was loaded. Viruses spread most quickly during the first 24 hours (due to lack of antiviral protection) so be sure to leave this interval low.

- **Update Now** A handy button to check your settings and to manually refresh your AV definitions if you've turned off automatic updates.

Below that first section there are a few configuration options for handling compressed files. Since a single compressed file can contain one or more files, and those files themselves can be compressed, in order to ensure that all content is checked, the NetScreen device will decompress zip files if possible and examine the results for viruses. This can be time and resource consuming, so some practical limits were introduced, but are user-configurable. Note that compressed file nesting is a common AV evasion technique. Another AV evasion technique is sending a very small compressed file that expands into an extremely large uncompressed file, attached with a second file that is malicious. The idea is that the AV scanner would max out on the benign, but extremely large file and then skip checking any other files after it, including the resulting malicious files. To prevent these kinds of evasion techniques you can adjust the following settings:

- **File Decompression** The number of recursions the scanner will go down into, from 1 to 4.

- **Drop/Bypass** and **Size Exceeds** This sets the limit for the size of uncompressed files to scan, and also an action if this limit is reached.

- **Drop/Bypass** and **Number of Files Exceeds** This sets the limit for the number of uncompressed files to scan, and also an action if this limit is reached.

The final section in the Scan Manager configuration screen covers which protocols will be inspected for viruses. Keep in mind, this is a *global* setting – any protocol turned off here will not be scanned, regardless of how the configuration of the policy that the AV is applied to. Protocol options include **HTTP** (with options for **Webmail** or **All HTTP**), **SMTP**, **POP3**, **FTP**, and **IMAP**. Disabling any of these options will relieve your NetScreen of some burden, but will also increase your likelihood of infection. Turn off these protocols *only* if you are certain they cannot be passed (for example, if you are using an explicit blocking policy).

For the webmail blocking option, the NetScreen has to have the URL path portion configured for relevant webmail systems in order to determine if it has to check attachments for viruses. By default, three popular webmail sites are pre-configured – AOL, Yahoo, and Hotmail. The settings for these sites may change as the developers for these sites add new features or make other changes. Also, any other webmail site you want filtered will have to be added manually and monitored for effectiveness due to changes later. I would recommend *not* using this feature unless the NetScreen device simply cannot pass HTTP traffic fast enough in **All HTTP** mode. Also keep in mind that if you do use this mode, you can set any URL path, not just webmail, to check for viruses, such as popular file download sites like TuCows, Freshmeat, or FilePlanet.

Figure 10.10 ScreenOS 5.1.0 Scan Manager Antivirus Parameters

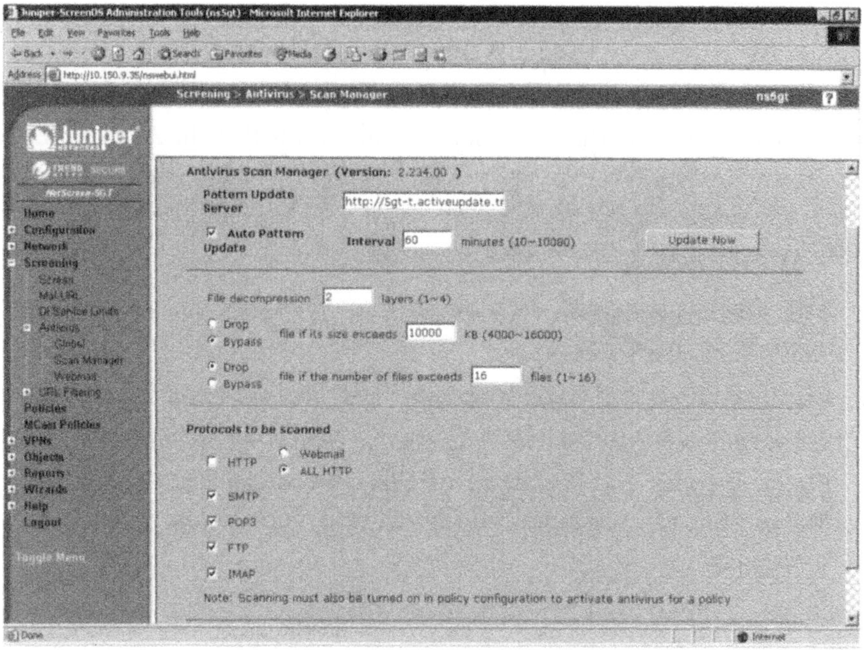

Activating Antivirus Scanning

Activating AV couldn't be easier. Currently, there is only one AV object on the device, so refer back to Figure 10.3 again and find the **Antivirus Objects** section. Select the scan-mgr object from the **Available AV Object Names** column and click the **<<** button to move it to the **Attached AV Object Names** column. Be sure to click the **OK** button to save the setting. Do this for each policy that needs antivirus scanning on any of the supported protocols.

Understanding Application Layer Gateways

Application Layer Gateways are algorithms within ScreenOS that handle dynamic firewall policies that certain protocols require, such as FTP. Many such protocols were designed without security or other access controls in mind, which can cause problems when firewalls are introduced.

For example, FTP uses multiple sessions to facilitate file transfers – a primary command channel, and secondary data channels for directory listings and file transfers. Often, these data channels will flow in the opposite direction than the original command channel. Since these data channels could connect on any port, it's almost impossible to create a static firewall policy that would permit these data channels, but still provide adequate protection.

The FTP ALG automatically solves this problem by monitoring the FTP command channel, looking for FTP *port* commands that specify which source and destination ports are being requested, and dynamically opening up that specific combination of source IP/port and destination IP/port firewall policy (called a *gate*) that permits the session to flow. Once the session is complete, the gate is immediately closed.

The FTP ALG also handles the special case where the FTP session flows through a NAT interface. In this circumstance, the endpoints don't always realize their addresses are being translated mid-stream. The FTP port commands use whatever IP the endpoint hosts' interfaces are configured for, which, in the case of a host behind a NAT firewall, will typically be unreachable from the Internet.

The ALG handles this at the application layer by modifying the ASCII port command in-situ, replacing the inside IP with the IP of the NAT interface. Since port commands are passed as ASCII text, including the IP address, the chances are high that the number of characters that represent the inside IP and the external IP won't exactly match (for example, an inside address of 192.168.1.5 contains 11 characters, which may be translated to something like 123.123.123.123 at 15 characters or something like 1.2.3.4, which contains only 7). The firewall cannot inject these extra bytes of data without modifying the TCP checksum as well as the TCP sequence numbers. It achieves this by essentially proxying the connection at the TCP layer. This is similar to the SYN proxy feature used by the TCP flood SCREEN setting.

NetScreen ALGs are different from many competitors' products. Many other firewall vendors utilize full protocol proxies, which themselves are vulnerable to attack, misconfiguration, or protocol obsolescence as new commands, options, and features are added to a protocol. CheckPoint's FireWall1 uses tiny proxies to validate data on protocols like HTTP, FTP, and SMTP. While this method is very flexible, it can still cause problems if the proxy encounters a valid command that it has not been programmed to handle, which could cause the session to break, since the proxy won't forward what it thinks is an invalid command. Furthermore, since the firewall is participating in the stream at the application layer, it's very possible (and has even happened) that the proxy itself is vulnerable to a security concern. Since FireWall1 runs on Windows, Linux, and Solaris, shellcode for these platforms is relatively easy to find. NetScreen firewalls do not participate in the exchange at the application layer, which isolates them from these sorts of attacks.

Some protocols just don't support being proxied. Microsoft's Server Message Block and Remote Procedure Call both require a real endpoint connection. While these are not commonly Internet-transiting protocols, a good defense-in-depth strategy would still have this traffic flowing through firewalls that need to know how to handle it. A new ALG found in ScreenOS 5.1 allows users to filter at the application layer for MS-RPC by parsing *globally unique identifiers* (GUIDs) —a unique 128-bit number used by Microsoft to label process endpoints. Custom-defined services are created based upon GUIDs, which are then used in a policy. This enables you to create policies that allow or prevent access to individual processes on a Windows system. This is very handy for protecting from attacks such as Blaster, Sasser, Agobot and others that use MS-RPC as one of their attack vectors.

Others vendors tend to cut corners and, for the sake of performance, will make a very simple ALG-like algorithm that should solve a problem, but has unexpected consequences. Just recently Symantec issued a security update for its DNS ALG. Apparently, the DNS ALG worked like so: if a UDP packet arrived with a source port of 53, it was a DNS reply to a DNS request that had already gone out through the firewall, and would permit the packet through without any session lookup. The ALG would also bypass any incoming policy explicitly blocking the packet, such as destination port, destination IP, or source IP. The flaw in the firewall was so fundamental that it would even bypass protections designed for its own management interface. When this oversight was made public, hackers discovered that sending management packets *to* the Simple Network Management Protocol (SNMP) port on the firewall *from* UDP port 53, they could successfully command the firewall and change the firewall's settings without being authenticated. A patch was later released. ScreenOS features are subject to security review at various stages of the development process to avoid fundamental logic flaws such as this.

ScreenOS currently has 26 ALGs, including FTP, DNS, and H.323, with more being released with every new version. These ALGs require little to no configuration to operate properly. They automatically detect appropriate traffic on the registered ports for the protocol they handle and then do their jobs. As mentioned earlier, these ALGs can be reapplied to arbitrary ports using custom service objects as needed.

Applying Best Practices

NetScreen firewalls have a wealth of security features to use, but even the best tool can be rendered ineffective through poor implementation. This section hopes to instill some good security practices to use with your NetScreen device.

Defense-In-Depth

How many locks do you have on your front door? Just one? Or do you have one lock for the doorknob, another for the deadbolt, and a chain? Do you have an alarm system as well? How about a bat by the bed? If you have all of this, then you already understand what *defense-in-depth* means. Network security is no different. Having a NetScreen firewall protecting your network is a good start to an overall effective network security system. However, it is the components of the whole system working together—internal firewalls, perimeter firewalls, IDPs, authentication services, management, antivirus software, and monitoring services—that make you more secure. The National Security Agency (NSA) has recently released a very informative paper on this subject, located at www.nsa.gov/snac/support/WORMPAPER.pdf.

Zone Isolation

An extension of the defense-in-depth concept, zone isolation involves placing different system types (for example, servers, end users, Engineering, Finance, Information Technology, etc) on different zones, which then allow for firewall policies between these dissimilar groups. Do your end users need access to the Finance department's systems? If so, what kind? Find out how to limit access to just what is necessary. Don't just assume that because a computer is inside your perimeter that it's safe. Keep access to specific areas, zones and data to the smallest possible number of computers.

Egress Filtering

Egress filtering is the process of putting restrictions on outgoing traffic as well as incoming traffic. Many locations only get half of the security picture straight – they block traffic from coming in except to specific Internet-facing servers (mail, Web, DNS, etc.) but let all inside traffic go back out completely unfiltered. Ideally, your outgoing policies should be as complex and stringent as your incoming policies. Or better yet, have *no* traffic initiated by your end users allowed out to the Internet, but rather have all traffic go through approved and configured proxy servers (such as HTTP or FTP. I highly recommend the highly-configurable open source proxy called *Squid* that comes with about every distribution of Linux out there) or internal-only servers (such as mail or DNS). This locks down infections since most backdoors don't support proxies, and those that do can be detected and blocked at your proxy.

Explicit Permits, Implicit Denies

The idiom of "You don't know what you don't know" is never truer than in the security business. Firewall administrators who block specific ports and let all others through are asking for trouble through their ignorance. Why Windows XP listens on 10 different ports to perform the same function, I'll never know. If there's just one port I miss, a worm or other malicious attack could slip by and tear up my network from the inside. Instead, permit what you *know* you want permitted, and block everything else—this keeps things simple and threats *known*.

Retain Monitoring Data

If something does happen, and it usually does, you need to know the breadth and width of the problem, when it started, and how it happened so that you can properly clean it all up and keep it from happening again. You're going to have enough trouble as it is from hackers hiding their activities through evasion and log file deletion on compromised systems. Don't compound this problem by not having dedicated, secure machines for logging and keeping the data for a historically significant period of time. This may be the only way to track a Black Hat attacker who spaces his attacks out over hours or days. It doesn't hurt to *look* at the logs from time to time as well to ensure things are copasetic.

Keep Systems Updated

If there's one thing 2004 has taught network security professionals, it's that automatic operating system updates are a good thing. Windows, MacOS, and many flavors of Linux now support some sort of automatic patching system to react to newly discovered security issues. *Use* these tools to your advantage, and keep your systems patched. Check in with Windows Update the first Tuesday of the month to see what new vulnerabilities Microsoft has 'fessed up to, and get to patching!

Summary

This chapter has covered a lot of ground in a short amount of space. Indeed, complete books are available just on subjects covered here. Despite this, we've managed to cover all SCREEN, Deep Inspection, URL filtering, and antivirus features, as well as the Application Layer Gateway functions enough to give you a good understanding of the capabilities of each, and how to set them up.

SCREEN features are the legacy security protection and cover things like SYN, UDP, and ICMP floods (with user-configurable thresholds), session-exhaustion attacks (with separate thresholds for source and destination), classic IP and TCP header manipulation, port scans and sweeps, and certain OS-specific DoS attacks. Enabling these attacks imposes almost no performance hit.

Deep Inspection takes security all the way to the application layer for selected protocols. Using stateful contexts to accurately isolate malicious traffic, you can minimize false positives and false negatives and maximize valid hits. Protocols covered in ScreenOS 5.0 included HTTP, FTP, DNS, SMTP, IMAP, and POP3, with a very limited set of contexts exposed to end users for use in their own signatures. ScreenOS 5.1 introduced several new protocols including SMB, MS-RPC, NetBIOS, Gnutella, AIM, and YMSG and included a significant increase in the number of contexts supported for end user's signatures.

We covered how ScreenOS uses contexts to break down a protocol stream into inspectable fields and uses a DFA to inspect traffic, and how to use customer available contexts and the DFA RegEx syntax to write our own custom signatures.

Also covered was ScreenOS' support for HTTP URL filtering with a variety of URL filtering options from WebSense and SurfControl, including a method of storing filtering profile right on the device with SurfControl Integrated Mode. The Integrated Mode requires a license key.

Antivirus is an important new feature in ScreenOS 5.0 that allows HTTP, FTP, SMTP, POP3 and IMAP protocols to be inspected for viruses. While there are a variety of settings to configure, the majority of the defaults work well, and with a few clicks AV can be up and running almost effortlessly. Antivirus also requires a license key.

Application layer gateways are the grease that allows certain security-impaired protocols to work through a firewall. FTP, H.323 and dynamic-channel protocols could play havoc with a firewall policy if it wasn't for ALGs and the gate feature that opens dynamic firewall policies automatically to allow data channels of already permitted command channels of these troublesome protocols.

Finally, we covered some security basics—how to put this all together into a more secure whole. Defense-in-depth, zone isolation, egress filtering, implicit permits, explicit denies, logging and keeping systems up to date aren't just topics in a CISSP book—they're real-world solutions for making your network more secure. Applying even just a few of these concepts will go a long way to making the Internet a safer place.

Solutions Fast Track

Introduction to the ScreenOS Security Features

- ☑ NetScreen firewall products pack a diverse range of features into a small, easy-to-use system.

- ☑ A firewall's primary function is always security.

- ☑ NetScreen firewall products have a variety of different security methods to stop many different types of attack.

- ☑ SCREEN features generally cover IP and TCP layer attacks.

- ☑ Deep inspection covers advanced IP, TCP/UDP, and Application Layer attacks.

- ☑ Content filtering enforces local usage policy.

- ☑ Antivirus keeps mass-mailing worms and other malware out of your network.

- ☑ Application Later Gateways handle problem protocols securely.

Understanding the Anatomy of a Hack

- ☑ Generally, there are three phases of an attack: recon, exploit, and consolidation.

- ☑ Different kinds of attackers require different methods for protection.

- ☑ Script Kiddies want publicity for their activities and will make their presence very well known.

- ☑ Black Hat hackers are more insidious and patient—it takes diligence and consistency to detect them.

☑ Self-propagating worms are becoming more aggressive and complex as time goes by. They will attack like a Kiddy but exploit like a Black Hat.

☑ Defense-in-depth, updated systems and signatures, event log vigilance, good social engineering awareness training and a sound security policy can keep these attacks at bay.

Configuring SCREEN Settings

☑ NetScreen legacy screen settings protect networks using a variety of detection methods.

☑ Network reconnaissance uses port scans, sweeps, and protocol option manipulation to avoid detection.

☑ Port scans and sweeps are detected, and can be tweaked with user-configurable threshold settings.

☑ Several TCP flag manipulation techniques are detected, including null scan, SYN/FIN scan, and others.

☑ A variety IP protocol option manipulation techniques are also detected, such as source-route, time-stamp and others.

☑ SYN, UDP, and ICMP flood attacks are prevented with user-definable thresholds to maximize throughput while still providing protection.

☑ Rudimentary HTTP content filtering is supported, with the optional blocking of ActiveX and JavaScripts, as well as EXE and ZIP file downloads.

☑ Other protocol attacks, such as WinNuke, Land, Ping of Death, and others are also covered.

Applying Deep Inspection

☑ Deep Inspection covers application layer attacks on selected protocols.

☑ With ScreenOS 5.0, 6 protocols are covered: HTTP, FTP, DNS, SMTP, POP3, and IMAP.

☑ Customer-exposed contexts were also extremely limited in ScreenOS 5.0

☑ ScreenOS 5.1 introduced several new protocols with new contexts: SMB, MS-RPC, NetBIOS, Gnutella, AIM, and YMSG

☑ ScreenOS 5.1 also added new contexts for ScreenOS 5.0 supported protocols for end users to write signatures with.

☑ Signatures use a custom subset of regular expressions and a DFA string-matching algorithm to detect attacks.

Setting up Content Filtering

☑ NetScreen firewall products support both URL filtering and, more recently, antivirus filtering.

☑ Starting with ScreenOS 5.1, NetScreen now also supports SurfControl as well as the legacy WebSense URL filtering system.

☑ On newer low to midrange NetScreens, SurfControl can also be used in Integrated Mode right on the device.

☑ NetScreen firewalls support off-loading as well as on-board antivirus inspection starting with ScreenOS 5.1.

☑ On-board antivirus inspection uses the Trend Micro engine.

Understanding Application Layer Gateways

☑ Many commonly used protocols, such as FTP, MS-RPC, or H.323, were never designed to be firewalled.

☑ ALGs enable these security-impaired protocols to work through a firewall by parsing the command channel.

☑ ALGs are *not* protocol proxies, which are limited to certain protocols and are subject to change.

☑ Other competitors' over-simplified ALGs can contain logic errors leading to security breaches.

Applying Best Practices

☑ Defense-in-depth distributes security across your infrastructure to prevent single-point-of-failure compromises.

- ☑ Zone isolation increases the granularity of control over devices in your network.

- ☑ Egress filtering ensures protects against unknown activity leaving your network.

- ☑ Explicitly permitting desired traffic and blocking everything else ensures you know what's allowed where.

- ☑ Keeping logging systems secure and monitored will help you isolate problems and keep security events from recurring.

- ☑ Most common operating systems now support automatic updates—*use them*!

Frequently Asked Questions

The following Frequently Asked Questions, answered by the authors of this book, are designed to both measure your understanding of the concepts presented in this chapter and to assist you with real-life implementation of these concepts. To have your questions about this chapter answered by the author, browse to **www.syngress.com/solutions** and click on the **"Ask the Author"** form. You will also gain access to thousands of other FAQs at ITFAQnet.com.

Q: What's a "Grey Hat" hacker?

A: A Grey Hat is someone who knows both sides of the security coin (Black Hat and White Hat) and will dabble with both. Like many things in life, 'good' and 'bad' distinctions are not so binary in the real world. Is it okay to use a malicious attack against an offensive site (hate crime, child porn, spam relay etc.)? Is it okay to attack a host that attacked you first? Computer ethics classes are now a regular component of most security certification courses.

Q: What's a good setting for the (SYN | UDP | ICMP) flood threshold?

A: There's no universal setting that could be applied effectively to every network. Network activity, purpose, and traffic are different for each segment, and they need to be tweaked appropriately. Ideally, you'd want a setting that's just above dropping normal volumes of legitimate flows, so when an actual flood occurs, the NetScreen can react immediately.

Q: Why doesn't DI have the same coverage as an IDP?

A: NetScreen firewall devices have purpose-built Application-Specific Integrated Circuits (ASICs) that handle the majority of firewall operations, such as policy matching and data encryption. These are physical devices—hardware accelerators—that can't be modified. Since DI is a relatively new feature, it has to run in software on the system's CPU. Older NetScreen firewall CPUs were generously sufficient for device management, but are significantly slower than the ~3 GHz single and dual CPUs found on an IDP. This difference in computing power means that a full IDP would be impractical on the currently available platforms. Juniper is actively investigating a new ASIC that incorporates IDP functionality in hardware, as well as ensuring that new generations of NetScreen firewalls have beefier CPUs.

Q: Why is SurfControl Integrated Mode only available on lower-end products?

A: Many users of these more inexpensive products don't have permanent or full-time onsite IT support personnel, and may not have the time, money, or expertise to configure, run, and maintain their own WebSense or SurfControl URL filtering software. Yet these customers still want (and need) URL filtering. The Integrated Mode utilizes SurfControl's public servers that SurfControl maintains and supports. Also at risk is the performance impact (including latency) of sending large volumes of URL look-up requests over the Internet to a public server. The high-end products support speeds well over 10 Gb/s of sustained traffic—to look up every URL requested in real-time would waste significant bandwidth.

Q: Why should I bother with egress filtering? It's a lot of work, and my users are bound to complain about something not working.

A: The initial effort of configuring egress filtering now will save you several orders of magnitude's worth of work later. The majority of business-related software supports proxying or other filtering. Chances are, complaints from some end users regarding connectivity problems generally arise from software you don't want running on your network anyway.

Q: Why are there so many different license keys for features?

A: Juniper, like any for-profit company, wants to make money. It also understands that it needs to be competitive in the market. If Juniper sold its devices at a high price with all features enabled (many of which you may or may not use), it would have a difficult time selling them to customers who only needed some of the features and were willing to buy them at a reduced price. This way, a compromise is reached—they will sell you a useful product for a reasonable price, but the flexibility is there for additional features, which you can then buy a la carte. Time-limited license keys also facilitate subscriptions.

Chapter 11

VPN Theory and Usage

Solutions in this Chapter:

- Understanding IPSec
- IPSec Tunnel Negotiations
- Public Key Cryptography
- How to Use VPNs in NetScreen Appliances
- Advanced VPN Configurations

☑ Summary

☑ Solutions Fast Track

☑ Frequently Asked Questions

Introduction

As you progress through this chapter, you will understand the concepts of virtual private networks (VPNs), how VPNs operate, and how to implement VPN tunnels using IPSec (Internet Protocol Security) on Netscreen appliances. At this time you may be thinking, "What is a VPN and why would I need to use one?" There are several good reasons to implement VPN technology in your infrastructure, starting with security. A VPN is a means of creating secure communications over a public network infrastructure. VPNs use encryption and authentication to ensure that information is kept private and confidential. This means that you can share data and resources among several locations without the worry of data integrity being compromised.

Alone, the ability to make use of a public network to transmit data is also an advantage of VPN technology. Without using the Internet as a transport mechanism you would have to purchase point-to-point T1s or some other form of leased line to connect multiple locations. Leased lines are traditionally expensive to operate, especially if the two points being connected are across a large geographic region. Using VPNs instead of leased lines reduces the operating cost for your company.

VPNs are also cost effective for traveling users. Without VPNs, a traveling salesperson working outside the office might have to dial into a modem bank at the office and incur long distance charges for the call. A dialup VPN is much more cost effective, allowing the salesperson to connect to a local ISP (Internet service provider) and then access the corporate network via a VPN.

Suppose your company's corporate office has a database-driven intranet site that it wants your branch offices to be able to access, but they do not want the rest of the world to have access to this site. Sure, you could just stick the application on an Internet-facing server and give each user a password-protected account, but the information will still be transmitted unencrypted to the user. Let's say you decide to encrypt the sessions using SSL (Secure Sockets Layer). Although this encrypts the communications, you could still face the risk of a user's login information being compromised or a possible SQL injection attack against the application itself. Wouldn't it make more sense to protect the application by not having it publicly available at all? By creating a VPN between the two sites, the branch office can access the intranet site and share resources with the corporate office, increasing productivity and maintaining a higher level of security all at the same time.

Understanding IPSec

IP Security is a collection of protocols for securing communications at the IP (Internet Protocol) layer. IPSec was engineered to provide several services: privacy and confidentiality of data, origin authentication, data integrity, access control, and protection against replay attacks. IPSec is widely used for VPNs. IPSec consists of two modes, transport and tunnel. IPSec also consists of two protocols, encapsulating security payload (ESP) and authentication header (AH). IPSec allows for manual or automatic negotiation of security associations (SAs). All of this information makes up the domain of interpretation, which is used to establish security associations and Internet key exchange.

IPSec Modes

As mentioned earlier, the IPSec protocol provides us with two modes of operation: *transport mode* and *tunnel mode*. Each of these modes provides us with similar end results, but work differently to get us there. For starters, transport mode requires that both endpoints of the VPN tunnel be hosts. *Tunnel mode* must always be used when one endpoint is a security gateway, such as a NetScreen appliance or router. NetScreen appliances always provide IPSec tunnels in tunnel mode.

Transport mode only encrypts the *payload*, or data portion, of the IP packet. The header of the packet is not encrypted or altered. Think of it as a sealed envelope. You are able to see the address of whom the letter is to, but you cannot view the message delivered within. Transport and tunnel mode packets are illustrated in Figures 11.1 and 11.2.

In tunnel mode the original packet, both header and payload, is encapsulated entirely into another IP packet. This new packet has its own header, containing source and destination address information. These addresses are the actual endpoints of the tunnel. Although both modes encrypt the actual payload, tunnel mode is generally thought of to be more secure than transport mode.

Figure 11.1 Transport Mode Packet Diagram

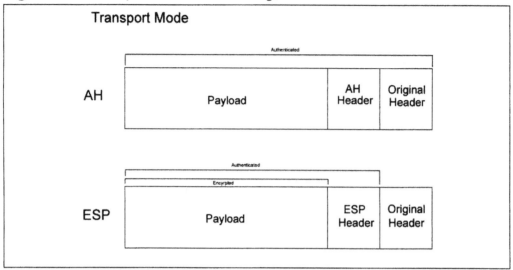

Figure 11.2 Tunnel Mode Packet Diagram

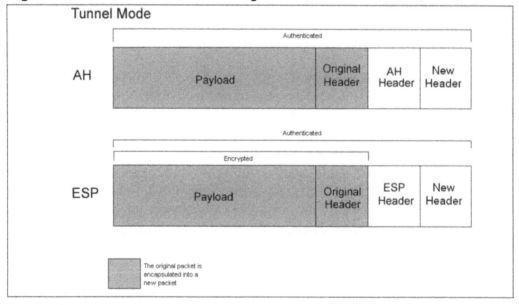

Protocols

As we previously mentioned, IPSec has two methods for verifying the source of an IP packet as well as verifying the integrity of the payload contained within – authentication header and encapsulating security payload.

Authentication header, or AH for short, provides a means to verify the source of an IP packet. It is also used to verify data integrity of the payload the packet contains. When used in transport mode, AH authenticates the IP packet's payload and portions of the IP header. When AH is used in tunnel mode, the entire internal IP header is authenticated as well as selected portions of the external IP header. AH can also protect against replay attempts. AH can be used by itself, or it can be used in conjunction with encapsulating security payload.

Encapsulating security payload, or ESP, provides methods to ensure data privacy, source authentication, and payload integrity. ESP may also protect against replay attacks. ESP, when used in tunnel mode, encrypts the entire IP packet and attaches a new IP header to the packet. The new IP header contains all of the information necessary to route your packet to its destination. ESP also allows you to choose what to do with the packet: encrypt the packet, authenticate the packet, or both. ESP, with transport mode, encrypts the IP payload, but not the IP header. Optionally with transport mode, ESP can also authenticate the IP payload. When using ESP with tunnel mode both the IP header and payload are encrypted. Like transport mode, ESP also optionally allows for authentication of the IP packet.

Key Management

Probably the most critical part of a VPN is key management and distribution. IPSec supports the use of both manual and automatic key distribution.

In manual key configurations, all security parameters are configured at both ends of the tunnel manually. Although this method works well in smaller networks, there are some issues with using manual keys. This can be especially troublesome when the key is initially distributed, since there may be no way to verify the key was not compromised before reaching its final destination. This also becomes cumbersome when you choose to change the key, which results in a need for redistribution. When using manual key VPN, the key is never changed unless the administrator chooses to change it.

To help lessen the burden on administrators, the IPSec protocol supports *Internet Key Exchange,* or IKE for short. IKE generates and negotiates keys and security associations automatically based on pre-shared secrets or digital certificates. A pre-shared secret is nothing more than a key both parties have prior to initiating the negotiations. Like manual key VPN, the pre-shared secret must be exchanged securely before use. However, unlike manual key VPNs, IKE can change the key automatically at a specified interval. This is seen as a significant security enhancement over that of manual key VPN. We will discuss the use of pre-shared secrets later in this chapter.

As mentioned, IKE can also use digital certificates. During IKE negotiation, both sides generate public and private key pairs, and acquire a digital certificate. If the issuing certificate authority is trusted by both parties, the participants can verify their peer's signature by retrieving the peer's public key.

There are also several other benefits of using IKE over the use of a manual key VPN. IKE eliminates the need to manually specify the IPSec security parameters at both peers, reducing the management load on the administrator. IKE also allows for the use of anti-replay services, certification authorities, and dynamic peer authentication in IPSec VPNs, which are discussed in more detail later in this chapter.

Security Associations

Security associations (SA) is the concept used by IPSec to manage all of the parameters required to establish a VPN tunnel. In simple terms, SA is a set of parameters describing how communications are to be secured. SAs contain the following components: security keys and algorithms, mode of operation (transport or tunnel), key management method (IKE or manual key), and lifetime of the SA. IPSec stores all active security associations in a database called the *security association database* (SAD). The SAD contains all parameters needed for IPSec operation, including the keys currently in use. In order to have bidirectional communication, you must have at least two SAs, one for each direction of traffic flow.

IPSec Tunnel Negotiations

When using a manual key VPN for communications, negotiations are not required between the two endpoints of the VPN tunnel. This is because all of the necessary security association parameters were defined during the creation of the tunnel. When traffic matches a policy using a manual key VPN, traffic is encrypted, authenticated, and then routed to the destination gateway.

An IPSec tunnel using IKE requires two phases to complete negotiation. Phase 1 of IKE negotiation establishes a secure tunnel for negotiation of security associations. Then, during phase 2, IPSec SAs are negotiated defining the method for encrypting and authenticating user data exchange. The next section explains what happens in each phase of negotiation in detail.

Phase 1

From our previous discussion you already know that phase 1 negotiations consist of exchanging proposals on how to authenticate and secure the communications channel. Phase 1 exchanges can be done in two modes: *main mode* or *aggressive mode.*

In main mode, three two-way exchanges, or six total messages, are exchanged. During a main mode conversation, the following is accomplished:

- **First exchange** Encryption and authentication algorithms for communications are proposed and accepted.

- **Second exchange** A Diffie-Hellman exchange is done. Each party exchanges a randomly generated number, or nonce.

- **Third exchange** Identities of each party are exchanged and verified.

NOTE

In the third exchange, identities are not passed in the clear. The identities are protected by the encryption algorithm agreed upon in the exchange of the first two sets of messages.

In aggressive mode, the same principle objectives are completed, but are done so in a much shorter conversation. Phase 1 negotiations in aggressive mode only require that two exchanges be made, and that a total of three messages are exchanged. An aggressive mode conversation follows the following pattern:

- **First message** The initiating party proposes the security association, starts a Diffie-Hellman exchange, and sends its nonce and IKE identity to the intended recipient.

- **Second message** During the second message, the recipient accepts the proposed security association, authenticates the initiating party, sends its generated nonce, IKE identity, and its certificate if certificates are being used.

- **Third message** During the third message, the initiator authenticates the recipient, confirms the exchange, and if using certificates, sends its certificate.

In an aggressive mode exchange, the identities of communicating parties are not protected. This is because the identities are sent during the first two messages exchanged prior to the tunnel being secured. It is also important to note that a dialup VPN user must use aggressive mode to establish an IKE tunnel.

Notes from the Underground…

What is Diffie-Hellman?

The Diffie-Hellman (DH) key exchange protocol, invented in 1976 by Whitfield Diffie and Martin Hellman, is a protocol allowing two parties to generate shared secrets and exchange communications over an insecure medium without having any prior shared secrets. The Diffie-Hellman protocol is consists of five groups of varying strength modulus. Most VPN gateways support DH Groups 1 and 2. NetScreen appliances, however, support groups 1, 2, and 5. The Diffie-Hellman protocol alone is susceptible to man-in-the-middle attacks, however. Although the risk of an attack is low, it is recommended that you enable *Perfect Forward Secrecy* (PFS) as added security when defining VPN tunnels on your NetScreen appliance. For more information on the Diffie-Hellman protocol, see www.rsasecurity.com/rsalabs/node.asp?id=2248   and RFC 2631 at ftp://ftp.rfc-editor.org/in-notes/rfc2631.txt

Phase 2

Once phase 1 negotiations have been completed and a secure tunnel has been established, phase 2 negotiations begin. During phase 2, negotiation of security associations of how to secure the data being transmitted across the tunnel is completed. Phase 2 negotiations always involve the exchange of three messages. Phase 2 proposals include encryption and authentication algorithms, as well as a security protocol. The security protocol can either be ESP or AH. Phase 2 proposals can also specify whether or not to use PFS and a Diffie-Hellman group to employ. PFS is a method used to derive keys that have no relation to any previous keys. Without PFS, phase 2 keys are generally derived from the phase 1 SKEYID_d key. If an attacker was to acquire the SKEYID_d key, all keys derived from this key could be compromised. During phase 2 each side also offers its proxy ID. Proxy IDs are simply the local IP, the remote IP, and the service. Both proxy IDs must match. For example, if 1.1.1.1 and 2.2.2.2 are using the SMTP (Simple Mail Transfer Protocol) service, then the proxy ID for 1.1.1.1 would be 1.1.1.1-2.2.2.2-25 and for 2.2.2.2 it would be 2.2.2.2-1.1.1.1-25.

Damage & Defense...

Key Lifetime – Short vs Long and PFS

When planning your VPN deployment, consideration should be given to the key lifetime and perfect forward secrecy in relation to security. Since enabling PFS requires additional processing time and resources some administrators choose not to use it, instead opting for a shorter key lifetime. This, however, can be a bad practice. If a successful man-in-the-middle attack were able to discover the SKEYID_d key, all keys derived from this key could be compromised. Enabling PFS, even with a longer key life, is actually a more secure practice than having a short key life with no PFS.

Public Key Cryptography

Public key cryptography, first born in the 1970s, is the modern cryptographic method of communicating securely without having a previously agreed upon secret key. Public key cryptography typically uses a pair of keys to secure communications – a private key that is kept secret, and a public key that can be widely distributed. You should not be able to find one key of a pair simply by having the other. Public key cryptography is a form of asymmetric-key cryptography, since not all parties hold the same key. Some examples of public key cryptography algorithms include RSA, Diffie-Hellman and ElGamal.

So how does public key encryption work? Suppose John would like to exchange a message securely with Chris. Prior to doing so, Chris would provide John with his public key. John would then take the message he wishes to share with Chris and encrypt the message using Chris' public key. When Chris receives the message, he takes his private key and decrypts the message. Chris is then able to read the message John had intended to share with him. But what if someone intercepts the message and has possession of Chris' public key? Absolutely nothing happens. When messages are encrypted using Chris's public key they can only be decrypted using the private key associated with that public key.

PKI

PKI is the meshing of encryption technologies, services, and software together to form a solution that enables businesses to secure their communications over the Internet. PKI involves the integration of digital certificates, certificate authorities (CAs), and public key cryptography. PKI offers several enhancements to the security of your enterprise.

PKI gives you the ability to easily verify and authenticate the identity of a person or organization. By using digital certificates, it is easy to verify the identity of parties involved in a transaction. The ease of verification of identity is also beneficial to access control. Digital certificates can replace passwords for access control, which are sometimes lost or easily cracked by experienced crackers.

Certificates

Digital certificates are nothing more than a way to verify your identity through a certificate authority using public key cryptography. NetScreen appliances support the use of digital certificates as a method of validating your identity during VPN negotiations. There are certain steps you must take before you can use a certificate to validate your identity. First, you must generate a certificate request from within the NetScreen appliance. When this is done, the NetScreen appliance generates a public/private key pair. You then send a request with the public key to your certificate authority. A response, which incorporates the public key, will be forwarded to you that will have to be loaded into the NetScreen appliance. This response generally includes three parts:

- The CA's certificate, which contains the CA's public key.
- The local certificate identifying your NetScreen device.
- In some cases a certificate revocation list (CRL). This lists any certificates revoked by the CA.

You can load the reply into the NetScreen device either through the WebUI or via TFTP (Thin File Transport Protocol) through the CLI (command line interface), whichever you prefer. Loading the certificate information into the NetScreen gives us the following:

- Your identity can be verified using the local certificate.

- The CA's certificate can be used to verify the identity of other users.

- The CRL list can be used to identify invalid certificates.

CRLs

A *certificate revocation list*, or CRL, is used to ensure that a digital certificate has not become invalid. NetScreen appliances use CRLs to check for invalid certificates before connecting VPN tunnels. When speaking in regards to the use of digital certificates with VPNs, the certificate is validated during phase 1 negotiations. In the event that no CRL has been loaded into the NetScreen, the appliance tries to retrieve a CRL via LDAP (Lightweight Directory Access Protocol) or HTTP (Hypertext Transfer Protocol), which is defined inside the CA certificate. NetScreen appliances also allow you to specify an address to refer to for the CRL. If you do not define an address, the default address within the CA's certificate is used.

How to Use VPNs in NetScreen Appliances

Site-to-Site VPNs

There are two ways to configure site-to-site VPNs when both endpoints have static IP addresses:

- Site-to-site VPN using a manual key.

- Site-to-site using an autokey.

Hosts behind either gateway can initiate the negotiations between the two gateways.

But what happens when you need to create a VPN between a gateway with a dynamically assigned address and a gateway with a static address? Does it mean you cannot create a VPN between the two? No, it doesn't. You can still create a VPN, but you need to create a dynamic peer site-to-site VPN tunnel using *autokey IKE*. Negotiation of a dynamic peer tunnel differs somewhat, though. Only hosts that are behind the dynamic gateway can initiate the VPN tunnel.

This is because the remote gateway has a static IP. After the VPN tunnel is established, parties behind either gateway can pass traffic across the tunnel.

Site-to-site VPN tunnels require the configuration of both gateways. Configuration at each endpoint is identical, except the gateways are in reverse order. The default phase 2 security level is set to *standard* when creating a new VPN tunnel. Standard security, when mentioned in regards to NetScreen appliances, is **nopfs-esp-des-md5**. Unless you are terminating a VPN to a device that does not support PFS, or any higher encryption and authentication methods, it is recommended that you do not use the default configuration. You should use at least **g2-esp-3des-sha**. Figures 11.3 and 11.4 show screenshots of the NetScreen WebUI VPN configuration and advanced configuration pages, respectively.

Figure 11.3 VPN Configuration Page

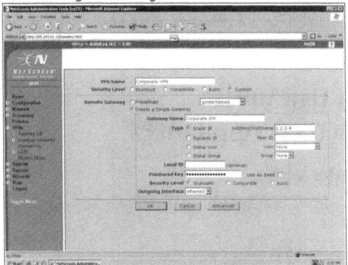

Figure 11.4 The Advanced Features Configuration Page

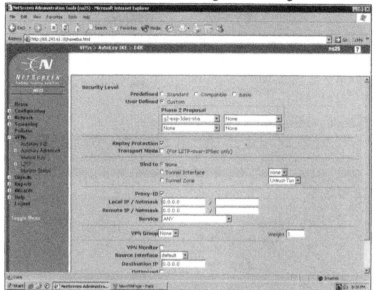

Policy-based VPNs

Policy-based VPNs are VPNs that route traffic based on specific policies within a NetScreen appliance. Policy-based VPNs can be either manual key or autokey IKE. A policy-based VPN works based on specific criteria that a packet matches as it reaches the gateway. First, before you can create a policy-based VPN you must configure the VPN tunnel. After creating the VPN tunnel you then create a policy, choose the action **Tunnel**, and select the VPN object you configured earlier. The action **Tunnel** works very similar to the **Permit** option, except it requires you to select a tunnel object that you have previously created so that it can properly handle the traffic. A policy-based VPN tunnel always permits the traffic so long as it matches all the criteria of the rule. With policy-based VPNs, each separate traffic policy will create its own security association, so using multiple policy-based VPNs will result in using more system resources. This is true even if the destination tunnel is the same for multiple policies.

Policy-based VPNs are best used in the following situations:

- When you do not need to filter specific traffic on the tunnel.

- When you are not using any dynamic routing protocols.

- When there is no need for conserving IPSec tunnels and security associations.

- When you are using the VPN tunnel in conjunction with a dialup VPN client.

With policy-based VPNs, you are limited in the number of tunnels you can create, depending on the number of tunnels the device can support. A sample of a configured policy using a VPN is shown in Figure 11.5.

Figure 11.5 Policy-based VPN Configuration

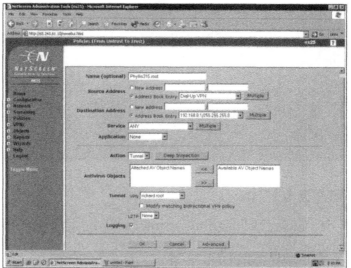

Creating a Policy-Based Site-to-Site VPN

Suppose your company has two offices and wants to share resources among the two via a VPN. Let's create a policy-based site-to-site VPN that does just that. Before we can begin, we need information about the sites. Site1 uses the network 192.168.0.0/24 and has a NetScreen appliance with a static address of 4.4.4.4. Site2 uses the network 10.10.10.0/24 and has a NetScreen appliance with a static address of 5.5.5.5. We will be using autokey IKE and the pre-shared key will be **dgL-I2G#U438^*gyG(6t!**. We also want to use Diffie-Hellman Group 2, AES-128, and SHA-1 for our encryption. Now that we have the necessary information, we can start to build our VPN tunnel.

First and foremost, we need to define our networks at each end of the tunnel. This can be done by accessing **Objects | Address | List**. Select **New** from the top of the screen. Choose a name for the address object, such as Site2, and then add the IP address, netmask, and zone. We also need to create an address object for the local network. Let's name it **Trusted LAN (192.168.0.x)**. Figure 11.6 shows the configuration page for the Site1 firewall. The configuration for Site2 would also be completed as shown here, substituting the network address for Site1's local network in for the IP address. Like Site1, Site2's firewall would also contain an address object defining the local network.

Figure 11.6 Configuring an Address Object

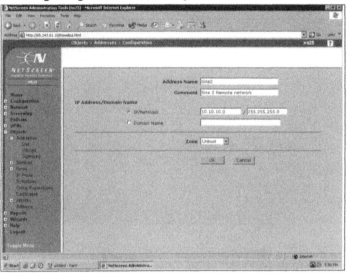

Once we have added the addresses to the address book, we can configure our VPN gateways. To do this, select **VPNS | AutoKey Advanced | Gateway**. Select **New** from the top of the screen. Enter a name for the gateway. Choose **Custom** for the **Security Level**, since we will be using pre-g2-aes128-sha. Later, we will configure this on the Advanced page of the gateway configuration. Since we know that Site2 has a static IP address of 5.5.5.5, we choose the default setting **Static IP**, and enter **5.5.5.5** in the available field. Now, enter the pre-shared key into the field labeled **Preshared Key**. We have completed the basic configuration for this end of the VPN tunnel, but we still need to set the correct proposals to be used. Click on the **Advanced** button to show the Advanced configuration page. Under Phase 1 Proposal, select **pre-g2-aes128-sha**. Because both endpoints have static IP addresses, we should leave our **Mode** set to **Main**. Once you have selected the correct proposal, scroll to the bottom of the page and select **Return** to go back to the basic configuration page. Once back at the basic configuration page, select **OK** to save the new gateway. Figures 11.7 and

11.8 show the basic and advanced configuration pages completed with our settings. To configure Site2's VPN gateway, we would use the same steps we just
completed, substituting the address **4.4.4.4** as the **Static IP**.

Figure 11.7 Basic VPN Gateway Configuration

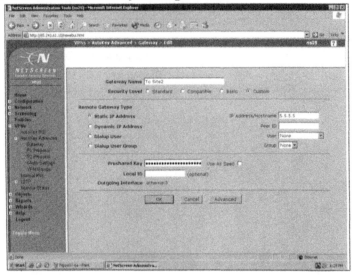

Figure 11.8 Advanced VPN Gateway Configuration

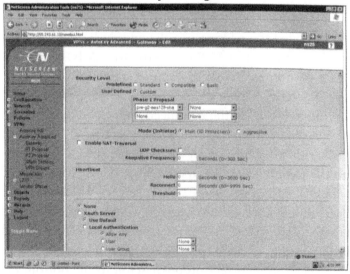

Now that we've created the VPN Gateway, we need to create an AutoKey
IKE entry that uses our gateway, and configure the security proposals for phase 2.

To do this, select **VPNs | AutoKey IKE** and select **New** from the top of the screen. Let's give the VPN a descriptive name, such as VPN To Site2. Again, we choose **Custom** as our security level. Access the drop-down menu to the right of Remote Gateway and choose the gateway we previously configured, To Site2. Click the **Advanced** button to bring up the advanced options for our IKE entry. Use the **Phase 2 Proposal** drop-down list to select **g2-esp-aes128-sha**. Click the **Return** button to go back to the basic configuration page. Choose **OK** to save the new IKE entry. Figures 11.9 and 11.10 show the basic and advanced configuration pages for creating an AutoKey IKE entry.

Figure 11.9 Basic AutoKey IKE Configuration

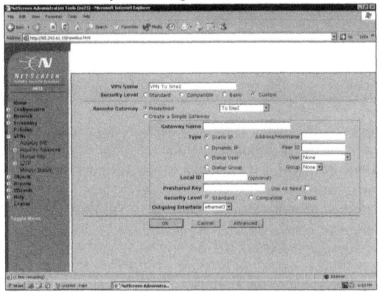

Figure 11.10 Advanced AutoKey IKE Configuration

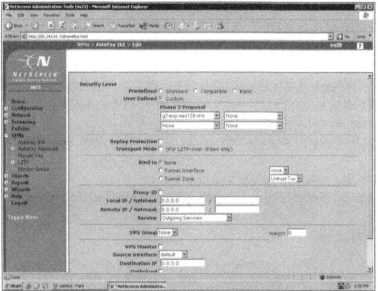

Once we've completed the above steps, we need to create a policy allowing traffic to use the VPN. Click **Policies**. At the top of the page choose the options **From: Trust To: Untrust** and click **New**. Name the policy **To / From Site2**. Use the **Source Address** drop-down list to select the local network address book entry we defined earlier. Choose **Site2** as the **Destination Address** from the drop-down menu. Since we want to allow all traffic to flow between the two sites, we will leave the **Service** as **ANY**. Choose the action **Tunnel** and select the IKE entry that we created earlier, **VPN to Site2**. Enable the Check the box to **Modify** matching bidirectional VPN policy. Also enable the **Position at Top** option. Figure 11.11 shows what our policy should look like once completed.

Figure 11.11 VPN Policy Configuration

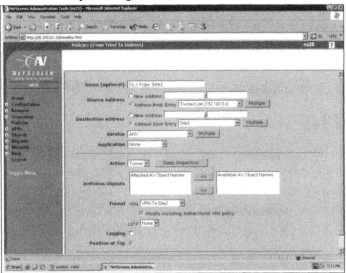

Keep in mind that the configuration for the other end of our tunnel can be completed as outlined above, but using Site1's network information in place of Site2's. Once both ends of the tunnel have been configured, the two NetScreen devices will negotiate security associations and establish a VPN tunnel. To the users, this process is transparent. In fact, most users only know they can use resources located at the other site; they have no clue as to what process allows them to do so.

Route-based VPNs

Route-based VPNs, like policy-based VPNs, can also use either manual key or autokey IKE, but are configured and function somewhat differently. Route-based VPNs do not make reference to a tunnel object, but rather the destination address of the traffic. When the NetScreen appliance performs a route lookup to see which interface it should use to send the traffic, it sees there is a route through a tunnel interface that is bound to a VPN tunnel and uses that interface to deliver the traffic.

There are some advantages to using a route-based VPN. Using route-based VPNs is a good way to conserve system resources. Unlike policy-based VPNs, you can configure multiple policies that allow or deny specific traffic to flow through a route-based VPN, and all of these policies will use a single security association. Route-based VPNs also offer the ability to exchange dynamic routing information, such as border gateway protocol (BGP), on the tunnel inter-face. Route-based VPNs allow you to create policies that have an action of deny, unlike policy-based VPNs. Route-based VPNs also have different limitations than policy-based VPNs. With route-based VPNs, you are limited by one of two things: the number of route entries your appliance supports, or the number of tunnel interfaces your appliance supports, whichever of the two is the least.

Dialup VPNs

NetScreen appliances support the use of dialup VPN. A dialup VPN is a VPN that connects using either the NetScreen remote VPN client, or another NetScreen appliance that does not have a static IP address (a dynamic peer). NetScreen appliances support dialup VPN configurations based on a per-user or per-group basis. Using a group saves time and makes things easier on the admin-istrator since there is only the need to configure one tunnel. You can also con-figure a group IKE user and use the IKE ID for the dialup users group.

One of the nifty things about using a dialup VPN is you can actually con-figure policy-based VPNs for the dialup users. For example, if you want a user to be allowed to connect to 10.11.12.13 to send e-mail, you can create a policy only allowing access to 10.11.12.13 on port 25. Later, if you want to allow that same user access to his POP3 (Post Office Protocol v3) mailbox on server 10.11.12.14, you can simply add another policy to the remote client allowing the user access to 10.11.12.14 on port 110.

For a dynamic peer, you can use either policy-based or route-based VPN. Just remember that in order to use a route-based VPN, you need to configure an internal virtual IP address. The NetScreen Remote client, which we will discuss a bit more in the next section, also supports having a virtual IP address and can be used with a route-based VPN as well.

NetScreen Remote

NetScreen Remote is Juniper Network's software VPN client. NetScreen remote can be installed onto most any Windows-based desktop PC. NetScreen Remote is primarily used for policy-based Dialup VPNs. It is also often used by home users working from a cable or DSL modem connection, which are still consid-ered dialup VPNs since the IP address of the client is usually dynamic. As previ-ously mentioned, NetScreen Remote also supports the use of route-based VPNs.

Once NetScreen Remote has been installed, it starts with each logon to Windows. Configuration of NetScreen Remote is easily completed using the GUI-based Security Policy Editor tool.

Let's walk through a scenario of configuring NetScreen Remote to connect to ABC Company's corporate network and allow us RDP access to a terminal server. Suppose we will be connecting to ABC's corporate network via a DSL modem with a dynamic IP address. ABC's firewall administrator has provided us with the following information to help us configure a policy in NetScreen Remote.

ABC's NetScreen IP:	1.2.3.4
IP Subnet:	10.10.10.0
Netmask:	255.255.255.0
Pre-shared key	NetScreen-Firewalls-Rule!

ABC's administrator has also told us that he would like us to use replay protection, perfect forward secrecy, Diffie-Hellman Group 2, AES-256 for encryption, and SHA-1 for the hashing algorithm in all applicable phases. During our conversation with ABC's administrator, he asked for our e-mail address to use as our identity and we provided him with the address clathem@domain.tld. Now that we have all the necessary information, let's create a policy in NetScreen Remote that will properly direct and secure our traffic.

Click on **Start | Programs | NetScreen-Remote | Security Policy Editor** to start the NetScreen Remote security policy editor. Choose **Edit | Add | New Connection** to add a new policy to the My Connections heading. Since the NetScreen Remote software can contain multiple security policies we should name this policy with a descriptive name so that in the future we can easily tell what this policy does. Right-click on this policy, choose **Rename**, and rename this policy **ABC Company RDP**. Highlight the name of the policy. We will start here, configuring the remote gateway and destination network on this screen. Under **Remote Party Identity and Addressing** change the **ID Type** to **IP Subnet**. For the **Subnet** enter in our destination network, **10.10.10.0**, and in the **Netmask** enter **255.255.255.0**. Leave **Protocol** as **All**. Next we need to enable the option **Connect Using Secure Gateway Tunnel**. Since we know that ABC's gateway IP is **1.2.3.4**, we enter it into the **IP Address** field. When completed, our initial screen should look as pictured in Figure 11.12.

Figure 11.12 Initial Configuration of NetScreen Remote

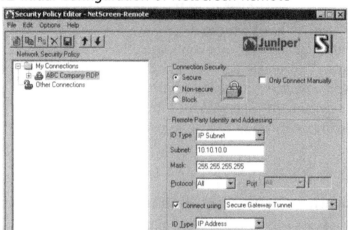

Next, click the plus sign to the left of the policy to expand it one level. You now see the option to configure **My Identity**, where you choose to use a pre-shared key or certificate, and **Security Policy**, in which you configure which encryption and authentication options you will use during communications. Start off by selecting **My Identity**. Since ABC's firewall admin has assigned us a pre-shared key, we will want to change the **Select certificate** option to **none**. Upon doing so, a button labeled **Pre-shared Key** appears. Click this button to bring up the Pre-shared key dialog box and then click **Enter Key**. Figure 11.13 shows an example the pre-shared key dialog box. Enter the key as assigned to us by ABC's administrator and click **OK**. Since ABC's administrator is using our e-mail address for our identity, we select the option for e-mail address under **ID Type** and enter our e-mail address, **clathem@domain.tld**, into the field. We will leave the fields **Virtual Adapter** and **Internet Interface** as the default choices. Figure 11.14 shows the settings completed in NetScreen Remote.

Figure 11.13 Entering the Pre-shared Key

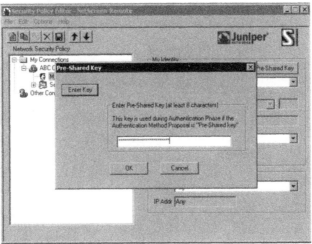

Figure 11.14 Configuring My Identity

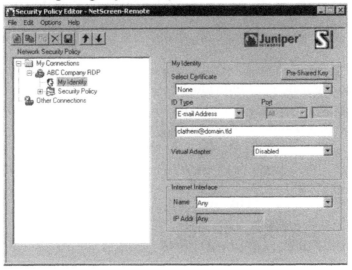

Now that we've completed the setup of our identity and pre-shared key, we need to complete the configuration of our security policies. Start off by selecting **Security Policy**. Since we will be connecting from a DSL modem with a dynamic IP address, we need to use **Aggressive Mode**, so let's select that option. ABC's administrator also specified that we use perfect forward secrecy, so we need to enable the **PFS** option. We were told to use Diffie-Hellman Group 2 in all phases, so the default selection of **DH group 2** is fine. Replay detection is also enabled by default. Figure 11.15 shows our Security Policy configuration.

Figure 11.15 Initial Policy Configuration

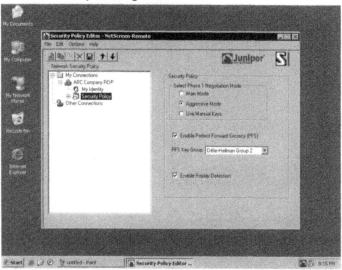

Now that we've completed the initial security policy configuration, we can move on to configuring each individual policy. Click the plus to the left of **Security Policies**. Here you will see the settings for Phase 1 and Phase 2 proposals. Start off by expanding **Authentication (Phase 1)** and then click on **Proposal**. Note that the default settings for Phase 1 negotiations in NetScreen remote is to use a Pre-shared key, Diffie-Hellman Group 2, Triple DES for Encryption, and SHA-1 for hashing, or as I and the NetScreen firewall like to refer to it, PRE-G2-3DES-SHA. Since ABC's administrator specifically noted the use of AES-256 for encryption, we change the **Encryption Alg** field to reflect his specifications. Figure 11.16 shows Phase 1 properly configured as specified.

Figure 11.16 Configuring Phase 1 Proposal

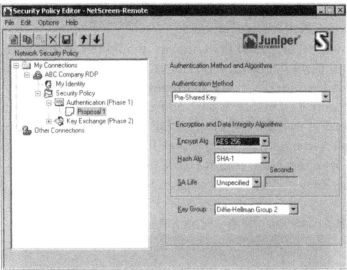

The last configuration modification we must make is under the **Key Exchange (Phase 2)** heading. Expand the heading and select **Proposal**. Look under the **Encapsulation Protocol (ESP)** label. Change the encryption algorithm to **AES-256**. Figure 11.17 shows the completed configuration for Phase 2.

Figure 11.17 Configuring Phase 2 Proposal

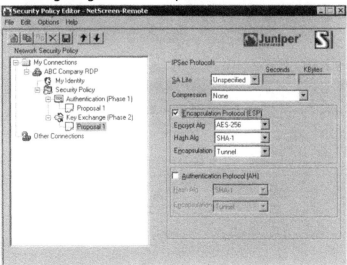

After completing the configuration of the policy, we need to save our changes. Click on **File | Save**. We're done! We've completed the setup of a security policy for NetScreen Remote.

Now that we've completed the setup, we should test to ensure that our policy works properly. Right-click on the NetScreen Remote icon in the system tray and choose **Connect… | My Connections\ABC Company RDP**, as illustrated in Figure 11.18. If all is well, you will see a dialog box notifying you that the connection to ABC Company RDP was successful. If negotiations fail you will receive a message notifying you of the failure to connect. It's probably a good time to open the NetScreen Remote Log Viewer, as shown in Figure 11.19. The Log Viewer is an excellent place to start troubleshooting the VPN.

Figure 11.18 Activating the NetScreen Remote Policy

Figure 11.19 NetScreen Remote Log Viewer

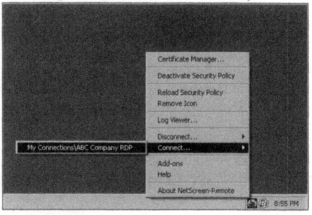

L2TP VPNs

NetScreen Appliances support the *layer 2 tunneling protocol,* or L2TP for short, when operating in layer 3 mode. The L2TP protocol works by sending PPP (Point to Point Protocol) frames through a tunnel between the LNS and the L2TP access concentrator. Originally L2TP was designed so that a dialup user could make a virtual PPP connection through a L2TP access concentrator (LAC) at an ISP. The LAC at the ISP would create a tunnel to the L2TP network server at either another ISP, or at a corporate network. The L2TP tunnel never actually extended to the client's desktop, only to the ISP's LAC.

L2TP tunnels are not encrypted, so they are not actually true VPN tunnels. The primary purpose for L2TP is so that a dialup user can be assigned an IP address that is known and can be referenced in policies. In order to encrypt an L2TP tunnel, you need to use an encryption scheme such as IPSec. Generally this is referred to as L2TP-over-IPSec. L2TP-over-IPSec requires two things: IPSec and L2TP tunnels to be set up with the same endpoints and then linked together in a policy, and the IPSec tunnel must be in transport mode.

NOTE

Modern operating systems, such as Windows 2000, can alone act as a LAC, so that an L2TP tunnel can extend all the way to the desktop. NetScreen devices can act as LNS servers, so a L2TP VPN can easily be created between a NetScreen appliance and a Windows 2000 desktop provided you don't mind tweaking your registry a bit. To use L2TP without IPSec, change the value of the registry key (or create if one does not exist) ProhibitIPSec at HKEY_LOCAL_MACHINE\System\CurrentControlSet\Services\RasMan\Para meters to hexadecimal 1 and reboot.

The NetScreen device does need to be configured with a group of IP addresses to assign to the L2TP clients, and these IP addresses must differ from the subnet in use on the LAN (local area network). For example, if your LAN address range is 10.0.0.0/24 then you would need to use something outside this range, such as 10.0.1.0 or 10.0.2.0. Note that you can use private address ranges that are not routable on the Internet. When the client connects to the NetScreen appliance, it is assigned an IP address for the L2TP tunnel, as well as DNS

(Domain Name Service) and WINS (Windows Internet Naming Service) servers if applicable. The NetScreen appliance can also perform PPP authentication for the client through RADIUS, LDAP, securID, or its own internal database. NetScreen appliances support the use of Challenge Handshake Authentication Protocol (CHAP) with RADIUS and its internal database. NetScreen appliances also support Password Authentication Protocol (PAP) with RADIUS, LDAP, securID, and its internal database.

Advanced VPN Configurations

VPN Monitoring

Suppose you want to monitor the status of VPN tunnels you've configured. By enabling VPN monitoring you can do just that. NetScreen offers the ability to monitor VPN tunnels via SNMP (Simple Network Management Protocol). ICMP (Internet Control Message Protocol) echos (widely known as *pings*) are sent through the tunnel at user-configurable intervals to monitor connectivity. Should the pings indicate a change in the state of the tunnel, an SNMP trap is triggered. A trap of *up to down* is triggered when the monitoring state of a tunnel is up, but a number of consecutive pings are sent without a reply, and there is no other VPN traffic flowing through the tunnel. A *down to up* trap is triggered when the tunnel monitoring state is down, but a ping request receives a reply. Note that it only takes one successful ping reply to change the state to up, and the rekey option must be disabled. The NetScreen WebUI also has a page that can show you the status of a tunnel. To view this page, click to expand the VPN tab and then click **Monitor Status**.

Netscreen appliances report the following information on VPN tunnels via SNMP.

- Number of active VPN sessions.
- Start time of each VPN session.
- The security associations for each session, including encryption and authentication method, IKE protocol, VPN type, peer and local IP addresses and gateway ID, security parameter index, and phase 1 authentication method.
- Tunnel state.

- VPN monitoring state.
- Phase 1 and 2 state and lifetime.

Gateway Redundancy

When you have the need for gateway redundancy and failover to provide contin-
uous connectivity, NetScreen has the answer. You can create a group of up to
four redundant VPN gateways that policy-based site-to-site VPNs can connect
to. These gateways can have the same parameters for phase 1 and 2 security associations, or they can be totally different.

NetScreen appliances use two mechanisms to monitor individual endpoints
of a VPN group: IKE heartbeats and recovery attempts. By combining these two
mechanisms with *TCP-SYN Flag checking*, NetScreen devices can failover to a
new gateway without any disruption in service. *TCP-SYN Flag checking* is a
check performed by NetScreen appliances to ensure that the TCP SYN flag is
set when an initial TCP (Transmission Control Protocol) session is attempted.
When a failover occurs, the gateway that picks up the communications assumes
the first packet received is the start of a new TCP session and expects the SYN
flag to be set. Since the packet is part of an existing TCP session, the SYN flag is
not set, and the packet is dropped. Thus when TCP-SYN flag checking is
enabled, all applications would have to reconnect after a failover. To allow a truly
successful failover without loss of connectivity, you should disable SYN flag
checking in VPN tunnels. Currently there is no way to disable SYN flag
checking via the WebUI; you must use the CLI command **unset flow tcp-syn-
check-in-tunnel**.

It is important to note that VPN groups do not support L2TP, dialup, manual
key, or route-based VPNs. NetScreen redundant gateway VPN groups also support policy-based dynamic peer IKE VPNs, provided that the members of the
VPN group have static addresses and the dynamic address is on the appliance
doing the monitoring.

"But how does it work?" you ask. When an appliance starts negotiation of a
VPN that points to a VPN group, negotiations are performed with all members
of the group. Traffic is then directed to the destination gateway with the highest
priority in the group. So what happens with the other members of the VPN
group? The initiating party keeps the tunnels in an active state, sending heartbeat
packets through them. If the higher priority active tunnel was to fail, the tunnel
with the next highest priority is quickly put into play by the VPN monitor, and
traffic continues to flow.

Back-to-Back VPNs

Back-to-back VPNs are used to enforce interzone policies between two spoke sites through the hub site. There are several advantages to using back-to-back VPNs. Using back-to-back VPNs can reduce the number of tunnels you need to create. This can be especially helpful on NetScreen appliances that support smaller numbers of VPN tunnels. Take a NetScreen 5XP for example, which supports only 10 tunnels. If you had to create multiple VPN tunnels to several different VPN gateways, you would quickly consume all your VPN resources. But if you use back-to-back VPNs, you can create a single tunnel from each site to the hub site, and then route traffic between all of the sites through the hub site. You've accomplished the same results as with multiple VPN tunnels, allowing traffic to pass between all of the sites, but have done so with only one VPN at each spoke's gateway.

Another advantage of back-to-back VPNs is the ability to define policies between sites. Enforcing policies between spoke sites can be accomplished by placing each of the sites into different zones. Since each site is located in a different zone, the NetScreen must perform a policy lookup before routing the traffic to the destination site. This effectively allows you to control which traffic is allowed between your spoke sites. Suppose both of the spokes terminate at the same interface, but you still want to be able to control traffic between the two. Simply enable intrazone blocking and then define policies between the tunnel interfaces.

The administrator of the hub site can also control the flow of all traffic from the remote sites. By defining a policy at each spoke site that passes all traffic from the trusted network destined for the outside world across the VPN to the hub site, the administrator can use policies at the hub site to filter traffic.

Hub and Spoke VPNs

Hub and spoke VPN tunnels route traffic directly from one spoke VPN tunnel to another spoke VPN tunnel terminated on the hub appliance. This is done by adding a pair of routes to the route table. When intrazone blocking is disabled, the hub site only needs to perform a route lookup in order to properly forward the traffic. The major advantage of using hub and spoke VPN technology is circuit aggregation. By using hub and spoke VPNs, the hub site can have as few as one circuit connecting it to the spoke sites and use this single circuit to route traffic to the spoke sites. When using another technology such as frame relay, the hub site will have several circuits terminating at the site and will need to use several ports and routers in order to interconnect the spoke sites.

Multi-tunnel Interfaces

NetScreen appliances support the ability to have multiple IPSec VPN tunnels bound to one interface. In fact, you can bind as many tunnels as your NetScreen appliance supports to the same interface, provided the route table is not filled first. NetScreen appliances use both the route table and next-hop tunnel binding to link a destination address to a specific tunnel on a tunnel interface.

Solutions Fast Track

Understanding IPSec

☑ IPSec was engineered to provide several services: privacy and confidentiality of data, origin authentication, data integrity, access control, and protection against replay attacks.

☑ The IPSec protocol provides two modes of operation: *transport mode* and *tunnel mode.*

☑ IPSec has two methods for verifying the source of an IP packet as well as verifying the integrity of the payload contained within - authentication header (AH) and encapsulating security payload (ESP). While ESP can encrypt and authenticate the entire packet, AH only authenticates the packet.

☑ IPSec supports the use of both manual keys and autokey IKE.

☑ Internet Key Exchange, or IKE, generates and negotiates keys and security associations automatically based on either pre-shared secrets or digital certificates.

☑ *Security associations* (SA) is the concept used by IPSec to manage all of the parameters required to establish a VPN tunnel, including security keys and algorithms, mode of operation (transport or tunnel), key management method (IKE or manual key), and lifetime of the SA. All of this information is stored in the security association database (SAD).

IPSec Tunnel Negotiations

☑ Because all security association is manually configured in a manual key VPN, negotiations are not required between the two endpoints. Traffic is simply encrypted, authenticated, and routed to the destination gateway.

☑ IPSec tunnels using IKE requires two phases to complete negotiation: phase 1 establishes a secure tunnel for negotiation of security associations and phase 2 IPSec SAs are negotiated defining the method for encrypting and authenticating user data exchange.

☑ Phase 1 exchanges can be done in two modes: *main mode* or *aggressive mode*. In main mode, six messages are exchanged, while in aggressive mode only three messages are exchanged.

☑ Main mode negotiations are considered more secure than aggressive mode negotiations, since the identities of the participating parties are not exchanged in the clear.

Public Key Cryptography

☑ Public key cryptography is the modern cryptographic method of communicating securely without having a previously agreed upon secret key.

☑ Public key cryptography uses a pair of keys to secure communications – a private key that is kept secret, and a public key that can be widely distributed.

☑ Some Examples of public key cryptography algorithms include RSA, Diffie-Hellman and ElGamal.

☑ PKI is the meshing of encryption technologies, services, and software together to form a solution that enables businesses to secure their communications over the Internet.

☑ Digital certificates are a way to verify identities through a certificate authority (CA) using public key cryptography.

☑ *Certificate revocation lists*, or CRLs, are used to ensure that a digital certificate has not become invalid

How to Use VPNs in NetScreen Appliances

☑ There are two ways to configure site-to-site VPNs when both endpoints have static IP addresses, site-to-site with AutoKey IKE and manual key VPN.

☑ A VPN can also be created between two NetScreen appliances when one endpoint has a dynamic IP address. The negotiations of the tunnel must be initiated by the end with the dynamic IP, and aggressive mode must be used for phase 1 negotiations.

☑ When creating VPN tunnels it is advisable to always use at least 3DES for encryption and SHA-1 for hashing.

☑ Policy-based VPNs route traffic based on specific policies within a NetScreen appliance, and can be either manual key or autokey IKE.

☑ When using policy-based VPNs each separate traffic policy will create its own security association, so using multiple policy-based VPNs will result in using more system resources, even if the destination tunnel is the same for multiple policies.

☑ Route-based VPNs can use either manual key or autokey IKE. They do not make reference to a tunnel object, but rather the destination address of the traffic. When the NetScreen appliance performs a route lookup to see which interface it should use to send the traffic, it sees a route through a tunnel interface bound to a VPN tunnel and uses that interface to deliver the traffic.

☑ Using route-based VPNs is a good way to conserve system resources over the use of a policy-based VPN.

☑ NetScreen appliances support dialup VPN configurations based on a per-user or per-group basis. Using the group VPN saves time by allowing the administrator to configure a single tunnel for the group.

☑ NetScreen Appliances support the *layer 2 tunneling protocol* (L2TP) when operating in layer 3 mode.

Advanced VPN Configuration

☑ NetScreen appliances support VPN monitoring via SNMP traps or through the WebUI.

☑ Netscreen appliances support the creation of a group of up to four redundant VPN gateways that policy-based site-to-site VPNs can connect to. These gateways can have the same parameters for phase 1 and 2 security associations, or they can be totally different.

☑ To allow a successful failover to a redundant gateway without loss of connectivity, you should disable SYN flag checking in VPN tunnels, using the CLI command **unset flow tcp-syn-check-in-tunnel**.

☑ Back-to-back VPNs are used to enforce interzone policies between two spoke sites through the hub site.

☑ The major advantage of using hub and spoke VPN technology is circuit aggregation, allowing multiple spoke sites to be terminated through a single circuit at the hub site.

☑ NetScreen appliances support the ability to have multiple IPSec VPN tunnels bound to one interface, allowing as many tunnels as your NetScreen appliance supports to be bound to the same interface (provided the route table is not filled first).

Links to Sites

- www.qorbit.net/nn/ - NetScreen Mailing List Archive - An excellent place to search for answers to common problems

- www.netscreenforum.com/ - Discussion forums dedicated to everything NetScreen.

- ftp://ftp.rfc-editor.org/in-notes/rfc2631.txt - RFC 2631 The Diffie-Hellman key exchange protocol

Mailing Lists

- www.qorbit.net/mailman/listinfo/nn - The qorbit mailing list dedicated to NetScreen products

Frequently Asked Questions

The following Frequently Asked Questions, answered by the authors of this book, are designed to both measure your understanding of the concepts presented in this chapter and to assist you with real-life implementation of these concepts. To have your questions about this chapter answered by the author, browse to **www.syngress.com/solutions** and click on the **"Ask the Author"** form. You will also gain access to thousands of other FAQs at ITFAQnet.com.

Q: Can NetScreen firewalls establish VPN tunnels between other manufacturer's firewalls, such as Cisco PIX or Snapgear?

A: Yes, NetScreen firewalls have a broad range of compatibility modes built in. By using different Phase 1 and Phase 2 proposals you can make NetScreen operate with any IPSec-based firewall on the market. NetScreen firewalls also support the ability to create custom Phase 1 and Phase 2 proposals, so you can tailor the proposals to your liking.

Q: What encryption and hashing algorithms do NetScreen appliances support?

A: NetScreen appliances support Diffie-Hellman Groups 1, 2, and 5. NetScreen appliances support DES, 3DES, AES-128, AES-192, and AES-256 for encryption algorithms. For hashing, NetScreen appliances support MD5 and SHA-1.

Chapter 12

Virtual Systems

Solutions in this Chapter:

- What Is a Virtual System?
- How Virtual Systems Work
- Configuring Virtual Systems

☑ Summary

☑ Solutions Fast Track

☑ Frequently Asked Questions

Introduction

The NetScreen firewall is a truly scaleable device. On the high-end firewalls, you can divide the firewall into multiple virtual firewalls or virtual systems. A virtual system (VSYS) is a logical firewall that is contained in a single physical firewall. Firewalls that support virtual systems allow you to create as many virtual systems as you are licensed for. Each virtual system can share components with other virtual systems or the root system.

Internet service providers (ISPs) or large organizations are the typical users of virtual systems. Both of these groups use virtual systems because of the need for many firewalls in a single location. For these users it would be impractical for them to have large numbers of firewalls. ISPs use the VSYS technology as a way to give customers access to their very own firewall while maintaining hundreds of virtual systems without the need for dedicated firewalls for each customer. Large organizations that require the use of many separate firewalls would benefit from the technology as well. The cost to use virtual systems is not an inexpensive proposition, but compared to maintaining many physical firewalls it can provide some cost benefits.

In this chapter, we will explore the virtual system technology and how to implement it. Together, we first will look at the virtual system technology and what it provides. Next, we will explore how virtual systems work. Looking deeply into how one physical device can differentiate traffic to dozens, if not hundreds, of different virtual systems. This is by far the most complex portion of virtual systems. There are two different methods to specify which traffic should be sent to which virtual system. We will look into each type of traffic classification and when to apply each one.

The last section of this chapter will be dedicated to creating virtual systems. This is the easiest part of the process of using a virtual system. Planning is always the biggest part of any battle. We will look at the creation, deletion, and administration of virtual systems.

What Is a Virtual System?

A virtual system is a unique security domain inside of a NetScreen firewall. Each virtual system contains its own address book, user lists, custom service definitions, VPNs, and policies. Virtual systems also have there own virtual system administrators. These administrators are limited to accessing a specific virtual system. This limits the VSYS administrator to their own virtual system, thus keeping them out of other virtual systems and the root system.

Virtual System Components

Each virtual system has three components that can be used either in a shared state or exclusively. Each of these components should already be familiar to you. When shared, the component is made available to other systems, virtual or root. If the component is exclusive to a virtual system, it can only be used by that specific system. The following are the three main components of a virtual system:

- **Virtual Routers** When a virtual system is created, it automatically gains access to all shared virtual routers. A new virtual router is created simultaneously and named "<vsys name>-vr". This VR is unable to be shared.

- **Zones** Just as with virtual routers, when a VSYS zone is created it has access to all shared zones. When a virtual system is created, three new zones are automatically created: Trust-<vsys name>, Untrust-Tun-<vsys name>, and Global-<vsys name>.

- **Network Interfaces (first type)** Untrust Zone Interface Types: You can use several types of interfaces for the Untrust zone on a virtual system: a Dedicated Physical Interface, Subinterface (with VLAN Tagging), and Shared Interface (Physical, Subinterface, Redundant Interface, Aggregate Interface) with the root system only.

- **Network Interfaces (second type)** Trust Zone Interface Types: Dedicated Physical Interface, Subinterface (with VLAN Tagging), and Shared Physical Interface with root system (using IP-based traffic classification).

Tools & Traps...

Sharing Nicely with Others

We have begun to discuss the idea of "shared" objects. A shared object is an object that can be used by multiple systems residing on the same physical firewall. On a virtual system, this consists of zones, interfaces, and virtual routers. Sharing the same objects across several virtual systems allows for the efficient distribution of resources.

In situations when you are using a NetScreen-500 and it is configured with the maximum eight Ethernet interfaces, you want to ensure that in the long term you have enough resources available to you. This is where efficient sharing amongst all of the available virtual systems and the root system is important. If you have long-term expansion goals, you will want your initial design to reflect this. You never want to be stuck in a situation where you need to redesign your network after several months of deployment because you failed to see the bigger picture in the beginning.

How Virtual Systems Work

When using virtual systems, you essentially have one physical firewall device and many virtual firewalls inside of that single firewall. Amazingly enough, the NetScreen-5400 firewall can support up to 500 virtual systems. To support this, Juniper has derived some amazing ways to support this type of architecture. In this section of the chapter, we will look into just how Juniper enables this to happen.

Classifying Traffic

There are two types of mechanisms that Juniper uses to determine where traffic entering the physical firewall should go. It decides this based upon the type of traffic entering the device. The first type of traffic is traffic that is destined for the virtual system itself. Because there is no other place for the traffic to go except for the configured component of the virtual system, the traffic goes to that particular virtual system. This type of traffic includes traffic destined for a virtual private network (VPN), mapped IP (MIP), or virtual IP (VIP).

However there is a second type of traffic that creates a great deal of difficulty when attempting to categorize it: through traffic. This is traffic destined for hosts beyond the firewall itself, thus it passes through your firewall. There are two methods of handling traffic of this type. The first method is to use virtual local area network (VLAN) tagging. This method determines which traffic is destined for particular virtual systems. The second method available is called IP traffic classification. This requires you to manually configure which subnets or IP ranges are destined for a particular virtual system.

VLAN-Based Classification

VLAN-based traffic classification employs the use of VLAN tagging to determine the destination of traffic. Each virtual system using a subinterface would require that interface to have its own specific VLAN dedicated to that interface. This requires not only configuring your firewall but configuring your network infrastructure as well. This requires that you divide your network into a configuration that encompasses VLANs. NetScreen firewalls support the IEEE 802.1Q standard tags.

VLANs are bound to virtual systems by a subinterface. A VSYS must be associated with a VLAN when it shares its Untrust interface with the root system and has an interface bound to its own "Trust-<vsys name>" zone. Also, if the VSYS has a subinterface bound to the Untrust zone, that particular VSYS must be associated with another VLAN in the Untrust zone.

IP-Based Classification

There will be times when it may not be possible to reconfigure your network so it encompasses a design with VLANs. If such is the case, another option can be used called IP-based classification. IP-based classification allows you to manually specify which traffic should be sent to which VSYS.

Virtual System Administration

Administering a virtual system is the same as administering a regular appliance. The only difference is that you can only have one read-write administrator and one read-only administrator. A read-write administrator for a VSYS has the same privileges as a read-write administrator for an appliance. As the name goes, the read-only administrator can only view the configuration of the virtual system.

The root administrator over the entire firewall device is allowed to create and delete virtual systems. The root administrator is required to give resources to virtual systems. If you wanted to give a virtual system access to interfaces or virtual routers, the root administrator is required to do this. These tasks cannot be done by a VSYS admin. Once the VSYS admin has the interfaces or VRs in the VSYS, it can do whatever it wants with them, but only after the root administrator gives the VSYS access to the resource.

Configuring Virtual Systems

As complicated as virtual systems sound, their configuration is actually quite easy. In this section, we'll discuss the creation of virtual systems. Creation of a virtual system is easy—the hardest part is in their planning. Due to the complexity of using multiple firewalls in the same unit, you should always have a complete plan when using virtual systems. The last thing you want is to have important questions arise at the zero hour. In fact, I firmly believe that success is 99% planning and 1% execution. Thus, everything should be so well mapped out beforehand that your project's execution feels seamless.

Creating a Virtual System

When initially creating a virtual system, you only have one decision to make. You must determine the name for your new virtual system. When you create a virtual system from the CLI, you will immediately enter the virtual system so you can continue configuring it. In the WebUI, you must click the button labeled Enter to access the VSYS.

When generating a VSYS, you must create an administrator for the newly created system. At login, this administrator will have access to that system only. In the WebUI, you create the virtual system and the administrator in one fell swoop. You can see the virtual system main page in Figure 12.1. When creating virtual system administrators from the CLI, it requires a few additional commands, just as any CLI configuration takes.

Figure 12.1 The Virtual System Main Page (WebUI)

From the WebUI:

VSYS

1. In the upper right-hand corner, click the button labeled **New**.

2. The VSYS | Edit page should appear.

3. The minimum needed for creating a new VSYS is simply a name.

4. You can enter the name in the text box labeled Vsys Name.

5. To create a read-write admin for this VSYS, enter the VSYS admin's name in the text box labeled **Vsys Admin Name**, and the new password in the boxes labeled **Vsys Admin New Password** and **Confirm New Password**.

6. You have several more options on the VSYS creation page. For instance, you can also create a read-only VSYS admin.

7. To create a read-only admin for this VSYS, enter the VSYS admin's name in the text box labeled **Vsys Read-Only Admin Name** and the new password in the boxes labeled **Vsys Read-Only Admin New Password** and **Confirm New Password**.

The last option lets you determine what type of virtual router to use. You have three options:

- The first is to create a new default virtual router. To do this, select the radio button labeled **Create a Default Virtual Router**.

- To select an existing virtual router, mark the radio button labeled **Select an Existing Virtual Router** and choose a virtual router from the drop-down box under that selection.

- The last option is to create a custom virtual router. To do this, select the radio button labeled **Create a Custom Virtual Router** and enter the new VR name in the text box labeled **vr name.**

From the CLI:

```
Ns500-> set vsys Syngress
Ns500(Syngress)-> set admin name Jamie
Ns500(Syngress)-> set admin password MasterCheif
Ns500(Syngress)-> save
Ns500(Syngress)-> exit
Ns500->
```

Figure 12.2 displays the virtual system creation page.

Figure 12.2 The Virtual System Creation Page (WebUI)

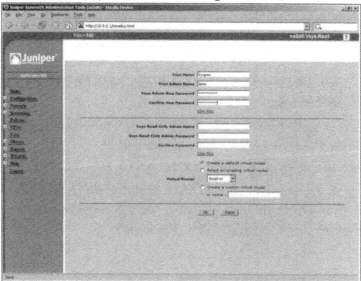

Network Interfaces

Because a virtual system is a firewall, its key components are its interfaces. Interfaces are required to pass traffic from one zone of your network to another. As we briefly discussed earlier, there are several types of interfaces that a virtual system can use:

- **Physical Interface** As the name states, a physical interface is an actual physical port that would connect directly to the network.

- **Subinterface** Subinterfaces are tied directly to a physical interface and require the use of VLAN tagging to differentiate which traffic is destined to which subinterface.

- **Shared Interface** Interfaces can only be shared with the root system. There are several types of shared interfaces you can configure (Physical, Subinterface, Redundant interface, Aggregate Interface). It would be normal to use a shared interface, for example, when you have an Internet connection you want to configure to share with your virtual systems. When using shared interfaces, you must also configure traffic classification to determine which virtual system should process the traffic. Multiple virtual systems can share the same interface with root. But don't think of this as two virtual systems sharing an interface with each other. Just think of it as the root system sharing the interface with each of the virtual systems.

Physical Interfaces

When you decide to dedicate a physical interface to a virtual system, that virtual system gets exclusive use of that interface. To do this, you must import the physical interface to the virtual system. When you want to import an interface, it must be bound to the Null zone at the root level before it can be imported. When you've finished using a physical interface, you must export it to give the interface back to the root system. In Figure 12.3, you can see the screen used during the importation process.

Figure 12.3 Interface Importation (WebUI)

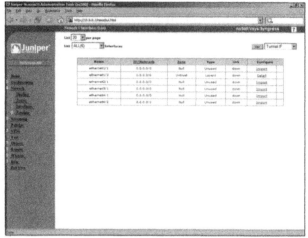

From the WebUI:

To import the physical interface to the virtual system, do the following:

1. Log in as the root administrator or read–write administrator for the root system.

2. Identify the Vsys you want to import a physical interface to.

3. In the Vsys row, click the link labeled **Enter**.

4. You should now be in the Vsys you have chosen. Select **Network | Interfaces**.

5. You are now presented with the list of interfaces for the device.

6. Identify the interface you want to use and import it into the virtual system.

7. Click the link labeled **Import**.

8. You will be prompted with a dialog that reads "You are about to import an interface. Are you sure you want to continue?" Click **OK**.

9. Once the interface is imported, you can add a zone to the interface and then an IP address, just as you normally would.

10. To export an interface, enter the virtual system as mentioned earlier and go to the **Network | Interfaces** location in the WebUI.

11. The interface must have the IP address removed and the zone removed before it can be exported. Identify the interface you want to export and then click the link labeled **Export**.

12. You will be prompted with a dialog that reads "You are about to export an interface. Are you sure you want to continue?" Click **OK**.

From the CLI:

```
Ns500-> set vsys Syngress
Ns500(Syngress)-> set interface ethernet4/2 import
Ns500(Syngress)-> set interface ethernet4/2 zone Trust-Syngress
Ns500(Syngress)-> set interface ethernet4/2 ip 10.10.10.1/24
Ns500(Syngress)-> save
Ns500(Syngress)-> exit
Ns500-> set vsys Syngress
Ns500(Syngress)-> unset interface ethernet4/2 ip 10.10.10.1/24
Ns500(Syngress)-> unset interface ethernet4/2 zone Trust-Syngress
Ns500(Syngress)-> unset interface ethernet4/2 import
Ns500(Syngress)-> save
Ns500(Syngress)-> exit
Ns500->
```

Figure 12.4 displays the screen used during the exportation process.

Figure 12.4 Exporting an Interface (WebUI)

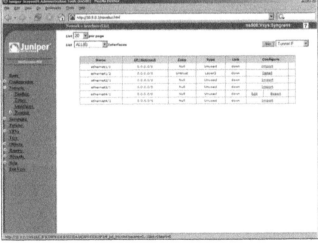

Subinterfaces

Subinterfaces are virtual interfaces that are bound to a specific physical interface. When using subinterfaces, you are also required to use VLANs. This means you may have to reconfigure your network to support VLANs. Figure 12.5 shows the WebUI Subinterface Configuration screen.

Figure 12.5 Subinterface Configuration (WebUI)

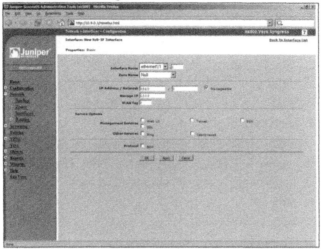

From the WebUI:

1. Log in as the root administrator or read–write administrator for the root system.

2. Identify the Vsys you want to create a subinterface for.

3. In the Vsys row, click the link labeled **Enter**.

4. Go to **Network | Interfaces**.

5. In the upper right-hand corner of the page, choose **Sub-If** from the drop-down menu.

6. Click the button labeled **New** in the upper right-hand corner.

7. Configuring a subinterface is similar to configuring a physical interface (as shown in Chapter 3). Enter your IP addressing, subnetting, and management configuration here.

8. Choose which physical interface you want to be bound to at the top of the page, and then set your VLAN tag in the text box labeled **VLAN Tag**.

9. Once you have completed your configuration, click **OK.**

From the CLI:

```
Ns500-> set vsys Syngress
Ns500(Syngress)-> set interface ethernet4/2.1 zone Trust-Syngress
Ns500(Syngress)-> set interface ethernet4/2.1 ip 10.10.10.1/24 tag 4
Ns500(Syngress)-> save
Ns500(Syngress)-> exit
Ns500-> set vsys Syngress
Ns500(Syngress)-> unset interface ethernet4/2.1 ip 10.10.10.1/24
Ns500(Syngress)-> unset interface ethernet4/2.1 zone Trust-Syngress
Ns500(Syngress)-> save
Ns500(Syngress)-> exit
Ns500->
```

Shared Interface

Configuring a shared interface relies on the configuration of a shared zone. Because of the zone hierarchy, you must create a zone that's shared. Once you apply that shared zone to an interface, it is then automatically shared to all virtual systems. In Figure 12.6, you can see the zone configuration screen with the option to share the zone.

Figure 12.6 Shared Zone Configuration (WebUI)

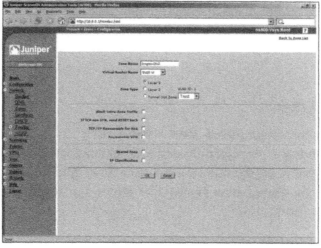

From the WebUI:

To configure a shared interface, do the following:

1. Log in as the root administrator or read-write administrator for the root system.

2. Go to **Network | Zones**.

3. Click the button labeled **New** in the upper-right hand corner.

4. In the text box labeled **Zone Name**, enter the zone name.

5. At the bottom of the page, check the box labeled "**Shared Zone**."

6. Go to **Network | Interfaces**.

7. Identify the interface you want to share and click the link titled **Edit**.

8. At the top of the page in the drop-down box labeled **Zone**, choose the shared zone you created.

9. Click **OK** at the bottom of the page.

From the CLI:

```
Ns500-> set zone name Syngress-DMZ
Ns500-> set zone Syngress-DMZ shared
Ns500-> set interface ethernet4/2 zone Syngress-DMZ
Ns500-> set interface ethernet4/2 ip 10.10.10.1/24
Ns500-> save
Ns500->
Ns500-> unset interface ethernet4/2 ip 10.10.10.1/24
Ns500-> unset interface ethernet4/2 zone Syngress-DMZ
Ns500-> save
Ns500-> exit
Ns500->
```

Traffic Classification

The second part to using a shared zone is traffic classification. By configuring traffic classification, you are explicitly defining which zone traffic is destined for. Traffic classification is configured on a per zone basis. You would configure traffic classification on the shared zone. Figure 12.7 shows the WebUI configuration screen for traffic classification.

Figure 12.7 Traffic Classification (WebUI)

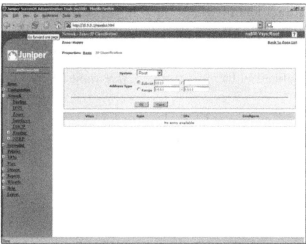

From the WebUI:

To configure traffic classification, do the following:

1. Log in as the root administrator or read-write administrator for the root system.

2. Go to **Network | Zones**.

3. Identify the zone you want to configure traffic classification for and click the link labeled **Edit**.

4. In the center of the top part of the page, click the link titled **IP Classification**.

5. In the drop-down box labeled System, choose which system you want to map the defined traffic to. You can choose either an IP subnet or an IP range.

6. If you want to define an IP subnet, select the radio button labeled Subnet and enter the IP subnet in the first text box to the right of the text **Subnet** and then the netmask in the text box labeled "/" in the same row as the text **Subnet.**

7. If you want to define an IP address range, select the radio button labeled **Range** in the first text box to the right of the text "Range" and enter the first IP address. In the text box next to the text "-", enter the last IP address in the specified range.

8. Once you have defined your range or subnet, click **OK**.

9. To remove the range or subnet from the Network | Zones (IP Classification), identify the subnet/IP range you want to remove and click the link titled **Remove**.

10. You will be prompted with a dialog that reads "You are about to remove an IP classification list. Are you sure you want to continue?" Click **OK**.

From the CLI:

```
Ns500-> set zone Syngress-DMZ ip-classification range 1.2.3.4-1.2.3.20 vsys
Syngress

Ns500-> set zone Syngress-DMZ ip-classification

Ns500-> save

Ns500->

Ns500-> unset zone Syngress-DMZ ip-classification range 1.2.3.4-1.2.3.20
vsys Syngress

Ns500-> unset zone Syngress-DMZ ip-classification

Ns500->
```

Tools & Traps…

So Many Configurations, So Little Time

As you can see, configuring an actual VSYS is an easy process. It contains many of the same elements used when configuring a regular NetScreen appliance. When deploying a NetScreen system that is capable of using virtual systems, you will be working with a product that costs tens of thousands of dollars. In some cases, the virtualization license that gives a system the ability to use virtual systems can cost tens of thousands of dollars as well.

This type of deployment, whether for one or for five hundred virtual systems, requires intense planning and great scrutiny to ensure a successful implementation. It's not because the configuration is complex; it usually has to do with the scale of the deployment. Make sure you have documented what you want to configure on each virtual system. Diagrams are always a great benefit to any deployment and are of great help in long-term documentation.

Summary

In this chapter, we looked at virtual systems. As you have learned, virtual systems are a powerful tool you can use to divide up your NetScreen firewall system into several firewalls or virtual systems. This lets you maximize the return on investment (ROI) of a single large firewall, allowing it to be divided into multiple independent firewalls. This provides several benefits.

It allows for separate management domains. You can divide your firewall into several smaller logical devices and thereby separate management resources from one another. Secondly, you can use it the same way you would if you had two or more separate firewalls. This is often done to logically separate two distinct parts of the network. In the case where you would use two separate physical firewalls, you could use just one NetScreen system that's capable of running virtual systems.

Virtual systems are just the next logical step in the evolution of firewall design, and show off Juniper's excellent product design by demonstrating that the NetScreen firewall is such a scalable device.

Solutions Fast Track

What Is a Virtual System?

- ☑ A virtual system is a unique security domain inside a NetScreen firewall.
- ☑ Virtual systems can use components shared by the root system.
- ☑ You can define a virtual system so it will use its own virtual router.

How Virtual Systems Work

- ☑ NetScreen firewalls have two ways of classify traffic, thereby deciding which virtual system to send it to.
- ☑ When using a subinterface, you must configure VLAN tagging to differentiate traffic.
- ☑ You can only have one read-write administrator and one read-only administrator per virtual system.

Configuring Virtual Systems

☑ Creating a virtual system is an easy one-step process.

☑ Physical interfaces that are dedicated to a virtual system must be imported into the virtual system.

☑ If you are going to use shared interfaces, you must configure IP classification to decide which virtual system will receive which traffic.

Frequently Asked Questions

The following Frequently Asked Questions, answered by the authors of this book, are designed to both measure your understanding of the concepts presented in this chapter and to assist you with real-life implementation of these concepts. To have your questions about this chapter answered by the author, browse to **www.syngress.com/solutions** and click on the **"Ask the Author"** form. You will also gain access to thousands of other FAQs at ITFAQnet.com.

Q: Virtual systems seem like a great idea, but are they practical for my environment?

A: Organizations very rarely use virtual systems. They are only practical to use when you require many separate firewalls. Only large organizations and ISPs have the type of environment that requires virtual systems. Even though the application of virtual systems may be beneficial to you, the cost may be prohibitive.

Q: Why would you want to share a resource instead of using a dedicated resource?

A: There are many valid reasons why you would want to share resources instead of using dedicated resources. The first good reason would be to conserve resources. You may require many resources and dedicating them may not be feasible. A great second reason would be practicality. It may be easier to have one physical interface connected to the Internet and share it amongst five virtual systems than to dedicate five interfaces to the same Internet connection. The great part about this device's design is that you could do either depending on your requirements.

Q: Configuring and managing many virtual systems seems complex. Is there a better way to manage all of this?

A: Juniper provides a platform called the NetScreen-Security Manager for all of your central management needs. The NSM is discussed in Chapter 16 and is a great investment in a heavy Juniper infrastructure.

Q: How do I get my network to support VLANs?

A: A network switch that uses VLANs is required to support VLAN architecture. Many switches today support the use of VLANs. Typically, a managed switch can support VLANs. Look to the documentation of your switch manufacturer to see what your switches can do.

Q: Can you give VSYS administrators the same name on different VSYSs?

A: Administrator names are unique. Once you specify an administrative user with a particular name, that name cannot be used a second time.

Chapter 13

High Availability

Solutions in this Chapter:

Introduction

As the reliance on data networks becomes greater, the importance of their availability increases. This chapter provides a comprehensive look at the features provided by the various NetScreen firewalls for achieving high availability (HA) networks. The effort involved in understanding and implementing the most highly available networks is significant and can be a daunting task. This chapter explores the available options in a progressive manner, building on the previous knowledge as much as possible. Juniper Networks have gone to great lengths to provide features that are both complete and appropriate for improving the availability of networks.

This chapter begins with a discussion about the nature of and justification for high availability networks. Having a feel for the multi-faceted nature of this topic is a great help, especially when trying to justify planned expenses to upper management.

Next, we examine how high availability can be achieved using the different methods and features available across the NetScreen range of firewalls. Several configuration examples are provided that can be used as a baseline to develop high availability solutions appropriate to your specific network.

Towards the end of the chapter, some of the more advanced issues are presented and ideas and recommendations are given on how to best approach them.

Throughout this chapter, there are examples with configuration instructions for both the command line interface (CLI) and the Web interface. Any instructions for configuration via the Web interface assumes that the firewall is already configured with an Internet Protocol (IP) address. It is recommended that you use the CLI for several reasons: it is always available via the console port regardless of configuration (unless explicitly disabled), some commands are only available via the CLI, and it is much easier to work with than the Web interface. However, if you have a large installation, the NetScreen Security Manager (NSM) platform is the better choice, because it offers a graphical user interface (GUI) and the ability to easily manage several firewalls. In the end, the interface you use to configure your NetScreen firewalls should be the one you feel most comfortable with and that can get the job done.

The Need for High Availability

Whether due to hardware or software faults, one fact cannot be disputed: network components fail. The only issues that can be debated are the frequency of

the failure and the impact that each type of failure will have. HA is about mitigating the risks of network failures and bringing them within acceptable bounds,
which are (or at least should be) dictated by your business strategy. Do you
depend on your e-commerce Web site to be available 24 hours a day, 365 days a
year? If so, your idea of acceptable network outages will be vastly different from
someone whose business only relies on the network for sending and receiving
occasional e-mails. Knowing your business strategy is the first step towards being
able to decide which HA measures, if any, you should add.

The next step in justifying HA is to understand the trade-off between the
cost and the improvement gained. Cost is not only measured in money, but also
in time and complexity. A highly available network takes longer to implement,
results in more maintenance work, takes longer to gain an understanding of, and
due to increased complexity, raises the risks of human error. Making an informed
decision is not as easy as you might think.

Depending on a businesses needs, HA can be anything from having a spare
unit in the storage room to having a fully meshed, fully redundant network
infrastructure with automatic failure detection and failover. Generally speaking,
the term HA is only used for situations where a standby device is already configured and can be brought into play at a moment's notice.

The NetScreen range of firewalls provides a large variety of different means to
achieving an HA network, from fall-back to dial-up on the small office, home
office (SOHO) appliances, to device redundancy using mid-range appliances, to
the heavy duty features of the Enterprise and Carrier class systems. Table 13.1
shows a matrix of the different HA categories provided by the NetScreen firewalls.

Table 13.1 HA Feature Matrix

HA Feature	SOHO	HA Category NSRP-Lite	NSRP
Fall-back to dial-up	Yes	No	No
Active/Passive setup	No	Yes	Yes
Active/Active setup	No	No	Yes
RTO synchronization	No	No	Yes

Improving Availability Using NetScreen SOHO Appliances

Of all of the SOHO range of firewall appliances available (HSC, NS-5XT, and NS-5GT), all but the HSC support providing a secondary path for untrusted traffic. That is, should the normal link fail, a backup link can be activated and thereby the connectivity restored. This is a very useful feature, as anyone who has suffered from unplanned Internet Service Provider (ISP) outages can attest to. Two different ways to make sure that redundant ISP links are available is either by using two Ethernet interfaces or using one Ethernet interface and the serial interface as the backup. In the first scenario, the common setup has two ADSL modems or routers connected to separate ISPs, with one being the preferred provider. In the second scenario, the typical setup has an ADSL (asymmetric digital subscriber line) modem or router as the preferred link, and a modem connected to the serial interface providing dial-up access if needed.

When setting up redundant links, there are two main issues that must be specified: what will cause the backup link to activate, and how is it activated?

The event of deciding that the primary link is dead and the backup link should be activated is called a *failover*. The deciding factors for a failover includes such things as physical link failure, virtual private network (VPN) failure, or an IP address becoming unreachable.

Once a failover is triggered, the backup link must be activated. How this happens depends on your setup. For example, you can have a second ADSL modem where the backup link is activated by setting up a Point-to-Point Protocol over Ethernet (PPPoE) session via that modem, or you can have a normal dial-up modem where the backup link is activated by dialing a configured phone number followed by a Point-to-Point Protocol (PPP) login.

Failing Over Between Interfaces

By default, you must manually initiate a failover. In many cases, this is sufficient and even recommended. You can initiate the failover from the CLI using the **exec failover force** command, or via the Web interface by going to **Network | Untrust failover | Force to failover**. To revert back to the primary untrust interface, use the **exec failover revert** command from the CLI, or go to **Network | Untrust failover | Force to revert** via the Web interface.

If you want to automate failovers, use the **set failover auto** command from the CLI or select **Network | Untrust failover | Automatic failover | Apply** via the Web interface.

Unless told otherwise, NetScreen firewalls determine whether to fail over to the backup interface by monitoring the status of the primary untrust port. If a link failure is detected, traffic is moved to the backup interface after a certain hold-down time has passed (30 seconds by default). This hold-down time is used to prevent rapid switching back and forth between the interfaces. Delaying the failover for a short time gives the interfaces a chance to stabilize. A failover is a serious action that should not be made without good cause. If you find that the 30-second default hold-down time is inappropriate in your situation, you can adjust it with the **set failover hold-down N** command, where **N** is the number of seconds to wait before initiating the failover.

The monitoring of the untrust port only detects a link failure between the NetScreen and the modem or router it is connected to; it does not detect failures beyond that modem or router. Hence, if you have an ADSL modem connected to your NetScreen and the Digital Subscriber Line (DSL) service is interrupted, it will not be detected by port monitoring on the firewall. To handle these types of problems, you must configure other types of monitoring such as VPN monitoring or IP tracking.

Using Dual Untrust Interfaces to Provide Redundancy

Using dual untrust interfaces is suited to any scenario where the untrusted network, generally the Internet, can be reached via two different paths with each path providing an Ethernet connection. This can be via:

- ADSL modem (using PPPoE on the NetScreen)
- ADSL router
- Ethernet Direct (using PPPoE on the NetScreen)
- Cable Ethernet (using PPPoE on the NetScreen)

Combinations of the above, or any service that uses PPPoE to provide access, can be used to establish the redundancy desired in this scenario.

To be able to use dual untrust interfaces, the port mode must be set to either *dual-untrust* or *combined*. The combined mode is only available on the NS-5XT

Elite model, but functions identically to the two untrust ports. For the remainder of this chapter, *dual-untrust* is used to refer to either of these two modes.

> ## ! WARNING
>
> If you change the port mode, the entire configuration will be erased. It is a good idea to back up the existing configuration before you continue. Also, because the configuration is lost (including assigned IP addresses), it is easier to use the CLI via the console port than the Web interface.

Bringing the NetScreen into *dual-untrust* mode is done using the **exec port-mode dual-untrust** command from the CLI, or going to **Configuration | Port Mode | Port mode** via the Web interface. Any previous configuration will be erased and must therefore be manually re-entered after the firewall has rebooted. If you do not know what mode the firewall is in, you can see it by using the **get system** command from the CLI or by going to **Configuration | Port Mode** via the Web interface.

Example: Configuration for Dual ADSL Modems

Once in *dual-untrust* mode, you can add the necessary configuration needed for the two separate untrusted paths. For example, imagine a scenario where the preferred path is via one ADSL modem, and the backup path is via a different ADSL modem (or other service relying on PPPoE authentication), as depicted in Figure 13.1 below.

Figure 13.1 Redundant ADSL Internet Connections

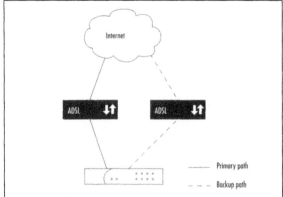

From the CLI:

```
set pppoe name "primary-adsl" username user1 password abc123
set pppoe name "primary-adsl" interface ethernet3
set pppoe name "primary-adsl" clear-on-disconnect
set pppoe name "primary-adsl" idle-interval 0
set pppoe name "primary-adsl" auto-connect 20
set pppoe name "backup-adsl" username user2 password bcd234
set pppoe name "backup-adsl" interface ethernet2
set pppoe name "backup-adsl" clear-on-disconnect
set pppoe name "backup-adsl" idle-interval 0
set pppoe name "backup-adsl" auto-connect 20
set failover auto
```

From the Web interface

1. Go to **Network | PPPoE | New**.
2. Name this instance **primary-adsl**.
3. Bind this instance to **ethernet3**.
4. Enter the ISP's **Username** and **Password**.
5. Enable the **Clear IP on disconnect** option.
6. Enable **Auto-connect** and specify **20 seconds**.
7. Click **OK** to save.
8. Return to **Network | PPPoE | New**.
9. Name this instance **backup-adsl**.
10. Bind this instance to **interface ethernet2**.
11. Enter the **ISP Username** and **Password**.
12. Enable **Auto-connect** and specify **20 seconds**.
13. Click **OK** to save.
14. Go to **Network | Untrust failover | Automatic Failover** and click **OK**.

The *clear-on-disconnect* option is used to ensure that any old interface IP address or default gateway is removed when the PPPoE session goes down. This ensures that packets are routed correctly after a failover, instead of being sent to the now unreachable gateway.

The *idle-interval* option allows you to automatically disconnect the PPPoE session after a certain period of inactivity. In this case, we do not want to do that. By setting it to zero, this feature is disabled and the PPPoE session will not be dropped due to inactivity.

The *auto-connect* option enables the NetScreen to attempt to re-connect to the PPPoE session if it is dropped. If this is not set, the connection must be manually brought up via the **exec pppoe connect** command, or by power-cycling the NetScreen. Clearly, this is not a desirable feature in our case; we use auto-connect.

Another interesting aspect of this option is how it interacts with the automatic failover (if enabled). To give the primary untrust interface a good chance of recovering before a failover is initiated, set the auto-connect value lower than the failover hold-down setting, which is 30 seconds by default. This way, the PPPoE connection on the primary interface is retried before the failover is triggered. This might be enough to prevent a failover altogether depending on the reason for the failure of the PPPoE session.

Example: Advanced Configuration for ADSL Modem Plus ADSL Router

For this example, imagine a setup where the primary link is via an ADSL modem and the backup is via an ADSL router to a different ISP. They are used in this order to get the IP address assigned directly to the NetScreen. This way any NAT can take place on the NetScreen. The NetScreen provides more power and flexibility in this area than most ADSL routers commonly do, so it is the sensible thing to do.

To make matters a bit more interesting in this example, also assume that the primary ISP has assigned a static IP address to us (1.1.1.1) that should always be used, even if the remote end attempts to assign a different IP address during the PPP negotiation. Any decent ISP should be able to assign static IP addresses via PPPoE itself, but for the sake of this exercise, let's assume that this ISP cannot. The ISP's equipment is really bad at responding to the Link Control Protocol (LCP) Echo requests that are used to verify that the link is up. Unless more conservative timings are used on our end, the link will keep getting dropped despite actually being up and working fine. Furthermore, this ISP supports only Password Authentication Protocol (PAP); the considerably more secure Challenge Handshake Authentication Protocol (CHAP) is not supported.

From the CLI:

```
# public IP address as assigned by the primary ISP
set interface ethernet3 ip 1.1.1.1/24
# private IP address used between the NetScreen and the backup DSL router
# the DSL router gets the public IP address via PPPoE and then NATs traffic
set interface ethernet2 ip 172.16.32.2/30
set pppoe name "adsl" username user1 password abc123
set pppoe name "adsl" interface ethernet3
set pppoe name "adsl" static-ip
set pppoe name "adsl" authentication PAP
set pppoe name "adsl" clear-on-disconnect
set pppoe name "adsl" auto-connect 20
set pppoe name "adsl" idle-interval 0
set pppoe ppp lcp-echo-retries 20
set pppoe ppp lcp-echo-timeout 600
# set a default gateway for the backup path, when in use
set vrouter trust-vr route 0.0.0.0/0 interface ethernet2 gateway
172.16.32.1
set failover auto
```

NOTE

Comments can be used in external NetScreen configuration files. Comments are removed when the configuration is loaded into the NetScreen, but can be really useful for documenting configurations in a non-interfering manner. Full-line comments start with a hash mark followed by a space (#). Half-line comments start with a space followed by a hash mark followed by a space (#).

From the Web interface:

1. Go to **Network | Interfaces | Edit | ethernet3**.
2. Enter **1.1.1.1/24** for the IP address.
3. Click **OK**.
4. Go to **Network | Interfaces | Edit | ethernet2**.

5. Enter **172.16.32.2/30** as the IP Address and Netmask.

6. Click **OK** to save.

7. Go to **Network | PPPoE | New**.

8. Name this instance **adsl**.

9. Enter the **Username** and **Password** for the ISP.

10. Bind it to interface **ethernet3**.

11. Select **PAP** as the Authentication type.

12. Check the **Static IP** option.

13. Select the **Clear-on-disconnect** option.

14. Set **Auto-connect** to **20 seconds**.

15. Click **OK** to save.

16. Go to **Network | PPPoE | PPP**.

17. Set LCP Echo Retries to **20**.

18. Set LCP Echo Timeout to **600**.

19. Click **OK**.

20. Go to **Network | Routing | Routing entries**.

21. Select **trust-vr**.

22. Click **New** to add a new route.

23. Enter **0.0.0.0/0** as the IP Address and Netmask.

24. Select **ethernet2** as the gateway interface.

25. Enter **172.16.32.1** as the gateway IP address.

26. Click **OK** to save the new route.

27. Go to **Network | Untrust failover | Automatic Failover** and click **OK**.

Falling Back to Dial-up

If you do not have two Ethernet-capable connections to the Internet, you can use a dial-up connection as the backup path. The modem is connected to the NetScreen's serial port, and the dial-up is configured using the modem settings and the serial interface. It is also possible to specify multiple phone numbers to dial in sequence, in effect giving you more fall-back possibilities; if the first ISP does not answer, the next in line can be dialed.

NOTE

The serial interface is only available when *trust-untrust* or *home-work* mode is used as the port mode. It is not possible to use the serial interface in any other mode.

Following are the steps needed to configure this :

1. Move the serial interface to the untrust zone to enable it.
2. Configure the modem settings.
3. Enter the ISP account details.
4. If using the CLI, add a default route for the serial interface (done automatically when using the Web interface).
5. Enable **automatic failover** (if desired).

Example: A Simple Backup Dial-up Configuration

Using an unspecified generic modem, we configure a backup dial-up setup for an ISP that has a single dial-up number. Figure 13.2 shows the setup.

Figure 13.2 Fall-back to Dial-up Internet Connection

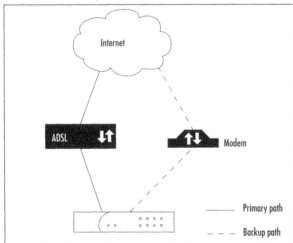

From the CLI:

```
set interface serial zone untrust
set modem settings "generic" init-strings AT&FS7=255S32=6
set modem settings "generic" active
set modem isp "myisp" account login user1 password abc123
set modem isp "myisp" primary-number 5550123
set modem isp "myisp" priority 1
set vrouter trust-vr route 0.0.0.0/0 interface serial
set failover auto
```

From the Web interface:

1. Go to **Network | Interfaces** and click **Edit** for the serial interface.
2. Select the **Untrust** zone.
3. Click **OK**.
4. Return to **Network | Interfaces | serial Edit** and click **Modem**.
5. Name the modem **generic**.
6. Specify an Init-string of **AT&FS7=255S32=6**.
7. Select it as **Active**.
8. Click **OK** when done.
9. Go to **Network | Interfaces | serial Edit | ISP**.
10. Name the ISP **myisp**.
11. Provide the **Login Name** and **Password** details as well as the **Primary telephone number**.
12. Set the Priority to **1**.
13. Click **OK**.

14. Go to **Network | Untrust failover | Automatic Failover** and click **Apply**.

Example: An Advanced Backup Dial-up Configuration

To demonstrate more of the flexibility provided with the dial-up ability, let's consider a more complex example. Here, we configure support for two different

ISPs, each with dual dial-up numbers. A Rockwell-based 56K modem will primarily be used; the settings on an old US Robotics 28800 are configured as a backup. Since we are more concerned with network availability than the phone bill, we will disconnect the call after 45 minutes of inactivity (inactivity being defined as a period where no packets are permitted by a policy through the firewall). We also want to dial rapidly until we successfully connect to an ISP, so the dial interval is lowered to 4 seconds (the default is 10 seconds). Be aware that you need to allow for sufficient time for the phone line to actually disconnect before the next dial attempt is made. Also, since we will have four different numbers that we can potentially connect via, there is little to be gained by retrying the same number many times before continuing to the next number (or ISP if there was no answer on either of the first ISP's numbers). Setting the number of retry attempts to one causes the NetScreen to only attempt to redial each number once before continuing on to the next.

From the CLI:

```
set interface serial zone untrust
set modem settings "rockwell" init-strings AT&FV1W1X4&C1&D3&K3&N3%C3S7=60
set modem settings "usr28800" init-strings AT&F&A3&B1&H1&R2&D0&C1X4S7=90
set modem settings "rockwell" active
set modem idle-time 45
set modem interval 4
set modem retry 1
set modem isp "isp1" account login user1 password abc123
set modem isp "isp1" primary-number 5550123 alternative-number 5550124
set modem isp "isp1" priority 1
set modem isp "isp2" account login user2 password bcd234
set modem isp "isp2" primary-number 5550198 alternative-number 5550199
set modem isp "isp2" priority 2
set vrouter trust-vr route 0.0.0.0/0 interface serial
set failover auto
```

From the Web interface:

1. Go to **Network | Interfaces|** and click **Edit** for the serial interface.
2. Select the **Untrust** zone.
3. Click **OK**.

4. Still under **Network | Interfaces | serial Edit**, click on **Modem**.

5. Name the modem **rockwell**.

6. Specify an Init-string of **AT&FV1W1X4&C1&D3&K3&N3%C3S7=60**.

7. Select it as **Active**.

8. Set the Idle-time to **45 minutes**.

9. Set the Retry Interval to **4 seconds**.

10. Specify the number of Retries as **1**.

11. Add a second modem named **usr28800**.

12. Set the Init-string to **AT&F&A3&B1&H1&R2&D0&C1X4S7=90**.

13. Click **OK** when done.

14. Go to **Network | Interfaces | serial Edit | ISP**.

15. Name the ISP **isp1**.

16. Provide the **Login Name** and **Password** details as well as the dial-up **Primary and Alternative telephone numbers**.

17. Set the Priority to **1** (the highest priority).

18. Click **OK**.

19. Add a second ISP named **isp2**.

20. Enter the **Login Name** and **Password** for this ISP, followed by the **Primary** and **Alternative phone numbers**.

21. Specify a priority of **2**.

22. Click **OK** to save these settings.

23. Navigate to **Network | Untrust failover | Automatic Failover** and click **Apply**.

NOTE

You can send AT commands to the attached modem using the **exec modem command** command in the CLI (e.g., **exec modem command ATZ** to reset the modem).

It is also possible to examine the state of the modem with the **get modem state** command (e.g., is it waiting, dialing, connected, and so forth).

Restricting Policies to a Subset When Using the Serial Interface

Since a dial-up link inherently has less bandwidth and more latency than a DSL line or similar, it is easy to end up with a seriously congested up-link after having failed over to the dial-up path. Fortunately, the wise NetScreen designers foresaw this problem and provided a means to avoid it. By tagging individual policies, it is possible to choose which policies should or should not be active while traffic is moving via the backup serial interface. Which policies you choose to disable, if any, is entirely up to you, but some common examples include File Transfer Protocol (FTP), Voice over IP (VoIP), and audio-streaming services, since they are capable of chewing up a lot of bandwidth very easily.

Example: Marking FTP as Not Allowed When Using the Serial Interface

Assume we want to add a policy allowing FTP traffic to move from the trust to the untrust zone, which is automatically disabled when traffic is failed over to the serial interface.

From the CLI:

```
set policy from trust to untrust any any ftp permit no-session-backup
```

From the Web interface:

1. Go to **Policies** and create a new policy from the Trust zone to the Untrust zone.
2. Select **any** as the source and destination address.
3. Select **FTP** as the service.
4. Set **Permit** as the action for the policy.
5. Click **Advanced**.
6. Deselect the **Valid For Serial** option, and click **Return**.
7. Click **OK** to save the new policy.

As can be seen, the keyword "no-session-backup" is added to the policy to indicate that the policy should not be active when the serial interface is in use.

Note that this has no impact if you are using *dual-untrust* mode as the port mode, since the serial interface is not used in that case.

Using IP Tracking to Determine Failover

Relying on link monitoring is insufficient, especially when using tunneled protocols such as PPPoE. Usually when an outage occurs, it is not because the Ethernet cable between the NetScreen and the ADSL modem failed, but because the PPPoE connection could not be established. If using a default configuration, this scenario would not result in a failover because the Ethernet link is working and that is all that is being monitored. Nevertheless, there is no disputing the fact that the Internet connectivity is non-existent in this case, and that a failover should happen.

To address this problem, NetScreen has introduced the concept of *IP tracking*. IP tracking works by regularly pinging specified IP addresses; if they do not reply within the defined bounds, the link is considered down and a failover can be triggered. Note that I say, "can be triggered" not "will be triggered." That is because it is possible to have IP tracking configured and in use without actually having it cause failovers. The value of doing so is questionable, however.

IP tracking is considered an interface-level setting. This means that full routing is not done for the ping packets that are sent; they are always sent out via the interface that the IP tracking is configured on. You have the option of either specifying the next hop (gateway) to use for the pings explicitly, or letting the NetScreen determine it automatically. In an environment where the IP address and the default gateway are dynamically assigned, it is not feasible to explicitly set the gateway address.

The IP addresses that can be tracked fall into two categories: those specified explicitly and those referred to by function. The latter includes only one type: the default gateway for the interface. This is very useful when the interface dynamically receives an IP address as well as the default gateway, as is the case with PPPoE and Dynamic Host Control Protocol (DHCP). In situations where you do not know the IP address you need to ping beforehand, being able to refer to it as a dynamic entity and let the NetScreen worry about the specifics of which IP it refers to is very handy.

Just being able to ping a few IP addresses and fail over if any single one of them does not respond, is not particularly helpful, and NetScreen has recognized this. A great deal of flexibility is provided by the *weighting* system offered by the IP tracking. Fine-grained control is possible by assigning different *weights* (importance) to different IP addresses and setting a failover *threshold*. For example, you could say something like, "If both Web Server A and Web Server B or Mail Server M are unreachable, then failover." It is generally a good idea to keep it as simple as possible.

The weighting system consists of two main components: the individual weights for the tracked IP addresses and the failover threshold value. If at any point the combined sum of the failed IP addresses weights equal or exceed the threshold, failover can be triggered. An IP address is considered to have failed if a certain number of pings have gone unanswered. It is possible to configure both the frequency of the pings and the number of missing replies that are needed for it to be classified as "failed."

Example: Tracking the Default Gateway

This example shows what is perhaps the most common scenario; tracking a dynamically assigned default gateway on interface ethernet3. Automatic failover is enabled and set to use IP tracking as the determining factor.

From the CLI:

```
set interface ethernet3 track-ip
set interface ethernet3 track-ip dynamic
set failover auto
set failover type track-ip
```

From the Web interface:

1. Go to **Network | Interfaces | Edit | Track IP**.
2. Select **Enable Track IP** to enable IP tracking on this interface.
3. Press **Apply**.
4. Go to **Network | Interfaces | ethernet3 Edit | Track IP**.
5. Select the **Dynamic** option to track the default gateway.
6. Select **Add** to add dynamic monitoring to the list.
7. Go to **Network | Untrust failover** and enable the **Automatic Failover** option.
8. Select **IP tracking** as the Failover Type.
9. Click **Apply** to confirm these settings.

Example: A More Complex IP Tracking Scenario

To expand on the previous example, consider a scenario where we always want to be able to reach at least one of two Web servers as well as our mail server. We also know that due to the amount of junk mail received these days, the mail server might be slow to respond to pings, so we make adjustments for this, pinging once every five seconds and allowing for six missed responses (the default is to ping every second and only allow three missed replies).

For this exercise, we assume that the Web server's IP addresses are 1.1.1.1 and 1.1.1.2, and that the mail server resides at 2.2.2.2. The weights are allocated thus: 1 for each of the Web servers, 2 (or greater) for the mail-server, and a failover threshold of 2. Thus, if both Web servers fail, the sum of the weight for the failed IP addresses will reach 2, which is the failover threshold.

From the CLI:

```
set interface ethernet3 track-ip
set interface ethernet3 track-ip 1.1.1.1 weight 1
set interface ethernet3 track-ip 1.1.1.2 weight 1
set interface ethernet3 track-ip 2.2.2.2 interval 5 threshold 6 weight 2
set interface ethernet3 track-ip threshold 2
set failover auto
set failover type track-ip
```

From the Web interface:

1. Go to **Network | Interfaces | ethernet3 Edit | Track IP**.
2. Select **Enable Track IP** to enable **IP tracking** on this interface.
3. Set the Failover Threshold to **2**.
4. Click **OK**.
5. Return to **Network | Interfaces | ethernet3 Edit | Track IP**.
6. Add IP address **1.1.1.1** with a Weight of **1** and click **Apply**.
7. Add IP address **1.1.1.2** with a Weight of **1** and click **Apply**.
8. Add IP address **2.2.2.2**, with an Interval of **5**, a Threshold of **6**, and a Weight of **2** and click **Apply**.
9. Go to **Network | Untrust failover** and enable the **Automatic Failover** option.

10. Select **IP tracking** as the Failover Type.

11. Click **Apply** to confirm these settings.

Monitoring VPNs to Determine Failover

If IP tracking does not provide you with sufficient control and you are reliant on VPN tunnels, you will be pleased to know that the status of VPN tunnels can also be used as a basis for initiating failovers. This feature works similar to IP tracking in that it adds up the weights for the VPN tunnels that are down, and if they reach the failover threshold, a failover is initiated. There are some differences such as the threshold is always 100 (think of it as 100 percent), and that in addition to the *working* and *failed* states, there is also a *halfway failed* state, in which half the weight of the tunnel is counted towards the threshold.

Such is the case for VPN tunnels that are in *inactive*, *ready*, and *indeterminate* states. For example, if the VPN weight is 60, it would be counted as 30 when that VPN tunnel was in an *inactive* state, and hence the NetScreen would be 30 percent towards failing over to the backup interface (assuming automatic failover is enabled).

Not all VPNs are monitored for failure. You have to enable monitoring on the VPN tunnels you wish to monitor, which enables you to monitor only the most important ones.

Be aware that once a failover is triggered due to failed VPN tunnels, it *will not revert back* to the primary interface by default. Once the failover has taken place, no attempts will be made to reestablish the failed VPN tunnels, and therefore the failover threshold will stay exceeded until you manually intervene. To avoid this, you must enable *re-keying* as well as monitoring. By doing this, the NetScreen will attempt to regularly restore the failed VPN tunnels and, if successful (and the failure value falls below the threshold), will revert traffic back to the primary interface. This is not enabled by default because if there were a continual attempt to bring the tunnels up, the second path would be open all the time, which is generally not desired. It is safer to have the firewall administrator explicitly enable re-keying where wanted, instead of hoping they will remember to disable it where appropriate.

Example: Monitoring One VPN Tunnel, with Fall-back to a Second Unmonitored Tunnel

In this example, under normal circumstances a single VPN tunnel is up and in use, which goes to corporate headquarters (HQ) and is therefore very important. If it fails for any reason, the NetScreen will fail over to the backup interface where a second VPN tunnel is also ready to connect to HQ. To achieve this, we use two tunnel interfaces and add routes to HQ through both of those tunnel interfaces. We also enable re-keying on the primary VPN so that the NetScreen will revert back to the primary interface once that VPN tunnel is up again. Figure 13.2 shows the set up for this scenario.

Figure 13.3 Redundant VPN Tunnels to HQ

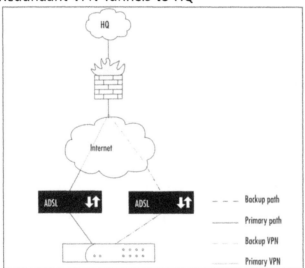

From the CLI:

```
# prepare tunnel interaces
set interface tunnel.1 zone untrust
set interface tunnel.1 ip unnumbered interface ethernet3
set interface tunnel.2 zone untrust
set interface tunnel.2 ip unnumbered interface ethernet2
# use two IKE gateways, bound to ethernet3 and ethernet2, respectively
set ike gateway hq-gw-eth3 ip 1.2.3.4 aggressive outgoing-interface
   ethernet3 preshare key123 sec-level standard
```

```
set ike gateway hq-gw-eth2 ip 1.2.3.4 aggressive outgoing-interface
   ethernet2 preshare key123 sec-level standard
# create the actual VPNs
set vpn to-hq-primary gateway hq-gw-eth3 sec-level standard
set vpn to-hq-primary bind interface tunnel.1
set vpn to-hq-primary monitor rekey
set vpn to-hq-primary failover-weight 100
set vpn to-hq-backup gateway hq-gw-eth2 sec-level standard
set vpn to-hq-backup bind interface tunnel.2
# routes to corporate HQ, via VPN tunnels
set vrouter trust-vr route 10.10.0.0/16 interface tunnel.1
set vrouter trust-vr route 10.10.0.0/16 interface tunnel.2
# enable automatic failover, based on VPN monitoring
set failover auto
set failover type tunnel-if
```

From the Web interface:

1. Go to **Network | Interfaces | New Tunnel IF**.
2. Name the new interface **tunnel.1**.
3. Set the Zone (VR) to **Untrust** (trust-vr).
4. Select **Unnumbered** and set the interface to **ethernet3**.
5. Click **OK**.
6. Return to **Network | Interfaces | New Tunnel IF**.
7. Name this interface **tunnel.2**.
8. Set the Zone (VR) to **Untrust** (trust-vr).
9. Select **Unnumbered** and specify **ethernet2**.
10. Click **OK**.
11. Go to **VPNs | Autokey Advanced | Gateway | New**.
12. Name this interface **hq-gw-eth3**.
13. Choose **standard** as the Security Level.
14. Select **Static IP Address** as the Remote Gateway Type.
15. Enter **1.2.3.4** as the Address/Hostname.
16. Specify **key123** as the Preshared Key.

17. Select **ethernet3** as the Outgoing Interface.

18. Click **OK**.

19. Return to **VPNs | Autokey Advanced | Gateway | New**.

20. Name this interface **hq-gw-eth2**.

21. Choose **standard** as the Security Level.

22. Select **Static IP Address** as the Remote Gateway Type.

23. Enter **1.2.3.4** as the Address/Hostname.

24. Enter **key123** as the Preshared key.

25. Select **ethernet2** as the Interface.

26. Click **OK** to save.

27. Go to **VPNs | Autokey IKE | New** to create a new VPN.

28. Name this VPN **to-hq-primary**.

29. Choose **standard** as the Security Level.

30. Select **Predefined** as the Remote Gateway and **hq-gw-eth3** as the actual gateway.

31. Click **Advanced** to enter additional settings for this VPN.

32. Select **tunnel.1** as the Interface.

33. Select **VPN Monitor** to enable monitoring of this VPN.

34. Enable the **Rekey** option.

35. Click **Return** followed by **OK** to save these settings.

36. Return to **VPNs | Autokey IKE | New** to create a new VPN.

37. Name this VPN **to-hq-backup**.

38. Choose **standard** as the Security Level.

39. Select **Predefined** as the Remote Gateway, and choose **hq-gw-eth2** from the list.

40. Click **Advanced**.

41. Bind this VPN to **tunnel.2**.

42. Click **Return** and then **OK** to save.

43. Go to **Network | Routing | Routing entries | trust-vr | New** to add a new route.

44. Enter **10.10.0.0/16** as the Network address/Netmask.

45. Select **tunnel.1** as the Interface.

46. Set the Gateway IP Address to **0.0.0.0**.

47. Click **OK**.

48. Return to **Network | Routing | Routing entries | trust-vr | New**.

49. Enter **10.10.0.0/16** as the Network Address/Netmask.

50. Select **tunnel.2** as the Interface.

51. Set the Gateway IP Address to **0.0.0.0**.

52. Click **OK**.

53. Go to **Network | Untrust Failover**.

54. Set the Failover Type to **Tunnel Interface**.

55. Enable **Automatic Failover**.

56. Click **Apply**.

57. Return to **Network | Untrust Failover** and click **Edit weights**.

58. Set the Weight to **100** for the VPN named **to-hq-primary**, if not done already.

59. Click **OK**.

Introducing the NetScreen Redundancy Protocol

It is time to focus on the more advanced features of NetScreen. Because the standard features are not strong enough for the more demanding environments, the mid- to high-range NetScreens provide support for the NetScreen Redundancy Protocol (NSRP). This protocol is the heart of all of the HA options covered here. NSRP has been available for several years, and was originally referred to as *HA*. With the introduction of NSRP version 2 in the ScreenOS 3.1 versions, this changed. HA setups are now commonly referred to as NSRP setups, or just referred to as "running NSRP."

Tools & Traps…

Using NSRP version 1

The features described here apply only to NSRP version 2. If you are using an older model of NetScreen (for example, the NS-100) for which ScreenOS 4.0 or later is not available, you will be limited to NSRP version 1, which has a very limited feature set, and the commands for configuring HA are different. Instead of using **get/set nsrp** commands you use **get/set ha** commands. While the syntax is very similar to the NSRP version 2 commands, most of the features covered here are not available. If you find yourself in this situation, you should consider upgrading your hardware.

NSRP is the protocol that redundant NetScreen devices use to talk to each other when running in various HA configurations. It is the language that allows them to exchange state information and make decisions. Before we detail the specifics of what type of information is exchanged over NSRP, we need to cover a bit more theory.

One of the main goals of HA is to have multiple redundant systems, where a second system can take over in case the first one fails. This is commonly achieved by duplicating the hardware. As with the NetScreen firewalls, any HA setup that is using NSRP implies that there are at least two firewalls of the same model working together. This group of firewalls is called an *NSRP cluster*, or simply, a *cluster* (see Figure 13.4). While conceptually NSRP has been engineered to allow for future expansion into clusters containing more than two members, this is not yet implemented and may never be.

Figure 13.4 A NetScreen Cluster

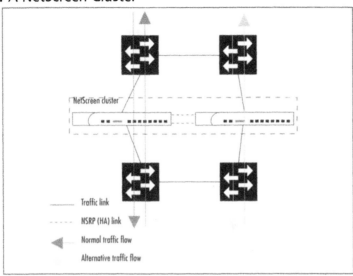

Virtualizing the Firewall

To minimize the amount of downtime caused when the first system in a cluster fails, it is important to ensure that the second system knows precisely what the first system is doing, so that it can pick up without any interruption. In effect, what you want to do is shift the entire running firewall onto new hardware. When looked at this way, it makes sense to turn the actual firewall into a virtual firewall that has some hardware associated with it. This is precisely what is done in NetScreen firewalls. When NSRP is enabled, a Virtual Security Device (VSD) is created, and the configuration for the physical interfaces change to apply to virtual interfaces called Virtual Security Interfaces (VSI). The fact that these virtual interfaces are in turn associated with actual hardware is not important; all of the configurations are done on the VSI. NSRP then takes care of associating the VSI to the correct physical interface (see Figure 13.5).

Figure 13.5 VSDs and VSIs

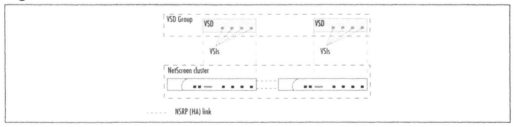

By abstracting the firewall in this manner, it becomes relatively easy to move the firewall between different hardware units as necessary. It also becomes possible to have more than one VSD per physical firewall. A VSD is not a stand-alone entity, but rather it is always part of a *VSD group*, which spans both of the NetScreens in the cluster. There is one VSD per VSD group on each cluster member, and the VSD configuration is identical everywhere. This sets the scene for when a failover is needed, as the configuration is already set up and ready to go. Note that the VSD only acts as a container for the VSIs. Other configuration items, such as policies and routing, apply across all VSDs on a NetScreen.

Within a VSD group, one VSD is the designated *master VSD*. This VSD is the currently active VSD that is processing and forwarding traffic. The other VSD in the VSD group is the *backup*, which is located on the other NetScreen. The backup VSD is not processing traffic, which means that only one of the firewalls is active and processing traffic at any given time. This is known as an *Active/Passive setup*.

It is important to note that IP addresses assigned to a VSI follow the master VSD. This is slightly different from how Virtual Router Redundancy Protocol (VRRP) works. In VRRP, the backup unit has its own IP address and simply acquires the primary IP address upon failover. With NSRP, there is only one interface IP address that floats between the NetScreens as necessary.

The *manage-ip* settings stay bound to the physical interface and do not follow the VSD. It would not be very useful if the IP addresses were also moved across to the active firewall, since that would render the backup firewall unreachable for management purposes. Thus, when the backup firewall becomes the master, it already has the manage IP address and then simply adds the VSI address (see Figure 13.6).

Figure 13.6 VSI IP Addresses vs Manage IP Addresses

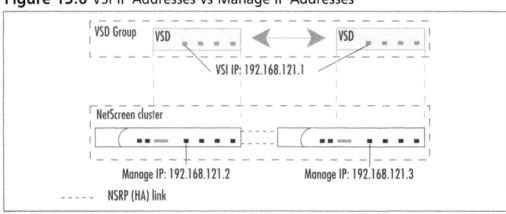

When talking about NSRP clusters, the opposite of a VSI is a *local interface*. A local interface is one that is not tied to a VSD, and therefore will not move across in case of a failover. There are a few select cases when this can be useful, which are covered later. For now all you need to be aware of is that it is possible, though uncommon, to have local interfaces that do not participate in the VSD.

Understanding NSRP States

As mentioned, the fundamental concept of NSRP is duplicating hardware—to be able to move the firewall functionality around as necessary using VSDs. As a consequence of this, at any given time each VSD is in one of six states, which determines the current role of the VSD. The possible states are:

- Master
- Primary Backup
- Backup
- Initial
- Ineligible
- Inoperable

Understanding which state is used for what purpose is central to monitoring and controlling your NSRP cluster. Instead of simply explaining what each state is, let's look at the order in which the VSD transitions between the states.

When a VSD is first created, either due to a reboot or a configuration change, it is put in the *initial* state. While in this state, the VSD learns which other NetScreens are participating in the VSD group, synchronizes that state with the other VSDs if needed, and possibly partakes in the election process for which VSD should become the master.

From the *initial* state, the VSD can move into either the *master* or *backup* state. If it wins the election process, this VSD takes on the task of processing traffic. If it does not win, it transitions into the *backup* state.

The election process used to determine the master VSD is reasonably straightforward. First, if there is no other VSD available, this VSD automatically wins the election. Second, if two VSDs are starting up at the same time, the winner is determined based on the configured priorities (**set nsrp vsd-group id X priority N**). The unit with the lowest priority value is the preferred VSD.

If both VSDs have the same priority, or the priority is not configured, the VSD with the lowest Media Access Control (MAC) address wins.

Normally, an election is only held if there is no master VSD in the VSD group. However, if the starting VSD has preemption enabled (**set nsrp vsd-group X preempt**), it can force an election, which it would probably win due to having a better priority than the old master VSD.

A VSD in the *backup* state checks to see if there is already a primary backup VSD, and if there isn't, makes itself the primary backup for the VSD group. As the primary backup, it is responsible for taking over the traffic processing should the master fail or step down. From the *primary backup* state there are generally two directions the VSD can take; it either ends up promoted to master due to the old master VSD disappearing, or it goes into the *inoperable* state.

A VSD puts itself into the *inoperable* state if it detects a failure that would prevent it from processing traffic. If this VSD were the master, any failure that resulted in a failover would result in this VSD becoming *inoperable*. In this state, the VSD does not participate in elections for the position of master VSD; however, it does continue to check for the failure condition. If that condition is remedied, as can be the case if the failure was caused by a monitored interface going down and subsequently is brought back up, the VSD will progress from the *inoperable* state back into the *initial* state again.

The *ineligible* state is only entered by manual intervention. It is the *administratively down* state of the VSD. If for any reason, you want to prevent the VSD from participating in the master election, thereby preventing it from processing traffic, you can put the VSD into the *ineligible* state by using the **set nsrp vsd-group id X mode ineligible** command. The VSD group stays in that state until you use the corresponding *unset* command, or the NetScreen is rebooted without having saved the configuration (the *ineligible* state can be kept across reboots if you save the configuration after entering the command).

This explains the various NSRP states that a VSD can be in. If you are confident in this knowledge, you will have no problem understanding what the VSDs in your cluster are doing.

The Value of Dual HA Links

Only a single link is needed for the NSRP traffic in an NSRP cluster; however, there are significant advantages to using dual HA links. To better understand these advantages, let's examine what types of packets are exchanged between the NetScreens in an NSRP cluster.

There are two categories of packets that are exchanged: *control messages* and *data packets*. Control messages are what enable NSRP to function. Data packets are simply normal user data packets that are passed on from one firewall to the other for processing. This packet forwarding occurs in certain cases, but it is not the norm and should be avoided if possible. Cases where it can occur are if an Active/Active setup is used or if the firewalls are operating in the now obsolete Network Address Translation (NAT) mode.

The control messages consist of various heartbeats and synchronization messages, such as physical link probes, VSD state information, and session synchronization information. These messages are always sent via HA link #1. If you have dual HA interfaces, #1 has the lower interface number. For example, if ethernet7 and ethernet8 are bound to the HA zone, ethernet7 would carry the control messages unless it becomes unavailable, in which case the control messages would be sent on ethernet8 instead.

Due to the bandwidth requirements of the data-forwarding function, data forwarding is not always available. Table 13.2 shows when and which HA link is used for data or control messages in the different scenarios.

Table 13.2 NSRP Control and Data Messages HA Link Usage

Message Type	Interfaces			
	Single 100MB	Dual 100MB	Single 1GB	Dual 1GB
Control	Yes (#1)	Yes (#1)	Yes (#1)	Yes (#1)
Data	No	Yes (#2)	Yes (#1)	Yes (#2)

On NetScreen models that do not contain dual dedicated HA interfaces, one or two interfaces can be bound to the HA zone to enable them to be used as HA links. This is done by assigning the interface to the HA zone just as you would with any other zone.

NOTE

If you find yourself in a situation where you do not have any unused interfaces on the firewall and you want to turn it into an NSRP cluster, you can still do so. NetScreens have the option of allowing NSRP traffic to co-exist with normal traffic on an interface. You will need to use an interface that is connected to a switch that provides a Layer 2 broadcast domain that is common to both firewalls. By using the **set nsrp inter-**

face command, you can direct NSRP to send the control messages on that particular interface. Be aware that the NSRP packets can use up a significant amount of bandwidth. Also, remember that in this scenario you should enable authentication and encryption of the NSRP traffic.

Building an NSRP Cluster

Before you can configure the NetScreens to be used in your NSRP cluster, you must do the cabling. There are a few options available; this section covers the advantages and disadvantages of the most common ones. What is presented here is not an exhaustive list; however, it should be enough for you to properly evaluate your own proposed setup, and then make an informed decision based on that evaluation.

The five different ways of cabling discussed here are grouped into two categories: *traffic links* and *HA links*. For the traffic links, the three main choices are to connect the firewalls directly to the routers, connect the firewalls to the routers via switches, or connect the firewalls in a full mesh. The HA links can either be directly connected between the NetScreens or connected via switches (see Figure 13.7).

Figure 13.7 Different Approaches to Cabling NetScreen Clusters

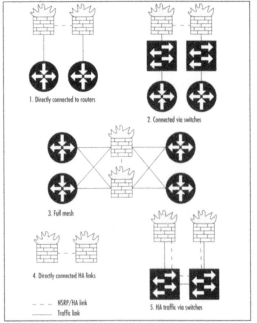

1. Directly connected to routers
2. Connected via switches
3. Full mesh
4. Directly connected HA links
5. HA traffic via switches

- - - NSRP/HA link
——— Traffic link

Connecting the Firewalls Directly to the Routers

This option reviews the advantages and disadvantages of cabling by connecting the NetScreens directly to the next hop routers.

Advantages

- Interface failure on the router is immediately detected, resulting in faster failover.
- There is less risk of failure (one less point of failure) without a switch in between.

Disadvantages

- It is not possible to have a secondary HA path.
- Tracking a VRRP primary IP address is slightly more complicated.

Most of these advantages are self-explanatory, but the disadvantages require some elaboration. A secondary HA path can be configured to use in case the HA links fail. It is useful in certain scenarios, and a full explanation of its value is included in the "Avoiding the Split-brain Problem" section later in this chapter. The issue of tracking VRRP IP addresses is a minor point. To negate this disadvantage, you only need to remember to use the Address Resolution Protocol (ARP) tracking method instead of the default method.

The typical use for this way of cabling is when firewalls act as transit nodes; that is, when there is no LAN directly behind the firewalls and you are using very small subnets for all interfaces (such as /30 or /29 subnets) (see Figure 13.8). Note that you cannot use IP tracking if you use a /30 subnet for a VSI, because it does not leave room for a managed IP, which is necessary in order for IP tracking to work.

Figure 13.8 Directly Connected Routers

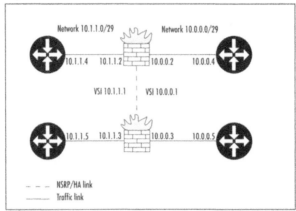

Connecting the Firewalls to Routers via Switches

This option covers connecting the NetScreens via Layer 2 switches, which in turn connect to the routers. The main pros and cons of using this approach are:

Advantages

- It is possible to use a secondary HA path.
- It is possible to avoid the need for another router if the firewalls are directly protecting a LAN, because the firewall can be the default gateway for the LAN hosts.

Disadvantages

- Interface failure on the router is not immediately detected—IP tracking must be used.
- Switches are additional points of failure that must be factored into availability calculations.

As must be expected, the advantages and disadvantages for this approach are almost the opposite of when you connect the firewalls directly to the routers.

This way of cabling is very common, simply because NetScreens are more commonly used for protecting LANs than for protecting transit-type traffic. A highly common scenario is where the NetScreens are cabled to switches on the inside, and directly to routers on the outside, typically Internet border routers (see Figure 13.9).

Figure 13.9 Firewalls Connected to Both Routers and Switches

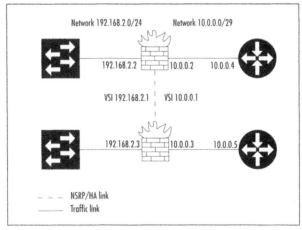

Cabling for a Full-mesh Configuration

Full-mesh cabling is for those who want very, very high levels of availability. A full mesh implies that each NetScreen has dual links to each of the neighboring nodes, be it routers or switches. This makes the network highly resilient not only to one device failure, but to two or even three simultaneous failures (see Figure 13.10).

Figure 13.10 Comparison Between a Non-Full-mesh and a Full-mesh Network

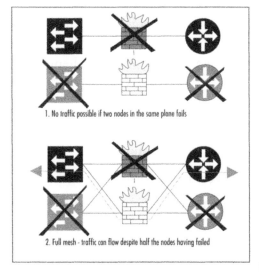

The main pros and cons of a full mesh setup are as follows:

Advantages

- Can survive multiple points of failure (as long as it is not both of the firewalls).

- It is possible to use a secondary HA path.

- "Full-mesh" is a good buzzword to use for making management happy (and convince them of approving the expenditure involved).

Disadvantages

- Requires substantially more resources—twice as many interfaces are used on all nodes.

- Configuring all of the nodes correctly is difficult, because there are many interactions to take into account.

- Testing all of the possible traffic paths is time consuming.

In many cases, a full mesh is unwarranted and simply overkill. Before deciding to implement a full mesh, do the math for the availability required, and compare it to the expenses involved. Do not forget the hidden items such as the time needed for proper design, the configuration, and the verification testing. Remember, if you have not tested and verified that your HA setup is working as intended, you do not have a highly available network—it is as simple as that.

Using Directly Connected HA Links

When deciding how to cable the HA links, there are two choices: either you connect them directly using crossover cables, or you connect them via switches. The advantages and disadvantages of connecting them directly are summarized below.

Advantages

- There is a minimum risk of link failure

- Link failure is detected immediately on both firewalls

- The NSRP data is not open for interception

- Uses less resources (no ports needed to be allocated on switches)

Disadvantages

■ None

Connecting HA Links via Switches

I do not recommend connecting HA links via switches, since there are significant drawbacks to doing it this way.

Advantages

■ Can be done, if necessary.

Disadvantages

■ Must configure separate virtual local area networks (VLANs) on the switches to prevent NSRP traffic from escaping into the LAN.

■ Must use port-based VLANs on the switches, because forwarded data packets may contain VLAN tags that could otherwise conflict with the switch configuration.

■ Authentication and encryption of NSRP packets should be enabled.

■ Must use HA link probes to detect link failures consistently.

■ Depending on cabling, a single switch failure could disrupt both HA links.

If there is more than one NetScreen cluster on the same network, the NSRP traffic could end up colliding if the same cluster ID was used for both clusters. NSRP packets are broadcast packets, and therefore easily use up significant bandwidth if not confined to their own VLAN. Depending on your setup, the NetScreens may need to forward data packets between each other, which is done over the HA data link. The packets are forwarded as is, and therefore can contain VLAN tags. Hence, the switches must be configured to use a port-based VLAN for the HA data link, and to accept and forward both tagged and untagged frames. Depending on your brand of switches, this may or may not be possible.

In addition, when sending NSRP traffic across switches it is good practice to both authenticate and encrypt the traffic, even if it is separated onto its own VLAN. There is a lot of sensitive information contained in the NSRP packets; you would not want someone to eavesdrop on them.

Finally, when cabling in this manner, the NetScreens are not able to detect a HA link failure directly; they have to rely on HA link probes to determine whether the link is still up or not. You have to explicitly enable these probes, and if you forget, you may find yourself in some "interesting" situations. (See "Avoiding the Split-brain Problem" later in this chapter).

Figure 13.11 shows two ways of cabling the HA links. In the first scenario, a single switch failure would disrupt both HA links, whereas in the second scenario, only one HA link would be affected.

Figure 13.11 Two Ways of Cabling HA Links Through Switches

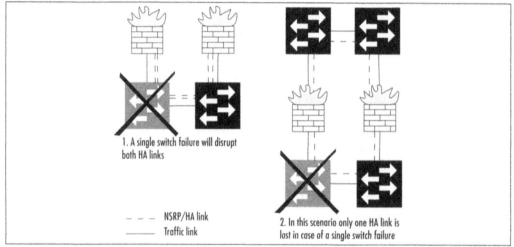

Adding a NetScreen to an NSRP Cluster

To add a NetScreen to an NSRP cluster, additional configuration is needed. The good news is that this is easy to do for a simple NSRP cluster. Once you have made it part of the cluster, you will probably want to add a few more configuration settings to make it fail over when appropriate. For now, let's focus on how to turn a stand-alone NetScreen into an NSRP cluster member.

The theory for this is simple. A NetScreen that has an NSRP cluster ID *greater* than zero is considered part of a cluster; valid cluster IDs range from 1 to 7. The following example shows you how to set the cluster ID.

Example: Setting the Cluster ID

In this example, we make the NetScreen part of NSRP cluster 1. By following these instructions for both firewalls when they are cabled for HA, you will see that they detect each other by looking at the output from the **get nsrp** command.

From the CLI:

```
set nsrp cluster id 1
```

From the Web interface:

1. Go to **Network | NSRP | Cluster**.
2. Enter **1** as the Cluster ID.
3. Press **OK**.

Example: Setting Both Cluster ID and Cluster Name

In addition to a cluster ID, each cluster can also be assigned a name, which is needed if you are using certificates and/or Simple Network Management Protocol (SNMP). The hostname used for those items should be the cluster name instead of the individual hostnames (which differ between the firewalls). If you do not do this, the certificates will only be valid on one of the firewalls, and the SNMP management system will most likely also refuse to acknowledge the second firewall. In this example we set the cluster name to **beowulf** and the cluster ID to **7**.

From the CLI:

```
set nsrp cluster id 7
set nsrp cluster name beowulf
```

From the Web interface:

It is not possible to set the cluster name from the Web interface.

Synchronizing the Configuration

Once you have cabled the NSRP cluster the way you want it, you must address the configuration side of things. Cluster members must have *near-identical* configurations in order to operate properly. The reason for near-identical and not *identical* is that some aspects must be unique to each NetScreen, including things such as the hostname and the management IP addresses.

While it is possible to copy the cluster configuration from another cluster member by using the **exec nsrp sync global-config** command, personal experience leads me to recommend a different approach to synchronizing the configurations initially. Unless you are highly familiar with the precise effects of this command, it will not do what you want or expect it to do. Take my advice on this one. If you want to experiment and find out for yourself how it works, by all means, go right ahead. If on the other hand you want to get your cluster set up as quickly and smoothly as possible, perform the following sequence of steps.

Initial Synchronization Procedure #1

1. Configure the first firewall fully, including the cluster configuration.

2. Back up the configuration to a Trivial File Transfer Protocol (TFTP) server using the **save config to tftp x.x.x.x netscreen1.cnf** command.

3. Open up the resulting file (*netscreen1.cnf*) in your favorite text editor.

4. Change the few things that should be different between the two firewalls. This typically includes: hostname, management IP addresses (*mgt* interface and/or *manage-ip*), VSD group priority and preemption, and physical interface settings.

5. Save the changed file under a new filename (e.g., *netscreen2.cnf*).

6. Download the new configuration file to the second NetScreen using the **save config from tftp x.x.x.x netscreen2.cnf to flash** command.

7. Once the configuration has been saved, reset the second firewall (remember to answer **n** when asked if you want to save the configuration—if you save it at this point you will overwrite the recently downloaded configuration).

8. When the firewall has rebooted, log in and issue the **exec nsrp sync file** command followed by **save all**. This will copy the various files (such as Public Key Infrastructure [PKI] information and Secure Shell [SSH] keys) from the first NetScreen and store it on the second NetScreen.

9. Reboot the second NetScreen to ensure it is using the new information that was just synchronized.

10. You should now have a fully working NSRP cluster. You can make further configuration changes at this point, which will automatically be propagated to all of the members of the clusters. See Table 13.3 for a list of commands that do not propagate within the cluster.

Table 13.3 Commands That Do Not Propagate to Other Cluster Members

Command
(un)set interface <int> manage -ip <ip>
(un)set interface <int> phy ...
(un)set interface <int> bandwidth ...
(un)set interface redundant<X> phy primary <int>
Commands for local interfaces
(un)set console ...
(un)set hostname <hostname>
(un)set snmp name <sysname>
(un)set vrouter <name> router -id
(un)set nsrp cluster ...
(un)set nsrp auth password <password>
(un)set nsrp encrypt password <password>
(un)set nsrp vsd -group id <X> mode ineligible
(un)set nsrp vsd -group id <X> preempt
(un)set nsrp vsd-group id <X> priority <prio>
(un)set nsrp vsd -group id <X> monitor track -ip ...
(un)set nsrp monitor ...

NOTE

Both the **clear ...** and **debug ...** commands do not by default propagate to other cluster members. To execute one of these categories of commands on all cluster members, use the form **clear cluster ...** and **debug cluster ...** commands.

The advantages of synchronizing the configuration using the above method are that you know precisely what is going on at all times, and there is no real risk of duplicate IP addresses conflicting with each other between the firewalls. This makes it possible to use this procedure safely when logged in remotely. Also, having the configuration files stored side-by-side makes it easy to compare them and see the differences (using the **diff** command for UNIX and the **WinDiff** application available for Windows.

If you do not have a TFTP server available, or for some other reason do not want to use the procedure outlined above, the following is the more official "cold start" approach.

Initial Synchronization Procedure #2

1. Configure the first firewall fully, including the cluster configuration.

2. Run the unset all command on the second firewall to clear any existing configuration, and to confirm the action when prompted to do so.

3. Reset the second firewall; do not save the configuration when prompted.

4. When it has rebooted, issue the **set nsrp cluster id X** command to make it part of the same cluster as the first firewall (X being the same cluster ID used on the first firewall). Alternatively, do this via the Web interface.

5. Synchronize the files between the firewalls with the **exec nsrp sync file** command, and run on the second firewalls.

6. Synchronize the cluster configuration using the **exec nsrp sycn global-config run** command, and run on the second firewall.

7. Configure all of the settings that were not synchronized automatically. Refer to Table 13.3 for a list of commands you will have to enter manually. Also enter them on the second firewall.

8. Save the newly built configuration with the **save all** command.

9. Reset the second firewall.

10. After it has rebooted, run the **exec nsrp sync global-config checksum** command and verify that the configurations are in sync. If they are not, manually inspect the two configurations and discern any differences that must be corrected.

As you can see, this procedure leaves more room for error. However, this does not necessarily mean that errors *will* occur. If you know the setup and configuration details intimately, you will be able to use this procedure and have it run smoothly, or at least be able to correct any problems quickly. Personally, I prefer to take the safer route and use procedure #1. The choice, however, is yours.

> **NOTE**
>
> If you are using the Network Time Protocol (NTP) for keeping time on the firewalls in the cluster, you should add the **set ntp no-ha-sync** command, which will enable both firewalls to clock off of the NTP server independently. If you do not use this command, the clocks will be synchronized using the built-in NSRP time synchronization feature, which has much lower accuracy than NTP.

Determining When to Failover – The NSRP Ways

Similar to the options provided on the low-end range of NetScreen firewalls, NSRP provides a number of different methods that can be used to determine when a failover should be initiated. While the options in some cases may seem identical to their low-end cousins, do not confuse them—they are distinctly different, albeit subtly so. Also, if you recall from the earlier discussion, the low-end range of NetScreen firewalls provided VPN monitoring as one of the many ways to determine the failover point. This particular feature is not present when using NSRP because it not considered necessary or appropriate at this level; it is only really useful on the small firewalls.

If you really like that feature, you can achieve almost the same thing using IP tracking towards one or many hosts that are reachable only through the VPN. For cases where there are no known hosts behind the VPN, simply tracking the VPN gateway may be sufficient.

Before going into detail about how to detect the need for a failover, let's look at a list of things that are already reason enough to fail over:

- Software crashes

- Hardware or power failure

- Link failure on monitored interfaces or zones

- Unavailability of one or more tracked IP addresses

The first two items, software and hardware failure, are detected automatically without any need for explicit configuration. The latter two items are available to provide flexibility in determining whether to fail over or not, and must be explicitly enabled to be in effect.

Using NSRP Heartbeats

Heartbeat monitoring is an integral part of NSRP, and is always active. It provides the mechanism to detect when a firewall becomes unresponsive for any reason, such as a software or hardware failure or cable faults. There are only two user-configurable settings for this feature: the frequency of the heartbeats and the number of missed heartbeats allowed before a failover is triggered.

By default, heartbeats are sent once every second, and the threshold for lost heartbeats is set to three, implying that a failover would happen in under four seconds in case the active firewall stops responding. That's quite impressive by most standards. It is however not the most aggressive setting – it is possible to lower the heartbeat frequency to a mere 200 milliseconds, giving us a sub-second failover time, in exchange for some added processing overhead due to the rapid heartbeats. In demanding environments it can be well worth the trade-off though. However, you will need to be very careful in selecting the equipment that the firewalls connects to—many, or even most, routers and switches are not capable of keeping up with such a quick failover, and may introduce additional delays before the network has stabilized.

If you do lower the heartbeat interval, it is also recommended that you increase the initial hold-down value. The reason for this is that the total time spent in the *initial* NSRP state should be of a sufficient period to allow synchronization of the state information before the unit makes itself available in the cluster. The actual hold-down time is calculated as *init-hold* x *hb-interval* millisec-onds, which by default resolves as 5 x 1000 = 5000 milliseconds, or 5 seconds. To compensate for lowering the heartbeat interval from 1000 to 200 milliseconds, it would be appropriate to set the *init-hold* value to 25, which would keep the actual time spent in the *initial* state at 5 seconds. You may need to adjust this to your particular setup, but this is a good starting point. Generally it doesn't hurt to have a high initial hold-down time, since the only time this will have an impact on the network is if both firewalls are powered on at the same time, in which case the initial hold-down time to some extent determines how long it takes before the firewalls can start passing traffic.

Example: Configuring More Aggressive Heartbeats

To show how the heartbeat settings are configured, we will use the above example with the exception of allowing for four lost heartbeats before triggering the failover. This still provides sub-second failover, and also shows how to adjust the threshold value (since the lower value, three, is the default value).

Using the CLI:

```
set nsrp vsd-group hb-interval 200
set nsrp vsd-group hb-threshold 4
set nsrp vsd-group init-hold 25
```

Using the Web interface:

It is not possible to adjust the heartbeat settings from the Web interface.

Using Optional NSRP Monitoring

NSRP provides options for monitoring other things beside NSRP heartbeats; specifically, interface link status (interface monitoring), zone availability (zone monitoring), and IP address reachability (IP tracking). The IP tracking provided by NSRP is basically a superset of the IP tracking feature provided for low-end NetScreen firewalls. It also ties in with the other monitoring methods in that a common threshold value is used. This means that the total weight of all failed objects (interfaces, zones, and IP addresses) is compared against a single value, and the outcome of that comparison determines whether a failover is triggered (see Figure 13.12). If you are using only a single monitoring method, this is of no sig-nificance, but once you begin mixing different methods, it can become tricky to keep track of all of the interactions. Proper planning is the key to being successful in those circumstances. Difficult as it may be to get it right, there is no doubt that it provides a lot of flexibility.

There are two levels of monitoring offered: *device level* and *VSD level*. Objects monitored on a device level affect all of the VSDs on that firewall, whereas objects monitored on a VSD level only affect that particular VSD. If the device level monitoring reaches the failover threshold, all VSDs on that device become inoperable. On the other hand, if a VSD failover threshold is reached, only that VSD becomes *inoperable*—other VSDs on that firewall may still be operable.

Figure 13.12 The Relationship Between the Monitoring Objects and the Failover Threshold

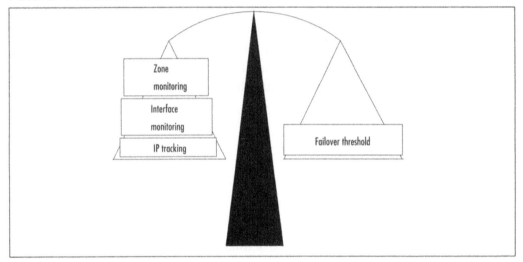

Example: Lowering the Failover Threshold

For this example, imagine that we want to work in percentages instead of the default failover threshold of 255. Setting the failover threshold to 100 makes it easier to think of conceptually and becomes easier to explain to others: "The loss of interface X counts as a 50 percent loss," rather than "Losing the link on interface X adds 127 to the weighted sum, and the failover threshold is at 255."

Using the CLI:

```
set nsrp monitor threshold 100
```

Using the Web interface:

It is not possible to adjust this setting from the Web interface.

Using NSRP Interface Monitoring

The easiest optional monitoring method is interface monitoring. By marking an interface as monitored, its link state becomes a deciding factor for triggering failovers. By default, any single monitored interface can cause a failover. This can be changed by adjusting the weight attached to the interface. Each failed interface's weight is added to the failover threshold (i.e., if there are two monitored interfaces both with a weight of 50 and both fail, it will be counted as 100 towards the failover threshold).

Example: A Simple Interface Monitoring Setup

Consider a simple setup where interfaces ethernet1 and ethernet3 are used. If either of them fail, we want them to fail over to the backup firewall. Device level monitoring is used here.

From the CLI:

```
set nsrp monitor interface ethernet1
set nsrp monitor interface ethernet3
```

From the Web interface:

1. Go to **Network | NSRP | Monitor | Interface | VSD ID: Device | Edit interface**.
2. Select **ethernet1**.
3. Set the Weight to **255**.
4. Select **ethernet3**.
5. Set the Weight to **255**.
6. Click **Apply**.

Example: A More Complex Interface Monitoring Setup

In this example, we configure the monitoring of three interfaces: ethernet1, ethernet2, and ethernet3. Due to the setup used, it is acceptable to lose either ethernet2 or ethernet3, but not both. If the ethernet1 link goes down at any time, a failover should be triggered. Since the monitor threshold cannot be changed via the Web interface, we use the default threshold value of 255 for this example.

From the CLI:

```
set nsrp monitor interface ethernet1 weight 255
set nsrp monitor interface ethernet2 weight 128
set nsrp monitor interface ethernet3 weight 128
```

From the Web interface:

1. Go to **Network | NSRP | Monitor | Interface | VSD ID: Device | Edit interface**.

2. Select **ethernet1**.

3. Set the Weight to **255**.

4. Select **ethernet2**.

5. Set the Weight to 128.

6. Select **ethernet3**.

7. Set the Weight to **128**.

8. Click **Apply**.

Using NSRP Zone Monitoring

Instead of monitoring individual links and juggling the weight of the interfaces, it is sometimes useful to monitor an entire *zone*. When monitoring a zone, the zone is not considered to have failed until there are no working interfaces left in that zone. The definition of "working" in this case is that its link state is "up." As such, zone monitoring provides a slightly more high-level approach to monitoring, compared to interface monitoring. Its main advantage shines through when you are working on firewalls where you have lots of interfaces (say 10+) bound to the same zone. It saves a lot of typing and clicking when you can ask the firewall to monitor the zone instead of every interface. Alternatively, if a monitored zone contains no interfaces at all, that zone will never fail.

Just as with interface monitoring, each zone has an assigned weight. If the zone fails, its weight is counted towards the failover threshold; once the failover threshold is reached, a failover is triggered. Keep in mind that the failover threshold is shared between all of the monitoring methods, and that it is possible to have a failover triggered as a result of a combination of failed interfaces and failed zones. Care must be taken to ensure that the interactions are what you want them to be.

Example: Monitoring the Untrust Zone

For this example, only a single zone is monitored and the default weight is used. This scenario means that the failure of the zone will cause a failover.

From the CLI:

```
set nsrp monitor zone untrust
```

From the Web interface:

1. Go to **Network | NSRP | Monitor | Zone | VSD ID: Device | Edit zone**.
2. Select the **Untrust** zone.
3. Set the Weight to **255**.
4. Click **Apply**.

Example: Using Combined Interface and Zone Monitoring

For this example, consider a fictional scenario where we do not want to cause a failover unless all of the interfaces in custom zone **Internet** as well as interface **ethernet6** have failed. To achieve this, we divide the total weight needed to trigger a failover (255) between the two objects, giving us a weight of 128 for the Internet zone, and the same for the ethernet6 interface. It would also have worked equally well with the weights set to 128 + 127 or 1 + 254 for the zone and interface, respectively, and variations thereof.

From the CLI:

```
set nsrp monitor zone Internet weight 128
set nsrp monitor interface ethernet6 weight 128
```

From the Web interface:

1. Go to **Network | NSRP | Monitor | Zone | VSD ID: Device | Edit zone**.
2. Select the **Internet** zone.
3. Set the Weight to **128**.
4. Click **Apply**.
5. Go to **Network | NSRP | Monitor | Interface | VSD ID: Device | Edit interface**.
6. Select **ethernet6**.
7. Set the Weight to **128**.
8. Click **Apply**.

Using NSRP IP Tracking

The third monitoring option is tracking IP address reachability. By regularly contacting the tracked IP address, its availability is determined. This is similar to the functionality provided by the low-end NetScreen firewalls, but with a few pointed differences such as the way that the weight associated with the IP address is used, and the method used to contact the IP address.

If you recall, all three optional NSRP monitoring features (interface monitoring, zone monitoring, and IP tracking) share the same failure threshold and counter. With IP tracking, another layer is introduced. While each monitored interface and zone counts as its own separate object with associated weight, IP tracking is only ever a single monitored object with one weight attached. The entire IP tracking object can either be failed or not. There is no in-between value indicating that some IP addresses have failed while others are still responding. To determine whether the IP tracking object is flagged as failed or not, another failure threshold is used internally. Each monitored IP address has an associated internal weight, which is added towards the internal IP tracking failover threshold. When enough IP addresses have failed, the internal threshold value is reached or exceeded and the IP tracking object will count as failed. With that, the weight associated to the IP tracking object will be counted towards the device failover threshold (see Figure 13.13).

Figure 13.13 The Relationship Between All Monitored Objects

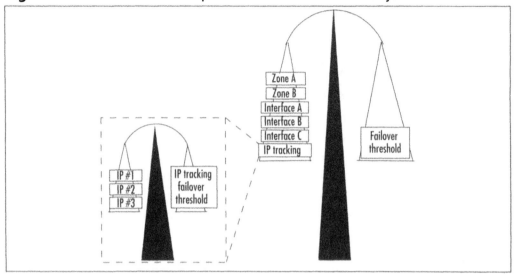

In addition to carrying its own internal failover threshold, IP tracking provides two different methods of contacting the tracked IP address: the traditional Internet Control Message Protocol (ICMP) ping approach and ARP requests. The latter are intended to be used mainly in instances where the tracked IP address is the virtual IP of a directly connected cluster of routers using the VRRP. Due to the workings of VRRP, it is not generally possible to use pings to determine whether it is or is not reachable. ARP request packets, however, always solicit a response from the router. The restriction when using ARP packets is that the tracked IP address must be in the same physical subnet as the NetScreen, since no IP routing is done for ARP packets.

It is possible to specify the interval for the probe packets as well as the failure threshold for each tracked IP address. The failure threshold determines how many responses can be lost before that IP address is considered down.

When using IP tracking, there are restrictions on which interface can be used as the source for the tracking packets. Of particular note is that a plain VSI cannot be used, since that IP address might move between different hardware units. Think about it. To be able to track an IP address, you must send the requests from an IP address that is available on the firewall regardless of whether it is the master of the cluster or a backup. Since the IP addresses assigned to VSIs follow the master unit, they are unsuitable for IP tracking purposes. In order to work around this problem, any interface that is the source of IP tracking packets must have a managed IP address specified. Since the managed IP does not move between units, it can be used.

Example: Using IP Tracking to Determine VPN Availability

As mentioned earlier, NSRP does not provide any explicit methods for tracking VPN states and triggering failovers based on those states. We can, however, simulate it by tracking IP addresses that are only available as long as the VPN tunnel is up (i.e., IP addresses that can only be reached *through* the tunnel). In this example, we configure things to do precisely that. We work on the assumption that IP addresses 172.16.5.1 and 172.16.5.2 are only reachable through the tunnel, and that they are both likely to always be available (i.e., they belong to routers, compared to a PC workstation which may or may not be powered on). Furthermore, we assume that the VPN tunnel is already configured and bound to the ethernet3 interface, which has an IP address of 1.1.1.1.

To enable IP tracking packets to be sent from the ethernet3 interface, a manage IP address is added onto each firewall (they must be different from each other and from the VSI IP address). We have decided that pinging each IP address every five seconds is sufficient, and we allow for four lost responses before flagging the IP address as down. Each IP address is assigned a weight that is half of the IP tracking failover threshold, meaning that both IP addresses must be unreachable before the IP tracking object itself is flagged as down. The default weight of 255 is used on the IP tracking object, which means that if it is marked as failed, a failover will be triggered. Figure 13.14 shows this network layout.

Figure 13.14 A VPN to Corporate HQ

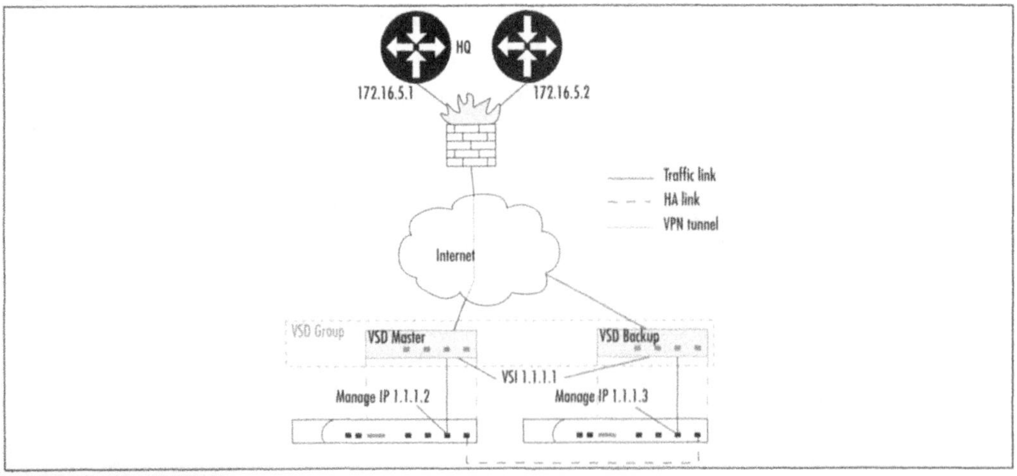

From the CLI:

```
# on firewall A, use this command
set interface ethernet3 manage-ip 1.1.1.2
# on firewall B, use this instead
set interface ethernet3 manage-ip 1.1.1.3
#
set nsrp monitor track-ip ip 172.16.5.1
set nsrp monitor track-ip ip 172.16.5.1 interval 5
set nsrp monitor track-ip ip 172.16.5.1 threshold 4
set nsrp monitor track-ip ip 172.16.5.1 weight 50
set nsrp monitor track-ip ip 172.16.5.2
set nsrp monitor track-ip ip 172.16.5.2 interval 5
set nsrp monitor track-ip ip 172.16.5.2 threshold 4
set nsrp monitor track-ip ip 172.16.5.2 weight 50
set nsrp monitor track-ip threshold 100
set nsrp monitor track-ip
# this command uses the default value, and is only shown for clarity's sake
set nsrp monitor track-ip weight 255
```

From the Web interface:

1. Go to **Network** | **Interfaces** | **ethernet3** | **Edit**.
2. Enter **1.1.1.2** or **1.1.1.3** as the Managed IP on Firewalls A and B, respectively.
3. Click **OK**.
4. Go to **Network** | **NSRP** | **Monitor** | **Track IP**.
5. Click **New**.
6. Enter **172.16.5.1** as the Track IP.
7. Set the Weight to **50**.
8. Specify an Interval of **5**.
9. Specify the Threshold as **4**.
10. Click **OK** to add this IP address to the list of tracked addresses.
11. Click **New** to add a second IP address.
12. Enter **172.16.5.2** as the Track IP.

13. Set the Weight to **50**.

14. Specify an Interval of **5**.

15. Specify the Threshold as **4**.

16. Click **OK**.

17. Go to **Network | NSRP | Monitor | Track IP | VSD: Device | Edit**.

18. Select **Enable Track IP**.

19. Specify the Failover Threshold as **100**.

20. Click **Apply**.

> **NOTE**
>
> If you use the **set nsrp monitor track-ip ...** commands, the IP tracking applies to all VSDs on this firewall. If you want per-VSD IP tracking, use the **set nsrp vsd-group id X monitor track-ip ...** commands.

Example: Combining Interface, Zone, and IP Tracking Monitoring

If you are working in high-end environments, you will probably wind up using multiple tracking methods within the same NSRP cluster. To give you a head start, let's review such an example.

In this scenario, we have two NetScreens directly connected to two VRRP routers on one side and four switches on the other. We use interface monitoring towards the routers, because that is the quickest way to determine a severe failure of a router, and also IP tracking using ARP. Either of these options should trigger a failover to minimize downtime. We use zone monitoring towards the switches, because we have dual interfaces in the *inside* zone. Spanning Tree Protocol (STP) is used within the inside network to prevent network loops, and is normally partitioned in two halves, each with a direct connection to the firewalls. This achieves the best use of bandwidth, but in the case of a switch failure, all inside traffic can be sent via one of the links to the firewall. While we could achieve the same monitoring effect by monitoring each of the links to the switch and giving that link a weight of 50 percent of the failover threshold, zone monitoring is the more elegant way to implement this (see Figure 13.15).

Interface ethernet1 is connected to the routers and bound to the *outside* zone. Interfaces ethernet2 and ethernet3 are connected to the two sets of switches and are bound to the *inside* zone. The routers' primary address is 192.168.77.1, and the backup IP address is 192.168.77.2. On the firewall side, 192.168.77.3 is the VSI address, and 192.168.77.4 and 192.168.77.5 are the managed IP addresses used for originating the IP tracking packets from. We use 100 as the failover threshold (for its value of enabling us to think in percentages), except for the internal IP tracking threshold where we use 101 instead (to make it clear which values are related).

Since the monitor threshold cannot be adjusted via the Web interface, weights of 255 are used throughout the configuration when using the Web interface.

Figure 13.15 Network Using STP

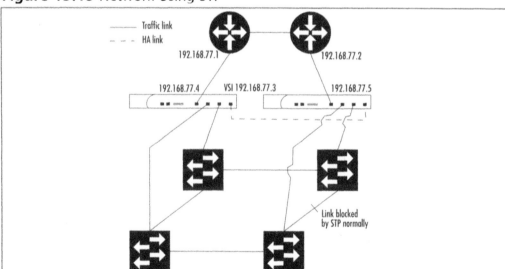

From the CLI:

```
set zone name outside
set zone name inside
set interface ethernet1 zone outside
set interface ethernet1 ip 192.168.77.3/29
set interface ethernet1 route
```

```
# on firewall A, use this command
set interface ethernet1 manage-ip 192.168.77.4
# on firewall B, use this command instead
set interface ethernet1 manage-ip 192.168.77.5
#
set interface ethernet2 zone inside
set interface ethernet3 zone inside
# IP address configuration for ethernet2 & 3 omitted
set arp always-on-dest
set nsrp cluster id 1
set nsrp monitor threshold 100
set nsrp monitor interface ethernet1 weight 100
set nsrp monitor zone inside weight 100
set nsrp monitor track-ip ip 192.168.77.1
set nsrp monitor track-ip ip 192.168.77.1 weight 101
set nsrp monitor track-ip threshold 101
set nsrp monitor track-ip weight 100
set nsrp monitor track-ip
```

From the Web interface:

1. Go to **Network | Zones**.
2. Click **New**.
3. Enter **outside** as the Zone Name.
4. Click **OK**.
5. Click **New**.
6. Enter **inside** as the Zone Name.
7. Click **OK**.
8. Go to **Network | Interfaces | ethernet1 | Edit**.
9. Enter **outside** as the Zone Name.
10. Enter **192.168.77.3** as the IP Address and **29** as the Netmask.
11. Click **Apply**.
12. Use **192.168.77.4** as the Managed IP on Firewall A, and **192.168.77.5** as the Managed IP on Firewall B.

13. Enter **Route** as the Interface Mode.

14. Click **OK**.

15, Go to **Network | Interfaces | ethernet2 | Edit**.

16. Enter **inside** as the Zone Name. (The IP address configuration for this interface is not shown in this example.)

17. Click **OK**.

18. Go to **Network | Interfaces | ethernet3 | Edit**.

19. Select **inside** as the Zone Name. (The IP address configuration for this interface is not shown in this example.)

20. Click **OK**.

21. Go to **Network | NSRP | Cluster**.

22. Select **Cluster ID** and enter an ID value of **1**.

23. Click **Apply**.

24. Go to **Network | NSRP | Monitor | Interface | VSD ID: Device | Edit interface**.

25. Select **ethernet1**.

26. Set the Weight to **255**.

27. Click **Apply**.

28. Go to **Network | NSRP | Monitor | Zone | VSD ID: Device | Edit zone**.

29. Enter **inside** as the Zone Name.

30. Set the Weight to **255**.

31. Click **Apply**.

32. Go to **Network | NSRP | Monitor | Track IP**.

33. Click **New**.

34. Enter **192.168.77.1** as the Track IP.

35. Set the Weight to **101**.

36. Click **OK**.

37. Go to **Network | NSRP | Monitor | Track IP | VSD: Device | Edit**.

38. Select **Enable Track IP**.

39. Specify the Failover Threshold as **101**.

40. Click **Apply**.

One command used in this example that we have not discussed is the **set arp always-on-dest** command. Whenever you connect your NetScreens to a load balancer or router running VRRP or similar protocol, it is wise to enable this option. What it does is force an ARP lookup for incoming sessions, instead of relying on the MAC address in the incoming frame. This can alleviate problems in cases where the load balancer or router sends packets from its virtual IP address with its physical MAC. Without this option enabled, you might end up with sessions "stuck to" one particular router, even after a failover has occurred. Be aware that this option can only be adjusted via the CLI, not via the Web interface. Note that enabling this option will not cause an ARP request for every single session. The ARP table is consulted first; only if an entry is not found there will it send an ARP query.

Reading the Output from "get nsrp"

Before we continue exploring the NSRP features, let's take a look at what sort of feedback to expect from the NetScreen in regards to the NSRP configuration. You will undoubtedly find yourself frequently using the **get nsrp** command whenever you are working with NSRP clusters. Therefore, being familiar with its output will make you more efficient at controlling your cluster.

In addition to the **get nsrp** command and all of its sub-commands, one other command that you should add to your arsenal is a simple **get config** filtered to only show NSRP settings (i.e., **get config | include nsrp** or, in its abbreviated form, **get conf | i nsrp**). This shows you all of the NSRP commands that have been entered into the configuration, and can often be easier to read than the **get nsrp** output. No state information is provided when you use this command, therefore it is not a replacement for **get nsrp**, but it is a very useful complement.

Looking into an NSRP Cluster

It would be impossible to provide listings of all of the possible outputs from **get nsrp**, and there is no attempt to do so here. Instead, we look at a single example that shows some of the NSRP features enabled, but not all. Also, there is a wealth of information available from the NSRP sub-command printouts; do a **get nsrp ?** to see the options.

Example: NS-500 Firewall and NSEP cluster

In this example, we examine a numbered output from one NS-500 firewall participating in an NSRP cluster.

From the CLI:

```
1. ns(B)-> get nsrp
2. nsrp version: 2.0

   cluster info:
3. cluster id: 2, no name
4. local unit id: 2071408
   active units discovered:
5. index: 0, unit id:   2071408, ctrl mac: 0010db1f9b75,
      data mac: 0010db1f9b76
6. index: 1, unit id:   2070976, ctrl mac: 0010db1f99c5,
      data mac: 0010db1f99c6
7. total number of units: 2

   VSD group info:
8. init hold time: 5
9. heartbeat lost threshold: 3
10. heartbeat interval: 200(ms)
    group priority preempt holddown inelig   master       PB other members
11.   0        50 no             3 no      2070976   myself
12. total number of vsd groups: 1
13. Total iteration=144,time=926517,max=16862,min=1355,average=6434

   RTO mirror info:
14. run time object sync:    enabled
15. ping session sync: enabled
16. nsrp data packet forwarding is enabled

   nsrp link info:
```

```
17. control    channel: ha1 (ifnum: 5)   mac: 0010db1f9b75 state: up
18. data       channel: ha2 (ifnum: 6)   mac: 0010db1f9b76 state: up
19. ha secondary path link not available

20. NSRP encryption: disabled
21. NSRP authentication: disabled
22. device based nsrp monitoring threshold: 255, weighted sum: 0, not
failed
23. device based nsrp monitor interface: ethernet1/1(weight 255, UP)
       ethernet3/1(weight 255, UP)
24. device based nsrp monitor zone:
25. device based nsrp track ip: (weight: 255, disabled)
26. number of gratuitous arps: 4 (default)
27. config sync: enabled

28. track ip: disabled
```

Following is an explanation of each numbered line of code.

1. The command being issued. As can be inferred from the prompt, it is done from the backup firewall.

2. The version of NSRP.

3. This line tells us that this firewall is participating in NSRP cluster 2, and does not have a cluster name assigned.

4. Here we learn what the ID number of this firewall is. This ID refers to the hardware itself, not a VSD. It can be used for correlation on other cluster members (see numbered line 11 in the printout).

5. This line states that this firewall has been found in the NSRP cluster. The unit ID here matches the ID printed on line 4. You can also see the virtual MAC addresses used by this firewall for its NSRP messages and forwarded data. This is different from the interface MACs, which you can obtain by running the **get interface** command.

6. On this line we learn that another firewall has been discovered in the cluster, this one with an ID of 2070976. If you were to log on to that firewall and run **get nsrp**, you would find that this is the same ID that is printed on line 4.

7. A count of the number of discovered cluster members. If this says 1, you know something is missing.

8. The *init-hold* value (discussed in "Determining When to Fail Over – The NSRP Ways").

9. The number of lost heartbeats before a failover is initiated.

10. The heartbeat interval, which in this case has been lowered to its minimum value. Worth noting is that the *init-hold* value on line 8 has not been adjusted to compensate for this.

11. This line presents a summary of VSD group 0. You can see that this firewall has a priority of 50 for this VSD (100 is the default), preemption is not enabled, but if it were, a 3-second hold-down would be in effect, preventing rapid failovers back and forth. You can also see that the VSD is not marked as ineligible, and that the firewall with ID 2070976 has the master VSD for this group, and that this firewall is the Primary Backup. If there are multiple VSD groups defined, you will get multiple lines printed, each with this summary.

12. This line shows the number of VSD groups defined on this firewall. Here it tells us that only one VSD group exists.

13. The output here is only intended for debugging purposes by Juniper/NetScreen, and can safely be ignored.

14. This line shows us that RTO mirroring is enabled (see the "Taking Advantage of the Full NSRP" section).

15. Here is more debug output, and again, you can simply ignore this line.

16. Here we learn that data forwarding across the HA data link is enabled.

17. This line shows us that the HA control link is up, and that interface ha1 is used for control messages.

18. Similar to the line above, this shows that the HA data link is up and available, and interface ha2 is the designated HA data link.

19. This shows us that no secondary NSRP path is configured on this firewall. Even if it were configured on the other firewall in the cluster, it would not help, because this firewall is not expecting NSRP messages on any interfaces other than ha1 and ha2.

20. Because NSRP encryption is not enabled, it likely means that the HA links are direct crossover cables between the two firewalls.

21. Just as with the encryption, authentication of NSRP messages is disabled.

22. This line is very useful; it not only tells us what the failover threshold is, but also shows us how far towards that threshold we have progressed. This can be valuable information when you are troubleshooting. If you do not like having to compare the weighted sum to the threshold, you can refer to the end of the line to see if enough things have failed to warrant a failover or not. Note that what is shown here is the *device* monitor settings. If you have set monitoring on VSD level, you need to use the **get nsrp vsd-group id X monitor** command to see the corresponding information for the VSD.

23. On this line, we find all of the device level interface monitoring that is configured, and the weight and state of those links. Again, this only shows interface monitoring configured on device level, not on VSD level.

24. Device level zone monitoring is shown on this line. In this case, no zones are monitored. To see VSD level zone monitoring, use the **get nsrp vsd-group id X monitor** command instead.

25. Similar to the preceding lines, this line shows whether IP tracking is enabled on device level, and the weight of that IP tracking. To get the details for the actual IP addresses tracked, you need to use the **get nsrp monitor track-ip** command. Similarly, if you have IP tracking on VSD level, use the **get nsrp vsd-group id X monitor track-ip** command.

26. This line shows the number of gratuitous ARPs that will be sent right after a failover.

27. Automatic configuration synchronization is enabled according to this line. This is almost always what you want. If you know that you do not want it, use the **unset nsrp config sync** command to change it.

28. This line is mainly a legacy leftover from older days. Line number 25 provides more information, so you can safely ignore this line, if you want.

Using NSRP-Lite on Mid-range Appliances

With all that theory under our belt it is time to see how we can implement a highly available network by using the NSRP-Lite feature available on some of the mid-range NetScreen appliances. NSRP-Lite is a slimmed-down variant of NSRP that does not support the full feature-set of NSRP. All of the features discussed so far are available, however, which makes NSRP-Lite a very formidable feature in and of itself.

The two main things that NSRP-Lite cannot do are the Active/Active setup and synchronization of Run-Time Objects (RTOs). The lack of RTO synchronization means that in case of a failover, any existing sessions and VPNs will be lost and must be re-established. If you are using VPNs with NSRP-Lite, remember to enable VPN monitoring with the *rekey* option to ensure that the VPNs are reestablished after a failover.

Since the mid-range NetScreen appliances are targeted towards small and medium enterprises (SMEs), we go through example setups fitting for that category. We start off with a simple but still fully usable example, followed by a more advanced setup where we make good use of local interfaces to provide redundant outgoing paths.

> **NOTE**
>
> By default, the NetScreen firewalls do not inspect TCP packets to verify that they are part of an existing TCP session; only source and destination information is matched against the policies. This is very helpful if you have asymmetric routing or are using NSRP-Lite, as it allows sessions to survive asymmetric routing as well as failovers.
>
> It does, however, mean that an attacker can introduce packets into your network easier. If you are concerned about that, you can force the NetScreen to verify each TCP session by using the **set flow tcp-syn-check** command. When TCP SYN-flag checking is active, only TCP packets with only the SYN flag set can create session entries, and only TCP traffic that is part of that session will be allowed through.

Basic NSRP-Lite Usage

Using only the features covered up to this point, let's see how we can provide an office network with highly available Internet access.

Example: Providing HA Internet Access

For this example, imagine that we have an office network in need of Internet access. The Internet access is delivered to the premises by a third party, which provides the Customer Premises Equipment (CPE) and is also responsible for said CPE. This particular CPE contains a built-in Ethernet switch with a few ports (say four) for good measure. Upper Management has decreed that Internet access is of utmost importance, and we should make it as highly available as we can, given our equipment. The equipment at our disposal includes a number of switches and two mid-range NetScreen firewalls capable only of NSRP-Lite.

After working through the possible options, the network layout shown in Figure 13.16 is decided upon and needs to be implemented. Based on this design, we produce the following configuration for the NetScreens.

Figure 13.16 Office Network with HA Internet Access

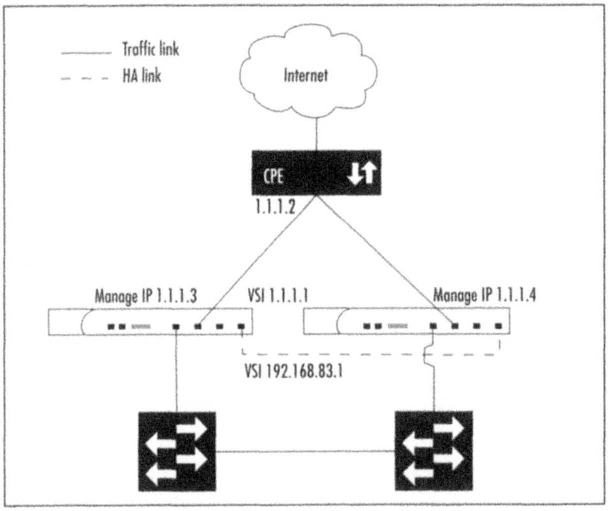

From the CLI:

```
set zone name office
set zone name internet
set zone office vrouter trust-vr
set zone internet vrouter trust-vr
set interface ethernet1 zone office
set interface ethernet2 zone internet
set interface ethernet3 zone ha
```

```
set interface ethernet4 zone ha
set interface ethernet1 ip 192.168.83.1/24
set interface ethernet2 ip 1.1.1.1/29
# on firewall A, use these commands
set interface ethernet2 manage-ip 1.1.1.3
set hostname sme-fwA
# on firewall B, use these commands instead
set interface ethernet2 manage-ip 1.1.1.4
set hostname sme-fwB
#
set vrouter trust-vr route 0.0.0.0/0 interface ethernet2 gateway 1.1.1.2
set nsrp cluster id 1
set nsrp cluster name sme
set nsrp monitor interface ethernet1
set nsrp monitor interface ethernet2
# configure aggressive IP tracking
set nsrp monitor track-ip ip 1.1.1.2
set nsrp monitor track-ip ip 1.1.1.2 weight 255
set nsrp monitor track-ip ip 1.1.1.2 threshold 2
set nsrp monitor track-ip
# prefer to have firewall #1 as the master, but do not preempt
# on firewall A, use this command
set nsrp vsd-group id 0 priority 1
# on firewall B, use this instead
set nsrp vsd-group id 0 priority 2
#
# configure for sub-second failover on lost heart-beats
set nsrp vsd-group hb-interval 200
set nsrp vsd-group hb-threshold 4
set nsrp vsd-group init-hold 25
```

From the Web interface:

1. Go to **Network | Zones | New** to create a new zone.
2. Enter **office** as the Zone Name.
3. Select **trust-vr** as the Virtual Router Name.

4. Click **OK**.

5. Click **New**.

6. Enter **internet** as the Zone Name.

7. Select **trust-vr** as the Virtual Router Name.

8. Click **OK**.

9. Go to **Network | Interfaces | ethernet1 | Edit**.

10. Enter **office** as the Zone Name.

11. Enter **192.168.83.1** as the IP Address and **24** as the Netmask.

12. Click **OK**.

13. Go to **Network | Interfaces | ethernet2 | Edit**.

14. Enter **internet** as the Zone Name.

15. Enter **1.1.1.1** as the IP Address and **29** as the Netmask.

16. Click **Apply**.

17. Use **1.1.1.3** as the Managed IP on Firewall A, and **1.1.1.4** on Firewall B.

18. Select **Route** as the Interface Mode.

19. Click **OK**.

20. Go to **Network | Interfaces | ethernet3 | Edit**.

21. Select **HA** as the Zone Name.

22. Click **OK**.

23. Go to **Network | Interfaces | ethernet4 | Edit**.

24. Select **HA** as the Zone Name.

25. Click **OK**.

26. Go to **Network | DNS**.

27. Enter **sme-fwA** as the hostname on Firewall A, and **sme-fwB** on Firewall B.

28. Click **Apply**.

29. Go to **Network | Routing | Routing Entries**.

30. Click **New** after selecting **trust-vr** as the virtual router to create the new routing entry in.

31. Enter **0.0.0.0** as the IP Address and **0.0.0.0** as the Netmask.

32. Select **Gateway** instead of Next Hop Virtual Router Name.

33. Set the Interface to **ethernet2**.

34. Enter **1.1.1.2** as the Gateway IP Address.

35. Click **OK**.

36. Go to **Network | NSRP | Cluster**.

37. Select **Cluster ID** and enter **1** as the ID.

38. Click **Apply**.

39. Go to **Network | NSRP | Monitor | Interface | VSD ID: Device | Edit interface**.

40. Select **ethernet1**.

41. Set the Weight to **255**.

42. Select **ethernet2**.

43. Set the Weight to **255**.

44. Click **Apply**.

45. Go to **Network | NSRP | Monitor | Track IP**.

46. Click **New**.

47. Enter **1.1.1.2** as the Track IP.

48. Set the Weight to **255**.

49. Set the Threshold to **2**.

50. Click **OK**.

51. Go to **Network | NSRP | Monitor | Track IP | VSD ID: Device | Edit**.

52. Select **Enable Track IP**.

53. Click **Apply**.

54. Go to **Network | NSRP | VSD Group | Group ID 0 | Edit**.

55. Set the Priority to **1** on Firewall A, and to **2** on Firewall B.

56. Click **OK**.

Note that the cluster name and heartbeat settings must be entered via the CLI even if you are using the Web interface, because they cannot be adjusted via the Web interface.

Working with Local Interfaces in an NSRP-Lite Setup

If we adjust one of the inputs from the scenario of only having a single Internet link, we end up with a more interesting example that is worth examining. In the case where we have two separate Internet links provided to the premises, each with its own CPE and only providing a single Ethernet port, our NetScreen setup becomes quite different. Let's take a closer look at how to deal with this new scenario.

Example: HA Internet via Dual Providers

While this example is similar to the previous one, the resulting configuration is quite different because in this case it is not possible to connect both of the NetScreens to each of the CPE routers (see Figure 13.17). Instead, the individual firewall must have a local configuration for talking to its connected CPE. To achieve this when running NSRP (or NSRP-Lite), you must use local interfaces so that the configuration of those interfaces does not move between the firewalls. You can create a local interface by removing the default VSD once NSRP is enabled, and then create a new VSD and only bind select interfaces to it. Any interfaces not bound to the new VSD remain as local interfaces.

For clarity's sake, we omit the configuration for sub-second failover on lost heartbeats as well as the more aggressive settings for the IP tracking. Also note that because the interfaces towards the CPE are local interfaces, there is no need to set a Managed IP for the IP tracking.

Figure 13.17 Network Layout Using Local Interfaces

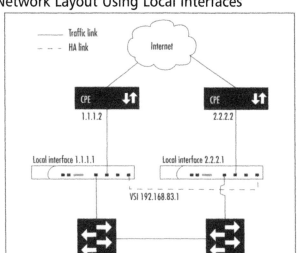

From the CLI:

```
set zone name office
set zone name internet
set zone office vrouter trust-vr
set zone internet vrouter trust-vr
set interface ethernet1 zone office
set interface ethernet2 zone internet
set interface ethernet3 zone ha
set interface ethernet4 zone ha
set nsrp cluster id 1
set nsrp cluster name sme
set nsrp monitor interface ethernet1
set nsrp monitor interface ethernet2
unset nsrp vsd-group id 0
set nsrp vsd-group id 1
# only ethernet1:1 is a VSI now
set interface ethernet1:1 ip 192.168.83.1/24
# on firewall A, use these commands
set interface ethernet2 ip 1.1.1.1/30
set hostname sme-fwA
set vrouter trust-vr route 0.0.0.0/0 interface ethernet2 gateway 1.1.1.2
```

```
set nsrp monitor track-ip ip 1.1.1.2
set nsrp monitor track-ip ip 1.1.1.2 weight 255
set nsrp monitor track-ip
set nsrp vsd-group id 1 priority 1
# on firewall B, use these commands instead
set interface ethernet2 ip 2.2.2.1/30
set hostname sme-fwB
set vrouter trust-vr route 0.0.0.0/0 interface ethernet2 gateway 2.2.2.2
set nsrp monitor track-ip ip 2.2.2.2
set nsrp monitor track-ip ip 2.2.2.2 weight 255
set nsrp monitor track-ip
set nsrp vsd-group id 1 priority 2
#
```

From the Web interface:

1. Go to **Network | Zones**.

2. Click **New** to create a new zone.

3. Enter **office** as the Zone Name.

4. Select **trust-vr** as the Virtual Router Name.

5. Click **OK**.

6. Click **New**.

7. Enter **internet** as the Zone Name.

8. Select **trust-vr** as the Virtual Router Name.

9. Click **OK**.

10. Go to **Network | Interfaces | ethernet1 | Edit**.

11. Enter **office** as the Zone Name.

12. Click **OK**.

13. Go to **Network | Interfaces | ethernet2 | Edit**.

14. Enter **internet** as the Zone Name.

15. Click **OK**.

16. Go to **Network | Interfaces | ethernet3 | Edit**.

17. Enter **HA** as the Zone Name.

18. Click **OK**.

19. Go to **Network | Interfaces | ethernet4 | Edit**.

20. Select **HA** as the Zone Name.

21. Click **OK**.

22. Go to **Network | NSRP | Cluster**.

23. Select **Cluster ID** and enter **1** as the ID.

24. Click **Apply**.

25. Go to **Network | NSRP | Monitor | Interface | VSD ID: Device | Edit interface**.

26. Select **ethernet1**.

27. Set the Weight to **255**.

28. Select **ethernet2**.

29. Set the Weight to **255**.

30. Click **Apply**.

31. Go to **Network | NSRP | VSD Group**.

32. Click **Remove** for Group ID 0.

33. Confirm the prompt to delete it.

34. Click **New**.

35. Set the Group ID to **1**.

36. Click **OK**.

37. Go to **Network | Interfaces**.

38. Click **New** after selecting **VSI IF**.

39. Select **ethernet1** as the VSI Base.

40. Select **VSD Group 1**.

41. Assign it an IP Address and Netmask of **192.168.83.1/24**.

42. Click **Apply**.

Do the following on Firewall A:

1. Go to **Network | Interfaces | ethernet2 | Edit**.

2. Enter **1.1.1.1** as the IP Address and **30** for the Netmask.

3. Click **OK**.

4. Go to **Network | DNS**.

5. Enter **sme-fwA** as the hostname.

6. Click **Apply**.

7. Go to **Network | Routing | Routing Entries**.

8. Click **New** after selected **trust–vr** as the virtual router.

9. Enter **0.0.0.0/0.0.0.0** as the Network Address/Netmask.

10. Select **Gateway** instead of Next Hop Virtual Router Name.

11. Pick **ethernet2** as the Interface.

12. Enter **1.1.1.2** as the Gateway IP Address.

13. Click **OK**.

14. Go to **Network | NSRP | Monitor | Track IP**.

15. Click **New**.

16. Enter **1.1.1.2** as the Track IP.

17. Set the Weight to **255**.

18. Click **OK**.

19. Go to **Network | NSRP | Monitor | Track IP | VSD ID: Device | Edit**.

20. Select **Enable Track IP**.

21. Click **Apply**.

22. Go to **Network | NSRP | VSD Group | Group ID 1 | Edit**.

23. Set the Priority to **1**.

24. Click **OK**.

Do the following on Firewall B:

1. Go to **Network | Interfaces | ethernet2 | Edit**.

2. Enter **2.2.2.1** as the IP Address and **30** for the Netmask.

3. Click **OK**.

4. Go to **Network | DNS** .

5. Enter **sme-fwB** as the hostname.

6. Click **Apply**.

7. Go to **Network | Routing | Routing Entries**.

8. Click **New**

9. Select **trust-vr** as the Virtual Router Name.

10. Enter **0.0.0.0/0.0.0.0** as the Network Address/Netmask.

11. Select **Gateway** instead of Next Hop Virtual Router Name.

12. Select **ethernet2**.

13. Enter **2.2.2.2** as the Gateway IP Address.

14. Click **OK**.

15. Go to **Network | NSRP | Monitor | Track IP**.

16. Click **New**.

17. Enter **2.2.2.2** as the Track IP.

18. Set the Weight to **255**.

19. Click **OK**.

20. Go to **Network | NSRP | Monitor | Track IP | VSD ID: Device | Edit**.

21. Select **Enable Track IP.**

22. Click **Apply**.

23. Go to **Network | NSRP | VSD Group | Group ID 1| Edit**.

24. Set the Priority to **2**.

25. Click **OK**.

Notes from the Underground…

Forcing Links Down on the Backup Firewall

In certain rare situations you might find that having all of the links up (but inactive) on the backup firewall causes problems. This is sometimes seen in cases where the NetScreens connect directly to a router instead of going via a switch, and the router uses only link state to adjust its routing, thereby sending packets to the inactive interface, which will simply be dropped.

Continued

www.syngress.com

> If you find yourself in this situation, the recommendation is to re-think the network design to avoid this scenario. If this is not possible, try re-thinking it again. If you still can't avoid it, be prepared for some headaches as you work around it on the firewall. This can be done with the **unset nsrp link-up-on-backup** command.
>
> As the name implies, when this is unset, the links are brought down on the backup unit (except for the HA interfaces and the Management interface, if applicable). Until recently, this command was a hidden, undocumented command (it also existed in NSRPv1 as **unset ha link-up-on-slave**). The reasons for it being hidden and undocumented are many, including: management via traffic interfaces become impossible, secondary NSRP paths are not available, failover time is greatly increased, especially in the presence of STP, and unless you are using a model that has a dedicated management interface, it is not possible to use NTP for clock synchronization (or any management features, for that matter).
>
> Where at all possible, avoid using this feature, even if it is now a documented option.

Creating Redundant Interfaces

In addition to providing HA using redundant firewalls, it is also possible to use *redundant interfaces*. The idea behind a redundant interface is that failing over to a different firewall is disruptive and should be avoided. By cabling the firewalls so that each one has redundant links to each network segment (such as the case of a full-mesh setup), interface redundancy can be used. Instead of failing over all traffic onto a different firewall, it is only failed over onto a different interface on the same firewall (see Figure 13.18).

Figure 13.18 Cabling for Redundant Interfaces

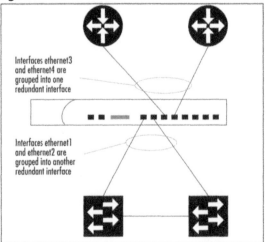

Interfaces ethernet3 and ethernet4 are grouped into one redundant interface

Interfaces ethernet1 and ethernet2 are grouped into another redundant interface

Redundant interfaces are not a part of NSRP, but are commonly used together with NSRP to build full-mesh setups. However, it is possible to create redundant interfaces without enabling NSRP.

If you are using redundant interfaces with NSRP, you need to know that you can bind VSIs to the redundant interfaces, just as you would with a physical interface. By the same token, you can also keep a redundant interface as a local interface instead of a VSI.

Grouping Physical Interfaces Into a Redundant Interface

To create a redundant interface, two or more physical interfaces are grouped together. Within a redundant interface group, one interface is considered the primary interface and will be used for sending and receiving traffic unless its link goes down. The secondary interface has its link up at all times, but is not active; traffic sent to it is simply discarded.

Once the redundant interface has been created, it can be configured like any other interface. It is assigned to a zone, given an IP address, and can be referred to in unnumbered VPN tunnels. An interesting aspect worth noting is that the physical interfaces do not need to be assigned to the same zone as the redundant interface.

Example: A Simple Redundant Interface Setup

To keep matters simple, consider only a partial setup in which redundant interfaces are used (see Figure 13.19). We will group the interfaces ethernet1 and ethernet2 together as a redundant interface, and bind the redundant interface to the *inside* zone.

With this configuration, all traffic normally passes over ethernet1. If that link fails, traffic is instantly moved to ethernet2.

Figure 13.19 Firewall with a Redundant Interface

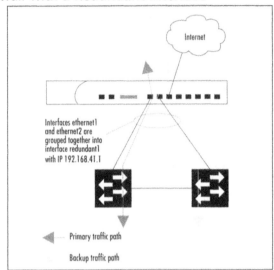

From the CLI:

```
set interface redundant1 zone inside
set interface redundant1 ip 192.168.41.1/24
set interface ethernet1 group redundant1
set interface ethernet2 group redundant1
```

From the Web interface:

1. Go to **Network | Interfaces | New Redundant IF**.
2. Enter **redundant1** as the interface name.
3. Enter **inside** as the Zone Name.
4. Specify **192.168.41.1/24** as the IP Address and Netmask.
5. Press **OK** to create the redundant interface.
6. Go to **Network | Interfaces | ethernet1 | Edit**.
7. Set As Member Of to **redundant1**.
8. Press **OK**.
9. Go to **Network | Interfaces | ethernet2 | Edit**.
10. Set As Member Of to **redundant1**.
11. Press **OK**.

Example: Changing the Primary Interface of a Redundant Interface

By default, the first physical interface added to the redundant interface group becomes the primary interface. It is possible to change this afterwards, if desired. For this example, we assume that interface redundant1 consists of physical interfaces cthernet1 and ethernet2, and that ethernet1 is currently the primary interface. To change the primary interface to ethernet2, use the following.

From the CLI:

```
set interface redundant1 phy primary ethernet2
```

From the Web interface:

It is not possible to change the primary interface of a redundant interface from the Web interface.

Taking Advantage of the Full NSRP

By now we have explored most aspects of NSRP, but there are still a few important areas remaining. One of the shortcomings of NSRP-Lite is that in the case of failover, any existing session and VPN information (among other things) is lost. Juniper/NetScreen has an answer to this problem as well. It is called RTO mirroring, and is only available with the full NSRP.

A second shortcoming of NSRP-Lite is that in an NSRP cluster, one firewall ends up sitting unutilized for most of the time. It can be hard to justify the purchase of an additional firewall when management counters with the argument, "It says here that it will not actually be used. Why do you expect me to spend $$$ on something that will not be used?" The setups we have looked at so far are what are referred to as Active/Passive setups—one firewall is active and the other is passive. NSRP provides the ability to create Active/Active configurations, in which both firewalls actively handle traffic. Designing the network for Active/Active setups requires careful consideration, but once you have it set up and working, your network will run very nicely.

In this section, we also examine a full-mesh setup, where we combine just about everything that has been discussed in this chapter into one concrete example. Let's start by looking at RTO mirroring.

Synchronizing State Using RTO Mirroring

As mentioned throughout this chapter, a failover between two firewalls can be very disruptive; session information is lost, VPNs are brought down, DHCP leases go missing, and so on. The solution to this problem is RTO mirroring, which means that all of this dynamic information (RTOs) is actively mirrored between the VSDs. In case of a failover, all of this state information is already available on the new master VSD, and can resume operations with a minimum of interference to the traffic flow.

Enabling RTO mirroring is easy to do, but depends on the configurations being in sync between the firewalls. Before you attempt to enable RTO mirroring, it is useful to run the **exec nsrp sync global-config checksum** command to verify that the configurations indeed are in sync.

Example: Enabling RTO Mirroring in an NSRP Cluster

To create a cluster that is using RTO mirroring, the following is needed.

From the CLI:

```
set nsrp cluster id 1
set nsrp rto-mirror sync
```

From the Web interface:

1. Go to **Network | NSRP | Cluster**.
2. Enter **1** as the Cluster ID.
3. Click **Apply**.
4. Go to **Network | NSRP | Synchronization**.
5 Select **NSRP RTO Synchronization**.
6. Select **NSRP Session Synchronization**.
7. Click **Apply**.

Example: Preventing Certain Sessions from Being Backed Up

Earlier in this chapter when discussing the SOHO range of NetScreens and their HA features, we mentioned the **no-session-backup** option that a policy can be tagged with. If you recall, we mentioned that this option has a different meaning when NSRP is used.

Instead of the entire policy being inactive after a failover, under NSRP, this option indicates that any sessions created as a result of this particular policy should *not* be mirrored by the other VSD. Hence, if a failover occurs, those unmirrored sessions are dropped and must be reestablished after the failover. This can sometimes be useful when dealing with denial of service (DOS) attacks against insecure protocols.

Let's reuse the same policy; however, here it implies that any existing FTP sessions are dropped in case of a failover.

From the CLI:

```
set policy from trust to untrust any any ftp permit no-session-backup
```

From the Web interface:

1. Go to **Policies** and create a new policy from the **Trust** zone to the **Untrust** zone.

2. Select **any** as the source and destination address.

3. Select **FTP** as the service.

4. Set **Permit** as the action for the policy.

5. Click **Advanced.**

6. Deselect the **HA Session Backup** option, and click **Return**.

7. Click **OK** to save the new policy.

Setting Up an Active/Active Cluster

Setting up an Active/Active NSRP cluster is not that different from setting up an Active/Passive cluster. The difference is that in an Active/Active cluster you have more than one VSD group. You configure the VSD groups so that under normal circumstances the first firewall has the master VSD for the first VSD group and the backup VSD for the second VSD group, and vice versa. Spreading the VSDs out like this is a simple matter of setting their priorities correctly (see Figure 13.20).

Figure 13.20 Multiple VSD Groups

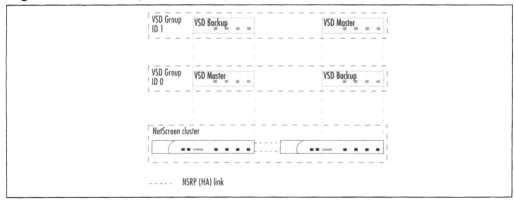

Since each VSD contains its own set of VSIs, you end up with multiple IP addresses in each network, compared to a single IP address per network (not counting Managed IP addresses) if you are using a single VSD. To benefit from this setup, you must configure the neighboring network nodes to load-balance between these IP addresses. With routers this is commonly done by having two routes with identical cost, each pointing to one of the VSI IP addresses. If the NetScreens are providing the default gateway for a LAN, then you can configure half the hosts on the LAN to use the IP address in the first VSD, and the second half to use the other VSD's IP address as their default gateway. This is the same approach as if you are using a pair of VRRP routers as the default gateway.

An important thing to remember when setting up Active/Active configuration is that you must duplicate the routes as well. If you do not have routes for the second VSD, it is forced to forward all traffic to the first VSD across the HA data link, which should be avoided (see Figure 13.21).

Figure 13.21 Network with Missing Route in VSD Group 1

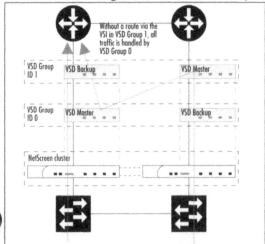

In addition to this, you must also take into account that the load you are putting on the firewalls may need to be handled by a single firewall. In other words, each firewall should run at 50 percent capacity at the most under normal conditions because in a failover scenario, everything goes through the remaining firewall; it cannot be expected to operate at more than 100 percent. If you attempt to put more traffic through it, be prepared to have some packets dropped.

Example: A Typical Active/Active Setup

Consider a scenario where you have two NetScreens providing a default gateway towards the Internet for an office LAN. The NetScreens are connected to redundant switches, as well as redundant Internet border routers (see Figure 13.22).

Figure 13.22 Network Layout for an Active/Active Setup

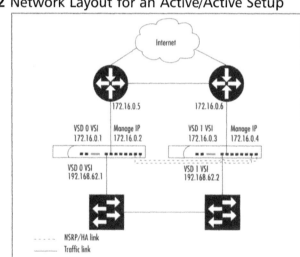

The client hosts in the office LAN have been configured so that half of them use the internal IP address of the first VSD, and the rest use the internal IP address of the second VSD as the default gateway. The routers run VRRP and the NetScreens use ARP-based IP tracking of their respective router's IP address.

From the CLI:

```
set zone name office
set zone name internet
set zone office vrouter trust-vr
set zone internet vrouter trust-vr
```

```
set interface ethernet1 zone office
set interface ethernet1 ip 192.168.62.1/24
set interface ethernet1 route
set interface ethernet2 zone internet
set interface ethernet2 ip 172.16.0.1/29
set interface ethernet2 route
# on firewall A, use this command
set interface ethernet2 manage-ip 172.16.0.2
# on firewall B, use this coammnd instead
set interface ethernet2 manage-ip 172.16.0.4
#
set interface ethernet7 zone ha
set interface ethernet8 zone ha
set nsrp cluster id 1
set nsrp cluster name deepthought
set nsrp vsd-group id 1
set interface ethernet1:1 ip 192.168.62.2/24
set interface ethernet2:1 ip 172.16.0.3/29
set vrouter trust-vr route 0.0.0.0/0 interface ethernet2
    gateway 172.16.0.5
set vrouter trust-vr route 0.0.0.0/0 interface ethernet2:1
    gateway 172.16.0.6
set nsrp monitor interface ethernet1
set nsrp monitor interface ethernet2
set nsrp vsd-group id 0 monitor track-ip ip 172.16.0.5
set nsrp vsd-group id 0 monitor track-ip ip 172.16.0.5 method arp
set nsrp vsd-group id 0 monitor track-ip ip 172.16.0.5 weight 255
set nsrp vsd-group id 0 monitor track-ip
set nsrp vsd-group id 1 monitor track-ip ip 172.16.0.6
set nsrp vsd-group id 1 monitor track-ip ip 172.16.0.6 method arp
set nsrp vsd-group id 1 monitor track-ip ip 172.16.0.5 weight 255
set nsrp vsd-group id 1 monitor track-ip
set nsrp rto-mirror sync
set nsrp secondary-path ethernet1
set nsrp vsd-group master-always-exists
set arp always-on-dest
```

```
# on firewall A, use these commands
set hostname deepthoughtA
set nsrp vsd-group id 0 priority 1
set nsrp vsd-group id 0 preempt
set nsrp vsd-group id 0 preempt hold-down 45
set nsrp vsd-group id 1 priority 2
# on firewall B, use these commands instead
set hostname deepthoughtB
set nsrp vsd-group id 0 priority 2
set nsrp vsd-group id 1 priority 1
set nsrp vsd-group id 1 preempt
set nsrp vsd-group id 1 preempt hold-down 45
#
```

From the Web interface:

1. Go to **Network | Zones | New** to create a new zone.
2. Enter **office** as the Zone Name.
3. Select **trust-vr** as the Virtual Router Name.
4. Click **OK**.
5. Click **New** again.
6. Enter **internet** as the Zone Name.
7. Select **trust-vr** as the Virtual Router Name.
8. Click **OK**.
9. Go to **Network | Interfaces | ethernet1 | Edit**.
10. Enter **office** as the Zone Name.
11. Assign **192.168.62.1/24** to the IP Address and Netmask.
12. Select **Route** as the Interface Mode.
13. Click **OK**.
14. Go to **Network | Interfaces | ethernet2 | Edit**.
15. Enter **internet** as the Zone Name.
16. Assign **172.16.0.1/29** to the IP Address and Netmask.

17. Select **Route** as the Interface Mode.

18. Click **Apply**.

19. Enter **172.16.0.2** as the Managed IP on Firewall A, and **172.16.0.4** on Firewall B.

20. Click **OK**.

21. Go to **Network | Interfaces | ethernet7 | Edit**.

22. Select **HA** as the Zone Name.

23. Click **OK**.

24. Go to **Network | Interfaces | ethernet8 | Edit**.

25. Select **HA** as the Zone Name.

26. Click **OK**.

27. Go to **Network | NSRP | Cluster**.

28. Select **Cluster ID** and enter **1** as the ID.

29. Click **Apply**.

30. Go to **Network | NSRP | VSD Group**.

31. Click **New**.

32. Set the Group ID to **1**.

33. Click **OK**.

34. Go to **Network | Interfaces**.

35. Click **New** after selecting **VSI IF**.

36. Select **ethernet1** as the VSI Base.

37. Select the VSD Group to **1**.

38. Assign **192.168.62.2/24** to the IP Address and Netmask.

39. Click **Apply**.

40. Click **New** after selecting **VSI IF**.

41 Select **ethernet2** as the VSI Base.

42. Select VSD Group **1**.

43. Assign **172.16.0.3/29** to the IP Address and Netmask.

44. Click **Apply**.

45. Go to **Network | Routing | Routing Entries**.

46. Click **New.**

47. Select **trust-vr** as the Virtual Router Name.

48. Enter **0.0.0.0/0.0.0.0** as the Network Address and Netmask.

49. Select **Gateway** instead of Next Hop Virtual Router Name.

50. Select **ethernet2**.

51. Enter **172.16.0.5** as the Gateway IP Address.

52. Click **OK**.

53. Click **New**

54. Select **trust-vr** as the Virtual Router Name.

55. Enter **0.0.0.0/0.0.0.0** as the Network Address and Netmask.

56. Select **Gateway** instead of Next Hop Virtual Router Name.

57. Select **ethernet2:1**.

58. Enter **172.16.0.6** as the Gateway IP Address.

59. Click **OK**.

60. Go to **Network | NSRP | Monitor | Interface | VSD ID: Device | Edit interface**.

61. Select **ethernet1**.

62. Set the Weight to **255**.

63. Select **ethernet2**.

64. Set the Weight to **255**.

65. Click **Apply**.

66. Go to **Network | NSRP | Monitor | Track IP**.

67. Click **New**.

68. Enter **172.16.0.5** as the Track IP.

69. Set the Weight to **255**.

70. Change the Method to **ARP**.

71. Set the VSD Group ID to **0**.

72. Click **OK**.

73. Click **New**.

74. Enter **172.16.0.6** as the Track IP.

75. Set the Weight to **255**.

76. Change the Method to **ARP**.

77. Set the VSD Group ID to **1**.

78. Click **OK**.

79. Go to **Network | NSRP | Monitor | Track IP | VSD ID: 0 | Edit**.

80. Select **Enable Track IP**.

81. Click **Apply**.

82. Go to **Network | NSRP | Monitor | Track IP | VSD ID: 1 | Edit**.

83. Select **Enable Track IP**.

84. Click **Apply**.

85. Go to **Network | NSRP | Synchronization**.

86. Select **NSRP RTO Synchronization**.

87. Select *NSRP Session Synchronization*.

88. Press **Apply**.

89. Go to **Network | NSRP | Link**.

90. Select **ethernet1** as the Secondary Link.

91. Click **Apply**.

On firewall A, do the following:

1. Go to **Network | DNS**.

2. Enter **deepthoughtA** as the hostname.

3. Click **Apply**.

4. Go to **Network | NSRP | VSD Group | Group ID 0 | Edit**.

5. Set the Priority to **1**.

6. Select **Enable Preempt**.

7. Set the Preempt Hold-Down Time to **45**.

8. Click **OK**.

9. Go to **Network | NSRP | VSD Group | Group ID 1 | Edit**.

10. Set the Priority to **2**.

11. Click **OK**.

Do the following on Firewall B:

1. Go to **Network | DNS**.

2. Enter **deepthoughtB** as the hostname.

3. Click **Apply**.

4. Go to **Network | NSRP | VSD Group | Group ID 0 | Edit**.

5. Set the Priority to **2**.

6. Click **OK**.

7. Go to **Network | NSRP | VSD Group | Group ID 1 | Edit**.

8. Set the Priority to **1**.

9. Select **Enable Preempt**.

10. Set the Preempt Hold-Down Time to **45**.

11. Click **OK**.

Not all settings can be adjusted from the Web interface. In this example, you need to enter the cluster name manually via the CLI, as well as enable the **nsrp master-always-exists** and **arp always-on-dest** options.

Implementing a Full-mesh Active/Active Setup

The grand masterpiece of HA with NetScreen firewalls is the full-mesh Active/Active setup. Such a setup typically includes redundant interfaces, RTO mirroring, and multiple VSD groups. As such, it can be a handful to set up, and even more of a challenge to test and verify properly. To give you a place to start, we go through a sample full-mesh setup, which will give you a good outline of what is required. Please remember that every network is different; you must adjust the settings so that they are right for your network. Once you are done, remember to test, test, and further test your setup. You will not know if it all works until you have tested all possible scenarios. Tedious work for sure, but if you are on a pager for network support, it is work that will pay off quite well.

Example: A Full-mesh Active/Active Setup

For this full-mesh example, we build on the previous example. The difference is that this time we have cabled the nodes in a full mesh, and therefore need to make configuration changes on the NetScreens. In particular, redundant inter-faces must be introduced. (See Figure 13.23.)

Figure 13.23 A Fully Meshed Active/Active Setup

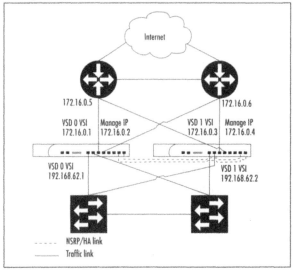

From the CLI:

```
set zone name office
set zone name internet
set zone office vrouter trust-vr
set zone internet vrouter trust-vr
set interface redundant1 zone office
set interface redundant1 ip 192.168.62.1/24
set interface redundant1 route
set interface ethernet1 zone office
set interface ethernet1 group redundant1
set interface ethernet2 zone office
set interface ethernet2 group redundant1
set interface redundant2 zone internet
set interface redundant2 ip 172.16.0.1/29
set interface redundant2 route
set interface ethernet3 zone internet
set interface ethernet3 group redundant2
set interface ethernet4 zone internet
```

```
set interface ethernet4 group redundant2
# on firewall A, use this command
set interface redundant2 manage-ip 172.16.0.2
# on firewall B, use this coammnd instead
set interface redundant2 manage-ip 172.16.0.4
#
set interface ethernet7 zone ha
set interface ethernet8 zone ha
set nsrp cluster id 1
set nsrp cluster name deepthought
set nsrp vsd-group id 1
set interface redundant1:1 ip 192.168.62.2/24
set interface redundant2:1 ip 172.16.0.3/29
set vrouter trust-vr route 0.0.0.0/0 interface redundant2
    gateway 172.16.0.5
set vrouter trust-vr route 0.0.0.0/0 interface redundant2:1
    gateway 172.16.0.6
set nsrp monitor interface redundant1
set nsrp monitor interface redundant2
set nsrp vsd-group id 0 monitor track-ip ip 172.16.0.5
set nsrp vsd-group id 0 monitor track-ip ip 172.16.0.5 method arp
set nsrp vsd-group id 0 monitor track-ip ip 172.16.0.5 weight 255
set nsrp vsd-group id 0 monitor track-ip
set nsrp vsd-group id 1 monitor track-ip ip 172.16.0.6
set nsrp vsd-group id 1 monitor track-ip ip 172.16.0.6 method arp
set nsrp vsd-group id 1 monitor track-ip ip 172.16.0.5 weight 255
set nsrp vsd-group id 1 monitor track-ip
set nsrp rto-mirror sync
set nsrp secondary-path redundant1
set nsrp vsd-group master-always-exists
set arp always-on-dest
# on firewall A, use these commands
set hostname deepthoughtA
set nsrp vsd-group id 0 priority 1
set nsrp vsd-group id 0 preempt
set nsrp vsd-group id 0 preempt hold-down 45
```

```
set nsrp vsd-group id 1 priority 2
# on firewall B, use these commands instead
set hostname deepthoughtB
set nsrp vsd-group id 0 priority 2
set nsrp vsd-group id 1 priority 1
set nsrp vsd-group id 1 preempt
set nsrp vsd-group id 1 preempt hold-down 45
#
```

From the Web interface:

1. Go to **Network | Zones | New** to create a new zone.
2. Enter **office** as the Zone Name.
3. Select **trust-vr** as the Virtual Router Name.
4. Click **OK**.
5. Click **New**.
6. Enter **internet** as the Zone Name.
7. Select **trust-vr** as the Virtual Router Name.
8. Click **OK**.
9. Go to **Network | Interfaces| New** after selecting **Redundant IF**.
10. Enter **office** as the Zone Name.
11. Assign **192.168.62.1/24** as the IP Address and Netmask.
12. Select **Route** as the Interface Mode.
13. Click **OK**.
14. Click **New** after selecting **Redundant IF**.
15. Enter **internet** as the Zone Name.
16. Assign **172.16.0.1/29** as the IP Address and Netmask.
17. Select **Route** as the Interface Mode.
18. Click **Apply**.
19. Enter **172.16.0.2** as the Managed IP On Firewall A, and **172.16.0.4** on Firewall B.
20. Click **OK**.

21. Go to **Network | Interfaces | ethernet1 | Edit**.

22. Enter **office** as the Zone Name.

23. Set As Member Of to **redundant1**.

24. Click **OK**.

25. Go to **Network | Interfaces | ethernet2 | Edit**.

26. Enter **office** as the Zone Name.

27. Set As Member Of to **redundant1**.

28. Click **OK**.

29. Go to **Network | Interfaces | ethernet3 | Edit**.

30. Enter **internet** as the Zone Name.

31. Set As Member Of to **redundant2**.

32. Click **OK**.

33. Go to **Network | Interfaces | ethernet4 | Edit**.

34. Enter **internet** as the Zone Name.

35. Set As Member Of to **redundant2**.

36. Click **OK**.

37. Go to **Network | Interfaces | ethernet7 | Edit**.

38. Select **HA** as the Zone Name.

39. Click **OK**.

40. Go to **Network | Interfaces | ethernet8 | Edit**.

41. Select **HA** as the Zone Name.

42. Click **OK**.

43. Go to **Network | NSRP | Cluster**.

44. Select **Cluster ID** and enter **1** as the ID.

45. Click **Apply**.

46. Go to **Network | NSRP | VSD Group | New**.

47. Set the Group ID to **1**.

48. Click **OK**.

49. Go to **Network | Interfaces | New**.

50. Select **VSI IF**.

51   Select **redundant1** as the VSI Base.

52. Select VSD Group **1**.

53. Assign **192.168.62.2/24** as the IP Address and Netmask.

54. Click **Apply**.

55. Click **New** after selecting **VSI IF**.

56. Select **redundant2** as the VSI Base.

57. Select VSD Group **1**.

58. Assign **172.16.0.3/29** as the IP Address and Netmask.

59. Click **Apply**.

60. Go to **Network | Routing | Routing Entries| New**

61. Select **trust-vr** as the Virtual Router Name.

62. Enter **0.0.0.0/0.0.0.0** as the IP Address and Netmask.

63. Select **Gateway** instead of Next Hop Virtual Router Name.

64. Select **redundant2**.

65. Enter **172.16.0.5** as the Gateway IP Address.

66. Click **OK**.

67. Select **trust-vr** as the Virtual Router Name.

68. Click **New**.

69. Enter **0.0.0.0/0.0.0.0** as the IP Address and Netmask.

70. Select **Gateway** instead of Next Hop Virtual Router Name.

71. Select **redundant2:1**.

72. Enter **172.16.0.6** as the Gateway IP Address.

73. Click **OK**.

74. Go to **Network | NSRP | Monitor | Interface | VSD ID: Device | Edit interface**.

75. Select **redudant1**.

76. Set the Weight to **255**.

77. Select **redundant2**.

78. Set the Weight to **255**.

79. Click **Apply**.

80. Go to **Network | NSRP | Monitor | Track IP | New**.

81. Enter **172.16.0.5** as the Track IP.

82. Set the Weight to **255**.

83. Change the Method to **ARP**.

84. Set VSD Group ID to **0**.

85. Click **OK**.

86. Click **New**.

87. Enter **172.16.0.6** as the Track IP.

88. Set the Weight to **255**.

89. Change the Method to **ARP**.

90. Set VSD Group ID to **1**.

91. Click **OK**.

92. Go to **Network | NSRP | Monitor | Track IP | VSD ID: 0 | Edit**.

93. Select **Enable Track IP**.

94. Click **Apply**.

95. Go to **Network | NSRP | Monitor | Track IP | VSD ID: 1 | Edit**.

96. Select **Enable Track IP**.

97. Click **Apply**.

98. Go to **Network | NSRP | Synchronization**.

99. Select **NSRP RTO Synchronization**.

100. Select **NSRP Session Synchronization**.

101. Press **Apply**.

102. Go to **Network | NSRP | Link**.

103. Select **redundant1** as the Secondary Link.

104. Click **Apply**.

Do the following on Firewall A:

1. Go to **Network | DNS**.

2. Enter **deepthoughtA** as the hostname.

3. Click **Apply**.

4. Go to **Network | NSRP | VSD Group | Group ID 0 | Edit**.

5. Set the Priority to **1**.

6. Select **Enable Preempt**.

7. Set the Preempt Hold-Down Time to **45**.

8. Click **OK**.

9. Go to **Network | NSRP | VSD Group | Group ID 1 | Edit**.

10. Set the Priority to **2**.

11. Click **OK**.

Do the following on Firewall B:

1. Go to **Network | DNS**.

2. Enter **deepthoughtB** as the hostname.

3. Click **Apply**.

4. Go to **Network | NSRP | VSD Group | Group ID 0 | Edit**.

5. Set the Priority to **2**.

6. Click **OK**.

7. Go to **Network | NSRP | VSD Group | Group ID 1 | Edit**.

8. Set the Priority to **1**.

9. Select **Enable Preempt**.

10. Set the Preempt Hold-Down Time to **45**.

11. Click **OK**.

Not all settings can be adjusted from the Web interface. You would need to enter the cluster name and enable the **nsrp master-always-exists** and **arp always-on-dest** options from the CLI.

Failing Over

A chapter on HA and NSRP would not be complete without a more in-depth dissection of what happens when a failover occurs. Things that can cause a failover are:

■ Software crashes (resulting in lost heartbeats)

- Hardware or power failure (resulting in lost heartbeats)
- Link failure on monitored interfaces or zones
- Unavailability of one or more tracked IP addresses
- Manually requested failover

Once the primary backup VSD has determined that it must become the master VSD, a few things happen. Firstly, the VSD promotes itself to master to prevent any other VSD from doing the same thing. Second, if the VSD has any links down, an attempt is made to bring them up. If a monitored link cannot be brought up, the VSD relinquishes its role as master and puts itself in the *inoperable* state. (See "Avoiding the No-brain Problem" in this chapter.)

Assuming the VSD is the newly promoted master VSD with all relevant links up, it proceeds to send out gratuitous ARP requests. This is a very important aspect of the failover. These ARP requests tell the neighboring network nodes that the IP addresses configured on the VSIs are now reachable via a different path than before. This will cause switches to update their forwarding tables, and routers to update their ARP tables. By default, four ARP packets are sent out on each interface, but this can be adjusted if needed (see the example below).

As soon as the neighboring nodes have adjusted to this change, traffic is sent to this VSD instead of the old one. If RTO mirroring was enabled before the failover, this VSD already has a copy of the *run-time* state, and proceeds to handle traffic with no further disruption. Note that some packets may have been lost during the time it takes for the neighboring nodes to reroute their traffic flows to the second NetScreen.

Example: Adjusting the Number of ARP Packets Sent After Failover

If you discover that some network elements do not notice that the VSD has failed over, you might want to try increasing the number of ARP requests sent out after the VSD has failed over. Here we increase it from the default four to nine.

From the CLI:

```
set nsrp arp 9
```

From the Web interface:

1. Go to Network | NSRP | Cluster.

2. Enter **9** for Number Of Gratuitous ARPs To Resend.

3. Press **Apply** to save these settings.

Failing Over Virtual Systems

Ensuring that virtual systems (VSYS') fail over takes some consideration and careful configuration. The key to making sure that a VSYS fails over correctly lies in remembering that only VSIs are moved across to the other VSD. Therefore, for a VSYS to fail over, its interfaces must be VSIs not local interfaces (or variations built on a local interface).

Example: Binding a VSYS to VSD Group 1

To illustrate the concept of using VSIs for the VSYS, consider a scenario where an NSRP cluster has been configured, and VSD group 5 is in use. To set up the VSYS in a way that ensures that it fails over as expected (VLAN 42 on ethernet1/1 and VLAN 3 on ethernet2/1), we use the following configuration. The important thing to note here is that the IP addresses are assigned to the VSI, not to the sub-interface.

From the CLI:

```
set vsys vsys4
set interface ethernet1/1.4 tag 42 zone untrust      # Sub-interface
set interface ethernet1/1.4:5 ip 1.1.1.42/24         # VSI
set interface ethernet2/1.3 tag 3 zone trust-vsys4 # Sub-interface
set interface ethernet2/1.3:5 ip 192.168.102.1/24  # VSI
set interface ethernet2/1.3:5 route                  # VSI
# more vsys configuration...
save
exit
```

From the Web interface:

1. Go to **VSYS | New**.

2. Enter **vsys4** as the VSYS Name.

3. Press **OK**.

4. Go to **VSYS | vsys4 | Enter | Network | Interface**.

5. Press **New Sub-IF**.

6. Enter **ethernet1/1.4**.

7. Select the **untrust** Zone.

8. Enter **42** as the VLAN Tag.

9. Press **OK** to create this interface.

10. Return to **VSYS | vsys4 | Enter | Network | Interface**.

11. Press **New VSI IF**.

12. Enter **ethernet1/1.4**.

13. Choose VSD Group **5**.

14. Enter **1.1.1.42/24** as the IP Address and Netmask.

15. Press **OK**.

16. Return to **VSYS | vsys4 | Enter | Network | Interface**.

17. Press **New Sub-IF**.

18. Enter **ethernet2/1.3** as the Interface Name.

19. Select the **trust-vsys4** Zone.

20. Enter **3** as the VLAN Tag.

21. Press **OK**.

22. Return to **VSYS | vsys4 | Enter | Network | Interface**

23. Press **New VSI IF**.

24. Enter **ethernet2/1.3** as the VSI Base.

25. Choose VSD Group **5**.

26. Use **192.168.102.1/24** as the IP Address and Netmask.

27. Select **Route** as the Interface Mode.

28. Press **OK**.

Avoiding the Split-brain Problem

Consider a scenario where two NetScreens are cabled together in a HA setup with single or dual HA links. Ordinarily, these two units send heartbeats back and forth, verifying each other's state and agreeing on who should be the master unit. When this is happening, all is well, but what if for some reason the HA link(s) were disconnected? The NetScreens would no longer be able to talk to each other, and even though the loss of the HA links would not have a direct impact on the surrounding network, the resulting events will have an impact on the rest of the network—a very bad one.

What happens in this scenario is that each of the NetScreens thinks the other unit fell over, and therefore there is only one NetScreen left, and hence this is the master. As such, the previous primary backup NetScreen promotes itself to master, and all of a sudden both firewalls are trying to persuade the surrounding network that it is the only place to send packets. Untold grief ensues, and sporadic connectivity through the firewalls is the best to be hoped for until at least one HA link is restored. This is commonly referred to as "split-brain."

Now that we know how and why it happens, let's look at ways we can mitigate the risk of this actually happening. The first option is to use dual HA links instead of a single link; it is less likely that both links fail simultaneously compared to a single link.

Second, if the HA links are connected via one of more switches, consider changing them to direct cross-over cables to avoid being dependent on the switch(es). Also, make sure you have enabled the HA link probes with the **set nsrp ha-link probe** command. Without the link probes, the firewalls may not be able to detect the link failure.

The third alternative is perhaps the most interesting, and warrants a more thorough discussion. In addition to one or two dedicated HA links, it is possible to specify a secondary path for the heartbeats. This secondary path is simply one of the traffic interfaces, which will be used as a fall-back option in case of total HA link failure (see Figure 13.24). Heartbeat packets will coexist with normal traffic on this interface. The important thing here is to ensure that the interface chosen is in the same Layer 2 broadcast domain as the corresponding interface on the second NetScreen. Or in plain English, the two interfaces must be part of the same VLAN. The reason for this is that the heartbeat packets are not IP packets, and are therefore not routable through the network. Generally, this works out well, since it is almost always the case for interfaces in the *trust* (or similar) zone. This is also good for security reasons. You would not want to send the heartbeats via the *untrust* (or similar) zone, since that part of the network is by definition, not trusted.

Figure 13.24 HA Link Failure

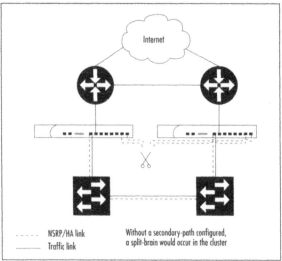

Example: Configuring a Secondary NSRP Path

Adding a secondary path to an existing NSRP setup is very easy. For this example, if you have confirmed that interface ethernet1 on both firewalls meets the criteria for being used as a secondary path, the following settings will achieve your goal.

From the CLI:

```
set nsrp secondary-path ethernet1
```

From the Web interface:

1. Go to **Network | NSRP | Link**.
2. Select **ethernet1** as the Secondary Link.
3. Press **Apply** to save these settings.

Avoiding the No-brain Problem

The opposite problem to "split-brain" is "no-brain," where neither of the firewalls wants to be the master. This can be just as problematic (and infuriating) as having them both want to be the master. Let's first take a look at how we can find ourselves in this situation, and then work out how to avoid it from happening. The good news is that there is a definite way around this problem. The bad news is that it might not always yield the best possible result. This will become apparent as we work through the cause and the solution.

To illustrate how this problem can occur, consider the following scenario (Figure 13.25) where two NetScreens in an NSRP cluster are used to provide the office with Internet connectivity and to make services available from the Demilitarized Zone (DMZ). Aiming for a highly available network, each NetScreen connects to a separate switch, both in the DMZ and in the *trust* zone (we are not interested in how things look on the *untrusted* side for this scenario). To ensure that a failover occurs, you need the firewalls to monitor the appropriate interfaces. This is a decent setup that will handle most failure situations quite well. However, there is always Murphy's Law, and in this particular case it could manifest itself as a power failure to both of the DMZ switches. A bit contrived? Perhaps; but if you are a seasoned network engineer, you already know that the most unlikely things happen at the most inopportune moments.

Figure 13.25 Network with Redundant DMZ and Office Switches

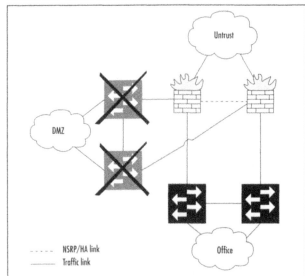

The failure of the DMZ switch that the current master firewall is connected to is detected by the firewall (thanks to interface monitoring), and goes into the *inoperable* state. This in turn prompts the backup NetScreen to promote itself to master, except for the fact that it just detected a link failure, and went into the *inoperable* state instead.

By now you see the problem. Because of a failure that originally affected only the DMZ, the entire office is left without Internet connectivity. Not quite what you had in mind when you set up the HA network.

Fear not, for there is a way to avoid this. You can force an NSRP cluster to always have a master by using the **set nsrp vsd-group master-always-exists** command. The good news is that there will always be a master with this set. The bad news is the way that the master is elected. If both NetScreens have failed, the master is elected based on the preempt settings and the priority values, which means that while a master is elected, it may not be the best one for the job. As a point in case, consider the scenario (Figure 13.26) where one of the switches in the *trusted* zone also lost power (in addition to the DMZ switches). If that happened to be the switch that the resulting master firewall is connected to, the office is still without Internet connectivity, despite the fact that the second firewall would be able to pass the traffic. In this scenario, there is nothing that can be done other than manually failing over to the other NetScreen.

Figure 13.26 Network with Three Failed Switches

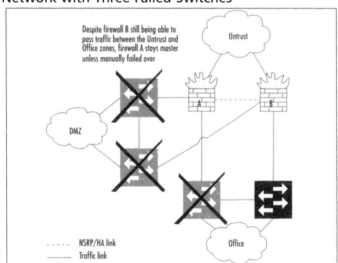

Despite firewall B still being able to pass traffic between the Untrust and Office zones, firewall A stays master unless manually failed over

Untrust

DMZ

NSRP/HA link

Traffic link

Office

HA, like security itself, always boils down to the same thing—risk management and mitigation. There is no such thing as perfection, only a decreasing likelihood of things going wrong in a service-impacting manner. However, that should not discourage you from grabbing the cheap gains where possible. So if you find yourself with a network that runs a risk of running across this particular problem, then adding the **master-always-exists** option makes sense.

Summary

HA is a hot topic, with more importance being placed on the availability of data networks across the globe. The NetScreen firewalls step up to the challenge by offering a wide range of different features designed for improving the overall availability of the networks in which they are deployed.

Many of the low-end SOHO firewalls come with features explicitly designed to make sure that Internet or other remote network connectivity is always available. While not spouting the same impressive range of features as the high-end NetScreen firewalls, the features provided are nevertheless highly useful and appropriate for the intended task of these firewalls. With the ability to automatically detect VPN failures and network host unavailability, and in that case automatically establish an alternative network path, the SOHO range leaves very little to be desired in this area.

On the mid-range and high-end firewalls, the NSRP is available, which provides plenty of different options for improving network availability. The concept of duplicating hardware to increase availability is present with the NetScreen firewalls, in which two firewalls are grouped into an NSRP cluster. Enabling NSRP on a NetScreen automatically creates an abstraction of some parts of the firewall, referred to as a VSD. This abstraction has the ability to move between the cluster members as needed. By also abstracting the Ethernet interfaces into VSIs, NSRP provides virtual IP addresses not unlike those you get when using the VRRP on routers.

NSRP also provides a range of monitoring features that enable you to precisely track the state of the network, and when determined to be necessary, automatically fail over to a second firewall or even just a second interface, if you are making use of redundant interfaces. Interface link state, zone availability, and IP address availability are all things that can be monitored. The ability to configure the monitoring either on a device level or on a VSD level gives you great flexibility and enables you to tailor the failover behavior to something that is suitable for your network.

If you find yourself with a network design that requires different configurations on the NSRP cluster members to cater for differing network paths connected to the firewalls, you can achieve this by using local interfaces instead of VSIs. An IP address assigned to a local interface will not move between the cluster members, making it the ideal candidate for such a scenario.

To provide a minimum amount of disruption when a failover occurs, you can use RTO mirroring, which means that the standby firewall synchronizes the run-time state of the active firewall, thus ensuring that the standby firewall can take over traffic processing without missing a beat. At most a few packets will need to be resent, but all sessions are kept alive.

By creating multiple VSDs, you can have both firewalls in an NSRP cluster processing traffic at the same time in an Active/Active setup, making the most of your hardware. Combining all of the HA features, you can achieve some remarkably available networks, as is the case of a fully meshed Active/Active setup.

Solutions Fast Track

Discussion About the Need for HA

☑ HA is all about risk mitigation.

☑ The level of availability should be dictated by your business strategy.

☑ Finding the right balance between availability and cost is not always easy.

Improving Availability Using NetScreen SOHO Appliances

☑ Many SOHO appliances provide the ability to fail over between interfaces.

☑ You can use either manual or automatic failover.

☑ Depending on the model, failover between two Ethernet interfaces or one Ethernet and the serial interface (with attached modem) is possible.

☑ You can restrict the policies to a subset while failed over the serial link.

☑ IP tracking can be used to determine when to fail over.

☑ You can track either the default gateway or explicit IP addresses.

☑ The state of VPNs can also be used to determine when to fail over. Remember to use the *monitor rekey* option if you are using automatic failover.

Introducing the NSRP

☑ NSRP is the protocol used between firewalls configured in redundant clusters.

☑ VSDs are the logical containers used when configuring NSRP.

☑ VSIs are logical interfaces belonging to a VSD, which are configured with the IP addresses that should be possible to transfer between the firewalls when a failover occurs.

☑ A VSD can be in any of the following states: Master, Primary Backup, Backup, Initial, Ineligible, or Inoperable.

☑ Where possible, use dual HA links.

Building an NSRP Cluster

☑ Several choices are possible in regards to the cabling of the NSRP cluster.

☑ Using directly connected HA links is preferred.

☑ To make a NetScreen part of an NSRP cluster, assign it a cluster ID between 1 and 7.

☑ Before the cluster can work properly, the configuration must be synchronized between the cluster members.

Determining When to Fail Over – The NSRP Way

☑ NSRP automatically uses heartbeats between the cluster members to monitor each other.

☑ The interface link state can be used to determine failover.

☑ The monitoring of zones provides a slightly higher level of interface monitoring.

☑ IP tracking provides a flexible way to determine when to fail over.

☑ Use the ARP method if tracking a VRRP IP address.

☑ Remember that the weighting involved in IP tracking is different than that of interface and zone monitoring.

Reading the Output from "get nsrp"

- ☑ In addition to the **get nsrp** command, **get config | include nsrp** is a useful command to remember.

- ☑ Remember to distinguish between monitoring on device level (which affects all VSDs) and monitoring on VSD level.

- ☑ Use the **get nsrp vsd-group id X monitor** command to examine per-VSD monitoring.

Using NSRP-Lite on Mid-range Appliances

- ☑ NSRP-Lite does not support RTO mirroring.

- ☑ Only Active/Passive setups are possible with NSRP-Lite.

- ☑ A local interface is an interface that is not bound to a VSI, and its IP address cannot fail over to another firewall.

- ☑ Local interfaces can be highly useful in setups with redundant but different traffic paths.

Creating Redundant Interfaces

- ☑ A redundant interface is created by grouping two or more physical interfaces together.

- ☑ Using redundant interfaces results in less risk of failing over between firewalls.

- ☑ Redundant interfaces are not dependent on NSRP being enabled.

- ☑ VSIs can be bound to a redundant interface, just as with a physical interface.

- ☑ Redundant interfaces are commonly used in full mesh setups.

Taking Advantage of the Full NSRP

- ☑ The use of RTO synchronization means that sessions will not be dropped in case of a failover occurring.

- ☑ In an Active/Active setup, both firewalls are actively processing traffic.

☑ Two VSD groups are used to achieve Active/Active setups.

☑ Equal-cost routes are commonly used for load balancing from the routers.

☑ If a cluster is providing the default gateway for a LAN, configure half of the hosts on the LAN to use the IP address of the first VSD, and the other half to use the IP address of the second VSD, to achieve rudimentary load sharing.

☑ Remember to provide routes for the second VSD, or you will most likely have problems.

☑ A full-mesh, Active/Active setup provides the best availability.

Failing Over

☑ When a failover occurs, the newly elected master VSD sends out gratuitous ARPs to announce the topology change to neighboring network nodes.

☑ In order for a VSYS to fail over, it must be using VSIs, not local interfaces or derivatives thereof.

Avoiding the Split-brain Problem

☑ A split-brain is where the firewalls in an NSRP cluster have lost the HA link(s) and both assume that it is the only firewall available in the cluster, and therefore both promote themselves to master.

☑ Use dual HA links where possible.

☑ Connect the HA link(s) directly via crossover cables instead of via a switch.

☑ Specify a secondary NSRP path, using a traffic interface, with the **set nsrp secondary-path Ethernet *X*** command.

Avoiding the No-brain Problem

☑ A no-brain scenario is where both firewalls in an NSRP cluster have determined that they are ineligible to become master, and the cluster is left without a master.

☑ To force an NSRP cluster to always have a master, use the **set nsrp vsd-group master-always-exists** command.

☑ When a master is elected in this scenario, only the preempt and priority settings are used; IP tracking and monitoring settings are ignored.

Frequently Asked Questions

The following Frequently Asked Questions, answered by the authors of this book, are designed to both measure your understanding of the concepts presented in this chapter and to assist you with real-life implementation of these concepts. To have your questions about this chapter answered by the author, browse to **www.syngress.com/solutions** and click on the **"Ask the Author"** form. You will also gain access to thousands of other FAQs at ITFAQnet.com.

Q: I'm working on setting up an NSRP cluster, but I'm having trouble getting it to work. Both the HA links are up on both sides and the NetScreens are members of the same cluster ID, but they still don't see each other. Each thinks it's the master unit, and there is no backup listed in the **get nsrp** output. Why would this be?

A: You have managed to cross the two HA links. HA link #1 is connected to port A on the first NetScreen, but to port B on the second NetScreen and vice versa. This causes both NetScreens to receive each other's heartbeats on the HA data link, where it is ignored. Make sure you connect the HA links from port A to port A and port B to port B. What A and B is depends of course on the model of NetScreen you are using.

Q: One of the firewalls in my NSRP cluster is complaining about the configuration being out of sync. How did this happen and how do I fix it?

A: The most probable cause of this is that you made a configuration change to the cluster when this firewall was not running or was otherwise not part of the cluster. Therefore, that configuration change was not propagated across to this firewall. To remedy this, use the **exec nsrp sync global-config run**

command. Make sure you save the configuration after doing this. If you want to verify that the configurations are indeed in sync, run the **exec nsrp sync global-config checksum** command.

Q: How do I force a failover?

A: On the current master device, execute the **exec nsrp vsd-group id X mode backup** command where *X* is the ID number of the VSD group (0 is the default VSD group if none have been specified).

Q: I am trying to set up an Active/Active NSRP cluster using a single HA link. I get no error messages, but all traffic from the LAN to the outside world going via the second VSD group is dropped. What is wrong?

A: You have most likely forgotten to add a default route for the second VSD. Since you do not have a HA data link, the packets cannot be forwarded between the VSDs, and are therefore dropped. Add a default route for the VSI in the second VSD, and traffic should flow normally.

Q: I have configured NSRP IP tracking, but it is not working. I do not see any pings sent out and the VSD fails over very quickly. What is up with this? Do I have a faulty ScreenOS version?

A: You forgot to set a Managed IP on the interface used for sending the IP tracking packets. Remember that IP tracking packets cannot be sent from a VSI; they need either a Managed IP or a local interface address. If you use the **get nsrp monitor track-ip** or **get nsrp vsd-group id X monitor track-ip** commands, you can see the statistics for the IP tracking as well as any error messages.

Chapter 14

Troubleshooting the NetScreen Firewall

Solutions in this Chapter:

- Troubleshooting Methodology
- Troubleshooting Tools
- Network Troubleshooting
- Debugging the NetScreen Device
- Debugging NAT
- Debugging VPNs
- Debugging NSRP
- Debugging Traffic Shaping
- NetScreen Logging

☑ Summary

☑ Solutions Fast Track

☑ Frequently Asked Questions

Introduction

Troubleshooting is a fact of life in computer networking. This chapter will cover different ways to track the status of packets going through your firewall. NetScreen firewalls offer a selection of tools to assist with troubleshooting network access.

When dealing with network firewalls, it is important to remember that they often change the content of the packets going through them. It is our task to keep track of the changes and make sure these changes are what we intended. Most firewalls do four main functions: packet forwarding, stateful filtering, address translation, and encryption. We tackle each of these functions differently. Troubleshooting packet forwarding can be as easy as inspecting the routing table. Address translation may require looking at a log of the traffic. Troubleshooting encryption may require analysis of a detailed packet dump. NetScreen firewalls offer specific troubleshooting tools built into the ScreenOS operating system. Commands such as ping and get route can help with simple connectivity troubleshooting. The firewall has a debug mode that has the capability to log packet headers or even the content of the packets themselves.

Remember that every firewall issue is resolvable. There is a reason behind every decision the firewall makes. We will begin by going through the process a packet makes as it makes its way through the firewall. Next we will go over the different tools available for troubleshooting. After that we will go over troubleshooting methods for VPNs (virtual private networks), NSRP (NetScreen Redundancy Protocol), and traffic shaping. Finally, we will cover the logs the firewall creates to help us determine what the firewall is doing with our packets.

Troubleshooting Methodology

So something is not going the way you expected it to. The first step is a sanity check. Is this a firewall issue? Are the packets making it to the firewall? Many firewall issues may actually be internal routing issues. Follow your packets from your computer through the internal network hubs, switches, and routers. It may be a good idea to sniff the traffic just outside of your firewall to see what the packets look like before they get to the firewall. Every troubleshooting session begins with a plan of action. Let's outline a plan of action to help us figure out what went wrong. Here are seven steps to follow when troubleshooting issues.

1. Describe the Problem
2. Describe the Environment
3. Determine the Location of the Problem
4. Identify the Cause of the Problem
5. Solve the Problem
6. Test the Solution
7. Document the Changes

We will go over each of these steps and describe how they can help is in the troubleshooting process.

Step One – Describe the Problem

Before we can start troubleshooting the process, we need to be able to describe the problem. It is important to tackle each problem individually in order to solve the problem at hand.

Step Two – Describe the Environment

Next we need to be able to describe which network devices we are dealing with. This step includes listing the hardware and software involved in the path of the network traffic.

Step Three – Determine the Location of the Problem

The location of the problem is not always apparent. We need to determine where the problem is occurring. There are several troubleshooting tools available to us to help locate the problem. This step can be tricky, as the problem might not be occurring where we thought it might be.

Step Four – Identify the Cause of the Problem

Once we determine where the problem exists, we need to identify the cause of the problem. This is normally done by analyzing the output of certain troubleshooting tools.

Step Five – Solve the Problem

Once the cause of the problem is identified, we need to actually resolve the problem. This might involve physically altering the network or issuing commands into network equipment by changing the configurations. Whatever you do, keep track of what you change.

Step Six – Test the Solution

Recreate the issue and see of the problem is fixed. As the fix may have affected other network traffic, make sure everything else is in working order as well.

Step Seven – Document the Changes

Documentation is one of the most important and most skipped steps. A good network administrator keeps a detailed log of what changes are made to the network infrastructure. Keeping track of what changes are made during troubleshooting is also important because the solution might create unintended problems in other areas of the network. Keep this log handy in case other issues arise.

Troubleshooting Tools

The NetScreen firewall has several troubleshooting tools built into it. This section will cover the tools in detail. Each tool has a specific purpose and should cover any troubleshooting need you have.

Tools & Traps...

Secure Troubleshooting

One thing you want to make sure of when troubleshooting your firewall is that you don't compromise your security during the troubleshooting process. If you are using HTTP (Hypertext Transfer Protocol) or Telnet to access your firewall, then someone may be able to sniff your packets while you are working on your issues.

The WebUI can be encrypted with SSL (Secure Sockets Layer) or tunneled through a VPN. It is recommended that this connection be secured

Continued

at all times. The certificate can be self-signed by the NetScreen firewall so no certificate has to be purchased.

The command line interface can be encrypted by using SSH (Secure Shell) to log into your firewall. Telnet should be disabled so it cannot be used by anyone. If Telnet access is required for some reason, be sure to encrypt the packets by a VPN tunnel. Serial console access requires physical access to the firewall. You can disable all CLI access if you wish and require serial access to manage the box. This may be a bit extreme, though.

Ping

Ping is probably the most well-known network troubleshooting utility in existence. The **ping** command is used to test for network connectivity. Every network operating system has a version of it pre-installed. Ping was written in December, 1983 by Mike Muuss for BSD UNIX. The BSD UNIX network stack has been ported to many operating systems, including every version of Microsoft Windows. Although the name was originally derived from a sonar analogy; it is now referred to as an acronym for Packet InterNet Groper.

The functionality is simple, send an ICMP (Internet Control Message Protocol) echo-request and wait for an ICMP echo-reply. The code shown in Figure 14.1 is an example of sending a ping to IP (Internet Protocol) address 192.168.0.1, and getting four replies in return. This is a connectivity check from a Windows machine to a router.

Figure 14.1 Ping Command in Windows

```
Command Prompt                                              _ □ X
C:\>
C:\>
C:\>
C:\>
C:\>
C:\>
C:\>
C:\>
C:\>
C:\>
C:\>ping 192.168.0.1

Pinging 192.168.0.1 with 32 bytes of data:

Reply from 192.168.0.1: bytes=32 time=24ms TTL=154
Reply from 192.168.0.1: bytes=32 time=7ms TTL=154
Reply from 192.168.0.1: bytes=32 time=9ms TTL=154
Reply from 192.168.0.1: bytes=32 time=7ms TTL=154

Ping statistics for 192.168.0.1:
    Packets: Sent = 4, Received = 4, Lost = 0 (0% loss),
Approximate round trip times in milli-seconds:
    Minimum = 7ms, Maximum = 24ms, Average = 11ms

C:\>
```

By default, the NetScreen device will send five ICMP echo requests of 100 bytes each with a two second timeout. Advanced settings can also be included on the command line:

```
ping <address> from <interface name>
ping <address> count <number of pings to send>
```

Figure 14.2 shows an example of using the ping command in ScreenOS 5.

Figure 14.2 Ping Command in ScreenOS-5

```
c:\ Telnet 192.168.0.3                                           _ □ ×
ns5gt->
ns5gt-> ping 192.168.0.1
Type escape sequence to abort

Sending 5, 100-byte ICMP Echos to 192.168.0.1, timeout is 2 seconds
!!!!!
Success Rate is 100 percent (5/5), round-trip time min/avg/max=2/2/2 ms
ns5gt-> ping 192.168.0.5
Type escape sequence to abort

Sending 5, 100-byte ICMP Echos to 192.168.0.5, timeout is 2 seconds
.....
Success Rate is 0 percent (0/5),
ns5gt-> ping
Target IP address:192.168.0.1
Repeat count [5]:
Datagram size [100]:
Timeout in seconds[2]:
Source interface:
Type escape sequence to abort

Sending 5, 100-byte ICMP Echos to 192.168.0.1, timeout is 2 seconds
!!!!!
Success Rate is 100 percent (5/5), round-trip time min/avg/max=2/2/3 ms
ns5gt->
```

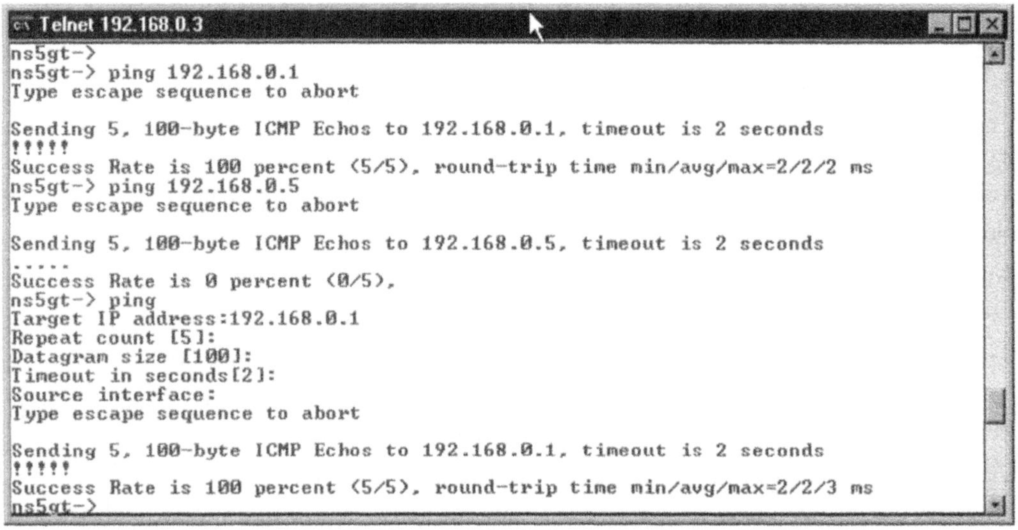

Keep in mind the results of ping are not always to be trusted. Some network traffic does not pass ping traffic and might even change the results of the command.

Traceroute

The **traceroute** command is useful to troubleshoot multi-hop routing. The traceroute command uses the TTL (Time to Live) field of the IP protocol in order to get an ICMP TIME_EXCEEDED response from each gateway the packet goes through to get to the destination. Figure 14.3 shows an example of traceroute in ScreenOS.

Figure 14.3 Traceroute in ScreenOS

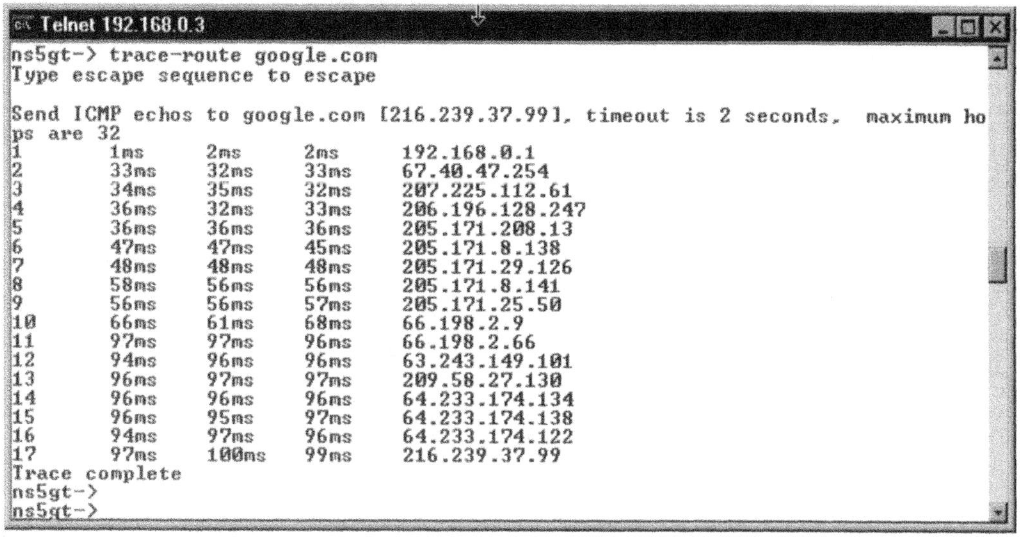

```
Telnet 192.168.0.3                                           _ □ ×
ns5gt-> trace-route google.com
Type escape sequence to escape

Send ICMP echos to google.com [216.239.37.99], timeout is 2 seconds,  maximum ho
ps are 32
1       1ms     2ms     2ms     192.168.0.1
2       33ms    32ms    33ms    67.40.47.254
3       34ms    35ms    32ms    207.225.112.61
4       36ms    32ms    33ms    206.196.128.247
5       36ms    36ms    36ms    205.171.208.13
6       47ms    47ms    45ms    205.171.8.138
7       48ms    48ms    48ms    205.171.29.126
8       58ms    56ms    56ms    205.171.8.141
9       56ms    56ms    57ms    205.171.25.50
10      66ms    61ms    68ms    66.198.2.9
11      97ms    97ms    96ms    66.198.2.66
12      94ms    96ms    96ms    63.243.149.101
13      96ms    97ms    97ms    209.58.27.130
14      96ms    96ms    96ms    64.233.174.134
15      96ms    95ms    97ms    64.233.174.138
16      94ms    97ms    96ms    64.233.174.122
17      97ms    100ms   99ms    216.239.37.99
Trace complete
ns5gt->
ns5gt->
```

```
ns5gt-> trace-route 192.168.0.1

Type escape sequence to escape


Send ICMP echos to 192.168.0.1, timeout is 2 seconds,   maximum hops are 32

1          67ms      2ms        3ms        192.168.0.1

Trace complete
```

Traceroute results should also be taken with a grain of salt. Since traceroute uses TTL fields in the packets, any devices that do not respond to that field will not return valid data.

Get Session

The **get session** command will show all current established sessions going through the NetScreen device. If an entry exists in the session table, the connection has passed through the routing table and the policy successfully.

Each session entry has three lines of information. The first line contains the policy rule number, which can be viewed by the **get policy** command. The **time** entry shows idle time and resets every time traffic goes through the firewall. Figure 14.4 illustrates these points.

Figure 14.4 Get Session in ScreenOS

```
Telnet 192.168.0.3                                                    _ □ ×
ns5gt->
ns5gt->
ns5gt->
ns5gt->
ns5gt->
ns5gt->
ns5gt-> get session
alloc 3/max 2064, alloc failed 0, mcast alloc 0, di alloc failed 0
id 223/s**,vsys 0,flag 00000040/0080/21,policy 320002,time 180, dip 0
  1(0601):192.168.0.2/42541->192.168.0.3/23,6,0011240349f8,3,vlan 0,tun 0,vsd 0,r
oute 3
  3(0010):192.168.0.2/42541<-192.168.0.3/23,6,000000000000,4,vlan 0,tun 0,vsd 0,r
oute 0
id 293/s**,vsys 0,flag 00000050/0080/21,policy 320002,time 1, dip 0
  1(0001):192.168.0.2/8704->192.168.0.3/42543,1,0011240349f8,3,vlan 0,tun 0,vsd 0
,route 3
  3(0010):192.168.0.2/8704<-192.168.0.3/42543,1,000000000000,4,vlan 0,tun 0,vsd 0
,route 0
id 294/s**,vsys 0,flag 00000050/0080/21,policy 320002,time 1, dip 0
  1(0001):192.168.0.2/8960->192.168.0.3/42543,1,0011240349f8,3,vlan 0,tun 0,vsd 0
,route 3
  3(0010):192.168.0.2/8960<-192.168.0.3/42543,1,000000000000,4,vlan 0,vsd 0
,route 0
Total 3 sessions shown
ns5gt->
```

Get Policy

The **get policy** command will display the current NetScreen policy. This command is useful as a reference to see which **policy ID** is assigned to each rule. Pay attention to the **From** and **To** fields, which indicate which zones each policy crosses, as shown in Figure 14.5.

Figure 14.5 Get Policy in ScreenOS

```
Telnet 192.168.0.3                                                    _ □ ×
ns5gt->
ns5gt->
ns5gt->
ns5gt->
ns5gt->
ns5gt->
ns5gt->
ns5gt->
ns5gt->
ns5gt->
ns5gt->
ns5gt->
ns5gt->
ns5gt->
ns5gt->
ns5gt->
ns5gt->
ns5gt->
ns5gt-> get policy
Total regular policies 1, Default deny.
    ID From      To       Src-address  Dst-address  Service        Action S
tate    ASTLCB
    1 Trust     Untrust   Any          Any          ANY            Permit e
nabled ---X-X
ns5gt->
```

Get Route

The **get route** command shows the current NetScreen routing table. There is a separate routing table for each virtual router. In the example below (Figure 14.6), there are no routes for the untrust-vr, which is the default configuration. Make sure you differentiate which routes are static and which routes are added by a routing protocol.

Figure 14.6 Get Route in ScreenOS

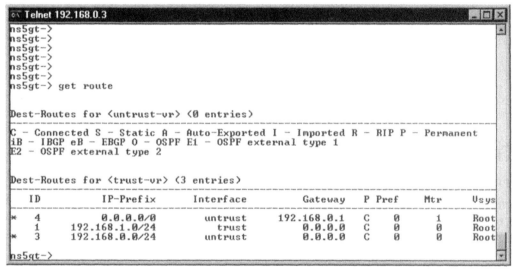

Get Interface

The **get interface** command shows detailed interface statistics. This command (shown in Figure 14.7) is useful to see which zone an interface is in and which hardware MAC (Media Access Control) address is assigned to each interface.

Figure 14.7 Get Interface in ScreenOS

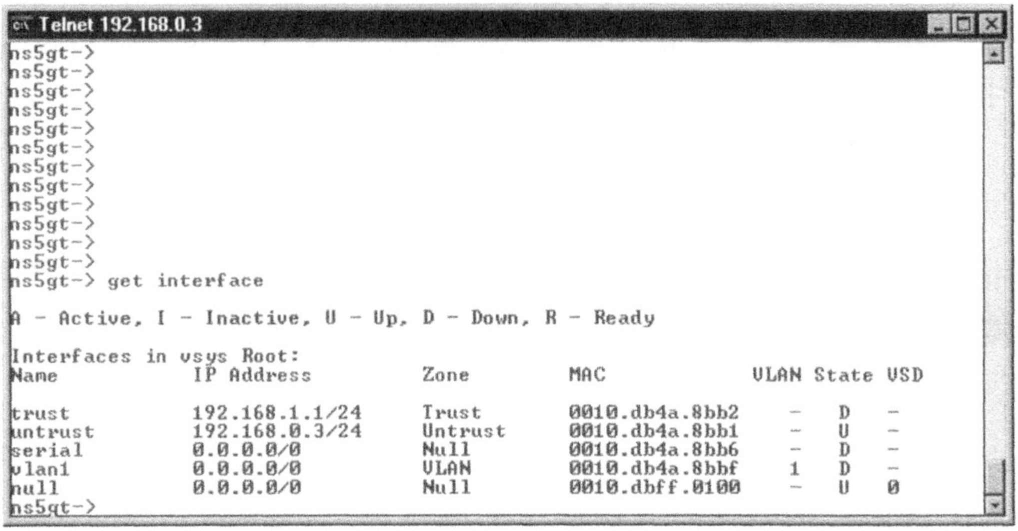

```
Telnet 192.168.0.3                                                    _ □ X
ns5gt->
ns5gt->
ns5gt->
ns5gt->
ns5gt->
ns5gt->
ns5gt->
ns5gt->
ns5gt->
ns5gt->
ns5gt->
ns5gt->
ns5gt-> get interface

A - Active, I - Inactive, U - Up, D - Down, R - Ready

Interfaces in vsys Root:
Name          IP Address        Zone       MAC             VLAN State VSD

trust         192.168.1.1/24    Trust      0010.db4a.8bb2   -   D   -
untrust       192.168.0.3/24    Untrust    0010.db4a.8bb1   -   U   -
serial        0.0.0.0/0         Null       0010.db4a.8bb6   -   D   -
vlan1         0.0.0.0/0         VLAN       0010.db4a.8bbf   1   D   -
null          0.0.0.0/0         Null       0010.dbff.0100   -   U   0
ns5gt->
```

Get ARP

The ARP (Address Resolution Protocol) table of the NetScreen firewall can be
viewed by using the **get arp** command. This can be useful when troubleshooting
OSI layer 1 and layer 2 issues. Figure 14.8 shows the ARP table of the NetScreen
firewall.

Figure 14.8 Get ARP in ScreenOS

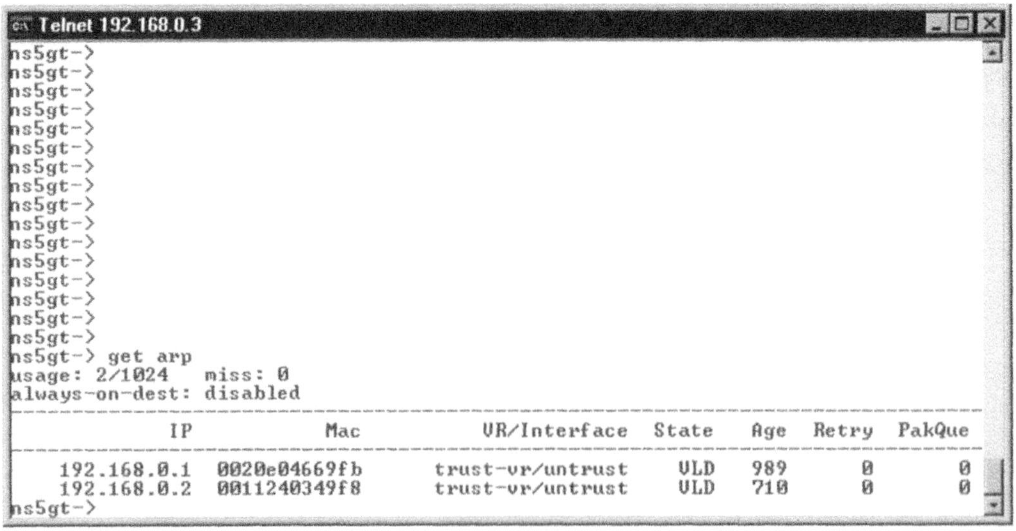

```
Telnet 192.168.0.3                                                    _ □ X
ns5gt->
ns5gt->
ns5gt->
ns5gt->
ns5gt->
ns5gt->
ns5gt->
ns5gt->
ns5gt->
ns5gt->
ns5gt->
ns5gt->
ns5gt->
ns5gt->
ns5gt->
ns5gt-> get arp
usage: 2/1024    miss: 0
always-on-dest: disabled
-------------------------------------------------------------------------
          IP          Mac            VR/Interface    State  Age  Retry PakQue
-------------------------------------------------------------------------
    192.168.0.1  0020e04669fb    trust-vr/untrust    VLD    989    0     0
    192.168.0.2  0011240349f8    trust-vr/untrust    VLD    710    0     0
ns5gt->
```

www.syngress.com

Get System

The **get system** command gives you several important pieces of information. Use this command to get an overview of your firewall and the setting for each interface. On an unknown firewall, this should be the first command you use.

- **Serial Number** This can be used to reset the device to the factory defaults. Use the serial number as the username and password when logging in on the serial interface. Be aware this will also wipe out any configuration changes you have made.

- **Software Version** The software version of the ScreenOS device in running memory.

- **Date and Time** of the NetScreen device.

- **Total Device Resets** Tracks the total number of asset recovery resets. This number counts the number of times the system has been reset to the factory defaults.

- **User Name** The username of the current user.

Debug

The debug utility in ScreenOS is a powerful troubleshooting tool that allows you to track sessions going through the NetScreen firewall. The firewall has a memory buffer set aside for the debug system. Packets can be captured in this memory for inspection. Here is a typical usage of the debug system:

- **debug flow basic** Enables the debugging system of the NetScreen firewall.

- **clear db** Clears the debug memory buffer.

- **Test network traffic** This can include any of the previous troubleshooting commands.

- **undebug all** Turns off the debug memory dump.

- **get dbuf stream** Displays the output for analysis.

A filter can also be put into place to limit what traffic gets sent to the debug buffer. The command **set ffilter** allows you to set the type of traffic that will be collected. The following filters are available:

- **dst-ip** Destination IP address
- **dst-port** Destination port
- **ip-proto** Internet Protocol number
- **src-ip** Source IP address
- **src-port** Source port

If multiple filters are specified in the **set ffilter** command, the filter will only collect traffic that matches all of the filters specified. The **set ffilter** command can be executed multiple times and traffic will be collected if it matches any of the filters. For example, to filter all tcp traffic from 192.168.0.1 to 10.1.1.1 issue the following command:

```
ns5gt-> set ffilter src-ip 192.168.0.1 dst-ip 10.1.1.1 ip-proto 6
```

To view current filters, use the **get ffilter** command. Each filter in place has an ID number to identify it. To remove a filter use the **unset ffilter** command followed by the ID number of the filter to be deleted.

Snoop

Snoop is a full packet sniffer. The output of **snoop** goes into the same memory buffer that debug sends to. The biggest difference between debug and snoop is that snoop can dump the actual contents of the packets to the memory buffer. Snoop output is more difficult to read than debug output and it is typically used when the contents of the packets need to be analyzed. Here are the commands for using snoop:

- **snoop** Starts the snoop capture.
- **snoop info** Displays current snoop status.
- **snoop detail** Enables full packet logging. This will log the full contents of the packets.
- **snoop off** Turns off the snoop capture.
- **snoop filter** Allows you to filter what gets captured. Uses syntax similar to that used for debug filtering.
- **clear db** Clears the debug memory buffer.
- **get dbuf stream** Displays the output for analysis.

Putting It All Together

When troubleshooting the NetScreen firewall, use any of the above commands necessary to resolve the issue. When a packet arrives at an interface of the firewall the following things happen.

1. The packet arrives at the NetScreen firewall.

2. The packet goes through a 'sanity check' to make sure it is not corrupt.

3. A session lookup is performed. If the packet is part of an existing session, it follows the rest of the packets in the same session.

4. The packet is routed, based on the routing table and zones.

5. The packet is checked against the firewall policy.

6. The ARP cache is referenced.

7. A session is created if one does not exist and the packet is forwarded.

Notice that the session is not created until the packet passes through the routing table and the firewall policy.

Network Troubleshooting

Before you blame the firewall, you need to determine whether or not the firewall is actually the root of the problem. There are several tools available for network troubleshooting. The first thing you will need is a decent packet sniffer. A packet sniffer is a network analyzer that will grab packets on the network and sometimes display them in a readable format. Ethereal (www.ethereal.com) is the best free sniffer available and will do the job nicely.

Make sure the firewall can ping the default gateway. The firewall should also be able to ping something on the Internet as well as internal resources. If the firewall cannot reach a host, then it will be difficult for a packet to reach it after going through the firewall, unless there is another firewall blocking the traffic from the firewall itself.

Debugging the NetScreen Device

When debugging traffic flowing through the NetScreen device, we need to keep in mind we might have more than one virtual router (VR) involved. ScreenOS has two VRs by default: a *trust-vr* and an *untrust-vr*. Each virtual router has its own routing table. By default, all of the zones, with the exception of the *null zone*, are associated with the trust-vr.

Let's start off with a NetScreen firewall with one virtual router in use, which is the default. Use the **get route** command to display the routing table. Make sure your added route belongs to the trust-vr. An asterisk (★) will appear next to all routes in use. The most common problems are due to incorrect routing. The **debug flow basic** command is useful when troubleshooting issues with routing. Use it if you cannot figure out where the packets are going. Ask yourself the following questions:

- Do you have a default route? A default route is a route to 0.0.0.0

- Is your default route going to the correct address and interface?

- Do you have a route to the network you are trying to get to? Do you need one?

- Is the added route going to the right interface?

When troubleshooting issues with multiple virtual routers, it is important to remember each virtual router needs a default gateway. For example, when using the **get route** command, look for a default route to the untrust-vr in the trust-vr. Also pay attention to added routes from routing protocols such as OSPF (Open Shortest Path First) and RIP (Routing Information Protocol). Are you getting OSPF routes added to the wrong virtual router?

Once the routing is taken care of, the next thing to look at is the policies. Use the command get policy to make sure your packets are going to the correct zone based on the policy. Take note of the policy ID number so you can reference it when using the debug command if needed. Intra-zone blocking may be enabled, which requires a policy for traffic to pass. You can see if this setting is enabled by looking at the zone details. For example, get zone trust.

You can also use the **get policy global** command to see if any global policies are getting in the way. The global zone is referenced if the packets pass through all the rules of the specific zone policy or there happen to be no rules in the specific zone policy. Adding a global zone rule that logs all dropped traffic can help the troubleshooting process.

Every packet that goes through the NetScreen firewall follows a path based on internal decisions that are, in turn, based on the contents of the packet and where it came from. When a packet arrives at an interface of the NetScreen firewall, the firewall first checks to see if the packet it part of an existing session. If it is, the packet is forwarded out the pre-determined interface. If the packet is not part of an existing session, then the packet is processed through the routing table. If the packet is not routable, it is dropped. If it is routable, a zone lookup is performed. If the packet does not traverse a zone, it is forwarded to its destination and added to the session table. If the packet does cross a zone, a policy lookup is done. Then the packet is either dropped, or added to the session table and forwarded. This is a simplified description of what happens when a packet is inspected, but it helps for troubleshooting purposes. Figure 14.9 shows a flowchart of the process that the NetScreen firewall follows with each packet that arrives at an interface.

Figure 14.9 NetScreen Traffic Process Flowchart

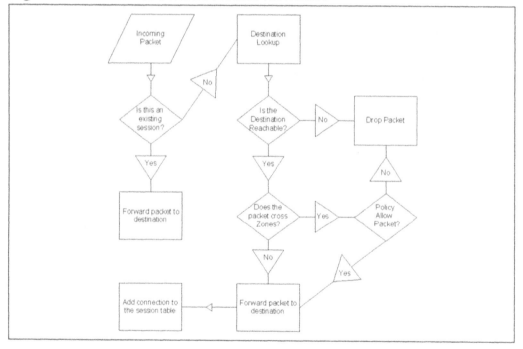

Damage & Defense...

Deep Inspection

Deep Inspection (DI) allows the NetScreen firewall to inspect layer 7 data in packets that transverse the firewall. Keep your DI signatures up to date to make sure you are making the best of this feature. DI signatures can be configured to automatically update.

DI does not replace a full-blown Intrusion Prevention System (IPS). A properly secured network should be multilayered and have security measures at every hop through the network. Make sure your IPS system is monitoring every segment of your network.

Debugging NAT

Troubleshooting Network Address Translation (NAT) requires a deep understanding of the network infrastructure. There are two types of NAT in the NetScreen firewall: *policy-based* and *interface-based*.

- **Interface-based NAT** is only applicable for trust zones to untrust zones. Interface-based NAT is configured by accessing **Network | Interfaces** in the WebUI. This method of translation is also referred to as *hide NAT*. Trust zone interfaces are in this mode by default. Interface-based NAT works by translating the source port of the packets to the egress interface IP address and changing the source port of the packets to keep track of the return traffic.

- **Policy-based NAT-src** is configured in the **Policies** section of the WebUI. Policy-based NAT-src is the most configurable way to setup address translation. There is no limitation to which zones can use policy-based NAT-src. Dynamic IP pools (DIPs) can be used using this method.

You can tell if the firewall is in interface-based NAT mode by typing **get config** and looking for the text, "System in NAT/route mode". The interface in NAT mode will say "mode nat". Use the **get session** and the **debug log** commands to troubleshoot issues with all types of NAT. When using DIP pools, the command **get dip** will show the status of all of the ip addresses available in the pool.

Here are common problems with source address translation:

- Invalid DIP address range
- Missing DIP pool

Here are common problems with destination address translation:

- VIP (Virtual IP) not mapped to correct internal host
- Route in the wrong zone
- Missing inbound policy

Debugging VPNs

Troubleshooting Virtual Private Networks can be easy if the right steps are followed. With NetScreen firewalls, there are actually two different types of VPNs. Policy-based VPNs are based on rules in the **Policies** page of firewall. Route-based VPNs are based on *tunnel* interfaces. Route-based VPNs can also have policies on top of the tunnel interfaces blocking certain types of traffic through the tunnel.

When troubleshooting VPNs, the most important thing to remember is that both ends of the VPN have to share the same encryption settings. Below is a listing of which VPN settings must be set the same on both ends of the tunnel. These settings are for both route-based and policy-based VPNs.

- Phase 1 key management protocol, for example, IKE.
- Phase 1 encryption algorithm to encrypt the key, for example, DES, 3DES, AES, or CAST.
- Phase 1 hash/authentication algorithm, for example, SHA1 or MD5.
- Phase 1 authentication, for example, PRE-SHARED SECRET or CERTIFICATE.
- Phase 1 mode, for example, MAIN or AGGRESSIVE.
- Phase 2 encryption algorithm to encrypt the data, for example, DES, 3DES, AES, or CAST.
- Phase 2 hash/authentication algorithm, for example, SHA1 or MD5.

- Phase 2 Perfect Forward Secrecy, for example, YES-GROUP1, YES-GROUP2, YES-GROUP5, or NO.

- Outgoing interface of the VPN tunnel.

- Encryption domain.

The Event log contains VPN events. When troubleshooting a VPN on a NetScreen firewall, you will want to keep an eye on the Event log for PKI (Public-key infrastructure) events. There are a couple of debug commands that are also useful during troubleshooting Phase 1 issues:

- **get ike cookie** This will display all completed Phase 1 negotiations.

- **debug flow basic** This will enable debugging.

- **debug ike** This will enable detailed VPN debug logs.

- **clear ike** This will force a VPN tunnel to renegotiate. It will clear Phase 1 and Phase 2 for the specified tunnel.

Here are troubleshooting commands useful for Phase 2 issues:

- **get sa active** This will display all completed Phase 2 negotiations.

- **unset ike policy-checking** This will tell the firewall to ignore the policy and allow all routed traffic through the VPN.

Policy-based VPN

Here are several common issues with policy-based VPNs:

- Policies are in the wrong order. Remember the rule base is parsed from top to bottom.

- Missing a rule in the other direction. VPN policies require a rule to allow inbound as well as outbound traffic.

- Wrong VPN tunnel is selected. Double-check the address book entries and the VPN tunnel selected.

- Policy is in the wrong zone. Make sure the traffic going into the VPN is allowed by a policy.

Route-based VPN

Troubleshooting route-based VPNs requires special attention to the routing table of the firewall. Since policies are optional, we should also make sure a policy is not blocking our VPN traffic. Here are several common issues with route-based VPNs:

- Route is not in place to send traffic to the tunnel interface.
- Policy is in place blocking VPN traffic.
- Policy is not in place when tunnel interface is not in the same zone as the originating traffic.

Debugging NSRP

The NetScreen Redundancy Protocol provides redundancy and failover functionality for NetScreen firewalls. NSRP allows for stateful failover, which means that connection will not be broken when the failover occurs. On some of the smaller NetScreen firewalls, such at the 5GT and the 25, this failover is not stateful, which is known as H/A Lite. A dedicated link is required for the session table to be synchronized. When troubleshooting NSRP use the following commands:

- **get nsrp cluster** Displays the cluster information.
- **get nsrp monitor** Displays a list of monitored interfaces.
- **get nsrp vsd id 0** Displays Virtual Security Device number 0.
- **exec nsrp sync global-config check-sum** Will tell you if the cluster members are synchronized.
- **exec nsrp sync global save** Will synchronize the configuration between cluster members; a reboot is necessary to complete the update.

There are several factors that can contribute to a slow failover. Auto-negotiation of the ports the firewall is plugged into should be manually set. The time it takes to negotiate the port speed and duplex might mean downtime. The heartbeat interval can be shortened. The default heartbeat interval is 1000ms, but it can be set as low as 200ms. Also keep in mind that a truly redundant configuration requires multiple switches, routers, and network connections.

Debugging Traffic Shaping

The NetScreen firewall has the ability to limit the bandwidth packet use on a per policy basis. If incorrectly configured, this can decrease the performance of the firewall significantly. When using traffic shaping, packets are placed into queues and released based on the shaping rules. Traffic shaping rules consist of guaranteed bandwidth, maximum bandwidth, and priority settings.

Each interface has a *traffic bandwidth* setting. To successfully use traffic shaping, this bandwidth setting should be configured for the most efficient bandwidth. Keep in mind these settings are full duplex. If you set a rule to allow 1500Kbps in one direction, the firewall will allow 1500Kbps in the reverse direction.

- **Guaranteed Bandwidth** reserves bandwidth in a policy rule.

- **Maximum Bandwidth** limits the bandwidth used in a policy rule.

- **Priority** settings allow you to give certain traffic higher priority over other traffic.

By default, all traffic is set to the lowest priority queue. Take note of the guaranteed bandwidth settings on your rules, as they cannot exceed the traffic bandwidth of the interface the traffic is flowing out of. You can get the traffic shaping rules from a policy using the **get policy id** command (see Figure 14.10).

Figure 14.10 Get Policy ID in ScreenOS

```
Telnet 192.168.0.3                                                    _ □ X
ns5gt->
ns5gt->
ns5gt->
ns5gt-> get policy
Total regular policies 1, Default deny.
    ID From       To       Src-address  Dst-address  Service       Action S
tate    ASTLCB
     1 Trust      Untrust  Any          Any          ANY           Permit e
nabled ---~X-X
ns5gt->
ns5gt->
ns5gt-> get policy id 1
name:"none" (id 1), zone Trust -> Untrust,action Permit, status "enabled"
src "Any", dst "Any", serv "ANY"
Policies on this vpn tunnel: 0
nat off, url filtering : disabled
vpn unknown vpn, policy flag 0000, session backup: on
traffic shapping off, scheduler n/a, serv flag 00
log yes, log count 0, alert no, counter no(0) byte rate(sec/min) 0/0
total octets 74722, counter(session/packet/octet) 0/0/0
priority 7, diffserv marking Off
tadapter: state off, gbw/mbw 0/-1
No Authentication
No User, User Group or Group expression set
ns5gt->
```

Notes from the Underground…

Advanced Syslog

As you know, the NetScreen firewall generates syslog messages. One of the best things you can do if you do not have a Netscreen Security Manager (NSM) server is to setup a syslog server to collect logs from your firewall.

There are several very good, free syslog filtering systems available. If you search for syslog on Freshmeat.net (http://freshmeat.net), you will find over 100 different free software products that can make your firewall administration much easier. I recommend that you install an Apache/PHP front end to the syslog server so you can easily search through the logs, sort them, and generate reports for those management types.

A dedicated syslog server should be locked down tight. This server can accept syslog from any servers you point to it. Typically this server should only answer on the syslog port, HTTPS port for reports, and possibly SSH for administration.

NetScreen Logging

The NetScreen firewalls have the ability to log network traffic. Looking at these logs can help the troubleshooting process immensely. Logs can be distributed via the following methods:

- **Console** Some log messages are sent to the console (serial, SSH, or Telnet).

- **Internal** The firewall can store a limited amount of logs for real-time troubleshooting.

- **E-mail** The NetScreen firewall can be set up to e-mail syslog-generated log files.

- **SNMP** Simple Network Monitoring Protocol will allow the NetScreen device to alert an SNMP management system.

- **Syslog** The UNIX standard for log messages.

- **WebTrends** A third-party log analyzer.

- **NSM** NetScreen Security Manager is a management system for NetScreen firewalls.

Traffic

Logging can be enabled on a per rule basis. You can access specific logs for a rule by clicking on the log icon in the policy editor. The syslog can output all of the traffic logs to a centralized syslog server. The traffic log has the following fields:

- Date/Time
- Source Address/Port
- Destination Address/Port
- Translated Source Address/Port
- Translated Destination Address/Port
- Service
- Duration
- Bytes Sent
- Bytes Received

Self

Logs sent to the NetScreen firewall itself are referred to as *self logs*. These logs are very similar to the traffic logs. The self log has the following fields:

- Date/Time
- Source Address/Port
- Destination Address/Port
- Duration
- Service

Event

Event logs are system logs generated when the NetScreen firewall performs or does not perform a function. This log is useful to see when users log into the WebUI or the status of PKI certificates. The event log has the following fields:

- Date/Time
- Level (the severity level of the event, including Emergency, Alert, Critical, Error, Warning, Notification, Information, and Debugging)
- Description

Summary

In this chapter we covered various ways to troubleshoot network traffic passing through the NetScreen firewall. We covered the path a packet makes as it goes through the firewall, various tools at our disposal, and tips for troubleshooting different functions available through ScreenOS.

There are several troubleshooting tools built into ScreenOS. Ping allows us to test connectivity. Traceroute allows us to find the path a packet takes through a network. Various **get** commands on the CLI show us internal tables in memory. ScreenOS also has a complete debugging system that allows us to view what happens to a packet as it goes through the firewall step by step. Snoop allows us to view the entire content of the packets that transverse the firewall.

The NetScreen firewall is unique in that it can have virtual routers. Troubleshooting these routers can be easy as long as we note which settings apply to which virtual routers. Each interface on the firewall belongs to one zone. Each zone on the firewall belongs to a virtual router. Policies determine what happens when a packet needs to cross a zone. Intra-zone blocking will force packets going to and from the same zone to go through a policy lookup.

Troubleshooting VPNs requires configuration settings to agree on both ends of the VPN. Most VPN issues are due to a misconfiguration of the VPN settings on one end of the tunnel. The outgoing interface of the VPN tunnel must be set in order for the VPN to work properly.

NSRP is the NetScreen method of high availability. The heartbeat interval of the cluster can be tweaked to improve failover performance. NetScreen firewalls support traffic prioritization. When troubleshooting traffic shaping, make sure the guaranteed bandwidth of the policy does not exceed the maximum bandwidth of the outgoing interface.

The firewall has a complete and detailed logging system. Traffic logs contain detailed logs of network traffic going through the firewall. Self logs contain detailed logs of traffic destined to the firewall itself. Event logs contain system logs and alerts.

Solutions Fast Track

Troubleshooting Tools

☑ **ping** is a connectivity tool.

☑ **traceroute** verifies the path the packets are taking.

624
Chapter 14 • Troubleshooting the NetScreen Firewall

☑ **get session** allows you to view the session table in real time.

☑ **get policy** allows you to view the rule base of the firewall.

☑ **get route** allows you to view the routing table.

☑ **get interface** allows you to view the interfaces of the firewall.

☑ **get arp** allows you to view the ARP table of the firewall.

☑ **get system** allows you to view the status of the firewall and various settings.

☑ **debug** can be used to follow traffic through the firewall.

☑ **snoop** performs a detail packet capture.

Network Troubleshooting

☑ Use packet sniffers in your network to assist with troubleshooting.

☑ Determine if the packets are even reaching the firewall interface.

Debugging the NetScreen Device

☑ Pay attention to the routing table.

☑ Pay attention to zone settings and policy settings.

Debugging VPNs

☑ Verify that the Phase 1 and Phase 2 settings are the same on both ends of the VPN tunnel.

☑ Verify that the outgoing interface of the VPN is set correctly.

☑ Verify that VPN traffic is routed to the tunnel interface for route-based VPNs.

☑ Verify that VPN policies are in place with correct address book entries for policy-based VPNs.

Debugging NSRP

☑ The **exec nsrp sync global-config check-sum** command will tell you if the cluster members are synchronized.

☑ Shorten the heartbeat interval if the firewalls are not failing over as quickly as you want them to.

☑ Verify that the speed and the duplex of the ports the firewall is plugged into are manually set.

Debugging Traffic Shaping

☑ Verify that each interface has its traffic bandwidth set.

☑ Make sure the guaranteed bandwidth settings do not exceed the traffic bandwidth for the interface.

NetScreen Logging

☑ Traffic logs contain logs of network traffic for rules with logging enabled.

☑ Self logs contain logs of network traffic terminated at the firewall.

☑ Event logs contain system events of the firewall.

Frequently Asked Questions

The following Frequently Asked Questions, answered by the authors of this book, are designed to both measure your understanding of the concepts presented in this chapter and to assist you with real-life implementation of these concepts. To have your questions about this chapter answered by the author, browse to **www.syngress.com/solutions** and click on the **"Ask the Author"** form. You will also gain access to thousands of other FAQs at ITFAQnet.com.

Q: What command is used to view the full contents of packets?

A: The **snoop** command will dump the entire contents of the packets.

Q: How are the default routes usually configured when using two virtual routers?

A: One zone has a default gateway of the other zone. The other zone has a default gateway of the internet router.

Q: What commands would typically you use to generate a debug log?

A: First **debug flow basic** would enable the debug log. **undebug all** will stop logging. **get dbuf stream** will display the results.

Q: How would you limit what gets logged with **debug** or **snoop**?

A: The **set ffilter** command allows you to set filters on what gets placed into the debug log.

Q: What commands would you use to verify Phase 1 and Phase 2 of a VPN tunnel were completed?

A: The command **get ike cookie** lists Phase 1 completions and **get sa active** lists Phase 2 completions.

Q: What is intra-zone blocking?

A: Intra-zone blocking blocks traffic within the zone unless there is a policy that allows the traffic to pass. By default intra-zone blocking is disabled.

## Chapter 15

Enterprise NetScreen Management

Solutions in this Chapter:

- Alternative Methods for Monitoring NetScreen Devices
- NetScreen Security Manager

- ☑ Summary
- ☑ Solutions Fast Track
- ☑ Frequently Asked Questions

Introduction

Now that you are an expert on NetScreen firewalls, you will probably want to start deploying these devices within your organization. As you start configuring and placing each firewall, you may start to think that this is a lot of work for one person and that there must be a better way. Tracking logs, configurations changes, VPNs (virtual private networks), and whether a device is properly functioning can be an overwhelming task for an administrator. Fortunately, there are options available to simplify this task. NetScreen devices provide support for tools like Syslog and SNMP (Simple Network Management Protocol). In addition, Juniper has developed a product called NetScreen Security Manager that provides a centralized method to manage and administer your firewalls across the distributed enterprise. NetScreen Security Manager (NSM) provides the ability to manage up to 1,000 devices from a single location. This includes the hardware configuration, policies, VPNs, logging, troubleshooting, and more.

Alternative Methods for Monitoring NetScreen Devices

Before we start to discuss NSM, it's important to understand the other options available to us from a monitoring perspective. If NSM is not an option for your organization, each firewall provides capability to monitor through the use of tools like Syslog, SNMP, Webtrends, or e-mail.

Syslog

Syslog is an industry standard and typically low-cost method used for capturing log files from devices, servers, or applications. Most often, Syslog is a service running on a UNIX host that has the capability to capture and store logging data that is sent to it over a network connection. Syslog is not included with Windows, but there options available. Since NetScreen firewall devices to not contain a hard drive, memory is allocated for storing logs. Once the memory fills up, newer entries overwrite the older entries. Administrators are typically required to keep this information for several reasons, among those being legal purposes, trending and usage reports, and troubleshooting. This is where Syslog comes in. NetScreen firewalls can be configured to send their logging data to a remote Syslog server.

NetScreen devices operate over the standard Syslog UDP (User Datagram Protocol) port 514. The Sylog protocol provides the ability to categorize traffic through what are referred to as *facilities*. NetScreen firewalls make use of two facilities, called *normal* and *security*. Within the normal and security facilities, logs can be sent to one of nine locations, Local0 through Local7 and Auth/Sec. A single firewall device can be configured to send logs to up to four Syslog servers. The following illustration (Figure 15.1) displays the configuration screen from the WebUI, which can be reached by accessing **Configuration | Report Settings | Syslog**.

Figure 15.1 Syslog Configuration

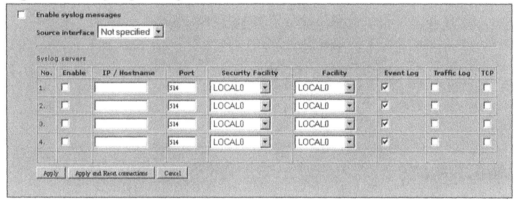

- **Enable Syslog messages** Turns on the Syslog capability of the NetScreen firewall.

- **Source Interface** Select the interface from where Syslog messages will be sent, such as **ethernet1**.

- **Syslog Servers**
  - **Enable** Turns on logging for Syslog servers 1 through 4.
  - **IP/Hostname** The IP (Internet Protocol) address or DNS (Domain Name Service) name of the Syslog server.
  - **Port** Override the default port, which is UDP port 514.
  - **Security Facility** The logging location within Syslog for the security facility.
  - **Facility** The logging location within Syslog for the normal facility.

- ■ **Event Log** Turns on event logging to the Syslog server.

- ■ **Traffic Log** Turns on traffic logging to the Syslog server.

- ■ **TCP** – This option will send the logs using TCP (Transmission Control Protocol) as the transmit protocol rather than the default UDP. The Syslog server must support TCP-based Syslog in order for this to work.

The following is an example of configuring Syslog from the command line. In the example, we will add two Syslog servers and override the default port. Server 1 is 10.10.10.99/1015 while server 2 is 10.20.20.144/2015.

```
set syslog config 10.10.10.99 port 1015
set syslog config 10.10.10.99 log all
set syslog config 10.10.10.99 facilities local0 local0
set syslog config 10.20.20.144 port 2015
set syslog config 10.20.20.144 log all
set syslog config 10.20.20.144 facilities local0 local0
set syslog enable
save
```

WebTrends

WebTrends offers a product called WebTrends Firewall Suite that allows you to create customized reports from Syslog data. NetScreen firewall devices have support for this product built into ScreenOS. The WebTrends configuration screen in the WebUI can be accessed by selecting **Configuration | Report Settings | WebTrends** (Figure 15.2)

Figure 15.2 WebTrends Configuration

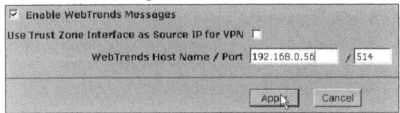

- **Enable WebTrends Messages** Enables WebTrends support in ScreenOS.

- **Use the Trust Zone Interface as Source IP for VPN** If data is being sent though a VPN tunnel to a server on the opposite end, enable this option.

- **WebTrends Host Name/Port** Hostname or address of the WebTrends server and the port.

The following commands will enable WebTrends support through the command line interface.

```
set webtrends enable
set webtrends host-name 192.168.0.56
set webtrends port 514
save
```

SNMP

SNMP is another industry standard for monitoring a network environment. An SNMP system is a fairly simple design that consists of a manager and agents. For a typical scenario, the administrator would configure an SNMP manager, like HP OpenView, to receive notifications, or traps, from the agent. The NetScreen agent supports SNMPv1 and v2c as well as Management Information Base II (MIB II). MIBs are a group of definitions that define properties within the managed device. In addition to the MIB-II information, Juniper provides private enterprise MIBs that can be loaded through a MIB browser on to the SNMP manager. The NetScreen MIBs can be downloaded from http://support.juniper.net.

NetScreen devices can be configured to support up to three SNMP communities, each of which can contain up to eight hosts. Communities can be granted read and read/write access. Due to security reasons, write access is only provided for sysName and sysContact in MIB-II, the rest are read-only. When defining SNMP hosts for the community, you can enter a specific host with a 32-bit subnet or you can define an entire subnet. Keep in mind that only specific hosts will be able to receive traps. Hosts defined as part of a subnet will not be able to receive traps, but will be able to query the device. MIB-II data or traps can be accessed through any physical interface. If virtual systems are being used, it's important to keep in mind that SNMP data cannot be implemented individually on each virtual system. Instead, it must be configured at the root virtual system.

In order to configure the SNMP report settings through the WebUI, select **Configuration | Report Settings | SNMP**. You will be presented with a screen similar to the one shown in Figure 15.3.

Figure 15.3 SNMP Agent Configuration

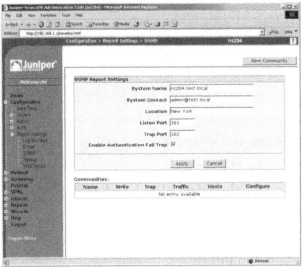

- **System Name** The host name of the device.

- **System Contact** The name of the administrator responsible for the device.

- **Location** The physical location of the device.

- **Listen Port** The UDP port that the NetScreen device listens on.

- **Trap Port** The UDP port that the NetScreen devices uses to send traps.

- **Enable Authentication Fail Trap** If this option is enabled, the NetScreen agent will send a trap when a device that is not a part of the community or with the wrong community string attempts to query the device.

Once the SNMP Report Settings have been configured, a community must be defined. Click the **New Community** button in order to enter this information. Figure 15.4 displays the community configuration screen.

Figure 15.4 SNMP Community Configuration Screen

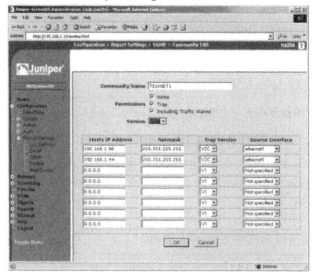

- **Community Name** The name of the SNMP group, or community, that has access to the device. Keep in mind that the community name acts like at password. Even though the name is sent over the network in clear text, it is still a good idea to keep this from being disclosed.

- **Permissions**

    - **Write** This provides write capability to the SNMP community data, sysName and sysContact.

    - **Trap** The agent will send traps to all hosts in the community set to receive them.

    - **Including Traffic Alarms** Sends traffic alarms to the SNMP community.

- **Version** You have the option to specify which version of SNMP to support, whether is it is v1, v2, or any.

- **Hosts IP Address/Netmask** By default, defined hosts are a 32-bit subnet mask. These specific hosts are able to query and receive traps from the NetScreen SNMP agent. If the host is defined as an entire subnet, for example 192.168.1.0/24, the NetScreen firewall will not generate traps to those hosts. However, hosts in the defined subnet will be able to query the device.

- **Trap Version** Must be specified for each host. If the supported version is specified, then the Trap Version cannot be different. In the example above, the supported version is specified as V2C. The traps for the hosts must also be defined as V2C. If the supported version was defined as ANY, then the administrator would have the option to select trap support for V1 or V2c for each defined host.

- **Source Interface** The interface from where the SNMP traps are sent.

The following example (Figure 15.5) displays a device with two communities defined. As you can see, the enabled options display a checkmark icon while disabled services display a red X. Each community is presented with its own name and respective hosts.

Figure 15.5 Defined SNMP Communities

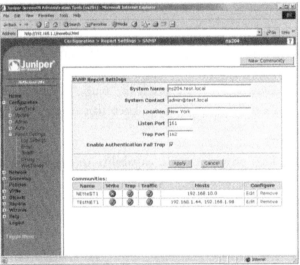

Finally, SNMP on the physical interface must be enabled as a management service. For this example, we will turn SNMP on for the Ethernet 1 interface (Figure 15.6).

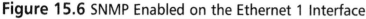

Figure 15.6 SNMP Enabled on the Ethernet 1 Interface

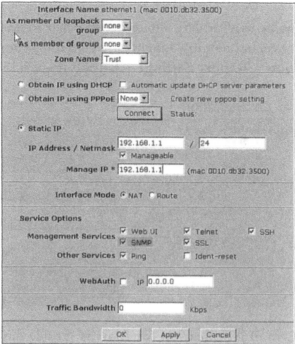

Taking the above examples from the WebUI, we can apply them to configuring SNMP through the command line interface.

```
set snmp name ns204.test.local
set snmp contact admin@test.local
set snmp location "New York"
set snmp port listen 161
set snmp port trap 162
set snmp auth-trap enable
set snmp community NEtteST1 Read-Only Trap-on  traffic version any
set snmp host NEtteST1 192.168.10.0 255.255.255.0 src-interface ethernet1
set snmp community TEstNET1 Read-Write Trap-on  traffic version v2c
set snmp host TEstNET1 192.168.1.98 255.255.255.255 src-interface ethernet1
trap v2
set snmp host TEstNET1 192.168.1.44 255.255.255.255 src-interface ethernet1
trap v2
set interface ethernet1 manage snmp
save
```

E-mail and Log Settings

E-mail messages can be used to alert administrators when an event is taking place on a NetScreen device. In order to configure e-mail settings through the WebUI, access **Configuration | Report Settings | E-mail** (Figure 15.7).

Figure 15.7 E-mail Configuration

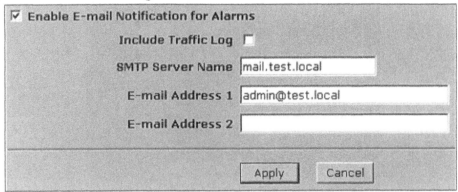

- **Enable E-mail Notification for Alarms** Enable this option to turn on support for e-mail alarms.

- **Include Traffic Log** Traffic log information can also be sent to an e-mail address.

- **SMTP Server Name** The hostname or address of the SMTP (Simple Mail Transfer Protocol) server that will be used to send alerts.

- **E-mail Address 1** and **2** Two addresses can be added for users to be notified.

The following example configures the options displayed in Figure 15.7 using the command line.

```
set admin mail alert
set admin mail server-name mail.test.local
set admin mail mail-addr1 admin@test.local
```

For all of the previous monitoring methods, as well as NetScreen Security Manager (which is discussed in the next section), administrators have the option to decide which types of alerts or events will be sent. The best way to understand these options would be to take a look at the log settings screen in the WebUI.

This can be accessed by going to **Configuration | Report Settings | Log Settings** (Figure 15.8).

Figure 15.8 Log Settings

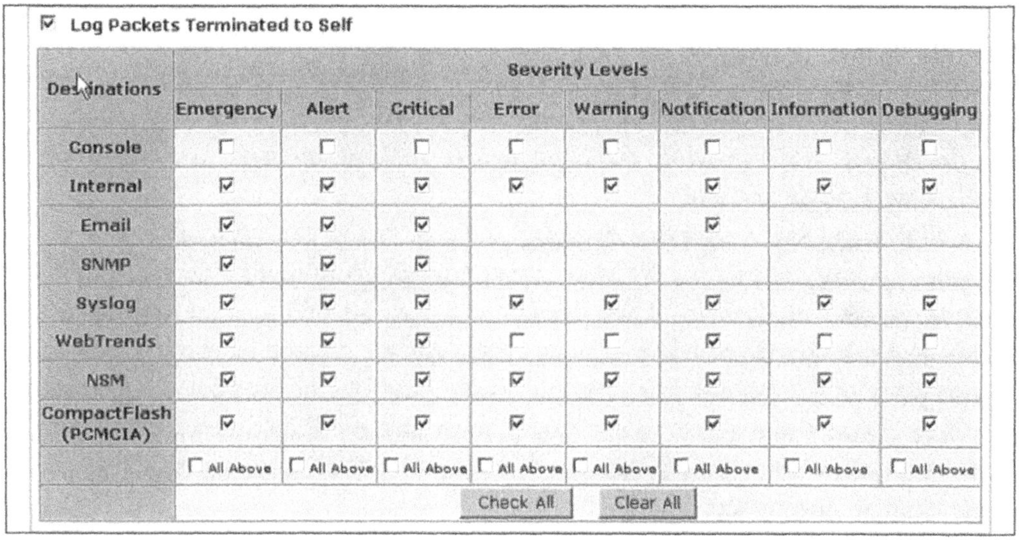

Destinations	Severity Levels							
	Emergency	Alert	Critical	Error	Warning	Notification	Information	Debugging
Console	☐	☐	☐	☐	☐	☐	☐	☐
Internal	☑	☑	☑	☑	☑	☑	☑	☑
Email	☑	☑	☑			☑		
SNMP	☑	☑	☑					
Syslog	☑	☑	☑	☑	☑	☑	☑	☑
WebTrends	☑	☑	☑	☐	☐	☑	☐	☐
NSM	☑	☑	☑	☑	☑	☑	☑	☑
CompactFlash (PCMCIA)	☑	☑	☑	☑	☑	☑	☑	☑
	☐ All Above	☐ All Above	☐ All Above	☐ All Above	☐ All Above	☐ All Above	☐ All Above	☐ All Above

☑ Log Packets Terminated to Self

Check All   Clear All

Security Levels:

- **Emergency** Includes attacks like SYN Attacks, Ping of Death, and Teardrop attacks.
- **Alert** Multiple user authentication errors and attacks not classified as emergency.
- **Critical** Traffic alarms, changes to high availability status, blocked URLs (Uniform Resource Locators).
- **Error** Events like admin name and password changes.
- **Warning** Logon failures, authentication failures, administrators that have logged on.
- **Notification** Changes to link status and traffic logs.
- **Information** Events not included in other categories.
- **Debugging** Logs associated with debugging.

NetScreen Security Manager

Up to this point in the chapter, several methods for monitoring the devices have been presented. This is useful for keeping informed about the traffic and status of devices, but what can be done to effectively manage policy and hardware configuration changes? In a small environment, managing each individual device is probably acceptable, but with large, distributed deployments, this model does not scale appropriately. It's for this environment that NetScreen Security Manager was developed. NSM provides the capability to manage multiple devices, up to 1000, from a single console.

Additionally, NSM supports domains and role-based administration. The domain capability allows for NSM to create logical groupings of devices and place them into subdomains. Each domain can have its own unique objects, VPNs, and policies. Within the domains, roles can be created to allow access to certain parts of the system. For example, a role could be created for the help desk that only allows them access to the Log Viewer and the Realtime monitor, while an administrative role could be assigned to firewall admin allowing that user to make changes and update policy.

Another feature of NSM that makes it such a powerful tool is the ability to model devices and configure with templates. By creating a model, an administrator has the ability to create a device that does not yet exist. The complete configuration can be created in advance, so once the device is deployed, it can be pushed to the firewall, making it immediately ready for application. Templates provide the capability to simplify the process further. With templates, common configuration elements can be predefined and applied to existing or modeled devices. For example, assume that all NetScreen devices in a network use the same DNS servers. A template for the DNS servers could be created and then applied to each device, reducing time and effort required for configuration.

NetScreen Rapid Deployment is a feature that simplifies the process of bringing a device online. Once the device is modeled, the administrator can create a small file, called a *configlet*, that can be sent to an onsite administrator who can then load the configlet onto the NetScreen device. The information in the configlet contains just enough information to get the device communicating on the network and to talk to NSM. Once NSM has been notified by the device that it is active, the administrator can then push the remaining configuration to make it fully functional.

The Anatomy of NSM

Before talking about how to use NSM, it's good to spend some time understand the design and implementation of the product. NSM is a three-tier architecture that includes a management server, client GUI (graphical user interface), and the firewall devices. Figure 15.9 presents a typical deployment, which is the focus in this chapter.

Figure 15.9 Typical NSM Deployment

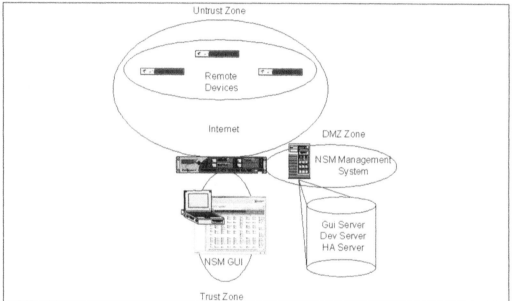

Following the example of a typical deployment, the first tier of NSM is the management server consisting of three components called the Gui Server, the Dev Server, and the HA Server. The Gui Server is responsible for managing the commands sent from the NSM graphical user interface as well as authentication and managing system resources. Up to 20 GUI clients can be connected at one time. The Dev Server, or Device Server, is responsible for all communications with the firewall devices, including logging and policy updates. For the purposes of performance and scalability, the Gui and Dev services can be separated between two different servers. The HA Server is a process that constantly monitors the status of the Gui Server and Dev Server. If it detects that either process has stopped, it will automatically restart the process.

The second tier of NSM is the GUI, a java-based application that connects to the Gui server running on the management system. From the GUI, the user is able to manage the devices, develop policy, and view logs. Later in this chapter, we will discuss the user interface and become familiar with its various functions.

The firewall devices comprise the third tier of NSM. Communication with each device needs to be established to the Dev server. Generally speaking, most of the communications between the devices and the Dev server are initiated by the devices. This makes it possible to manage firewalls with dynamic IP addresses since these devices inform NSM when an IP address change has occurred. Like all other management services on the device, NSM support is turned on at the interface. This means that a policy or VPN is not needed in order to manage the firewalls and that communication takes place over a secure TCP-based communications channel called Secure Server Protocol (SSP).

All three tiers of NSM make use of the SSP protocol in order to communicate. SSP contains encryption and authentication mechanisms that are provided by RSA public key cryptography, AES symmetric encryption, and HMAC-SHA-1 hashing. For NetScreen devices running ScreenOS v5.0 or later, two ports are used for communication, ports 7800 and 7801. Port 7800 is used by the device to communicate with the Dev server while port 7801 is used by the user interface to communicate with the Gui server. This means that any firewalls placed between the NSM management system, the user interface, and remote firewall devices, must open the appropriate ports to facilitate communication with NSM. Figure 15.10 expands on the example to show what policy would be like in order for the NSM deployment to work properly.

Figure 15.10 Deployment Policy

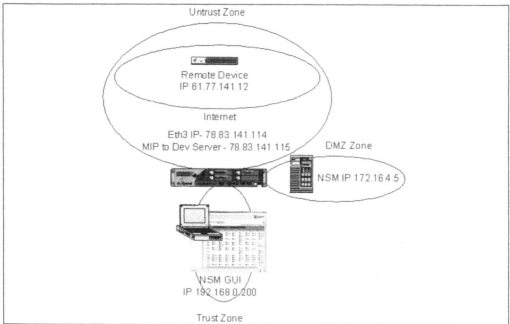

Table 15.1 Deployment Policy

From Zone	From Source	To Zone	To Source	Service	Action
Untrust	61.77.141.12	DMZ	MIP (78.83.141.115)	NSM (7800)	Permit
DMZ	172.15.4.5	Untrust	61.77.141.12	NSM (7800)	Permit
Trust	192.168.0.200	DMZ	172.15.4.5	NSM GUI (7801)	Permit

One of the advantages of using NSM with ScreenOS 5.0 is the simplicity of the SSP protocol. Policy and device changes, logging, and firmware updates are all managed through this mechanism. SSH and Telnet are still used for importing an existing device and for troubleshooting, so it is recommended that one of these management services is enabled as well, with SSH being the preferred method.

NSM also supports devices running ScreenOS 4.0, but since the SSP protocol is not supported by that version of ScreenOS, the port requirements are different. Device configuration updates are sent through SSH or Telnet while logging takes place using the Juniper Networks Server Protocol (TCP port 15400). Additionally,

TFTP (Thin File Transfer Protocol) and NetScreen Address Change Notification (TCP port 11122) are required. Since most of these protocols are not encrypted, it is recommended that you manage these remote devices through a VPN. Obviously, ScreenOS 5.0 simplifies the administration quite a bit.

As mentioned, we are focusing on a typical deployment of NSM, but it is worth mentioning two more items that are common for the larger enterprise deployments. First, NSM can be deployed in a high availability cluster, with one server in an *active* mode while the other is in *standby*. Replication between both Gui Servers takes place using the rsync utility on UNIX systems. The Dev Servers would then be configured to access an external shared disk for log access. Second, while NSM does have some built in reports that are useful, a complete historical reporting package called the Statisical Report Server (SRS) is available as option. SRS can be used to store data generated by the NetScreen devices and create reports for analysis and management requirements.

Installing NSM

For the management services, NSM is supported on Solaris 8 or 9, Red Hat Linux 8.0 or 9.0, and Red Hat Enterprise Linux ES 3.0. The following is a list of the minimum system requirements:

- **CPU** Sun Microsystems UltraSPARC IIi 500MHz (or higher), OR Linux 1GHz (x86) processor (or higher).
- **RAM** 1GB or higher.
- **Swap Space** 4GB for both the Gui Server and Dev Server.
- **Storage** 10K rpm, 18GB drive (at least 40GB recommended).
- **Network Connection** 100MBps Ethernet Adaptor.

NSM can be resource intensive, so it is required that it runs on a dedicated server. Keep in mind that what is listed are the minimum requirements for the server and that sizing and capacity planning should be considered.

Installing the management services is a fairly straightforward process, but some planning should be considered. Questions that should be asked need to be focused around how many devices will be supported, how much logging will take place, if high availability of the NSM server is a requirement, and the size of the firewall configs. For this book, we will focus on simple installation of NSM on a running Red Hat Linux Enterprise ES 3.0 server. By default, the NSM installation creates directories in /usr and /var. /var contains the logs and policy information, so this drive will have to have a fairly large portion of the disk space allocated. The following steps assume that the operating has been installed and that access to the console has been provided.

1. Login to the server as root. By default, the NSM processes run as the root user. Later in the installation, we will change this to provide a more secure configuration.

2. Copy the installation package to the server. Most often, this is accomplished through FTP (File Transfer Protocol) or secure copy (scp). At the time of this book, the current version of NSM is Feature Pack 2, Release 3 (fp2r3), so that is the package we will place on the server (nsm04_fp2r3_linux.zip).

3. For this installation, the package was placed in the /tmp directory. This file will have to be extracted in order to get access to the installation scripts.

```
[root@NSM root]# cd /tmp
 [root@NSM tmp]# ls
nsm04_fp2r3_linux.zip
[root@NSM tmp]# unzip nsm04_fp2r3_linux.zip
Archive:  nsm04_fp2r3_linux.zip
  inflating: systemupdate-nsm-linux.tar.gz
  inflating: nsm04fp2r3_servers_linux_x86.sh

[root@NSM tmp]# ls
nsm04_fp2r3_linux.zip            systemupdate-nsm-linux.tar.gz
nsm04fp2r3_servers_linux_x86.sh
```

4. The package systemupdate-nsm-linux.tar.gz will update or install packages required by NSM. First, extract the package by entering **tar xvf systemupdate-nsm-linux.tar.gz**. Once this is done, a new directory will be created, called systemupdate-nsm-linux. Change to this directory and execute the update.sh script.

```
[root@NSM systemupdate-nsm-linux]# ls
README.txt  rh8  rh9  rhes3  update.sh

[root@NSM systemupdate-nsm-linux]# sh ./update.sh
```

```
Checking if user is root...................................ok
Checking version of RedHat.................................ok
In order for NSM to be installed properly, the following Linux
RPMs are needed from the following list:

 compat-libstdc++-7.3-2.96.118.i386.rpm

Hit ENTER to continue or Ctrl-C to stop...



Cleaning up RPM database (this may take a while)...........ok
Running Linux System Update for RedHat Enterprise Server 3.0 (Stage
1)
Stage 1....................................................ok
Running Linux System Update for RedHat Enterprise Server 3.0 (Stage
2)
Stage 2....................................................ok
```

Refer to /tmp/systemUpdate-InstallLog.20041114170748 for more information. In this case, one required RPM package was needed and installed by the system update utility.

5. Now, change back to the /tmp directory and run the NSM installation script.

```
[root@NSM systemupdate-nsm-linux]# cd ..



[root@NSM tmp]# sh ./nsm04fp2r3_servers_linux_x86.sh
```

The script will perform a series of pre-installation tasks to verify that requirements are met. Once that is completed, the administrator is presented with the option to install the Gui and Dev servers independently, or to install them together on the same server. Continuing with our typical example, both services will be installed on the same server.

```
                  Creating staging directory...ok


########## PERFORMING PRE-INSTALLATION TASKS ##########
Running preinstallcheck...
Checking if platform is valid..............................ok
```

```
Checking for correct intended platform.....................ok
Checking if all needed binaries are present................ok
Checking for platform-specific binaries....................ok
Checking if user is root...................................ok
Checking if user root exists...............................ok
Checking if system meets RAM requirement...................ok
Checking for sufficient disk space.........................ok
Noting OS name.............................................ok
Stopping any running servers
########## GATHERING INFORMATION ##########


1) Install Device Server only
2) Install GUI Server only
3) Install both Device Server and GUI Server
Enter selection (1-3) []> 3
```

6. At this point, the script will ask if the machine is going to participate in an HA cluster. For this example, we will answer **no**.

```
########## GENERAL SERVER SETUP DETAILS ##########


Will this machine participate in an HA cluster? (y/n) [n]>n
```

7. The installation script provides the option to select what directories will be used for storing log and configuration data. This directory can grow quite large, so be sure to allocate enough space. By default, both the Gui and Dev servers have directories created in /var/netscreen.

8. Enter the IP address of the management server that the software is being installed on.

```
Enter the management IP address of this server [172.15.4.5]>
```

9. NSM creates a default user account called **super**. The installation script will prompt for a password.

```
Please enter a password for the 'super' user
Enter password (password will not display as you type)>
Please enter again for verification
Enter password (password will not display as you type)>
```

10. NSM must be informed if a Statistical Report Server will be used. For this example, enter **no**.

    ```
    Will a Statistical Report Server be used with this GUI Server?
    (y/n) [n]>
    ```

11. If you decide to use the HA server, which will act as a watchdog process to verify that the Gui and Dev servers are operating, enter **yes**.

    ```
    ########## HIGH AVAILABILITY (HA) SETUP DETAILS ##########


    Will server processes need to be restarted automatically in caseof
    a failure? (y/n) [y]>
    ```

12. Provide the directories in which the Dev and Gui serices will be installed.

    ```
    ########## DEVICE SERVER SETUP DETAILS ##########
    Enter data directory location [/var/netscreen/DevSvr]>


    ########## GUI SERVER SETUP DETAILS ##########
    Enter data directory location [/var/netscreen/GuiSvr]>
    ```

13. NSM can perform a nightly backup of the database. If required, enter **yes** at the prompt. A two digit number (00-23) will have to be entered to indicate the time of the back up as well as the IP address of the remote backup server, if one is being used. The final steps of this section will ask for the number of backups to store and the path to rsync and ssh.

    ```
    ########## BACKUP SETUP DETAILS ##########


    Will this machine require local database backups? (y/n) [y]>


    Enter hour of day to start the database backup (00 = midnight, 02
    = 2am, 14 = 2pm ...)[02]>


    Will daily backups need to be sent to a remote machine? (y/n) [n]>
    y


    Enter the IP address of the remote backup machine []> 172.15.4.3
    ```

```
Enter number of database backups to keep [7]>


Enter database backup directory [/var/netscreen/dbbackup]>


The database backup server(s) requires that you have previously
installed the rsync program.
Enter the full path to rsync [/usr/bin/rsync]>


The database backup server(s) requires that you have previously
installed the ssh program.
Enter the full path for the ssh command [/usr/bin/ssh]>
                    Note: A trust relationship between this machine
and the
remote machine, via ssh-keygen, is a requirement for the
remote replication to work properly.
Here are sample commands:
cd /root
ssh-keygen -t rsa
chmod 0700 .ssh
                    -- then copy .ssh/id_rsa.pub to the peer
machines' .ssh/authorized_keys
```

14. Finally, you will be asked if the NSM services should start after the script is finished and if the choices made are correct.

```
########## POST-INSTALLATION OPTIONS ##########


Start server(s) when finished? (y/n) []> y


########## CONFIRMATION ##########


About to proceed with the following actions:
- Install Device Server
- Install GUI Server
- Install High Availability Server
- This machine does not participate in an HA cluster
- Store Device Server data in /var/netscreen/DevSvr
```

```
- Store GUI Server data in /var/netscreen/GuiSvr
- Use IP address 192.168.0.125 for management
- Connect to GUI Server at 172.15.4.5:7801
- Set password for 'super' user
- Servers will be restarted automatically in case of a failure
- Local database backups are enabled
- Start backups at 02
- Daily backups will be sent to a remote machine
- IP address of the remote backup machine: 172.15.4.3
- Number of database backups to keep: 7
- Create database backup in /var/netscreen/dbbackup
- Use rsync program at /usr/bin/rsync
- Path for the ssh command: /usr/bin/ssh
- Start server(s) when finished: Yes


Are the above actions correct? (y/n)>y
```

15. The script will display the installation tasks as they are completed.

```
########## EXTRACTING PAYLOADS ##########
Extracting payload.......................................ok
Decompressing payload....................................
gzip: payload.tgz: unexpected end of file
ok


########## PERFORMING MIGRATION TASKS ##########


########## PERFORMING INSTALLATION TASKS ##########
----- INSTALLING Device Server -----
Looking for existing RPM package..........................ok
Removing DevSvr files from default location...............ok
Installing Device Server RPM..............................ok
Installing JRE............................................ok
Creating var directory....................................ok
Creating /var/netscreen/dbbackup..........................ok
Putting NSROOT into start scripts.........................ok
Filling in Device Server config file(s)...................ok
```

```
Setting permissions for Device Server......................ok
Installation of Device Server complete.


----- INSTALLING GUI Server -----
Looking for existing RPM package...........................ok
Removing GuiSvr files from default location................ok
Installing GUI Server RPM..................................ok
Installing JRE.............................................ok
Creating var directory.....................................ok
Putting NSROOT into start scripts..........................ok
Filling in GUI Server config file(s).......................ok
Setting permissions for GUI Server.........................ok
Running generateMPK utility................................ok
Running fingerprintMPK utility.............................ok
Installation of GUI Server complete.


----- INSTALLING HA Server -----
Looking for existing RPM package...........................ok
Removing HaSvr files from default location.................ok
Installing HA Server RPM...................................ok
Creating var directory.....................................ok
Putting NSROOT into start scripts..........................ok
Filling in HA Server config file(s)........................ok
Setting permissions for HA Server..........................ok
Installation of HA Server complete.


----- SETTING START SCRIPTS -----
Enabling Device Server start script........................ok
Enabling GUI Server start script...........................ok
Enabling HA Server start script............................ok


########## PERFORMING POST-INSTALLATION TASKS ##########
Running nacnCertGeneration..................................ok
Removing staging directory..................................ok
Starting GUI Server.........................................ok
```

```
                           Starting Device
Server...................................ok
Starting HA Server...............................................ok


NOTES:
- Installation log is stored in
/usr/netscreen/DevSvr/var/errorLog/netmgtInstallLog.20041114214046


- This is the GUI Server fingerprint:
   83:23:83:F7:3A:6E:24:C1:08:3B:D4:54:05:88:6E:6B:31:85:69:27
   You will need this for verification purposes when logging into
the GUI
   Server. Please make a note of it.


- To enable firmware updates to ScreenOS 4.x devices, the TFTP
server on
   this machine needs to be enabled.


- To enable firmware updates to ScreenOS 4.x devices, the TFTP
server on
   this machine must have its root directory set to
   '/usr/netscreen/DevSvr/var/cache'.
```

16. When installation is completed, you will be returned to the command prompt. Verify that the Dev, Gui, and HA services are running.

```
[root@NSM tmp]# cd /usr/netscreen/GuiSvr/bin
[root@NSM bin]# ./guiSvr.sh status
Retrieving status...
guiSvrManager (pid 11179)..........................ON
guiSvrMasterController (pid 11315).................ON
guiSvrDirectiveHandler (pid 11448).................ON
guiSvrStatusMonitor (pid 11572)....................ON


[root@NSM bin]# cd ../../DevSvr/bin
[root@NSM DevSvr]# ./devSvr.sh status
Retrieving status...
devSvrManager (pid 11778)..........................ON
```

```
devSvrLogWalker (pid 11903)........................ON

devSvrDataCollector (pid 12030)....................ON

devSvrDirectiveHandler (pid 12214)................ON

devSvrStatusMonitor (pid 12367)...................ON


[root@NSM bin]# cd ../../HaSvr/bin

[root@NSM bin]# ./haSvr.sh status

Retrieving status...

highAvail.........................................off

highAvailSvr (pids 12664).........................ON
```

Installation of the graphical user interface is a straight-forward process. The GUI is supported on Windows XP, 2000, and NT 4.0 with service pack 6a, as well as Red Hat Linux 8.0 or 9.0 and Red Hat Enterprise Linux ES 3.0. For this example, the GUI will be installed on a Windows system.

1. Starting the installation executable will present the user with the introduction screen (Figure 15.11). Select **Next** to continue.

Figure 15.11 NSM Introduction Screen

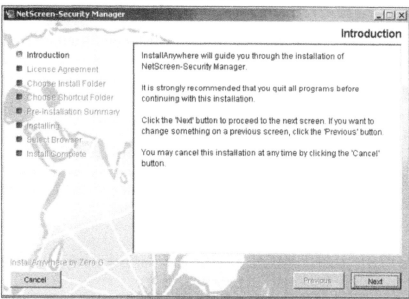

2. The next screen is the end user license agreement. Accept the terms and select **Next**.

3. Choose the installation directory (Figure 15.12). By default, the directory is C:\Program Files\NetScreen-Security Manager.

Figure 15.12 Installation Directory

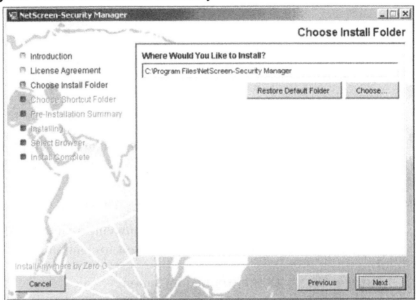

4. Choose the location for the icon installation (Figure 15.13). Select **Next** to continue.

Figure 15.13 Icon Installation

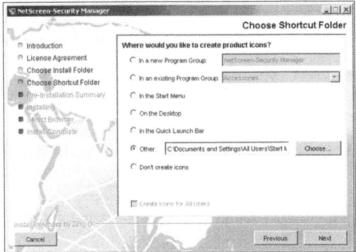

5. The final screen reviews the options selected and extracts the files to the install folder (Figure 15.14). Select **Install** to finish.

Figure 15.14 Pre-Installation Summary

With the management server configured and the GUI installed, let's take a look at using NSM to manage the NetScreen FW/VPN devices.

Using the GUI for the First Time

Now that the NSM server and GUI are installed, it is time to start using it. When the user interface is started, a prompt will appear asking for a user login, password, and server address or hostname. For the first login, you will want to use the "super" account and password that was created during the installation of the management server.   Once logged in, the administrator will be presented with the user interface (Figure 15.15).

Figure 15.15 NetScreen Security Manager User Interface

NetScreen Security Manager presents a clean, user-friendly interface that is broken down into several components that focus on various tasks and aspects of managing the firewall devices.

- **Log Viewer** Displays logs generated by the firewall devices as well as those from tasks performed by NSM. Logs are presented by rows and columns that can then be filtered to view specific information. In addition, new log views can be created. Each view can have its own filters to create a quick and easy method to get to important information.

- **Report Manager** Contains predefined reports that can be viewed as bar and pie charts, which can present a summary of events and traffic. These reports can be exported and printed, if needed.

- **Log Investigator** If using the Deep Inspection capability, the Log Investigator provides a way to correlate the data regarding which attacks or anomalies have been triggered, sources and destination, ports attacked, and time reference.

- **Device Manager** Contains the device objects that are used by NSM. This includes production firewalls, modeled devices, virtual systems, and high availability clusters. In addition, templates and extranet devices (VPN devices that are not a NetScreen device) are included. Hardware configuration takes place in these objects as well as associating policy.

- **Security Policies** Firewall and VPN policies are developed in this section, as well as changes, deletions and updates. This includes all features of NetScreen policy including items like Quality of Service (QoS), authentication, Deep Inspection, and address translation.

- **VPN Manager** Provides a method to quickly build and manage virtual private networks. Administrators can also create custom phase 1 and phase 2 proposals and configure policy for remote access.

- **Object Manager** Contains all objects that are used to build policy and VPNs. This includes things like network and hosts, services, NAT (network address translation) objects, users, and more.

- **Server Manager** This provides the capability to monitor the status of the servers and services running NetScreen Security Manager.

- **Realtime Monitor** This monitors the status of the NetScreen devices, VPNs, and high availability clusters. Administrators can also use tools for troubleshooting and viewing real-time statistics.

- **Job Manager** Every time NSM is used to initiate a function, like pushing policy, importing a device, or verifying a configuration, a historical entry is created in the Job Manager. Administrators can review the entries to verify successes and failures, and to view the errors generated by a failed job.

- **Audit Log Viewer** Contains log entries for activities and changes performed by NSM administrators.

Adding and Managing a Device in NSM

Since NSM offers enough capability to fill a book of its own, we are going to cover a few key features to help get you familiar with the system. Continuing on with our example (Figure 15.10 above), we will add a new firewall in order to create a policy-based VPN. Looking in the Device Manager, we can see that the headend firewall, called Headquarters, has already been added (Figure 15.16).

Figure 15.16 Headquarters Firewall

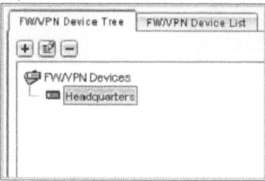

The remote office firewall is a 5XT and will be named "New York". When NSM imports a device, it first communicates with the device over Telnet or SSH. Since the remote device is on the Internet, SSH support has been enabled on the untrust interface. In order to add the firewall, click on the plus sign and select **Device**. The New Device dialog box will be presented (Figure 15.17).

Figure 15.17 New Device Dialog Box

Since the New York firewall is already in production, under the Device Exists section, select **Device is Reachable** and then click **Next**. The dialog box will then ask for the IP address, the username and password, and the service to use to establish communication (Figure 15.18).

Figure 15.18 Specify Connection Settings

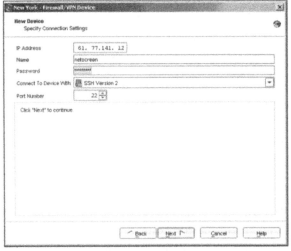

At this point, NSM will attempt to connect to the device through SSH and retrieve the RSA fingerprint (Figure 15.19). If the fingerprint is displayed, then communication was successful.

Figure 15.19 RSA Fingerprint

The final screen of the import dialog will verify the IP address, the ScreenOS version, and the serial number of the device (Figure 15.20). Since the device is remote and the Headquarters firewall is using NAT, the remote firewall must communicate with NSM through a MIP (Mapped IP). Under the primary tab, select **Use Device Server Through MIP**, which in this case is the address 78.83.141.136. The secondary tab is used if a backup device server is available. In this case, a single device server exists, so the secondary tab will not be used. Notice that a message states that the firewall has to be imported manually once the device has been added. The Add Device procedure essentially creates the device in NSM, verifies the device exists, and configures the device to communicate with NSM using the SSP protocol. Once that is accomplished, the device configuration can be imported through SSP.

Figure 15.20 Finish Adding New Device

Importing the configuration of the New York firewall is a simple process. Simply access the Device Manager, right click on the New York firewall, and select **Import Device** (Figure 15.21). Another dialog box will open and display the status of the job. Also, an entry will be created in the Job Manager for the device import.

Figure 15.21 Import Device

We can verify that the device is managed and functioning by going to the Realtime Monitor and viewing the current status (Figure 15.22). Notice that the New York firewall's connection status is **Up** and its first and last connect times to NSM are displayed.

Figure 15.22 Realtime Monitor

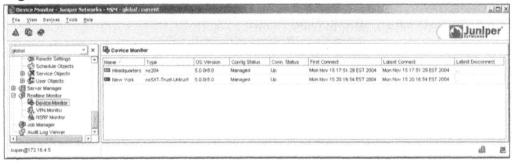

Now that the device has been added, all aspects of the configuration can be managed through NSM. By double-clicking on the New York object in the Device Manager, a configuration screen will be presented (Figure 15.23).

Figure 15.23 Device Configuration Screen

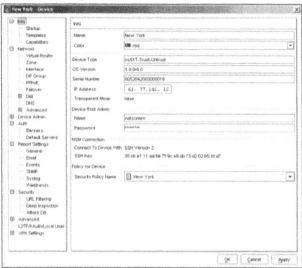

- **Info** Presents an overview of device parameters, like ScreenOS version, port mode, and serial number. In addition, policy can be selected and templates can be applied.

- **Network** All network settings can be modified, including things like interface IP addresses, virtual interfaces, virtual routers, and zones.

- **Device Admin** Provides the ability to set NTP servers, create local device administrators, and enable management services like the WebUI and SSH.

- **Auth** Define banners for services used to authenticate users, like Webauth, Telnet, and FTP. Administrators can also select which servers are used for authentication.

- **Report Settings** Essentially provides access to items discussed in this chapter, like Syslog, SNMP, and e-mail monitoring.

- **Security** Configure Websense for URL filtering and Deep Inspection options.

- **Advanced** Tune features like service timeouts and packet flow.

- **L2TP/Xauth/Local User** Manage user accounts for remote access.

- **VPN Settings** Much of this can be handled using the VPN Manager, but access is granted for granular control over VPN configurations.

Once a change is made to the configuration, the device will have to be updated. This can be done by going to the menu bar and selecting **Devices | Configuration | Update Device Config**. This process will push any changes made in the device configuration.

Using the Logs

One of the key strengths of NSM is the logging capability. As a centralized repository for logging up to 1,000 devices, NSM can greatly simplify the constant task of monitoring traffic and events across multiple firewalls in a distributed enterprise environment. NSM is capable of logging up to 20,000 logs per second. Figure 15.24 displays the Log Viewer.

Figure 15.24 NSM Log Viewer

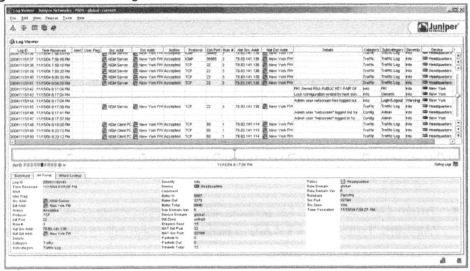

NSM logs are broken out by rows and columns, which can be manipulated in a number of ways. You can reorder the columns by selecting a column header and dragging it to the desired placement. Columns can be hidden or added to the viewer by clicking the **Choose Columns** icon in the menu bar. Rows can be filtered by clicking the **Filter Summary** icon. Across the bottom of the Log Viewer, three tabs provide a way to quickly take in information by providing summary views, as well as a useful Whois lookup utility. The bar across the middle allows an administrator to quickly jump to a specific point in the logs. Just like the logging capability described in earlier sections, the information presented in the Log Viewer is determined by the administrator on each device. The administrator determines which policies and traffic will be logged, and what alarms and events will be sent.

Now that the New York firewall is managed by NSM, let's create a log view that will only present logs generated by that device. First, access **File | New View** and enter a name, in this case, **New York Firewall**. In the menu tree, underneath the Log Viewer component, and entry will appear with the name of the new view. Select the new view and open the Filter Summary window by clicking its icon. Figure 15.25 displays the Filter Summary.

Figure 15.25 Filter Summary

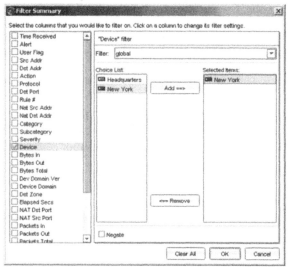

Since we only want to view the log entries for the New York firewall, scroll down and enable the **Device** option. In the filter window, select **New York** and add it to the **Selected Items** column. Click **OK** and note that a new view has been created based on the requirements.

In addition to the Log Viewer, the Audit Log Viewer (Figure 15.26) monitors administrative activities in NSM. The logs provide information regarding the time of the event, the action taken, and which device was affected. The Audit Log Viewer also contains two detailed views, called the *Target* view and the *Device* view. The Target view displays changes made to a device configuration, like going into the Device Manager and updating the DNS server on the New York firewall. The Device view displays information about when a change was made to the device itself. Double-clicking on the entry in the Target and Device views will open a window that displays what changes were made for that specific Audit Log entry.

Figure 15.26 Audit Log Viewer

Time Generated	Admin Name	Action	Targets	Devices	Miscellaneous	Log Id
11/15/04 6:16:45 PM	super/global	Update object	Headquarters/device/global			20041115/29
11/15/04 6:18:22 PM	super/global	Update object	^rb_Headquarters_100v702q0/rb_firewall/global			20041115/30
11/15/04 6:18:33 PM	super/global	Update device		Headquarters/device/global		20041115/31
11/15/04 6:19:01 PM	super/global	User logout				20041115/32
11/15/04 7:56:22 PM	super/global	Update object	^rb_Headquarters_100v702q0/rb_firewall/global			20041115/35
11/15/04 7:56:45 PM	super/global	Update device		Headquarters/device/global		20041115/36
11/15/04 7:58:06 PM	super/global	Not specified		Headquarters/device/global		20041115/37
11/15/04 8:00:32 PM	super/global	Autodetect device		Headquarters/device/global		20041115/38
11/15/04 8:04:05 PM	super/global	Autodetect device		Headquarters/device/global		20041115/39
11/15/04 8:15:02 PM	super/global	Not specified		Headquarters/device/global		20041115/40
11/15/04 8:16:24 PM	super/global	Insert object	New York/device/global			20041115/41

Target Name		Table	Domain		Device Name	Table	Domain
New York	device		global				

Creating and Using Objects

NSM stores most of its objects in the Object Manager (Figure 15.27), which are then used in when creating policy or VPNs.

Figure 15.27 Object Manager

Network and Address Translation:

- **Address Objects** Individual hosts or networks.
- **Global DIP** Dynamic IP NAT Objects.
- **Global MIP** Mapped IP NAT Objects.
- **Global VIP** Virtual IP NAT Objects.
- **IP Pools** IP address ranges that are used by remote access users.
- **Remote Settings** DNS and WINS settings.

Services and Schedules:

- **Predefined Service Objects** Service objects that have been provided in the default installation of NSM, such as HTTP, FTP, and SMTP.
- **Custom Service Objects** Service objects defined by the administrator, such as custom application protocols.
- **Schedule Objects** Objects that can be used to determine when a policy is active.

Application Layer Protection:

- **Predefined Attack Objects** Stateful Signature and Protocol Anomaly objects for Deep Inspection.
- **Custom Attack Objects** Attack objects created by the administrator.
- **AntiVirus Objects** Defines the Trend Micro server used for gateway antivirus.

Users and Authentication:

- **Local Users** Remote access users stored in the local firewall database.
- **External Users** Remote access users stored in an external database.
- **External User Groups** Remote access user group stored in an external database.
- **Group Expressions** Objects that allow expressions to be used for user authentication.
- **Authentication Servers** Servers used for authentication.

Certificates:

- **Certificate Authorities** Certificate authority certificates.
- **CRLs** Certificate authority's revocation list.

For our example, a host object must be created that will only allow the NSM GUI client computer (192.168.0.200) to access a single website on the Internet, www.juniper.com. An object already exits for the GUI client, so one must be created for www.juniper.net. In the NSM menu tree, access **Object Manager | Address Objects**. Click the plus sign to create a new host object (Figure 15.28).

Figure 15.28 Create a New Host Object

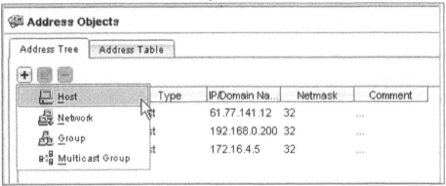

You will be presented with a dialog box for creating a new host object (Figure 15.29). You can enter a host object using the IP address or the DNS name.

Figure 15.29 New Host Object

Now, in the menu tree, go to the **Policy Manager**. Since the NSM GUI client computer is located behind the Headquarters firewall, we will need to modify that policy. Looking at our policy for Headquarters, we can see that there are four rules already in place (Figure 15.30). Since the first rule list allows any networked device in the Trust zone to go any where on the Internet (Untrust zone) over HTTP, Ping, and SSH, this is the rule that must be modified.

Figure 15.30 Policy for Headquarters Firewall

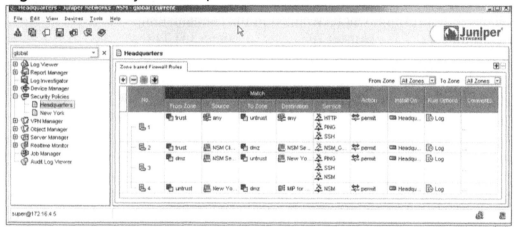

On rule 1, right click on the **From Zone Source** column and select the **NSM Client PC** bject. On the **To Zone Destination** column, right click and select the **www.juniper.net** object. Right click on the **Service** column and disable **Ping** and **SSH**. Figure 15.31 displays the modified rule.

Figure 15.31

Once this is complete, push the new policy by going to the menu and selecting **Devices | Configuration | Update Device Config**. The Job Information dialog box will appear and you will be able to view the progress of the update.

Creating VPNs

It can be a complex task to manage a large, multi-site VPN deployment. The VPN Manager can make this easier by providing a central utility that can create and monitor the tunnels, encryption mechanisms, and policy. Both route-based and policy-based VPNs are supported, as well as the transport modes of autoKey IKE (Internet Key Exchange), manual key, L2TP (Layer 2 Tunneling Protocol), and L2TP-over-autokey IKE. For our example, we will create a policy-based site-to-site VPN between Headquarters and New York using autoKey IKE. The following information will be required in the configuration:

Headquarters	Untrust IP:	78.83.141.114
	Source Interface:	Ethernet 3
	Private Network:	192.168.0.0/24
New York	Untrust IP:	61.77.141.12
	Source Interface:	Untrust
	Private Network:	10.10.10.0/24

1. In the NSM menu tree, access the Object Manager and create a Network Object for both private networks using the following fields:

   Name: HQ_Lan

   IP Address: 192.168.0.0

   Netmask: 24

   Name: New_York_Lan

   IP Address: 10.10.10.0

   Netmask: 24

2. In the NSM menu tree, access **VPN Manager | Protected Resources**. This will allow you to create objects to identify which networks will be accessible through the VPN. Click on the plus sign to add a resource. Figure 15.32 displays configuration information for the Headquarters LAN, while Figure 15.33 displays the protected resource for New York.

Figure 15.32 Headquarters Protected Resource

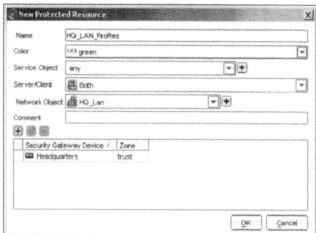

Figure 15.33 New York Protected Resource

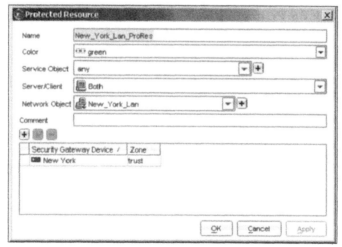

3. In the NSM menu tree, access **VPN Manager | VPNs**. Click on the plus sign and create an autoKey IKE VPN. Enter the name **Corp_VPN**, ensure the **Enable** box is checked, and ensure that the **Termination Point** is the **Untrust** interface. You will be presented with the VPN management interface (Figure 15.34).

Figure 15.34 VPN Management Interface

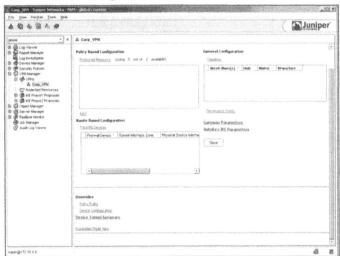

4. Click on **Protected Resources** and add the two objects created in step 3.

5. Click on **Topology** and a window will open. Click on the plus sign to add a new topology (Figure 15.35). Since this is a simple deployment involving only two sites, we will add both firewalls in the **Mains** column.

Figure 15.35 Add a Topology

6. Click **OK** in the New Topology window and again in the Topology window.

7. Select **Gateway Parameters**. Click the **Security** tab and make sure the **Security Level** is **Predefined** and that the **Predefined** field is set to **Standard** (Figure 15.36).

Figure 15.36 Gateway Security

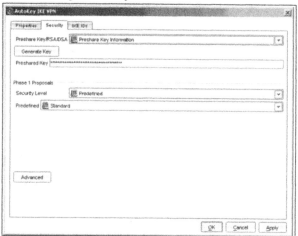

8. Select AutoKey IKE Parameters. Under the Properties tab, select Rekey and VPN Monitor. Under the Security tab, make sure the Security Level is Predefined and that the Predefined field is set to Standard (Fig 15.37).

Figure 15.37 VPN Security

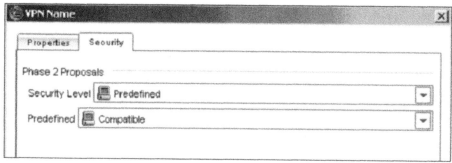

9. Click Save. Click on Policy Rules to view the VPN policy that will be applied to the Headquarters and New York firewalls (Figure 15.38).

Figure 15.38 Policy Rules

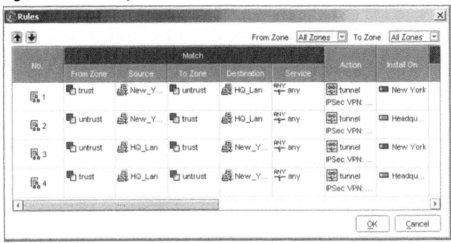

10. At this point, you can push the policy to both firewalls by going to the menu bar and selecting Devices | Configuration | Update Device Config. Once the job is complete, the active VPN tunnel can be verified by going to the menu tree and selecting Realtime Monitor | VPN Monitor (Figure 15.39)

Figure 15.39 VPN Monitor

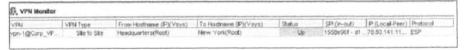

Summary

As you can probably tell, there is quite a bit of capability provided by NetScreen Security Manager, too much to effectively cover in a single chapter. As you become more familiar with NetScreen and as your enterprise deployment grows, NSM will become a component that should definitely be considered. In fact, it is one of the key strengths of a Juniper NetScreen solution. However, if your environment does not justify NSM, the alternative methods for managing and monitoring your devices are still fairly easy to use and deploy. Syslog and SNMP are common throughout all networked environments, and odds are that these will fit into management systems already in place.

Solutions Fast Track

Alternative Methods for Monitoring NetScreen Devices

- ☑ By default, Syslog operates over UDP port 514.
- ☑ NetScreen devices can Syslog information a total of four servers.
- ☑ WebTrends is supported by ScreenOS and can provide reports based on Syslog data.
- ☑ NetScreen devices support SNMPv1 and v2.
- ☑ ScreenOS can communicate with up to three communities consisting of up to eight hosts.
- ☑ Juniper provides private MIBs that can be loaded with an SNMP browser.

NetScreen Security Manager

- ☑ NSM services consist of three primary components: Gui, Dev, and HA servers.
- ☑ The management system can be installed on Red Hat or Solaris, while the GUI is supported on Windows or Red Hat.

☑ Nearly every aspect of managing NetScreen firewalls can be completed through a single user interface.

Frequently Asked Questions

The following Frequently Asked Questions, answered by the authors of this book, are designed to both measure your understanding of the concepts presented in this chapter and to assist you with real-life implementation of these concepts. To have your questions about this chapter answered by the author, browse to **www.syngress.com/solutions** and click on the **"Ask the Author"** form. You will also gain access to thousands of other FAQs at ITFAQnet.com.

Q: What is the Auth/Sec facility in Syslog?

A: Auth/Sec is a user-definable facility for storing logs. There are no differences between is and facilities 0 through 7.

Q: Can Syslog information be sent over TCP instead of UDP?

A: Yes, this is an option in the Syslog configuration. The Syslog server must support this communication as well.

Q: What versions of SNMP does a NetScreen firewall support?

A: SNMP v1 and v2.

Q: When using NetScreen Rapid Deployment in Security Manager, what is a configlet?

A: A configlet is an encrypted file that contains just enough information to get the firewall on the network and communicating with the NSM device server. Once this is working, the administrator can push the rest of the configuration and policy to the device.

Q: What ports are used by NSM?

A: TCP port 7800 is used for the device communications with the Device server, while TCP port 7801 is used by the graphical user interface to communicate with the Gui server.

Q: What operating systems are supported by NSM?

A: Solaris 8 or 9 and Red Hat Enterprise 3.

Appendix

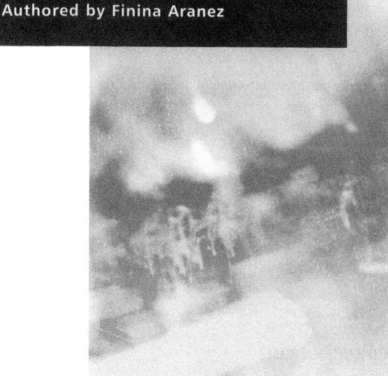

ScreenOS 5.1.0 Enhancements and New Features

Authored by Finina Aranez

Introduction

As we were writing this book, Juniper released ScreenOS 5.1.0 to the public. This release is a major milestone for Juniper. It provides many new features and enhancements. It also is one of many upcoming and planned releases which will take Juniper's NetScreen security products to new heights in support for emerging technologies and features.

Appendix A was developed in coordination and with the support of the ISG Technical Publications team at Juniper. Special thanks to Finina Aranez who authored the NetScreen Migration content. The information presented below is provided and taken from the NetScreen Migration 5.1.0 publication, available at www.juniper.net.

New Features in ScreenOS 5.1.0

This chapter provides brief descriptions of all the new features introduced in this Beta release of ScreenOS 5.1.0. For detailed information on each feature, refer to the *NetScreen Concepts & Examples ScreenOS Reference Guide* and the *NetScreen CLI Reference Guide*.

This chapter is organized into the following sections:

- Attack Protection
- Authentication
- DHCP
- DNS
- Interfaces
- L2TP
- Network Management
- NSRP
- Policies
- PortModes
- PPPoE
- Routing
- Services
- SNMP
- Traffic Shaping
- URL Filtering
- VPNs

Attack Protection

Deep Inspection Enhancements

A NetScreen device can now perform Deep Inspection (DI) on packets using several popular peer-to-peer (P2P) and instant messenger protocols, Microsoft-Remote Procedure Call (MSRPC), and Server Message Block running on

NetBIOS (SMB/NetBIOS). In addition, there are some new user-configurable contexts for previously supported protocols. You can also individually disable pre-defined attack objects in an attack object group, enable or disable logging per attack group in a policy referencing multiple groups, and apply negation so that the NetScreen device treats everything not matching a specific attack object as an attack.

GPRS Overbilling Attack

You can protect subscribers of a PLMN (Public Land Mobile Network) by configuring a NetScreen device to prevent GPRS (General Packet Radio Service) Overbilling attacks. Only NetScreen-500 and NetScreen-5000 Series devices support this feature.

Antivirus

The NetScreen device can now scan FTP and IMAP traffic, and HTTP uploads. In addition, you can enable and disable the scanning of a set of predefined MIME content types in HTTP traffic.

TCP Reset

When you execute the **set flow check tcp-rst-sequence** command, the NetScreen device checks that the TCP sequence number in a TCP segment with the RST bit enabled matches the previous sequence number for a packet in that session or is the next higher number incrementally. If the sequence number does not match either of these expected numbers, the NetScreen device drops the packet and sends the host a TCP ACK segment with the correct sequence number. By default, this check is disabled. (Note: The NetScreen-5000 series does not support this option.)

Authentication

Extra Banner

You can add a second banner line for administrative console and Telnet connection logins.

WebAuth via SSL Only

Configuring the NetScreen device for WebAuth using "SSL only" directs the device to allow only SSL-based (HTTPS) WebAuth user authentication. WebAuth via clear text HTTP is disabled.

Self-Signed Certificates

When a NetScreen device first powers up, it automatically creates a self-signed certificate for use with a Secure Sockets Layer (SSL) connection to the device. If you configure the NetScreen device to redirect an administrator's connection attempt to SSL, the device uses the auto-generated self-signed certificate to authenticate itself to the administrator. You can also manually generate additional self-signed certificates with attributes that you define.

DHCP for VoIP

This feature is related to the VoIP features in this release. To enable a NetScreen device that is acting as a DHCP server to work with some IP phones, you can now define custom DHCP options based on the IP phones you use.

DIP

DIP is enhanced to support dynamic destination address and port translation for sessions initiated by incoming traffic. Previously, in NAT mode, DIP could be used to dynamically create source address and port translation for sessions initiated by outgoing traffic, but not for incoming traffic. For incoming traffic, MIP or VIP, which statically create destination address and port translation, had to be used. Some applications, such as SIP and H.323, require a mechanism to support dynamic destination address and port translation for sessions initiated by incoming traffic. DIP can now be used to dynamically create destination address and port translation for incoming traffic.

Domin Name Service

Dynamic DNS

Dynamic DNS (DDNS) is a mechanism that allows clients to dynamically update IP addresses for registered domain names. This is useful when an ISP uses PPP, DHCP, or XAuth to dynamically change the IP address for a CPE router (such as a NetScreen device) that protects a web server. Thus, any clients from the internet can access the web server using a domain name, even if the IP address of the CPE router previously changed dynamically. This is made possible by a DDNS server such as dyndns.org or ddo.jp, which contains the dynamically-changed addresses and their associated domain names. The CPE updates these DDNS servers with this information, periodically or in response to IP address changes.

Proxy DNS

The DNS proxy feature provides a transparent mechanism that allows clients to make split DNS queries. Using this technique, the proxy selectively redirects the DNS queries to specific DNS servers, according to partial or complete domain names. This is useful when VPN tunnels or PPPoE virtual links provide multiple network connectivity, and it is necessary to direct some DNS queries to one network, and other queries to another network.

Interfaces

MTU on Tunnel Interface

You can configure the Maximum Transmission Unit (MTU) size for tunnel interfaces. When a NetScreen device receives a packet on a tunnel interface, the device fragments the packet only if it exceeds the configured MTU size.

Generic Routing Encapsulation (GRE)

NetScreen devices now support terminating GRE tunnels, which are used to encapsulate multicast traffic inside of VPNs between two NetScreen devices.

Layer 2 Transport Protocol

Outgoing Dialup Policy for L2TP and L2TP over IPSEC

In conjunction with incoming policies, you can now configure outgoing dialup policies to create bidirectional L2TP and L2TP-over-IPSec tunnels.

Network Management

Configuration Synchronization

The NetScreen device notifies NetScreen-Security Manager when the configuration has changed from the last time it was synchronized (had an import or update).

Configuration Timestamp

A NetScreen device provides a timestamp for saved and running configurations to view synchronized configurations.

Bulk CLI

Setting the bulk-CLI determines how and when the device performs rollback if the NetScreen-Security Manager connection drops during an update session.

Multiple Firmware

You can now use the Boot/OS Loader to load multiple firmware images on some NetScreen devices.

NetScreen Redundancy Protocol - NSRP

Interface Monitoring

You can configure an interface to monitor the logical and physical link status of one or more interfaces and zones. Each monitored object (monitored interface, zone, and set of tracked IP addresses) has a weight contribution. If the total weight of all monitored objects exceeds a specified threshold, then the interface changes its state from up to down and all its associated routes become inactive. (The state change of the monitoring interface can also be from down to up.)

NSRP Active/Active enhancements

In an Active/Active NSRP configuration, the Backup device could prematurely age out a session that is currently in the Master device. To prevent this, use the **set nsrp rto session ageout-ack** command. When you configure this command, the backup device notifies the Master device before it ages out a session. If the Backup device receives an ageout acknowledgement from the Master, it resets the timer of the session and does not age out the session. If the Backup device does not receive an acknowledgement, it ages out the session. In addition, you can also execute the command **set nsrp rto session non-vsi** command to synchronize the sessions of a non-VSI interface.

Policies

New Policy Action – Reject

When you specify "reject" as the action of a policy, the NetScreen device drops any packet to which the policy applies and sends a TCP reset (RST) segment to the source host for TCP traffic and an ICMP "destination unreachable, port unreachable" message (type 3, code 3) for UDP traffic. For types of traffic other than TCP and UDP, the NetScreen device drops the packet without notifying the source host, which is also what occurs when the action is "deny".

Port Modes

DMZ/Dual Untrust Port Mode

The NetScreen-5GT supports the DMZ/Dual Untrust port mode which binds interfaces to the Untrust, Trust, and DMZ security zones, allowing you to pass traffic simultaneously from the internal network.

Point to Point Protocol over Ethernet

Multiple PPPoE Sessions Over a Single Interface

You can configure a NetScreen device to allow multiple PPPoE sessions over the same physical interface. This is possible because the device supports creation of multiple PPPoE sub-interfaces (each with the same MAC address) for a given physical interface. Therefore, you can bind each sub-interface to a different PPPoE instance and make a PPPoE connection on each instance.

PPPoE and NSRP

Two NetScreen devices that support PPPoE in Active/Passive mode can handle failover of a PPPoE connection. Upon initiation of the connection, the Master device synchronizes its PPPoE state with the Backup device. Because the Passive device uses the same IP address as the Master device, it does not have to make a new PPPoE connection once it becomes the Master. Therefore, it can maintain communication with the Access Concentrator after failure of the Master. This is necessary when the PPPoE interface supports VPN connections, and these connections must continue, using the same interface IP after failover.

Routing

Equal Cost Multi Path (ECMP)

ECMP routing allows multiple routes to the same destination with the same cost to be used to load balance routed traffic. Traffic is distributed on a per-flow basis between routes with equal cost. ECMP routes are applied to both static and dynamic routes. ECMP is supported by all dynamic routing protocols.

Source Interface-Based Routing (SIBR) and Source-Based Routing (SBR)

In the virtual router you can enable and disable source interface-based routing as well as source-based routing and establish the order of route lookups in the various routing tables. For static routes, you can also configure the route as static or permanent.

BGP Enhancements

BGP supports up to 40K routes and 256 peers in high-end platforms such as the NetScreen-5200 and NetScreen-5400. BGP supports additional options for adding static routes into BGP and for aggregating routes.

OSPF Enhancements

OSPF supports two new interface types, point-to-multipoint and demand circuits. These interface types are applicable to tunnel interfaces.

RIP Enhancements

RIP supports the new demand circuit interface type, point-to-multipoint, prefix summarization, and the use of alternate routes. In high-end platforms, a RIP instance can support up to 256 neighbors per interface or 256 interfaces with one neighbor on each interface. For large numbers of virtual systems, up to 500

RIP instances and 1000 neighbors are supported, with each RIP instance having 2 interfaces and 1 neighbor per interface. In addition, NetScreen devices now support RIP versions 1 and 2.

Multicast Routing

NetScreen devices support the following multicast protocols: Internet Group Management Protocol (IGMP) versions 1, 2, and 3; Protocol Independent Multicast - Sparse Mode (PIM-SM); and Protocol Independent Multicast - Source Specific Multicast (PIM-SSM).

Services

Sun RPC ALG—Remote Procedure Call Application Layer Gateway

Sun RPC—also known as Open Network Computing (ONC) RPC—provides a way for a program running on one host to call procedures in a program running on another host. NetScreen devices support Sun RPC as a predefined service, and allow and deny traffic based on a policy you configure. The ALG provides the functionality for NetScreen devices to handle the dynamic transport address negotiation mechanism of Sun RPC, and to ensure program number-based firewall policy enforcement. You can define a firewall policy to permit or deny all RPC requests, or to permit or deny by specific program number. The ALG also supports Route and NAT mode for incoming and outgoing requests.

Microsoft RPC ALG—Remote Procedure Call Application Layer Gateway

MS RPC is the Microsoft implementation of the Distributed Computing Environment (DCE) RPC. NetScreen devices support MS RPC as a predefined service, and allow and deny traffic based on a policy you configure. The ALG provides the functionality for NetScreen devices to handle the dynamic transport address negotiation mechanism of MS RPC, and to ensure UUID-based firewall policy enforcement. You can define a firewall policy to permit or deny all RPC requests, or to permit or deny by specific UUID number. The ALG also supports Route and NAT mode for incoming and outgoing requests.

RTSP ALG—Real Time Streaming Protocol Application-Layer Gateway

RTSP is an application-layer protocol used to control delivery of one or more synchronized streams of multimedia, such as audio and video. NetScreen devices support RTSP as a service, and allow or deny RTSP traffic based on a policy you configure. The ALG is needed because RTSP uses dynamically assigned port numbers that change during delivery of the stream. The ALG keeps track of the changing port numbers and opens pinholes accordingly. In NAT mode, the ALG translates IP addresses and ports if necessary. NetScreen devices support RTSP in Route mode, Transparent mode, and in both interface-based and policy-based NAT mode.

NAT Support for SIP ALG

NetScreen devices support the Session Initiation Protocol (SIP) Application Layer Gateway (ALG) in Network Address Translation (NAT) mode. NAT makes it possible for a private subnet to share one public IP address to access the Internet by concealing the private (illegal) addresses of the subnet. Replacement of IP addresses and port numbers in SIP messages is done depending on the direction of the message. For outbound messages, the client's private IP addresses and port numbers are replaced with the firewall's public IP addresses and port numbers. For inbound messages, the firewall's public IP addresses and port numbers are replaced with corresponding private IP addresses and port numbers. Some SIP NAT devices translate just enough IP addresses to allow the application to work. Because of the ScreenOS firewall, however, the NetScreen implementation of SIP NAT translates all IP addresses—in the SIP header as well as in the SIP body—both to provide application functionality, and to hide information. It translates IP addresses in SIP headers in order to hide that information, and it translates Session Description Protocol (SDP) headers in the SIP body in order to allocate resources—that is, port numbers for where the media is expected to arrive. The allocated port resources are used for translating packets forwarded to the server, and for creating pinholes that wait on the device for matching media packets.

H.323

H.323 protocol lets you to secure Voice-over-IP (VoIP) communication between terminal hosts, such as IP phones and multimedia devices. In such a telephony system, gatekeeper devices manage call registration, admission, and call status for VoIP calls. Gatekeepers can reside in the two different zones, or in the same zone. In ScreenOS version 5.10 you can configure a NetScreen device to accept incoming calls over a NAT boundary. To do this, you create a DIP address pool for dynamically allocating destination addresses. This differs from most configurations, where a DIP pool provides source addresses only. In addition, version 5.1.0 provides default settings that are automatically compatible with Avaya telecommunications equipment and infrastructure.

SIP Attack Protection

The ability of the SIP proxy server to process calls can be impacted by repeat SIP INVITErequests, whether malicious or through client or server error, that it initially denied. To prevent the SIP proxy server from being overwhelmed by such requests, you can use the sip protect deny command to drop repeat requests to all or specific proxy servers for configurable periods of time.

SNMP

The following tables were added to the NS-VPN-L2TP.mib. The tables are used to monitor the L2TP tunnels and calls.

- NsVpnL2tpMonTunnelEntry
- NsVpnL2tpMonCallEntry

The following traps were added to the NS-TRAPS.mib. The traps are used to detect call and tunnel termination.

- vpn-l2tp-tunnel-remove(43), — VPN tunnel removed
- vpn-l2tp-tunnel-remove-err(44), — VPN tunnel removed and error detected
- vpn-l2tp-call-remove(45), — VPN call removed
- vpn-l2tp-call-remove-err(46), — VPN call removed and error detected

Traffic Shaping

DiffServ Code Point Marking

NetScreen devices support DSCP marking on the first three bits of the DSCP fields in the IP header. NetSCreen devices now provide a global option to zero out the second 3 bits of the DSCP field. When this feature is on, the device changes the DS field values to 'xxx000|yy', ensuring that priority levels you set in policies are preserved and handled correctly by downstream routers.

URL Filtering

Integrated URL Filtering

Some NetScreen devices support a URL filtering solution that uses the Content Portal Authority (CPA) protocol from SurfControl. The NetScreen device intercepts each HTTP request and sends the requested URL to the SurfControl server for categorization. Then the device determines whether to block or permit the request based on the category of the URL.

Redirect URL Filtering

The NetScreen device sends the first HTTP request in a TCP connection to either a Websense server or a SurfControl server, enabling you to block or permit access to different sites based on their URLs, domain names, and IP addresses.

VPN's

NAT-Traversal

NAT-Traversal (NAT-T) allows Internet Key Exchange (IKE) and IP Security (IPSec) packets to traverse network address translation (NAT) devices that are also IKE/IPSec-aware. ScreenOS now supports NAT-T based on *draft-ietf-ipsec-nat-t-ike-02.txt* and *draft-ietf-ipsec-udp-encaps-02.txt*, as well as NAT-T based on version 0 of these drafts.

Index

Printed and bound by CPI Group (UK) Ltd, Croydon, CR0 4YY

03/10/2024

01040341-0019